Praise for *The WEIRDest People in the World*

"Henrich brings to the argument the same intensity of detail that made the WEIRD article stand out like neon among its peers . . . These days, few anthropologists are willing to put their data on the table, make a claim, and welcome challengers. We need more big books like this one. It is very much worth reading."

—T. M. Luhrmann, *The American Scholar*

"The rare case of a volume that deserves all its many accolades . . . Overall, it's a remarkable tome that makes a powerful case."

—Stephen L. Carter, *Bloomberg* (Best Nonfiction Books of 2020)

"*The WEIRDest People in the World* is one of the most consumingly fascinating books I've read in years." —James Marriott, *The Sunday Times* (London)

"A fascinating, vigorously argued work that probes deeply into the way 'WEIRD people' think." —*Kirkus Reviews*

"Ambitious and fascinating . . . This meaty book is ready-made for involved discussions." —*Publishers Weekly*

"[A] sweeping and magisterial book, likely to become as foundational to cultural psychology as the WEIRD acronym [Henrich] and his colleagues coined a decade ago." —Alex Mackiel, *Quillette*

"Joseph Henrich's *The WEIRDest People in the World* . . . makes for stunning reading. (It is also written with such wit and humor, and luminous clarity.) Probably an understatement to say that it is one of the most important books of the year."

—Cass R. Sunstein, author of
The World According to Star Wars, on Twitter

"Joseph Henrich has undertaken a massively ambitious work that explains the transition from kin-based societies to the modern world, drawing on a wealth of data across disciplines that significantly contributes to our understanding of this classic issue in social theory."

—Francis Fukuyama, author of
The Origins of Political Order and *Political Order and Political Decay*

"This delightful and thought-provoking book argues that there is nothing natural about most of the values, attitudes, and priorities of WEIRD (Western, Educated, Industrialized, Rich, and Democratic) people. They have evolved over time, in response to specific historical, institutional, and environmental circumstances. It is more vital than ever to understand how we can improve living standards throughout the world and deal with spectacular global challenges. Understanding where humanity's diversity has come from and in what way it matters for confronting our problems is vital. This fascinating book is a must-read for everybody who cares about these questions."

—Daron Acemoglu, coauthor of *Why Nations Fail:*
The Origins of Power, Prosperity, and Poverty and
The Narrow Corridor: States, Societies, and the Fate of Liberty

"A dazzling achievement. In the course of explaining how modern Western culture differs from all others past and present, Joseph Henrich has both altered and unified the fields of anthropology, history, psychology, and economics. He destroys the assumption, common in psychology and endemic in economics, that human nature is everywhere the same. His account makes it possible to understand why some cultures have readily adopted Western tools to transform their societies, economies, and politics, while others reject those tools."

—Richard E. Nisbett, author of *Mindware: Tools for Smart Thinking*

"Joseph Henrich's book combines a startling account of the mental and social oddities of Westerners with a persuasive new explanation for them. The concept of a universal human psyche will never be the same again."

—Richard Wrangham, author of *The Goodness Paradox:*
The Strange Relationship Between Virtue and Violence in Human Evolution

"This is a deep and important book of tremendous erudition, engagingly written with vivid examples, that highlights at once the ways in which human beings are similar and dissimilar the world over."

—Nicholas A. Christakis, author of
Blueprint: The Evolutionary Origins of a Good Society

"This book is a tour de force. It seamlessly combines ideas from evolutionary biology and cultural evolution with data from the psychology laboratory, field experiments in remote villages, high-tech econometrics, and ethnographic anecdotes to explain why people in Western societies think differently than other people, and how these differences culturally evolved over the last fifteen hundred years. *The WEIRDest People in the World* sets a new standard in the human sciences." —Robert Boyd, coauthor of *How Humans Evolved*

"There's nothing so fascinating as a social anthropologist's analysis of his own tribe. Joseph Henrich shows how strange and exceptional Western society is when compared with most of the world, and links it with features of the WEIRD brain."

—John Barton, author of
A History of the Bible: The Book and Its Faiths

"In the past five hundred years, Westerners have become more educated, industrialized, rich, and democratic than any other society in history—which, says Joseph Henrich, has made Westerners think differently about the world from everyone else. Drawing on anthropology, economics, history, and psychology, this magnificent book measures and even explains just how different Westerners are. It is a major contribution to the debates over why the West rules. It will make you think even more differently about the world than you already do."

—Ian Morris, author of *War! What Is It Good For?:*
Conflict and the Progress of Civilization from Primates to Robots

"Joseph Henrich has thought more deeply about cultural evolution than anybody alive. His fascinating insights into just how weird people like him and me are, with our Western lifestyles—and the implications of that, for better and for worse—are a great contribution to scholarship and literature."

—Matt Ridley, author of *How Innovation Works:*
And Why It Flourishes in Freedom

"Written in clear and vivid prose, Joseph Henrich's new book argues that the psychological characteristics of populations in modern prosperous countries are not universal to human societies. They were the result of institutional changes brought about by the Catholic Church in Europe during the Middle Ages, which laid the foundation for almost everything else that followed. Whether or not you agree, this bold and original book will shape the debate about the origins of modern society for years to come."

—Paul Seabright, author of
The Company of Strangers: A Natural History of Economic Life

"Reading this book feels like digging in your backyard and discovering a lost city. What Joseph Henrich has unearthed is truly astonishing: the modern West owes its prosperity to strange ways of thinking, created by accident centuries before the European Enlightenment. If that sounds improbable to you, prepare to meet a mountain of evidence, compiled by one of the great systematic thinkers of our time. This book is at once monumental and thrilling."

—Joshua Greene, author of *Moral Tribes: Emotion, Reason, and the Gap Between Us and Them*

"In this brilliant synthesis of cultural evolution and social psychology, Joseph Henrich explores the deep historical roots of individualism, generalized trust, impersonal prosociality, and analytical thinking—in short, the psychological traits that make people WEIRD."

—Peter Turchin, author of *Ultrasociety: How 10,000 Years of War Made Humans the Greatest Cooperators on Earth*

"The polymath and pioneering thinker Joseph Henrich has made a major contribution to the social sciences by demonstrating, through careful study, how Western societies are psychologically odd relative to the rest of humanity. Now, in this engaging and accessible text, Henrich elaborates on these important ideas by explaining how the West got to be WEIRD in the first place, and how the peculiar psychology of Western countries proved instrumental to their success. Along the way, Henrich makes a compelling case that human minds are not fated to think in a universal manner, but tune themselves surprisingly flexibly to the idiosyncrasies of local culture."

—Kevin N. Laland, coeditor of *Evolutionary Causation: Biological and Philosophical Reflections*

"Generations of scholars have grappled with the question of why the West rose. Joseph Henrich's intriguing new answer reveals how history shaped psychology and psychology changed history. Western Europe's shift from traditional kinship networks to voluntary associations fostered the individualism and literacy that opened up a uniquely WEIRD path to transformative progress. Propelled by a bold vision, this landmark study is required reading for anyone curious about the origins of modernity."

—Walter Scheidel, author of *Escape from Rome: The Failure of Empire and the Road to Prosperity*

"The most absorbing, provocative, and compelling book I have read in a long time. Joseph Henrich's thrilling exposé of cultural variety and evolution is grounded in meticulous science, and his arguments go beyond the milestone of Jared Diamond's *Guns, Germs, and Steel*. You will never look again in the same way at your own seemingly universal values."

—Uta Frith, author of *Autism: Explaining the Enigma*

"If you are considering reading this book, you are almost certainly WEIRD. Henrich lucidly explains how and why you got that way. Going beyond blank slate, social constructivist, and naïve models of common human psychology, he also makes a powerful case that, for human beings, culture and biology are always inextricably intertwined."

—Edward Slingerland, Distinguished University Scholar and professor of Asian studies at the University of British Columbia and author of *Trying Not to Try: Ancient China, Modern Science, and the Power of Spontaneity*

"*The WEIRDest People in the World* is a novel and fascinating look at our democratic, Western societies. The book presents a wealth of evidence that cultural learning and specific cultural rules of kinship relations generated the psychological foundations underlying the economic success of 'the West.' It is an exciting read that covers economics, sociology, psychology, history, and neuroscience."

—Ernst Fehr, professor of economics at the University of Zurich and coeditor of *Neuroeconomics: Decision Making and the Brain*

Natalie Henrich

JOSEPH HENRICH

The WEIRDest People in the World

Joseph Henrich is the author of *The Secret of Our Success: How Culture Is Driving Human Evolution, Domesticating Our Species, and Making Us Smarter*, among other books. He is the chair of the Department of Human Evolutionary Biology at Harvard University, where his research focuses on evolutionary approaches to culture, psychology, social status, religion, cooperation, and decision-making.

THE **WEIRD**EST PEOPLE IN THE WORLD

How the West Became Psychologically
Peculiar and Particularly Prosperous

JOSEPH HENRICH

PICADOR | FARRAR, STRAUS AND GIROUX | NEW YORK

Picador
120 Broadway, New York 10271

The Library of Congress has cataloged the Farrar, Straus and Giroux hardcover
edition as follows:

Names: Henrich, Joseph Patrick, author.
Title: The WEIRDest people in the world : how the West became psychologically
   peculiar and particularly prosperous / Joseph Henrich.
Description: New York : Farrar, Straus and Giroux, 2020 | Includes bibliographical
   references and index.
Identifiers: LCCN 2020012447 | ISBN 9780374173227 (hardcover)
Subjects: LCSH: Cognitive psychology. | Developmental psychology. | Social interaction. |
   Human evolution.
Classification: LCC BF201 .H46 2020 | DDC 153—dc23
LC record available at https://lccn.loc.gov/2020012447

Picador Paperback ISBN: 978-1-250-80007-7

To Natalie

20 years, 6 cities, and 3 children

CONTENTS

Part IV: Birthing the Modern World

PREFACE

In 2006, I unwittingly set off down the path leading to this book when I moved from the Department of Anthropology at Emory University to the University of British Columbia (UBC) in Vancouver, where I became a professor in the Departments of both Psychology and Economics. This was indeed an unlikely port of call, since I'd never taken a course in either field. Soon after arriving at UBC, two seemingly independent developments laid the foundation for this book. First, the Head of the Department of Economics, Anji Redish, suggested that I might teach a course called "The Wealth and Poverty of Nations" to fulfill my teaching obligation in the department. She'd noticed that when I was a graduate student at UCLA, I had taught a seminar based on Jared Diamond's book *Guns, Germs, and Steel*. This teaching opportunity led me deep into the literature in economics on why countries differ in prosperity, and why the Industrial Revolution occurred in Europe but not elsewhere. Topically, this research naturally fit my long-running anthropological interest in the evolution of human societies, although anthropologists usually didn't try to explain things that occurred after the rise of ancient states. Economists, by contrast (at that time), rarely looked back more than about 500 years from the present. Each time I taught the course, I modified the readings, which provided me with a chance to explore and critique the field. While this was fun, I didn't realize just how important this knowledge would be to my ongoing efforts to understand human psychological variation.

The second important development arose as I got to know two UBC social psychologists, Ara Norenzayan and Steve Heine. Ara, an Armenian who had emigrated from war-torn Lebanon to Fresno, California, when he was 18 years old, had spent the early part of his scientific career studying cultural differences in perception, thinking styles, and reasoning. Steve, whose research was (I suspect) often inspired by interactions with his Japanese wife, had been comparing how Canadians and Japanese think about themselves in relation to others and how that affects their motivations, decision-making, and sense of self. Independently, all three of us had noticed—within our separate domains of expertise—that Western populations were often unusual when compared to two or more other populations. Over Chinese takeout, in a basement food court where the famed psychologists Daniel Kahneman and Amos Tversky had purportedly hatched their plans to examine rational decision-making, we decided to compile all the cross-cultural studies that we could locate on important aspects of human psychology. After carefully reviewing all the research that we could locate, we arrived at three striking conclusions:

1. *Massively biased samples*: Most of what was known experimentally about *human* psychology and behavior was based on studies with undergraduates from Western societies. At the time, 96 percent of experimental participants were drawn from northern Europe, North America, or Australia, and about 70 percent of these were American undergraduates.
2. *Psychological diversity*: Psychological differences between populations appeared in many important domains, indicating much greater variation than one might expect from reading the text-

books or major journals in either psychology or behavioral economics.

3. *Psychological peculiarity*: When cross-cultural data were available from multiple populations, Western samples typically anchored the extreme end of the distribution. They were psychologically weird.

Taken together, these three findings meant that almost everything we—scientists—knew about human psychology derived from populations that seemed to be rather unusual along many important psychological and behavioral dimensions. Crucially, there was no obvious way to tell whether a psychological pattern found in Western undergraduates would hold cross-culturally, since existing research going back over a half century had revealed differences across populations in people's susceptibility to visual illusions, spatial reasoning, memory, attention, patience, risk-taking, fairness, induction, executive function, and pattern recognition.

Four years after our lunch in the basement, Ara, Steve, and I finally published "The weirdest people in the world?" in the journal *Behavioral and Brain Sciences* (2010), along with a commentary in *Nature* magazine. In these publications, we dubbed the populations so commonly used in psychological and behavioral experiments as "W.E.I.R.D." because they came from societies that are Western, Educated, Industrialized, Rich, and Democratic. Of course, we suspected there was likely important psychological variation among Western populations and within Western countries, but even this variation wasn't showing up very often in published studies or textbooks.

Although our publication in *Behavioral and Brain Sciences* did succeed in highlighting the narrowness of sampling within the psychological and behavioral sciences, I've always found it unsatisfying, because it doesn't explain anything. How can we account for all this psychological variation? And why are WEIRD people so unusual? In fact, without guiding theories or explanations, we couldn't even be sure that WEIRD people were indeed unusual. We wondered if WEIRD researchers—who entirely dominate the relevant scientific disciplines—might have unknowingly gravitated toward those aspects of psychology or behavior on which they themselves—their populations—were likely to stand out. Steve wondered aloud at lunch about what Japanese psychology might look like if Japanese researchers had developed their own version of this discipline, without first importing Western concepts, interests, and emphases.

In the aftermath of our paper, my mental gears began to turn on the question of how to explain the broad patterns of psychological variation that Ara, Steve, and I had discerned. The current effort documents my progress to date. However, in constructing this book, I ended up first producing another book, called *The Secret of Our Success* (2016). Originally, the ideas that I developed there were supposed to form Part I of this book. But, once I opened that intellectual dam, a full book-length treatment flooded out, and nothing could stop it. Then, with *The Secret of Our Success* tempered and ready, I could confidently synthesize the elements necessary for this book. Thanks to my publisher, Farrar, Straus and Giroux, for understanding that sometimes you need to forge the proper tools before tackling a big job.

This project required me to draw on and integrate research from across the social and biological sciences, and for that I had to rely on a vast network of friends, colleagues, and fellow scientists who pitched in with their knowledge, wisdom, and insights over a decade. I could never thank everyone who helped me, in countless conversations and emails.

As a wayward cultural anthropologist who washed up on the academic shores of psychology and economics at the University of British Columbia, I'd like to thank the truly amazing group of scholars and friends there who took me in. The contributions of Steve and Ara were, of course, foundational. I also learned a tremendous amount from Ted Slingerland, Patrick Francois, Siwan Anderson, Mauricio Drelichman, Ashok Kotwal, Kiley Hamlin, Mark Schaller, Mukesh Eswaran, Jessica Tracy, Darrin Lehman, Nancy Gallini, Andy Baron, Sue Birch, and Janet Werker. Special thanks to Siwan and Patrick for providing comments on my draft chapters.

Just as I was officially embarking on the intellectual journey to this book, I was invited to become a fellow in the Canadian Institute for Advanced Research (CIFAR) in the Institutions, Organizations, and Growth (IOG) group. This serendipitous lightning bolt brought me into continuous contact with leading economists and political scientists who were working on questions of direct relevance. My thanks to CIFAR and the entire IOG, since I learned from everyone. Early on, my conversations with the economic historians Avner Greif and Joel Mokyr contributed to forming the backbone of this book. Special thanks to Joel, who provided chapter-by-chapter feedback and always responded to my naïve questions about economic history. I also learned much from interacting with Guido Tabellini, Matt Jackson, Torsten Persson, Roland Bénabou, Tim Besley, Jim Fearon, Sara Lowes, Suresh Naidu, Thomas Fujiwara, Raul Sanchez de la Sierra, and Natalie Bau. Of course, my ongoing debates with Daron Acemoglu and James Robinson were essential, as they forced me to sharpen my arguments and spot gaps in my evidence. When James and I co-taught a course at Harvard, he made sure the students carefully inspected each of my arguments.

In 2013–14, I was fortunate to spend a year at New York University's Stern School of Business as part of the Business and Society Program. My time at Stern was incredibly productive, and I benefited greatly from weekly conversations and an opportunity to co-teach with the psychologist Jon Haidt. During this time, I also enjoyed helpful advice from the economists Paul Romer and Bob Frank.

After I arrived at Harvard, sections of this book underwent dramatic improvements with input from a group of young economists. In 2016, I first told Benjamin Enke about my book over several pints during our weekly pub gatherings. He got excited about the ideas and, over the next year, put together an impressive paper that I draw heavily on in Chapter 6. At roughly the same time, I'd invited Jonathan Schulz to give a talk in my lab, since I'd heard from one of my postdocs that he was working on something about "cousin marriage and democracy" at Yale. For most people, especially most economists, "cousin marriage and democracy" would probably sound a bit wacky. But to me, it was obvious that he and I had probably ended up on converging scientific tracks. After his talk, I immediately invited him to become a postdoc in my lab and join a collaboration that I'd begun with another economist, Jonathan Beauchamp, who was leaving his post at the International Monetary Fund to return to academic life. To our trio we soon added the Iranian-born economist Duman Bahrami-Rad. The intellectual fruit of our teamwork is now published in *Science* magazine and forms the core of Chapters 6 and 7. Thanks to all these guys for reading drafts of this book and providing helpful comments.

During this same period, I also benefited immensely from weekly interactions with the economists Nathan Nunn and Leander Heldring. In courses that we co-instructed, Leander and Nathan provided feedback on my ideas, lecture by lecture, as I presented them.

Members of my laboratory group have had to endure my obsession with the topics covered in this book. For their comments and insights over the years, thanks to Michael Muthukrishna, Rahul Bhui, Aiyana Willard, Rita McNamara, Cristina Moya, Jennifer Jacquet, Maciek Chudek, Helen Davis, Anke Becker, Tommy Flint, Martin Lang, Ben Purzycki, Max Winkler, Manvir Singh, Moshe Hoffman, Andres Gomez, Kevin Hong, and Graham Noblit. Special thanks to Cammie Curtin and Tiffany Hwang, who, during the time each spent as my lab manager, contributed to this book in myriad ways.

Along the way, I benefited from conversations in interactions with many researchers and authors, including Dan Smail, Rob Boyd, Kim Hill, Sarah Mathew, Sascha Becker, Jared Rubin, Hans-Joachim Voth, Kathleen Vohs, Ernst Fehr, Matt Syed, Mark Koyama, Noel Johnson, Scott Atran, Peter Turchin, Eric Kimbrough, Sasha Vostroknutov, Alberto Alesina, Steve Stich, Tyler Cowen, Fiery Cushman, Josh Greene, Alan Fiske, Ricardo Hausmann, Clark Barrett, Paola Giuliano, Alessandra Cassar, Devesh Rustagi, Thomas Talhelm, Ed Glaeser, Felipe Valencia Caicedo, Dan Hruschka, Robert Barro, Rachel McCleary, Sendhil Mullainathan, Lera Boroditsky, Michal Bauer, Julie Chytilová, Mike Gurven, and Carole Hooven, among many others. Several people supplied me with data, and I've tried to specifically thank them for that in the endnotes. During two visits to the University of Pennsylvania, I was particularly inspired by in-depth discussions with one of my fellow travelers, Coren Apicella, whose work with Hadza hunter-gatherers is featured in Chapter 11.

I would also like to extend my thanks to my editor at FSG, Eric Chinski, for his helpful comments on the penultimate draft of my manuscript, and to my literary agent, Brockman Inc., for their early and consistent encouragement of this project.

Finally, my greatest gratitude goes to my family, Natalie, Zoey, Jessica, and Josh, who have for a decade lovingly supported my efforts on this demanding project.

Joe Henrich
Cambridge, Massachusetts
August 1, 2019

The WEIRDest People in the World

Prelude:
Your Brain Has Been Modified

Your brain has been altered, neurologically rewired as it acquired a skill that your society greatly values. Until recently, this skill was of little or no use and most people in most societies never acquired it. In developing this ability, you have:[1]

1. Specialized an area of your brain's left ventral occipito-temporal region, which lies between your language, object, and face processing centers.

2. Thickened your corpus callosum, which is the information highway that connects the left and right hemispheres of your brain.

3. Altered the part of your prefrontal cortex that is involved in language production (Broca's area) as well as other brain areas engaged in a variety of neurological tasks, including both speech processing and thinking about others' minds.

4. Improved your verbal memory and broadened your brain's activation when processing speech.

5. Shifted your facial recognition processing to the right hemisphere. Normal humans (not you) process faces almost equally on the left and right sides of their brains, but those with your peculiar skill are biased toward the right hemisphere.[2]
6. Diminished your ability to identify faces, probably because while jury-rigging your left ventral occipito-temporal region, you impinged on an area that usually specializes in facial recognition.
7. Reduced your default tendency toward holistic visual processing in favor of more analytical processing. You now rely more on breaking scenes and objects down into their component parts and less on broad configurations and gestalt patterns.

What is this mental ability? What capacity could have renovated your brain, endowing you with new, specialized skills as well as inducing specific cognitive deficits?

The exotic mental ability is reading. You are likely highly literate.

Acquiring this mental ability involves wiring in specialized neurological circuitry in various parts of the brain. For processing letters and words, a *Letterbox* develops in the left ventral occipito-temporal region, which connects with nearby regions for object recognition, language, and speech. Brain injuries that damage the *Letterbox* cause illiteracy, though victims retain the ability to recognize numerals and make mathematical calculations, indicating that this region develops specifically for reading.[3]

The *Letterbox*'s circuitry is tuned to specific writing systems. For example, while Hebrew characters activate the *Letterbox* in Hebrew readers, English readers deal with these characters as they would any other visual object—and not like they do Roman letters. The *Letterbox* also encodes deeper, nonvisual patterns. For example, it registers the similarity between "READ" and "read" even though the two words look quite different.[4]

Let me show you something: there will be some large symbols at the top of the next page. Don't read them, but instead only study their shapes. I'll tell you when you should read them.

White Horse
白　馬

If you are literate in English, I bet you couldn't help but read "White Horse" above. Your brain's reading circuitry is superfast, automatic, and, as we just demonstrated, out of your conscious control. You can't help reading what you see. By contrast, unless you are also literate in Chinese, you probably had no trouble simply admiring the interesting markings that form the Chinese characters above, which also mean "White Horse" (*bai ma*). In highly literate populations, psychologists like to flash words at experimental participants so quickly that they don't consciously realize that they have just seen a word. Yet we know that they not only saw the flashed word but also read it, because its meaning subtly influences their brain activation and behavior. Such subliminal priming demonstrates both our inability to switch off our reading circuitry and the fact that we don't even know it when we are in fact reading and processing what we read. Although this cognitive ability is culturally constructed, it's also automatic, unconscious, and irrepressible. This makes it like many other aspects of culture.[5]

Learning to read forms specialized brain networks that influence our psychology across several different domains, including memory, visual processing, and facial recognition. Literacy changes people's biology and psychology without altering the underlying genetic code. A society in which 95 percent of adults are highly literate would have, on average, thicker corpus callosa and worse facial recognition than a society in which only 5 percent of people are highly literate. These biological differences between populations will emerge even if the two groups were genetically indistinguishable. Literacy thus provides an example of how culture can change people biologically independent of any genetic differences. Culture can and does alter our brains, hormones, and anatomy, along with our perceptions, motivations, personalities, emotions, and many other aspects of our minds.[6]

The neurological and psychological modifications associated with literacy should be thought of as part of a cultural package that includes practices, beliefs, values, and institutions—like the value of "formal education" or institutions such as "schools"—as well as technologies like alphabets, syllabaries, and printing presses. Across societies, a combination of practices, norms, and technologies has jury-rigged aspects of our genetically evolved neurological systems to create new mental abilities. To understand the psychological and neurological diversity we find around the world, in domains ranging from verbal memory to corpus callosum thickness, we need to explore the origins and development of the relevant values, beliefs, institutions, and practices.

The case of literacy illustrates why so many psychologists and neuroscientists have broadly misread their experimental results and repeatedly made incorrect inferences about *human* brains and psychology. By studying the students attending their home universities, neuroscientists found a robust right-hemisphere bias in facial processing. Following good scientific practice, different researchers replicated these results using different populations of Western university students. Based on these successful replications, it was inferred that this hemispheric bias in facial processing was a basic feature of human neurocognitive functioning—not a cultural by-product of deep literacy. Had they done what psychologists usually do to look for cultural differences—run experiments on East Asian students attending American universities—they would have further verified their prior results and confirmed a right-hemisphere bias. This is because all university students must be highly literate. Of course, there's no shortage of illiterate people in the world today, with estimates placing the number somewhere north of 770 million, which is more than twice the population of the United States. They just don't make it into university labs very often.

Here's the thing: highly literate societies are relatively new, and quite distinct from most societies that have ever existed. This means that modern populations are neurologically and psychologically different from those found in societies throughout history and back into our evolutionary past. If you unwittingly study these peculiar modern populations without realizing the powerful impact that technologies, beliefs, and social norms related to literacy have on our brains and mental processes, you can get the wrong answers. This can happen even when you study seemingly basic features of psychology and neuroscience, like memory, visual processing, and facial recognition.

If we want to explain these aspects of brains and psychology as they appear in modern societies, we need to understand the origins and spread of high rates of literacy—when and why did most people start reading? Where and why did the beliefs, values, practices, technologies, and institutions emerge to create and support this new ability? This turns a question about neuroscience, and global psychological diversity, into one about cultural evolution and history.

What God Wants

Literacy does not come to pervade a society simply because a writing system emerges, though having such a system certainly helps. Writing systems have existed for millennia in powerful and successful societies, dating back some 5,000 years; yet until relatively recently, never more than about 10 percent of any society's populations could read, and usually the rates were much lower.

Suddenly, in the 16th century, literacy began spreading epidemically across western Europe. By around 1750, having surged past more cosmopolitan places in Italy and France, the Netherlands, Britain, Sweden, and Germany developed the most literate societies in the world. Half or more of the populations in these countries could read, and publishers were rapidly cranking out books and pamphlets. In examining the spread of literacy between 1550 and 1900 in Figure P.1, remember that underneath this diffusion are psychological and neurological changes in people's brains: verbal memories are expanding, face processing is shifting right, and corpus callosa are thickening—in the aggregate—over centuries.[7]

It's not immediately obvious why this takeoff should have occurred at this point in history and in these places. The explosion of innovation and economic growth known as the Industrial Revolution wouldn't hit

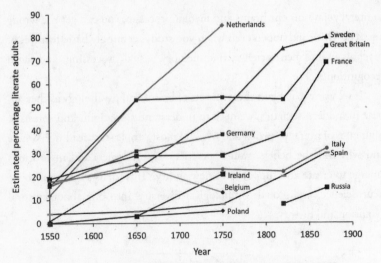

FIGURE P.1. Literacy rates for various European countries from 1550 to 1900. These estimates are based on book publishing data calibrated using more direct measures of literacy.[8]

England, and later the rest of Europe, until the late 18th century (at the earliest), so the initial spread of literacy isn't a response to the incentives and opportunities created by industrialization. Similarly, it wasn't until the late 17th century, with the Glorious Revolution in Britain, that constitutional forms of government began to emerge at the national level, so literacy isn't purely a consequence of political representation or pluralism in state politics. In fact, in many places in Europe and America, high levels of literacy emerged and persisted long before the advent of mandatory state-funded schools. Of course, this doesn't mean that literacy wasn't eventually spurred along by wealth, democracy, and state funding. These developments, however, are too late to have sparked popular literacy. So, what did?

It began late in 1517, just after Halloween, in the small German charter town of Wittenberg. A monk and professor named Martin Luther had produced his famous Ninety-Five Theses, which called for a scholarly debate on the Catholic Church's practice of selling indulgences. Catholics at the time could purchase a certificate, an "indulgence," to reduce the time that their dead relatives had to spend in purgatory for their sins, or to lessen the severity of their own Penance.[9] Luther's Ninety-Five Theses marked the eruption of the Protestant Reformation. Elevated by his excommunication and bravery in the face of criminal charges, Luther's subsequent writings on theology, social policy, and living a Christian life reverberated outward from his safe haven in Wittenberg in an expanding wave that influenced many populations, first in Europe and then around the world. Beyond the German lands, Protestantism would soon develop strong roots in the Netherlands and Britain, and later spread with the flows of British colonists into North America, New Zealand, and Australia. Today, variants of Protestantism continue to proliferate in South America, China, Oceania, and Africa.[10]

Embedded deep in Protestantism is the notion that individuals should develop a personal relationship with God and Jesus. To accomplish this, both men and women needed to read and interpret the sacred scriptures—the Bible—for themselves, and not rely primarily on the authority of supposed experts, priests, or institutional authorities like the Church. This principle, known as *sola scriptura*, meant that everyone needed to learn to read. And since everyone cannot become a fluent Latin scholar, the Bible had to be translated into the local languages.[11]

Luther not only created a German translation of the Bible, which rapidly came into broad use, but he began to preach about the importance of literacy and schooling. The task ahead for him was big, since estimates suggest that only about 1 percent of the German-speaking population was then literate. Beginning in his own principality, Saxony, Luther pushed rulers to take responsibility for literacy and schooling. In 1524, he penned a pamphlet called "To the Councilmen of All Cities in Germany That They Establish and Maintain Christian Schools." In this and other writings, he urged both parents and leaders to create schools to teach children to read the scriptures. As various dukes and princes in the Holy Roman Empire began to adopt Protestantism, they often used Saxony as their model. Consequently, literacy and schools often diffused in concert with Protestantism. Literacy also began spreading in other places, like Britain and the Netherlands, though it was in Germany that formal schooling first became a sacred responsibility of secular rulers and governments.[12]

The historical connection between Protestantism and literacy is well documented. Illustrating this, Figure P.1 shows that literacy rates grew the fastest in countries where Protestantism was most deeply established. Even as late as 1900, the higher the percentage of Protestants in a country, the higher the rate of literacy. In Britain, Sweden, and the Netherlands, adult literacy rates were nearly 100 percent. Meanwhile, in Catholic countries like Spain and Italy, the rates had only risen to about 50 percent. Overall, if we know the percentage of Protestants in a country, we can account for about half of the cross-national variation in literacy at the dawn of the 20th century.[13]

The problem with these correlations and many similar analyses that link Protestantism to either literacy or formal schooling is that we can't tell if Protestantism caused greater literacy and education or whether literacy and education caused people to adopt Protestantism. Or maybe both Protestantism and literacy tended to emerge in the wake of economic growth, representative governments, and technological developments like the printing press. Fortunately, history has provided a kind of natural experiment in Prussia, which has been explored by the economists Sascha Becker and Ludger Woessmann.

Prussia provides an excellent case study for a couple of reasons. First, it developed incipient notions of religious freedom early on. By 1740, Prussia's King Frederick (the Great) declared that every individual should find salvation in his own way—effectively declaring religious freedom. This meant that Prussians could pick their religion unconstrained by the top-down dictates of political leaders. Second, Prussia had relatively uniform laws and similar governing institutions across regions. This mitigates concerns that any relationship observed between literacy and Protestantism might be due to some unseen linkage between religion and government.

Analyses of the 1871 Prussian census show that counties with more Protestants had higher rates of literacy and more schools, with shorter travel times to local schools. This pattern prevails, and the evidence is often stronger, when the effects of urbanization and demographics are held constant. The connection between Protestantism and schools is even evident in 1816, prior to German industrialization. Thus, the relationship between religion and schooling/literacy isn't due to industrialization and the associated economic growth.[14]

Still, the relationship between Protestantism and literacy/schooling is just an association.[15] Many of us learned that causal links can never be inferred from mere correlations, and that only experiments can identify causation. This isn't entirely true anymore, however, because researchers have devised clever ways to extract quasi-experimental data from the real world. In Prussia, Protestantism spread from Wittenberg like the ripples created by tossing a stone in a pond (to use Luther's own metaphor). Because of this, the further a Prussian county was from Wittenberg in 1871, the smaller the percentage of Protestants. For every 100 km (62 mi) traveled from Wittenberg, the percentage of Protestants dropped by 10 percent (Figure P.2). The relationship holds even when we statistically remove the influence of all kinds of economic, demographic, and geographic factors. Thus we can take proximity to ground zero of the Reformation—Wittenberg—as a cause of Protestantism in Prussia. Obviously, lots of other factors matter, including urbanization, but being near Wittenberg—the new center of action after 1517—had its own independent effect on Protestantism within the Prussian context.

The radial patterning of Protestantism allows us to use a county's proximity to Wittenberg to isolate—in a statistical sense—that part of the variation in Protestantism that we know is due to a county's proximity to Wittenberg and not to greater literacy or other factors. In a sense, we can think of this as an experiment in which different counties were experimentally assigned different dosages of Protestantism to test for its effects. Distance from Wittenberg allows us to figure out how big that experimental dosage was. Then, we can see if this "assigned" dosage of Protestantism is still associated with greater literacy and more schools. If it is, we can infer from this natural experiment that Protestantism did indeed *cause* greater literacy.[16]

The results of this statistical razzle-dazzle are striking. Not only do Prussian counties closer to Wittenberg have higher shares of Protestants,

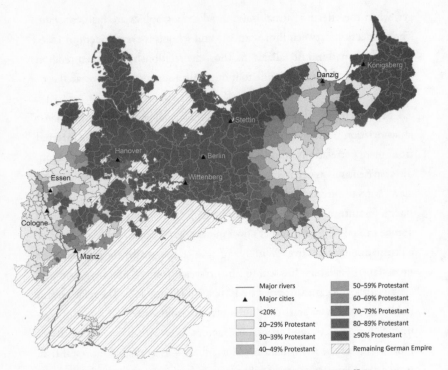

FIGURE P.2. The percentage of Protestants in Prussian counties in 1871.[17] The map highlights some German cities, including the epicenter of the Reformation, Wittenberg, and Mainz, the charter town where Johannes Gutenberg produced his eponymous printing press.

but those additional Protestants are associated with greater literacy and more schools. This indicates that the wave of Protestantism created by the Reformation raised literacy and schooling rates in its wake. Despite Prussia's having a high average literacy rate in 1871, counties made up entirely of Protestants had literacy rates nearly 20 percentile points higher than those that were all Catholic.[18]

These same patterns can be spotted elsewhere in 19th-century Europe—and today—in missionized regions around the globe. In 19th-century Switzerland, other aftershocks of the Reformation have been detected in a battery of cognitive tests given to Swiss army recruits. Young men from all-Protestant districts were not only 11 percentile points more likely to be "high performers" on reading tests compared to those from all-Catholic districts, but this advantage bled over into their scores in math, history, and writing. These relationships hold even when a district's population density, fertility, and economic complexity are kept constant. As in Prussia, the closer a community was to one of the two epicenters of the Swiss Reformation— Zurich or Geneva—the more Protestants it had in the 19th century. Notably, proximity to other Swiss cities, such as Bern and Basel, doesn't reveal this relationship. As is the case in Prussia, this setup allows us to finger Protestantism as driving the spread of greater literacy as well as the smaller improvements in writing and math abilities.[19]

While religious convictions appear central to the early spread of literacy and schooling, material self-interest and economic opportunities do not. Luther and other Reformation leaders were not especially interested in literacy and schooling for their own sake, or for the eventual economic and political benefits these would foster centuries later. *Sola scriptura* was primarily justified because it paved the road to eternal salvation. What could be more important? Similarly, the farming families who dominated the population were not investing in this skill to improve their economic prospects or job opportunities. Instead, Protestants believed that people had to become literate so that they could read the Bible for themselves, improve their moral character, and build a stronger relationship with God. Centuries later, as the Industrial Revolution rumbled into Germany and surrounding regions, the reservoir of literate farmers and local schools created by Protestantism furnished an educated and ready workforce that propelled rapid economic development and helped fuel the second Industrial Revolution.[20]

The Protestant commitment to broad literacy and education can still be observed today in the differential impacts of Protestant vs. Catholic missions around the globe. In Africa, regions that contained more Christian missions in 1900 had higher literacy rates a century later. However, early Protestant missions beat out their Catholic competitors. Comparing them head-to-head, regions with early Protestant missions are associated with literacy rates that are about 16 percentile points higher on average than those associated with Catholic missions. Similarly, individuals in communities associated with historical Protestant missions have about 1.6 years more formal schooling than those around Catholic missions. These differences are big, since Africans in the late 20th century had only about three years of schooling on average, and only about half of adults were literate. These effects are independent of a wide range of geographic, economic, and political factors, as well as the countries' current spending on education, which itself explains little of the variation in schooling or literacy.[21]

Competition among religious missions makes a big difference. Both Catholic and Protestant missionaries were more effective at instilling literacy when they were directly competing for the same souls. In fact, in the absence of competition from the literacy-obsessed Protestants, it's not entirely clear that Catholic missionaries had much effect on literacy at all. Furthermore, detailed analyses of the African data reveal that Protestant missions not only built formal schools but also inculcated cultural values about the importance of education. This is consistent with 16th- and 17th-century Europe, where the Catholic interest in literacy and schooling was fueled in part by the Protestants' intense focus on it.[22]

Besides shaping the Catholic Church through competition, Luther's Protestantism also inadvertently laid the foundation for universal, state-funded schooling by promoting the idea that it was the government's responsibility to educate the populace. From the beginning, Luther's writings not only emphasized the need for parents to ensure their children's literacy but also placed the obligation for creating schools on local princes and dukes. This religiously inspired drive for public schools helped make Prussia a model for state-funded education that was later copied by countries like Britain and the United States.

Notably, *sola scriptura* specifically drove the spread of female literacy, first in Europe and later across the globe. In 16th-century Brandenburg, for example, while the number of boys' schools almost doubled, from 55 to 100, the number of girls' schools increased over 10 times, from 4 to 45. Later, in 1816, the higher the percentage of Protestants in a county or town, the larger the percentage of girls who were enrolled in schools relative to boys. In fact, when a county's distance to Wittenberg is used to extract only that quasi-experimental fraction of the variation in religious affiliation (Catholic or Protestant) that was caused by the early ripples of the Reformation, the relationship still holds—indicating that Protestantism likely caused a rise in female literacy. Outside of Europe, the impact of Protestantism on educating girls continues to play out as Christianity spreads globally. In both Africa and India, for example, early Protestant missions had notably larger effects on the literacy and schooling of girls compared to their Catholic competitors. The impact of Protestantism on women's literacy is particularly important, because the babies of literate mothers tend to be fewer, healthier, smarter, and richer as adults than those of illiterate mothers.[23]

When the Reformation reached Scotland in 1560, it was founded on the central principle of a free public education for the poor. The world's first local school tax was established there in 1633 and strengthened in 1646. This early experiment in universal education soon produced a stunning array of intellectual luminaries, from David Hume to Adam Smith, and probably midwifed the Scottish Enlightenment. The intellectual dominance of this tiny region in the 18th century inspired Voltaire to write, "We look to Scotland for all our ideas of civilization."[24]

Let's follow the causal chain I've been linking together: the spread of a religious belief that every individual should read the Bible for themselves led to the diffusion of widespread literacy among both men and women, first in Europe and later across the globe. Broad-based literacy changed people's brains and altered their cognitive abilities in domains related to memory, visual processing, facial recognition, numerical exactness, and problem-solving. It probably also indirectly altered family sizes, child health, and cognitive development, as mothers became increasingly literate and formally educated. These psychological and social changes may have fostered speedier innovation, new institutions, and—in the long run—greater economic prosperity.[25]

Of course, just as the great German sociologist Max Weber theorized, there's much more to the story of Protestantism than literacy. As we'll see in Chapter 12, Protestantism also likely influenced people's self-discipline, patience, sociality, and suicidal inclinations.[26]

The Histories of Religions, Biologies, and Psychologies

This book is not primarily about Protestantism or literacy, though I will endeavor to explain why European populations at the close of the Middle Ages were so susceptible to the unusually individualistic character of Protestant beliefs. The very notion that every individual should read and interpret ancient sacred texts for himself or—worse—herself, instead of simply deferring to the great sages, would have seemed somewhere between outrageous and dangerous in most premodern societies.[27] Protestantism, which was actively opposed by many religious and secular elites, would have gone nowhere in most places and during most epochs. To explain the unusual nature of Western Christianity, as well as our families, marriages, laws, and governments, we'll be going much deeper into the past to explore how a peculiar set of religious prohibitions and prescriptions reorganized European kinship in ways that altered people's social lives and psychology, ultimately propelling the societies of Christendom down a historical pathway not available elsewhere. You'll see that Protestantism and its important influences are much closer to the end of the story than to the beginning.

Nevertheless, the case of literacy and Protestantism illustrates, in microcosm, four key ideas that will run through the rest of this book. Let's go through them:

1. Religious convictions can powerfully shape decision-making, psychology, and society. Reading the sacred scripture was primarily about connecting with the divine, but the unintended side effects were big, and resulted in the survival and spread of some religious groups over others.

2. Beliefs, practices, technologies, and social norms—culture—can shape our brains, biology, and psychology, including our motivations, mental abilities, and decision-making biases. You can't

separate "culture" from "psychology" or "psychology" from "biology," because culture physically rewires our brains and thereby shapes how we think.[28]

3. Psychological changes induced by culture can shape all manner of subsequent events by influencing what people pay attention to, how they make decisions, which institutions they prefer, and how much they innovate. In this case, by driving up literacy, culture induced more analytic thinking and longer memories while spurring formal schooling, book production, and knowledge dissemination. Thus, *sola scriptura* likely energized innovation and laid the groundwork for standardizing laws, broadening the voting franchise, and establishing constitutional governments.[29]

4. Literacy provides our first example of how Westerners became psychologically unusual. Of course, with the diffusion of Christianity and European institutions (like primary schools) around the world, many populations have recently become highly literate.[30] However, if you'd surveyed the world in 1900, people from western Europe would have looked rather peculiar, with their thicker corpus callosa and poorer facial recognition.[31]

As you'll see, literacy is no special case. Rather, it's the tip of a large psychological and neurological iceberg that many researchers have missed. In the next chapter, I'll begin by probing the depths and shape of this iceberg. Then, after laying a foundation for thinking about human nature, cultural change, and societal evolution, we'll examine how and why a broad array of psychological differences emerged in western Europe, and what their implications are for understanding modern economic prosperity, innovation, law, democracy, and science.

PART I

The Evolution of Societies and Psychologies

1

WEIRD Psychology

The Western conception of the person as a bounded, unique, more or less integrated motivational and cognitive universe; a dynamic center of awareness, emotion, judgment, and action organized into a distinctive whole and set contrastively both against other such wholes and against a social and natural background is, however incorrigible it may seem to us, a rather peculiar idea within the context of the world's cultures.
—anthropologist Clifford Geertz (1974, p. 31)

Who are you?

Perhaps you are WEIRD, raised in a society that is Western, Educated, Industrialized, Rich, and Democratic. If so, you're likely rather psychologically peculiar. Unlike much of the world today, and most people who have ever lived, we WEIRD people are highly individualistic, self-obsessed, control-oriented, nonconformist, and analytical. We focus on ourselves— our attributes, accomplishments, and aspirations—over our relationships and social roles. We aim to be "ourselves" across contexts and see inconsistencies in others as hypocrisy rather than flexibility. Like everyone else, we are inclined to go along with our peers and authority figures; but, we are less willing to conform to others when this conflicts with our own beliefs, observations, and preferences. We see ourselves as unique beings, not as nodes in a social network that stretches out through space and back in time. When acting, we prefer a sense of control and the feeling of making our own choices.

When reasoning, WEIRD people tend to look for universal categories and rules with which to organize the world, and mentally project straight lines to understand patterns and anticipate trends. We simplify complex phenomena by breaking them down into discrete constituents and assigning properties or abstract categories to these components—whether by imagining types of particles, pathogens, or personalities. We often miss the relationships between the parts or the similarities between phenomena that don't fit nicely into our categories. That is, we know a lot about individual trees but often miss the forest.

WEIRD people are also particularly patient and often hardworking. Through potent self-regulation, we can defer gratification—in financial rewards, pleasure, and security—well into the future in exchange for discomfort and uncertainty in the present. In fact, WEIRD people sometimes take pleasure in hard work and find the experience purifying.

Paradoxically, and despite our strong individualism and self-obsession, WEIRD people tend to stick to impartial rules or principles and can be quite trusting, honest, fair, and cooperative toward strangers or anonymous others. In fact, relative to most populations, we WEIRD people show relatively less favoritism toward our friends, families, co-ethnics, and local communities than other populations do. We think nepotism is wrong, and fetishize abstract principles over context, practicality, relationships, and expediency.

Emotionally, WEIRD people are often racked by guilt as they fail to live up to their culturally inspired, but largely self-imposed, standards and aspirations. In most non-WEIRD societies, shame—not guilt—dominates people's lives. People experience shame when they, their relatives, or even their friends fail to live up to the standards imposed on them by their communities. Non-WEIRD populations might, for example, "lose face" in front of the judging eyes of others when their daughter elopes with someone outside their social network. Meanwhile, WEIRD people might feel guilty for taking a nap instead of hitting the gym even though this isn't an obligation and no one will know. Guilt depends on one's own standards and self-evaluation, while shame depends on societal standards and public judgment.

These are just a few examples, the tip of that psychological iceberg I mentioned, which includes aspects of perception, memory, attention, reasoning, motivation, decision-making, and moral judgment. But, the questions I hope to answer in this book are: How did WEIRD populations become so psychologically peculiar? Why are they different?

Tracking this puzzle back into Late Antiquity, we'll see that one sect of Christianity drove the spread of a particular package of social norms and beliefs that dramatically altered marriage, families, inheritance, and ownership in parts of Europe over centuries. This grassroots transformation of family life initiated a set of psychological changes that spurred new forms of urbanization and fueled impersonal commerce while driving the proliferation of voluntary organizations, from merchant guilds and charter towns to universities and transregional monastic orders, that were governed by new and increasingly individualistic norms and laws. You'll see how, in the process of explaining WEIRD psychology, we'll also illuminate the exotic nature of WEIRD religion, marriage, and family. If you didn't know that our religions, marriages, and families were so strange, buckle up.

Understanding how and why some European populations became psychologically peculiar by the Late Middle Ages illuminates another great puzzle: the "rise of the West." Why did western European societies conquer so much of the world after about 1500? Why did economic growth, powered by new technologies and the Industrial Revolution, erupt from this same region in the late 18th century, creating the waves of globalization that are still crashing over the world today?

If a team of alien anthropologists had surveyed humanity from orbit in 1000 CE, or even 1200 CE, they would never have guessed that European populations would dominate the globe during the second half of the millennium. Instead, they probably would have bet on China or the Islamic world.[1]

What these aliens would have missed from their orbital perch was the quiet fermentation of a new psychology during the Middle Ages in some European communities. This evolving proto-WEIRD psychology gradually laid the groundwork for the rise of impersonal markets, urbanization, constitutional governments, democratic politics, individualistic religions, scientific societies, and relentless innovation. In short, these psychological shifts fertilized the soil for the seeds of the modern world. Thus, to understand the roots of contemporary societies we need to explore how our psychology culturally adapts and coevolves with our most basic social institution—the family.

Let's begin by taking a closer look at the iceberg.

Really, Who Are You?

Try completing this sentence in 10 different ways:

    I am _____.

. . .

If you are WEIRD, you probably answered with words like "curious" or "passionate" and phrases like "a scientist," "a surgeon," or "a kayaker." You were probably less inclined to respond with things like "Josh's dad" or "Maya's mom," even though those are equally true and potentially more central to your life. This focus on personal attributes, achievements, and membership in abstract or idealized social groups over personal relationships, inherited social roles, and face-to-face communities is a robust feature of WEIRD psychology, but one that makes us rather peculiar from a global perspective.

Figure 1.1 shows how people in Africa and the South Pacific respond to the "Who am I?" (Figure 1.1A) and the "I am_____" tasks (Figure 1.1B), respectively. The data available for Figure 1.1A permitted me to calculate both the percentage of responses that were specifically individualistic, referring to personal attributes, aspirations, and achievements, and those that were about social roles and relationships. At one end of the spectrum, American undergraduates focus almost exclusively on their individual attributes, aspirations, and achievements. At the other end are the Maasai and Samburu. In rural Kenya, these two tribal groups organize themselves in patrilin-

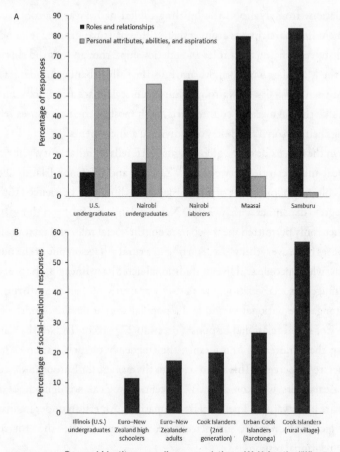

A

B

FIGURE 1.1. Personal identity across diverse populations. (A) Using the "Who am I?" task, the upper figure shows the tendencies for people in different populations to focus on their roles and relationships vs. their personal attributes and achievements. The bars show the average percentages of responses for each person in each place. (B) Using the "I am _____" sentence completion task, the lower panel illustrates the average percentage of people's answers that were social-relational in nature.[2]

eal clans and maintain a traditional cattle-herding lifestyle. Their responses referenced their roles and relationships at least 80 percent of the time while only occasionally highlighting their personal attributes or achievements (10 percent or less of the time). In the middle of this distribution are two populations from Nairobi, the bustling capital of Kenya. Nairobi laborers, including participants from several different tribal groups, responded mostly by referencing their roles and relationships, though they did this less than the Maasai or Samburu. Meanwhile, the fully urbanized undergraduates at the University of Nairobi (a European-style institution) look much more like their American counterparts, with most of their responses referencing their personal attributes or individual achievements.[3]

On the other side of the globe, Figure 1.1B tells a similar story. The close political and social ties between New Zealand and the Cook Islands allow us to compare populations of Cook Islanders who have experienced differing degrees of contact with WEIRD New Zealanders. Unlike in Kenya, the data here only permitted me to separate out the social roles and relationship responses from everything else. Starting in a rural village on one of the outer islands, where people still live in traditional hereditary lineages, the average percentage of social-relational responses was nearly 60 percent. Moving to Rarotonga, the national capital and a popular tourist destination, the frequency of social-relational responses drops to 27 percent. In New Zealand, among the children of immigrants, the frequency of such responses falls further, to 20 percent. This stands close to the average for European-descent New Zealanders, who come in at 17 percent. New Zealand high school students are lower yet, at 12 percent. By comparison, American undergraduates are typically at or below this percentage, with some studies showing zero social-relational responses.

Complementing this work, many similar psychological studies allow us to compare Americans, Canadians, Brits, Australians, and Swedes to various Asian populations, including Japanese, Malaysians, Chinese, and Koreans. The upshot is that WEIRD people usually lie at the extreme end of the distribution, focusing intensely on their personal attributes, achievements, aspirations, and personalities over their roles, responsibilities, and relationships. American undergraduates, in particular, seem unusually self-absorbed, even among other WEIRD populations.[4]

Focusing on one's attributes and achievements over one's roles and relationships is a key element in a psychological package that I'll clump together as the *individualism complex* or just *individualism*. Individualism is best thought of as a psychological cluster that allows people to better navigate WEIRD social worlds by calibrating their perceptions, attention, judgments, and emotions. I expect most populations to reveal psychological packages that similarly "fit" with their societies' institutions, technologies, environments, and languages, though as you'll see the WEIRD package is particularly peculiar.

MAPPING THE INDIVIDUALISM COMPLEX

To understand individualism, let's start at the other end of the spectrum.[5] Throughout most of human history, people grew up enmeshed in dense family networks that knitted together distant cousins and in-laws. In these regulated-relational worlds, people's survival, identity, security, marriages, and success depended on the health and prosperity of kin-based networks, which often formed discrete institutions known as clans, lineages, houses, or tribes. This is the world of the Maasai, Samburu, and Cook Islanders. Within these enduring networks, everyone is endowed with an extensive array of inherited obligations, responsibilities, and privileges in relation to others in a dense social web. For example, a man could be *obligated* to avenge the murder of one type of second cousin (through his paternal great-grandfather), *privileged* to marry his mother's brother's daughters but tabooed from marrying strangers, and *responsible* for performing expensive rituals to honor his ancestors, who will shower bad luck on his entire lineage if he's negligent. Behavior is highly constrained by context and the types of relationships involved. The social norms that govern these relationships, which collectively form what I'll call *kin-based institutions*, constrain people from shopping widely for new friends, business partners, or spouses. Instead, they channel people's investments into a distinct and largely inherited in-group. Many kin-based institutions not only influence inheritance and the residence of newly married couples, they also create communal ownership of property (e.g., land is owned by the clan) and shared liability for criminal acts among members (e.g., fathers can be imprisoned for their sons' crimes).

This social interdependence breeds emotional interdependence, leading people to strongly identify with their in-groups and to make sharp in-group vs. out-group distinctions based on social interconnections. In fact, in this world, though you may not know some of your distant cousins or fellow tribal members who are three or four relationship links removed, they will remain in-group members as long as they are connected to you through family ties. By contrast, otherwise familiar faces may remain, effectively, strangers if you cannot link to them through your dense, durable social ties.[6]

Success and respect in this world hinge on adroitly navigating these kin-based institutions. This often means (1) conforming to fellow in-group members, (2) deferring to authorities like elders or sages, (3) policing the behavior of those close to you (but not strangers), (4) sharply distinguishing your in-group from everyone else, and (5) promoting your network's collective success whenever possible. Further, because of the numerous obligations, responsibilities, and constraints imposed by custom, people's motivations tend not to be "approach-oriented," aimed at starting new relationships or meeting strangers. Instead, people become "avoidance-oriented" to minimize their chances of appearing deviant, fomenting disharmony, or bringing shame on themselves or others.[7]

That's one extreme; now, contrast that with the other—individualistic— end of the spectrum. Imagine the psychology needed to navigate a world with few inherited ties in which success and respect depend on (1) honing one's own special attributes; (2) attracting friends, mates, and business partners with these attributes; and then (3) sustaining relationships with them that will endure for as long as the relationship remains mutually beneficial. In this world, everyone is shopping for better relationships, which may or may not endure. People have few permanent ties and many ephemeral friends, colleagues, and acquaintances. In adapting psychologically to this world, people come to see themselves and others as independent agents defined by a unique or special set of talents (e.g., writer), interests (e.g., quilting), aspirations (e.g., making law partner), virtues (e.g., fairness), and principles (e.g., "no one is above the law"). These can be enhanced or accentuated if a person joins a like-minded group. One's reputation with others, and with themselves (self-esteem), is shaped primarily by their own individual attributes and accomplishments, not by nourishing an enduring web of inherited ties that are governed by a complex set of relationship-specific social norms.[8]

For our first peek at global psychological variation, let's squash the individualism complex down into a single dimension. Figure 1.2 maps a well-known omnibus measure of individualism developed by the Dutch psychologist Geert Hofstede based initially on surveys with IBM employees from around the world. The scale asks about people's orientation toward themselves, their families, personal achievements, and individual goals. For example, one question asks, "How important is it to you to fully use your skills and abilities on the job?" and another, "How important is it to you to have challenging work to do—work from which you can get a personal sense of accomplishment?" More individualistically oriented people want to fully harness their skills and then draw a sense of accomplishment from their work. This scale's strength is not that it zeroes in on one thin slice of psychology but rather that it aggregates several elements in the individu-

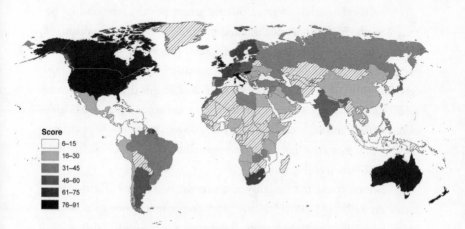

FIGURE 1.2. Global map of individualism based on Hofstede's omnibus scale covering 93 countries. Darker shading indicates greater individualism. Hatched areas indicate a lack of data.[9]

alism package. At the high end of the scale, you won't be shocked to find Americans (score 91), Australians (90), and Brits (89)—no doubt these are some of the WEIRDest people in the world. Beneath these chart-toppers, the most individualistic societies in the world are almost all in Europe, particularly in the north and west, or in British-descent societies like Canada (score 80) and New Zealand (79). Notably, Figure 1.2 also reveals our ignorance, as swaths of Africa and Central Asia remain largely terra incognita, psychologically speaking.[10]

This omnibus measure of individualism converges strikingly with evidence from other large global surveys. People from more individualistic countries, for example, possess weaker family ties and show less nepotism, meaning that company bosses, managers, and politicians are less likely to hire or promote relatives. Further, more individualistic countries are less inclined to distinguish in-groups from out-groups, more willing to help immigrants, and less firmly wedded to tradition and custom.

More individualistic countries are also richer, more innovative, and more economically productive. They possess more effective governments, which more capably furnish public services and infrastructure, like roads, schools, electricity, and water.[11]

Now, it's commonly assumed that the strong positive relationships between psychological individualism and measures like national wealth and effective governments reflect a one-way causal process in which economic prosperity or liberal political institutions cause greater individualism. I certainly think that causality does indeed flow in this direction for some aspects of psychology, and probably dominates the economic and urbanization processes in much of the world today. We've seen how, for example, moving to urban areas likely affected the self-concepts of Cook Islanders and Nairobi laborers (Figure 1.1).[12]

However, could the causality *also* run the other way? If some other factor created more individualistic psychologies first, prior to economic growth and effective governments, could such a psychological shift stimulate urbanization, commercial markets, prosperity, innovation, and the creation of new forms of governance? To summarize, my answers are yes and yes. To see how this could happen, let's first look at the broader psychological package that has become historically intertwined with the individualism complex. Once you see the key psychological components, it should be clearer how these changes could have had such big effects on Europe's economic, religious, and political history.

Before continuing our global tour of psychological variation, let me highlight four important points to keep in mind:[13]

1. We should celebrate human diversity, including psychological diversity. By highlighting the peculiarities of WEIRD people, I'm not denigrating these populations or any others. My aim is to explore the origins of psychological diversity and the roots of the modern world.

2. Do not set up a WEIRD vs. non-WEIRD dichotomy in your mind! As we'll see in many maps and charts, global psychological variation is both continuous and multidimensional.

3. Psychological variation emerges at all levels, not merely among nations. I'm sometimes stuck comparing country averages, because that's the available data. Nevertheless, throughout the book, we'll often examine psychological differences within countries— between regions, provinces, and villages, and even among second-generation immigrants with diverse backgrounds. Even though WEIRD populations typically cluster at one end of global distributions, we'll explore and explain the interesting and important variation within Europe, "the West," and the industrialized world.

4. None of the population-level differences we observe should be thought of as fixed, essential, or immutable features of nations, tribes, or ethnic groups. To the contrary, this book is about how and why our psychology has changed over history and will continue to evolve.

CULTIVATING THE WEIRD SELF

Adapting to an individualistic social world means honing personal attributes that persist across diverse contexts and relationships. By contrast, prospering in a regulated-relational world means navigating very different kinds of relationships that demand quite different approaches and behaviors. Psychological evidence from diverse societies, including populations in the United States, Australia, Mexico, Malaysia, Korea, and Japan, reveals these patterns. Compared to much of the world, WEIRD people report behaving in more consistent ways—in terms of traits like "honesty" or "coldness"—across different types of relationships, such as with younger peers, friends, parents, professors, and strangers. By contrast, Koreans and Japanese report consistency only *within* relational contexts—that is, in how they behave separately toward their mothers, friends, or professors across time. *Across* relational contexts, they vary widely and comfortably: one might be reserved and self-deprecating with professors while being joking and playful with friends. The result is that while Americans sometimes see behavioral flexibility as "two-faced" or "hypocritical," many other populations see personal adjustments to differing relationships as reflecting wisdom, maturity, and social adeptness.[14]

Across societies, these differing expectations and normative standards incentivize and mold distinct psychological responses. For example, in a study comparing Koreans and Americans, both parents and friends were asked to make judgments about the characteristics of the study participants. Among Americans, participants who had reported greater behavioral consistency across contexts were rated as both more "socially skilled" and more "likable" by parents and friends than those who reported less consistency. That is, among WEIRD people, you are *supposed* to be consistent across relationships, and you will do better socially if you are. Meanwhile, in Korea, there was no relationship between the consistency measure across relationships and either social skills or likability—so, being consistent doesn't buy you anything socially. Back in the United States, the degree of agreement between parents and friends on the characteristics of the target participants was twice that found in Korea. This means that "the person" "seen" by American friends looked more similar to that seen by American parents than in Korea, where friends and parents experience the same individuals as more different. Finally, the correlation between personal consistency across relationships and measures of both life satisfaction and positive emotions was much stronger among Americans than among Koreans. Overall, being consistent across relationships—"being yourself"—pays off more in America, both socially and emotionally.[15]

Such evidence suggests that the immense importance assigned by the discipline of psychology to notions of self-esteem and positive self-views is probably a WEIRD phenomenon. In contrast, in the few non-WEIRD societies where it has been studied, having high self-esteem and a positive view of oneself are *not* strongly linked to either life satisfaction or subjective well-being. In many societies, it's *other-esteem* ("face") that matters, not self-esteem rooted in the successful cultivation of a set of unique personal attributes that capture one's "true self."[16]

In WEIRD societies, the pressure to cultivate traits that are consistent across contexts and relationships leads to *dispositionalism*—a tendency to see people's behavior as anchored in personal traits that influence their actions across many contexts. For example, the fact that "he's lazy" (a disposition) explains why he's not getting his work done. Alternatively, maybe he's sick or injured? Dispositionalism emerges psychologically in two important ways. First, it makes us uncomfortable with our own inconsistencies. If you've had a course in Social Psychology, you might recognize this as *Cognitive Dissonance*. The available evidence suggests that WEIRD people suffer more severely from *Cognitive Dissonance* and do a range of mental gymnastics to relieve their discomfort. Second, dispositional thinking also influences how we judge others. Psychologists label this phenomenon the *Fundamental Attribution Error*, though it's clearly not that fundamental; it's WEIRD. In general, WEIRD people are particularly biased to attribute actions or behavioral patterns to what's "inside" others, relying on inferences about dispositional traits (e.g., he's "lazy" or "untrustworthy"), personalities (she's "introverted" or "conscientious"), and underlying beliefs or intentions ("what did he know and when did he know it?"). Other populations focus more on actions and outcomes over what's "inside."[17]

GUILT-RIDDEN BUT SHAMELESS

Based on data from 2,921 university students in 37 countries, people from more individualistic societies report more guilt-like and fewer shame-like emotional experiences. In fact, students from countries like the United States, Australia, and the Netherlands hardly ever experience shame. Yet they had more guilt-like experiences than people in other societies; these experiences were more moralized and had a greater impact on both their self-esteem and personal relationships. Overall, the emotional lives of WEIRD people are particularly guilt-ridden.[18]

To understand this, we first need to consider shame and guilt more deeply. Shame is rooted in a genetically evolved psychological package that is associated with *social devaluation in the eyes of others*. Individuals experience shame when they violate social norms (e.g., committing adultery), fail to reach local performance standards (e.g., flunking a psychology course), or when they find themselves at the low end of the dominance hierarchy. Shame has a distinct universal display that involves downcast gaze, slumped shoulders, and a general inclination to "look small" (crouching). This display signals to the community that these poor performers recognize their violation or deficiency and are asking for leniency. Emotionally, those experiencing shame want to shrink away and disappear from public view. The ashamed avoid contact with others and may leave their communities for a time. The public nature of the failure is crucial: if there's no public knowledge, there's no shame, although people may experience fear that their secret will get out. Finally, shame can be experienced vicariously. In regulated-relational societies, a crime or illicit affair by one person can bring shame to his or her parents, siblings, and beyond, extending out to cousins and other distant relations. The reverberation of shame through kin networks makes sense because they are also judged and potentially punished for their relative's actions.[19]

Guilt is different; it's an internal guidance system and at least partially a product of culture, though it probably integrates some innate psychological components like regret. The feeling of guilt emerges when one measures their own actions and feelings against a purely personal standard. I can feel guilty for eating a giant pizza alone in my house or for not having given my change to the homeless guy that I encountered early Sunday morning on an empty Manhattan street. I feel this because I've fallen below my own personal standard, not because I've violated a widely shared norm or damaged my reputation *with others*.

Of course, in many cases we might experience both shame and guilt because we publicly violated a social norm—e.g., smacking a misbehaving son. Here, the shame comes from believing that others will now think less of us (I am the kind of person who hits children) and the guilt from our own internalized standards (e.g., don't hit children, even in anger). Unlike shame, guilt has no universal displays, can last weeks or even years, and seems to require self-reflection. In contrast to the spontaneous social "withdrawal" and "avoidance" of shame, guilt often motivates "approach" and a desire to mitigate whatever is causing the guilt. Guilty feelings from letting a friend or spouse down, for example, can motivate efforts to apologize and repair the relationship.[20]

It's easy to see why shame dominates many regulated-relational societies. First, there are many more closely monitored social norms that vary across contexts and relationships, and consequently more chances to screw up and commit shame-inducing errors, which are more likely to be spotted by members of people's dense social networks. Second, relative to individualistic societies, people in regulated-relational societies are expected to fulfill multiple roles over their lives and develop a wide set of skills to at least some minimum threshold. This creates more opportunities to fall below local standards in the eyes of others. Third, social interdependence means that people can experience shame even if they themselves never do anything shameful. Of course, guilt probably also exists in many societies dominated by shame; it's just less prominent and less important for making these societies function.[21]

By contrast, guilt rises to prominence in individualistic societies. As individuals cultivate their own unique attributes and talents, guilt is part of the affective machinery that motivates them to stick to their personal standards. Vegetarians, for example, might feel guilty for eating bacon even when they are traveling in distant cities, surrounded by nonvegetarians. No one is judging them for enjoying the bacon, but they still feel bad about it. The idea here is that, in individualistic societies, those who don't feel much guilt will struggle to cultivate dispositional attributes, live up to their personal standards, and maintain high-quality personal relationships. Relative to guilt, shame is muted, because the social norms governing diverse relationships and contexts in individualistic societies are fewer, and often not closely monitored in these diffuse populations.[22]

LOOK AT ME!

Psychologists have been fascinated for over half a century by people's willingness to conform to peers and obey authority figures.[23] In Solomon Asch's famous experiment, each participant entered the laboratory along with several other people, who appeared to be fellow participants. These "fellow participants," however, were actually confederates who were working for the researchers. In each round, a target line segment was shown to the group alongside a set of three other segments, labeled 1, 2, and 3 (see the inset in Figure 1.3). Answering aloud, each person had to judge which of the three line segments matched the length of the target segment. On certain preset rounds, the confederates all gave the same *incorrect* response before the real participant answered. The judgment itself was easy: participants got the correct answer 98 percent of the time when they were alone. So, the question was: How inclined were people to override their own perceptual judgments to give an answer that matched that of others?

The answer depends on where you grew up. WEIRD people do conform to others, and this is what surprised Solomon. Only about one-quarter of his participants were never influenced by their peers. WEIRD people, however, conform less than all the other populations that have been studied. The bars in Figure 1.3 illustrate the size of the conformity effect across samples of undergraduates from 10 different countries. The power of confor-

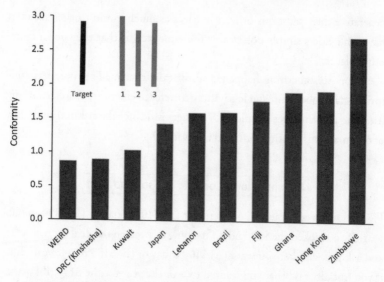

FIGURE 1.3. Strength of the conformity effect in the Asch Conformity Experiment across 10 diverse populations. The bars for WEIRD societies, Japan, and Brazil represent averages from multiple studies.[24]

mity goes up by a factor of three as we move from WEIRD societies, at one end, to Zimbabwe, at the other end.[25]

Further analyses of these experiments reveal two interesting patterns. First, less individualistic societies are more inclined to conform to the group (correlating the data in Figures 1.2 and 1.3). Second, over the half century since Solomon's initial efforts, conformity motivations among Americans have declined. That is, Americans are even less conforming now than in the early 1950s. Neither of these facts is particularly shocking, but it's nice to know that the psychological evidence backs up our intuitions.[26]

The willingness of WEIRD people to ignore others' opinions, preferences, views, and requests extends well beyond peers to include elders, grandfathers, and traditional authorities. Complementing these controlled studies of conformity, I'll discuss global survey data in later chapters showing that, relative to other populations, WEIRD people don't value conformity or see "obedience" as a virtue that needs to be instilled in children. They also don't venerate either traditions or ancient sages as much as most other societies have, and elders simply don't carry the same weight that they do in many other places.[27]

Suppose something happened historically that made people less conforming, less obedient, and less willing to defer to elders, traditional authorities, and ancient sages. Could such changes influence the cultural evolution of organizations, institutions, and innovation?

Marshmallows Come to Those Who Wait

Here's a series of choices. Do you prefer (A) $100 today or (B) $154 in one year? If you picked the $100 now, I'm going to sweeten the deal for next year and ask you whether you want (A) $100 today or (B) $185 in one year. But, if you initially said that you wanted to wait the year for the $154, I'll make the delayed payment less appealing by asking you to pick between (A) $100 today or (B) $125 next year. If you now switch from the delayed payment (B) to $100 now (A), I will sweeten the delayed payment to $130. By titrating through these kinds of binary choices, researchers can triangulate in on a measure of people's patience, or what is variously called "temporal discounting" or "delay discounting." Impatient people "discount" the future more, meaning they weight immediate payoffs over delayed payoffs. More patient people, by contrast, are willing to wait longer to earn more money.

Patience varies dramatically across nations, among regions within nations, and between individuals. Using the titration method just described, along with a survey question, the economists Thomas Dohmen, Benjamin Enke, and their collaborators measured patience among 80,000 people in 76 countries. Figure 1.4 maps this variation at the country level, using darker shades to indicate countries in which people are—on average—more patient. While those in lightly shaded countries tend to go for the quick $100 today (calibrated to the local currency and purchasing power), those in the darkly shaded countries tend to wait the year for the bigger payoff. For example, people from the most patient country, Sweden, can resist the immediate $100 and are willing to wait a year for any amount of money over

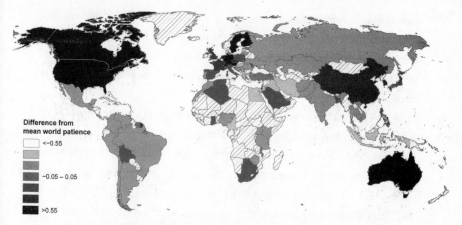

FIGURE 1.4. Global distribution of patience across 76 countries. Darker shades indicate greater patience. Hatched regions indicate a lack of data.[28]

$144. In contrast, in Africa, Rwandans require at least $212 in a year before they are willing to pass up $100 today. On average, around the globe, people won't defer gratification for a year until the delayed amount exceeds $189.

This map nicely highlights a continuous spread of global national-level variation in patience, including some variation within Europe. Starting with the most patient, the countries in black are: Sweden, the Netherlands, the United States, Canada, Switzerland, Australia, Germany, Austria, and Finland.[29]

Greater patience in these experiments is associated with better economic, educational, and governmental outcomes across countries, between regions within countries, and even among individuals within regions. At the national level, countries with more patient populations generate greater incomes (Gross Domestic Product, or GDP, per capita) and more innovation. These populations have higher savings rates, more formal schooling, and stronger cognitive skills in math, science, and reading. Institutionally, more patient countries have more stable democracies, clearer property rights, and more effective governments. The strong relationship between patience and these outcomes emerges even when we look at each world region separately. In fact, the data suggest that greater patience is most strongly linked to positive economic outcomes in less economically developed regions like sub-Saharan Africa, Southeast Asia, and the Middle East. That is, inclinations to defer gratification may be even more important for economic prosperity where the formal economic and political institutions operate less effectively.[30]

The same patterns emerge if we compare regions within countries or individuals within local regions. Within countries, regional populations possessing greater average patience generate higher incomes and attain more education. Similarly, comparing individuals within the same local area, more patient people get paid more and stay in school longer.

Delay-discounting measures are related to what psychologists call *self-regulation* or *self-control*. To measure self-control in children, researchers sit them in front of a single marshmallow and explain that if they wait until the experimenter returns to the room, they can have two marshmallows instead of just the one. The experimenter departs and then secretly watches to see how long it takes for the kid to cave and eat the marshmallow. Some kids eat the lone marshmallow right away. A few wait 15 or more minutes until the experimenter gives up and returns with the second marshmallow. The remainder of the children cave in somewhere in between. A child's self-control is measured by the number of seconds they wait.[31]

Psychological tasks like these are often powerful predictors of real-life behavior. Adults and teenagers who were more patient in the marshmallow task as preschoolers stayed in school longer, got higher grades, saved more money, earned higher salaries, exercised more, and smoked less. They were also less likely to use drugs, abuse alcohol, and commit crimes. The effect of steely marshmallow patience on adult success holds independent of IQ and family socioeconomic status, and even if you only compare siblings within the same families—that is, a more patient child does better than her sibling when they are adults.[32]

As with individualism, guilt, and conformity, a person's patience and self-control are calibrated to fit the institutional and technological environments that they confront across their lives. In some regulated-relational societies, there's little personal payoff to self-control, so we shouldn't expect the association between patience and adult success to be universal. Nevertheless, when local social norms reward self-control or penalize impatience, all manner of psychological tricks develop that ratchet up people's self-control. As we go along, we'll see how cultural learning, rituals, monogamous marriage, markets, and religious beliefs can contribute to increasing people's patience and self-control in ways that lay the groundwork for new forms of government and more rapid economic growth.

UN Diplomats Get Parking Tickets

Representing 149 countries, diplomats to the United Nations in New York City were immune from having to pay parking tickets until November 2002. With diplomatic immunity, they could park anywhere, double-park, and even block driveways, business entrances, and narrow Manhattan streets without having to pay fines. The effect of this immunity was big: between November 1997 and the end of 2002, UN diplomatic missions accumulated over 150,000 *unpaid* parking tickets totaling about $18 million in fines.

While bad for New Yorkers, this situation created a natural experiment for two economists, Ted Miguel and Ray Fisman. Because nearly 90 percent of UN missions are within one mile of the UN complex, most diplomats faced the same crowded streets, rainy days, and snowy weather. This allowed Ted and Ray to compare the accumulation of parking tickets for diplomats from different countries.

The differences were big. During the five years leading up to the end of immunity in 2002, diplomats from the UK, Sweden, Canada, Australia, and a few other countries got a total of zero tickets. Meanwhile, diplomats from Egypt, Chad, and Bulgaria, among other countries, got the most tickets, accumulating over 100 *for each member* of their respective diplomatic delegations. Looking across nations, the higher the international corruption index for a delegation's home country, the more tickets those delegations accumulated. The relationship between corruption back home and parking behavior in Manhattan holds independent of the size of a country's

UN mission, the income of its diplomats, the type of violation (e.g., double-parking), and the time of day.[33]

In 2002, diplomatic immunity for parking violations ended and the New York Police Department clamped down, stripping the diplomatic license plates from vehicles that had accumulated more than three parking violations. The rate of violations among diplomats plummeted. Nevertheless, despite the new enforcement and overall much lower violation rates, the diplomats from the most corrupt countries still got the most parking tickets.

Based on real-world data, this study suggests that the delegations from diverse countries brought certain psychological tendencies or motivations with them from home that manifested in their parking behavior, especially when there was no threat of external sanctions.[34] This is not, however, a tightly controlled laboratory experiment. Diplomatic scofflaws, for example, may have been influenced by the opinions of their passengers or by a greater desire to annoy police who they may have perceived as xenophobic. So, those from less corrupt countries like Canada might appear to be acting impartially and in favor of anonymous New Yorkers, but we can't be totally sure.

Now, consider this experiment, the Impersonal Honesty Game: university students from 23 countries entered a cubicle with a computer, a die, and a cup. Their instructions were to roll the die twice using the cup and then report the first roll on the computer screen provided. They were paid in real money according to the number that they rolled: a roll of 1 earned $5; 2, $10; 3, $15; 4, $20; 5, $25; and 6, $0. Basically, the higher the number they rolled, the more money they got, except for a 6, which paid nothing.

The goal of this experimental setup was to assess participants' inclinations toward impersonal honesty while minimizing their concerns about the watchful eyes and judgments of other people, including the experimenters. Participants were alone in a cubicle and could simply cover the die with their hand if they were concerned about secret surveillance. Of course, this meant that no one, including the experimenters, could really know what number a person rolled. But, while there's no way to know what any single person actually did, we have probability theory, which tells us what should happen at the group level, if people follow the rules.

Let's consider the percentage of people from each country who reported rolling a "high-payoff" number, a die roll of 3, 4, or 5. Since a die has six sides, half of the rolls should be these "high-payoff" values if people are reporting honestly. Thus, 50 percent is our *impartial benchmark*. By contrast, self-interested individuals should just report a 5. If everyone in a country were self-interested, we'd expect 100 percent of reported rolls to be high-payoff. This is our *self-interested benchmark*.

Not surprisingly, all countries fall between our two benchmarks. In WEIRD countries like Sweden, Germany, and the UK, the reported high-payoff rolls are about 10 to 15 percentile points above the impartial benchmark of 50 percent. Across countries, however, the percentage reporting higher rolls goes up from there to nearly 85 percent in Tanzania. As expected, every population breaks impartial rules; but, it turns out that some populations break such rules more than others.[35]

Figure 1.5 shows the strong relationship between the percentage of high-payoff reports in this simple experiment and an index of corruption for each country. As with parking violations around the UN, people from more corrupt countries were more likely to violate an impartial rule. Unlike with the diplomats, however, this is a controlled experimental situation in which even the experimenters can't figure out what any one person did. The difference must thus lie in what people bring into the cubicle with them.

It's important to realize that this is a quintessentially WEIRD experiment. The task measures people's motivation to follow an impartial and arbitrary allocation rule over one's own self-interest (why does 6 result in zero, anyway?). Extra money one obtains by misreporting a die roll doesn't obviously take money away from another person, but only vaguely from some impersonal institution—the research team or their funders. No one is directly hurt if you report a 5 instead of a 6, and anonymity is virtually assured. At the same time, any extra money you get by inflating your die roll, or by merely entering a 5 into the computer, could be shared with your children, parents, friends, or needy cousins. In fact, misreporting could be seen as an opportunity to help your family and close friends at the expense

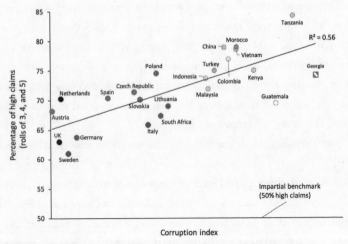

FIGURE 1.5. Relationship between the percentage of people reporting dice rolls of 3, 4, or 5 for each country and the corruption index. The darker the circle, the higher the country's score on psychological individualism, as shown in Figure 1.2. The hatched box for the Republic of Georgia indicates missing data on individualism.[36]

of some impersonal organization. In some places, it would be considered irresponsible not to violate such a silly rule to help one's family.

Why do so many WEIRD people act against their families' interests to follow this arbitrary, impartial rule, and expect others to follow it as well? Could this dimension of psychology influence the formation and functioning of formal governing institutions?

WEIRD PEOPLE ARE BAD FRIENDS

You are riding in a car driven by a close friend. He hits a pedestrian. You know that he was going at least 35 mph in an area of the city where the maximum allowed speed is 20 mph. There are no witnesses, except for you. His lawyer says that if you testify under oath that he was driving only 20 mph, it may save him from serious legal consequences.

Do you think:

a. that your friend has a definite right to expect you to testify (as his close friend), and that you would testify that he was going 20 mph, or

b. that your friend has little or no right to expect you to testify and that you would not falsely testify that he was only going 20 mph?

This is the Passenger's Dilemma, which has been done with managers and businesspeople around the world. If you picked response (b), you're probably pretty WEIRD, like people in Canada, Switzerland, and the United States, where more than 90 percent of participants prefer not to testify and don't think their friend has any right to expect such a thing. This is the *universalistic* or nonrelational response. By contrast, in Nepal, Venezuela, and South Korea, most people said they'd willingly lie under oath to help a close friend. This is the *particularistic* or *relational* response, which captures people's loyalty to their family and friends. Figure 1.6 maps the percentage

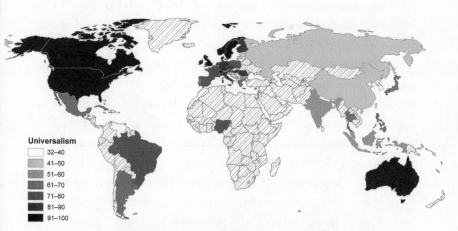

Universalism

32–40
41–50
51–60
61–70
71–80
81–90
91–100

FIGURE 1.6. Universalistic or nonrelational responses to the Passenger's Dilemma among managers in 43 countries around the globe. The darker shading captures the percentage of people who gave the universalistic response and were thus unwilling to help their friends. Cross-hatching indicates that no data are available.[37]

of universalistic responses across 43 countries, with darker shades indicating more universalistic and fewer particularistic responses.[38]

There's nothing special about the content of the Passenger's Dilemma. In places where people would help their friends by testifying, they also report a willingness to (1) give their friends insider company information, (2) lie about a friend's medical exam to lower his insurance rates, and (3) exaggerate the quality of the cuisine at a friend's restaurant in a published review. In these places, the "right" answer is to help your friend. People aren't trying to distinguish themselves as relentlessly honest individuals governed by impartial principles. Instead, they are deeply loyal to their friends and want to cement enduring relationships, even if this involves illegal actions. In these places, being nepotistic is often the morally correct thing to do. By contrast, in WEIRD societies, many people think badly of those who weight family and friends over impartial principles and anonymous criteria like qualifications, merit, or effort.

TRUSTING STRANGERS

How would you answer the famous Generalized Trust Question (GTQ): "Generally speaking, would you say that most people can be trusted or that you can't be too careful in dealing with people?"

The percentage of those surveyed who say that most people can be trusted provides us with a crude assessment of *impersonal trust* that we can use to map the globe. The GTQ has been so widely used that we can distinguish not only countries but also regions, provinces, and U.S. states. The darker the shading in Figure 1.7, the higher the percentages of people in that region who say that most people can be trusted.

WEIRD populations have among the highest levels of impersonal trust, although there's interesting variation within both the United States and Europe. Across countries, the percentage of people who generally think most people can be trusted ranges from 70 percent in Norway to 4–5 percent in Trinidad and Tobago. In the United States, people in North Dakota and New Hampshire are the most trusting, with around 60 percent of people generally trusting others; meanwhile, at the other end, only about

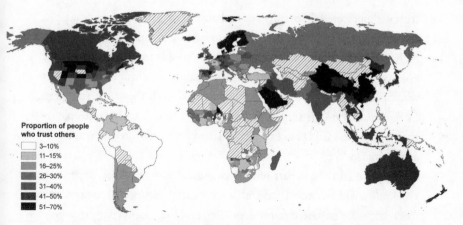

FIGURE 1.7. Impersonal Trust Map. This maps responses to the Generalized Trust Question across countries and among regions within certain larger countries. Darker shading indicates greater impersonal trust. Specifically, the higher the percentage of people in the area who said that most people could be trusted, the darker the shading. Hatched areas reveal our ignorance. For the United States, the shading gives the average percentage of "trusters" from 1973 to 2006 in different states.[39]

20 percent of people are generally trusting in Alabama and Mississippi. In Europe, regional variation is also substantial. For example, trust is twice as high in Trento, in northern Italy (49 percent), than in Sicily (26 percent), in the south. A similar pattern distinguishes northern from southern Spain.[40]

While the GTQ is useful, because it has been put to hundreds of thousands of people around the world, we should worry that it might not capture people's actual decisions when they confront a stranger in a situation involving real money. To explore this, researchers have combined data from hundreds of experiments in which they paired strangers, put cash on the line, and then observed how much trust was extended in making an investment. The data, from over 20,000 participants in 30 countries, confirm that in places where people actually do trust strangers in anonymous experimental settings, they also tend to say, when asked the GTQ, that most people can be trusted.[41]

However, although the GTQ often does tap *impersonal* trust, it can be misleading in places where a dense network of relational ties sustains broad trust without fostering sociality and exchange among strangers. For example, the dense social networks in China allow many populations to maintain high levels of trust with those around them ("people around here") without possessing much *impersonal* trust. The signature for this pattern emerges when people are specifically asked about how much they trust strangers, foreigners, and people they've met for the first time. In China, people report trust on the GTQ but explicitly distrust strangers, foreigners, and new acquaintances.[42]

Impersonal trust is part of a psychological package called *impersonal prosociality*, which is associated with a set of social norms, expectations, and motivations for impartial fairness, probity, and cooperation with strangers, anonymous others, or even abstract institutions like the police or government. Impersonal prosociality includes the inclinations we feel toward a person who is not tied into our social network at all. How should I treat this person? It's like a baseline level of prosociality with anonymous others, or a default strategy.[43]

Impersonal prosociality also includes motivations, heuristics, and strategies for punishing those who break impartial norms. In places where people trust strangers and cooperate with those they've just met, they are also more inclined to punish anyone who violates their impartial norms of fairness or honesty even if the violation isn't directly against themselves. At the same time, they are less inclined to seek revenge against those who've personally crossed them.

These psychological differences are strongly associated with national outcomes around the globe. Countries where people show more impersonal prosociality have greater national incomes (GDP per capita), greater economic productivity, more effective governments, less corruption, and faster rates of innovation. Of course, if formal institutions like courts, police, and governments are well functioning, it's a lot easier to develop impersonal prosociality, but how do you get there in the first place? Won't in-group loyalty, nepotism, cronyism (i.e., loyalty to friends), and corruption always undermine any effort to build formal governing institutions that are impersonal, impartial, and effective? What if a psychology favorable to impersonal prosociality arose first, prior to any complementary formal governing institutions?[44]

Obsessed with Intentions

Two men, Bob and Andy, who did not know one another, were at a very busy outdoor market. There were lots of people. It was very crowded and there was not very much room to walk through the crowd. Andy was walking along and stopped to look at some items on display, placing a bag that he was carrying on the ground. Bob noticed Andy's bag on the ground. While Andy was distracted, Bob leaned down and picked up Andy's bag and walked away with it.

How good or bad was what Bob did? (use this scale)

VERY BAD   BAD   NEITHER GOOD NOR BAD   GOOD   VERY GOOD

Now, try this one:

Two men, Rob and Andy, who did not know one another, were at a very busy outdoor market. There were lots of people there. It was very crowded and there was not very much room to walk through the crowd. Rob was walking along and stopped to look at some items on display, placing a bag that he was carrying on the ground. Another very similar bag was sitting right next to Rob's bag. The bag was owned by Andy, whom Rob did not know. When Rob turned to pick up his bag, he accidentally picked up Andy's bag and walked away with it.

How do you judge Rob in this situation? How good or bad was what Rob did? (Use the above scale.)

Most Americans judge Rob less harshly than Bob, seeing him only as "bad" instead of "very bad." Similarly, judgments of how much Bob and

Rob should be punished drop from "very severely" (Bob) to only "severely" (Rob). The sole difference between Rob and Bob in these stories is their mental states—their intentions. Bob stole Andy's bag while Rob took it by accident. In both cases, equal harm was done to Andy.

To explore the role of intentions in moral judgments, a team led by the anthropologist Clark Barrett and the philosopher Steve Laurence (and including me) administered a battery of vignettes like those above to several hundred people in 10 diverse populations from around the globe, including traditional societies in Amazonia, Oceania, Africa, and Southeast Asia. We aimed not for broad samples from whole countries or regions, as with much of the data discussed above, but for remote, rural, and relatively independent small-scale societies that still maintain traditional lifeways. Economically, most of these groups produce their own food, whether by hunting, fishing, farming, or herding. For comparison, we also included people living in Los Angeles. The various vignettes that people responded to focused on theft, poisoning, battery, and food taboo violations, and examined a wide range of factors that might influence people's judgments of someone like Bob or Rob.[45]

It turns out that how much people rely on others' mental states in judging them varies dramatically across societies. As usual, WEIRD people anchor the extreme end of the distribution, relying heavily on the inferences we make about the invisible states inside other people's heads and hearts.

Figure 1.8 summarizes people's responses to the above vignettes—our theft scenario. The height of the bars represents the difference between how harshly people judged Bob (intentional theft) vs. Rob (accidental theft). These scores combine measures of goodness and badness with how much the participants thought the perpetrators' reputations should be damaged and how much they should be punished. The results reveal the importance of intentions across these populations—taller bars mean that people weighted Rob's and Bob's intent more heavily for punishment and reputation as well as badness. On the right side, the populations in Los Angeles and eastern Ukraine gave the greatest weight to Bob's intentions, judging him much more harshly than they did Rob. At the other end of the distribution, the

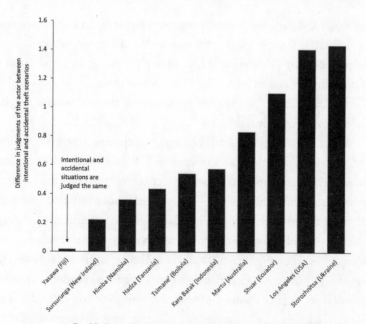

FIGURE 1.8. For 10 diverse societies, this plot shows the differences between the severity of judgments for the intentional vs. accidental theft scenarios (as presented for Rob and Bob, above). The judgments combine measures of badness, reputational damage, and punishment. The taller the bar, the larger the impact of intentions on the severity of judgments.

people of Yasawa Island (Fiji) made no distinction between Bob and Rob. Other groups, like the Sursurunga in New Ireland (Papua New Guinea) and Himba herders (Namibia), used intentions to shade their judgments of perpetrators, but the overall impact of intentions was small.

Patterns similar to those shown for theft in Figure 1.8 emerge for crimes like battery and poisoning, as well as for taboo violations. The importance of intentionality varies from zero in Yasawa, Fiji, to its maximum among WEIRD people.[46]

Differences such as these—in the use of mental states for making moral judgments—have been confirmed in subsequent research and aren't confined to comparing small-scale societies to WEIRD people. The Japanese, for example, are less inclined than Americans to weigh intentionality when making moral and legal judgments of strangers, especially in more traditional communities. The application of intentionality in judgment depends heavily on the nature of the relationships among the parties involved. Japan is noteworthy because its formal legal institutions are nearly an exact replica of America's, but those institutions operate very differently because people's underlying psychology is different.[47]

Many WEIRD people find these results surprising. Intentions, beliefs, and personal dispositions are so central to WEIRD moral judgments that the idea that people in other societies judge others based mostly or entirely on what they did—the outcome—violates their strong intuition that mental states are primary. But, putting relatively little importance on mental states is probably how most people would have made moral judgments *of strangers* over most of the last 10 millennia. This expectation comes directly out of how kin-based institutions operate in regulated-relational societies. As you'll see in later chapters, kin-based institutions have evolved culturally to create tight-knit and enduring social units by diffusing responsibility, criminal culpability, and shame across groups like clans or lineages, which downgrades and sometimes eliminates the importance of individual mental states in making moral judgments.[48]

Missing the Forest

In the year 2000, I had returned to the communities of the Mapuche, an indigenous population in rural Chile that I studied in 1997–98 as part of my doctoral dissertation. Living on small farms nestled among rolling hills in the shadow of the snowcapped Andes, the Mapuche still use oxen and steel plows to cultivate wheat and oats along with small vegetable plots. Extended families work together in activities like sowing and threshing that culminate in yearly harvest rituals, bringing together otherwise scattered households. I'd spent almost a year wandering around these fields and communities, often evading the angry dogs that protect people's homesteads, so that I could interview Mapuche farmers and sometimes administer psychological and economic experiments. I learned, among other things, that an oxen team can reliably pull your four-wheel-drive Subaru out of deep mud, and that it's possible to outrun a pack of guard dogs because they wear out before you do, as long as you're prepared to do seven-minute miles for several miles.[49]

On this trip, I had brought along some experimental tasks that I'd learned about while hanging out with the psychologist Richard Nisbett at the University of Michigan. Nisbett and some of his students, now all accomplished psychologists, had uncovered substantial differences between East Asians and Euro-Americans in their reliance on "analytic" vs. "holistic" thinking. The key distinction is between focusing on "individuals" or their "relationships." When thinking analytically, people zoom in on and isolate objects, or component parts, and assign properties to those objects or parts to explain actions. They look for strict rules or conditions that permit them to place individuals, including animals or people, into discrete categories with no overlap. They explain things by coming up with "types" (what type of person is she?) and then assign properties to those types. When thinking about trends, analytic thinkers tend to "see" straight lines and assume things will continue in their current direction unless something happens. In contrast, holistic thinkers focus not on the parts but on the whole, and specifically on the relationships between the parts or on how they fit together. And, as part of a larger web of complex relationships, they expect time trends to be nonlinear or even cyclical by default.[50]

Various experimental tasks tap different aspects of analytic vs. holistic thinking. In administering one of these tasks—the Triad Task—I presented individuals with a target image and two other images, labeled A and B. For example, I presented a target image of a rabbit, along with an image of a carrot (A) and a cat (B). After verifying what participants saw in the images, I asked them whether the target (e.g., the rabbit) "goes with" A or B. Matching the target to one of the pair indicates a rule-based, analytic approach, while matching it to the other points to a holistic or functional orientation. If the participants matched the rabbit and the cat, they are *probably* matching them using an abstract rule-based category—rabbits and cats are both animals. However, if they matched the rabbit and the carrot, they are probably prioritizing a specific functional relationship—rabbits eat carrots.

Seating the Mapuche within a global distribution, Figure 1.9 shows the results of a similar Triad Task administered through the website yourmorals .org to over 3,000 people from 30 countries. As usual, WEIRD populations pile up at one end of the distribution—in black—while the rest of the world spreads out across the spectrum. WEIRD people are highly analytical compared to most other societies. As for the Mapuche, taking their choices at face value, they were the most holistic, having picked the analytic choice only a fifth of the time, on average.[51]

Based on my Mapuche ethnography, I think that these percentages may mask even larger psychological differences. When I went back and interviewed each of my Mapuche participants, I learned that most of their seemingly "analytic choices" were in fact derived from holistic reasoning. For example, when the target image was a pig that could "go with" either

FIGURE 1.9. Analytic vs. holistic thinking across 30 countries using the Triad Task with 3,334 individuals. WEIRD countries appear in black. The Mapuche data derive from a slightly different version of the Triad Task.[52]

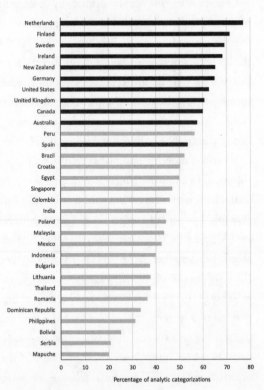

Percentage of analytic categorizations

a dog (analytic, both are animals) or a cornhusk (holistic, pigs eat corn), some Mapuche who'd picked the dog explained that the dog "protects" or "guards" the pig. Of course, this makes perfect sense: most farmers rely on dogs to protect their homes and livestock from rustlers (and pesky anthropologists). The Mapuche ferreted out a variety of contextually appropriate holistic relationships to support their seemingly "analytic choices." Truly analytic responses from them are likely below 10 percent.

Across societies, inclinations toward analytic over holistic thinking influence our attention, memory, and perception, which in turn influence our performance even on tasks with objectively correct answers. For example, after watching video clips of underwater scenes, East Asians remembered the backgrounds and context in memory tests better than Americans. Eye-tracking measurements reveal why: East Asians spent more time visually exploring parts of the scene beyond the focal or central animals and objects.[53] By contrast, Americans zeroed in on and tracked the center of attention while ignoring the context and background. These patterns of attention shaped what participants remembered.

If a population became more inclined toward analytic thinking and the use of intentions in moral or legal judgments, how might that influence the subsequent development of law, science, innovation, and government?

The Rest of the Iceberg

Self-focused, individualistic, nonconforming, patient, trusting, analytic, and intention-obsessed capture just a small sampling of the ways in which WEIRD people are psychologically unusual when seen in a global and historical perspective. We also overvalue the things we ourselves own (the *endowment effect*), overestimate our valued talents, seek to make ourselves look good (self-enhancement), and love to make our own choices. Table 1.1 lists some of the key psychological peculiarities discussed in this book, some of which I've already mentioned and others that we'll encounter in later chapters.

If you're surprised that WEIRD people are psychologically unusual,

TABLE 1.1. KEY ELEMENTS IN WEIRD PSYCHOLOGY

Individualism and Personal Motivation

- Self-focus, self-esteem, and self-enhancement
- Guilt over shame
- Dispositional thinking (personality): Attribution Errors and Cognitive Dissonance
- Low conformity and deference to tradition/elders
- Patience, self-regulation, and self-control
- Time thrift and hard work (value of labor)
- Desire for control and love of choice

Impersonal Prosociality (and Related Worldviews)

- Impartial principles over contextual particularism
- Trust, fairness, honesty, and cooperation with anonymous others, strangers, and impersonal institutions (e.g., government)
- An emphasis on mental states, especially in moral judgment
- Muted concerns for revenge but willingness to punish third parties
- Reduced in-group favoritism
- Free will: notion that individuals make their own choices and those choices matter
- Moral universalism: thinking that moral truths exist in the way mathematical laws exist
- Linear time and notions of progress

Perceptual and Cognitive Abilities and Biases

- Analytical over holistic thinking
- Attention to foreground and central actors
- Endowment effect—overvaluing our own stuff
- Field independence: isolating objects from background
- Overconfidence (of our own valued abilities)

you're in good company. Researchers in both the disciplines of psychology and economics, along with much of the rest of the behavioral sciences, were also rather surprised when experimental studies from around the world began to reveal striking patterns of psychological variation. Many had simply assumed that they could confidently make claims about *human* brains, hormones, motivations, emotions, and decision-making based on studies with American college students or any other WEIRD sample.[54]

Despite the growing evidence, many psychologists and economists remain either in shock or denial, as it turns out that much of the material in textbooks and academic journals, as well as in popular works of nonfiction, don't actually tell us about *human* psychology, but merely reflect WEIRD cultural psychology. Even now, over 90 percent of participants in experimental studies remain WEIRD, long after the alarm was raised. Nevertheless, the good news is that the gears of science are beginning to turn, as researchers from several disciplines are putting their shoulders to this mill wheel.[55]

Let's close by returning to the core questions of this book:

1. How can we explain the global psychological variation highlighted above?
2. Why are WEIRD societies particularly unusual, so often occupying the extreme ends of global distributions of psychology and behavior?
3. What role did these psychological differences play in the Industrial Revolution and the global expansion of Europe during the last few centuries?

To tackle these questions, we'll examine how the medieval Catholic Church inadvertently altered people's psychology by promoting a peculiar set of prohibitions and prescriptions about marriage and the family that dissolved the densely interconnected clans and kindreds in western Europe into small, weak, and disparate nuclear families. The social and psychological shifts induced by this transformation fueled the proliferation of voluntary associations, including guilds, charter towns, and universities, drove the expansion of impersonal markets, and spurred the rapid growth of cities. By the High Middle Ages, catalyzed by these ongoing societal changes, WEIRDer ways of thinking, reasoning, and feeling propelled the emergence of novel forms of law, government, and religion while accelerating innovation and the emergence of Western science.

Before getting to this main event, however, we first need to develop an understanding of human nature and societal evolution. What kind of animal are we? How should we think about the role of culture and cultural evolution? What's an institution, and where do they come from? How do culture, institutions, and psychology interact and coevolve? Why have kinship, marriage, and ritual been so central in most human societies? How and why do societies scale up in size and complexity, and what's the role of religion in this process?

2

Making a Cultural Species

Nature, when she formed man for society, endowed him with an
original desire to please, and an original aversion to offend his
brethren. She taught him to feel pleasure in their favourable, and
pain in their unfavourable regard. She rendered their approbation
most flattering and most agreeable to him for its own sake; and their
disapprobation most mortifying and most offensive.

—Adam Smith (1759), *The Theory of Moral Sentiments* (I.III.34)

As they howled and beat on his chest, William Buckley figured they were
going to kill him. Gradually, however, he realized that this small band of
Australian hunter-gatherers was rejoicing because they had mistaken him
for one of their deceased kinsmen. His rescuers believed that adults returning from the afterlife were light-skinned, like their newborns. Feeding the
band's misperception, Buckley had picked up the dead man's spear a few
days earlier, which the band had left implanted at the foot of his burial
mound. With this lucky stroke, Buckley effectively slotted himself directly
into their kinship network. His inability to speak, weakness, and general
ineptness were written off as the unfortunate side effects of death.[1]

Weeks earlier, in late December of 1803, Buckley and a few of his fellow
prisoners had escaped from an Australian penal colony and fled along the
wild coast of Victoria. He soon split from his companions, who all eventually died. On the verge of death himself, unable to forage food, locate fresh
water, or make fire, Buckley was rescued and restored to health by his new
Aboriginal family.

Buckley's band was one of several that together formed a patrilineal clan, which was one of about two dozen clans that composed the Wathaurung tribe. Clans in the region owned and controlled specific territories, which contained valuable resources like clam beds, quartz deposits, and spawning grounds. Territories were owned corporately by all clan members, and membership was inherited automatically through one's father.

Threaded together by marital and ritual ties, the Wathaurung were enmeshed in a tribal confederation that spoke related languages and possessed similar customs. Each clan belonged to one of two marriage groups. Everyone had to marry someone in the other marriage group, and sex with members of one's own marriage group was considered incest. Men arranged marriages for their daughters or sisters, often when they were children or even infants. As in most hunter-gatherer societies, men could marry polygamously, with prestigious hunters and great warriors sometimes accumulating five or even six wives, leaving lesser men with no wives and few prospects.[2] Buckley also described the white-streaked bodies, rhythmic drumming, synchronous dancing, and roaring fires at large ceremonies that periodically brought together diverse clans and neighboring tribes. These rituals sometimes included circumcision rites that initiated adolescent boys from scattered communities.[3]

Despite the ties of marriage and ritual, the most striking feature of Buckley's three decades with the Wathaurung were the violent conflicts that occurred among bands, clans, and tribes. In his life story, Buckley recounted 14 conflicts, which included several deadly night raids as well as pitched battles involving hundreds of warriors. In one instance, 300 enemy tribesmen amassed at the far side of a clearing. Buckley's band fled for their lives but eventually had to regroup, assemble allies, and defend their territory at great cost. In another horrifying scene, his band stumbled across the bloody remnants of a friendly band that had been massacred the day before. The dominant justifications for most of this violence involved disagreements over women—over who would marry whom—though in a few cases the attacks were revenge for the use of sorcery to cause "unnatural" deaths (e.g., sorcery-induced snakebites).

In describing one of these conflicts, Buckley gives us a glimpse of corporate guilt. A man from another clan had "lured away" one of the wives of Buckley's band. By "lured away," it seems that she simply preferred to live with a different man. When Buckley's band happened across the "thief's" band, the escaped wife was forcibly taken back. She ended up residing in Buckley's lodgings, much to his distress. Months later, in the middle of the night, the woman's jealous lover suddenly appeared, stabbed the sleeping husband, who was lying next to a snoozing Buckley, and fled with his mistress. A few weeks later, Buckley's band again encountered this group, but this time the murderer and "stolen" wife were elsewhere. To Buckley's horror, his band wreaked vengeance, killing both the murderer's adult brother and four-year-old daughter, who seemed completely innocent, from Buckley's point of view.

After 25 years with his band, saddened by the violent deaths of those closest to him, Buckley began to live independently from his tribe. Like other hunter-gatherers, he'd learned to fear and distrust strangers, since lone travelers could be scouts for raiding parties. Following standard practice, Buckley surrounded his little camp with low turf-and-bark fences to conceal his campfires at night.

After seven years of living on his own, having actively avoided contact with ships and sailors, Buckley finally decided to reenter the European world, at a new settlement called Melbourne.

Evolved to Learn

Buckley's experience in Aboriginal Australia highlights two central questions for understanding human nature. First, Buckley and the other fugitives utterly failed to survive by hunting and gathering despite starting with about four days' worth of supplies and entering one of Australia's most bountiful ecologies. They couldn't find enough food, start fires, build shelters, or make the necessary spears, nets, or canoes. That is, these men couldn't survive as hunter-gatherers on a continent where humans had lived as foragers for nearly 60,000 years. Why not? Since our species has spent most of the last two million years living as hunter-gatherers, one might think that the one thing our big primate brains should be good at is surviving by hunting and gathering. If they didn't evolve to make us better at hunting and gathering, then what did our big brains evolve for?

The second important question highlighted by Buckley's experience arises from the social world he encountered. After falling in with his Aboriginal family, he hardly mentions hunger, thirst, or the other deprivations that dominate the first part of his story. Instead, the action shifts to a world structured by social norms that organize people into clans and tribes, threaded into interdependent webs of culturally-prescribed obligations and responsibilities. Social norms prescribed arranged marriages, encouraged men to marry multiple wives, and effectively placed half of the local population under an incest taboo. Alongside marital ties, psychologically-potent rituals helped solidify the bonds within and between clans and tribes. However, despite these social bonds, violent intergroup conflict remained a constant threat and a major cause of death. In this world, people's survival depended heavily on the size and solidarity of their social groups. But, where did all these clans, marriage groups, rituals, and tribes come from?

The key to addressing both of these questions is to recognize that humans are a cultural species. Unlike other animals, we have evolved genetically to rely on learning from others to acquire an immense amount of behavioral information, including motivations, heuristics, and beliefs that are central to our survival and reproduction. This ability to learn from one another is so powerful compared to other species that we alone can accumulate increasingly complex bodies of cultural knowledge, related to everything from sophisticated projectile technologies and food-processing techniques to new grammatical tools and expanding packages of social norms. These topics form the core of my last book, *The Secret of Our Success: How Culture Is Driving Human Evolution, Domesticating Our Species, and Making Us Smarter*. There I lay out in detail how we can understand our species' origins, psychology, and culture from an evolutionary perspective. Here, I'll briefly sketch some of the foundations of this approach before applying it to the origins of WEIRD psychology and the modern world.

The way to approach the centrality of culture in human nature is not by opposing "evolutionary" or "biological" explanations with those based on "learning" or "socialization." Instead, researchers have incorporated culture under an expanded evolutionary approach by asking how natural selection has shaped our primate brains to allow us to most effectively learn the ideas, beliefs, values, motivations, and practices we'll need to survive and thrive in whatever ecological or social environments we end up in. Thus, we have evolved genetically to learn adaptively in ways that calibrate our minds and behavior to the environments we encounter.

Specifically, our evolved capacities for cultural learning have been honed to figure out *who* to learn from, *what* to learn, and *when* to use cultural learning over other informational sources like individual experience or innate intuitions. This is the *who*, *what*, and *when* of cultural learning. Let's quickly go through this triad.

To figure out who to learn from, adults, children, and even infants integrate cues related to a potential role model's skill, competence, reliability, success, prestige, health, age, sex, and ethnicity, among others. By preferentially attending to more successful or prestigious people, learners focus their attention and memory on those individuals most likely to possess useful information, practices, motivations, values, etc., that lead to greater success and status. By combining cues like prestige and success with self-similarity cues like sex and ethnicity (e.g., speaking the same dialect), learners can target their attention on those who possess the skills, strategies, and attitudes most likely to be useful to them in their future roles or communities.[4]

Besides influencing who we learn from, natural selection has also shaped what we pay attention to—like food, sex, and gossip—and how we process, store, and organize particular kinds of beliefs and preferences. For example, when given information about the diet, habitat, and dangerousness of novel animals, children from places as diverse as Fiji, Amazonia, and Los Angeles implicitly assume that this information applies to an entire category—say, "cobras"—and then preferentially remember the dangerousness of these species over information about their habitats, diets, or names. When they make mistakes, children err in adaptive ways, mistaking harmless species for dangerous ones instead of mistaking dangerous animals for safe ones. These kinds of *what-cues* influence our inferences, memory, and attention in ways that help us filter out, structure, and recall the really important information while avoiding costly mistakes.[5]

Of course, the cultural elements we acquire can themselves influence what we subsequently attend to, remember, and believe. One source of these culturally induced what-cues comes from the "fit" between newly encountered beliefs or practices and those previously acquired. For example, if you grew up believing both that the tribe in the next valley was evil and that eating human flesh is evil, then you're predisposed to believe it when someone tells you that the tribe in the next valley engages in cannibalism. Evil tribes do evil things. It all fits, psychologically speaking.[6]

This brings us to the question of *when* learners should rely on cultural learning over their own experience, personal information, or instincts. The answer is straightforward: when problems are difficult, situations are ambiguous, or individual learning is costly, people should rely more heavily on learning from others. To put these ideas to the test, my favorite experiments manipulate both the difficulty of a task and the size of cash payoffs for correct responses. Participants, for example, might be paid different amounts of money for correctly identifying which of a set of curvy lines is the longest. They can rely on their own direct perception or on cultural learning—on the decisions of others. The harder the task is—i.e., the closer the curvy lines are in length—the more people rely on observing other people's decisions and aggregating this information into their own judgments. In practice, this often involves ignoring one's perceptions and going with the choice made by a majority or plurality of other people. Further, as long as the task isn't too easy, putting more cash on the line for correct answers only *increases* people's reliance on cultural learning over their own direct assessments or perceptions. This implies that cultural learning will tend to dominate our experiences and intuitions in domains that are important but too costly or impossible to explore through personal experience or trial and error. Think religion and ritual.[7]

Crucially, these genetically evolved learning abilities aren't simply downloading a cultural software package into our innate neurological hardware. Instead, culture rewires our brains and alters our biology—it renovates the firmware. When learners watch others, they are actively calibrating their neurocircuitry in ways that move their perceptions, preferences, behaviors, and judgments closer to those of their chosen models. Consider the delay-discounting measures for patience from the last chapter (Figure 1.4). When given the opportunity to learn patience from another person by observing their choices, learners gradually adjust their delay discounting to match their model. To implement these psychological adjustments, brain scanning studies reveal that the striatum, which is part of the brain's reward and reinforcement learning system, processes any deviations between learners and their models and then induces proportionate plastic changes in the medial prefrontal cortex, which appears to encode the most appropriate reactions for a given context. Similar studies reveal how cultural learning neurologically shapes our preferences for, and perceptions of, expensive wine, handsome men, and good songs. By selectively attending to particular kinds of ideas and individuals under particular circumstances, our cultural learning abilities adaptively rewire our brains and biology to better calibrate them for navigating our culturally constructed worlds.[8]

By selectively filtering and recombining the beliefs, practices, techniques, and motivations acquired from others, our species' learning abilities give rise to a process called *cumulative cultural evolution*. Operating over generations, cumulative cultural evolution can generate increasingly sophisticated technologies, complex languages, psychologically-potent rituals, effective institutions, and intricate protocols for making tools, houses, weapons, and watercraft. This can, and often does, happen without anyone understanding how or why practices, beliefs, and protocols work, or even that these cultural elements "do" anything. In fact, in some cases, cultural products operate more effectively when people don't understand how or why they work, as will become clear when I discuss rituals and religions.[9]

What's amazing about the products of cumulative cultural evolution is that they are often smarter than we are—much smarter. These practices, which range from poison recipes to incest taboos, have evolved culturally to embody a tacit knowledge of the world that we—the practitioners—often lack. To see this, let's begin with a case in which there's a well-understood goal: making a deadly arrow poison used by Congo Basin hunter-gatherers. This is perhaps the deadliest hunting poison known, dropping prey in their tracks before they can vanish into the bush. The recipe combines 10 different plant varieties, including three powerful poisons—nightshade, poison rope, and sassy bark. Poison rope alone can bring down a hippo in 20 minutes. These ingredients are first thickened with fig latex and yam juice. Saliva is then stirred in until the mixture turns brownish red. Then, a marsh toad is added, presumably for its toxic skin. This concoction is brought to a boil before crushed beetle grubs and stinging ants are blended in. The resulting dark paste is set into a bark envelope, which is then placed inside the body of a dead monkey and buried for several days. Once it is unearthed, sap from the euphorbia tree is added to this deadly adhesive paste, which can then be applied to arrows.[10] Do NOT try this at home.

If you are a young learner, or a new arrival like Buckley, are you going to modify this protocol? Which plant, insect, amphibian, or processing step are you going to drop or change? Can you drop the monkey burial? Maybe; but perhaps that step catalyzes a chemical reaction that intensifies the poison. You'd be wise to first copy all the steps. Then, later, if you are particularly well stocked with game and a bit bored, you might experiment with procedural variations. But most of the time, you'll end up with less effective concoctions, meaning your prey may vanish into the bush. I suspect that it would take hundreds of experiments by a team of ethnobotanists to both understand what's going on chemically and eventually improve on this traditional recipe.[11]

Unfortunately, we don't know precisely how this ancient poison recipe culturally evolved. However, we do know something about cultural learning among Congo Basin hunter-gatherers and have explored the implications of different learning strategies for cumulative cultural evolution. The evidence suggests that aspiring hunters first learn from their fathers how to make arrow poisons. About a third of these foragers then update their fathers' recipes with insights from others, probably from the most successful and prestigious hunters. When transmission patterns like these are placed into cultural evolutionary computer simulations, or carefully manipulated in experiments with real people trying to learn new things, the results reveal how cultural evolution can assemble highly adaptive and complex recipes, procedures, and tools over generations without anyone understanding how or why various elements are included. In *The Secret of Our Success*, I lay out a broad range of other examples, from the use of particular spices in hot climates, which reduces the threat posed by foodborne pathogens, to a repertoire of fish taboos in Fiji that protect pregnant and breastfeeding women and their offspring from the dangerous reef toxins that accumulate in certain marine species.[12]

Over at least two million years, our species evolved in a world in which we were becoming ever more reliant on tapping into a growing body of complex cultural know-how to acquire the skills, practices, and preferences that were crucial for finding food, making tools, and navigating the social world. To thrive in this world, natural selection favored expanding brains that were increasingly capable of acquiring, storing, organizing, and retransmitting valuable cultural information. As part of this, natural selection beefed up both our motivations and our capacities for cultural learning, including the mentalizing abilities that allow us to copy other people's motor patterns and infer their underlying beliefs, heuristics, preferences, motivations, and emotional reactions. These abilities increasingly connected us with other minds.[13]

The sharpening of our cultural learning abilities further fueled cumulative cultural evolution to generate an ever-broadening array of more complex adaptations, thereby generating autocatalytic feedback between genes and culture. As the importance, diversity, and complexity of cultural products ratcheted up, natural selection gradually strengthened our inclinations to rely on cultural learning over our instincts and individual experiences because the tools, protocols, and practices that we acquired from others became far superior to anything that any single individual could possibly figure out on their own. Eventually, our species became obligate cultural learners, dependent on the inheritance of our communities for our very survival. We thus evolved as a species to put faith in the accumulated wisdom of our forebearers, and this "faith instinct" is at the core of our species' success.[14]

Understanding how our adaptive cultural learning abilities generate the process of cumulative cultural evolution helps illuminate the origins of our complex tools, nuanced practices, and sophisticated languages; but, what about the social world? How can we explain the clans, incest taboos, arranged marriages, and intergroup violence that dominated Buckley's Aboriginal life? At their core, these are questions about human sociality, about why we associate and cooperate with some people but avoid—and sometimes kill—others. To get a grip on this, we first need to understand what institutions and social norms are, and how they emerge. Then, with that under our belts, we'll explore the most fundamental of human institutions, those based on kinship and marriage. Understanding these primordial institutions and their psychological underpinnings will prepare the ground for examining why and how human societies scale up in political and social complexity in the ways they do, and why the path taken by Europe in the last millennia is so peculiar.

Evolving Societies

Human societies, unlike those of other primates, are stitched together by culturally transmitted social norms that cluster into institutions. For example, marriage institutions around the world are composed of social norms that regulate things like who individuals can marry (e.g., not stepchildren), how many spouses they can have (e.g., one at a time), and where the married couple lives after marriage (e.g., with the husband's family). For now, we aren't yet talking about *formal* institutions or written laws. We need to thoroughly understand the cultural evolution of institutions built on social norms like marriage and kinship before we can develop an understanding of what formalizing and codifying does to institutions.

If institutions are packages of social norms, what are social norms? To dig into this, let's focus on societies without governments, police, or courts— societies that possess hunting-and-gathering lifeways that provide insights into our Paleolithic ancestors. This will give us a baseline, so that in the next chapter we can consider how the spread of food production—agriculture and animal husbandry—shaped our social worlds and institutions.[15]

Social norms arise directly from cultural learning and social interaction— that is, via cultural evolution. Just as we can learn the proper way to mix hunting poisons, we can culturally acquire certain social behaviors or practices as well as the standards for judging others on those behaviors or practices. Once a practice coexists with the standards for judging violations, cultural evolution can generate a widely shared rule that, if violated or exceeded, will provoke a reaction from the community in some way. Many social norms prescribe or proscribe certain behaviors, and violation of them incurs the wrath of the community. Other norms are social standards that, if exceeded, inspire affirmation or respect from the community.

Here's one simple way that small-scale societies create stable norms: people learn that you shouldn't steal from those with a good reputation. If someone does steal from a person with a good reputation, then they earn a bad reputation. Having a bad reputation means that others can opportunistically exploit or steal from you with impunity. If the norm violator is a hunter, anyone can steal his arrows, bowstrings, or arrowheads when he's asleep, sick, or visiting other camps. If the violator demands to know who stole his stuff, other people just say they didn't see anyone. Here, envy, greed, and plain-old self-interest provide the motivations for punishing those with a bad reputation while a good reputation acts like a magical cloak that shields the well-reputed from the darker angels of their neighbor's nature. This produces a situation in which individuals have strong incentives to avoid breaking norms, lest they get a bad reputation and risk exploitation.

Everyone also has incentives to punish norm-breakers—people can steal stuff from their neighbors with impunity as long as they only target those with bad reputations.[16]

Building on such anti-theft or anti-exploitation norms, cultural evolution can support other cooperative norms, such as those related to food sharing. For example, norms in some hunter-gatherer societies forbid hunters from eating certain parts of their kills and demand that these parts be shared with others. This motivates hunters to share their kills, since they cannot eat the tabooed parts, and enforces any violations by assigning a bad reputation to deviant hunters, which means others can steal from them with impunity. Often these norms include other motivational beliefs, such as the notion that taboo violations will cause the entire band to experience poor hunting, or that violators are "tainted" by a kind of contamination that can pass to anyone who interacts with the norm-violator in any way, including by having sex with the person. Related beliefs like these encourage others to monitor their fellow band members—lest their entire group suffer poor hunting—and enforce ostracism of violators, lest they catch some of the meaty taint.[17]

The harnessing of meat taboos by cultural evolution to promote food sharing is not just an odd coincidence. To the contrary, our species' long evolutionary history with meat—a source of pathogens and illness as well as valuable fat and protein—has probably left us with a psychological readiness to learn meat-related avoidances and think about contamination. Cultural evolution has exploited this piece of our evolved psychology for its own cooperative ends. This is how cultural evolution often works, by tapping and repurposing our species' psychological idiosyncrasies in new ways.[18]

Taboos represent just one way to foster the band-wide food sharing that is central to the survival of mobile hunter-gatherers. What's impressive about food sharing in these populations is that while it's essentially universal as an outcome—all such foraging populations widely distribute at least some important foods—the patterns are maintained by diverse sets of norms. These variously involve ritualized distributions, transfers of ownership, and marital obligations (especially to in-laws), as well as taboos linking food, sex, and hunting success. In different populations, cultural evolution has mixed and matched many of the same elements to achieve similar outcomes at the group level.[19]

Broadly, then, norms are stable, self-reinforcing sets of culturally-learned and interlocking beliefs, practices, and motivations that arise as people learn from each other and interact over generations. Norms create social rules or standards that prescribe, forbid, or sometimes endorse some set of actions. These actions are incentivized and sustained by their reputational consequences—by the evaluations and reactions of the community. Notably, norms often include beliefs, such as the consequences of taboo violations for hunting success, that help motivate norm adherence, monitoring, and the sanctioning of norm-breakers.

INNATE ANCHORS AND CORE INSTITUTIONS

While cultural evolution can create an immense range of arbitrary norms, related to, for example, sex, rituals, and dress (e.g., wearing neckties), not all social norms are equally likely to evolve or remain stable. When the first social norms began to emerge, we were apes that had long possessed an endowment of social instincts about mating, parenting, social status, and alliance formation. The impact of cultural evolution, which was likely already up and running to some degree, would have only built on our primate psychology by sharpening and reinforcing our instincts for helping close relatives, caring for offspring, bonding with mates, and avoiding inbreeding (incest). Emerging norms would have tended to anchor on and extend these instincts. Tethered to more solid psychological moorings, such norms would have tended to outlast more arbitrary, free-floating alternatives.

This psychological tethering explains why our most fundamental institutions are rooted in kinship. Like other primates, humans possess innate altruistic inclinations toward our close genetic relatives—*kin altruism*. This evolved aspect of our psychology explains why mothers love their babies and siblings usually stick together. Kinship norms not only reinforce these powerful motivations, by creating social expectations in communities (e.g., siblings *should* help each other), but extend these expectations outward from the nuclear family to more distant relatives, and even to strangers. When more distant relatives get called "mom," "dad," "brother," and "sister," sets of norms and perhaps even some internalized motivations about the relationships get stretched outward along with the labels, effectively pulling more distant kinfolk closer over time. However, unlike many agricultural societies where norms tighten social networks, the norms of mobile hunter-gatherer societies allow—even compel—individuals and families to weave extensive, far-flung kin networks that stretch out for tens or hundreds of miles.[20]

In many societies, the innate anchor derived from our close genetic kin can be combined with the psychological power of personal names to create an institution that helps people stitch together broad individual networks. In Africa, among Ju/'hoansi hunter-gatherers in the Kalahari Desert, the names of people's close kin are used to establish analogous relationships with distant kinfolk, and even strangers, to effectively draw them closer. For example, if you meet a young woman named Karu and your daughter is named Karu, you can tell this new Karu to call you "mother" or "father." This pulls her closer and means that you should treat her like a daughter, which of course automatically implies that Karu is off-limits in the marriage department. This naming practice pulls people closer, both psychologically and socially, and provides a flexible way to enmesh everyone within a kinship network. Based on one calculation, people's naming networks stretched out in a radius of 60 to 115 miles. As in many such populations, Ju/'hoansi want to encompass everyone within a circle of kinship, and they get nervous around people outside of that circle.[21]

Alongside kin altruism, kin-based institutions also tap into our pair-bonding instincts, which form the core of marriage. In many ways, marriage represents the keystone institution for most—though not all—societies and may be the most primeval of human institutions. Pair-bonding is an evolved mating strategy found scattered around the natural world, from penguins and seahorses to gorillas and gibbons. It permits males and females to team up to rear offspring. In evolutionary terms, there's a kind of swap here. Females grant males preferred sexual access and stronger guarantees that her kids are in fact his kids. In return, males invest more time and effort in protecting, and sometimes providing for, her and her offspring.

By anchoring on these pair-bonding instincts, marriage norms can dramatically expand family networks in a couple of interrelated ways. For example, marriage norms in many societies constrain women's behavior and sexuality in ways that increase the confidence of both her husband and his family that her children are also his (genetic) children. Thus, many marriage norms increase *paternity certainty*. By exploiting our instincts for parental investment and kin altruism, greater paternity certainty not only induces more fatherly investment in children, but also firms up the kids' links to their entire paternal side. By recognizing and highlighting these links, marriage norms can effectively double the size of a new baby's kindred. Putting this into broader perspective, individuals in most other primate species don't know their fathers and thus effectively miss half of their genetic relatives.[22]

By firming up the links between children and their fathers, as well as between spouses, marriage creates in-laws, or what anthropologists call *affines*. Interestingly, even when affines are not genetically related, their evolutionary fitness is still intertwined in the children of the couple that connects them. For example, my wife's sisters and my mother's brother aren't related at all, but both share a genetic interest in my kids. By creating affines, cultural evolution has harnessed a shared genetic interest that no other species has managed to exploit. In many societies, these otherwise weak affinal ties are highlighted and nourished by social norms involving gifts, rituals, and mutual obligations. Among hunter-gatherers, meat-sharing norms often specify that some of the first portions of a hunter's kill go to his wife's parents.[23]

The effect of marriage bonds on kinship ties are big: a married man with just one brother and one daughter not only has affinal connections to his father's family and his wife's relatives, but he also has a connection to his brother's wife's family and eventually his daughter's husband's family. Consequently, within hunter-gatherer bands, over half of the average person's relatives are affines of some kind, not blood relatives. Without affines, hunter-gatherer bands would not consist of mostly relatives.[24]

In harnessing our pair-bonding instincts to build up larger societies and broader social networks, cultural evolution has often favored *lifelong* marital bonds because these bonds stitch large kin networks together. During his hunter-gatherer life in Australia, William Buckley's closest companion was his "brother-in-law," a relationship that survived both the death of the man he socially replaced and his sister, who created the affinal tie. By contrast, when natural selection built our pair-bonding instincts, the bonds were only "designed" to hold for as long as fatherly investment paid off in the health and survival of the kids. When it evaporates, the emotional or motivational door opens to forming new pair-bonds. Here, cultural and genetic evolution are often at odds, favoring enduring vs. temporary unions (respectively), and many modern couples find themselves caught in the crossfire between norms that prescribe lifelong unions and the ephemeral emotions of pair-bonding.

Marriage norms also regulate who can marry and reproduce with whom, which subtly structures societies in ways most people don't realize. One common way that cultural evolution has repeatedly managed this is by harnessing our innate aversion to incest to create sexual and marriage taboos that apply much more broadly than the small circle of close relatives circumscribed by inbreeding concerns. Natural selection has endowed humans with psychological adaptations that suppress our sexual attraction toward close relatives because of the likelihood of unhealthy offspring. By using a few simple cues, this psychological mechanism generates a sense of disgust that usually causes us to avoid sex with siblings, parents, and children. One important cue is growing up together. Tellingly, this developmental "proximity alert" sometimes misfires, leading to sexual repulsion between unrelated boys and girls who happen to grow up together. This effect is interesting, because you might think that siblings or other people who grow up together would be more inclined to fall in love, since they share so much already.[25]

The existence of innate incest aversion provides a psychological anchor on which cultural evolution has constructed potent incest taboos. By harnessing our disgust reaction at the idea of sex with siblings or parents, cultural evolution need only "figure out" ways to (1) stretch this feeling out to other individuals and (2) deploy it in judging others. It's that uncomfortable feeling you (might) get when you imagine consensual sex between stepsiblings. They aren't genetically related, but it still seems wrong. Among mobile bands of hunter-gatherers like the Ju/'hoansi, incest taboos prohibit everyone from marrying their first, second, or third cousins as well as anyone closer, like a niece. This pattern contrasts with norms in many agricultural societies, where only some cousins fall under incest taboos while others are preferred marriage partners.[26]

In her account of Ju/'hoansi marriage norms, the ethnographer Lorna Marshall shows how incest taboos extend our innate incest aversion. Despite having no knowledge of the health risks, Ju/'hoansi felt that the idea of sex with a parent or sibling was horrible, disgusting, and dangerous. In fact, it was so awful that some women refused to discuss it. However, when asked about sex with cousins, Ju/'hoansi didn't show the same strong emotional reactions; they nevertheless felt that it would be "like" having sex with a brother or sister. Essentially, they described a discomfort with the idea of sex with cousins based on an extension of the disgust they experienced at the idea of sibling incest. As we'll see, although these broad prohibitions on marrying all cousins are relatively rare in agricultural societies, they oddly reemerged in early medieval Europe, with substantial long-term consequences.[27]

By providing psychological anchors, our instincts for kin altruism, pair-bonding, and incest aversion help explain why marriage and family have long been our most persistent institutions. I'll refer to institutions rooted in the above-described instincts as *kin-based institutions*. Notably, however, included in these institutions are also norms that cultivate enduring interpersonal connections and relationships with non-kin, often by tapping other aspects of our evolved psychology in the same ways that marriage norms are built around our instincts for pair-bonding and inbreeding avoidance. Communal rituals provide a nice example.

COMMUNAL RITUALS

Describing the Ju/'hoansi trance dance, the ethnographer Megan Biesele observes: "The dance is perhaps the central unifying force in Bushman [Ju/'hoansi] life, binding people together in very deep ways which we do not fully understand."[28] Such psychologically-potent communal rituals, which forge enduring interpersonal ties, mend existing relationships, and enhance group solidarity, have been documented in most small-scale societies.

Inspired by such ethnographic insights, psychological scientists have begun to systematically decompose rituals into their key elements. Rituals can be thought of as ensembles of "mind hacks" that exploit the bugs in our mental programs in subtle and diverse ways. Let's consider three of the most common active ingredients found in communal rituals: synchrony, goal-oriented collaboration, and rhythmic music.

Synchrony seems to exploit both our evolved action-representation system and our mentalizing abilities. When moving in step with others, the neurological mechanisms used to represent our own actions and those used for others' actions overlap in our brains. This is a neurological by-product of how our body's own representational system is deployed to help model and predict others' movements—it's a glitch. The convergence in these representations blurs the distinction between ourselves and others, which leads us to perceive others as more like us and possibly even as extensions of ourselves. For evolutionary reasons, this illusion draws people closer together and creates a feeling of interdependence.[29]

Tapping our mentalizing abilities, synchrony also harnesses the fact that we humans unconsciously track who is mimicking us and use it as a cue that they like us and want to engage with us. This arises in part because mimicry is one of the tools we use to help us infer other people's thoughts and emotions—if someone frowns, you automatically micro-frown to better intuit their feelings. During synchronous dances, drills, or marches, our mental tracking system is flooded with false mimicry cues, suggesting that everyone likes us and wants to interact. Since we're usually positively inclined to such affiliative cues, and the synchronous patterns cause all participants to feel similarly, a virtuous feedback loop can emerge.[30]

In addition to synchrony, rituals also nurture relationships, enhance cooperation, and elevate interpersonal trust by bringing people together to work collaboratively on a joint goal, which often involves completing a sacred ceremony. Research with both children and adults confirms that working together on a shared goal deepens group solidarity and strengthens interpersonal connections.

Complementing synchronous movement and joint action, rhythmic music contributes to the psychological potency of rituals in three different ways. The first is practical: it provides an effective mechanism for individuals, at least those with rhythm, to sync up their physical movements. Second, making music together can serve as the joint goal for the group. And third, by operating through a second modality—sound added to movement—music provides a means to enhance the ritual experience by influencing our mood.[31]

Although the systematic experimental work on these ritual elements remains far from complete, the existing findings are beginning to suggest that these three effects are synergistic. That is, working together in highly orchestrated ways, in sync to rhythmic music, magnifies our sense of solidarity and willingness to cooperate more powerfully than simply the sum of the effects of each separate element. This "orchestrated teamwork effect" likely harnesses our *interdependence psychology*, which I'll discuss below.

These insights from psychological research converge with the observations of anthropologists. Enriching Megan Biesele's account of Ju/'hoansi trance dances (above), Lorna Marshall elaborates on the effects of this communal dance ritual:

> People bind together subjectively against external forces of evil,
> and they bind together on an intimate social level . . . Whatever
> their relationship, whatever the state of their feelings, whether
> they like or dislike each other, whether they are on good

terms or bad terms with each other, they become a unit, singing, clapping, moving together in an extraordinary unison of stamping feet and clapping hands, swept along by the music.[32]

The Ju/'hoansi dance is an explicitly collaborative effort to banish troublesome spirits that—as a by-product—heals social wounds and festering grudges.[33]

Synchronous movement, rhythmic music, and goal-oriented teamwork all interact to endow rituals with their power to infuse participants with communal feelings and an expansive sense of interconnectedness and interdependence. However, these are just a few of the psychologically active ingredients found in rituals. In later chapters, we'll encounter other ways in which rituals tap into and manipulate aspects of our psychology, and see how ritual has been one of the basic tools used by cultural evolution to hold human societies together.[34] Like many such "mind hacks," it turns our psychological bugs into social technologies.

Incidentally, if all this business about incest taboos, cousin marriage, and communal rituals seems weird, it's not. These practices are all commonplace in many or most human societies. You are the WEIRD one. Keep that in mind.

INTERGROUP COMPETITION AND COEVOLVED SOCIAL PSYCHOLOGY

Though I've given you only a glimpse of some of the institutions of mobile hunter-gatherers, it may already be clear that they are remarkably well designed for surviving in the marginal and unpredictable environments that have dominated our species' evolutionary history. Ju/'hoansi incest taboos, for example, compel parents to arrange marriages for their children with distant kinfolk, dramatically extending their social networks. These distant connections pay off by providing a safe haven when droughts, floods, injuries, raiding parties, or other disasters strike. Similarly, food taboos foster broad meat sharing, which mitigates the threat posed by streaks of bad luck for hunters. Communal rituals nurture social harmony, both within and across bands. These institutions create diverse safety nets, open trading opportunities, and firm up alliances.

How did groups develop institutions that effectively compelled individuals to bear personal costs like sharing meat or not marrying attractive cousins? There's no evidence that people designed these institutions or even understand what they do. When asked about their incest taboos, for example, no Ju/'hoansi suggested that they foster the formation of sprawling networks that interconnect distant families and thereby create a kind of social insurance. As you'll see, this is typical. Even WEIRD people, despite their immense confidence in the rational construction of their institutions, have little inkling of how or why their institutions really work.

Of course, not all norms are beneficial, and groups do indeed regularly develop arbitrary norms as well as those that favor powerful constituencies, like old men. Sometimes groups even develop maladaptive norms that are harmful to both individuals and their communities. However, social norms are put to the test when groups with different norms compete. Norms that favor success in competition with other groups tend to survive and spread. Such intergroup competition can occur through violent conflict, as Buckley experienced, but it can also occur when less successful groups copy the practices and beliefs of more successful groups or when more prosperous groups simply grow faster, through higher fertility, lower mortality, or greater net immigration. These and related forms of intergroup competition create a countervailing force that can favor group-beneficial norms over other cultural evolutionary pushes and pulls. Further, by mixing and matching different social norms, these processes can gradually assemble and spread increasingly effective, cooperative institutions.

This kind of competition has certainly driven the scaling up of human societies over the last 12,000 years, but its importance likely extends well back into our evolutionary history, before the origins of agriculture. The richest insights into the nature and extent of this ancient competition come from analyses of ethnographically and historically known hunter-gatherers. Wherever we look, from the Arctic to Australia, hunter-gatherer populations compete, and those with the best combinations of institutions and technologies expand and gradually replace or assimilate those with less effective cultural packages. For example, around 1000 CE, a population speaking an Inuit-Inupiaq language and carrying a new set of cooperative institutions, which included potent rituals and broad food-sharing norms, fanned out from the northern slope of Alaska and spread across the Canadian Arctic. Over several centuries, this population gradually replaced the fragmented and isolated hunting communities who had lived there for millennia.[35]

When detailed cases like these are combined with genetic and archaeological findings from ancient Stone Age populations, the emerging picture indicates that our preagricultural ancestors were likely embroiled in intergroup competition, including violent conflicts, that would have profoundly shaped their institutions, just as it has continued to do in more recent millennia. This suggests that during much of our species' evolutionary history, the social environments that we had to adapt to genetically were culturally constructed by the kinds of institutions that survived these ancient forms of intergroup competition.[36]

Here, I'll briefly describe three features of human psychology that have likely been shaped by this culture-gene coevolutionary process. First, the reputational damage and punishment associated with norm violations would have favored a psychology that rapidly recognizes the existence of social rules, accurately infers the details of these rules, readily judges the compliance of others, and, at least partially, internalizes the local norms as fast-and-frugal heuristics for navigating the social world. These selection pressures were likely powerful. In anthropologically known hunter-gatherer societies, norm-violators lost skilled hunting partners, fertile mates, and valuable allies. When such sanctions failed to bring violators into line, hunter-gatherers escalated to ostracism, beatings, and even executions. Among the Wathaurung, for example, Buckley notes that if a woman refused to marry her husband's brother after the death of her own husband (called levirate marriage), she would be killed.[37]

The second important feature of our coevolved social psychology arose because social norms increasingly wove webs of interdependence among the individuals within groups. Driven by intergroup competition, norms created social safety nets, enforced widespread food sharing, and fostered communal defense. To see how interdependence is produced, consider the food-sharing norms discussed above. Imagine we live in a small band of five hunters, our spouses, and two children per couple—20 people in total. The hunting is difficult, so we hunters only make kills on 5 percent of all days. Consequently, each nuclear family would go without meat for an entire month during one out of every five months, on average. However, if we share our kills, our band will almost never go a month without meat (less than 0.05 percent of months). Interestingly, now that we are sharing, the survival of you and your family will partly depend on me—on my health and survival. If I die, the chances that you and your family go a month without meat will increase by a factor of four. Even worse, my absence increases the chances that one of the other hunters or his spouse will die in the coming years—poor nutrition leads to sickness, etc. If another hunter dies, or leaves the band because his spouse dies, your chances of going a month without meat will increase by 22 times from the original situation, and now the chances of someone else falling ill or dying further escalates. From an evolutionary point of view, social norms like those that create food sharing mean that an individual's fitness—their ability to survive and reproduce— is intertwined with the fitness of everyone else in the band. This entangles even band members who don't directly contribute to each other's welfare: if your spouse nurses you back to health when you are ill, and you share your game with me and my kids, I need to worry about your spouse's welfare. The same point applies to many other norms, such as those related to common defense. In fact, the threat posed by violent intergroup conflict may be the most important domain of interdependence. Overall, the greater the number of domains such as food sharing and defense that are governed by cooperative norms, the greater the degree of fitness interdependence among group members.

The outcome is that social norms create communities in which the health and survival of each individual depend on almost everyone else. Psychologically, natural selection has shaped our minds to assess our interdependence with others, and to use these assessments to motivate affiliation, personal concern, and support for others. Cues of interdependence probably include eating together, sharing social ties, collaborating on joint projects, and co-experiencing traumatic events. And although people continue to assess interdependence throughout their lives, many of these cues operate most powerfully on children, adolescents, and young adults, when they are building their lifelong social networks. As you've seen and will see again, cultural evolution has fashioned rituals, marriage systems, economic exchanges, and other institutions in order to activate, manipulate, and extend aspects of our interdependence psychology.[38]

On a larger scale, beyond people's interdependent networks, cultural evolution also created a mosaic of diverse communities that generated selection pressures favoring a tribal psychology. Because of how we learn from others, cultural evolution frequently produces ethnolinguistic communities. These populations are marked both by a cluster of easily identifiable traits related to language, dialect, and dress ("ethnic markers") as well as by a set of underlying social norms governing domains such as exchange, child-rearing, kinship, and cooperation that foster interaction among group members. To help individuals adroitly navigate social landscapes populated by a diversity of such groups, natural selection has favored a suite of mental abilities and motivations for acquiring and using information about diverse tribal communities—those with ethnic markers and norms different from one's own—and for preferentially interacting with and learning from those who share one's own ethnic markers. Over the long term, these ways of learning and interacting have often influenced marriage norms, leading to prohibitions against marrying people from other tribal or ethnic groups—those not sharing one's dialect, dress, or other customs. Such marriage norms foster the formation of distinct tribes, ethnic groups, or castes built around similar institutions and shared notions of identity.[39]

Avenues into Your Mind

In the chapters ahead, I'll lay out how institutions related to kinship, commercial markets, and voluntary associations induced important psychological shifts that contributed to creating both WEIRD psychology and economic prosperity. The key to explaining how and why all this happened lies in exploring how our psychology shapes institutions and how institutions shape our psychology. By looking at marriage and kinship, including norms like incest taboos, I've begun to illustrate how evolved aspects of our psychology influence these most fundamental institutions. Now I want to turn the causal arrow around by briefly highlighting three ways in which institutions can feed back to shape our brains, psychology, and behavior.

1. *Facultative effects*: These are "online" ways that different institutional configurations shape our perceptions, judgments, and emotions on the fly, as it were, by altering the cues used by our brains to interpret our situation and calibrate our reactions. Such cues change people's behavior *in the moment* without altering their psychology in lasting ways. For example, we'll see that unconscious reminders that "God is watching" cause believers to be fairer and more cooperative with strangers.

2. *Cultural learning and direct experience*: In adapting to the incentives created by institutions, we use our evolved cultural learning abilities to acquire motivations, heuristics, mental models, and attention patterns from other people. For example, I discussed how cultural learning can alter our brains to adjust our willingness to wait for cash payments—patience. Of course, individuals may also learn through their own direct experience, as they get punished for norm violations or praised for excelling in culturally-valued domains like reading.

3. *Developmental impact*: Because much of our brain development occurs during adolescence, childhood, and even earlier, the social norms that shape our early life experiences may have particularly large effects on our psychology. For example, a growing body of evidence suggests that we may have evolved to make enduring calibrations to aspects of our physiology, psychology, and motivations based on stress and other environmental cues experienced

before age five. As adults, these early calibrations may influence our self-control, risk-taking, stress responses, norm internalizations, and relationships. By shaping our early lives, cultural evolution can manipulate our brains, hormones, decision-making, and even our longevity.[40]

Beyond these direct avenues into our psychology, cultural evolution also may help us successfully adapt to our institutional worlds by assembling practices or "training regimens"—often in the forms of games, stories, rituals, sports, and socialization practices—that hone our minds and bodies in ways that promote future success in our culturally constructed worlds. For example, reading bedtime stories may be a cultural practice that helps children train their brains in ways that promote success—culturally defined—in both school and work in WEIRD societies.

In considering this, keep in mind that intergroup competition and cultural evolution act on the entire psychological-institutional package, which includes all these avenues into our heads. Strong food-sharing norms, for example, may guarantee that fewer people experience acute food shortages as children or infants, thereby avoiding the long-term psychological shifts induced by such shocks. That is, the evolution of social norms that create well-functioning social safety nets ensures that a smaller percentage of children will experience the stressful nutritional deficits that trigger changes in their lifelong impulsivity, self-control, and response to stress. At the level of the community, these induced psychological shifts may improve the functioning of certain kinds of institutions such as banking and credit organizations. Thus, some institutions may spread in part because of how they ontogenetically shape a population's psychology.[41]

Perhaps the most important impact of the coevolutionary duet between psychology and institutions lies in how these mental shifts influence the kinds of new norms, ideas, practices, and beliefs that emerge and spread. Norms or beliefs spurned by a population with one psychology can be adored and adopted by a population with a different cultural psychology. As you'll see, the particular idea of endowing individuals with "rights" and then designing laws based on those rights only makes sense in a world of analytical thinkers who conceive of people as primarily independent agents and look to solve problems by assigning properties, dispositions, and essences to objects and persons. If this approach to law sounds like common sense, you are indeed WEIRD.

INSTITUTIONS CHANGE AND PSYCHOLOGY ADAPTS

All efforts to explain human psychology, politics, economics, and historical patterns rely on assumptions about human nature. Most treatises assume that people are either rational, self-interested agents or blank slates that await the inscription of their marching orders by murky cultural forces. Even approaches that take evolution and psychology seriously still typically adopt the "doctrine of psychic unity," the idea that everyone is more or less psychologically indistinguishable. Because they are rooted in WEIRD folk-models of individuals and society, these assumptions can usually be slipped in, unstated and unnoticed. Instead, here, I've outlined and grounded some of the key aspects about human nature that I'll be putting to work in later chapters.[42] The most important points to keep in mind as we head down the runway are:

1. Humans are a cultural species. Our brains and psychology are specialized for acquiring, storing, and organizing information gleaned from the minds and behaviors of others. Our cultural learning abilities directly reprogram our minds, recalibrate our preferences, and adapt our perceptions. As we'll see, culture has devised many tricks for burrowing into our biology to alter our brains, hormones, and behavior.

2. Social norms are assembled into institutions by cultural evolution. As powerful norm-learners, we can acquire a wide range of arbitrary social norms; however, the easiest norms to acquire and internalize tap deeply into aspects of our evolved psychology. I've highlighted a few aspects of our evolved psychology, including those related to kin-based altruism, incest aversion, pair-bonding, interdependence, and tribal affiliation.

3. Institutions usually remain inscrutable to those operating within them—like water to fish. Because cultural evolution generally operates slowly, subtly, and outside conscious awareness, people rarely understand how or why their institutions work or even that they "do" anything. People's explicit theories about their own institutions are generally post hoc and often wrong.

3

Clans, States, and Why You Can't Get Here from There

I believe that if our philosophers had lived among the Machiguengas [Matsigenkas] . . . they would have greatly doubted the concept of Man as a social animal.

—Padre Andres Ferrero (1966), a Catholic missionary who ministered to the Matsigenka in the Peruvian Amazon[1]

To understand the roundabout cultural evolutionary pathway that led to WEIRD psychology and modern societies, we first need to explore the more general processes that have driven the emergence of larger-scale cooperation, greater political integration, and broader exchange networks over the last 12 millennia. How has our species, since the origins of agriculture and animal husbandry—"food production"—managed to scale up from the relatively egalitarian, fluid networks of most Paleolithic hunter-gatherers to the vast societies of the modern world? As you'll see, the underlying processes are essentially the same as those sketched in the last chapter and were likely operating for tens or even hundreds of thousands of years before food production developed. Occasionally, these processes likely led some Paleolithic societies to scale up in size and complexity for a few centuries or more before collapsing under pressure from the rapidly changing climate. The crucial difference lies in how the emergence of food production altered and intensified the influence of intergroup competition on cultural evolution and how this shaped our institutions and psychology.

By laying out the pathways along which societies have *typically* scaled up, I'm setting the stage for showing how and why certain European populations during Late Antiquity and the Early Middle Ages were knocked off the usual trajectories and ended up on an entirely new pathway, one that hadn't been accessible before in human history.

At the dawn of agriculture, all societies were built on institutions rooted in family ties, ritual bonds, and enduring interpersonal relationships. New institutional forms always built on these ancient foundations by variously augmenting, extending, or reinforcing the inherited forms. That is, social norms related to family, marriage, ritual, and interpersonal relationships—kin-based institutions—only became more complex and *intensive* as societies began to scale up. Later, once purely kin-based institutions were insufficient to scale up societies any further, additional non-kin-based, non-relational institutions did develop. But, crucially, these institutions were always built atop a deep foundation of kin-based institutions. The fact that people couldn't simply wipe away their ancient kin-based institutions when building these new nonrelational or impersonal institutions creates what researchers call a strong *path-dependence*. That is, given that new forms always build on older forms, and these older forms are anchored in our evolved primate psychology, there are a limited number of pathways along which these new institutions can develop.[2]

How Ilahita Got Big

In the mid-20th century, anthropologists working in the remote Sepik region of New Guinea noticed that villages rarely exceeded about 300 people, of whom about 80 were men. The 300 were divided into a handful of patrilineal clans. When communities exceeded this size, cracks inevitably began to appear, and eventually social ruptures occurred along clan lines. Larger villages fractured into feuding hamlets and pushed away from each other to reduce conflicts. Though these explosions were typically sparked by disagreements about marriage, adultery, or witchcraft-induced deaths, they often ignited a pyre of nagging grievances.[3]

The relatively small size of these communities is puzzling, since warfare and raiding posed a persistent and deadly threat. Because different villages had roughly the same weapons and military tactics, greater numbers could make all the difference. Larger communities were safer and more secure, so people had life-and-death incentives to "make it work" and grow larger. Nevertheless, there seemed to be an invisible ceiling on the scale of cooperation.[4]

There was one striking exception to the "300 rule": an Arapesh community called Ilahita had integrated 39 clans into a population of over 2,500 people. Ilahita's existence put to rest simple explanations for the 300 rule based on ecological or economic constraints, since Ilahita's environment and technology were indistinguishable from those of surrounding communities. As elsewhere, villagers used stone tools and digging sticks to grow yams, taro, and sago (the starchy pith of palms) and used nets to hunt pigs, wallabies, and cassowaries.[5]

In the late 1960s, the anthropologist Donald Tuzin set off to investigate. His questions were simple: How was Ilahita able to scale up? Why didn't this community break up like all the others?

Tuzin's detailed study reveals how Ilahita's particular package of social norms and beliefs about rituals and gods built emotional bridges across clans, fostered internal harmony, and nurtured solidarity across the entire village. This cultural package stitched Ilahita's clans and hamlets into a unified whole, one capable of larger-scale cooperation and communal defense. The nexus of Ilahita's social norms centered on its version of a ritual cult called the Tambaran. The Tambaran had been adopted by a number of Sepik groups over several generations, but as you'll see, Ilahita's version was unique.

Like most communities in the region, Ilahita was organized into patrilineal clans, which usually consisted of several related lineages. Clan members saw themselves as connected by descent through their fathers from an ancestor god. Each clan jointly owned land and shared responsibility for each other's actions. Marriages were arranged, often for infant daughters or sisters, and wives moved to live in their husbands' hamlets (patrilocal residence). Men could marry polygynously, so older and more prestigious men typically married additional, younger wives.[6]

Unlike other Sepik communities, however, Ilahita's clans and hamlets were crosscut by a complex organization of eight paired ritual groups. As part of the Tambaran, these groups organized all rituals, along with much of daily life. The highest-level pairing divided the village into two parts, which we'll call ritual groups A and B. Groups A and B were each then divided in half; label these halves 1 and 2. Crucially, these second-tier divisions crosscut the first-tier ritual groups, so at this point, we have subgroups A_1, B_1, A_2, and B_2. Hence, people in A_2 have a link with those in B_2: both are in subgroup 2, and social norms dictated that they would sometimes need to work together on ritual tasks. Each subgroup was then further divided into two sub-subgroups that crosscut the higher levels. This continued down for five more tiers.

These ritual groups possessed a variety of reciprocal responsibilities that together threaded a network of mutual obligations that crisscrossed the entire village. For example, while every household raised pigs, it was considered disgusting to eat one's own pigs. People felt that eating one's own pigs would be like eating one's own children. Instead, members of one ritual group (e.g., group A) gave pigs to the other half (group B). This imbued even simple activities like pig rearing with sacred meaning while at the same time threading greater economic interdependence through the population. At communal ceremonies, ritual groups alternated administering initiation rites to the men of their paired ritual group. Ilahita males had to pass through five different initiation rites. Only by completing these rites could boys become men, earn the privilege to marry, acquire secret ritual knowledge, and gain political power. However, sacred beliefs required that these rites be performed by the opposite ritual group. So, to become a respected man and ascend the ritual (and political) hierarchy, all males were dependent on those in other Ilahita clans.

Alongside these ritual obligations, Tambaran norms also called for the entire village to work together in large community projects. Vastly larger than other structures in the community, the spirit house in Figure 3.1 was one such project.

Consistent with much psychological research on rituals, Tuzin's ethnography suggests that these mutual obligations and joint projects built emotional bonds among individuals and—most importantly in this context—across clans and hamlets. Much of this effect probably comes from tapping our evolved interdependence psychology. Interestingly, this isn't "real" interdependence, as in modern societies, where none of us would survive without massive economic exchange, but a kind of culturally constructed interdependence. Clans alone, as they did elsewhere in the Sepik, could have been economically independent, growing yams, raising pigs, and conducting initiation rites all on their own. However, Ilahita's Tambaran gods forbade such activities, and thus imposed a kind of "artificial" interdependence.[7]

Ilahita's Tambaran also incorporated psychologically potent communal rituals. Along with joint music-making and synchronous dance, the Tambaran gods demanded what anthropologists call *rites of terror*. Often administered to adolescent boys, these rites put participants through pain, isolation, deprivation, and frightening experiences involving darkness, masked figures, and unnatural sounds. Here again, new psychological evidence confirms old anthropological hunches: experiencing terror *together* forges powerful memories and deep emotional connections that bind participants for a lifetime. This creates the "band of brothers" phenomenon that emerges among soldiers who have faced combat together. In this institutionalized form, however, such rituals draw together young males from different clans and actively induce these binding psychological effects—thereby forging enduring interpersonal bonds in each new generation.[8]

Though rites of terror have evolved independently in small-scale societies all over the world, Ilahita had a particularly intense package, with five initiation levels. The sequence began at around age five. After being taken from their mothers, boys were introduced to the high-pageantry world of all-male rites by having stinging nettles rubbed on their scrota. They were then

FIGURE 3.1. Ritual dancing in front of the Tambaran spirit house. In this ritual, the Nggwal Bunafunei, some women are carrying spears and several—wives of the initiates—are dancing backward, praising the beauty magic of their husbands, who are at the left side of the circle. The wives are holding up shell rings in praise. On their backs, some of the women are wearing fiber bags filled with shells that jingle in rhythm as they dance.[9]

warned never to reveal anything about these special rituals to women, under pain of death. At around age nine, their second initiation culminated in the slashing of their penises with a bamboo razor. During adolescence, initiates were isolated in a secret village for months and prohibited from eating several desirable foods. In the most senior rites, initiates had to hunt down and kill men from enemy communities in order to "feed" the Tambaran gods. These emotionally intense rites further galvanized the bonds holding Ilahita's clans and hamlets together.[10]

This social and ritual system was infused with a powerful set of supernatural beliefs. Unlike their ancestor gods, who presided narrowly over particular clans, the Tambaran gods governed the entire community—they were village-level gods. Villagers believed that their community's prosperity and prestige derived from the proper performance of the Tambaran rituals, because those rituals satisfied the Tambaran gods, who, in return, blessed their community with harmony, security, and success. When village amity waned, the elders assumed that people hadn't been diligently performing the rituals properly and would call for supplemental rites to better satiate the gods. Although the elders had the causality wrong, performing additional rituals still would have had the desired psychological effect—mending and solidifying social harmony. By Tuzin's account, this was indeed what happened when such special rituals were performed.

The Tambaran gods also fostered greater harmony through their perceived willingness to punish villagers. Unlike the broad-based punishing powers of the powerful and moralizing gods found in today's world religions, the Tambaran gods were only believed to punish people for inadequate ritual performances. This supernatural punishment, however, would have helped guarantee that villagers conscientiously attended to the rituals, which is crucial since the rituals were doing important social-psychological work in bonding the community.

The Tambaran gods' supernatural punishment may have also suppressed sorcery accusations and their associated cycles of violence. In New Guinea, as in many societies, people don't see most deaths as accidental. Deaths that WEIRD people would consider as due to "natural causes" (e.g., infections or snakebites) are often perceived as caused by sorcery—i.e., murder by magic. An unexpected death, especially of someone in their prime, often provoked sorcery accusations, and sometimes led to revenge-driven slugfests between clans that could persist over years or even generations. After the Tambaran arrived in Ilahita, many of the deaths that villagers would have previously perceived as sorcery-induced were instead attributed to the anger of the Tambaran gods, who were believed to strike people down for failing in their ritual obligations. This possibility reoriented people's suspicions away from their fellow villagers and toward the gods. These new supernatural beliefs thus short-circuited one of the prime fuses that would have otherwise led to community disintegration.[11]

Overall, the Tambaran was a complex institution that integrated new organizational norms (ritual groups), routine practices (e.g., raising pigs), potent initiation rites, and beliefs about supernatural punishment in a manner that restructured social life. These cultural elements tapped into several aspects of innate human psychology in ways that strengthened and sustained the emotional bonds among Ilahita's clans. This enabled Ilahita to maintain a large community of many clans while other villages fractured and fell apart.

But, where did Ilahita's Tambaran come from?

Let's start with where it didn't come from. Tuzin's investigation reveals that the Tambaran wasn't designed by any individual or any group. When Tuzin showed the elders how elegantly the Tambaran partitioned and integrated their community, they were as surprised as he was. They'd followed simple prohibitions, prescriptions, and rules of thumb about people's roles, responsibilities, and obligations that created the system without anyone having a global understanding of how it all fit together. As in nearly all societies, individuals don't consciously design the most important elements of their institutions and certainly don't understand how or why they work.[12]

Instead, the Tambaran evolved over generations, morphing into diverse forms as it diffused across the Sepik. Ilahita just happened to end up with the best working version. Here's the story that Tuzin pieced together:

In the mid-19th century, a Sepik tribe called the Abelam began aggressively expanding, seizing territory, and sending families and clans fleeing from their villages. Because they were more militarily successful than other groups, it was widely assumed that the Abelam had developed some new rituals that had permitted them to tap into powerful supernatural forces. Around 1870, Ilahita's elders learned about the Tambaran from some of these refugees. It was decided that Ilahita's best chance to withstand the coming onslaught from the Abelam was to copy the Tambaran from them—to fight fire with fire. Piecing together the refugees' descriptions of the Tambaran, Ilahita assembled its own version.

Crucially, while Ilahita's Tambaran did end up resembling that of the Abelam, a number of consequential "copying errors" were inadvertently introduced during the reconstruction. There were three key errors. First, Ilahita "misfit" the ritual group organization to their clan structures, accidentally producing a greater degree of crosscutting and integration. The Ilahita system, for example, put brothers in different ritual groups and partitioned clans. The Abelam version, by contrast, left brothers together and clans fully encompassed within single ritual groups. Second, a misunderstanding created bigger, more powerful Tambaran gods. The Tambaran gods have specific names. Among the Abelam, they are the names of their clans' ancestor gods—so their Tambaran gods are just an ensemble of their ancestor gods. In Ilahita, the clans each already had their own ancestor gods. Not recognizing the divine Abelam names, Ilahita's elders superimposed the Tambaran gods over their own clan gods, effectively creating village-level gods where none had previously existed. Although it might seem odd to measure the size of a god, this copying error swelled the Tambaran gods by a factor of 39—instead of sitting at the apex of only one clan, these gods ascended to preside over 39 clans. Finally, Ilahita's elders simply appended the Abelam's four initiation rites to their own single Arapesh rite, giving them five initiation levels. By pushing up the age at which senior men passed out of the Tambaran system, this change effectively made the most powerful elders a decade older, and hopefully wiser, than among the Abelam.[13]

With this retrofit of the Tambaran, Ilahita halted the relentless advance of the Abelam and expanded its own territory. Ilahita swelled further over the subsequent decades as refugees from other villages flooded in. Despite their lack of kinship or marital ties to Ilahita's clans, immigrants were woven into the community through the Tambaran ritual system.

SCALING UP

Ilahita highlights how hard it is to sustain broad cooperation and scale up societies. Even when facing mortal threats, most Sepik communities couldn't get more than about 80 men to live, work, and fight together. Instead, people were killed, captured, or driven off their lands. Moreover, while the 300 rule represented a glass ceiling on cooperation, even this degree of cooperation wasn't easy, automatic, or effortless. Elsewhere in the Sepik, where warfare and raiding were less intense, other Arapesh populations preferred to live in smaller hamlets, with fewer than 90 people.

This case gives us a glimpse of the two key processes that drive up the scale and intensity of cooperation: (1) intergroup competition and (2) the "fit" between different social norms and institutions. Intergroup competition operates through at least five different processes, three of which appear in the Sepik:[14]

1. *War and raiding*: Any social norms, beliefs, or practices that generate greater cooperation, stronger in-group solidarity, or other technological, military, or economic advantages can spread via intergroup conflict, as groups with more competitive institutions drive out, eliminate, or assimilate those with less competitive institutions. Abelam institutions were spreading via this process in the Sepik.[15]

2. *Differential migration*: Whenever possible, people will migrate from less prosperous or secure communities to more prosperous and secure ones. Since immigrants, and especially their children, adopt the local customs, this differential migration drives the

spread of institutions that generate prosperity and security, as more successful communities grow at the expense of less successful ones. This is what happened as the refugees created by the Abelam onslaught fled into Ilahita's secure embrace.[16]

3. *Prestige-biased group transmission*: Individuals and communities preferentially attend to and learn from more successful or prestigious groups. This causes social norms and beliefs to diffuse from more successful groups to less successful ones and can drive the spread of more competitive institutions. However, since people often cannot distinguish what makes a group successful, this also results in the transmission of many norms and practices that have nothing to do with success, including things like hairstyles and music preferences. In Ilahita, the elders decided to explicitly copy the Tambaran from the successful Abelam. Along the way, Ilahita and other communities also copied the Abelam's elaborate yam-growing magic, which probably didn't contribute to anyone's success.[17]

4. *Differential group survival without conflict*: In hostile environments, only groups with institutions that promote extensive cooperation and sharing can survive at all. Groups without these norms either retreat into more amicable environments or go extinct during droughts, hurricanes, floods, or other shocks. The right institutions allow groups to thrive in ecological niches where other groups cannot. This process can operate even if groups never meet each other.[18]

5. *Differential reproduction*: Norms can influence the rate at which individuals have children. Since children tend to share the norms of their community, any norms that increase birth rates or slow death rates will tend to spread. Some world religions, for example, have spread rapidly due to their fertility-friendly beliefs, such as those involving gods that eschew birth control or nonreproductive sex.[19]

Once a new norm emerges in one group that improves cooperation, intergroup competition can grab ahold of it and spread it widely through one or more of the above processes. As we saw with the Tambaran, these competitive intergroup processes will aggregate and recombine social norms over generations in ways that permit societies to integrate, unite, and expand.

However, in thinking about cultural evolution, it's important to realize that intergroup competition is just one force among many, and that competition occurs at all levels—among individuals, families, and clans within larger populations. Clans provide a psychologically potent means to generate solidarity among members, in part by reducing internal conflicts. But, as happened in the Sepik, clans often can't get along, so scaling up to larger societies requires either unifying them or dissolving them. In fact, the more effectively norms galvanize cooperation within subgroups, the more challenging it can be to unite them and scale up.

The process of scaling up is also influenced by the social and psychological "fit" between existing institutions and new norms and beliefs. Novel norms and beliefs must emerge from a group's existing cultural repertoire, or, if copied from other groups, they must mesh with the indigenous institutions. Channeling and constraining the effects of intergroup competition creates the path-dependence I mentioned: any given set of institutions has only a limited number of likely "next moves" because of the "fit" between social norms, beliefs, and existing institutions. Ilahita, for example, was probably susceptible to adopting the Abelam's four levels of initiation because they already had one such rite and could simply append the new rituals. Similarly, their dual ritual-group institution would have been unsustainable except for Ilahita's flexible adoption norms, which permitted each ritual group and subgroup to maintain a viable number of members. In many matrilineal societies, by contrast, identity and inheritance are strictly determined by blood descent (no adoption), so Ilahita's ritual-group system may have collapsed without a means to redistribute members.[20]

There's nothing inevitable, irreversible, or unilineal about this scaling-up process. Populations on different continents, and in different regions, scaled up to varying degrees at different rates, either because intergroup competition was weak, often due to ecological or geographic constraints, or because the constellation of social norms didn't provide any easily accessible pathways to constructing higher-level institutions. And, of course, complex societies always collapse as the higher-level institutions that integrate and unify them eventually deteriorate and crumble. As you'll see, the institutional pathways to premodern states are relatively narrow, and the hidden footpath to WEIRD states requires a special maneuver, a kind of doubling back that allows for an end run around premodern state formations. To prepare for our descent from the smallest-scale human societies to premodern states, let's start where my intellectual journey began, among the Matsigenka in the Peruvian Amazon.[21]

TRUE INDIVIDUALISTS

Human minds adapt, through ontogeny and via cultural evolution, to the social worlds they confront. Because of this, most of us underestimate the degree to which the psychology and behavior of those around us are products of centuries of cultural evolution, with minds honed to navigate the modern world. What are people like when their society has long lacked courts, police, governments, contracts, and even leaders, like mayors, chiefs, and elders?

During my first few months in the Peruvian Amazon, I attended a community meeting in a Matsigenka village along the Urubamba River. At the meeting, the mestizo schoolteachers and an elected community leader spoke urgently about the need for everyone in the village to work together to build a new primary school. The villagers seemed vaguely supportive, though no one really said much. The next morning, I showed up at the agreed-upon time at the construction site with my camera, water bottle, and notebooks, ready to record the day's activities. No one was there. About a half hour later, one of the schoolteachers wandered by and then a Matsigenka man appeared. We moved some logs around and started to cut one of the logs with a handsaw. A few other men trickled in to help, but by lunch it was just me again. This went on for a few weeks and then apparently continued over several months. Eventually, the teachers stopped teaching and had the students build the new school. Over about six months of fieldwork in several villages, I observed this kind of strong independence repeatedly. From my perspective, Matsigenka appeared hardworking, brave, peaceful, soft-spoken, independent, and self-reliant. But, they didn't take orders, not from the schoolteachers or the elected village leaders, nor did they acquiesce to the general will of the community.

These weren't just the idiosyncratic impressions of a naïve graduate student. When my PhD advisor, Allen Johnson, arrived in another Matsigenka community some 27 years earlier, the first thing the schoolteacher who greeted him said was, "We are not very united here," by which he meant that the Matsigenka couldn't or wouldn't cooperate as a community. Similarly, the epigraph opening this chapter captures the experience of Catholic missionaries living among the Matsigenka during the mid-20th century.[22]

This population provides a fascinating case, because their society is both highly individualistic and entirely rooted in kin-based institutions. Matsigenka nuclear families are economically independent and fully capable of producing whatever they need. Each household maintains its own gardens, where they grow manioc (a potato-like root crop), plantains, and papaya, among other crops. Men make bows and a variety of arrows to hunt peccaries (pigs), tapirs ("forest cows"), fish, and birds. Women cook, brew manioc beer, mix medicines, and weave cotton clothes. Every few years, new gardens are cleared by slashing and burning a fresh patch of forest. Traditionally, Matsigenka nuclear families lived alone or in small extended family hamlets scattered throughout Peru's tropical forests. Socially, Matsigenka life is highly egalitarian and organized by kin ties. People track relations bilaterally, through both mothers and fathers. However, unlike most sedentary agricultural societies, there are no lineages, clans, chiefs, marriage groups, or communal rituals. Above the household, there are no decision-making or organizational institutions. Aside from incest taboos on certain cousins, people are free to pick their mates and to marry or divorce as they choose. It's acceptable, even desirable, for people to marry someone from their own hamlet. Ownership depends on labor or gifting, so most things are personally owned. If you made it, you own it unless you give it away. Men own the houses they construct, and women own the clothes they weave. Land can't really be owned, although gardens are temporarily controlled by whoever cuts and cultivates them.[23]

Unlike larger Sepik villages, Matsigenka hamlets traditionally maxed out at about 25 people. When disputes arose, hamlets split into nuclear families, who moved away to their distant gardens. Would-be leaders who did occasionally push themselves forward were usually just ignored or cut down to size through public joking. Since World War II, North American missionaries and the Peruvian government have been trying to settle Matsigenka in permanent villages, built around primary schools. But, even after three generations, these villages remain uneasy agglomerations of distinct family hamlets. When they can, families return to the isolation and tranquility of their remote gardens. The nature of Matsigenka social life is highlighted by the fact that, traditionally, people lacked personal names. Everyone was referred to by a kinship term like "brother," "mother," or "uncle." It was only in the 1950s that American missionaries began assigning Spanish names, plucked from the Lima phonebook, to the Matsigenka who settled in villages.[24]

Matsigenka lifeways represent a kind of cultural adaptation to both the ecology of tropical forests and the dangers posed by larger-scale societies. Looking back into the pre-Columbian period, more complex tribal populations living along the major rivers raided the Matsigenka for slaves. Before the Spanish arrived, Matsigenka slaves were sold to the Inca. Later, the Spanish replaced the Inca, but slave sales continued. Even in the 20th century, the rubber boom meant that any strangers coming upriver were probably trouble.[25]

By living in tiny hamlets or as solitary nuclear families, and vanishing at any sign of intruders, Matsigenka populations survived and eventually grew. No doubt their lack of large settlements reduced the payoffs to slave raiding. Scattered households hidden along remote tributaries are difficult and expensive to exploit. Even in recent decades, when an anthropologist approaches a remote Matsigenka house, she may find a still-smoldering fire, but no one home.

This set of institutions and lifeways has shaped Matsigenka psychology. Matsigenka are independent, self-reliant, emotionally controlled, industrious, and generous with close kinfolk. Individuals need to cultivate these traits to become well respected and successful in their society. Like WEIRD people, when they look for explanations, they tend to see the behavior of other people as well as that of animals and spirits as resulting from dispositional traits, desires, or character attributes. They also believe that individuals' actions matter and can influence their fate.[26]

The nature of Matsigenka psychology is underlined by the ineffectiveness of shame. In many traditional societies, shame emerges as the dominant emotion in social control. However, anthropologists and missionaries have long noted how difficult it is to shame a Matsigenka. Capturing this sentiment, Padre Ferrero explains: "The Matsigenka permits neither repression nor criticism. Should someone, even the missionary whose moral authority he recognizes, try to orient, correct or prevent his behavior, he departs immediately with the phrase: 'Here one can't live; nothing but gossip and rumors; I'm going where no one will bother me and I will bother no one.'"[27]

In many ways, the Matsigenka are even more individualistic and independent than WEIRD people, but socially they are rather different. The circle of trust among many Matsigenka begins to decline rapidly at the edge of their hamlets. They are even suspicious of distant kinfolk and will discuss the hidden motives of seemingly friendly visitors. At large social gatherings, many Matsigenka remain noticeably uneasy, especially if strangers are present; instead, most prefer a solitary life among intimate family members.[28]

The Matsigenka and other similar populations, which can be found sprinkled around the globe, provide important insights into the nature of human societies and the role of institutions and history in shaping our sociality and psychology. These groups are important because WEIRD researchers, as noted in the Padre's epigraph, often claim that humans are "ultrasocial," vastly more cooperative than other species. My response is always "Which humans?"—because so much of our sociality and psychology depends on our institutions. To understand contemporary sociality and human diversity, we need to explore the history of human institutions.[29]

When, How, and Why Did Societies Scale Up?

For much of our species' evolutionary history, going back at least a million years, the climate has been cooler, drier, and more volatile. From roughly 130,000 years ago until the origins of farming and herding, dramatic temperature swings every few centuries inhibited the domestication of plants, since crops need to adapt to specific climates. At the same time, lower CO_2 levels depressed plant growth, making early efforts at farming unproductive and leaving wild plant foods widely scattered. In these marginal environments, the expansive social networks created by the extensive kin-based institutions described for mobile hunter-gatherers in the last chapter would have permitted Paleolithic foragers to range over large territories, access scattered resources like waterholes, flint quarries, and fruit groves, and survive weather shocks like hurricanes and droughts. Populations with these kinship institutions were able to out-survive and often thrive relative to more insular populations.[30]

Things began to change around 20,000 years ago, following the zenith of the last ice age. Driven in part by cyclical changes in the earth's orbit, the climate gradually became warmer, more seasonal, and more stable, as the amount of CO_2 in the atmosphere rose. Grasses, fruits, legumes, and other plants became more productive and abundant, though less available during certain seasons. This opened an ecological door to farming that hadn't existed for over 100,000 years.[31]

To begin investing in certain crops in fertile regions, people needed to be able to secure and hold land. At the very least, farming communities had to be able to reap what they sowed, months or even years later. This gave a substantial edge to groups with any social norms, including rituals or religious beliefs, that made them better able to defend territory. As in pre-contact Australia and the Sepik, a group's ability to hold territory depended primarily on its size and solidarity. Similarly, large domesticated herds are easy pickings for hunters, so communities had to defend them. This suggests that the potential for agriculture and herding—food production—created the conditions for fierce intergroup competition to drive up the scale and complexity of societies, generating a coevolutionary interaction between agriculture and societal complexity: the more societies relied on agriculture and herding, the more they needed to scale up (and vice versa). Larger and more unified societies were simply better able to defend their territories.[32]

People didn't start farming because it was individually better for them. To the contrary, it was probably less productive than hunting and gathering, at least initially, and only worked when mixed with foraging. As populations increasingly relied on farming, archaeological studies reveal that the less nutritious diets derived from cereals and other crops produced people who were shorter, sicker, and more likely to die young. However, the effects of sedentism and the productivity of unskilled (young) labor were such that farmers reproduced more quickly than did mobile hunter-gatherers. With the "right" set of institutions, farmers could spread across the landscape like an epidemic, driving out or assimilating any hunter-gatherers in their path. Thus, early farming spread not because rational individuals prefer to farm, but because farming communities with particular institutions beat mobile hunter-gatherer populations in intergroup competition.[33]

The shift from extensive mobile networks to sedentary or semi-sedentary communities capable of controlling territory increasingly favored dense, intensive networks formed by community-level cooperative institutions. Naturally, cultural evolution retrofitted the existing kin-based institutions, modifying them in new ways to harness the same old social instincts to forge tighter and more cooperative communities, as we saw in Ilahita.

One common change was from kinship systems based on bilateral descent, where relatedness is tracked through both mother and father, to institutions favoring some degree of *unilineal descent*, where relatedness is either matrilineal or patrilineal. I'll call all of these unilineal kinship institutions *clans*. Of course, there's immense variation in the strength of these genealogical "side biases." Some societies, at the patrilineal extreme, even have beliefs that explicitly deny any blood relationships between children and their mothers.[34]

FORGING CLANS

Clans evolved culturally to foster greater cooperation and internal cohesion in order to defend territories and organize economic production. Many of the social norms that form clans can be understood by considering how they mitigate conflicts of interest to foster tightly knit units with clear lines of authority. By favoring one line of descent, clans ameliorate many of the internal conflicts found in bilateral kin-based institutions, especially as groups expand. To see these conflicts, suppose we start with a father who is putting together a defensive party of 10 men to drive some interlopers off their community's land. The father, Kerry, starts by drafting his two adult sons. This is a nice trio, evolutionarily speaking, since not only are all three closely related but they are also equally related—fathers and sons are genetically related at the same distance as brothers. This parity minimizes conflicts of interest within the trio.

Now, Kerry also recruits his older brother's two sons, and their sons, who are just old enough to tag along. This makes Kerry twice as closely related to his nephews and grandnephews as his own sons are to the same individuals. The nephews are four times more related to their own sons, and to each other, than they are to Kerry's sons. Still short three men, Kerry recruits his wife's brother, Chuck, and his two sons. This tight-knit trio is related neither to Kerry nor his nephews, though at least Kerry shares some genetic interest with Chuck through his own sons. As you can see, this is a mess of potential conflicts with several possible cleavages, including between the tightly-knit trios. What if Chuck faces a choice between saving one of his own sons in the melee or Kerry's two nephews? What if Kerry's nephew gets one of Chuck's sons killed?[35]

To mitigate such conflicts, clans elevate one side of a person's genealogy over the other and shift the focus of kinship reckoning from one centered on each individual to one centered on a shared ancestor. Thus everyone from the same generation is equally related to a shared ancestor, and everyone has the same set of relatives. This notion is amplified in how these societies label and refer to their relatives in their kinship terminologies. In patrilineal clans, for example, your father's brother is often also called "father"—or sometimes distinguished as "big father" if he's older than your father. "Big fathers" are often the bosses. Similarly, your father's brother's sons are called "brothers" and his daughters are "sisters." These extensions of primary kin typically extend outward for as far as we can track: if our grandfathers or great-grandfathers were brothers or even "brothers," then we're classificatory siblings and incest taboos kick in. The upshot is that members of patrilineal clans often call all the men of their father's generation "father" and all of the daughters of these men "sisters." For clarity, I'll follow my Fijian friends and refer to genealogical cousins who are called "brothers" and "sisters" as "cousin-brothers" and "cousin-sisters."[36]

This reorganization of how people think about relatedness and descent typically coevolved with a variety of complementary social norms governing arenas related to residence, marriage, security, ownership, authority, responsibility, rituals, and supernatural beings. These norm packages fostered cooperation and sustained internal harmony in a variety of clever ways. Here are some of the most common norms and beliefs, which I'll lay out from the point of view of patrilineal clans.[37]

1. *Residence after marriage*: Newly married couples must set up residence at, or near, the groom's father's house—*patrilocal residence*. The new couple's children will grow up living around, and working with, their father's brother's children and other patrilineal relatives. Co-residence and frequent interaction during childhood and adolescence strengthens these interpersonal bonds, builds trust, and reduces sexual attraction.

2. *Inheritance and ownership*: Norms specify the shared inheritance of land and other valuable resources (e.g., cows) through one's father. By endowing all clan members with an equal stake and shared responsibility, such inheritance norms tap our interdependence psychology—our psychological inclinations to help

those with whom our fitness is intertwined (if they prosper, we prosper).[38]

3. *Corporate responsibility*: Norms also foster interdependence through how they protect clan members. If anyone in your clan is harmed by someone from another clan, your honor depends on seeking compensation from the other clan. This often involves corporate responsibility: if someone injures or kills someone from your clan—accidentally or on purpose—the perpetrator's entire clan is held culpable, and thus is responsible for paying blood money. If satisfactory payment is not made, you are expected to take vengeance by killing a member of the perpetrator's clan—usually one of his cousin-brothers.[39]

4. *Incest taboos*: Norms often prohibit people from marrying within their own clan and promote marriages to cousins just outside the clan. As I noted, many of the females in one's own clan are cousin-sisters or "daughters," and thus covered under incest taboos. This suppresses sexual competition among men of the same clan for the women around them and instead focuses their mating efforts outward, on nearby clans. This builds alliances with other clans while avoiding most of the health costs of inbreeding.[40]

5. *Arranged marriages*: Norms about arranged marriages empower patriarchs to strategically use their daughters' marriages to nourish their clan's network of alliances and relationships. These alliances are reinforced by norms specifying what happens if either the husband or the wife dies. For example, levirate marriage norms specify that when the husband dies, his surviving wife must marry one of his brothers or cousin-brothers. This sustains the marital links and thus the alliances between clans.[41]

6. *Command and control*: Authority within the clan often depends on age, gender, and genealogical position. Harnessing our inclinations to defer to our older, wiser elders, these norms create clear lines of command and control that promote expeditious collective action. Such lines of authority are reinforced in daily practices,

including by norms specifying that men sit in rank order at meals and ceremonies.[42]

7. *Gods and rituals*: Ancestors often evolved into supernatural agents—ancestor gods. These beings typically demand ritual performances and sometimes punish clan members for failing to perform such rites. Since they are buried locally, ancestors are literally infused into the soil, thereby making clan lands sacred.[43]

These elements of intensive kinship provide just a sampling of some of the ways engineered by cultural evolution to scale up societies by creating dense networks of interdependent relatives. Of course, cultural evolution also devised novel ways to create and scale up institutions rooted in matrilineal clans and *bilateral* descent groups, called *kindreds*. Kindreds operate somewhat differently from clans (unilineal descent groups), but the underlying target remains the same: to forge a tightly knit, cooperative network or group. Intensive kin-based institutions like these permitted groups to take and defend territory as well as laying a foundation for cooperative labor, corporate ownership, and mutual insurance against injuries, illnesses, and the infirmities of old age.[44]

As we saw in the Sepik, scaling up by intensifying interpersonal bonds through clans or kindreds hits a ceiling. Individuals within tightly bound kin-groups can cooperate effectively in controlling territory and organizing production; but then the same kind of social dilemmas and cooperative conflicts reemerge when these kin-based units need to unify in larger communities, such as in villages or tribes (ethnolinguistic groups). Typically, while clans and kindreds usually possess some degree of internal hierarchy and authority, they don't tend to see themselves as inferior to other kin-groups. Given this equality among clans, how can societies scale up from here?[45]

UNITING THE CLANS

Building atop intensive kin-based institutions, cultural evolution has fashioned a variety of integrative higher-level institutions that forge disparate and often squabbling family groups into coherent communities and formidable political units. Here, I'll discuss two such institutions, segmentary lineages and age-sets, which have emerged independently in a variety of forms around the world.

Segmentary lineages provide an institutional mechanism to directly scale up from single clans. Typically, clans recognize few or no relationships between each other: unless rituals or other norms focus people's attention, no one remembers more than a few generations back. In a segmentary lineage, however, ritual obligations and other social norms create a broad consensus on what the purported genealogical relationships are among different clans. Crucially, norms demand that more closely related clans, who usually control adjacent territories, ally themselves against more distantly related segments. For example, if a man from clan 16 in Figure 3.2 gets into a cattle dispute with someone from clan 9, then everyone in minor segment IV could end up clashing with all of minor segment III. Similarly, if clan 16 attacks clan 1, a conflict arises between major segments A and B. Most importantly, if any of the clans find themselves in a conflict with an outside group, the entire maximal lineage (I) stands ready to defend their "brothers" and could go to war. In some cases, maximal lineages encompass an entire tribe or ethnolinguistic group, often involving hundreds of thousands of people. These alliances are triggered independently of who attacks whom, or for what reason. One unfortunate consequence of this is that any particularly feisty or aggressive clan could drag the entire maximal lineage into an enduring conflict.[46]

Psychologically, this descent-based institution is built around personal and corporate honor. A man's safety, security, and status—and his family's—are linked to his reputation. Acts of dishonor can dissolve the reputational shield that protects his property and family from thieves or avengers, and they can reduce his children's marital prospects and affect the reputation of his entire clan, not to mention other members of his immediate family. Hence, relatives closely monitor one another (out of self-interest) and will punish each other in order to restore the honor of their family or clan. Supporting one's lineage allies, including enacting vengeance when necessary, is central to each man's honor and his clan's reputation.

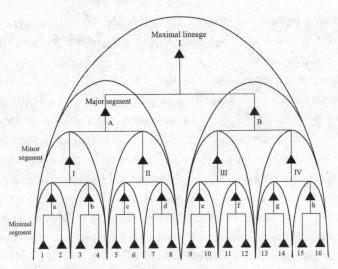

FIGURE 3.2. The prototypical segmentary lineage institution. The triangles with arabic numerals represent individual lineages. The lowercase letters and roman numerals label intermediate segments; the uppercase roman numerals mark the largest major segments; and the triangle at the top is the maximal lineage, which often represents the entire tribe or ethnolinguistic group.[47]

Segmentary lineages have spread by competing with other groups and expelling them from their territory (or assimilating them). For example, using 19th-century historical data from Sudan, anthropologists have illustrated this expansionary process by examining how the Nuer used their superior segmentary lineage institutions to assemble fighting forces of over 10,000 warriors to systematically drive out, or sometimes assimilate, the Dinka over several generations. Despite a large population, the Dinka could never put more than a few thousand warriors into battle. The Nuer expansion was halted only when the British military imposed a temporary peace. Deeper historical analyses reveal these processes playing out over centuries, as segmentary lineages spread widely across Africa.[48]

Even today, in a world dominated by territorial states, the impact of segmentary lineages can still be felt. In 21st-century Africa, tribal populations with segmentary lineages still experience significantly higher rates of violence and civil war than populations without these kin-based institutions. Based on surveys, these groups also report less trust in outsiders than other nearby communities lacking these institutions.[49] Many familiar cases of chronic conflict in Africa are associated with populations organized by segmentary lineages. In South Sudan, for example, the Dinka and Nuer continue slugging it out in a civil war after nearly two centuries of conflict. On the other side of the world, the echoes of the culture of honor that were part of Scotland's segmentary lineages still affect life and death: in counties of the U.S. South, the higher the percentage of Scottish or Scotch-Irish residents in the first U.S. census in 1790, the higher the murder rate is today. The cultural descendants of these migrants still tend to respond aggressively when their honor, family, or property is threatened. Globally, researchers have argued that the character of "Islamic terrorism" may be best explained by the honor psychology fermented in segmentary lineages. Boko Haram, Al Shabab, and Al Qaeda, for example, all recruit heavily from populations with segmentary lineages, and the character of their kin-based institutions may have shaped the particular religious creeds adopted by these groups.[50]

In contrast to segmentary lineages, age-set institutions provide a distinctive ritual-centered approach to integrating kin-based groups. As we saw in Ilahita, psychologically potent initiation rituals bring together cohorts of males from different kin-groups or residential communities. After an initiation or series of initiations, norms specify that this cohort—an age-set—is endowed with a new set of privileges, responsibilities, and obligations. Age-sets often work, play, and feast together as a unit, and usually police themselves internally. Failure to meet their cohort's collective obligations could threaten to delay their next ritual promotion. After their first initiation, for example, boys or teens might be charged with assisting the warriors in the next higher age-grade. Under the command of the senior age-set, warriors often train together and get tasked with tribal defense or tactical raiding. After graduating from the warrior grade, men in their 30s typically attain the privilege of taking a wife and starting a family. Years later, fathers and grandfathers get initiated into a senior level, where they gain political authority as part of a council of elders who make decisions for the entire organization.[51]

Age-sets are interesting because they create a degree of centralized political authority while (usually) helping to maintain egalitarian relationships among the underlying kin-based organizations. Psychologically, senior members of the governing age-grade are bound by their shared experience in multiple initiation rites, communal responsibilities, and long histories of working together in joint activities, including in war. This allows them to transcend their clan loyalties and kin-based commitments to act as a larger corporate group.

As with other widespread institutions, intergroup competition has spread age-sets in a variety of ways. Because of their military advantages, age-sets have expanded when their more cooperative societies have driven out or assimilated less unified populations. In both Africa and New Guinea, age-sets also spread as one ethnic group joined the age-set system of a neighboring group or when one group simply copied the institution wholesale from another, as happened in Ilahita.[52]

Segmentary lineages and age-sets allow egalitarian societies to scale up beyond clans and kindreds, but their success in competition with other forms of political organization is constrained because they lack centralized, stable, and hierarchical authorities. Such authorities allow societies not only to respond decisively to changing circumstances, such as encroaching neighbors, dwindling resources, and natural disasters, but also to strategically pursue the conquest of other societies. Any society that managed to centralize authority could potentially have an advantage in intergroup competition. What clever contrivances did cultural evolution cook up to improve command and control?[53]

Getting to Premodern States

Premodern states—in contrast to modern states—were built on an underlying social and psychological foundation formed by intensive kin-based institutions. As best we can tell, states first arose from what anthropologists call *chiefdoms*. The simplest version of a chiefdom is a single village consisting of a handful of clans in which one clan is set above the others. By virtue of shared norms and beliefs, affirmed routinely through rituals, the chiefly clan makes decisions for the community. Often the senior member of the senior lineage within the chiefly clan is the "chief." Social norms specify how this office passes down from one generation to the next. The chief, in consultation with senior members of the other clans, makes decisions for the community. These other clans may themselves be ranked relative to each other and possess different responsibilities and privileges. For example, in the Fijian communities where I do research, one clan is responsible for conducting the ritual for installing the chief. This gives him his full authority. A different clan is responsible for administering punishments to miscreants based on the decisions of the chief and his council of elders. Notably, the chiefly clan continues to intermarry with all of the other clans and maintains a full set of kin-based relationships with the entire community. Because male chiefs typically marry multiple wives, their kinship relations run wide across their communities. At this point, it's still kinship all the way down.[54]

To be clear, this political power is not coercive, at least at its core; it is legitimate authority built on social norms and sacred beliefs. In Fiji, as in many places, the chiefly clan is believed to be descended from the eldest brother of the founding ancestors of the community, who are perceived to be ancestor gods. In this kinship system, elder brothers must be conferred respect and deference by younger brothers. Tapping this intuition, many believe that disrespecting the chiefly clan's authority would anger the ancestors. Even when they are disappointed in the current chief, most people from nonchiefly clans still believe that his clan is special and must be the source of authority in their community. Think of this as a segmentary lineage system with ranked clans.

But, how does one clan gain authority or privileges over the others? Though these transitions have occurred independently on different continents over human history, they're relatively rare. What doesn't happen is that rational parties sit down, put their heads together, and hash out an effective institutional design. To see what *does* happen, let's return to New Guinea, where the anthropologist Simon Harrison stumbled onto one of these transitions in progress.

STEALING THE ANCESTORS' NAMES

At the confluence of the Sepik and Amoku Rivers, the community of Avatip consists of 16 patrilineal clans dispersed across three villages. In many ways, Avatip's villages resemble many others in the region, including those of the Arapesh. Households hunt, gather, farm, and fish. Clans build relationships with other clans through marriages, and males navigate through three initiation rites as part of an age-set system.[55]

Avatip, however, has evolved a unique set of religious beliefs and ritual institutions, mostly by copying and recombining elements from successful neighboring communities. Each clan was endowed with a set of ritual powers that it used to "nourish" the other clans. Some clans "owned" special rituals that fostered healthy yam crops or reliable fishing yields. Other clans conducted rituals to bring favorable weather, control storms, or limit flooding. Some clans administered the male initiation rites or conducted yearly harvest ceremonies. Of course, it was within each clan's power to withhold their rituals. Although all clans possessed at least some ritual powers, they were far from equal, because some clans controlled major rituals crucial to male initiation rites or fishing, while others possessed only minor rituals related to activities like harvesting crayfish or frogs.

The ritual inequality among these clans developed slowly over the 20th century. Avatip's largest clan had been systematically consolidating ritual powers from the smaller clans for at least 60 years. Changes in the ownership of ritual powers occurred at public debates in which one clan would challenge the true ownership of a ritual and its accompanying link to a powerful ancestor. The details of these debates are complex, but gaining control of another clan's ritual powers hinged mainly on acquiring their secret ancestral names. This knowledge could be gained through marital ties, as the sons and husbands of a clan's daughters were sometimes given access to these secrets despite their membership in other clans. Or sometimes clans extracted the information through bribery, extortion, or other skullduggery.

In the debates, larger and more powerful clans had several advantages. First, they usually had a handful of accomplished orators with deep ritual knowledge, affording more opportunities to obtain the secret names. Smaller clans had fewer opportunities and often they had no one with the standing or expertise necessary to participate. To meet challenges from the bigger clans, they sometimes had to tap the sons of the daughters they'd married off to other clans. Second, because of both their ritual powers and their economic strength, larger clans attracted more marriage offers. Since men could take multiple wives, larger clans accumulated more women and thus reproduced faster than smaller clans—and the rich got richer. Additional wives created affinal connections that entrepreneurial men could exploit to acquire the secret ritual knowledge of other clans.

The debates provided a legitimate means for one clan to gradually aggregate important ritual powers while slowly altering the underlying cosmology in ways that justified its own superiority. After a few generations, as disputes faded in memory, a clan's enlarged repertoire of privileges and powers was legitimated in the ongoing ritual cycles and became fully accepted by the community.

These ritual powers had real material bite. In one instance, the clan owning the fishing ritual placed a taboo on Avatip's fishing grounds that prevented all the clans from fishing for seven months. In another instance, after a young man had inadvertently shamed a group of ritual elders, the clan who owned the initiation rituals decided that he'd never pass through the higher rites, effectively rendering him a permanent adolescent (preventing him from ever marrying or possessing any political influence). When a clan accumulates enough of these rituals, it starts looking an awful lot like a chiefly clan with real power, political legitimacy (powerful ancestors), and sacred authority.[56] By institutionalizing inequality through ritual, Avatip was on the road to transforming into a chiefdom.[57]

A NARROW PATHWAY

Although Avatip might seem like a peculiar example, both anthropological and historical evidence suggest that the manipulation and accumulation of ritual powers and offices has been one of the main ways in which some clans have set themselves above others. Importantly, the creation of an elite clan doesn't necessarily result in the creation of a single hereditary ruler or chief. Sometimes the senior lineage heads within the elite clan form a council of elders that makes decisions by consensus. Other times, a chief may be selected from among the clan's senior members, especially during war, but then the lineage heads reassert themselves and take back power in an ongoing cycle.[58] It's the chiefly clans that endure, not the individual chiefs.

By providing a means to make and enforce community-level decisions, chiefdoms often have a substantial edge in competition with more egalitarian societies. This political centralization raises the level of cooperation among the clans in warfare and facilitates the provision of public goods such as temples, defensive walls, and moats. Perhaps most saliently, chiefdoms can cooperate militarily to expand their territory. As in Ilahita and Avatip, clans can pull together for their common defense, but active assaults and raids are initiated by individual clans or voluntary coalitions and thus usually remain relatively small-scale. Chiefdoms, however, often have enough command and control to unify large armies for military campaigns. Consequently, chiefdoms tend to spread through conquest and assimilation as well as by inspiring other groups to emulate their political organization. Of course, facing potent military threats, surrounding communities sometimes "voluntarily" join powerful chiefdoms.[59]

Since chiefdoms often grow by conquering or assimilating other communities, intergroup competition tends to produce a paramount system in which tens or even hundreds of communities unite under a hierarchy of chiefs, with the paramount chief at the top. Conquered villages might be led by the paramount chief's relatives, including his wives' brothers or fathers. Or a village's existing elite clan might be kept in power and begin intermarrying with the paramount chief's clan.[60]

Despite their size and political hierarchy, the simple chiefdoms I've been describing were still largely family affairs. Apart from the slaves (yes, there are usually slaves), most individuals could trace a pathway through a social network made up of blood and marital ties to the chief. This remained true as long as the elite clans continued to intermarry with everyone else. True social stratification didn't emerge until the upper strata stopped intermarrying with the lower strata. This isolated the upper strata and allowed them to claim that they were fundamentally different from the lower strata—truly divine, superior, and deserving. Psychologically, this permitted the elite to be (i.e., claim to be) a separate category of person, with special attributes and privileges.[61]

Under the right conditions, such *stratified* chiefdoms can evolve into premodern states—kingdoms—as they interpose new bureaucratic institutions between the elite ruling families and the clans or other kin-groups that dominate the rest of the population (Figure 3.3). The line between stratified chiefdoms and states is notoriously fuzzy—it comes down to a question of which and how many of these society-wide bureaucratic institutions need to be introduced before the whole is "a state." These institutions variously collect taxes, adjudicate disputes between clans, conduct long-distance trade, orchestrate public rites, and marshal armies.[62]

To run these organizations, elites intuitively wanted to rely on their family connections, presumably because they distrusted those outside their kin-based networks. However, chiefs and chiefly families had learned, and relearned the hard way, that they must promote competent non-elites into state institutions. Not only did this facilitate the effective functioning of government institutions such as tax collection (which rulers love), but it also protected rulers from other elite families who could consolidate power through these institutions and eventually take over. Unlike the elites, who had some claim to divine connections and ritual prerogatives, commoners and foreigners were much less of a threat. The sharp separation between the elites and everyone else in stratified societies meant that even the most capable non-elites were unlikely usurpers. Interestingly, perhaps the biggest threats to elites were the "illegitimate" sons

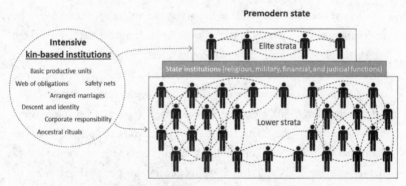

FIGURE 3.3. Premodern states were built on a foundation of intensive kin-based institutions. These institutions were infused with many of the norms and beliefs encircled on the left. Non-kin-based (nonrelational) institutions developed at the interface between the elite and everyone else. Note that slaves are excluded here.

that rulers everywhere seem to produce (e.g., William the Conqueror and Shaka Zulu).[63]

Despite the formation of these societal-level institutions, which were often at least somewhat meritocratic, premodern states remained rooted in intensive kin-based institutions, both in the lower strata and at the elite level (Figure 3.3). That is, even when premodern states had effective, impersonal bureaucratic institutions like armies or state religions, these were sandwiched between upper and lower strata that were both enmeshed in intensive kin-based institutions.[64]

To get a sense of how the first state-level institutions emerged, consider how chiefly clans can harness (exploit?) age-set institutions to create a well-functioning military. This begins when, in consolidating various ritual powers, a chiefly clan gains control over the male initiation rites that lie at the core of age-set institutions. With this leverage, chiefs can deploy the warrior age-grade as a tightly bonded army regiment that must obey (if they don't, they won't be initiated into the next age-grade). In 18th-century Africa, for example, some chiefs began deploying the warrior age-grade to collect tribute and raid surrounding groups. In the 19th century, after conquering several groups, the Zulu chief, Shaka, reorganized these age-sets so that they crosscut the many chiefdoms that were now united under his rule—thereby establishing an army composed of ritually-bonded young men drawn from diverse clans and tribes. This created the first state-level institution—the military—of the embryonic Zulu state. The powerful Zulu army struck terror into surrounding populations and would soon give the mighty British Empire much trouble.[65]

As state institutions multiplied and expanded, they often undermined the kin-based institutions of the lower strata, mostly by usurping some of their functions. For example, during Hawaii's transition from a chiefdom to a state in the 18th century, the elite had accumulated so much ritual, military, and supernatural power that they took the ownership of land away from the clans of the commoners and reallocated it to suit their own political purposes. Clans had to renew their "use rights" each year by paying tribute to the elites in pigs, dogs, mats, labor, and much more. Similarly, clans were also prevented from keeping deep genealogies, which was presumably meant to limit their size by making it harder for people to unify around common ancestors. These steps didn't end Hawaii's tradition of kin-based institutions, although they did sap some of their strength in favor of the elite.[66]

Premodern states still needed clan and tribal institutions to govern effectively, and sometimes the state even buttressed or augmented the power of kin-based institutions. Typically, premodern states left it to the clans or tribes to police and adjudicate their own internal affairs, including theft, assault, and even murder. States were most likely to intervene in disputes *between* clans or tribes within their territories, but often this was only if standard blood money payments or other customary judicial procedures had failed to thwart a cycle of violence. Legally speaking, individuals were rarely recognized in a state's courts and had no rights. Only kin-based organizations had legal standing. Even in powerful premodern states, the lives of most people—including the elite—remained infused with the relationships, identities, obligations, and privileges that derived from their kin-based institutions.[67]

Of course, there's no steady descent to chiefdoms and states: societal evolution is a rocky roller coaster in the dark, with lots of unexpected drops, turns, loops, and especially dead-ends. Clans resist subordination into chiefdoms, and chiefdoms resist conquest and assimilation by other chiefdoms and states. In the face of intergroup competition, any institutional elements and recombinations that increase a group's economic productivity, security, fertility, or military effectiveness tend to spread in the various ways described above. This means that once one community scales up in some way, perhaps through its own quirky internal dynamics (e.g., Avatip or Ilahita), a chain reaction is initiated. Surrounding communities will be wiped out, assimilated, or driven out unless they also somehow scale up.[68]

Once intergroup competition wanes, which often happens when states or empires manage to eliminate their competition, things slowly fall apart. Without the looming threats posed by competing societies, the competition among ruling families within a society will intensify and gradually tear the state-level institutions apart. Cracks, gaps, and loopholes appear even in the best institutions, allowing narrow elite interests to flood in, as lineages, clans, and sometimes entire ethnic communities devise ways to exploit state institutions for their own ends. For example, what if venerable customs dictate that the king's firstborn son will take the throne, but the king's firstborn turns out to be with a woman other than his wife, or with one of his secondary wives? Is it his firstborn, or the firstborn of his leading wife? When the Spanish conquistadors arrived in Peru, the Inca were weak because they were just emerging from a civil war that was caused by an ambiguity in succession between two half-brothers (both sons of the prior Inca). As institutions fail and centralized political organizations collapse, inequality rises and larger societies break down into their sturdiest constitutive parts, which are usually tribes, clans, or residential communities. Even when kin-based institutions have been suppressed by state institutions, their fundamental grounding in our evolved psychology enables them to readily reassemble themselves—in the advent of a state collapse—to resume the functions previously usurped by the state.[69]

Going End Around

This exploration of societal evolution leads us to one big question: How did we get from premodern states to modern WEIRD societies?

It turns out there's no direct path because WEIRD societies are organized on an entirely different institutional foundation. Instead of intensive kinship up and down the social strata, we have norms and beliefs, often backed by laws, that actively inhibit such kin-based institutions from forming. In most WEIRD societies, you can't marry your stepson, take multiple spouses, or arrange the marriage of your teenage daughter to your business partner. Similarly, you could tell your son that he must move into your house after he gets married, but he and his wife may have other ideas, and you have little leverage. You are compelled by custom and law to build relationships by other means and to depend on impersonal markets, governments, and other formal institutions (e.g., to provide safety nets for injuries, disasters, and unemployment).

How were WEIRD societies institutionally rebuilt from the ground up? Notions of family, kinship, and interpersonal relations infused all premodern states, and the mental models furnished by experience in kin-based institutions often shaped the formulation and construction of state institutions. Chinese emperors, for example, were often seen as strong, caring, and authoritarian fathers to their subjects, who, as his children, owed their emperor submission, respect, and devotion. So, how do you get individuals from both the upper and lower strata of premodern societies to leave their clans, kindreds, lineages, age-sets, and tribes to move to cities and join voluntary associations like companies, churches, guilds, unions, political parties, and universities? How do you get people to eschew the obligations, responsibilities, and protections of their extended kin networks and depart their ancestral homelands to join groups of strangers? Today, in the WEIRD world of (relatively) well-functioning hospitals, police departments, businesses, schools, and unemployment insurance, this might seem easy. But, there's a chicken-and-egg problem. In a world without at least some semblance of these modern secular institutions, people would have been crazy to abandon their kin-based organizations. If people won't or can't extricate themselves from their kin-based institutions, how could cultural evolution ever build modern states and related formal institutions in the first place? How do you get here from there?

4

The Gods Are Watching. Behave!

It will also be seen by those who pay attention to Roman history, how
much religion helped in the control of armies, in encouraging plebs,
in producing good men, and in shaming the bad . . . And truly there
never was any extraordinary institutor of laws among a people who
did not have recourse to God, because otherwise he would not have
been accepted.

—Niccolò Machiavelli (1531), *Discourses on Livy*, Book 1, Chapter 11

Upon entering a psychology laboratory in Vancouver, Canada, participants
were asked to first complete a sentence-unscrambling task and then to make
an economic decision about how to allocate $10 between themselves and
a stranger. For the unscrambling task, people were randomly assigned to
either a set of 10 sentences that were secretly laced with five God-related
words or a control group in which none of the words were divinely flavored.[1]
Try creating a sentence from these words:

divine dessert the was = _____

(answer: "the dessert was divine")

After completing this task, each person was assigned an anonymous
partner for a onetime interaction. Their job was to decide how to divide $10
between themselves and this other person. In this, the Dictator Game, most
WEIRD people agree that participants *should* give half the money to the recipient. Of course, purely selfish individuals will keep all $10 for themselves.

This two-stage experimental design, first developed by the psychologists Ara Norenzayan and Azim Shariff, asks a simple question: Do unconscious reminders of God influence people's willingness to comply with norms of impersonal fairness?

Yes, they do. In the control task—with no reminders of God—participants gave the stranger only $2.60 on average of the $10. The most common amount given here was zero dollars: nothing for the stranger. By contrast, when unconsciously reminded of God, participants suddenly became more generous, increasing their average allocation to $4.60; here, the most common single amount given was half the money, $5. The percentage of participants who gave nothing to the stranger dropped from 40 percent in the control task to only 12 percent among those reminded of God.[2]

Now, experiments involving such unconscious reminders, which psychologists call "primes," are notoriously delicate, because the primes need to be strong enough to be psychologically detectable by participants but not so strong that they bubble up into conscious awareness. Fortunately, Ara and Azim's experiments made a big splash, so we now have many such experiments using different approaches to measure prosocial norm compliance. Compiling all of the "God-priming" studies they could find—26 in total from many different laboratories and populations—Azim, Ara, and their collaborators found that participants reminded of God not only give more equal offers in Dictator Games but also cheat less on tests and cooperate more with strangers in group projects. Of course, not every study showed these effects; but across all the studies, the effects of God-primes came through loud and clear.[3]

What exactly is going on here? Maybe WEIRD people associate religion with Christianity and Christianity with charity, so the God-primes cause an unconscious association with charity that results in people giving more. Alternatively, maybe religious people are intuitively worried that God will see them violating some norm about cooperation or fairness and count it against them in some heavenly tally—that is, maybe believers have an implicit inclination to comply with moralized norms out of an internalized fear of divine judgment.

Which explanation is correct, if either? Our first piece of evidence comes from analyses of the religious commitments of the participants across the priming studies. When Ara and Azim's team looked at nonreligious people, the effect of priming God on social behavior went to zero. That is, God-primes don't work on atheists. By contrast, when nonbelievers were dropped from the analysis, the effects of priming God got stronger. The same pattern emerges when all 26 studies are analyzed together. It turns out the nonbelievers were diluting the potency of God's influence.

But, maybe atheists are a bit hardheaded, and thus difficult to influence with priming?

Ara and Azim also looked at the impact of "secular primes" by creating a sentence-unscrambling task involving words like "police," "court," and "jury." Figure 4.1 shows their results: secular primes elevate Dictator Game allocations for *both* religious people and atheists, while *God-primes only work on believers*. Notably, in the control group, there was no difference between believers and atheists. It seems that atheists are only resistant to

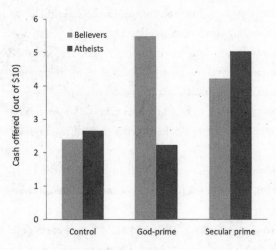

FIGURE 4.1. Average offers in the Dictator Game for three treatments for both believers and atheists.[4]

the influence of primes when they cue supernatural beings that the atheists believe don't exist.

This indicates that the impact of God-primes depends on people's supernatural commitments and not on vague secondary associations between "religion" and concepts like charity, which would be held by atheists and believers alike. Such religious faith should be especially important in expanding the sphere of cooperation in places that lack the well-functioning courts, governments, and police forces found in Vancouver—that is, it would have been particularly important in most places throughout human history.

The "priming" approach used in the above experiments represents a methodological technique that helps researchers figure out what causes what, psychologically. Of course, being much smarter than we are, cultural evolution figured out the power of priming long ago and has embedded God-primes into daily life in all of the world's major religions. Religious dress (Jewish kippahs), adornments (Catholic crosses), holy days, daily devotions, and temples on the market square all remind people of their gods and religious commitments. To see such primes in action, let's head into the medina of Marrakesh, in Morocco. Inside the old city walls, among the maze-like streets, Muslim shopkeepers played a modified Dictator Game. Here, the Muslim call to prayer sounds five times per day for 5 to 10 minutes from minarets around the city. That's our prime. In the experiment, 69 shopkeepers chose from among three ways to allocate the local currency—dirhams—between themselves and a charity. They could: (A) keep 20 dirhams for themselves and give 0 to charity; (B) keep 10 for themselves and give 30 to charity; or (C) take nothing and give 60 to charity. Twenty dirhams was about enough money to buy lunch or take a 15-minute taxi ride. The experiment was administered either during the call to prayer or between calls.[5]

Here's the key question: Did hearing the call to prayer in the background while considering their choice in this experiment influence these small business owners?

You bet. During the call to prayer, 100 percent of shopkeepers gave all of the money to charity (choice C). At other times, the percentage of participants giving it all to charity dropped to 59 percent. This is surprising, because these shopkeepers earn a living by hawking goods like dried fruits, local crafts, and handwoven rugs, and spend their days haggling over much smaller sums. Nevertheless, although they routinely hear the call, it still influences their behavior in significant ways.[6]

Such embedded primes influence Christians as well, creating the *Sunday effect*. In a study conducted over two months, Christians were more likely to participate in charitable efforts via email on Sundays (with some spillover into Mondays) than on other days of the week. By Saturday, the charitable inclinations of Christians hit their weekly low, and were not distinguishable from those of nonreligious people. But, then Sunday came, and many Christians got a ritualized booster shot that elevated their charitable inclinations. Unlike the faithful, nonreligious people reveal no such weekly cycle.

The Sunday effect also shows up in the use of online pornography across U.S. states. While on average there's little variation across states in porn usage, states with more religious populations reveal a weekly cycle that tracks the charity patterns above. People from more religious states apparently watch *less* porn on Sundays, but then compensate for this "porn deficit" by watching more over the rest of the week. These results are predictable, since the Christian God is famously obsessed with both charity and sex—i.e., not having it or even thinking about it.[7]

By giving us a glimpse into the subtle power of religion in our daily decision-making, studies like these uncover the psychological footprints left by cultural evolution. They reveal how, operating outside of our conscious awareness, supernatural beliefs and ritual practices can motivate the faithful to make personally costly decisions, treat strangers more fairly, and contribute to public goods like charities (and avoid porn).

Now, if you are WEIRD, you may think that religion always involves morally concerned gods who exhort people to behave properly, perhaps with threats to their soul in the next life. However, the character of gods, afterlives, rituals, and universal morality common to today's world religions is unusual, the product of long-running cultural evolutionary processes. To explore this, we'll venture back into the fog of prehistory to see how and why cultural evolution has shaped humanity's supernatural beliefs, rituals, and related institutions in ways that helped societies to scale up or hold together. Religions have fostered trade by increasing trust, legitimized political authority, and expanded people's conceptions of their communities by shifting their focus from their own clans or tribes to larger imagined communities like "all Muslims." This background will set the stage for understanding how the Western Christian Church of the Middle Ages shaped European families, cultural psychology, and communities in ways that opened a pathway to the political, economic, and social institutions of the modern world.

Moralizing Gods and Contingent Afterlives

To explain the evolution of supernatural beliefs and rituals, we need to consider three key ingredients: (1) our species' willingness to put faith in what we learn from others over our own direct experiences and intuitions, (2) the existence of "psychological by-products" from the kludgy evolution of our brains, and (3) the impact of intergroup competition on cultural evolution. The first ingredient, discussed in Chapter 2, arose in response to the power of cumulative cultural evolution to generate subtle but highly adaptive packages of nonintuitive beliefs and practices, like the use of pathogen-killing spices in culinary recipes. Because of these complex adaptive products, natural selection has often favored relying on cultural learning over other sources of information, especially when uncertainty was high and getting the right answer was important. The possible existence of supernatural beings, hidden powers, and parallel worlds represents precisely the sort of high-stakes but uncertain situations in which our cultural learning abilities often overrule our mundane intuitions and common experience in favor of our learning from others. Our evolved inclinations to rely heavily on cultural learning (at least under some circumstances) create a kind of "faith instinct" that opens the door to religion, making us susceptible to ideas and beliefs that violate our worldly expectations.

However, although our faith instinct does crack the door open, different supernatural beliefs and practices still need to compete to occupy our minds. In this competition, the advantage often goes to those beliefs or practices that most effectively penetrate our mental defenses—defenses that aim to filter out dangerous, implausible, or otherwise useless cultural junk. This is the second ingredient: cultural evolution will seek out back doors into our minds by locating glitches in our psychological firewalls. To see what I mean, consider one of the by-products of our sophisticated mentalizing abilities. These crucial abilities likely evolved as a key psychological adaptation in our species for more efficiently learning the accumulating bodies of cultural information related to tools, norms, and languages. They allow us to represent the goals, beliefs, and desires of other minds; but—here's the back door—they also allow us to represent the minds of nonexistent beings, like gods, aliens, and spirits, as well as Santa Claus and the tooth fairy.[8]

In fact, mentally representing the mind of a being that one never observes, or actually interacts with, may require particularly potent mentalizing abilities. This suggests that not only do our mentalizing abilities allow us to think about supernatural beings, but that those with superior mentalizing abilities may be more inclined to believe in gods, ghosts, and spirits because they are better at conjuring the richness of their minds. One piece of evidence for this idea is that Americans, Czechs, and Slovaks with better mentalizing abilities and greater empathy are more likely than others to believe in God. The impact of mentalizing accounts for the common observation from global surveys that women are more likely to believe in God than men. Across societies, women are better than men at mentalizing and empathy. Once we adjust for men's inferior abilities, women and men don't differ in their belief in God or other supernatural agents. Women's greater religious faith in many populations may be a by-product of their superior capacity for empathy.[9]

The evolution of our potent mentalizing abilities may also account for our species' tendency toward dualism—thinking of minds and bodies as separable and potentially independent. Dualistic inclinations leave us susceptible to beliefs in ghosts, spirits, and an afterlife in which your body goes in the ground and your soul departs for heaven. Of course, the best available science says that our minds are produced entirely by our bodies and brains, so they can't have an independent existence. Nevertheless, in the process of hot-wiring our brains, natural selection inadvertently created a cognitive glitch—another back door into our minds—that left us susceptible to believing that minds and bodies are separable. This probably occurred because our sophisticated mentalizing abilities for understanding other minds evolved relatively recently, long after the evolution of an ancient cognitive system for tracking the movements of other bodies, which we share with many other species. The disjointed evolution of these semi-independent mental systems produced a cognitive by-product, a capacity to entertain the notion that "minds" can separate from bodies.

If an omniscient engineer had crafted an integrated cognitive system for us, she certainly would have ruled out mind-body separations, since they are impossible. Dualistic conceptions like souls or ghosts should make about as much sense to us as a person who exists only on Tuesdays and Thursdays. Instead, stories about mind-body switches are easy to understand, even for young children in societies as diverse as Fiji and Canada. The popularity of movies portraying mind-body switches, like *Freaky Friday*, along with widespread cultural phenomena like demonic possessions and séances, testify to the readiness of our dualistic intuitions.[10]

To see the impact of cognitive bugs like dualism, consider how diverse beliefs compete to insinuate themselves into our minds and societies by getting repeatedly remembered, recalled, and retransmitted over generations. Many ideas will be too bizarre, complex, or counterintuitive to survive this competition, and will be systematically forgotten, misremembered, or otherwise mutated in ways that make them more amenable to our psychology.[11] The survivors will be those that best fit the quirks of our jury-rigged brains without violating our intuitions too drastically. This process helps explain the striking cross-cultural uniformities in people's beliefs about souls and ghosts, which seem to flow directly from our dualistic glitches. In the United States, for example, nearly half of adults believe in ghosts, and these beliefs persist despite consistent and long-running efforts by both scientific and religious organizations to dissuade people from such beliefs.[12]

These two ingredients—our faith instinct and cognitive bugs—help account for many of the supernatural beings found among mobile hunter-gatherers and presumably our Stone Age ancestors. The gods of hunter-gatherers tended to be weak, whimsical, and not particularly moral. They could be bribed, tricked, or scared off with powerful rituals. Among the Aboriginal hunter-gatherers of Japan, for example, people bribed the gods with offerings of millet beer. If things didn't improve, they'd threaten to cut the god off from his beer supply. Sometimes such gods did punish people with their supernatural powers, but this was usually because of some divine pet peeve rather than a moral conviction. In the Bay of Bengal, for example, the Andaman Islanders' storm god would rage against anyone who melted beeswax during the cicadas' songs. The islanders thought that melting beeswax was perfectly fine, and would sometimes do it anyway, but only if they thought the storm god couldn't see them. Even in rare cases when the gods did punish people for violating widely shared social norms, this usually involved an arbitrary taboo rather than something like murder, theft, adultery, or deception.[13] Although hunter-gatherers often believed in some form of afterlife, there was rarely any connection between proper behavior in this life—e.g., not stealing food—and the quality of one's afterlife.[14]

Of course, the smallest-scale human communities did, and still do, possess strong moral norms about how to treat other community members. The key difference is that these prescriptions and prohibitions are not strongly linked to universal cosmic forces or the commandments of mighty supernatural beings. For example, in discussing the Ju/'hoansi's creator god, ≠Gao!na (the "≠" and "!" represent click sounds), Lorna Marshall writes: "Man's wrong-doing against man is not left to ≠Gao!na's punishment nor is it considered to be his concern. Man corrects or avenges such wrong-doings himself in his social context. ≠Gao!na punishes people for his own reasons, which are sometimes quite obscure."

Marshall goes on to recount one story in which ≠Gao!na makes two men sick because they had burned some bees while using smoke to drive them away—it's apparently well-known that ≠Gao!na hates it when people burn bees. In terms of both their powers and morality, the gods of the smallest-scale human societies are much more like people than the later gods of larger-scale societies. That is, sometimes these gods are indeed morally concerned, but usually their concerns are local, even idiosyncratic, while their interventions are generally unreliable and ineffective.[15]

A fundamental question is: How did these weak, whimsical, and often morally ambiguous gods ever evolve into the big, powerful moralizers of modern religions? How did morality ever get all tied up with supernatural beings, universal justice, and the afterlife?

Enter our third ingredient: the influence of intergroup competition on the evolution of religious beliefs and rituals. Suppose some communities happened—by chance—to have gods or ancestor spirits that punished people for refusing to share food or for running away in the face of enemy raiders. Suppose still other communities came to share a belief in gods who punished people for breaking sacred oaths taken during key transactions, such as when trading valuable goods or affirming peace treaties. Over time, intergroup competition can gradually filter, aggregate, and recombine such diverse supernatural beliefs. If it's sufficiently intense, intergroup competition can assemble integrated cultural packages that include gods, rituals, afterlife conceptions, and social institutions that together expand the sphere of trust, intensify people's willingness to sacrifice in war, and sustain internal harmony by reducing assault, murder, adultery, and other crimes within groups.

We've already seen this process at work in Ilahita. There, a set of psychologically potent communal rituals did much of the work, but the actions and desires of the Tambaran gods also played a role. These village gods imposed the ritual-group system and demanded ritual observances. It was also believed that they punished those who failed in their ritual obligations, which may have motivated greater ritual adherence. Ilahita's combination of gods, rituals, and social organization allowed the community to scale up from a few hundred to a few thousand people. This case, however, also illustrates the limitations of relying primarily on the solidarity-building powers of communal rituals. Ilahita's powerful rituals, as well as those widely used in other small-scale societies, do forge potent social bonds, but their effectiveness is constrained by the need for individuals to interact with each other face-to-face. To scale up further, to construct and sustain complex chiefdoms and states, cultural evolution needed to somehow fashion *imagined communities*—broad networks of strangers connected by shared beliefs in supernatural beings, mystical forces like karma, or other worlds such as heaven and hell. How would intergroup competition have shaped people's beliefs about their gods?

WHAT GODS WANT, AND WHY

One of the primary ways that cultural evolution has managed to turn our cognitive bugs into potent social technologies has been by favoring deep commitments to supernatural beings who punish believers for violating social norms that are beneficial to the community. If people believe that their gods will punish them for things like stealing, adultery, cheating, or murder, then they will be less likely to commit these actions even when they could get away with them. Communities devoted to such gods are more likely to prosper, expand, spread, and provide models for other communities to copy. They are also less likely to collapse or disintegrate. Under these conditions, we should expect gods to evolve specific kinds of concerns about human actions and greater powers to both monitor adherents and punish or reward proper behavior. Let's take a deeper look at each of these.

Concerns about human action: Under the pressure of intergroup competition, gods should become increasingly concerned about those aspects of behavior that promote cooperation and harmony within groups. This includes any divine commands or prohibitions that expand the sphere of cooperation and trust. Gods should focus on those aspects of social interactions where cooperation and trust are difficult but potentially most beneficial for the community. This will often favor divine concerns about the treatment of socially distant coreligionists, and focus on acts like stealing, lying, cheating, and murder. In scaling up, societies can stretch the sphere of trust to include strangers from other clans or tribes when they too believe in a god who tends to the faithful. Gods should also worry about adultery, for two reasons: (1) sexual jealousy is a major source of social disharmony, violence, and murder (even between neighbors and relatives), and (2) the uncertainty about paternity created by adultery suppresses fatherly investments in children. Curbing adultery should both foster greater harmony within larger communities and improve the welfare of children. Below, we'll see why the gods should also be concerned about ritual performances, devotional adherence (e.g., to food taboos), and costly sacrifices.[16]

Divine monitoring: Intergroup competition should favor gods who are better at monitoring people's adherence to divine demands and prohibitions. Supernatural beings seem to first emerge with roughly human abilities for monitoring others, but then over millennia some became omniscient, eventually even gaining the ability to see into people's hearts and minds. Where I work in Fiji, the ancestor gods watch villagers from "dark places," but they can't watch everyone at the same time, track people when they travel to other islands, or see into people's hearts. By contrast, the villagers have no doubt that the Christian God, whom they also believe in, can do all this and more.

Supernatural sticks and carrots: Intergroup competition selects for gods with the power to punish and reward individuals and groups. Notably, because of how our norm psychology operates, punishment threats may be substantially more potent than rewards, but both can play a role in motivating behavior. Over time, the gods evolved from peevish pranksters to divine judges capable of inflicting injuries, illness, and even death. Eventually, some gods seized control over the afterlife, acquiring the power to dispense everlasting life or eternal damnation.

Does believing in a god who is more willing and able to monitor and punish norm violations actually influence people's decision-making? Can such gods "expand the circle" of cooperation by fostering fair and impartial interactions with strangers who share their faith? We've already seen that God-primes evoke more prosociality toward strangers; now, let's zero in on some of the specific channels through which belief operates.

THE ACTIVE INGREDIENTS

About a dozen years ago, over a few pints in our local pub, Ara Norenzayan, the religious studies scholar Ted Slingerland, and I designed a project to study the evolution of religions. As part of this, we assembled an international team with expertise in diverse populations of hunter-gatherers, subsistence farmers, cattle herders, and wage laborers from communities around the globe, from Siberia and Mauritius to Vanuatu and Fiji. Across these 15 populations, we tapped not only communities deeply enmeshed in world religions like Hinduism, Christianity, and Buddhism but also those actively participating in local traditions, including ancestor worship and animism (e.g., belief in mountain spirits). In each population, we conducted extensive anthropological interviews about people's supernatural beliefs and administered a set of decision-making tasks in which participants had to allocate substantial sums of real money.[17]

To begin our study, we first located two locally important gods at each field site. The first was the deity who best approximated the biggest and most powerful god possible—the omnipotent, omnipresent, and all-benevolent GOD. This is our "Big God." Then we looked for an important but less powerful supernatural agent, which we called our "Local God." For each god, we asked participants to rate their abilities to surveil mortals, read their minds, punish various violations, and grant an afterlife (among many other questions). From these ratings, we developed indices for each god that measured people's belief in that god's power to monitor and punish norm-violators.

To measure people's notions of fairness and impartiality, we used a decision task called the Random Allocation Game (RAG). In the RAG, each participant was seated in a private area—like a room or tent. In front of each were two cups, a pile of 30 coins, and a six-sided die colored black on three sides and white on the other three. Participants were told that they had to roll the die to allocate each coin to one of the two cups. The cash put into each cup was earmarked for a different recipient at the end of the game. In the most important versions of this setup, participants allocated the coins to (1) an anonymous coreligionist from a distant town or village and either (2A) themselves (Self Game) or (2B) another coreligionist from the participant's home community (Local Coreligionist Game). Once players' understanding of the game was verified, they were left alone to allocate the coins.[18]

Since we were interested in the effects of people's beliefs in supernatural surveillance, and not about the influence of earthly social pressures, participants were instructed to allocate the coins in the following manner: (1) pick one of the two cups *in your mind*; (2) roll the die and if one of the black-colored sides comes up, put the coin in the cup you *picked in your mind*; but if one of the white sides comes up, place the coin in *the other cup*, the one you didn't pick in your mind; (3) repeat this until you run out of coins.

This protocol ensures secrecy since, short of mind reading, no one can be sure which cup a player mentally selected on a given roll. Even if someone like the experimenter was spying on them, there's simply no way to tell if they actually cheated. Of course, while we experimenters can't be positive whether someone cheated on any specific die roll, we do have probability and statistics, which permits us to infer the amount of bias in people's allocations. On average, after 30 die rolls, there should be 15 coins in each cup. The further a person's allocations are from 15 per cup, the more likely they are to be biased in some way. Now, we expect people to be biased toward both themselves and members of their local communities. So, the question is whether Big Gods, through their monitoring and threat of punishment, can reduce this natural selfishness and parochialism by moving people closer to an equal split (15 coins on average for the distant coreligionist).

We found that Big Gods can indeed expand the circle and that this is influenced by people's beliefs about (1) divine monitoring and (2) supernatural punishing power. For example, when people believed that their Big God was more willing and able to punish bad behavior, they were *less biased against distant coreligionists*. Figure 4.2 plots our index of God's punishing power for both allocation tasks. Keeping in mind that a perfectly unbiased person will allocate 15 coins on average, the data show that people who thought their Big God was the fire-and-brimstone type (index = "1") allocated an average of 14.5 coins to a distant coreligionist. Meanwhile, people who thought that their Big God was an all-loving softy (index = "0") allocated only about 13 coins to the stranger.

Figure 4.2 includes, on the far left, people who said they "don't know" about their god's powers. These agnostics came almost exclusively from our two smallest-scale societies, the Hadza hunter-gatherers in Tanzania and the inland villagers on the island of Tanna in Vanuatu. In both places, researchers did their best to match a god from the local pantheon to our Big God concept, but the available gods just weren't particularly moralizing or powerful. This pattern is useful because it gives us a glimpse into how people behave when supernatural punishment from a potent moralizing god isn't part of their worldview. In this situation, favoring one's self and one's home community got even stronger, with average allocations dropping to between 12.5 and 13 coins. Overall, moving from little or no belief in supernatural punishment to the strongest beliefs in punishment *reduced the bias against strangers* by a factor of four to five times. These relationships hold even when we only compare individuals from the same communities, and statistically hold constant the effects of people's material security (wealth) and other demographic factors like schooling, age, and gender.[19]

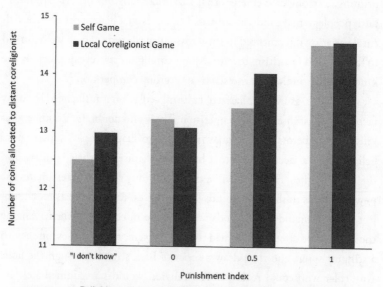

FIGURE 4.2. Belief in more punishing Big Gods in the Random Allocation Game is associated with more impartial treatment of distant coreligionists (strangers) in both the Self Game and the Local Coreligionist Game. Higher values on the punishment index indicate stronger beliefs in a more punishing Big God.[20]

Our team also did Dictator Games in the same fashion as the RAG, by allowing people to allocate coins between (1) themselves and a distant coreligionist and (2) a local coreligionist and a distant coreligionist. These results tell the same story as the RAG, although the impact of monitoring and punishment by Big Gods is even stronger.[21]

We also analyzed whether people's beliefs about their Local Gods influenced their allocations. Unlike with the Big Gods, people's beliefs about their Local Gods had no impact on their allocations. This patterning eliminates many alternative explanations, including the concern that people's anxiety about social punishment influenced both their experimental behavior and their beliefs about supernatural punishment. If this were the case, we'd expect people's beliefs about both Big Gods and Local Gods to be associated with their experimental behavior. But, it was only the Big Gods that mattered.[22]

When we put findings like these together with those involving God-priming, a strong case emerges that *particular* religious beliefs can indeed push people to make individually costly choices that benefit others. The cultural variation documented in this cross-cultural study, which we've linked to fairness and favoritism toward distant coreligionists, reveals precisely the kind of variation that's harnessed by intergroup competition.[23]

Of course, as I've emphasized, cultural evolution is influenced by many factors, not just intergroup competition. There's no doubt, for example, that kings and emperors have intentionally tried to shape people's supernatural beliefs and practices in ways that benefited themselves, their families, and their fellow elites. However, while this is certainly true, it overestimates the power of elites to shape the minds of the masses. Rulers were as much subject to the demands of the gods as they were in control of them. Among the Maya, for example, rulers had to ritually pierce their penises, often with a stingray spine, and then draw a series of bark strands through the hole. Any ruler who could really control religion would have immediately received a divine revelation tabooing any mutilation of the royal penis; yet this practice endured for at least two centuries. Similarly, on the other side of the world, in 16th-century India, the powerful Mughal emperor Akbar the Great tried to unify his Muslim and Hindu subjects by making up his own highly tolerant religious creed—a syncretic mix of elements from Islam, Hinduism, Zoroastrianism, and Christianity. Unfortunately, this bit of conscious, top-down divine engineering backfired. Orthodox Muslims promptly denounced Akbar's efforts as heresy and a fierce resistance solidified. At its peak, the powerful emperor's religion accumulated a total of only 18 prominent adherents before vanishing into history.[24]

My point is that throughout human history, rulers needed religions much more than religions needed rulers.

Just to be clear, I'm not praising either world religions or big gods. To me, they are simply another interesting class of cultural phenomena that demands explanation. The idea here is that cultural evolution, driven by intergroup competition, favored the emergence and spread of supernatural beliefs that increasingly endowed gods with concerns about human action and the power to punish and reward. These beliefs evolved not because they are accurate representations of reality but because they help communities, organizations, and societies beat their competitors. While this competition can be relatively benign, involving the preferential copying of more successful groups, it has also often involved the slaughter, oppression, and/or forced conversion of nonbelievers. These evolving gods have justified war, blessed genocide, and empowered tyrants (see the Bible). Intergroup competition favors expanding the circle, but it's still a circle that places some people on the outside.[25]

Drawing on comparative psychological evidence, we've seen how religious beliefs and rituals can ratchet up people's cooperative inclinations. Now, let's consider how gods and rituals actually evolved across diverse societies and over history.

The Evolution of Gods and Rituals

Under the pressure of intergroup competition, especially since the origins of agriculture, cultural evolution has shaped people's supernatural beliefs and rituals in ways that have facilitated and/or stabilized the scaling up of societies. As a point of departure, we can begin with the weak and morally ambiguous gods found in the smallest-scale societies, including hunter-gatherers. While some evidence now indicates that these gods probably did sometimes foster food sharing and intergroup relationships, they likely did little to promote the overall scaling up of societies or large-scale cooperation. However, as we saw with clans and ancestor gods in the last chapter, cultural evolution began seriously harnessing supernatural beliefs and rituals as societies began forging larger and tighter social units using kin-based institutions.

Around the globe and back into history, clans have frequently deified their mysterious founders. Since clan institutions usually endow elders with greater authority as they rise in seniority, it's perhaps natural that after important elders die, and their stories are told and retold, respect for them deepens and eventually develops into a mixture of awe, reverence, and fear. Although ancestor gods mostly punish people for failing to conduct proper ancestral rites, they do occasionally also punish those who violate the clan's customs, usually by striking the violators or their relatives with illnesses, injuries, or even death. The concerns of ancestor gods were, and still are, limited to their clans.[26]

Bigger gods can emerge from clan gods in many ways, one of which we saw when Ilahita's elders misconstrued the Abelam's ancestor gods as village-level deities. Similarly, the ancestor gods of conquering chiefdoms have sometimes been assimilated by the subjugated populations as powerful generic gods rather than deified ancestors. The question is, when events like these generate bigger gods with more power to punish, does this facilitate the scaling up of societies, or at least inhibit the usual forces that tear societies apart?[27]

To get a look at how gods evolved as nonliterate societies expanded their political integration from clans to complex chiefdoms, let's focus on the Pacific. We'll consider the development of supernatural punishment, the broadening of divine moral concerns, the legitimation of political leadership, and the nature of afterlife beliefs. As Austronesian populations spread across the islands of Southeast Asia and into the uninhabited regions of the Pacific over the course of only a few thousand years, they created a natural laboratory for studying societal evolution. At the time of European contact, these widely scattered populations varied in their size and political complexity from small-scale egalitarian communities to quite complex chiefdoms and even a couple of states.

Using this natural experiment to examine the coevolution of societal complexity and supernatural punishment, a team led by Joseph Watts, Russell Gray, and Quentin Atkinson used data from 96 Pacific societies before European contact to reconstruct the likely historical pathways of these societies. The team estimated the probability that a society scaled up in complexity in situations in which beliefs in broad supernatural punishment already existed and when they did not. The estimated probability of a historical transition to a complex chiefdom when no such punishment existed was—surprisingly—close to zero. By contrast, when ancestral communities already had beliefs in supernatural punishments for important moral violations, there was roughly a 40 percent chance of scaling up in complexity every three centuries or so. Seen in the light of the psychological experiments above, the role of religion in the scaling up of societies grows clearer.[28]

The broadening importance of supernatural punishment seems to have been accompanied by changes in what the gods cared about, how angry they got at violations of their demands, and who was part of their realm. Essentially every Austronesian society had gods that punished people for ritual violations, broken taboos, and other divine pet peeves. The comparative data, however, suggest that the gods in some places began to care about people's actions toward unrelated members of their society, those outside their own clans or communities. In Tonga, for example, the gods of this complex chiefdom inflicted shark attacks on those who stole from other Tongans. These beliefs had real bite: the anthropologist H. Ian Hogbin noted that thieves avoided swimming during the season when sharks were common. Nearby, Samoans believed that thieves were punished with ulcerous sores and swollen stomachs. In both Samoa and Tonga, some gods also punished adultery, although other gods helped conceal it.

Of course, these societies were rooted in intensive kin-based institutions, so divine punishment often included corporate guilt and shared responsibility. In Samoa, personal injuries, accidents, illness, and even death were believed to arise from supernatural punishments, often traceable to the actions of one's kinfolk. When a father became sick, his sons would often disappear to distant villages for fear that the divine punisher would soon target them as well. Notably, this example reveals the gods' limited powers—the sons apparently believed they could escape divine wrath by going far away. Eventually, cultural evolution would thwart such escape maneuvers by extending the reach of the gods to the entire universe.[29]

Alongside supernatural punishment and growing moral concerns, cultural evolution also interwove religious and political institutions in ways that more effectively linked chiefly authority with the gods. This divine legitimacy endowed chiefs with greater command and control, allowing them to govern larger populations, build temples, dig canals, plant yams, and conduct military operations. At the same time, the gods increasingly demanded human sacrifices, and sometimes these sacrifices included the chief's own children. Such ritualized acts no doubt enhanced social control while at the same time publicly demonstrating both the chief's power and his submission to the gods.[30]

Of course, while the Polynesian gods did sometimes punish antisocial behaviors, like theft and adultery, they were otherwise rather human. They enjoyed food, drink, and sex. They could be bribed or cajoled by worshippers who lay prostrate in prayer and by extravagant sacrifices. Invading armies would even make sacrifices to their enemies' gods to buy them off or at least curry some favor.[31]

While beliefs about divine punishment, moral concern, and political legitimacy were coevolving in ways that supported the scaling-up process, there's little evidence for the importance of a *contingent afterlife* in which a person's behavior during life leads to either a better or worse condition after death. For example, in the Society Islands, which include Tahiti and Bora Bora, if someone was killed at sea, they would enter a shark; but if they died in battle, they'd linger as a ghost on the battlefield. By virtue of their birth, members of elite clans often got to enter paradise in the afterlife (supposedly), so there was a heaven of sorts; but, people couldn't get there merely through exemplary behavior.

However, scattered around Oceania, there were a few afterlife beliefs that could have provided fuel for the engine of intergroup competition. In the Cook Islands, for example, the souls of brave warriors on Mangaia would "ascend to the upper region of the sky world, where they continued to dwell in everlasting happiness, clothed in fragrant flowers, dancing and enjoying the full gratification of all their desires." Wow, that's a big incentive to be a brave warrior. But, more importantly, such a belief provides a cornerstone upon which cultural evolution can build. If people believe that bravery matters for the afterlife, the door opens for cultural evolution to augment the list of heavenly virtues and earthly vices. Alas, this regional cultural evolutionary process was gradually curtailed by the arrival of Christians and Muslims in the middle of the second millennium.[32]

THE GODS MAKE HISTORY

The cultural evolutionary process just described above, which can only be inferred in the Pacific through a combination of anthropological, linguistic, and archaeological evidence, can be seen historically when the gods first begin to appear in the written record over 4,500 years ago in Sumer (Mesopotamia). At this point, the gods weren't much different from those just highlighted in the complex chiefdoms of Polynesia. They were a lot like us, but with superpowers. The god Enki, for example, got too drunk one night and mistakenly gave the secret knowledge of civilization to the seductive Inanna, the goddess of love and sex (and also war). Inanna, who gradually merged with Ishtar, was also the goddess of prostitutes and sometimes assisted adulterous women. Wives pregnant by their lovers prayed to Ishtar for their baby to resemble their husbands. The god Enlil, like the later god of the Israelites, ordered a giant flood to wipe out humanity. But, instead of believing that humanity had become a den of iniquity that needed cleansing, Enlil just found us too noisy.[33]

From this tumultuous hodgepodge of diverse supernatural agents, we see the action of intergroup—often intercity—competition shaping people's beliefs about the gods' role in politics and trade, among other domains. When ancient kings didn't actually transform into demigods, as they did in Egypt, kings still cultivated a close connection with the gods to give them greater legitimacy and a degree of divine authority. At the opening of his famous code, King Hammurabi of Babylon lays out the source of his divine mandate, beginning at the top of the hierarchy with the supreme creator god and the lord of heaven and earth. Hammurabi then declares, "I should rule over the black-headed people like Shamash, and enlighten the land, to further the well-being of humankind."[34]

Mesopotamian gods also promoted commerce and suppressed perjury. For example, the sun god and Inanna's twin brother, Shamash, emerged as the patron of truth and justice, presiding over the oaths taken during business transactions and treaty negotiations. Evidence for this appears early in the second millennium BCE when two merchant families in Ur (modern Iraq) signed a contract containing an oath to Shamash. Similarly, in the marketplace, statues of Shamash were erected, presumably to encourage fair trading practices using "Shamash-primes." Hammurabi's law code formalized this by requiring the use of divine oaths to enforce contracts and market exchanges as well as to ensure honest testimony during legal inquiries.[35]

The later gods of ancient Greece and Rome, contrary to the popular impressions created by later Christian spin doctors, were the upholders of public morality and would bestow divine favor on individuals, families, and cities. Though subject to the same moral shortcomings as their Mesopotamian forebearers, the Greek gods legitimized rulers, inspired armies, and policed corrupt practices. As with nearly all gods, they especially favored those who performed the ancient rituals, including costly sacrifices offered in elaborate rites. However, they did some degree of active monitoring and punishing, specifically for neglecting one's parents and for worshipping foreign gods. In Athens, murder was probably also divinely suppressed, but the pathway was indirect. The act of murder was believed to pollute the murderer. Should a tainted individual enter a sacred place, such as a temple, market, or certain other public spaces, the gods would be angered and might punish the entire city. Collective punishment would have motivated third parties—witnesses—to alert the authorities to the murderer's tainted condition, lest they all become collateral damage in some divine temper tantrum.[36]

By far the most important source of divine punishment arose from the violation of sacred oaths taken in the name of particular gods while signing commercial contracts, making sales, or assuming public offices. In Athens, as in many parts of the Greek world, the marketplace was filled with altars to various gods. Merchants were required to swear sacred oaths before these altars to affirm the authenticity and quality of their goods. Athenians' intense reliance on the gods, and on such oaths, may help explain their enduring reputation for trustworthiness in both business and treaty-making.[37]

In the later Roman world, sacred oaths were similarly used in sales, legal agreements, and contracts. These oaths, for example, were taken to discourage harvesters and millers from colluding on prices. Similarly, wine sellers were prepared to swear an oath on the quality and integrity of their products. And, of course, people swore oaths against perjury while giving testimony in court cases. Notably, the gods themselves weren't directly concerned about lying, cheating, and stealing per se. They were focused on the violation of oaths taken in their names—that is, like both the Greeks and the Romans themselves, the gods were concerned about their honor. Cultural evolution merely put this psychological intuition—personal and family honor—to work for the larger society.[38]

The centrality of the gods to Mediterranean commerce and trade is illustrated on the Aegean island of Delos, an epicenter for Roman maritime trade during the second century BCE. As a religious center and trading hub, the ancient marketplace was filled with altars and idols for various gods, but both Mercury and Hercules were central. In this sacred place, merchants swore oaths to these deities to establish trading fraternities and solidify contractual bonds that effectively networked the Mediterranean. Pausanias, a famous Greek traveler, observed that "the presence of the god made it safe to do business there." If you're skeptical that such oaths could matter, recall the psychological evidence above on the effects of priming deities on economic decision-making. In light of such evidence, it's hard to imagine that such explicit oaths, taken in a place of known spiritual power, didn't elevate people's trust and trustworthiness, thereby greasing the wheels of economic exchange.[39]

Hell, Free Will, and Moral Universalism

From this swirling cauldron of beliefs about gods and divine sanctions, which washed back and forth from the Mediterranean to India for centuries, new religions with universal gods (or cosmic forces) fully equipped to reward and punish particular behaviors began to emerge after about 500 BCE. The modern survivors of this competition include Buddhism, Christianity, and Hinduism. Later, Islam would join the list, along with many other religions.[40]

By roughly 200 BCE, universalizing religions included variants of three key features, which were psychological game changers. First, *contingent afterlives*: at the core of these religions were beliefs about life after death or some form of eternal salvation that was contingent on adhering to specific moral codes during one's life—these are notions of heaven, hell, resurrection, and reincarnation. Second, *free will*: most universalizing religions highlighted the ability of individuals to choose "moral actions" even when this meant violating local norms or resisting traditional authorities. Here, individuals' free choices shape their fate in the afterlife. Third, *moral universalism*: the moral codes of some of these religions evolved into divine laws that adherents believed were universally applicable to all peoples. These laws were either derived from the will of all-powerful gods (e.g., Christianity and Islam) or from the metaphysical structure of the universe (e.g., Buddhism and Hinduism). This was a big innovation, since in most places and times it was taken as a fact of life that different peoples—ethnolinguistic groups— had their own distinct social norms, rituals, and gods. All three of these features would have independently affected how people thought and behaved in ways that would have given the faithful an edge in competition with traditional communities and small-scale religions. Let's look at contemporary data to examine how such religious convictions might provide this edge.[41]

Across countries, the belief in a contingent afterlife is associated with greater economic productivity and less crime. Based on global data from 1965 to 1995, statistical analyses indicate that the higher the percentage of people in a country who believe in hell and heaven (not just heaven), the faster the rate of economic growth in the subsequent decade. The effect is big: if the percentage of people who believe in hell (and heaven) increases by roughly 20 percentile points, going from, say, 40 percent to 60 percent, a country's economy will grow by an extra 10 percent over the next decade. This pattern holds even after removing the usual factors that economists think influence economic growth. The data also suggest that it's specifically beliefs about a contingent afterlife that fuel economic growth. Believing in just heaven (but not hell) doesn't increase growth; neither does believing in God once the influence of contingent afterlife beliefs have been accounted for. Since many people seem keen to believe in heaven, it's really adding hell that does the economic work (believing only in hell is rare).[42]

On its own, this analysis doesn't show that contingent afterlife beliefs indisputably cause economic growth. However, seen in the light of all the above evidence, it suggests that certain religious beliefs—but not "religion" in general—probably do cash out in consequential ways that impact economic prosperity.[43]

Contingent afterlife beliefs may also influence global crime rates. The higher the percentage of people who believe in a contingent afterlife (hell and heaven) in a country, the lower the murder rate. By contrast, the greater the percentage of people who believe in only heaven, the *higher* the murder rate. That's right, believing *only in heaven is associated with more murder.* The same pattern appears for nine other crimes, including assault, theft, and robbery. But, we should be cautious in putting too much weight on these other crimes because of differences across countries in how often various crimes are reported. I've focused on murder because it's the most reliable crime statistic across countries. These relationships hold even after the factors usually associated with differences in crime rates across countries, like national wealth and inequality, are statistically held constant.[44]

Alongside afterlife beliefs, notions of *free will* may also influence people's decision-making, though unfortunately most of this research has been restricted to WEIRD societies. Laboratory psychological experiments suggest that Americans who believe more strongly in free will are *less* likely to cheat on math tests, take unearned cash payments, or conform to group opinions, and *more* likely to resist temptation, help strangers, and solve problems creatively. They are also more likely to make dispositional attributions—that's the bias toward explaining people's behavior based on dispositional traits (e.g., "he's lazy") over relevant contexts (e.g., "he's tired from work"). Because much of this research induces behavioral shifts in the laboratory by exposing some participants to scientific arguments that temporarily suppress their belief in free will and agency, we can infer that people's beliefs are driving the behavioral changes.[45]

Though research on moral universalism remains even more limited than research on free will, two studies suggest that commitments to moral universalism over moral relativism promote greater impersonal honesty and more generous charitable donations. As with free will, researchers have sought to demonstrate the causal influence of people's commitment to moral universalism by experimentally priming them with either moral universalism or moral relativism and then watching whether they cheat for money or donate more to the poor. The results show that cuing up moral universalism suppresses cheating and raises charitable donations.[46]

Taken together, this research supports the view that beliefs in contingent afterlives, free will, and moral universalism altered people's decision-making and behaviors in ways that fostered success in competition among religious groups or societies. So, cultural evolution may have favored adding these three enhancers to a supernatural concoction that included powerful, morally-concerned supernatural punishers (or other cosmic forces). But, what other ingredients are crucial in these social recipes?

Persuasive Martyrs and Boring Rituals

At the core of universalizing religions were, and still are, deeply-held emotional commitments to particular supernatural beliefs and worldviews. The long-term success of these new religious communities rested not so much on the ancient ritual formula—rooted in the binding power of emotionally-potent "imagistic" rites (as in Ilahita)—but instead on the enduring psychological impact of people's faith in their gods, moral codes, and conceptions of the universe. As part of this process, cultural evolution favored new ritual forms—termed "doctrinal" rituals—because they more effectively transmitted both the content of religious beliefs and deep commitments to those beliefs. Rituals gradually evolved to exploit aspects of our innate capacities for cultural learning. They became more frequent and more repetitious, using prayers, hymns, poems, creeds, and parables to carry the content of belief in memorable formats. Harnessing our attentional biases, these beliefs were (and still are) routinely transmitted by particularly prestigious or successful individuals—priests, prophets, and community leaders—or sometimes spoken in unison by the entire congregation to give young learners a sense of unified commitment (conformity). Psychological research suggests that these elements, among others, sharpen people's learning and memory, thereby fostering widely shared beliefs in large religious communities.[47]

To more effectively instill deep commitments to professed beliefs, the new doctrinal rituals also harnessed what I call *Credibility-Enhancing Displays* (CREDs). CREDs are actions that attest to people's underlying beliefs or true commitments, actions that they'd be very unlikely to perform if they didn't firmly hold their verbally stated beliefs. The clearest example of a CRED is martyrdom. Dying for our professed beliefs provides a convincing demonstration that we actually held those beliefs as deep convictions. Observers who see or hear about the actions of a martyr are more likely to acquire the martyr's expressed beliefs or deepen their own faith. Over the course of human evolution, natural selection has favored a psychological tendency to rely on CREDs as a way to avoid being exploited by manipulative individuals who might convey false beliefs to us for their own benefit. CREDs thus evolved to act as a kind of immune system against charlatans and purveyors of snake oil. Relying on CREDs would have become especially important after the emergence of complex languages, which would have given influential individuals the ability to cheaply spread false information or maladaptive beliefs for their own benefit. By using CREDs, especially for potentially costly beliefs, individuals can filter out true convictions from efforts at manipulation.[48]

Universalizing religions, ironically, have evolved to exploit our reliance on CREDs by building in ritualized opportunities for individuals to voluntarily perform costly acts or provide credible displays. Martyrs, of course, have played a central role in Christianity, Islam, and Buddhism, among other faiths, but this provides just the most glaring case of CREDs. Universalizing religions feature a full slate of more subtle CREDs, including scarification, food taboos, sexual prohibitions, fasts, animal sacrifices, and charitable donations that deepen the faith of both participants and observers, especially children and adolescents. Religions have also evolved to deploy CREDs to make religious leaders—priests, monks, and prophets—into more effective transmitters of the faith, through their vows of celibacy, poverty, and other demonstrations of their deep commitments.[49]

To tighten the synergy between beliefs and rituals, the gods evolved desires and commandments that motivated people to participate in rituals, stick to fasts, maintain taboos, and make credible vows. The new doctrinal rituals more effectively transmit the faith, and, in turn, the new faith motivates the reinforcing rituals through the threat of supernatural punishment. This interlocking cycle helps perpetuate the faith from one generation to the next.[50]

In addition to implanting specific beliefs and commitments, some doctrinal rituals may also promote greater self-regulation or delay discounting. Unlike the extravagant, emotional, and often painful rites of tribal religions, doctrinal rituals involve the performance of repetitious and often tedious devotions. Such practices require consistent and sustained attention, typically demanding some small but repeated costs in time or effort. Common examples include daily prayers, grace before meals, charitable giving, ritual attendance, fasts, and food taboos. Motivated by a combination of supernatural concerns (e.g., Allah wants all Muslims to pray at sunrise) and social norms enforced by reputation within religious communities (those who sleep in are "bad" Muslims), individuals cultivate greater self-regulation by performing these routine rituals.[51]

One key consequence of the broad dissemination and standardization of widely shared religious beliefs and rituals is the creation of what we might think of as "super-tribes" that tap our evolved psychology for thinking about symbolically-marked ethnic groups (Chapter 2). Religious groups evolved to use identity markers, including specialized dress, religious ornaments, obscure languages, and food taboos to delineate group boundaries and fire up our tribal instincts. Even in ancient Mesopotamia, the sharing of religious beliefs and deities may have permitted greater exchange over broader regions, just as it has throughout history and does in the modern world. At the beginning of the Common Era, some of the new universalizing religions were even better equipped to create large "imagined" super-tribes, which anyone could join (at least in principle). Their moral universalism and doctrinal rituals, combined with some literacy among leaders, opened the door to disseminating and maintaining a broadly shared set of supernatural beliefs and practices across much larger populations than was previously possible. The social circle expanded as these religious packages were favored by intergroup competition.[52]

The Launchpad

Because religions can powerfully shape our behavior and psychology, they've played a central role in the formation of higher-level political and economic institutions as societies have scaled up. Religion's power derives from the myriad ways in which cultural evolution has subtly shaped our supernatural beliefs and ritual practices to expand the social circle, nurture greater internal harmony, and intensify competitive advantages against out-groups. The psychological impacts of beliefs about godly desires, divine punishment, free will, and the afterlife combine with repetitive ritual practices to suppress people's tendencies toward impulsivity and cheating while increasing their prosociality toward unfamiliar coreligionists. At a group level, these psychological differences result in lower crime rates and faster economic growth. Of course, none of this helps us explain the peculiarity of WEIRD psychology, since universalizing religions of one sort or another have long taken over most of the world.[53]

With this backdrop now complete, the stage is set for the emergence of WEIRD psychology. It's the start of the first millennium of the Common Era, and universalizing religions are competing, mutating, and spreading around the Old World. What would happen if cultural evolution harnessed the power of one of these new universalizing religions to undermine and then transform the most fundamental of human institutions, those related to marriage, family, lineage, identity, and inheritance?

PART II

The Origins of WEIRD People

5

WEIRD Families

The families found in WEIRD societies are peculiar, even exotic, from a global and historical perspective. We don't have lineages or large kindreds that stretch out in all directions, entangling us in a web of familial responsibilities. Our identity, sense of self, legal existence, and personal security are not tied to membership in a house or clan, or to our position in a relational network. We limit ourselves to one spouse (at a time), and social norms usually exclude us from marrying relatives, including our cousins, nieces, stepchildren, and in-laws. Instead of arranged marriages, our "love marriages" are usually motivated by mutual affection and compatibility. Ideally, newly married couples set up residence independent of their parents, establishing what anthropologists call *neolocal residence*. Unlike patrilineal clans or segmentary lineages, relatedness among WEIRD people is reckoned *bilaterally*, by tracking descent equally through both fathers and mothers. Property is individually owned, and bequests are personal decisions. We don't, for example, have claims on the land owned by our brother, and we have no veto on his decision to sell it. Nuclear families form a distinct core in our societies but reside together only until the children marry to form new households. Beyond these small families, our kinship ties are fewer and weaker than those of most other societies. Though kinship does assert itself from time to time, such as when U.S. presidents appoint their children or in-laws to key White House posts, it usually remains subordinate to higher-level political, social, and economic institutions.[1]

Let's begin by putting some numbers on the kinship patterns described above using the Ethnographic Atlas, an anthropological database of over 1,200 societies (ethnolinguistic groups) that captures life prior to industrialization. Table 5.1 shows five of the kinship traits that characterize WEIRD societies: (1) *bilateral descent*, (2) *little or no cousin marriage*, (3) *monogamous marriage only*, (4) *nuclear family households*, and (5) *neolocal residence*. The frequencies of these WEIRD kinship traits vary from a high of 28 percent, for bilateral descent, to a low of 5 percent, for neolocal residence. This suggests that most societies have long lived in extended family households, permitted polygamous marriage, encouraged cousin marriage, and tracked descent primarily through one parent. Taken separately, each trait is uncommon, but in combination, this package is extremely rare—WEIRD.[2]

TABLE 5.1

FIVE WEIRD KINSHIP TRAITS IN GLOBAL-HISTORICAL PERSPECTIVE

WEIRD Traits	% of Societies
1 Bilateral descent—relatedness is traced (roughly) equally through both parents	28%
2 Little or no marriage to cousins or other relatives	25%
3 Monogamous marriage—people are permitted to have only one spouse at a time	15%
4 Nuclear families—domestic life is organized around married couples and their children	8%
5 Neolocal residence—newly married couples set up a separate household	5%

To see just how rare these patterns are, we can count how many of these kinship traits are possessed by each society in the Atlas. This gives us a score from zero to five that tells us how WEIRD a society is in terms of kinship. Figure 5.1 shows the results: over half of the societies in the Atlas (50.2 percent) possess *zero* of these WEIRD kinship traits, and 77 percent possess either zero or only one of these traits. At the other end, fewer than 3 percent of societies possess at least four of them, and only 0.7 percent possess all five traits. Notably, these tiny percentages include a small sampling of European societies, like the Irish and French Canadians of 1930. So, 99.3 percent of societies in this global anthropological database deviate from the WEIRD pattern.[3]

The aspects of traditional kinship found in the Atlas open a window not only on the world prior to industrialization but also on the social norms that remain important even today. Consider this question: How many people do you personally know who married their cousins?

If you know none, that's WEIRD, since 1 in 10 marriages around the world today is to a cousin or other relative. Based on data from the latter half of the 20th century, Figure 5.2 maps the frequency with which people

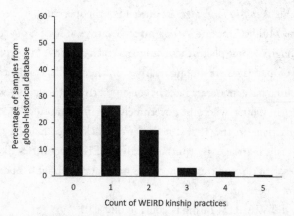

FIGURE 5.1. The percentage of societies with different numbers of WEIRD kinship practices from Table 5.1, ranging from zero to all five traits (based on data from the Ethnographic Atlas).

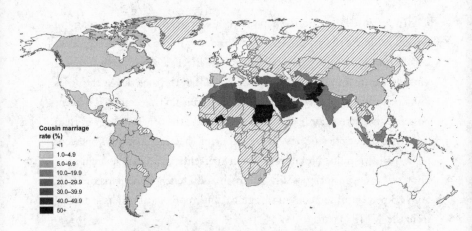

FIGURE 5.2. Cousin marriage rates. Rates of marriage between second cousins and closer relatives across countries based on data from the latter half of the 20th century. The darker the shading of a country, the higher the percentage of marriages among blood relatives. Hatched regions indicate that no data are available.[4]

marry their first or second cousins or other close relatives (uncles, nieces). Remember that second cousins share a pair of great-grandparents. For the sake of simplicity, and because most marriages to relatives involve cousins, I'll refer to this as *cousin marriage*. At one end of the spectrum, we see that people in the Middle East and Africa marry relatives at least a quarter of the time, though in some places these numbers reach up above 50 percent—so over half of marriages are among relatives. In the middle, countries like India and China have moderate rates of cousin marriage, though it's worth knowing that in China, when the government began promoting "modern" (Western) marriage in the 1950s, it outlawed uncle-niece marriage and, later, first cousin marriage. By contrast, really WEIRD countries like the United States, Britain, and the Netherlands have rates of about 0.2 percent, or one-fifth of 1 percent.[5]

So, how did WEIRD kinship become so unusual?

Many assume that the peculiar nature of WEIRD families is a product of the Industrial Revolution, economic prosperity, urbanization, and modern state-level institutions. This is sensible, and certainly appears to be what's happening in much of the world today, through globalization. As non-WEIRD societies have entered the global economy, urbanized, and adopted the formal secular institutions of WEIRD societies (e.g., Western civil codes, constitutions, etc.), their intensive kin-based institutions have often begun to slowly deteriorate, resulting in the spread of WEIRD kinship practices, particularly among educated urbanites. Nevertheless, against this onslaught of global economic and political forces, intensive kin-based institutions have proven themselves to be remarkably resilient.[6]

In Europe, however, the historical order was reversed. First, between about 400 and 1200 CE, the intensive kin-based institutions of many European tribal populations were slowly degraded, dismantled, and eventually demolished by the branch of Christianity that evolved into the Roman Catholic Church—hereinafter the Western Church or just the Church. Then, from the ruins of their traditional social structures, people began to form new voluntary associations based on shared interests or beliefs rather than on kinship or tribal affiliations. In these European regions, societal evolution was blocked from the usual avenues—intensifying kinship—and then shunted down an unlikely side road.[7]

The key point for now is that the dissolution of intensive kin-based institutions and the gradual creation of independent monogamous nuclear families represents the proverbial pebble that started the avalanche to the modern world in Europe. Now let's look at how this pebble was first inadvertently kicked by the Church.

Dissolving the Traditional Family

The roots of WEIRD families can be found in the slowly expanding package of doctrines, prohibitions, and prescriptions that the Church gradually adopted and energetically promoted, starting before the end of the Western Roman Empire. For centuries, during Late Antiquity and well into the Middle Ages, the Church's marriage and family policies were part of a larger cultural evolutionary process in which its beliefs and practices were competing with many other gods, spirits, rituals, and institutional forms for the hearts, minds, and souls of Europeans. The Church vied against ancestor gods, traditional tribal deities such as Thor and Odin, the old Roman state religion (Jupiter, Mercury, etc.), and various Mediterranean salvation cults (Isis and Mithras, among others), as well as diverse variants of Christianity. These other Christian sects were serious competition and included the Nestorian, Coptic, Syrian, Arian, and Armenian Churches. The Goths, for example, who played a role in the fall of the Western Roman Empire, were not pagans but Arian Christians. Arians, major heretics in the Western Church, held the astonishing view that God the Son (Jesus) was created by God the Father at a particular point in time, making the Son subordinate to the Father.

Today, it's clear that the Western Church won this religious competition hands down. Christianity is the world's largest religion, having captured over 30 percent of the global population. However, 85–90 percent of modern Christians trace their cultural descent through the Roman Catholic Church, back to the Western Church in Rome, and not through the many other branches of Christianity such as the Orthodox or Oriental Churches. This outcome was far from clear when the Western half of the Roman Empire broke up. The Eastern Orthodox Church, as the state religion of the Byzantine Empire, was backed by powerful Roman state institutions and military might. The Nestorian Church, based in cosmopolitan Persia, had established missions in India by 300 CE and in China by 635, many centuries before the Roman Catholic Church would arrive in these places.[8]

Why did the Western Church so dominate in the long run, not only exterminating or commandeering all of Europe's traditional gods and rituals but also outpacing other versions of Christianity?

There are many important elements to this story. For example, Rome's geographic location far from the main political action in Europe may have provided the pope—the bishop of Rome—with some freedom to maneuver. In contrast, other leading bishops, such as those in Constantinople, were under the thumb of the emperors of the Eastern Roman Empire. Similarly, much of northern Europe was relatively technologically backward and illiterate at this point, so the pope's missionaries might have had an easier job of making converts there, for the same reasons that North American missionaries were so successful at making converts in Amazonia during the 20th century. The locals were just more inclined to believe new religious teachings when missionaries showed up with fancy technologies and seemingly miraculous skills, like reading.[9]

Complexities aside, the most important factor in explaining the Church's immense success lies in its extreme package of prohibitions, prescriptions, and preferences surrounding marriage and the family. Despite possessing only tenuous (at best) roots in Christianity's sacred writings, these policies were gradually wrapped in rituals and disseminated wherever possible through a combination of persuasion, ostracism, supernatural threats, and secular punishments. As these practices were slowly internalized by Christians and transmitted to later generations as commonsense social norms, people's lives and psychology were altered in crucial ways. These policies slowly transformed the experience of ordinary individuals by forcing them to adapt to, and reorganize their social habits around, a world without intensive kin-based institutions.

Throughout this process, the Church was competing not only with other religious complexes, but also with intensive kin-based institutions and tribal loyalties. By undermining intensive kinship, the Church's marriage and family policies gradually released individuals from the responsibilities, obligations, and benefits of their clans and houses, creating both more opportunities and greater incentives for people to devote themselves to the Church and, later, to other voluntary organizations. The accidental genius of Western Christianity was in "figuring out" how to dismantle kin-based institutions while at the same time catalyzing its own spread.[10]

UP TO THE STARTING LINE

What did kinship look like among the tribes of Europe before the Church went to work? Unfortunately, we don't have the kind of detailed studies of kinship and marriage that anthropologists have provided for traditional societies in the 20th century. Instead, researchers have cobbled together insights from diverse sources, including (1) early law codes; (2) Church documents, including the many letters exchanged by popes, bishops, and kings; (3) travelers' reports; (4) saints' biographies; (5) Nordic and German sagas; (6) ancient DNA analysis (applied to burials); and (7) kinship terminologies preserved in ancient writings. Broadly speaking, these sources make it clear that prior to the Church's efforts to transform marriage and the family, European tribes had a range of intensive kin-based institutions that looked a lot like what we see elsewhere in the world.[11] Here are some broad patterns in the tribal populations of *pre-Christian* Europe:

1. People lived enmeshed in kin-based organizations within tribal groups or networks. Extended family households were part of larger kin-groups (clans, houses, lineages, etc.), some of which were called *sippen* (Germanic) or *septs* (Celtic).

2. Inheritance and postmarital residence had patrilineal biases; people often lived in extended patrilineal households, and wives moved to live with their husbands' kinfolk.

3. Many kinship units collectively owned or controlled territory. Even where individual ownership existed, kinfolk often retained inheritance rights such that lands couldn't be sold or otherwise transferred without the consent of relatives.[12]

4. Larger kin-based organizations provided individuals with both their legal and their social identities. Disputes within kin-groups were adjudicated internally, according to custom. Corporate responsibility meant that intentionality sometimes played little role in assigning punishments or levying fines for disputes between kin-groups.[13]

5. Kin-based organizations provided members with protection, insurance, and security. These organizations cared for sick, injured, and poor members, as well as the elderly.

6. Arranged marriages with relatives were customary, as were marriage payments like dowry or bride price (where the groom or his family pays for the bride).

7. Polygynous marriages were common for high-status men. In many communities, men could pair with only one "primary" wife, typically someone of roughly equal social status, but could then add secondary wives, usually of lower social status.[14]

Even at the core of the Roman Empire, intensive kin-based institutions remained central to social, political, and economic life. Roman families were organized around patriarchal patrilineages in which each man saw himself sandwiched in time between his great-grandfather and his great-grandsons. Even when they lived separately and had their own wives and children, adult men remained under the dominion of their fathers. Only male citizens without living fathers had full legal rights, control of family property, and access to tribunals; everyone else had to operate through the patriarch. It was within a father's power to kill his slaves or children. Inheritance rights, incest prohibitions, and exemption from giving legal testimony all extended out, along the patrilineal branches, to the descendants of one's father's father's father. Of course, the empire did develop legal mechanisms for inheritance by testament (wills), but during the pre-Christian period such testaments almost always followed custom and thus mostly came into play when matters were murky or disputes likely. Women remained under the control of either their father or their husband, although over time fathers increasingly retained control of their daughters even after marriage. Marriages were arranged (dowries paid) and adolescent brides went to reside in their husbands' homes (patrilocal residence). Marriage was monogamous by default, but Roman men had few sexual constraints on their behavior save for those that might conflict with other Roman men. Divorce became common in the empire when elites began ending their daughters' marriages in order to remarry them to ever more powerful families. Any children born during the marriage stayed with their father's family, though the wife's dowry returned with her to her father. As for cousin marriage, the details are complex, and both law and custom changed over time; but in short, cousin marriage in some form was socially acceptable, and some elites did marry their cousins in Roman society (Brutus, St. Melania, and Emperor

Constantine's four children). This continued until the Church started its relentless opposition.[15]

THE MONKEY WRENCHES

Around 597 CE, Pope Gregory I—Gregory the Great—dispatched a mission to the Anglo-Saxon Kingdom of Kent in England, where King Æthelberht had married a Frankish Christian princess (eventually St. Bertha) some 17 years earlier. After only a few years, the missionary team had succeeded in converting Æthelberht, had begun to convert the rest of Kent, and had made plans to expand into nearby realms. These papal missionaries, unlike earlier Christian missionaries in places such as Ireland, had definite instructions regarding proper Christian marriage. Apparently, these policies did not go down well with the Anglo-Saxons, since the mission's leader, Augustine (later known as St. Augustine of Canterbury), soon wrote to the pope seeking clarification. Augustine's letter consisted of nine questions, four of which were focused on sex and marriage. Specifically, Augustine queried: (1) How distant must a relative be in order for a Christian marriage to be permissible (second cousins, third cousins, etc.)? (2) Can a man marry his stepmother or his brother's wife? (3) Can two brothers marry two sisters? (4) Can a man receive Communion after a sex dream?[16]

Pope Gregory responded to each question in turn. To the first, after acknowledging its legality under Roman law, Gregory affirmed that first cousins, and certainly not anyone closer, were strictly prohibited from marrying. He then also confirmed that a man could not marry his stepmother or his dead brother's wife (no levirate marriage), even if they weren't related by blood. Although these responses meant that Augustine had his work cut out for him, the reply wasn't all bad news. The pope was fine with a pair of brothers marrying a pair of sisters, as long as the sets of siblings weren't related.[17]

Almost two centuries later, in 786, a papal commission again arrived in England, this time to assess the progress on Christianizing the Anglo-Saxons. Their report indicates that, although many had been baptized, there were serious issues among the faithful surrounding (1) incest (i.e., cousin marriage) and (2) polygyny. To uproot these stubborn customs, the Church promulgated the notion of "illegitimate children," which stripped the inheritance rights from all children except those born within legal—i.e., Christian—marriages. Prior to this, as in many societies, the children of secondary wives in polygynous unions had possessed some inheritance rights. For royalty, the sons of secondary wives could be "raised up" to succeed their father as king, especially if the king's primary wife was childless. Fighting this, by promoting the notion of "illegitimacy" and endowing itself with the power to determine who is legitimately married, the Church had seized a powerful lever of influence. These interventions made it substantially less appealing for cousins to marry or for women to become secondary wives.

Imposing these policies took centuries, in part because enforcement on the ground was so difficult. Throughout the ninth century, popes and other churchmen continued to complain to Anglo-Saxon kings about incest, polygyny, and illegitimacy, as well as the crime of having sex with nuns. In response, the Church could and sometimes did excommunicate elite men for marrying multiple women. By about 1000 CE, through its relentless efforts, the Church had largely prevailed in reshaping Anglo-Saxon (English) kinship.[18]

The Anglo-Saxon mission is just one example of a much broader effort that reaches back before the fall of the Western Roman Empire (476 CE). Beginning in the fourth century, the Church and the newly Christian Empire began to lay down a series of new policies, again in fits and starts, that gradually corroded the pillars that supported intensive kinship. Keep in mind, however, that there is no single coherent program here, at least in the beginning. Things look scattershot and idiosyncratic for centuries; but slowly, the successful bits and pieces coalesced into what I'll call the Church's Marriage and Family Program—the MFP. In undermining the intensive kin-based institutions in Europe, the MFP:

1. Prohibited marriage to blood relatives. These prohibitions were gradually extended to include quite distant relatives, up to sixth

cousins. This essentially tabooed marriage or sex between those who shared one or more of their 128 great-great-great-great-great-grandparents.

2. Prohibited marriage to affinal kin within the circle of tabooed blood relatives. If your husband died, you couldn't then marry his brother, your brother-in-law. In the eyes of the Church, your husband's brother became like your real brother (incest!).

3. Prohibited polygynous marriage, including the taking of secondary wives, as well as the use of sex slaves and publicly supported brothels. Brothels were both legal and common in the Roman Empire, which may explain why Latin has 25 words for "prostitute."[19]

4. Prohibited marriage to non-Christians (unless they have converted).

5. Created spiritual kinship, which established the institution of godparents. This institution provided a means to form new social bonds to care for children. Of course, you couldn't marry or have sex with spiritual kinfolk.[20]

6. Discouraged the adoption of children. Mothers were to care for their own children; if they couldn't, the Church or godparents would provide.[21]

7. Required both the bride and groom to publicly consent ("I do") to marriage. This suppressed arranged marriages and began to more firmly hitch marriage to romantic love.

8. Encouraged, and sometimes required, newly married couples to set up independent households—neolocal residence. The Church also encouraged the use of traditional marriage payments (e.g., dowry) to help fund this new residence.

9. Encouraged the individual ownership of property (land) and inheritance by personal testament. This meant that individuals could personally decide where their property went after their death.

To anyone other than an anthropologist, this might all sound boring or inconsequential, hardly the spark that ignited the blaze of Western civilization or the source of a major shift in people's psychology. However, by looking more closely, we can see how the Church's policies threw a barrage of monkey wrenches into the machinery of intensive kinship while simultaneously catalyzing its own spread. We'll first look at how the Church dismantled traditional marriage, then consider how it sapped the vigor of Europe's clans and kindreds, and finally see how it got rich on death, inheritance, and the afterlife.

EXPANDING THE INCEST TABOOS

In pre-Christian Europe, as in much of the world until recently, marriage customs had evolved culturally to empower and expand large kin-based organizations or networks. Marital bonds establish economic and social ties between kin-groups that foster trade, cooperation, and security. To sustain such ties, long-term marital exchanges are necessary, which usually means that new marriages must occur between blood or affinal relatives (in-laws). In patrilineal societies, senior males—the patriarchs—administer these ongoing spousal exchanges and thus use the marriage of their sisters, daughters, nieces, and granddaughters to cement relations with other kin-groups and nourish important alliances. Arranged marriages thus represent a key source of patriarchal power.[22]

The Church dramatically undercut the potency of marriage as a social technology and a source of patriarchal power by prohibiting polygynous unions, arranged marriages, and all marriages between both blood and affinal kinfolk. Illustrating this with just a sampling of the relevant decisions and decrees, Table 5.2 reveals the slow but relentless development of the taboos and punishments surrounding marriage within the Church from the fourth century onward. These policies sapped the lifeblood from Europe's kin-based institutions, weakened traditional authorities, and eventually dissolved Europe's tribes.[23]

TABLE 5.2. KEY MILESTONES IN THE MARRIAGE AND FAMILY PROGRAM (MFP)[24]

Year	Prohibitions and Declarations on Marriage from the Church and Secular Rulers
305–6	Synod of Elvira (Granada, Spain) decrees that any man who takes the sister of his dead wife as his new wife (sororate marriage) should abstain from Communion for five years. Those marrying their daughters-in-law should abstain from Communion until near death.[25]
315	Synod of Neocaesarea (Turkey) forbids marrying the wife of one's brother (levirate marriage) and possibly also sororate marriage.
325	Council of Nicaea (Turkey) prohibits marrying the sister of one's dead wife as well as Jews, pagans, and heretics.
339	The Roman Emperor Constantius prohibits uncle-niece marriages, in accordance with Christian sentiments, and imposes the death penalty on violators.
384/7	The Christian Roman Emperor Theodosius reaffirms prohibitions against sororate and levirate marriages and bans first cousin marriage. In 409, the Western emperor Honorius softens the law by allowing dispensations. It is not clear how long this persisted in the West. The dissolving Western Empire makes continued enforcement unlikely.
396	The Eastern Roman Emperor Arcadius (a Christian) again prohibits first cousin marriage, but without the harsh penalties. In 400 or 404, however, he changes his mind, making cousin marriage legal in the Eastern Empire.
506	Synod of Agde (France, Visigoth Kingdom) prohibits first and second cousin marriage, and marriage to a brother's widow, wife's sister, stepmother, uncle's widow, uncle's daughter, or any kinswoman. These are defined as incest.
517	Synod of Epaone (France or Switzerland, Burgundian kingdom) decrees that unions with first and second cousins are incestuous and henceforth forbidden, although existing unions are not dissolved. The synod also forbids marriage to stepmothers, widows of brothers, sisters-in-law, and aunts by marriage. Many subsequent synods in the area of what would become the Carolingian Empire refer to this synod for incest regulations.
527/31	Second Synod of Toledo (Spain) prescribes excommunication for all engaged in incestuous marriages. The number of years of excommunication should equal the number of years of the marriage. This is affirmed by synods in 535, 692, and 743.
538	First documented letter between a Frankish king and the pope is about incest (marriage to the wife of a deceased brother). The pope disapproves, but he leaves decisions about Penance to the bishops.
589	Reccared I, the Visigothic King (Spain), decrees the dissolution of incestuous marriages, punishing offenders with exile, and the transfer of their property to their children.

TABLE 5.2. KEY MILESTONES IN THE MARRIAGE AND FAMILY PROGRAM (MFP) *(cont.)*

Year	Prohibitions and Declarations on Marriage from the Church and Secular Rulers
596	The Frankish King Childebert II decrees the death penalty for marriage to one's stepmother but leaves the punishment of other incest violations to the bishops. If the convicted resists the Church's punishment, his property will be seized and redistributed to his relatives (creating incentives to report violators).
627	Synod of Clichy implements the same punishment and enforcement procedures as those decreed by King Childebert II in 596. A systematic collection of incest legislation is compiled around this time and becomes part of the *Collectio vetus Gallica*, the oldest collection of canons from Gaul.
643	Lombard laws of Rothari forbid marriage to one's stepmother, stepdaughter, and sister-in-law.
692	At the Synod of Trullo (Turkey), the Eastern Church finally forbids marriage to one's first cousins and corresponding affinal kin. This prohibits a father and a son marrying a mother and a daughter or two sisters, and two brothers marrying a mother and a daughter or two sisters.
721	Roman Synod (Italy) prohibits marriage to one's brother's wife, niece, grandchild, stepmother, stepdaughter, cousin, godmother, and all kinfolk including anyone ever married to any blood relative. In 726, Pope Gregory II specifies that for missionary purposes the prohibitions are up to first cousins, but for others the prohibitions extend to all known relatives. His successor, Gregory III, clarifies this prohibition such that marriages of third cousins are allowed but marriages to all affinal kin within the prohibited degree are not. These decisions are widely disseminated.
741	Under the Byzantine Emperor Leo III, the prohibitions in the Eastern Church are increased to include marriage of second cousins and, slightly later, second cousins once removed. The penalty for cousin marriage becomes whipping.
743	Roman Synod under Pope Zacharias orders Christians to refrain from marrying cousins, nieces, and other kinfolk. Such incest is punishable by excommunication and, if necessary, anathema (see text).
755	The Synod of Verneuil (France), convened under the Frankish King Pepin, commands that marriages be performed publicly.
756	Synod of Verbier (France) prohibits the marriage of third cousins and closer and decrees existing marriages between second cousins are to be ended. Those married to third cousins need only do Penance.
757	Synod of Compiègne (France) rules that existing marriages of second cousins or closer must be nullified. The Frankish king, Pepin, threatens secular punishments for any who disagree.

(continued)

TABLE 5.2. KEY MILESTONES IN THE MARRIAGE AND FAMILY PROGRAM (MFP) *(cont.)*

Year	Prohibitions and Declarations on Marriage from the Church and Secular Rulers
796	Synod of Friuli (Italy) directs attention to prenuptial investigations into potentially incestuous marriages and prohibits clandestine unions. The synod prescribes a waiting time before marriage during which neighbors and elders can examine whether a blood relationship exists that would prohibit marriage. The decree also stipulates that although infidelity by the wife is a legitimate reason for divorce, remarriage is impossible as long as both spouses live. Charlemagne puts his secular authority behind these rulings in 802.
802	Charlemagne's capitulary insists that nobody should attempt to marry until the bishops and priests, together with the elders, have investigated the blood relations of the prospective spouses.
874	Synod of Douci (France) urges subjects to refrain from marrying third cousins. To strengthen the ruling, the synod makes the children of incestuous unions ineligible for succession to an estate.
909	Synod of Trosle (France) clarifies and affirms the Synod of Douci, deeming that children born in an incestuous marriage are ineligible to inherit property or titles.
948	Synod of Ingelheim (Germany) prohibits marriage with all kin as far back as memory goes.
1003	At the Synod of Diedenhofen (Germany), Emperor Heinrich II (St. Henry the Exuberant) substantially widens the incest ban to include sixth cousins. He may have done this to weaken his political rivals.
1023	Synod of Seligenstadt (Germany) likewise forbids cousin marriage to sixth cousins. Bishop Burchard of Worms's *Decretum* also extends the definition of incestuous marriages to include sixth cousins.
1059	At the Synod of Rome, Pope Nicholas II forbids marriage to sixth cousins or as far back as relatives can be traced. His successor, Pope Alexander II, likewise decrees that marriages to sixth cousins or closer relatives are forbidden. The Kingdom of Dalmatia gets a temporary dispensation, forbidding marriages only out to fourth cousins.
1063	Synod of Rome forbids marriages up to sixth cousins.
1072	Synod of Rouen (France) forbids non-Christian marriages and decrees a priestly inquiry into all those about to wed.
1075	Synod of London (England) forbids marriages up to sixth cousins, including affinal kin.
1101	In Ireland, the Synod of Cashel introduces the incest prohibitions of the Catholic Church.

TABLE 5.2. KEY MILESTONES IN THE MARRIAGE AND FAMILY PROGRAM (MFP) (cont.)

Year	Prohibitions and Declarations on Marriage from the Church and Secular Rulers
1102	Synod of London nullifies existing marriages between sixth cousins (and closer) and decrees that third parties who knew of marriages among relatives are implicated in the crime of incest.
1123	The First Lateran Council (Italy) condemns unions between blood relatives (without specifying the relatedness) and declares that those who contracted an incestuous marriage will be deprived of hereditary rights.
1140	*Decretum* of Gratian: marriages of up to sixth cousins are forbidden.
1166	Synod of Constantinople (Turkey) reinforces the earlier Eastern Church's prohibitions on cousin marriages (second cousins once removed and closer), and tightens enforcement.
1176	The Bishop of Paris, Odo, helps introduce "the bans of marriage"—that is, the public notice of impending marriages in front of the congregation.
1200	Synod of London requires publication of the "bans of marriage," and decrees that marriages be conducted publicly. Kin marriages are forbidden, though the degree of kinship is not specified.
1215	Fourth Lateran Council (Italy) reduces marriage prohibitions to third-degree cousins and all closer blood relatives and affines. All prior rulings are also formalized and integrated into a constitution of canons. This brings prenuptial investigations and marriage bans into a formal legislative and legal framework.
1917	Pope Benedict XV loosens restrictions further, prohibiting only marriage to second cousins and all closer blood and affinal relatives.
1983	Pope John Paul II further loosens incest restrictions, allowing second cousins and more distant relatives to marry.

Appendix A supplies a more complete version of this table.

The importance of marriage norms for sustaining intensive kinship can be observed in the practices of *levirate* and *sororate* marriage. In many societies, social norms govern what happens to wives or husbands after their spouses die. Under levirate marriage, a widow marries her husband's brother (her brother-in-law), who can be either a real brother or a cousin-brother. Such marriages sustain the alliance between the kin-groups created by the original union. Conceptually, this works because brothers usually occupy the same role within a kinship network, so they are interchangeable, from the kin-group's point of view (though probably not from the wife's point of view). Marrying your brother-in-law might sound strange, but it is both cross-culturally common and biblically approved—check out Deuteronomy 25:5–6 and Genesis 38:8. Similarly, in sororate marriage, if a wife dies, she should be replaced by her unmarried sister or sometimes her cousin-sister, which similarly sustains the marital links that bind kin-groups together.

When the Church banned marriage to in-laws, classifying them as "siblings" to make such unions incestuous, the bonds between kin-groups were broken by the death of either spouse, since the surviving wife or husband was prohibited from incestuously marrying any of their affines. Moreover, not only were the marital ties severed, but the surviving spouses were often freed (or forced) to look elsewhere. Any wealth a wife brought with her into the marriage (e.g., her dowry) often then left with her. This meant that marriages couldn't permanently enrich kin-groups the way they traditionally had.

The banning of sororate and levirate marriages were among the first actions taken as the Church began to restructure European families (Table 5.2). In 315 CE, for example, the Synod of Neocaesarea (now Niksar, Turkey) banned men from marrying the wife of a dead brother—no levirate marriage. A decade later, in 325, the Council of Nicaea prohibited men from marrying the sister of a dead wife—no sororate marriage—and from marrying Jews, pagans, and heretics. These early decrees were modified in the eighth century to include prohibitions against marrying all affines, since they had only initially prohibited remarriage to "true" brothers.[26]

The Church gradually extended its marriage prohibitions—the circle of incest—from primary relatives (e.g., daughters) and key in-laws (e.g., son's wife) to include first cousins, siblings-in-law, and godchildren. The process first accelerated in the sixth century, under the Merovingian (Frankish) kings. From 511 to 627 CE, 13 of 17 Church councils addressed the problem of "incestuous" marriage. By the beginning of the 11th century, the Church's incest taboos had swollen to include even sixth cousins, which covered not only blood relatives but also affines and spiritual kin. For all practical purposes, these taboos excluded everyone you (or anyone else) believed that you were related to by blood, marriage, or spiritual kinship (god relatives). However, probably because these broad-ranging taboos were used to make bogus accusations of "incest" against political opponents, the Fourth Lateran Council in 1215 narrowed the circle of incest to encompass only third cousins and closer, including the corresponding affinal and spiritual relations. Third cousins share a great-great-grandparent.[27]

Over the same centuries, the penalties for incest violations tended toward greater severity. Punishments for incestuous marriages evolved from suspending the perpetrators from the Communion rite to excommunication and anathema—a solemn ritual promoted in the eighth century in which the soul of the excommunicant was formally handed over to Satan. Initially, existing marriages to forbidden relatives were grandfathered in as acceptable. Later, however, preexisting marriages were nullified as part of new decrees. Those who refused to separate when their marriages were suddenly nullified faced excommunication and anathema.[28]

Medieval excommunication was a major penalty, especially as the Church gained influence. Excommunicants were perceived as tainted by a kind of spiritual contagion, and thus Christians were forbidden to employ, or even interact with, them. Legally, excommunicants were restricted from entering into contracts with other Christians, and existing contracts were rendered void, or at least suspended until the excommunication was lifted. Debts to an excommunicated creditor could be ignored. The Council of Tribur in 895 even decreed that excommunicants, unless they were actively pursuing absolution, could be murdered without penalty. Those who didn't eschew the excommunicated risked catching the sinner's taint and other serious penalties, including ostracism. Violators who refused to pursue absolution by dissolving their incestuous marriages went to hell for eternity.[29]

If an excommunicant repeatedly refused to pursue absolution for their incestuous marriage, the Church could declare an anathema. Besides the obvious problem of going to hell, losing one's soul to Satan exposed excommunicants to all kinds of pains, accidents, and illnesses during their remaining life. It was as if, through its ritual powers, the Church had lowered its protective shield from around these incestuous "sinners," leaving them unprotected in a demon-haunted world. Clearly the Church had wheeled in the heavy supernatural artillery to defend its expanding incest taboos.

Although the Church's policies were clear, much remains unknown about how effectively MFP policies were implemented. We don't, for example, have any statistics on the declining rates of cousin marriage in different regions from 500 to 1200. Nevertheless, the historical record does make a few things evident: (1) these new policies were not merely after-the-fact codifications of existing customs; and (2) there were active efforts by the Church, though uneven across space and time, to get people to comply with the MFP. These inferences are supported by a continuous stream of policy reversals, reiterations, and long-running disputes associated with the Church's prohibitions. Early on, for example, we know that entire tribes actively sought more relaxed incest restrictions. In the eighth century, the Lombards lobbied the pope to permit them to marry their more distant cousins (second cousins and beyond).[30] The pope said no (also see Table 5.2: 1059 in the Kingdom of Dalmatia). Similarly, when the option became available, Christians willingly paid to purchase dispensations to marry their relatives. In Iceland just after Christianization, for example, the only paid political position—the Lawspeaker—was funded by these payments. Later records show Europeans in Catholic regions continued to pay for papal dispensations to marry their cousins well into the 20th century. And, though popes and bishops strategically picked their battles, these policies were sometimes imposed on kings, nobles, and other aristocrats. In the 11th century, for example, when the Duke of Normandy married a distant cousin from Flanders, the pope promptly excommunicated them both. To get their excommunications lifted, or risk anathema, each constructed a beautiful abbey for the Church. The pope's power is impressive here, since this duke was no delicate flower; he would later become William the Conqueror (of England).[31]

Now, although I can't cite any medieval statistics on cousin marriage, there is an elegant method to detect the MFP's imprint in fossilized kinship terminologies. By studying European languages in their earliest written sources, we see that they possessed kin terminologies that match the characteristics of the terminological systems used by societies with intensive kinship around the world. These linguistic systems, for example, possess special terms for "mother's brother" or "father's brother's son." At some point during the last 1,500 years, however, most of the languages of western Europe adopted the terminological system used for kinship in modern English, German, French, and Spanish, among other languages. This transformation in kin terminology occurred first in the Romance languages (Spanish, Italian, and French), roughly around 700 CE. In German and English, the transformation was well underway by 1100. Meanwhile, in remote parts of Scotland, people continued to use intensive kinship terminology late into the 17th century. Given that changes in kinship terminologies are thought to lag behind the "on-the-ground" changes in people's lives by a few centuries, this timing seems to roughly match the rolling implementation of the MFP.[32]

The Church's footprints can be seen even more directly in modern European languages, such as English. What do you call your brother's wife?

She's your "sister-in-law." What's with the "in-law" bit? Why is she like a sister, and what law are we talking about?

The "in-law" bit means "in canon law," so from the Church's point of view, she's like your sister—no sex or marriage, but treat her sweetly. At roughly the same time that "in-law" appeared in English, the terms for affines used in German changed to combine a prefix that means "affinal" with the appropriate term for the equivalent blood relative. So, the term for "mother-in-law" went from "*Swigar*" in Old High German (a unique term, not related to "mother") to "*Schwiegermutter*," or roughly "affinal-mother."

The role of the Church is obvious in English ("in-law"), but how do we know the Church was involved in German? Perhaps there's a subpopulation of German speakers who resisted the Church's influence and thus preserved the ancient kinship terminology in their dialect?

Yiddish, the Jewish dialect of German that split off from High German in the Middle Ages, still uses terms for in-laws derived from Old High German, before the transformation in affinal terminology that yoked affines to blood relatives and thereby imposed incest taboos. This fingers the Church as the cause of the transformation.[33]

Taken together, there seems little doubt that the Church's efforts gradually transformed the kinship organizations of European populations in ways that were eventually reflected in language. But why?

WHY THESE TABOOS?

Why did the Church adopt these incest prohibitions? The answer to this question has multiple layers. The first is simply that the faithful, including Church leaders, came to believe that sex and marriage with relatives was against God's will. For example, a plague in the sixth century was seen as God's punishment for incestuous marriages, which would have involved mostly marriages between cousins and affines. This form of incest was also seen as tainting the blood in ways that could contaminate others, both morally and physically. Given that many held these beliefs, the Church's efforts can be seen as a kind of public health campaign. But, this just backs the question up to why people might come to see incest in this expansive way. Incest taboos are psychologically palatable, in part because of our innate aversion to inbreeding, but most people across human history haven't believed this extends to affines, spiritual kin, and distant cousins.

To see the second layer, we now need to "zoom out" and remember that there were many religious groups competing in the Mediterranean and Middle East, each with different and often idiosyncratic religious convictions. The Church was just the "lucky one" that bumbled across an effective recombination of supernatural beliefs and practices. The MFP is a mixture that peppers a blend of old Roman customs and Jewish law with Christianity's own unique obsession with sex (i.e., not having it) and free will. Early Roman law, for example, prohibited close cousin marriage, though the law of the Roman Empire—where Christianity was born—permitted it without social stigma. Jewish law prohibited marriage (or sex) with some affines but permitted cousin marriage, polygynous marriage, and uncle-niece marriage. Roman law only recognized monogamous marriages, but basically ignored secondary wives and sex slaves (until Christianity took over). The Church blended these customs and laws with new ideas, prohibitions, and preferences in creating the MFP. At the same time, other religious groups experimented with their own combinations of customs, supernatural beliefs, and religious taboos. Then, equipped with their different cultural packages and divine commitments, these groups competed for adherents. Winners and losers were sorted out in the long run (Chapter 4).[34]

In this cauldron of competition, let's take a look at what other religious communities were doing with marriage during this epoch.[35] Table 5.3 summarizes the marriage policies for a few of the Western Church's competitors. Zoroastrianism, a potent universalizing religion in Persia, favored marriage to relatives, especially cousins, but including siblings and other close relatives. Today, Zoroastrianism survives, but with only a few hundred thousand adherents. The other Abrahamic religions all build off Mosaic law in various ways. All permitted cousin marriage for centuries after the Church's ban began, and some still permit it today. Cousin marriage is by far the most common form of kin marriage, so if you aren't banning cousin marriage, you're missing a pillar of intensive kin-based institutions. Similarly, both levirate and polygynous marriage were permitted in Judaism and Islam. This is interesting because it means that, although the Church's policies also built on Mosaic law, the MFP overruled implicit biblical endorsements of levirate, cousin, and polygynous marriage.[36]

The Eastern Orthodox Church (hereinafter the Orthodox Church) provides an important comparative case since it was officially united with the Western Church in Late Antiquity but slowly diverged until finally splitting formally in the Great Schism in 1054. However, by comparison with the Western Church's expanding set of marital prohibitions and escalating sanctions, the Orthodox Church only sluggishly followed the MFP, especially as it developed in the Merovingian Dynasty. Marriage to first cousins wasn't prohibited until 692. This prohibition was expanded to include second cousins in the eighth century, but never to third cousins. At the same time, the Eastern Church's monitoring and enforcement efforts didn't keep pace with those of the Western Church. The Orthodox Church's policy

TABLE 5.3. MARRIAGE PROHIBITIONS FOR SOME MAJOR RELIGIOUS COMMUNITIES[37]

Religious Tradition	Marriage Policies and Patterns in Late Antiquity and the Early Middle Ages
Zoroastrianism (Persia)	Advocated marriage with close relatives, including cousins, nieces, and even siblings. When a man died without a son, he couldn't enter heaven unless his surviving wife had a son with his brother. Both levirate and sororate marriage were permitted, as was polygyny.
Judaism	Followed Mosaic law, which forbids marriage to primary relatives and close affines (within the household, mostly). Cousin marriage was permitted, and both levirate and uncle-niece marriage were encouraged. Polygynous marriage was permitted until the beginning of the second millennium of the Common Era.
Islam	Built on Mosaic law, but explicitly prohibited uncle-niece marriage. Muslim societies in the Middle East promoted a nearly unique marriage preference in which a son married his father's brother's daughters. Levirate marriage was permitted, with the wife's agreement. Polygynous marriage was permitted but constrained to a maximum of four wives with equal status.
Orthodox Christianity	Followed Mosaic law but prohibited levirate and sororate marriage. Cousin marriage was permitted until 692 (Table 5.2), and later bans never extended to third cousins. Uncle-niece marriage was often tolerated. Polygynous marriage was prohibited under Roman law. This is essentially an "MFP-light."

decisions are shaded in gray in Table 5.2. We can think of the Orthodox Church as implementing an MFP-light.[38]

The bigger point is that different religious groups developed a broad range of divinely endorsed forms of marriage, ranging from Zoroastrianism's brother-sister unions to the Western Church's blanket ban on marriage to even the most remote affinal relatives (sixth cousins). The Western Church came to hold an extreme set of incest taboos, perceived to be rooted in their God's will, that had big downstream consequences and eventually opened the door to WEIRD psychology.

In trying to figure out where the Church's incest taboos came from, you might suspect that Latin Christians had somehow deduced the long-term social or genetic effects of various marriage prohibitions. While a few scattered Muslim and Christian writers did indeed speculate on these effects, such vague speculations about the possible impacts of various marriage customs don't seem to have anchored the religious debates surrounding incest or motivated the abolition of venerable marriage customs. Even in the modern world, where detailed scientific data are available, debates about both cousin marriage and polygamy persist. Moreover, neither a dim recognition of the health effects of inbreeding nor the social benefits of monogamously marrying strangers can explain the incest taboos on affines, stepsiblings, and godparents (and godparents' children)—they aren't genetically related and needn't be socially close.[39]

Ultimately, the Western Church, like other religions, adopted its constellation of marriage-related beliefs and practices—the MFP—for a complex set of historical reasons. Yet what matters for us here is how different sets of religiously-inspired beliefs and practices actually impacted life on the ground, in comparison with the alternatives and in competition with other societies over the long run. In the next two millennia, how did the societies influenced by the MFP fare relative to other groups, who adopted or maintained more intensive ways of organizing kinship?[40]

The MFP's overall impact on medieval European societies was far-reaching, as we'll see below and in the coming chapters. For now, just consider that someone looking for a spouse in the 11th century would have had to theoretically exclude on average 2,730 cousins and potentially 10,000 total relatives as candidates, including the children, parents, and surviving spouses of all those cousins. In the modern world, with bustling cities of millions, we could easily handle such prohibitions. But, in the medieval world of scattered farms, intimate villages, and small towns, these prohibitions would have forced people to reach out, far and wide, to find Christian strangers from other communities, often in different tribal or ethnic groups. These effects were, I suspect, felt most strongly in the middle economic strata, among those successful enough to be noticed by the Church but not powerful enough to use bribery or other influence to circumvent the rules. So, the MFP likely first dissolved intensive kinship from the middle outward. The elites of Europe would be the last holdouts, as the MFP silently and systematically reorganized the social structure beneath them (Figure 3.3).[41]

ENDING LINEAGES: ADOPTION, POLYGAMY, AND REMARRIAGE

Though clans and lineages are psychologically potent institutions, they have a weakness: they must produce heirs every generation. A single generation without heirs can mean the end of a venerable lineage. Mathematically, lineages with a few dozen, or even a few hundred, people will eventually fail to produce an adult of the "right" sex—e.g., males in a patrilineal clan or dynasty. In any given generation, roughly 20 percent of families will have only one sex (e.g., girls), and 20 percent won't have any children. This means that all lineages will eventually find themselves without any members of the inheriting sex. Because of this, cultural evolution has devised various *strategies of heirship* that involve adoption, polygamy, and remarriage. Adoption, common in many societies, permits families without heirs of the appropriate sex to simply adopt an heir, usually from a relative. With polygynous marriage, males who fail to produce an heir with their first wife can simply take a second or third wife and keep trying. In monogamous societies, such as Rome, those desperate for an heir can divorce and remarry in hopes of getting a more fertile partner.[42]

The Church relentlessly blocked these strategies at every turn. Adoption had been an important element in Europe's pre-Christian societies, and laws regulating adoption existed in both ancient Greece and Rome. Yet by the middle of the first millennium, the law codes of Christianized tribes were devoid of legal mechanisms for formally transferring kinship assignments, inheritance rights, and ritual responsibilities. The Church's efforts effectively bound all forms of inheritance directly to the genealogical line of descent. As a result, legal adoption makes no appearance in English law until 1926, where it followed the legalization of adoption in France (1892) and Massachusetts (1851).[43]

The Church, as noted above, undermined polygynous marriage as an heirship strategy not only by flatly banning additional wives of any kind but also by promoting the notion of illegitimacy. In pre-Christian Europe, various forms of polygynous unions were widespread, if we judge by the stream of concerns expressed by the bishops and missionaries who were working to stamp out the practice. Wealthy men could often take one primary wife and then add secondary wives. To supply an heir, the children of secondary wives could be "raised up" to continue the lineage, make crucial ritual sacrifices to the ancestors, and inherit the estate and titles. By only recognizing the children of a man's legal wife (married in the Church) as legitimate, and thus eligible for inheritance and succession, the Church stymied the practice of "raising up" and closed this common avenue to heirship.[44]

If you can't add wives to your household via polygyny, perhaps you can divorce and remarry a younger wife in hopes of producing an heir?

No, the Church shut this down, too. In 673 CE, for example, the Synod of Hertford decreed that, even after a legitimate divorce, remarriage was impossible. Surprisingly, even kings were not immune from such prohibitions. In the mid-ninth century, when the king of Lothringia sent his first wife away and took his concubine as his primary wife, two successive popes waged a decade-long campaign to bring him back into line. After repeated entreaties, synods, and threats of excommunication, the king finally caved in and traveled to Rome to ask for forgiveness. These papal skirmishes continued through the Middle Ages. Finally, in the 16th century, King Henry VIII turned England Protestant in response to such papal stubbornness.[45]

The Church's constraints on adoption, polygamy, and remarriage meant that lineages would eventually find themselves without heirs and die out. Under these constraints, many European dynasties died out for the lack of an heir. As with the MFP's incest prohibitions, these extinctions benefited the Church by freeing people from the constraints of intensive kinship and generating a flow of wealth into Church coffers. The new revenues were created by selling *annulments*: Yes, remarriage was impossible . . . but under some conditions, first marriages could be annulled—rendered invalid, never to have existed. Of course, this kind of powerful magic was expensive.

Now, let's look at how these policies, along with some adjustments to people's norms about ownership and inheritance, made the Church the largest landowner in Europe while at the same time decimating Europe's intensive kin-based institutions, thereby gradually altering the social worlds that each successive generation had to confront.[46]

INDIVIDUAL OWNERSHIP AND PERSONAL TESTAMENTS

Intensive kin-based institutions often possess social norms that regulate inheritance and the ownership of land or other important resources. In lineage- or clan-based societies, for example, lands are often corporately owned by all members of a kin-group. Inheritance in these situations is straightforward: the new generation of clan members collectively inherits from the previous generation, so there's no individual ownership. Often, the notion of selling clan lands is unthinkable because these territories are the home of the clan's ancestors, and deeply tied into the clan's rituals and identity. Even when such links aren't an issue or can be overcome, it's still the case that everyone in a kin-group, or at least every head of household, must consent to any sale, thus making such sales rare. In kindreds, where more individualized notions of ownership are common, brothers, half-brothers, uncles, and cousins usually retain residual claims on the deceased's lands or other wealth. These claims are firmly grounded in custom and thus cannot be easily overridden by any preferences the deceased owner may have expressed. That is, a father simply cannot disinherit his brothers or even his cousins in favor of his servant or priest. Inheritance isn't left to individual preference. In such societies, WEIRD notions of ownership and personal testaments may be nonexistent, or limited to a narrow set of circumstances. In this world, the Church maneuvered to benefit itself by promoting individual ownership and inheritance by personal testaments (wills).

To see how this worked, let's start in the Roman Empire during Late Antiquity, when individual ownership and testamentary inheritance were legally available to the elite. With these tools, Christian leaders such as Ambrose of Milan developed a doctrine that gave wealthy Christians a way to solve the otherwise intractable "camel-through-the-eye-of-a-needle" problem.

This dilemma arises from the Gospel of Matthew (19:21–26), where Jesus challenges a rich young man:

> "If you would be perfect, go, sell what you possess and give to the poor, and you will have treasure in heaven; and come, follow me." When the young man heard this, he went away sorrowful; for he had great possessions. And Jesus said to his disciples, "Truly, I say to you, it will be hard for a rich man to enter the kingdom of heaven. Again, I tell you, it is easier for a camel to go through the eye of a needle than for a rich man to enter the kingdom of God."

Molding this parable into a cornerstone, Ambrose erected a treasury for the Church by promulgating the idea that the wealthy could indeed get into heaven by giving their wealth to the poor, through the Church. Ideally, rich Christians should give their wealth to the poor and put themselves into God's service. But, the Church also provided a psychologically easier alternative: rich people could bequest some or all of their wealth to the poor at the time of their death. This allowed the wealthy to stay rich all their lives, but to still thread the proverbial needle, by giving generously to the poor at their death.[47]

This charitable doctrine was genius. For wealthy Christians, the idea provided a powerful incentive firmly rooted in the words of Jesus. It inspired a few Roman aristocrats to renounce their immense wealth and pursue lives of religious service. In 394 CE, for example, the super-rich Roman aristocrat Pontius Paulinus announced that he would follow Jesus's advice and give all of his wealth to the poor. Later that year in Barcelona, Paulinus was ordained a priest by popular acclaim. Such costly actions, especially when done by prestigious individuals like Paulinus, operate on our psychology as Credibility Enhancing Displays (CREDs, Chapter 4). Early Church leaders, including Ambrose of Milan, Augustine of Hippo, and Martin of Tours, all recognized the power of Paulinus' demonstration, and immediately promoted him as a paragon. Martin apparently went around exclaiming, "There is someone to imitate." The psychological effects of such costly renunciations of wealth would have: (1) implanted or deepened the faith in impressed observers, (2) sparked copycats who would also give away their wealth (further fueling the fire), and (3) enriched the Church, as the renounced wealth flowed to the poor through Church coffers.[48]

Unsurprisingly, most rich Christians were not sufficiently inspired to give all their wealth away, at least while they were still alive. However, paragons like Paulinus helped the Church convince people to give some or all of their wealth to the poor at their deaths. This charitable act, they were told, would provide them with the "treasure in heaven" mentioned by Jesus without all the hassle of living in poverty. Providing this back door into heaven was so effective in enriching the Church that secular rulers eventually had to enact laws to curb the wealthy from giving too much. The Visigoth king, for example, decreed that widows with any children or nephews were limited to giving away only a quarter of their estate, thereby leaving three-quarters to their children and kinfolk.[49]

The Church's focus on ministering to the sick and dying—a centerpiece of Christianity—explained, in part, why this doctrine was so effective. When rich Christians were dying, priests were summoned, as they still are today. These priests dutifully spent time with the dying, comforting them and preparing their immortal souls for the afterlife. An attentive priest, combined with the fear of an imminent death and some uncertainty about heaven vs. hell, apparently rendered the wealthy remarkably willing to bequest huge amounts of wealth to the poor (via the Church).

For the Church, this bequest strategy worked relatively well for the elite citizenry during Late Antiquity, as long as the governing institutions that enforced property rights, ownership, and testaments were still functioning. However, with the collapse of the Western Empire, the Church had to operate in a world where local tribal customs were just being codified and formalized. Since the earliest legal codes of tribal populations like the Anglo-Saxons and Franks reveal strong influences from intensive kinship, including customary inheritance rights, the Church had potent incentives to promote individual ownership and testamentary inheritance. Working with secular rulers, the Church pushed for laws supporting individual ownership, default inheritance rules favoring strictly lineal inheritance (cutting out brothers, uncles, and cousins), and greater autonomy in making bequests by testament.[50]

This drive for individual ownership and personal testaments would have weakened kin-based organizations, because these corporate groups would have continually lost their land and wealth to the Church. Lying on their deathbeds, Christians gave what they could to the Church to improve their prospects for the afterlife. Those without heirs, unable to adopt or remarry, could give all of their wealth to the Church once they were freed from the constraints of customary inheritance and corporate ownership. Kin-based organizations and their patriarchs were slowly bled to death as the Church phlebotomized their normal inheritance flows. Ancestral lands became Church lands.

These modifications to inheritance and ownership catalyzed and financed the Church's expansion. The spread of charitable donations would have both attracted new members through the persuasive power of expensive gifts—CREDs—and deepened the faith of existing members. At the same time, these bequests generated torrential revenues. The Church became immensely wealthy during the medieval period through a combination of bequests, tithes, and payments for services such as annulments and dispensations for cousin marriage. Among these, bequests made up by far the biggest portion of revenue. By 900 CE, the Church owned about a third of the cultivated land in western Europe, including in Germany (35 percent) and France (44 percent). By the Protestant Reformation in the 16th century, the Church owned half of Germany, and between one-quarter and one-third of England.[51]

By undermining intensive kinship, the MFP probably also dissolved the tribal distinctions among Europeans before the High Middle Ages. Tribal and ethnic communities, as noted in Chapter 2, are sustained in part by our inclinations to interact with and learn from those who share our language, dialect, dress, and other ethnic markers, as well as by the ease of interacting with those who share our social norms. Marriage is thus frequently a powerful force that reifies and reinforces tribal boundaries. The Church's

MFP operated to dissolve European tribes by (1) establishing a pan-tribal social identity (Christian), (2) compelling individuals to look far and wide to find unrelated Christian spouses, and (3) providing a new set of norms about marriage, inheritance, and residence that would have set a foundation on which diverse tribal communities could begin to interact, marry, and coordinate.[52]

By undermining Europe's kin-based institutions, the Church's MFP was both taking out its main rival for people's loyalty and creating a revenue stream. Under intensive kinship, loyalty to one's kin-group and tribal community comes first and requires much investment. With the weakening of kinship and dissolution of tribes, Christians seeking security could more fully dedicate themselves to the Church and other voluntary associations. The MFP also generated immense revenues—through marital dispensations, annulments, and bequests—that contributed to missionary work, new cathedrals, and poor relief (charity). Along with these social and financial contributions to the Church's success, the MFP's marriage prohibitions and inheritance prescriptions also altered the faithful's psychology in ways that fed back on the Church, altering it from within.[53]

The Carolingians, Manorialism, and the European Marriage Pattern

Beginning in the late sixth century, the Church found common cause with the Frankish rulers. Like many kings before and after, the Franks were constantly at odds with influential aristocratic families as well as numerous powerful clans. The MFP, by undercutting their ability to forge enduring alliances through marriage, constrained the size and solidarity of these noble families and rural kin-groups. Consequently, the Church and Frankish rulers teamed up, which put some secular authority and military punch behind the MFP (Table 5.2). In 596 CE, for example, the Merovingian king Childebert II decreed the death penalty for those who would marry their stepmothers but left the punishments for other incest violations up to the bishops. Any who resisted the bishops would have their lands seized and redistributed among their relatives—which created a potent incentive for kinfolk to keep tabs on each other. This alliance between the popes and the Frankish kings continued through Charles Martel and into the Carolingian Empire. Both King Pepin (the Short) and Emperor Charlemagne put incest prohibitions, policing, and punishments on the forefront of their political agendas.[54]

During his long rule, Charlemagne expanded his realm into Bavaria, northern Italy, Saxony (Germany), and parts of Muslim-controlled Spain. Sometimes leading and sometimes following, the Church grew in tandem with the Empire. This interdependence was highlighted on Christmas Day in 800 CE, when the pope crowned Charlemagne "Emperor of the Romans." Figure 5.3 shows the extent of the Carolingian Empire in 814, the year Charlemagne died.

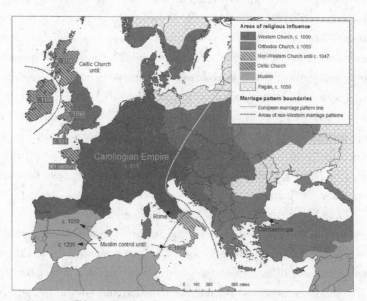

FIGURE 5.3. This map shows the boundaries of the Carolingian Empire in 814 CE and the territories claimed by the Western and Eastern Churches during the Great Schism (1054). The map also shows the lands under the Celtic Church and those controlled by Islamic powers. After roughly 1500, the European Marriage Pattern could be firmly documented in many of the regions that are interior to the dashed lines. For reference, the map marks the contemporary borders of modern European nations.[55]

Carolingian support for the Church's MFP reshaped European populations in ways that opened the door to new forms of organization and production. The first of these social and economic institutions, manorialism, emerged in the heartland of the Frankish empire as well as in England. Unlike the superficially similar institutions seen elsewhere, manorialism wasn't primarily rooted in either intensive kinship or slavery, as with the Roman villas of Late Antiquity. Instead, peasant couples entered into economic exchange relationships with large landowners and other peasant households. Although some of these farmers were serfs, tied to the land, many were free people. If their household needed labor, the couple hired teenagers or young adults from other households rather than tapping their own limited kin networks. A couple's children, depending on labor demands, often moved out during adolescence or young adulthood to begin working in either the lord's household or some other household that needed labor. When a son married, he could take over his parents' household or set up his own under his parents' lord or some other landowner. Or he could move to a town or city. If he took over his parents' farm, he'd become the head of household rather than working under his father; his parents then moved into a semiretirement phase. By allocating labor independent of kin ties, this economic system cemented neolocal residence and further curtailed patriarchal authority. Unrelated households in these manors provided a flexible labor pool and often cooperated by sharing water, mills, beehives, woodlands, orchards, vineyards, and stables.[56]

From a global and historical perspective, this form of manorialism is odd. In China during the same era, land and other resources were typically owned corporately by patrilineal clans. Clan-owned facilities included granaries, ancestor halls, and schools built to help prepare clan members for civil service examinations, which were required to enter government service. In Ireland, which was Christianized under the Celtic Church prior to the consolidation of the Western Church's MFP, manorialism was dominated by clans and reliant on slaves. Irish clans owned and controlled both the mills and the kilns. Cross-culturally, the reliance of Frankish manorialism on unrelated household helpers was unusual, as were nuclear households and neolocal residence. The weak kin ties of these manors meant that individuals and couples could (sometimes) leave for better options elsewhere, on other estates or in towns and monasteries (of course, landowners often resisted this).[57]

The complementarities between the Church's missionary interests, manorial organizations, and the Church's secular allies resulted in the injection of a particularly strong dosage of the MFP into the Carolingian Empire and England.[58] By roughly 1000 CE, manorial censuses confirm that peasant farming families lived in small, monogamous nuclear households and had two to four children. Young couples often formed independent neolocal households, sometimes moving to new manors. The age of marriage, however, remained young for girls, with estimates ranging from 10 to 15 years. This may have been because elite males were slow to relinquish their secondary wives. For example, with his 10 known primary or secondary wives, Charlemagne had 18 children. Among other royal families, these children sired three European dynasties: the Habsburgs, Capetians, and Plantagenets.[59]

By the end of the Middle Ages and into the Early Modern Period, the demographic data become plentiful enough that historians can begin to statistically delineate the European Marriage Pattern. This pattern is marked by certain key characteristics:

1. *Monogamous nuclear families with neolocal residence*, with males becoming heads of households at younger ages and new wives moving out from under the thumb of their mothers or mothers-in-law. Of course, nuclear families and neolocal residence were merely the ideal; economic circumstances still compelled many into extended families. By contrast, the ideal in China remained large, patrilocal multigenerational households, though sometimes circumstances forced people into nuclear households.[60]

2. *Late marriage*, with the average ages of both men and women often rising into the mid-20s. Many factors likely influence this pattern, including the importance of personal choice (no arranged

marriages), the challenge of finding nonrelatives (incest taboos), and the financial demands of setting up an independent household (neolocal residence).[61]

3. *Many women never marry*: By age 30, some 15–25 percent of northwestern European women remained unmarried. The Church provided a respectable alternative institutional mechanism to evade marriage: women could enter the convent. By contrast, in most societies close to 100 percent of females married, and usually at young ages. In traditional China, for example, only 1–2 percent of women remained unmarried at age 30.[62]

4. *Smaller families and lower fertility*: Smaller families were likely influenced by many factors, including fewer kin ties (less childcare), neolocal residence (less pressure from in-laws), a later age of marriage, and a lack of polygyny.

5. *Premarital labor period*: Between late childhood and early adulthood, young people often moved to work in the homes of other families, where they could earn money, learn new skills, and see how other households operated. The use of nonrelatives as "life-cycle servants" is rare in a global and historical perspective.[63]

The rough boundaries suggested for the European Marriage Pattern are sketched in Figure 5.3. The regions not showing this pattern are instructive. The Irish, having been Christianized too early, didn't experience the full force of the MFP until they were conquered by England in the 12th century. Similarly, southern Spain was under Muslim rule from 711 until 1492, though their territorial holdings gradually shrank during the period. Southern Italy, unlike the northern regions, was never consolidated within the Carolingian Empire (where the MFP was imposed early and forcefully), and various parts were governed by Muslim sultans or Byzantine emperors. In the east, the European Marriage Pattern is much closer to the borders of the old Carolingian Empire than to official borders mapped during the Great Schism between the Eastern and Western Churches.[64] This is because, though the Church did eventually expand eastward, the MFP arrived much later. In Chapter 7, we'll see that much of the variation in cousin marriage that persisted in Europe into the 20th century can be explained by knowing when the MFP arrived on the scene.[65]

Downstream Transformations

As their intensive kin-based institutions dissolved, medieval Europeans became increasingly free to move, both relationally and residentially. Released from family obligations and inherited interdependence, individuals began to choose their own associates—their friends, spouses, business partners, and even patrons—and construct their own relational networks. Relational freedom spurred residential mobility, as individuals and nuclear families relocated to new lands and growing urban communities. This opened a door to the development and spread of voluntary associations, including new religious organizations as well as novel institutions such as charter towns, professional guilds, and universities.[66] Such developments, underpinned by the psychological changes that I'll highlight over the next seven chapters, ushered in the Urban, Commercial, and Legal Revolutions of the High Middle Ages.[67]

The impact of societal change on the Church itself is interesting, as it represents a kind of feedback between the social and psychological shifts wrought by the MFP and the subsequent evolution of Catholic institutions. For example, the early monasteries in Anglo-Saxon England, before Pope Gregory's team arrived around 600 CE, tended to be family affairs. The offices of abbot and abbess passed among brothers or from mother to daughter. In Ireland, these practices continued for centuries, as monasteries were run by wealthy Irish clans and passed down as communal property.[68] However, the destruction of kin-based institutions, combined with the eventual delegitimization of priests' children, gradually suppressed the strong intrusion of intensive kinship into the Church's organizations. Many monasteries required aspiring monks to cut their kin ties as a condition of membership, making them choose between the Church and their families. Beginning with Cluny Abbey (910 CE) and accelerating with the emergence of the Cistercian Order (1098 CE), monasteries became less like clan businesses and more like NGOs, with the democratic election of abbots, written charters, and a hierarchical franchise structure that began to balance local independence with centralized authority.[69]

The Church's MFP reshaped the European family in a process that was largely complete 500 years ago. But, does this really influence psychology today? Does growing up in less intensive kin-based institutions influence our motivations, perceptions, emotions, thinking styles, and self-concepts in significant ways? Is there a way to trace contemporary psychological variation back to the Church?

6

Psychological Differences, Families, and the Church

Families represent the first institution we encounter upon arriving in the world, and, in most societies until recently, they have provided the central organizing framework for most people's lives. So, it makes sense that they might play a foundational role in shaping our minds and behavior. In Chapter 1, I showed global patterns of psychological variation in domains ranging from individualism, conformity, and guilt to impersonal trust, analytical thinking, and the use of intentionality in moral judgments. Here, I begin to lay down the evidence that this psychological variation arises, in part, as our minds adapt and calibrate to the culturally-constructed environments we confront, especially while growing up. We'll examine how intensive kin-based institutions influence people's psychology and, more specifically, how the Church's dismantling of intensive kinship in medieval Europe inadvertently pushed Europeans, and later populations on other continents, toward a WEIRDer psychology.

To accomplish this, I'll first lay out two ways of measuring the intensity of kin-based institutions for different ethnolinguistic groups and countries around the world. Then, using a wide-angle lens, I'll show that kinship intensity can explain significant chunks of the cross-national psychological variation highlighted in Chapter 1. You'll see that the weaker a population's traditional kin-based institutions, the WEIRDer their psychology is today. Next, I'll use the historical spread of the Church to create a measure of the duration of the Marriage and Family Program for every country in the world. Think of this as a time-release dosage of the MFP, measured in centuries of exposure to the Church. Using this historical dosage measure, we'll first see that the stronger the MFP dosage ingested by a population, the weaker their kin-based institutions. Finally, we'll directly connect these MFP dosages to contemporary psychological differences. Strikingly, the stronger the historical MFP dosage for a population, the WEIRDer their psychology is today.

In the next chapter, I'll focus on the psychological variation *within* Europe, and even within European countries, as well as within China and India. These analyses not only confirm the expected relationships between psychological variation and both kinship intensity and the Church, but should also fully immunize you against setting up the dichotomy of West vs. the Rest, or WEIRD vs. non-WEIRD in your mind. We are not observing fixed or essential differences among peoples but watching an ongoing cultural evolutionary process—influenced by multiple factors—playing out across geography and over centuries.

Kinship Intensity and Psychology

The relationship between kinship intensity and psychology has been systematically studied by my team, which includes the economists Jonathan Schulz, Duman Bahrami-Rad, and Jonathan Beauchamp, as well as by my colleague Benjamin Enke, who was inspired by the ideas in this book. Following these efforts, we'll measure kinship intensity using both an index of traditional kin-based norms as well as actual rates of cousin marriage for different populations. The first approach aggregates anthropological data from the Ethnographic Atlas into a single number for each population, which I'll call the Kinship Intensity Index, or KII. The KII combines the data that you saw summarized in Table 5.1 about cousin marriage, nuclear families, bilateral inheritance, neolocal residence, and monogamous marriage (vs. polygyny) with information on clans and customs about marrying within a certain community (endogamy). It thus captures the *historical* or *traditional* intensity of kin-based institutions for populations around the world, not 21st-century practices. The average date assigned to the anthropological data in the Atlas is about 1900 CE, so there's roughly a century between when our historical measures of kinship were observed and when our psychological measures were taken.

Historical institutions like kinship can influence contemporary psychology through multiple pathways. The most obvious pathway is through persistence, and kin-based institutions are notoriously durable. Using recent global surveys, my collaborators and I confirmed that the marriage and residence patterns reported in the Atlas have persisted to some degree into the 21st century. However, even when institutional practices have been abandoned, the values, motivations, and socialization practices that were wrapped around these traditional institutions can stick around for generations, sustained by cultural transmission. This creates a pathway through which even extinct historical institutions influence contemporary minds. For example, a population may have developed a whole set of values (e.g., filial piety), motivations (e.g., deference to elders), preferences (e.g., sons over daughters), and rituals surrounding their patrilineal clans, but then have their clan organizations legally banned and officially suppressed by the state (as happened in 1950s China). In this situation, cultural transmission can perpetuate a clannish psychology for generations, even after clan organizations have vanished. In fact, because people's psychology may not have had time to adapt to recently adopted kinship practices, measures of traditional kin-based institutions may even be better at explaining psychological variation than are contemporaneous family institutions.[1]

FIGURE 6.1. The Kinship Intensity Index (KII) for ethnolinguistic groups around the world. Darker shading indicates more intensive kin-based institutions. Hatching indicates that no data were available.[2]

Figure 6.1 maps the Kinship Intensity Index for over 7,000 ethnolinguistic groups around the globe, with darker shading indicating more intensive kin-based institutions. The Americas, for example, are now populated mostly by people whose kin-based institutions derive from historical European communities. Hence much of the Americas are assigned KII values traceable to Europe. The darker patches in South America, however, generally represent contemporary indigenous populations.[3]

This index has two main shortcomings. First, the underlying Atlas data derive from anthropological reports of local social norms. Consequently, the KII doesn't necessarily capture what people were actually doing on the ground—their behavior. To check that the ethnographic data captured in the Atlas actually do represent enduring behavioral patterns, we studied the relationship between our KII and the genetic relatedness among these populations based on DNA samples from a few hundred groups. We found that the higher a group's KII value, the higher their genetic relatedness (even after statistically controlling for other factors that might influence relatedness). This is precisely what we'd expect if the reported stable social norms were really influencing people's behavior over centuries—culture leaves fingerprints in the genome.[4]

The second shortcoming is that, as an index, the KII rolls together several different aspects of kin-based institutions, so we can't tell which features of intensive kinship are doing the psychological work. Is it the prohibitions on cousin marriage, or the ban on polygynous unions? Of course, I suspect that all of the elements in our index play some role (that's why we put them in there), but it would be nice to see the effects of individual customs. To address this issue, I'll also use data on the percentage of actual marriages to cousins or other close relatives. When we compare countries, we'll use the percentage of marriages to blood relatives who are second cousins or closer (mapped in Figure 5.2). I'll call this measure the "prevalence of cousin marriage," or just "cousin marriage." These rates are based on data from the 20th century and usually predate our psychological measures by at least a few decades.

Cousin marriage is particularly important, and worth singling out, because it represents one of the key differences that distinguish the Western Church's marriage policies from those of the Orthodox Church. While the Western Church obsessively sought to stamp out all marriages to even distant relatives for centuries during the Early and High Middle Ages, the Orthodox Church only sluggishly imposed some constraints and seemed unenthusiastic about enforcement.

To link these measures of kinship intensity to psychological differences, we'll look at three kinds of psychological outcomes. First, whenever possible, I'll analyze laboratory experiments or carefully crafted psychological scales. These provide our best measures of psychological variation, though they aren't usually available for many countries. To supplement these measures, we'll examine questions from global surveys that tap similar aspects of psychology. These surveys provide lots of data, often from hundreds of thousands of people in many countries, so we can statistically control for the effects of potentially important factors besides kinship intensity that might influence people's psychology, such as those related to climate, geography, religion, and disease prevalence. In some cases, we'll also be able to compare the psychology of immigrants living in the same country by using the kinship intensity from either their country of origin (where they emigrated from) or their ethnolinguistic groups. Finally, whenever possible, we'll look at real-world behavioral patterns related to the psychological attributes captured in the experiments and surveys. This is important because it shows that the psychological differences we are studying influence real life in important ways.

INDIVIDUALISM, CONFORMITY, AND GUILT

The nature of kin-based institutions affects how we think about ourselves, our relationships, our motivations, and our emotions. By embedding individuals within dense, interdependent, and inherited webs of social connections, intensive kinship norms regulate people's behavior in subtle and powerful ways. These norms motivate individuals to closely monitor themselves and members of their own group to make sure that everyone stays in line. They also often endow elders with substantial authority over junior members. Successfully navigating these kinds of social environments favors conformity to peers, deference to traditional authorities, sensitivity to shame, and an orientation toward the collective (e.g., the clan) over oneself.

By contrast, when relational bonds are fewer and weaker, individuals need to forge mutually beneficial relationships, often with strangers. To accomplish this, they must distinguish themselves from the crowd by cultivating their own distinct set of attributes, achievements, and dispositions. Success in these individual-centered worlds favors the cultivation of greater independence, less deference to authority, more guilt, and more concern with personal achievement.

This sounds plausible, but is it indeed true that societies with intensive kin-based institutions have tighter norms? A research team led by the psychologist Michele Gelfand has developed a psychological scale to assess the normative "tightness" of societies. Societies that are relatively "tighter" (vs. "looser") are governed by numerous and contextually sensitive norms that are strictly enforced. The team's questionnaire asks for people's level of agreement or disagreement with statements like "There are many social norms that people are supposed to abide by in this country" and "In this country, if someone acts in an inappropriate way, others will strongly disapprove." Based on data from thousands of participants, Figure 6.2 shows that the greater the KII (Panel A) or the higher the prevalence of cousin marriage (Panel B), the "tighter" the society feels. The variation captured on these plots runs from "loose" places like Venezuela to "tight" spots like Pakistan.

You are about to see a bunch of paired plots like these, so here are some guidelines for understanding them. First, for this entire section on kinship intensity, the vertical axes on each set of plots will always be the same, making it easy to compare the psychological effects of the KII and cousin marriage side by side. Second, when the actual values being represented are only meaningful relative to other values, as with the KII, I've left them off the plot to avoid distraction. What matters in these cases are the relative positions of different populations on the plot. However, whenever the values can be easily understood or add concreteness, I've left the numbers on.

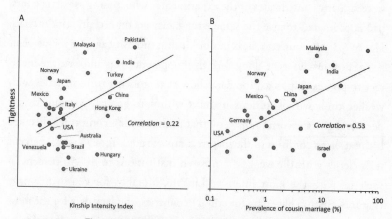

FIGURE 6.2. The relationship between psychological "tightness" and the (A) Kinship Intensity Index (30 countries) and (B) prevalence of cousin marriage (the percentage of marriages to relatives who are second cousins or closer, 23 countries). Note that the prevalence of cousin marriage is plotted on a logarithmic scale.[5]

Cousin marriage, for example, uses the actual percentages of marriages to close relatives, so those appear on all plots. Third, because of how cousin marriages bind communities together, the effects are best seen on a logarithmic scale. If you don't know much about logarithmic scales, don't worry; you can read the actual percentages on the horizontal axis. The simplest way to understand what the logarithmic scale does is to realize that the impact (on both the social world and people's psychology) of increasing the prevalence of cousin marriage from zero to 10 percent is much bigger than the effect created by increasing it by the exact same amount from 40 percent to 50 percent. A little cousin marriage goes a long way. Using a logarithmic scale allows us to visualize this more easily.[6]

Do kin-based institutions—perhaps through the tightness that they create—influence people's inclination toward conformity, such as that assessed by the Asch Conformity Experiment (Figure 1.3)? In Asch's line judgment task, university students from diverse countries had to decide if they'd publicly give the objectively correct answer, based on judging the lengths of line segments, or conform to the incorrect views expressed by those who had responded just before them—recall that these individuals were actually confederates of the experimenter who, posing as participants, had coordinated to give the same wrong answers on certain critical trials. Figure 6.3 plots our two measures of kinship intensity against the percentage of people who went along with their apparent peers and gave the incorrect responses in public. The data show that students from societies with weaker kin-based institutions are more willing to publicly contradict their peers and give the correct answer—that is, they are less conformist. People's inclination to conform to the incorrect answer goes from about 20 percent in societies with the weakest kin-based institutions to 40–50 percent in societies with the most intensive kinship. Notably, for cousin marriage (Figure 6.3B), we have data for only 11 countries, and lack data for the most conformist populations (seen in Figure 6.3A). Despite this truncated sample, a strong relationship still shows through.

The problem with the data on Asch Conformity and "tightness" is that they come from a small number of countries. To capture a broader swath of

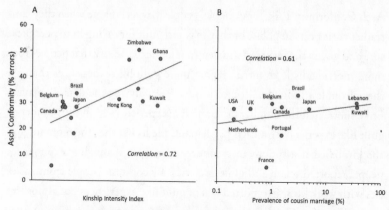

FIGURE 6.3. Relationship between Asch Conformity and the (A) Kinship Intensity Index (16 countries) and (B) prevalence of cousin marriage (11 countries). Asch Conformity is measured here using the percentage of participants' responses that were incorrect but conformed to those given by their peers. Cousin marriage is plotted on a logarithmic scale.[7]

humanity, let's consider two questions about people's adherence to tradition and the importance of obedience from a global survey—the World Values Survey. The first question asks people to rate on a scale from 1 to 7 how similar they are to the person described in this statement: "Tradition is important to her/him. She/he tries to follow the customs handed down by her/his religion or her/his family." The second question allows us to calculate the percentage of people in each country who think that it's important to inculcate "obedience" in children. The data show that countries with higher KII values or more cousin marriage report on-average stronger adherence to tradition and place greater value on inculcating obedience in children—the correlations range from 0.23 to 0.52 (Appendix Figure B.1). The effects are substantial: e.g., cutting the cousin marriage rate from 40 percent to near zero takes us from Jordan, where most of those surveyed (55 percent) report "obedience" as crucial for children, to the United States, where less than a third of people (31 percent) highlight obedience.[8]

The emotional underpinnings of conformist behavior, obedience to authority, and adherence to tradition likely involve shame and guilt. In the

Asch Conformity Task, for example, people may feel shame when they contradict their peers in public or they may feel guilt for caving in to peer pressure and giving the incorrect answer. In Chapter 1, we saw that people from more individualistic countries report more guilt-like experiences than do those from less individualistic countries. Re-analyzing the data, Benjamin Enke subtracted the number of shame-like experiences from the number of guilt-like experiences for each participant. He found that the more intense the kin-based institutions in a country, the more shame-like experiences people reported relative to guilt-like ones. By contrast, people from societies with weak kinship reported lots of guilt-like experiences but almost no shame-like ones. Guilt seems to be the primary emotional-control mechanism in societies lacking intensive kinship.[9]

The data on shame and guilt are based on self-reports by university students and may not capture the actual (unspoken) emotional experiences of most people from those populations. To tackle these issues, Benjamin analyzed data based on Google searches that included words for "shame" and "guilt." Studying Google searches allows us to aggregate a wider range of people than is otherwise possible, although we don't know exactly how wide. In addition, something about the online environment seems to remove people's concerns about being monitored by others, even though everything you do on the internet is logged. Prior work shows that people will ask Google just about anything, from questions about "having sex with stuffed animals" to concerns about the shape of their penis or the smell of their vagina.

With this as background, Benjamin used translations of "guilt" and "shame" from nine languages to gather data on the frequency of Google searches involving these terms in 56 countries over the preceding five years. By comparing only people searching in the same languages but from different countries, Benjamin's analysis reveals that countries with more intensive kin-based institutions searched for "shame" more frequently than "guilt" compared to those living in countries with less intensive kin-based institutions (Appendix Figure B.2). In short, societies with weak family ties seem guilt-ridden but nearly shameless.[10]

Pulling together several elements in the individualism complex, let's close this section by looking at Hofstede's famed measure of individualism, which is mapped in Figure 1.2. Recall that this omnibus measure of individualism integrates questions about personal development, achievement orientation, independence, and family ties. Figure 6.4 shows that countries with less intense kin-based institutions are more individualistic. To see the power of kinship, consider that pushing down cousin marriage prevalence from 40 percent to zero is associated with an increase of 40 points on individualism (going from India to the United States, say).

Notice that in Figure 6.4A, countries high on KII are always low on individualism, but those low on KII span the full range of individualism. Many of the countries that have both low KII and low individualism are in Latin America. This suggests that breaking down intensive kinship opens the door to developing the full individualism complex, but that other institutions—and perhaps other factors—are necessary to really drive up individualism. We'll explore some of these additional factors beginning in Chapter 9.[11]

The associations I've shown you so far, between psychology and kinship

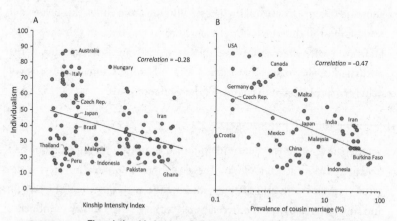

FIGURE 6.4. The relationship between individualism and the (A) Kinship Intensity Index (98 countries) and (B) prevalence of cousin marriage (57 countries). This omnibus measure of individualism comes from research among IBM employees and others around the world. Cousin marriage is plotted on a logarithmic scale.

intensity, are precisely the kinds of relationships predicted by the ideas I've been developing in this book. However, such simple correlations in cross-country data should be regarded with skepticism. To begin to chip away at concerns that such correlations might be misleading, our team took advantage of the larger samples available for outcomes such as individualism, adherence to tradition, and obedience. We wanted to statistically control for potential confounding factors—variables that might create the observed correlations by, for example, making people more conformist while also intensifying kinship. Building on prior work, we studied the impact of over a dozen different control variables. To deal with differences in geography, ecology, and agricultural productivity, we considered measures of terrain ruggedness, distance to navigable waterways, agricultural productivity, irrigation, disease prevalence, latitude, and time since the adoption of agriculture. To address the possibility that religion might be the real driver, we controlled for religiosity and only compared major religious denominations to each other—Catholic countries with Catholic countries, etc. Of course, as I'll show below, the Church has indeed had a major impact on kinship intensity, but these analyses nevertheless confirm that we can still detect the impact of kinship intensity even when we only look within religions and compare countries of similar religiosity. I'll say more about this below, but overall, most of the simple correlational results you'll see in this chapter remain even when these control variables are statistically held constant. In the next chapter, the analyses of variation within Europe, China, and India will help further pin down the nature of these relationships.

IMPERSONAL PROSOCIALITY

By the start of the first millennium CE, universalizing religions had emerged across the Old World. These religions were now, to varying degrees, outfitted with ethical codes, afterlife incentives, notions of free will, and some degree of moral universalism. However, their ability to influence behavior was restrained because both the masses and the elite remained fully embedded in, and dependent on, intensive kin-based institutions. These tight kinship networks instill people with a sense of identity and strong loyalties that often outweighed those of universalizing religions. My favorite expression of this hierarchy of personal commitments comes from Wali Khan, a Pashtun politician in Pakistan. At a time of national instability in 1972, Khan was asked about his personal identity and "first allegiance" during an interview. He replied, "I have been a Pashtun for six thousand years, a Muslim for thirteen hundred years, and a Pakistani for twenty-five."[12]

The Pashtun are a segmentary lineage society, and thus what Khan was saying is that his lineage comes well before both Islam and Pakistan. In fact, his dates suggest that his lineage was four to five times more important than his universalizing religion, Islam, and 240 times more important than his country, Pakistan. It's also worth highlighting his poetic phrasing, "I have been a Pashtun for six thousand years . . ." Since Khan was only in his 50s at the time of the interview, he apparently sees himself as merged into a continuous chain of being that stretches back for some six millennia.

Khan's comment underlines a point that I made in Chapter 3: clans and other intensive kin-groups have norms and beliefs that foster in-group solidarity, intense cooperation within a relatively tight circle, and duties that persist across generations. Many features of kin-based institutions promote a sense of trust that depends on interconnectedness through a web of personal relations and strong feelings of in-group loyalty toward one's network. People come to rely heavily on those they are connected to while fearing those they aren't. Intensive kinship thus breeds a sharper distinction between in-groups and out-groups, along with a general distrust of strangers.[13]

In light of these institutional differences, we should expect people from communities with more intensive kinship to make sharper distinctions between their in-groups and everyone else, resulting in a general distrust of strangers and anyone outside of their relational networks. To assess this, we used an approach from economics that integrates six questions from global surveys that ask people how much they trust (1) their families, (2) their neighbors, (3) people they know, (4) people they've met for the first time, (5) foreigners, and (6) adherents of religions other than their own. Using these data, we created an in-group trust measure by averaging people's responses to the first three questions, about family, neighbors, and people

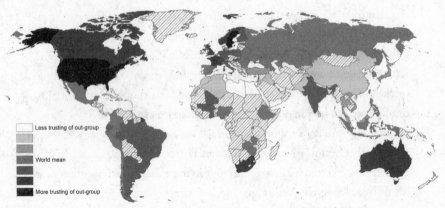

FIGURE 6.5. Map of Out-In-Group Trust based on six questions from the World Values Survey covering 75 countries. Darker shading indicates less distrust of strangers, foreigners, and adherents of other faiths relative to a person's family, neighbors, and people they know. Hatched areas indicate a lack of data.

they know. Then, we created an out-group trust measure by averaging the second three questions, about new people, foreigners, and adherents of other religions. By subtracting the first measure, in-group trust, from the second measure, we arrived at what I'll call Out-In-Group Trust. Mapped in Figure 6.5, Out-In-Group Trust provides the best measure of impersonal trust from surveys. To be clear, the actual values of Out-In-Group Trust are generally negative, meaning that everyone trusts their family, neighbors, and people they know more than strangers, foreigners, etc. But in some places, strangers are treated relatively more like family and friends than in other places. Unfortunately, we are again lacking data for most of Africa and much of the Middle East, which means that we are surely not capturing the full spectrum of global variation.

The higher a country's KII or cousin marriage, the more people distrust strangers, new people, and adherents of other religions (Figure 6.6). The relationship is particularly strong for cousin marriage, where going from the lowest to the highest rates takes you from the impersonal trust levels in the United States to those lying somewhere between Kuwait and Iraq. As

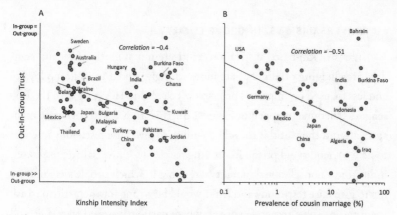

FIGURE 6.6. Relationship between Out-In-Group Trust (impersonal trust) and the (A) Kinship Intensity Index (75 countries) and (B) prevalence of cousin marriage (44 countries). The figure shows that countries with greater KII or more cousin marriage trust out-group members (people they've just met, foreigners, and adherents of other religions) substantially less than in-group members (family, neighbors, and people they know). Cousin marriage is plotted on a logarithmic scale.[14]

with the individualism measures above, these relationships persist even after statistically holding constant the influence of a host of ecological, climatic, and geographic factors as well as those related to religion and national wealth.

Exploring this more deeply, here's a cool trick that allows us to compare the Out-In-Group Trust expressed by individuals currently living in the same country who originally came from different countries. From the global survey, Benjamin pulled out the 21,734 first-generation immigrants. Then, using their reported ethnicity, he matched each immigrant to the KII of their ethnolinguistic group from the Atlas. His results tell the same story as that illustrated in Figure 6.6: immigrants living in the same country show higher levels of trust in strangers, foreigners, and people from other religions compared to their family, neighbors, and acquaintances if they originally came from populations with less intensive kinship. These relationships are unlikely to be due to economic or demographic differences among immigrants, because they persist even when individual differences in income and education are statistically held constant.[15]

UNIVERSALISM VS. IN-GROUP LOYALTY

Intensive kin-based institutions cultivate moral motivations and standards for judging others that are more strongly rooted in in-group loyalty and less focused on impartial principles. To see this, let's start with the Passenger's Dilemma (mapped in Figure 1.6). This study asked corporate managers around the world if they'd be willing to give false testimony in court to help a friend avoid prison for driving recklessly. Universalistic responses, indicating a nonrelational morality, are those in which people were unwilling to give false testimony and felt it would be wrong for their friend to ask them to lie. The alternative answer, where participants said they'd lie and felt it was fine for their friend to ask, is labeled as the *particularistic* or relational response, though it's also about in-group loyalty.

Figure 6.7 shows that the higher the rate of cousin marriage in a country, the more willing managers were to give false testimony in court. Here, cutting the rate of cousin marriage from 10 percent to near zero increases the percentage of corporate managers who would refuse to help a friend. The number goes from under 60 percent to about 90 percent. Note, I've dropped the companion KII plot here because there's little variation in the KII across this small sample, so there's not much to see.

Complementing these results, data from the World Economic Forum reveal that executives from countries with stronger kin-based institutions hire more relatives into senior management. WEIRD people call this "nepotism," but others call it "family loyalty" and consider it a smart way to get trustworthy employees.[16]

To get beyond the elite—managers and executives—let's also look at data collected at yourmorals.org using the Moral Foundations Questionnaire (MFQ) developed by the psychologists Jon Haidt and Jesse Graham to study differences in morality. Using the MFQ, Jon and Jesse have shown that you can capture much of human morality along five major dimensions, or what they call "foundations." The five foundations involve people's concerns about (1) fairness (justice, equity), (2) harm/care (not harming others),

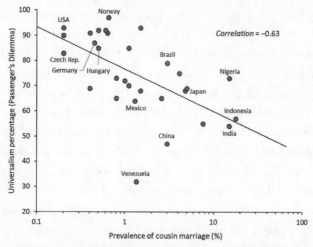

FIGURE 6.7. The relationship between universalism, captured as the percentage of universalistic responses to the Passenger's Dilemma, and the prevalence of cousin marriage. Cousin marriage is plotted on a logarithmic scale.[17]

(3) in-group loyalty (helping one's own), (4) respect for authority, and (5) sanctity/purity (adhering to rituals, cleanliness, taboos, etc.).

Using MFQ data collected online from 285,792 respondents from 206 countries, Benjamin conducted three kinds of analyses. First, he pulled out the in-group loyalty foundation. This foundation is based on asking people to specify their degree of agreement with statements like "People should be loyal to their family members, even when they have done something wrong." The results show that people from countries with higher KII scores were more morally concerned about in-group loyalty. Second, Benjamin created a measure by combining people's scores on the two universal dimensions of morality, involving the fairness and care/harm dimensions, and then subtracted the two more tribal dimensions, in-group loyalty and deference to authority. The idea here is that kin-based institutions strongly favor both in-group loyalty and deference to traditional authorities while suppressing universalizing or impartial notions of fairness as well as care and harm. Here, those with more intensive kinship cared relatively less about universal morality and focused more on in-group loyalty and deference to authority.[18] Finally, Benjamin pulled out the 26,657 immigrants (from nearly 200 countries) who had responded to the MFQ online. By matching each person to the KII of their country of origin, he compared only those currently living within the same country—facing the same governments, police, safety nets, etc. This analysis confirms the above cross-country comparisons: even within the same countries, people coming from places with more intensive kinship continued to care more about in-group loyalty and less about nonrelational morality.[19]

Overall, these findings from the Moral Foundations Questionnaire converge with those we examined using both the Passenger's Dilemma and nepotism surveys. From these results, a picture is emerging. But, this could be just how people talk about morality. We need to know if these apparent psychological differences, based on surveys, hold up when money, blood, and other precious things are on the line.

MONEY, BLOOD, AND PARKING SPOTS

Upon entering the economics laboratory, you are greeted by a friendly student assistant who takes you to a private cubicle. There, via a computer terminal, you are given $20 and placed into a group with three strangers. Then, all four of you are given an opportunity to contribute any portion of your endowment—from nothing to all $20—to a "group project." After everyone has had an opportunity to contribute, all contributions to the group project are increased by 50 percent and then divided equally among all four group members. Since players get to keep any money that they don't contribute to the group project, it's obvious that players always make the most money if they give nothing to the project. But, since any money contributed to the project increases ($20 becomes $30), the group as a whole makes more money when people contribute more of their endowment. Your group will repeat the interaction for 10 rounds, and you'll receive all of your earnings in cash at the end. Each round, you'll see the anonymous contributions made by others and your own total income. If you were a player in this game, how much would you contribute in the first round with this group of strangers?

This is the Public Goods Game (PGG). It's an experiment designed to capture the basic economic trade-offs faced by individuals when they decide to act in the interest of their broader communities. Society benefits when more people vote, give blood, join the army, report crimes, follow traffic laws, and pay taxes. Individuals, however, may prefer to skip voting, dodge taxes, develop "bone spurs" (dodge military service), and ignore posted speed limits. Thus there's conflict between the interests of individuals and those of the larger society.[20]

When researchers first did the PGG among WEIRD university students, they found that players contributed much more than would be expected if everyone was rational and self-interested. In other words, the canonical expectation from game theory, or what I'll call the *Homo economicus* prediction, substantially underestimated people's cooperative inclinations. This was a key insight, but the problems arose when researchers quickly generalized their student findings to our entire species—*Homo economicus* transformed into *Homo reciprocans*, in one memorable coinage.[21]

As you might anticipate, the behavior of WEIRD students turned out to be particularly unusual when placed in a broader perspective. In 2008, Benedikt Herrmann, Christian Thöni, and Simon Gächter took the PGG global, administering it to university students in 16 cities around the world. In every city, participants faced the same computer screens (with the content appropriately translated) and made anonymous decisions about the same sums of money, which were matched in "buying power" across countries. Despite creating essentially identical contexts and monetary incentives in these different cities, the research team still found substantial variation in people's willingness to cooperate anonymously with strangers.

Using these PGG data, Figure 6.8 reveals that societies with more intensive kin-based institutions contribute less on average to the group project in the first round. I like to look at people's initial contributions, because players make these decisions without seeing what the other players will do. The vertical axis gives the average contributions in each country as a percentage of participants' endowments (100 percent is giving all their endowment). For both KII and cousin marriage, increasing kinship intensity

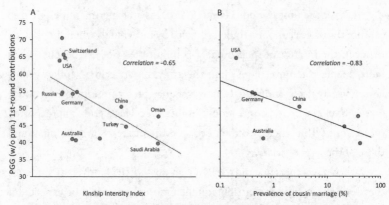

FIGURE 6.8. The relationship between average contributions (as a percentage) in the first round of the Public Goods Games and the (A) Kinship Intensity Index and (B) prevalence of cousin marriage. Countries with more intensive kinship cooperate less in the first round. Cousin marriage is plotted on a logarithmic scale.

from its lowest to highest value drops people's initial cooperative contributions from about 57 percent down to nearly 40 percent. Although these differences might not seem particularly big, they anticipate the much larger differences that develop and compound over several rounds of interaction, especially when individuals have opportunities to punish each other—as we'll see.[22]

Let's turn from carefully controlled laboratory economic games to a real-world public good, blood donations. Such donations represent a classic public good, since they are voluntary, costly, anonymous, and helpful to strangers. Everyone potentially benefits from well-stocked blood banks, as we never know when we might suddenly need a transfusion. However, giving blood is costly in terms of time, energy, and pain, so it's easy for individuals to skip doing it, but then later free-ride on everyone else's donations when they or their family get injured or sick and need blood. To examine blood donations, our team pulled data from the World Health Organization on unpaid voluntary blood donations for the years 2011–2013. We then calculated the frequency of donations per 1,000 people per year for 141 countries.[23]

Figure 6.9 shows that people from countries with intensive kinship rarely contribute blood anonymously and voluntarily. In fact, while those

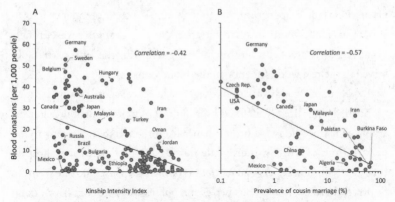

FIGURE 6.9. **Relationships between voluntary blood donations per 1,000 individuals (per year, 2011–2013) and the (A) Kinship Intensity Index and (B) prevalence of cousin marriage. Cousin marriage is plotted on a logarithmic scale.**

from countries with weak family ties give about 25 donations per 1,000 people (per year), countries with the highest KII donate almost no blood to strangers. Similarly, countries with low rates of cousin marriage give about 40 donations per 1,000 people, while those with high rates of cousin marriage make few donations. Notably, these results hold independent of the geographic, ecological, and religious variables discussed above.[24]

Figure 6.9A reveals a similar pattern to that shown for individualism in Figure 6.4. While intensive kinship is strongly associated with quite low frequencies of blood donations, weak family ties do not guarantee high rates of donations—societies without intensive kinship show a great deal of variation. Thus less intensive kinship opens the door to impersonal norms rooted in a universalizing morality—about blood donations, in this case—but weak kinship alone doesn't get you through the door.

It's easy to think up economic or other nonpsychological reasons why people might not donate much blood in places like Burkina Faso and China; but, what is clear is that the patterns for blood donations parallel those we find for contributions in the PGG, where most of these nonpsychological explanations don't apply. In the PGG, everyone was well educated, understood the situation, faced the same monetary incentives, and was explicitly given a convenient opportunity to contribute. Yet people's tendency to contribute to public goods involving strangers in the laboratory was strongly negatively correlated with kinship intensity, following the same pattern observed in the real world for anonymous blood donations.

Many public goods situations don't feel like "real cooperation," because no one is being directly affected by people's failure to contribute. For example, when people swipe printer paper from their employer's copy room, park in front of a fire hydrant while they dash into a pharmacy, cheat on their taxes, or submit personal receipts as business expenses, no one seems to be overtly harmed, though businesses and public safety are collectively damaged. To isolate this in the laboratory, let's return to the Impersonal Honesty Game (Chapter 1), where participants rolled a six-sided die and were paid cash in proportion to their *reported* outcome. A roll of 1 was worth the smallest amount of money, 5 was worth the most, and 6 was worth nothing at all. Analyzing this data, Figure 6.10 shows that university students from countries with more intensive kin-based institutions reported many more high rolls. Following the trend line, the percentages of high rolls go

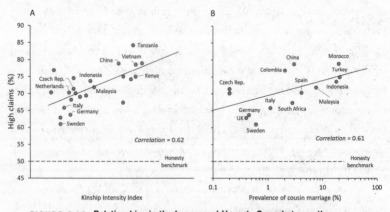

FIGURE 6.10. Relationships in the Impersonal Honesty Game between the percentage of high claims (rolls of 3, 4, or 5) and the (A) Kinship Intensity Index and (B) prevalence of cousin marriage. The dashed horizontal line at the bottom gives the honesty benchmark—this is the percentage of high claims that we'd expect if everyone always reported their rolls accurately. Cousin marriage is plotted on a logarithmic scale.

from about 65 percent in populations without intensive kinship to nearly 80 percent on average in places with intensive kinship.

The Impersonal Honesty Game mirrors real situations in which people can either follow impartial rules or break them for direct personal benefits. Capturing this dilemma in the real world, Chapter 1 described the natural experiment created by bringing diplomats from countries around the world to the United Nations in New York City and giving them diplomatic immunity from parking violations. By blocking narrow streets, driveways, and fire hydrants, parking scofflaws gain personal benefits in time and money while at the same time inconveniencing and sometimes even endangering the rest of the populace (strangers). Can the kinship intensity of the diplomats' home countries explain their parking behavior?

Indeed, diplomats from countries with strong kin-based institutions accumulated many more unpaid parking tickets than diplomats from countries with weak kin-based institutions (Figure 6.11). In fact, using either the KII or cousin marriage, countries with weak family ties received about 2.5 tickets on average per member of their diplomatic delegations, while those from countries with powerful kin-based institutions received 10 to

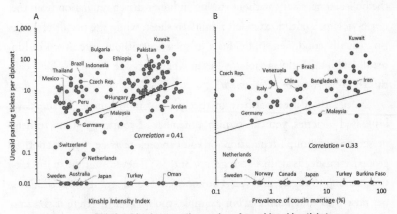

FIGURE 6.11. Relationships between the number of unpaid parking tickets per diplomat from each country and the (A) Kinship Intensity Index and (B) prevalence of cousin marriage in those countries. Both of the vertical axes and the prevalence of cousin marriage are plotted on logarithmic scales.

20 tickets per member of their delegations—so 5 to 10 times more unpaid parking tickets.[25]

IMPERSONAL PUNISHMENT AND REVENGE

All known societies depend on some form of sanctioning to sustain social norms. In kin-based institutions, norm-violators are typically punished either by their own family members or by traditional authorities, such as clan elders. For example, in many clan communities, if a young man steals from another village or a young woman repeatedly dresses inappropriately, they might be beaten by their father's older brother as punishment. Clans often protect their collective reputation by punishing misbehaving members—older brothers and uncles have strong incentives to not only beat their errant subordinates but also to leave some visible marks, so that other clans can notice and feel confident that the misdeed was punished. However, if someone from *another* clan were to merely yell at the thief or sartorial offender, we'd have a problem that could end in violence. An outside attack on, or even a criticism of, one clan member can constitute an insult to all members. By contrast, in societies with weak kinship, strangers can reprimand each other as individuals, point out violations, and even call the police, if necessary, without risking an honor-driven retaliation from the norm-violator's entire extended family. In short, while the use of violence isn't usually condoned, individuals in societies without intensive kinship readily admonish norm-violators, even when they are strangers. Let's call this *third-party norm enforcement.*

Notice the difference here in the types of punishment. In intensive kin-based societies, you can punish a member of your own group to help preserve your group's reputation, or you can seek revenge against another group for misdeeds against your group. But, you'd never interfere in interactions among strangers, and you'd be annoyed if some stranger poked his or her nose into your business. For example, you'd never interfere if you saw one stranger stealing from a different stranger—for all you know, it's payback for a prior affront between families. By contrast, in societies with weak family ties, seeking revenge is frowned upon and certainly not a source of honor or status. However, people think it's appropriate, or even admirable, to trip a purse snatcher fleeing from the police, or to physically constrain an unknown husband from beating his wife. When it comes to punishing strangers or out-group members, we need to distinguish *third-party norm enforcement* from *revenge-driven actions*. Both can be honorable and moral acts within their cultural milieus.

In the Public Goods Game described above, Herrmann, Thöni, and Gächter stumbled across these differences in motivations for punishment. In addition to the experiment discussed, they also conducted another version, one that gave players a chance to punish others in their group. In this version, after participants had all made their contributions to the group in a particular round, everyone got to see (anonymously) the amounts contributed by others and were given the opportunity to pay to take money away from other players. Specifically, for each dollar a person paid from their own account, the experimenter would take three dollars away from the targeted player.

When this experiment is done with WEIRD people, these punishment opportunities have a potent effect on cooperation. Some WEIRD people punish free riders, and then these low contributors respond by contributing more. Over repeated rounds, people's willingness to punish drives up contributions along with the group's total payoffs. In the long run, these peer-punishing opportunities lead to higher overall payoffs.[26]

This, however, isn't what happens at universities in the Middle East or eastern Europe. Indeed, some participants in these places did punish low contributors. But, low contributors who got punished often retaliated in later rounds, apparently seeking vengeance by trying to strike back at the high contributors whom they suspected had punished them. Of course, the experiment was designed to make this difficult—punishments were delivered anonymously. Undeterred and fired up, however, low contributors from these places still struck out blindly at high contributors, punishing them in later rounds. This phenomenon, it turns out, is actually common around the globe, but so rare among WEIRD students that it was initially written off as just part of the randomness inherent in human behavior. The consequences of this retaliatory response were sometimes so powerful that opportunities to punish entirely inhibited the cooperation-inducing effects of allowing peers to monitor and sanction each other.[27]

People's inclinations toward these two styles of punishment are strongly associated with kinship intensity. The easiest way to analyze these patterns is to take the amount of third-party norm enforcement from each population, where individuals punished those making contributions lower than their own, and then subtract it from the amount of vengeful punishment, where individuals punished those who made *higher* contributions than themselves. As expected, the higher the kinship intensity in a country, the more revenge-driven punishment people engage in relative to the amount of third-party norm enforcement.[28]

These differences in motivations to punish generate even bigger differences in cooperative contributions over repeated interactions. The greater a country's KII or prevalence of cousin marriage, the lower the average levels of cooperative contributions in the Public Goods Game over 10 rounds (Figure 6.12). Average contributions go from about 40 percent in places with the most intensive kinship, such as Saudi Arabia or the Sultan-

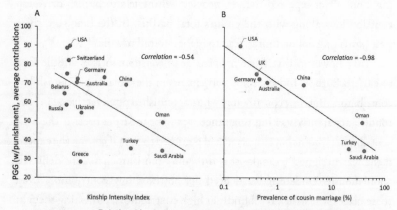

FIGURE 6.12. Relationships between average cooperative contributions over 10 rounds in the Public Goods Game with punishment and the (A) Kinship Intensity Index and (B) prevalence of cousin marriage. Cousin marriage is plotted on a logarithmic scale.

ate of Oman, to 70–90 percent in places with the weakest families, like the United States or Switzerland.[29]

There's a deep lesson in these results. By adding the option to punish fellow group members in the PGG, economists had thought they'd figured out a way to generate high levels of cooperation *in humans*. But, this "policy fix" worked best on WEIRD populations because, psychologically speaking, it fits their motivations, expectations, and worldviews. By contrast, in other populations, adding peer punishment to a PGG was a disaster because it provoked revenge cycles, even in the laboratory. These populations did better without this particular "policy fix." The lesson is simple: policy prescriptions and formal institutions need to fit the cultural psychology of the population in question.

INTENTIONALITY IN MORAL JUDGMENT

Intensive kin-based institutions bind communities together by intertwining individuals in webs of shared identity, communal ownership, collective shame, and corporate responsibility. In this world, scrutinizing a person's intentions or other mental states may be less relevant or even counterproductive. In predicting people's behavior, many contexts are so constrained by social norms and the watching eyes of others that intuiting people's personal beliefs or intentions won't help very much. Instead, it's better to know their social relationships, allies, debts, and obligations. Similarly, in making moral or criminal judgments, the importance of intentions depends on the relationship among the parties involved. In the extreme, intentions may be irrelevant for judging the penalty when someone from one clan murders someone from another clan. If you murder someone in another clan, your fellow clan members will be responsible for paying blood money to the victim's clan, and the size of this payment won't depend on whether you killed the guy by accident—your arrow deflected off the deer you were hunting—or by executing a carefully planned homicide. Moreover, if your clan doesn't pay the prescribed blood money, the victim's clan will hold all members culpable and seek revenge by killing someone from your clan without regard to the victim's intentions. By contrast, when ripped from the binding ties of their relational networks, an actor's intentions, goals, and beliefs become much more important. Without the constraints imposed by intensive kinship, people's intentions or other mental states tell you a lot more about why they did something or what they are likely to do in the future—so they matter more, and it's worth attending to them with greater scrutiny.[30]

In Chapter 1, I told you about a study in which a team of anthropologists gave people living in traditional communities around the world vignettes about characters who either accidentally or intentionally took someone's bag at a market ("theft"), dumped poison into their village well ("attempted murder"), punched someone ("battery"), or violated a food taboo. We saw that the importance of a person's intentions in judging a "theft" ranged from a maximum in Los Angeles and Ukraine down to near zero among the Sursurunga on New Ireland in Papua New Guinea and Yasawa Island in Fiji. These judgments combined people's assessments about how "good" or "bad" the action was, how much it should hurt the perpetrator's reputation, and how much the perpetrator should be punished. We subtracted their judgments of the perpetrator when the action was intentional from those when it was accidental.[31]

Now, we can explain much of the variation in the importance of intentionality in judging others. Societies with stronger kin-based institutions at the time of the research paid relatively little attention to people's intentions in making moral judgments in our vignettes. Figure 6.13 shows the relationship between our measure of the importance of intentionality in judging someone who took something at a busy market ("theft") and a contemporary measure of kinship intensity that I created to match the KII as closely as possible using data supplied by our team's anthropologists. This index captures about 90 percent of the variation across these societies in their use of intentions in judging the perpetrator for taking a bag ("theft"). Similar relationships hold for the other domains, particularly for battery and attempted murder. These patterns hold even after accounting for individual differences in formal schooling and the uncertainty of local environments. The impressive strength of these relationships becomes less surprising

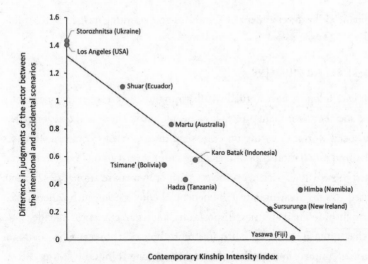

FIGURE 6.13. Relationship between the importance of intentionality in judging a "theft" and my contemporary Kinship Intensity Index. This index was formulated to match the KII. Like the KII, it's based mostly on ethnographic observations. Unlike the KII, it's not historical but captures contemporary practices.

when we consider that, unlike the businesspeople, online survey takers, and university students in so many of our studies above, people in many of these communities remain embedded in fully functioning kin-based institutions. Yasawans in Fiji, for example, still live in patrilineal clans, obey elders, marry cousins, and corporately control land.[32]

Consistent with their high levels of kinship intensity, pre-Christian European populations likely also lived in a world regulated by shame, not guilt, and placed much less importance on intentionality in moral judgments. Ancient sources like the Scandinavian sagas and the earliest law codes of barbarian tribes make little explicit reference to internal mental states like personal intentions or private guilt, yet they highlight shame or "face" as the central emotion of social control. By dissolving the kin-based institutions of Europe's tribes, the medieval Church would have bolstered people's use of mental states in making both moral and legal judgments of others. Later, we'll consider how these psychological shifts may have influenced the development of Western Law beginning in the High Middle Ages.[33]

ANALYTIC THINKING

Psychologists have argued that learning to effectively navigate a tightly knit social environment affects how people think about and categorize the nonsocial world. Growing up enmeshed in kin-based institutions focuses the mind on relationships and the interconnections among people; by contrast, those who experience a society with only weak relational ties become biased toward creating mutually beneficial connections with others based on their individual abilities, dispositions, and characteristics. The idea here is that intensive kinship cultivates more holistic thinkers who focus on broader contexts and on the relationships among things, including the interconnections among individuals, animals, or objects. By contrast, societies with less intensive kinship foster more analytically-oriented thinkers who tend to parse the world by assigning properties, attributes, or personalities to people and objects, often by classifying them into discrete categories according to presumed underlying essences or dispositions. In Chapter 1, I discussed the Triad Task, which is used to differentiate analytic from holistic thinking styles. In the task, participants saw sets of three images, such as a hand, winter glove, and wool hat. For each trio, they said whether the target object—for example, the glove—goes with either the hand or the hat. Analytic thinkers like discrete, rule-governed categories, so they're inclined to put the glove with the hat, as examples of winter clothing. Holistic thinkers, by contrast, look first for relationships, so they're more inclined to put the hand in the glove.[34]

People from countries with higher rates of cousin marriage reveal a more holistic thinking style (Figure 6.14). Going from a population where about 30 percent of marriages involve relatives to one in which there's almost no cousin marriage takes us from communities who engage in predominately holistic thinking (60 percent holistic) to those favoring mostly analytic approaches (62 percent analytic). Note, I've omitted the plot using the KII

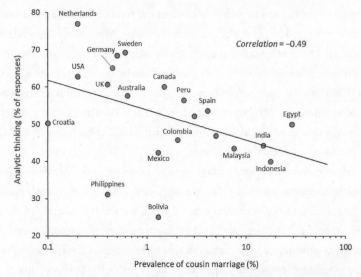

FIGURE 6.14. The relationship between analytical thinking based on the Triad Task and the prevalence of cousin marriage. Cousin marriage is plotted on a logarithmic scale.

because the 30 industrialized countries for which we have Triad Task data show little variation in KII, so there's not much to see.[35]

The relationship between kin-based institutions and analytic thinking may illuminate a long-recognized cross-cultural pattern in a perceptual ability called "field independence" (vs. "field dependence"). Field independence captures how good a person is at accurately assessing the size and position of objects in space *independent* from their background or context. This notion is closely related to the analytic visual processing that I discussed in relation to literacy in the Prelude. Using the Rod and Frame Task, for example, individuals from diverse societies were seated in front of a rod, which was surrounded by a square frame. The experimenter then gradually turned a knob that rotated the rod in space, like the hand on a clock. The participant's job was to tell the experimenter when the rod reached the vertical position (12 o'clock). The task is made more difficult by first rotating the frame so that it is askew relative to the ground. People who are more "field dependent" struggle to get the rod perpendicular when the frame is askew, and instead are drawn toward aligning the rod with the frame. More field independent people are better at ignoring the frame and aligning the rod vertically. The experiment gives an objective score, the rod's deviation from the vertical. In the 1960s and '70s, psychologists found that while traditional farming populations were quite field dependent, there were two distinct populations in the world that were particularly field independent. The first were WEIRD people. Can you guess the other one?

Mobile hunter-gatherers, who possess *extensive* (not intensive) kin-based institutions, are field independent. Consistent with this, anthropologists have long argued that, compared to farmers and herders who have more intensive kin-based institutions, hunter-gatherers emphasize values that focus on independence, achievement, and self-reliance while deemphasizing obedience, conformity, and deference to authority. Marking this, the kinship terminology adopted in European languages like English, German, French, and Spanish in the wake of the Church's expansion is the same as that found among many mobile hunter-gatherer populations.[36]

Overall, the evidence presented above indicates that global psychological variation covaries with intensive kinship in precisely the ways we'd expect if our minds have been adapting and calibrating to the social worlds created by these institutions. For now, it's enough to appreciate the extent of the psychological variation around the world and to recognize that it patterns in the expected ways. In the next chapter, we'll look more closely at these relationships and consider a variety of lines of evidence that, when taken together, support the idea that changes in kin-based institutions have indeed driven important psychological differences. But, before we get to that, let's consider the global relationships between the Church, intensive kinship, and psychological differences.

The Church Altered Kinship and Changed Psychology

The links between intensive kinship and psychological differences pose a key question: Why does kinship intensity vary so much around the world?

You've already seen part of the answer in Chapter 3: certain ecological conditions favored the development and spread of different forms of food production, including animal herding and irrigation agriculture. Rising populations and the pressure to control territory for food production energized competition among societies, which in turn favored norms that permitted larger communities, broader cooperation, greater production, and better command and control. Eventually, cultural evolution would generate complex chiefdoms and states; but, throughout much of this scaling-up process, kinship intensified in a host of ways. The premodern states that emerged in some places were always built atop a foundation of intensive kinship. So, the differing intensities of kin-based institutions are traceable through a variety of historical pathways back to differences in biogeography, climate, disease prevalence (e.g., malaria), soil fertility, navigable water-ways, and the availability of domesticable plants and animals. Of course, the historical details surrounding premodern states matter too, since some states harnessed kin-based institutions and others sought to "push back" against them. These factors, along with others, contribute to global differences in kin-based institutions.[37]

Here, however, we are interested in the question of whether, and how much, the Church has shaped the global variation in kin-based institutions by examining the relationship between kinship intensity and the duration of exposure to the Church. Then, we'll ask whether psychological variation can be tracked directly back to medieval Church exposure.

To assess the amount of exposure to the Church's MFP experienced by different populations, we mapped the expansion of the Church across Europe from roughly 500, when the MFP began to consolidate, to 1500 CE. In compiling this database, we relied primarily on the founding of bishoprics, which were often linked to the conversion of various kings or tribal chiefs to Christianity. Using this information, we calculated the duration of exposure to both the Western and Orthodox Churches. This is important because while the Orthodox Church didn't go to the extremes of the Western Church and lacked the enthusiastic enforcement often pursued by the Western Church, it did have its own program, a kind of MFP-light

(Table 5.3). By subtracting the year when the MFP began from 1500, we get two measures of "church dosage," one for the Western Church and the other for the Orthodox Church.[38]

These MFP dosages for Europe permit us to calculate MFP dosages for the rest of the world. To accomplish this, we used a "migration matrix" that estimates the total flux of populations, from country to country, between 1500 and 2000 CE.[39] For each country in the world, we (1) look at the composition of its modern national population, (2) track each subpopulation back to where their ancestors were living in 1500, (3) assign this subpopulation an MFP dosage based on its 1500 location, and (4) roll all of these subpopulations back together to generate an aggregate MFP dosage for each modern country. If this seems crude, it is. Fortunately, the MFP's effect was so big that it still shows through this messiness.[40]

Let's first connect the Church to kinship intensity. The data show that the longer a country's population was exposed to the Church, the weaker its kin-based institutions. Together, the dosages of both the Western and Orthodox Churches explain about 40 percent of the global differences across countries in the KII and 62 percent of the differences in cousin marriage. For comparison, the time since the origins of agriculture accounts for only an additional 18 percent of the variation in KII, and for 10 percent of the differences in cousin marriage across countries. In fact, of all the agricultural, ecological, climatic, geographic, and historical factors that we explored in trying to understand the global variation in kinship intensity, the biggest factor—though not the only—was historical exposure to the Church.[41]

The effects of the Western Church on reducing the KII are generally stronger than those of the Orthodox Church, but only a little stronger. However, as expected, the Orthodox Church had no effect on the frequency of cousin marriage, so the Western Church is doing all the work there. Each century of Western Church exposure cuts the rate of cousin marriage by nearly 60 percent. This finding fits nicely with the historical record, since cousin marriage—but not polygynous marriage or bilateral inheritance—

represents a core difference between the full MFP and the Orthodox Church's MFP-light.[42]

Now, let's look directly at the relationship between Church exposure and psychology. Figure 6.15 shows the effects of higher MFP dosages on the psychological measures examined above. National populations that collectively experienced longer durations under the Western Church tend to be (A) less tightly bound by norms, (B) less conformist, (C) less enamored with tradition, (D) more individualistic, (E) less distrustful of strangers, (F) stronger on universalistic morality, (G) more cooperative in new groups with strangers, (H) more responsive to third-party punishment (greater contributions in the PGG with punishment), (I) more inclined to voluntarily donate blood, (J) more impersonally honest (toward faceless institutions), (K) less inclined to accumulate parking tickets under diplomatic immunity, and (L) more analytically minded.

These effects are large. For example, a millennium of MFP exposure is associated with nearly a 20-percentile-point drop in people's willingness to go along with the group to give the same wrong answer in the Asch Conformity Task (Figure 6.15B), and a 30-percentile-point drop in people's willingness to lie in court to help a friend—particularism over universalism (6.15F). Similarly, a millennium of the MFP also raises a population's individualism from the intensity found in contemporary Kenya to that of Belgium (6.15D), increases voluntary blood donations fivefold (6.15I), cuts people's willingness to exaggerate their die rolls by half (6.15J), and reduces the number of unpaid parking tickets from nearly seven per member in a diplomatic delegation to only one ticket for every 10 members (6.15K). Similarly, every century of MFP exposure raises people's inclinations toward analytical thinking by just over 3 percent, taking it from about 40 percent to 74 percent over a millennium (6.15L). Our analyses also show that populations that experienced higher dosages of the Western Church's MFP are less concerned about inculcating obedience in children and less inclined to hire family into senior management positions (low on family loyalty).[43]

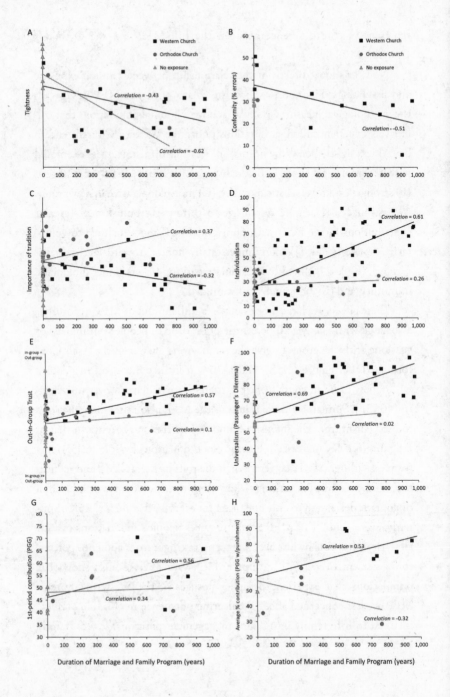

Duration of Marriage and Family Program (years)

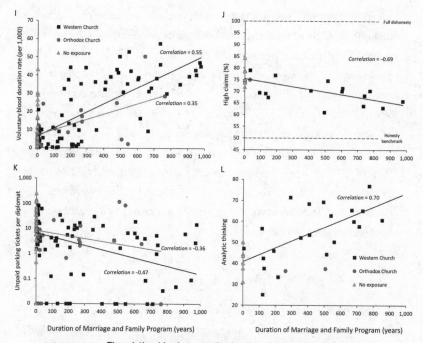

FIGURE 6.15. The relationships between the duration of exposure to both the Western and Orthodox Churches on psychology for: (A) "tightness" scores, (B) Asch Conformity using the percentage of incorrect judgments, (C) adherence to tradition, (D) individualism, (E) impersonal trust (Out-In-Group Trust), (F) universalism in the Passenger's Dilemma, (G) average first-round contributions in the Public Goods Game without punishment, (H) average contributions over all 10 rounds in the PGG with punishment, (I) voluntary blood donations per 1,000 people (per year), (J) percentage of high claims in the Impersonal Honesty Game, (K) unpaid parking tickets to UN diplomats, and (L) analytical thinking from the Triad Task.

The duration of exposure to the Orthodox Church reveals some similar patterns, but its effects are generally muted compared to those of the Western Church. In some cases, we lacked any data from countries exposed to the Orthodox Church—so you'll see only data points for the Western Church and one corresponding line in Figure 6.15. In other cases, for tightness and analytical thinking, we had a few data points and plotted them, but the lines shouldn't be taken too seriously, because they're based on so little data. The most complete data can be found in Figures 6.15I and 6.15K, for blood donations and unpaid parking tickets. In these cases, Orthodox Church exposure has effects like those of the Western Church, only weaker. The difference between the Orthodox and Western Churches is important, because it shows that psychological variation, and later economic and political differences, aren't due to something about exposure to Roman institutions or Christianity per se. The Orthodox Church remained the official church of the Roman Empire (Eastern) until 1453 CE and promoted supernatural beliefs and rituals that were very similar to those of the Western Church. These findings support the idea that the key difference in the long-term impact of the Western vs. Orthodox Churches lies in policies about, and implementation of, marriage and family practices, especially those related to incest taboos.

Opening the Floodgates

My goal in this chapter has been to convince you that the broad patterns of global psychological variation are consistent with a causal pathway that goes like this:

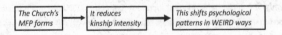

Given the roughness of our data, the strength of the relationships between so many aspects of psychology and both kinship intensity and MFP dosages is striking. Of course, it's always possible that the global psychological variation we've seen is caused by some other hidden factor that just happens to parallel the pathway that I've now highlighted. In the next chapter, I'm going to provide good evidence against this.

Nevertheless, it's worth underlining that for each aspect of psychology discussed above, whenever we had enough data, both Benjamin Enke and our team did dozens of supplementary analyses in which we sought to statistically account for the influence of an immense range of other factors that might somehow have created the relationships we've seen throughout this chapter. Collectively, we looked at agricultural fertility, ruggedness, religiosity, distance from the equator, navigable waterways, parasite stress, malaria, irrigation potential, and European colonization. We also isolated the psychological variation among countries on the same continent and only compared countries with the same dominant religious denominations. Under this analytical onslaught, the relationships I've shown you above mostly hold up, although often they get a bit weaker. Occasionally, the relationships do vanish, but there's no pattern to this—it's not that religiosity or agricultural fertility consistently overpowers either kinship intensity or MFP dosages. Taken together, our analyses strongly suggest that there's no lightning-bolt factor out there that demolishes these findings and illuminates an alternative pathway to account for global psychological variation. The problem is that, while comparing countries is a convenient way to illuminate the broad patterns of global variation, it's not a great way to unearth "what causes what," because too many factors remain hidden. In the next chapter, we'll dig deeper to uncover the pathway more clearly.

Before grabbing our spades, however, let's pause and step back. Taking them at face value, the analyses I've laid out above give us some sense of how the Church might have altered people's psychology in regions of Europe by the High Middle Ages (1000–1250 CE). By this time, some European communities had already experienced nearly five centuries of the MFP. By 1500, a time considered the dawn of the modern world, some regions had experienced the MFP for nearly a full millennium. The psychological changes induced by the shift in the organization of families and social networks help us understand why the newly forming institutions and organizations developed in certain ways. New monastic orders, guilds, towns, and universities increasingly built their laws, principles, norms, and rules in ways that focused on the individual, often endowing each member with abstract rights, privileges, obligations, and duties to the organization. To thrive, these voluntary organizations had to attract mobile individuals and then cultivate an adherence to, and preferably an internalization of, their mutually agreed upon principles and rules. With intensive kinship in a straitjacket, the one thing that medieval Europeans had in common was Christianity, with its universalizing morality, sense of individual responsibility, and strong notions of free will. From this peculiar soil, an impersonal suite of social norms germinated and gradually began to spread.

7

Europe and Asia

Due to the complex history of Europe, some regions received relatively small dosages of the Church's Marriage and Family Program. For example, we saw in Chapter 5 (Figure 5.3) that while Ireland, Brittany, and southern Italy have long been Christian, they weren't brought under the papal umbrella—and the full force of the MFP—until later than England and regions within the Carolingian Empire, including northern Italy and most of France and western Germany. This means that if the ideas I've presented hold water, we should be able to explain psychological variation just within Europe, and even within what was Christendom in 1500.

Exploring this is crucial because, while the cross-country relationships I presented in the last chapter are plentiful and often strong, there's potentially an immense range of other hidden forces that vary from country to country. These include factors related to religion, history, colonialism, ancestry, language, and much more. Of course, we tried to statistically control for all of them in some way, but you can never be totally sure. Here, by zeroing in on Europe, I'll show that it's still possible to detect the footprints of the Western Church as it lumbered across medieval Europe—both in the psychology of contemporary Europeans and in the last remnants of Europe's kin-based institutions. If we find patterns that parallel those found cross-nationally in the last chapter, now by comparing small regions within European countries, we can eliminate many alternative explanations.

Here's the key question: Are individuals from European regions with longer exposure to the Church and the MFP more individualistic and independent, less obedient and conformist, and more impersonally trusting and fair today than those from less exposed regions?

The Church's Footprints

Throughout this section, we'll rely on a set of four measures drawn from the European Social Survey, which contains data from 36 countries. In each of the questions used to create the first two psychological measures, participants were asked to say how similar the individuals described were to themselves using a six-point scale from "not like me at all" to "very much like me." The gendered pronouns in these statements were adjusted to fit the respondent. Here are the first two measures:

1. *Conformity and obedience*: This index represents an average of participants' responses to four related statements, including "It is important to her always to behave properly. She wants to avoid doing anything people would say is wrong" and "She believes that people should do what they are told. She thinks people should follow rules at all times, even when no one is watching."

2. *Individualism and independence*: This index averages responses to these two statements: "It is important to her to make her own decisions about what she does. She likes to be free and not depend on others" and "Thinking up new ideas and being creative is important to her. She likes to do things in her own original way."

To assess people's impersonal prosociality, participants were asked to respond to these questions on an 11-point scale (from 0 to 10):[1]

1. *Impersonal Fairness*: "Do you think that most people would try to take advantage of you if they got the chance, or would they try to be fair?" This scale ranged from 0 ("Most people would try to take advantage of me") to 10 ("Most people would try to be fair").
2. *Impersonal Trust*: "Generally speaking, would you say that most people can be trusted or that you can't be too careful in dealing with people?" This scale ranged from 0 ("You can't be too careful") to 10 ("Most people can be trusted").

To examine whether the MFP can still be detected in European psychology, our team assembled a database that tracked the spread of 896 bishoprics across Europe. Using these data, we calculated the average Church exposure for Europe's 442 regions, which I've mapped in Figure 7.1. In assessing a region's dosage, we specifically focused on the presence of bishoprics under papal administration. In southern Spain and Italy, for example, some bishoprics were established early but were subsequently "disconnected" from the Western Church when the regions were conquered by powers unfriendly to the bishop of Rome. Islamic societies, for example, conquered much of Spain and parts of Italy over a period of several centuries. As these regions were later conquered and reincorporated under the Western Church, the bishoprics became "active" again in our dosage measures. Similarly, while Ireland was Christianized early, the Celtic Church didn't enforce the MFP, so these regions didn't come under papal administration—and the MFP—until around 1100.

Strikingly, our results show that individuals living in regions that experienced a longer duration of the MFP possess weaker inclinations toward conformity-obedience, stronger motivations for individualism-independence, and greater impersonal fairness and trust. Because we only compared regions within countries, these patterns can't be due to contemporary differences

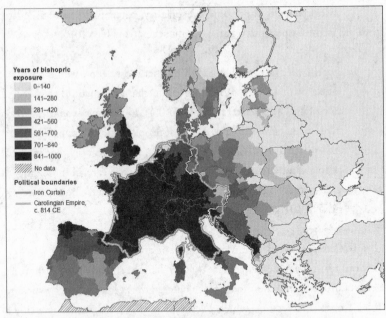

FIGURE 7.1. Regional dosages of the Marriage and Family Program based on tracking the diffusion of papally controlled bishoprics across Europe from 500 to 1500 CE. Dosages are measured in years of exposure to the Western Church and range from zero to 1,000 years. The darker the shading, the stronger the MFP dosage. Because of the relevance of the Carolingian Empire (Chapter 5), which teamed up with the Church during the Early Middle Ages to impose the MFP, the borders in 814 (at the death of Charlemagne) are highlighted. For reference, the Iron Curtain boundary, based on Churchill's 1946 speech, is highlighted to demarcate socialist Europe in the 20th century.

among European countries in their national wealth, governments, or social safety nets. These results also hold after statistically removing the effects of people's income, education, religious denominations, and reported religiosity. The fact that the local MFP dosage remained just as strong after statistically accounting for people's religious denominations (Catholic, Protestant, Muslim, etc.) and personal religiosity is important, because we might worry that the effects of bishoprics operate through their influence on people's supernatural beliefs or ritual attendance.

Of course, the founding of bishoprics in different places might have been influenced by some hidden forces that are actually doing the real work in shifting people's psychology. So, we also statistically held constant the influence of many different geographic, ecological, and climatic factors, including agricultural fertility, rainfall, irrigation, temperature, and the ruggedness of the terrain. To capture various other historical forces, we statistically controlled for the presence of old Roman roads, monasteries, and medieval universities as well as for the region's population density in 500. This should deal with differences in economic development and Roman influence at the start of the MFP. Even after all this, all four of our psychological measures still show a reliable relationship with the Church's MFP dosage. To summarize, European communities in regions that spent longer under the sway of the MFP are psychologically WEIRDer today.

This connects the Church to contemporary psychology. However, if the causal pathway I'm tracking is correct, we should also expect places in Europe with less exposure to the Church to have stronger kin-based institutions.

THE LAST REMNANTS OF INTENSIVE KINSHIP

Connecting a region's Church exposure to the presence of intensive kinship is challenging, because detailed data from Europe on kinship are hard to come by, and the Ethnographic Atlas's coverage of Europe is particularly poor (anthropologists avoid Europe—too WEIRD). The best source that my team has been able to locate, ironically, derives from papal dispensations that granted people permission to marry their first cousins. As noted earlier, the Church began permitting people to apply for special permission to marry their cousins during the latter half of the Middle Ages. Collating a variety of historical sources, our team gathered rates of first cousin marriages based on dispensation records for 57 different regions in France, Spain, and Italy in the 20th century. To highlight how powerful these effects are, we added data from regions in Turkey. Turkey is included in the European Social Survey because it's partially in Europe, and our team was able to locate cousin marriage data for Turkey in another survey. Adding Turkey's regions allows us to see that the insights extend outside of what was Latin Christendom. As expected, having never experienced the MFP, Turkey's regions maintain higher rates of cousin marriage than those in Spain, Italy, and France.

Here's the result: in regions with less MFP exposure during the Middle Ages, people were much more likely to still be asking for permission to marry their cousins in the 20th century. In fact, knowing the local MFP dosage allows us to explain nearly 75 percent of the variation in rates of first cousin marriage across regions in Italy, France, Turkey, and Spain. If we drop Turkey, MFP exposure still accounts for nearly 40 percent of the regional variation in cousin marriage. Put another way, for every century of MFP exposure, a region's rate of cousin marriage drops by nearly a quarter.

Further confirming the historical narrative developed in Chapter 5, our analyses show that if a region was inside the Carolingian Empire during the Early Middle Ages, its rate of first cousin marriage in the 20th century was minuscule, and probably zero. If the region was outside the Carolingian Empire, as were southern Italy, southern Spain, and Brittany (France's northwestern peninsula), the rate was higher. In Sicily, there were so many requests for dispensations to marry cousins in the 20th century that the pope delegated special power to the bishop of Sicily to allow marriages between second cousins without the Vatican's permission. Normally, dispensations were (and remain) a papal privilege, but the demand was so high that an exception was necessary.[2]

To complete this picture, let's examine the relationship between the prevalence of first cousin marriages—standing in as our proxy for intensive kinship—and our four dimensions of psychology from the European Social Survey. Based on responses from over 18,000 individuals from 68 different regions across four countries, people from regions with higher rates of cousin marriage in the 20th century show greater conformity-obedience, less individualism-independence, and lower levels of both impersonal trust and fairness. As Figure 7.2 shows, the effects are big. Simply knowing the rate

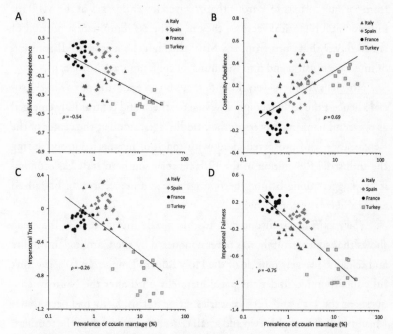

FIGURE 7.2. The relationships between the prevalence of first cousin marriage in regions of Spain, Italy, France, and Turkey and four dimensions of psychology: (A) Individualism-Independence, (B) Conformity-Obedience, (C) Impersonal Trust, and (D) Impersonal Fairness.

of cousin marriage allows us to explain between 36 percent (conformity-obedience) and 70 percent (impersonal fairness) of the regional differences in our four psychological dimensions, from cosmopolitan France to the remotest parts of southeastern Turkey. The figure illustrates—and our statistical analyses confirm—that although the variation in cousin marriage is much smaller within European countries, the broader trends mostly hold. Our analyses also confirm that these findings cannot be accounted for by differences in individual income, schooling, religiosity, or religious denomination.[3]

Although the analyses displayed in Figure 7.2 are based on sparse data from various corners of Europe that received lower dosages of the MFP for idiosyncratic historical reasons, they nevertheless illuminate a portion of the pathway that runs from the MFP through the historical dissolution of intensive kinship and into the minds of contemporary Europeans.

Now let's zoom in even closer to focus on an enduring puzzle in the social sciences: the Italian enigma. While northern and central Italy emerged as powerful banking centers in the Middle Ages, stood at the center of the Renaissance, and prospered along with much of northern Europe during the Industrial Revolution in the 19th century, southern Italy has economically slogged along behind, becoming instead an epicenter for organized crime and corruption. Why?

You've already seen one clue to this puzzle in Figure 5.3. That map shows that southern Italy was never conquered by the Carolingian Empire and remained largely outside of the Holy Roman Empire. In fact, it wasn't fully incorporated under the papal hierarchy until after the Norman conquests of the 11th and 12th centuries. Prior to this, Sicily had been under Muslim rule for roughly two and a half centuries, and much of the southern mainland had been under the control of the Eastern Empire and the Orthodox Church.

The imprint of this history can be seen in the prevalence of cousin marriages across Italian provinces in the 20th century, based again on Church dispensations for cousin marriage (Figure 7.3A). In northern Italy, which has been largely under the Western Church since the MFP began, the frequency of cousin marriage is less than 0.4 percent, and sometimes as low as zero. As we look south, rates of cousin marriage increase, rising to over 4 percent at the tip of the Italian boot and in much of Sicily. Keeping in mind that cousin marriage is both an important element of intensive kinship by itself and a proxy for other social norms, have a look at Figure 7.3B, which maps the frequency of voluntary (unpaid) blood donations across 93 Italian provinces in 1995. Remember, voluntary anonymous blood donations provide an important public good and a way of helping strangers. Notice any patterns when you compare panels A and B of Figure 7.3?

Strikingly, the lower the prevalence of cousin marriage in a province,

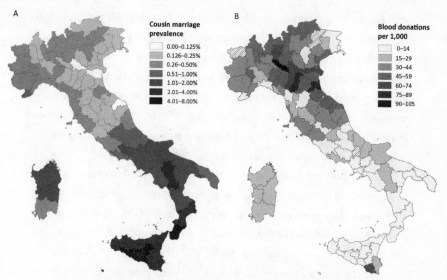

FIGURE 7.3. Panel A (left) shows the prevalence of first cousin marriage across 93 Italian provinces. The darker the shading, the higher the rate of cousin marriage. Panel B (right) shows the frequency of blood donations per 1,000 people for each province. Provinces with lower rates of cousin marriage made many more voluntary blood donations in 1995.

the higher the rate of voluntary blood donations to strangers. In southern Italy, including almost all of Sicily, the rates of blood donations are near zero. In some northern provinces, they reach 105 donations (16-ounce bags) per 1,000 people per year. Knowing just the rate of first cousin marriage allows us to account for about one-third of the variation in donations across Italian provinces. Put another way, doubling the rate of cousin marriage from, say, 1 percent to 2 percent reduces blood donations by 8 bags per 1,000 people. That's a big effect, given that the average donation for a province is only 28 bags per 1,000 people.[4]

Similar patterns emerge when we use real-world measures of people's trust in impersonal organizations and strangers. Italians from provinces with more cousin marriage (1) use fewer checks, instead favoring cash; (2) keep more of their wealth in cash instead of putting it into banks, stocks, etc.; and (3) take more loans from family and friends than from banks. The effects are striking: the use of checks plummets from over 60 percent in Italian provinces with low cousin marriage to just above 20 percent in provinces with relatively high rates of cousin marriage (Figure 7.4A). Similarly, the percentage of wealth that households keep in cash goes from about 10 percent in provinces with rates of cousin marriage near zero to over 40 percent in provinces with high rates of cousin marriage (Figure 7.4B). Using detailed data on individuals, these relationships hold even after statistically controlling for the influence of income, wealth, formal schooling, and family size.[5]

Corruption and Mafia activity reflect the same patterns seen for blood donations and impersonal trust. The greater the rate of cousin marriage in a province, the higher the rates of corruption and Mafia activity. There's a reason why the Mafia is often referred to as "the family" or "the clan" and the boss is sometimes called "the godfather." The strength of in-group loyalty and the power of nepotism in societies with intensive kinship create precisely the kind of psychology and social relations that foster graft and fuel organized crime. These patterns have developed despite Italy's formal governing and educational institutions, which are like those in other western European countries.[6]

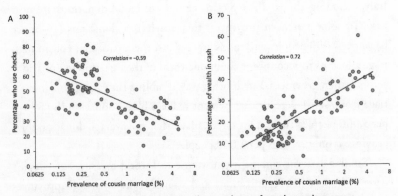

FIGURE 7.4. The relationship between the prevalence of cousin marriage across Italian provinces and (A) the percentage of people who use checks and (B) the percentage of household wealth kept in cash instead of banks, stocks, etc. These are both real-world measures of impersonal trust.

THE CHILDREN OF IMMIGRANTS

Every year, people from all over the world immigrate to different European countries. Eventually, many of these first-generation immigrants have children, who grow up entirely in Europe, speak the national language perfectly, and attend the local schools. We can learn a lot by comparing these second-generation immigrants. Using data from the European Social Survey from roughly 14,000 second-generation immigrants spread across 36 countries, we can compare the psychological outcomes of individuals who were born and raised in the same European country but whose parents arrived from diverse places. We assigned each individual a value for the Kinship Intensity Index (KII) and the prevalence of cousin marriage based on either their parents' countries of origin or the languages spoken in their homes. Then we analyzed the same four psychological dimensions studied above.

The results are illuminating: individuals whose parents came from countries with higher Kinship Intensity Indices or more cousin marriage were more conformist-obedient, less individualistic-independent, and less inclined to trust or expect fair treatment from strangers. These relationships remain strong even after we statistically accounted for differences in income, education, religious denomination, religiosity, and even people's personal experience of discrimination. They even hold if we only compare individuals living within the same small regions that we used above in examining the impact of different MFP dosages (Figure 7.1).[7]

The consistent and robust impact of historical kinship intensity on the psychology of second-generation immigrants reveals that an important component of these psychological effects is transmitted from one generation to the next, and not simply due to people's direct exposure to poor governments, social safety nets, particular climates, endemic diseases, or oppression by the native population in the immigrant's new home. Rather, these psychological differences persist in the adult children of immigrants both because migrants often re-create the intensive kin-based institutions found in their countries of origin (e.g., arranged marriages with cousins) and because particular ways of thinking and feeling are learned from parents, siblings, and those in newly formed social networks. Culturally transmitted aspects of psychology can persist long after the actual kinship practices related to polygyny, cousin marriage, and clans have disappeared.[8]

The same patterns emerged when we linked second-generation immigrants to the dosage of Church exposure experienced back in their parents' countries of origin. Individuals whose parents' native countries had been under the Western Church for longer were more individualistic-independent, less conformist-obedient, and more inclined toward impersonal trust and fairness.

The idea here is that the medieval Church shaped contemporary psychology through its demolition of Europe's kin-based institutions. However, as I've noted, the intensity of kinship has also been shaped by other factors, including ecology and climate. A powerful way to test the ideas I've developed is to step away from Europe to consider how, in the absence of the Church, ecological factors might have intensified kin-based institutions and in turn induced similar psychological patterns.

Psychological Differences Within China and India

Kinship intensity in China, and probably much of Asia, is linked to a combination of ecological and technological factors related to rice cultivation and irrigation. Specifically, in the preindustrial world, rice paddies could be incredibly productive—in terms of their yield per acre of land—compared to crops like wheat, corn, or millet. However, sustaining a high level of productivity for wet rice agriculture required the cooperation of relatively large groups. A single farming household simply couldn't construct, maintain, and defend the irrigation canals, dikes, and terraced fields, or handle the labor demands involved in weeding, fertilizing, and replanting seedlings from germination beds. As you now know, clan-based organizations foster precisely the kind of tight-knit, top-down organizations needed to tackle such cooperative challenges.[9]

Historically, the relative importance of paddy rice in China rose substantially after the 10th century, sparked by the arrival of new, quick-ripening varieties of wet rice from Southeast Asia. This was further fueled by the migration of northern farmers to the south and east, propelled by a combination of climatic shifts and increasing raids by Mongolian herders. Over about 800 years, this resulted in the gradual spread and intensification of patrilineal clans in various regions of China, but particularly in regions with the greatest potential for paddy rice. By the early 20th century, clans corporately owned about a third of the cultivated land in Guangdong Province and roughly 44 percent in the Pearl River delta.[10]

Today, China's provinces vary dramatically in the amount of agricultural land devoted to paddy rice (Figure 7.5). Moving from the south to the north, regional populations gradually decrease their reliance on paddy rice while increasing their cultivation of other staples, such as wheat and corn. The darker the shading in Figure 7.5, the greater the proportion of cropland devoted to paddy rice. This situation provides a natural experiment by creating variation in the intensity of kinship—and specifically in the importance of clans—that can be traced to an environmental factor: the ecological suitability of an area for paddy rice. We can link this ecological variation to psychological differences across China.[11]

To date, I have not obtained and analyzed detailed statistical data on features like cousin marriage, polygyny, and postmarital residence within China, so I can't produce a historical Kinship Intensity Index for China like the one used in the last chapter. However, data on the historical importance of clans across provinces confirm that the greater the percentage of agricultural land devoted to paddy rice cultivation within a province, the more prevalent and important were patrilineal clans.[12]

Directly linking agricultural practices to psychological differences, the psychologist Thomas Talhelm and his team administered a package of three different experimental tasks to over a thousand Han participants from 27 Chinese provinces at six different universities. The three tasks they administered are set out on the next page.[13]

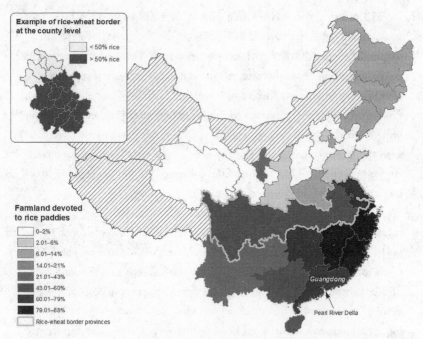

FIGURE 7.5. Map of China showing the variation in land devoted to paddy rice cultivation. Darker shades of gray represent regions in which a higher percentage of agricultural land is devoted to paddy rice. The inset illustrates how Talhelm's team analyzed the counties within provinces along the north-south border (see text).[14]

1. *In-group favoritism*: Participants were told to imagine that they'd gone into business with (1) a friend or (2) a stranger. Then, for each case, participants answered questions about their willingness to reward or punish the friend or stranger if they behaved (a) honestly or (b) dishonestly. People from regions that traditionally engaged in intensive paddy rice cultivation, whose social life was likely more strongly imbued with intensive kinship, should more strongly favor their friends and family. By contrast, those with weaker relational connections should be open to both finding new relationships and reassessing old ones; old bonds may have to break, and today's strangers are potentially tomorrow's friends.

2. *Self-focus*: Participants were asked to draw a sociogram of themselves and their friends, making sure to label the circles accordingly. Participants' self-focus was assessed by measuring how much bigger their self-circle was than the average size of their friend-circles. More self-focused individuals tend to draw themselves larger than everyone else. Because participants aren't told why they need to draw a sociogram, they can't figure out what's being tested or what the researchers want. This avoids concerns that people are presenting themselves in certain ways or just doing what they think the experimenter wants. Here, participants from communities that were historically less dependent on rice paddies, and presumably less clannish, should inflate their self-circles relative to their friend-circles.

3. *Analytic thinking*: Participants responded to the Triad Task, as discussed in earlier chapters. People from communities less dependent on paddy rice, where clans never became as important, should make more analytical choices in the task.

The results that Talhelm and his team found largely converge. In the In-group Favoritism Task (involving the "business partner"), Han Chinese participants from provinces that put a higher percentage of cropland under paddy rice cultivation tended to reward their friends *more* for honesty and punish them *less* for dishonesty than did those from other provinces. That is, those from more intensive paddy rice regions revealed greater loyalty (or more cronyism) toward their friends. Those from regions less reliant on paddy rice treated strangers and friends more similarly.

In the Self-focus Task, those from provinces with less paddy rice cultivation tended to inflate their self-circles more than they did their friend-circles. Cutting the data into two groups starkly reveals the effect: those from provinces where less than half of the agricultural land is under paddy rice cultivation inflated their circle by 1.5 millimeters (on average) relative to their friends, while those from provinces where over half of the cultivated land is rice paddies represented themselves as roughly the same size as their friends (approximately 0 mm difference). Less wet rice cultivation is associated with greater self-focus. Of course, by WEIRD standards, a self-inflation of 1.5 mm isn't that "impressive": Americans inflate themselves by 6.2 mm, Germans by 4.5 mm, and Brits by 3 mm. In Japan, another place with lots of rice paddies, people draw themselves as slightly smaller than their friends (−0.5 mm).[15]

In the Triad Task, people from provinces less dependent on paddy rice cultivation were more inclined to think analytically (Figure 7.6A). The effects were substantial: the average percentage of analytic matches for a person from a "paddy rice province" like Jiangxi or Shanghai ranged from 10 to 20 percent—they are strongly holistic. Meanwhile, those from low-rice-production provinces like Qinghai or Ningxia preferred analytic matches just over 40 percent of the time. That is, in provinces that grow primarily wheat, corn, and millet ("non-rice" crops), people make almost as many analytic as holistic matches. This places these non-rice-growing populations right in the range typical of WEIRD undergraduates but still below the WEIRD adults at yourmorals.org (Figure 1.9). Overall, knowing the percentage of land devoted to paddy rice in a province allows us to account for about half of the variation among Chinese provinces in their analytic vs. holistic thinking.[16]

The breadth of these psychological differences, captured in three different experimental tasks, is particularly impressive, given that all the participants were Han Chinese university students (not farmers) at one of six universities. Despite this homogeneity in age, education, nationality, and ethnicity, Talhelm and his team uncovered substantial psychological differences.

These correlations between people's psychology and paddy rice agriculture don't tell us what causes what. Maybe certain aspects of psychology *cause* people to disdain rice, or to disdain the cooperative activities that are required to grow wet rice? Or, since rice growing varies roughly from south to north, perhaps some other economic or geographic factor that also varies from south to north causes people to both think more analytically and grow less rice. Taking advantage of the larger sample they gathered using

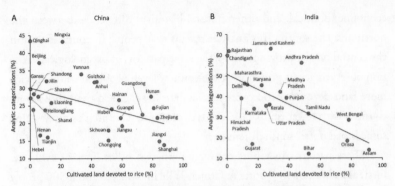

FIGURE 7.6. The relationship between analytic (vs. holistic) thinking, as measured using the Triad Task, and the percentage of land under rice paddy cultivation in (A) China and (B) India. The vertical axis gives the average percentage of analytic responses for individuals from each province (China) or state (India). The participants in China were all university students and ethnically Han. In India, the participants were recruited online and spanned a wide range of ages and ethnic backgrounds.[17]

the Triad Task, Talhelm's team tackled these concerns in two ways. First, rather than using the actual prevalence of paddy rice farming—a behavior—they used a measure of a region's "suitability for paddy rice" based purely on ecological variables like rainfall. Unlike *the activity* of cultivating rice, such rice-suitability measures cannot be *caused by* psychological differences among provinces. This measure of rice suitability, and a little statistical razzle-dazzle, allowed them to trace causal links from ecological conditions through agricultural practices to analytic thinking. That is, more holistic thinking probably cannot make it rain. This approach is not foolproof, but it's a nice step toward establishing a causal link that runs from paddy rice to analytic thinking.[18]

Second, to better deal with potentially hidden factors associated with China's north-south differences, Thomas's team narrowed their focus to only those five central provinces right along the north-south divide (Figure 7.5). Here, they obtained data on paddy rice growing for all the counties within each province, which allowed them to compare counties that are side by side but differ in their reliance on wet rice. Comparing adjacent or nearby counties within the same province minimizes concerns about broader climatic, economic, political, and other cultural-historical differences between the north and the south. This analysis reveals that people in counties within the central border provinces show the same patterns of psychological variation observed across provinces at the country level: people in counties with more land devoted to rice were less analytically inclined than those from counties with fewer rice paddies. This confirms that we aren't simply seeing some broad north-south difference.[19]

These patterns in China converge with two other lines of evidence. First, as a check on his efforts in China, Talhelm sampled about 500 people online from different states in India and administered both the Triad Task and his In-group Favoritism ("business partner") Task. Crucially, India's ecological gradient for paddy rice was similar to China's, except that it runs east-west across the subcontinent instead of south to north. If the conclusions about the psychological variation in China are correct, we should see similar psychological differences.

Sure enough, Indians from regions that engage in less paddy rice cultivation are more analytic on the triads and less nepotistic (friend-favoring) on the business partner tasks, just like in China. Figure 7.6B shows the relationship between cropland devoted to rice for different Indian states and their percentage of analytic choices on the Triad Task. This relationship in India holds independent of the age, gender, income, and education of participants. Now, I don't want to make too much of this one online study in India, but the fact that it confirms the same pattern seen in China, except now running east to west instead of south to north, makes idiosyncratic alternative explanations based on the details of Chinese history or geography seem unlikely.

The second piece of confirmatory evidence comes from a global study showing that the historical reliance of populations on irrigation—regardless of whether it's for rice paddies or not—is related to psychological measures of individualism, tightness, and obedience. Those whose ancestors were more reliant on irrigation agriculture are now less individualistic, more concerned about adhering to social norms, and more serious about inculcating obedience in their children.[20]

Taken together, this evidence from China and India confirms that important psychological variation exists within large countries, and it bolsters the notion that more intensive kinship generates certain predictable patterns. Here, the Church wasn't the cause of the variation in intensive kinship or psychology. Instead, certain ecological conditions created the potential for intensive agriculture, which in turn fueled the cultural evolution of highly cooperative, top-down, intensive kin-based institutions. Notably, however, the variation in intensive kinship created by this ecological variation is relatively small compared to the impact of the MFP—the Church nearly annihilated Europe's clans, kindreds, cousin marriage, polygamy, and inheritance norms.

Nevertheless, for Europe, this suggests that the path to weak kin ties and WEIRD psychology may have been shorter in some regions, where ecological conditions didn't favor super-strong kin-based institutions. That is, in the rain-fed, wheat-growing regions of northern Europe, the Church's MFP may have faced somewhat less resistance in dismantling the more diffuse kin-based institutions of some northern European tribes. Of course, we statistically controlled for all known ecological and economic contributors to psychological variation (such as irrigation and disease prevalence), so the results you've seen above hold independent of these factors.[21]

In thinking about China, especially considering its massive economic growth since the market reforms of 1979, let me plant a mental seed that we'll harvest later. Until the mid-20th century, many intensive kinship practices were common in China. Then, in 1950, at the culmination of a three-decade-long campaign to adopt/impose "modern" (European) marriage, the new communist government instituted the Marriage Law of the People's Republic of China. Legally speaking, Articles 1, 2, and 3 of this law ended polygamy, arranged marriage, concubinage, child betrothal, forced remarriage of widows (levirate marriage), and marriage payments (e.g., dowry). Infanticide was also prohibited, and wives gained the right to both own property and inherit it from their husbands. In terms of marriage among relatives, only uncle-niece marriage was banned in 1950 (second-degree relatives, Article 5), but this expanded to include first cousins in

1980 (third-degree relatives, Article 6a). This Marriage and Family Program should sound familiar: the powerful Chinese state has been doing over the last seven decades what the Church required centuries to accomplish in medieval Europe.[22]

Fertile Ground

Let's summarize the three major points in this chapter.

1. The patterns we've seen in Europe parallel those we saw globally in the last chapter. The longer a population was exposed to the Western Church, the weaker its families and WEIRDer its psychological patterns are today. Except now, our comparisons within European countries leave much less room for alternative explanations. These patterns can't be explained by colonialism, "European genes," democratic institutions, economic prosperity, or individual-level differences in income, wealth, education, religious denomination, or religiosity.

2. The effect of kin-based institutions on people's psychology is culturally persistent. The adult children of immigrants, who grow up entirely in Europe, still manifest the psychological calibrations associated with the kin-based institutions linked to their parents' native countries or ethnolinguistic groups.

3. Some similar patterns of psychological variation can also be detected in other large regions, including in China and India. Crucially, while this psychological variation probably traces to regional differences in kinship intensity, its underlying causes relate not to the Church but to ecological and climatic factors that made irrigation and paddy rice cultivation particularly productive over the population's history.

By 1000 CE, several regions of Europe had already experienced five centuries of the MFP. In these regions, which can be identified using our bishopric dosages (Figure 7.1), the Western Church had inadvertently induced a series of social and psychological shifts. Without intensive kin-based institutions to organize production, provide security, and endow people with a sense of meaning and identity, individuals were both socially compelled and personally motivated to relocate, seek out like-minded others, form voluntary associations, and engage with strangers. The relevant psychological shifts likely emerged in multiple ways: facultatively (on the fly), developmentally, and culturally. Research on the impact of relational and residential mobility suggests some role for both rapid psychological recalibrations to new circumstances and the enduring imprints of childhood experience. Psychologists have shown, for example, that priming people with settling down in a city vs. visiting it briefly immediately evokes different preferences: settling down causes people to facultatively value loyal friends, while shorter visits spark more egalitarian motivations. Meanwhile, research also points to developmental effects: young adults who moved geographically as children make less of a distinction between friends and strangers. Overall, greater residential mobility and more relational freedom (i.e., fewer constraints on new relationships) lead individuals to form larger social networks, favor new experiences, prefer novelty, and perhaps even think more creatively (see Appendix C).[23]

These psychological effects, some of which could be induced simply by increasing residential mobility and relational freedom, would have been especially strong among those moving into the towns, cities, and religious organizations that began growing in the 10th and 11th centuries. In assembling these new associations and organizations, the emerging proto-WEIRD psychology—analytic thinking, individualism, and a nonrelational morality—would have favored the development of both impartial rules that granted privileges and obligations to *individuals* (not clans) and impersonal mechanisms for enforcing trust, such as accounting records, commercial laws, and written contracts.

Of course, people are terrible at designing well-functioning formal institutions *de novo*. But, because this same process was occurring in many different European towns and cities, from northern Italy to England, cultural evolution could do the work. When a community or organization bumbled onto an effective combination of new formal institutions, norms, and beliefs, they prospered and consequently expanded by attracting new members. Such successful expansions led other organizations and communities to copy their practices and norms, which eventually spread in the form of written laws, organizational policies, and urban charters. As the most useful institutional elements were copied and recombined in different ways over centuries, effective formal institutional forms, which fit the developing proto-WEIRD psychology of the era, began to emerge for organizing and governing *individuals* (not families, kindreds, etc.). The new formal institutions increasingly fostered cooperation and mutually-beneficial exchanges among Christian strangers.

Before moving forward to examine the emergence of impersonal markets and their effects on psychology, I want to pause briefly to put one element of the Church's MFP under the microscope so we can see something of how and why it works. Let's take a close look at the social, psychological, and hormonal impacts of monogamous marriage and consider its role in the origins of WEIRD psychology and inclusive democratic institutions.

8

WEIRD Monogamy

In 1521, two expanding empires collided when Hernán Cortés and his Spanish conquistadors arrived in Mexico and began conquering the Aztecs. These two powerful empires had developed in isolation from each other for at least 15 millennia, and their common ancestors were Stone Age hunter-gatherers. Despite their independent development, the two empires were strikingly similar. Both were highly stratified agricultural societies governed by complex state bureaucracies, led by hereditary rulers, and infused with powerful religions that both fueled and justified their subjugation of other societies. Nevertheless, there were some key differences.

Just a few years after his daring and cutthroat conquest, Cortés greeted New Spain's Twelve Apostles, the first Catholic missionaries to arrive in Mexico. One member of the 12, the Franciscan friar Toribio de Benavente Motolinía, became an astute observer of the indigenous beliefs and customs within his new ministry. His writings give us a glimpse of one of the institutions that distinguished 16th-century Europeans from their Aztec contemporaries. Regarding marriage, Friar Toribio wrote:

For three or four years the Sacrament of Matrimony was not administered, except to those who were educated in the house of God. All other Indians lived with as many women as they cared to have. Some had two hundred women and others less, each one as many as suited him. Since the lords and chiefs stole all the women for themselves, an ordinary Indian could scarcely find a woman when he wished to marry. The Franciscans sought to uproot this evil; but they had no way of doing so because the lords had most of the women and refused to give them up. Neither petitions nor threats nor arguments, nor any other means which the Friars resorted to were sufficient to induce the Indians to relinquish their women and, after doing so, enter marriage with only one, as the law of the church demands ... This state of affairs continued until, after five or six years, it pleased the Lord that some Indians of their own accord began to abandon polygamy and content themselves with only one woman, marrying her as the Church required ... The Friars did not find it easy to have the Indians renounce polygamy. This was very hard to achieve because it was hard for the Indians to quit the ancient carnal custom that so greatly flattered sensuality.[1]

As an eyewitness, albeit not an unbiased one,[2] the friar zeroes in on three key aspects of polygynous marriage that recur across diverse societies. First, when men are permitted by custom to marry multiple women, elite men take multiple wives. Second, polygynous marriage has powerful social dynamics that create a glut of poor, low-status men with few prospects for mating and marriage, because most of the women marry "up." And third, the high-status men, often accompanied by their wives, resist the notion that each person should have no more than one spouse at a time.

Friar Toribio's writings show something else central to our story: Christian missionaries are relentless. Whether in Anglo-Saxon Kent around 600 CE, the Aztec Empire in 1530, or the Peruvian Amazon in 1995, they never stop and never give up; when proselytizing preachers fail or get themselves killed, they are soon replaced by fresh recruits who continue to push the Church's package of supernatural beliefs, rituals, and family practices.

To illustrate the inexorable dynamics of polygynous marriage, consider these observations by another ethnographer in a rather different community in the New World:

> There is a shortage of eligible women to marry in every
> polygynous society, and this is a primary factor responsible for
> intergenerational conflict in Colorado City/Centennial Park.
> Senior males are always on the marriage market and thus compete
> with younger men for mates in a limited pool of eligible women.
> The tension between married and unmarried men influences
> the perceptions of teenagers. For example, in the 1960s, a local
> policeman . . . would threaten to arrest unmarried males who did
> not leave the community . . . The competition for mates is acute.
> Young men realize that without the support and financial backing
> of their families (especially their fathers), they will not be able to
> compete with older males. Young men know, however, that if they
> do not find a girlfriend before they graduate from high school,
> they probably never will have one. Without a girlfriend, they will
> leave the community to find a wife.[3]

This situation bears an eerie similarity to the Aztec situation described by Toribio. But, far from 16th-century Mexico, this description comes from a small town on the Utah-Arizona border in late 20th-century America. Here, the anthropologist William Jankowiak gives us a look at the social life of a polygynous Mormon community associated with the Fundamentalist Church of Jesus Christ of Latter-Day Saints. In many ways, these fundamentalist Mormons aren't much different from most Americans. For example, after a day visiting national parks or hanging out at the mall, their dinner conversations range from the "entertainment value of *The Lord of the*

Rings" to the health benefits of flaxseed oil. Nevertheless, polygyny's math problem (see below) still plays out, creating a pool of disaffected, unmarried young men with few prospects and no stake in the future. These "lost boys," as the Mormons call them, become society's problem as they turn to crime, violence, and drugs instead of marrying to become reliable, hardworking fathers.[4]

To understand the power of polygynous marriage and its social dynamics, we first need to consider human nature and ponder WEIRD marriage from a species-level perspective.

A "Peculiar" Institution

By now you probably know what I'm going to say: it's not the fundamentalist Mormons or ancient Aztecs who possess an exotic form of marriage; it's us—WEIRD people. As with our kin-based institutions more generally, the peculiarity of WEIRD monogamy can be seen from both an evolutionary and a global-historical perspective. As you'll see, even among monogamous societies, WEIRD marriage is peculiar.[5]

From among our closest evolutionary relatives—apes and monkeys—guess how many species both live in large groups like *Homo sapiens* and have only monogamous pair-bonding?

That's right, zero. No group-living primates have the noncultural equivalent of monogamous marriage. Based on the sex lives of our two closest relatives, chimpanzees and bonobos, the ancestor we share with these apes was probably highly promiscuous and likely didn't form pair-bonds at all, let alone enduring, monogamous pair-bonds. Nevertheless, since we diverged from our ape cousins, our species has evolved a specialized psychological suite—our pair-bonding psychology—that can foster strong emotional bonds between mates that remain stable for long enough to encourage men to invest in their mate's children. This pair-bonding psychology provides the innate anchor for marital institutions. However, the nature of this anchor biases marital institutions toward polygynous pair-bonding. In contrast, our innate mating psychology doesn't usually favor widespread polyandrous marriage—that's one wife with multiple husbands—although there are good evolutionary reasons to expect this to pop up at low frequencies in societies lacking prohibitions against it.[6]

Our "polygyny bias" arises in part from fundamental asymmetries in human reproductive biology. Over our evolutionary history, the more mates a man had, the greater his reproduction, or what biologists call his "fitness." By contrast, for women, simply having more mates didn't directly translate into greater reproduction or higher fitness. This is because, unlike men, women necessarily had to carry their own fetuses, nurse their own infants, and care for their toddlers. Given the immense input needed to rear human children compared to other mammals, an aspiring human mother required help, protection, and resources like food, clothing, shelter, and cultural know-how. One way to obtain some of this help was to form a pair-bond with the most capable, resourceful, and highest status man she could find by making it clear to him that her babies would be his babies. The greater his paternal confidence, the more willing he was to invest time, effort, and energy in providing for her and her children. Unlike his wife, however, our new husband could "run in parallel" by forming additional pair-bonds with other women. While his new wife was pregnant or nursing, he could be "working" on conceiving another child with his second or third wife (and so on, with additional wives).

Moreover, as long as he can attract fertile mates, a man can continue to reproduce over his entire life span, unlike his wives, who have to stop at menopause. Thus men can potentially get a big fitness benefit from adding more mates—both long- and short-term partners—to their reproductive portfolios. For these reasons, natural selection has shaped our evolved psychology in ways that make men, particularly high-status men, favorably inclined toward polygynous marriage.[7]

I suspect you're not shocked by this revelation, that men have certain psychological inclinations toward polygyny. What might be more surprising is that the evolved psychological push toward polygynous marriage doesn't come just from men. Because women reproduce "in serial," having and investing in only one baby (usually) at a time, their selection of a really good mate can be crucial. Not only do their chosen mates supply half of their children's genes, but they may also provide protection, resources (e.g., meat, animal skins, flint, etc.), and other investments, such as teaching. In a world with polygynous marriage, young women and their families get a much larger selection of potential husbands to choose from than are available in a purely monogamous society; they can select either a married or an unmarried man. The best move for a particular woman in a hunter-gatherer society might be to become the second wife of a great hunter instead of being the first wife of a poor hunter; this helps guarantee that children get both excellent genes and a steady supply of meat (a valuable source of nutrition). Moreover, by joining a polygynous household, a woman might learn from her older co-wives, share resources like tools, honey, and cooking fires, and get help with babysitting or even nursing. Of course, in a perfect world, such a woman might prefer an *exclusive* arrangement with the great hunter; but, faced with the real-world choice between marrying polygynously for a better overall deal with the prestigious guy or marrying monogamously for a worse deal, she'll often prefer to marry a married man. Thus monogamous norms constrain women's choices as well as men's and can prevent people from marrying whom they really want.[8]

As a result, polygynous marriage will appeal to both men and women under many conditions, including in societies in which women are free to select their own husbands. Polyandrous marriage, by contrast, won't appeal psychologically to either men or women, except under relatively narrow social, economic, and ecological circumstances.[9] Consistent with this picture, most anthropologically known hunter-gatherer societies permit polygynous marriage, and, statistically speaking, it usually persists at low to medium frequencies. In the most comprehensive study, 90 percent of hunter-gatherer populations around the globe had some degree of polygynous marriage, while just 10 percent had only monogamous marriage. Of the societies with polygyny, about 14 percent of men and 22 percent of women were polygynously married. Even among highly egalitarian hunter-gatherers, such as those living in the Congo Basin, 14 to 20 percent of men married polygynously.[10] Not surprisingly, across all groups, it's always the prestigious men—the great shamans, hunters, and warriors—who attract multiple wives, though few marry more than about four women. Polyandrous marriage, by contrast, is statistically invisible, though many isolated cases have been reported.[11]

As societies adopted farming and began to scale up in size and complexity, the emergence of large inequalities among men greatly exaggerated the intensity of polygynous marriage. The Ethnographic Atlas reveals that 85 percent of agricultural societies had polygynous marriage. In many populations, taking additional wives remains a sign of a man's prestige and success, with the highest-status men having many more than four wives; in fact, a successful man who doesn't take additional wives could raise eyebrows. Meanwhile, only 15 percent of societies in the Atlas are described as "monogamous" and a mere 0.3 percent as "polyandrous." By creating social strata, hereditary wealth, inherited political power, and occupational castes, cultural evolution magnified the impact of our innate polygynous biases on marriage and mating as societies scaled up.[12]

During this scaling-up process, polygyny got so extreme that it can be difficult to comprehend the magnitude. The easiest way to get a glimpse of what was going on is by looking at the size of elite harems at different places and times around the globe. In the South Pacific at the time of European contact, Tongan chiefs had a few high-ranking wives who helped solidify alliances with other powerful families, and a few hundred secondary wives. In Africa, Ashante and Zulu kings each had 1,000 or more wives. However, these are just the paramount chiefs or kings; there was usually a fleet of lesser elites who maintained smaller harems for themselves. Zande kings, for example, each had more than 500 wives, but their chiefs also each maintained about 30 or 40 wives, and sometimes as many as 100. In Asia, things were often even more extreme: medieval Khmer kings in Cambodia possessed five elite wives and several thousand secondary wives who were themselves graded into various classes. In early China (1046–771 BCE), Western Zhou kings had one queen, three consorts, nine wives of secondary rank, 27 wives of third rank, and 81 concubines. By the second century CE, Han emperors had harems of 6,000 women.[13]

The parallels are striking: on different continents, and during distinct historical epochs, similar institutions emerged to provide elite men with vast numbers of exclusive mates. As societies scaled up, political and economic power often became concentrated in particular houses, clans, ethnic groups, or other coalitions. When unchecked by intergroup competition, these elites gradually pushed customs and laws in directions that benefited themselves at the expense of their societies.[14]

The key point is that, in a world without norms, beliefs, laws, or gods that inhibit successful and powerful men from taking many exclusive mates, our evolved psychological biases and inclinations often gave rise to extreme levels of polygyny that slowly insinuated themselves into the formal institutions of large, complex societies.

Okay, but how did we get here? Well, first, where's here?

Polygynous marriage remains legal in much of Africa, Central Asia, and the Middle East. At the same time, nearly all modern legal prohibitions on polygynous marriage derive from WEIRD foundations, ultimately rooted in Christian doctrines. In Japan and China, the adoption of "modern" (Western) marriage began in the 1880s and 1950s, respectively. In both cases, new governments explicitly copied Western secular institutions and laws, including prohibitions on polygynous marriage. In the 1920s, the new Republic of Turkey copied a whole set of WEIRD formal institutions and new laws, including prohibitions on polygynous marriage. In India, the Hindu Marriage Act of 1955 prohibited polygynous marriage for everyone except Muslims, who were still permitted to have up to four wives in accordance with their religious tradition. Naturally, this led some prestigious Hindu men to convert to Islam, thinking they'd found a legal loophole. In 2015, however, the Indian Supreme Court ruled that the law applies to everyone, no exceptions. Thus WEIRD monogamy is a relatively new import in most of the world.[15]

What drove the spread of monogamous marriage, first within Europe and later across the globe?

At a superficial level, the main drivers seem to be the successful spread of the Church in Europe and then the subsequent expansion of European societies around the globe, which paved the way for a flood of missionaries seeking converts and "saving" souls. Underlying these historical patterns are two standard forms of intergroup competition. In some cases, the European expansion involved military conquest, as among the Aztecs, where missionaries arrived to minister to newly subjugated peoples. Other times, and especially in more recent centuries, sophisticated societies responded to the evident economic and military power of European and European-descent societies (e.g., the United States) by voraciously copying their formal institutions, laws, and practices, ranging from democratic elections to the bizarre habit of wearing neckties. So, the question is whether monogamous marriage is more like contract law, which provides a foundation for commercial markets, or more like donning neckties, a ridiculous sartorial custom that spread globally by piggybacking on European prestige.

Below, I'll make the case that monogamous marriage norms—which push upstream against our polygynous biases and the strong preferences of elite men—create a range of social and psychological effects that give the societies that possess them a big edge in competition against other groups. Let's see how this works.

Polygyny's Math Problem[16]

Polygynous marriage tends to generate a large pool of low-status unmarried men with few prospects for marriage or even sex. Responding to this situation, men's psychology shifts in ways that spark fiercer male-male competition and, under many conditions, foment greater violence and more crime. To see this, consider the situation illustrated in Figure 8.1. Here, we compare two hypothetical communities, one monogamous and the other polygynous, each with 20 men (black circles) and 20 women (gray circles). I've ordered the men from top to bottom according to their social status, from CEOs to high school dropouts or from emperors to peasants. In the monogamous community (left side), the pool of unmarried low-status men is empty. Every man can find a wife, have children, and get a stake in the future. In the polygynous community (right side), the highest-status man, who represents the top 5 percent of wealth or status, has four wives. The next two men below him, representing those from the 85th to the 95th percentile in status, have three wives each. Below them, the guy representing the 80th–85th percentile range has two wives. From the 80th on down to the 40th percentile, everyone is monogamously married. Below this, the bottom 40 percent of men lack mates, possess few prospects for mating or marriage, and are thus unlikely to ever become husbands or fathers. It's this 40 percent that presents the math problem: the pool of "excess men" created by polygyny who have nothing to lose, from an evolutionary point of view. The degree of polygyny in my hypothetical community is not extreme, and not much different from what has been observed in many hunter-gatherer societies. No man has more than four wives. Only the top 20 percent of males marry polygynously. Most married men have only one wife, and most women have only one husband. Yet you still end up with 40 percent of the male population as involuntary lifetime bachelors. The level of polygyny in this stylized example is in fact substantially below that observed today in many African societies as well as in the polygynous Mormon communities of North America.[17]

The math problem in Figure 8.1 illustrates that men in polygynous communities usually face much greater male-male competition than those in monogamous communities. Consider the situation of Samu, the guy in our hypothetical polygynous community who represents the men in the bottom 5th to 10th percentile. Samu must somehow leap up past the 40th percentile if he wants even a shot at getting a single wife. If he plays it safe and works hard on his small farm, he'll climb no more than 25 percentile points. This won't get him above the 40th percentile, so he'll have little shot at attracting a wife and will likely end up an evolutionary zero. This is a fate worse than death for natural selection. Samu's only hope is to take risky actions that will catapult him up the ladder of social status 35 or more percentile points—he needs a big jump.

To put this in stark terms, suppose Samu happens upon a drunk mer-

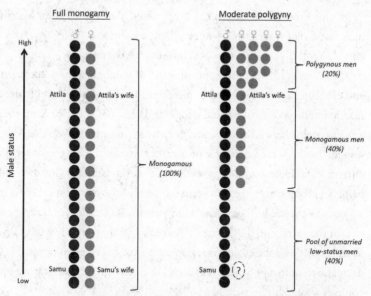

FIGURE 8.1. Polygynous marriage creates a pool of low-status unmarried men. Each side represents the same community of 40 adults, with 20 men and 20 women. The men are aligned vertically according to social status, from the lowest at the bottom to the highest at the top. Women prefer higher-status men, so under polygynous marriage the lowest-status men don't get any mates. The result is that many women enter into polygynous arrangements with the highest-status men, and many of the lowest-status men (40 percent) never marry.

chant in a dark alley late at night. He can either rob the rich merchant and use the money to expand his farm or do nothing (let's set aside the option of helping the merchant). If he does nothing, his chances of getting into the marriage and mating market remain low at, say, 1 percent. This means there's a 99 percent chance that he'll end up an evolutionary zero. However, if he robs the merchant, he'll increase his chances of finding a wife by 10 percent, but he'll face a 90 percent chance of getting caught and executed—once again, he'll end up an evolutionary zero. What should he do? Well, doing nothing means he has only a 1 percent chance of mating and having kids, while robbing the merchant increases his chances to 10 percent. Overall, for Samu, robbing the merchant looks 10 times better than doing nothing.

With this kind of calculus in the background, natural selection has tilted male psychology such that—under these conditions—men are more inclined to roll the evolutionary dice and commit the crime.

Now, instead, suppose Samu lived in our monogamous community and encountered the same drunk merchant. In this world, Samu is already married and has a two-year-old daughter. If he robs the merchant, there's a 90 percent chance he'll be executed, which means he won't be able to provide for his young daughter or continue expanding his family with his current wife. Here, Samu has a stake in the future and has already avoided being an evolutionary zero. Of course, if he robs the merchant, there is that 10 percent chance he'll get richer, and that would be nice for him (though not for the merchant); but, Samu is limited to having only one wife at a time in this society, so the evolutionary upside to any big economic payoff is less dramatic than in a polygynous society. He can't, for example, add a second, younger wife to his household.

Key here is that the biggest threat men face is ending up an evolutionary zero—having no mating prospects at all. To see this, realize that if you have one child, he or she might give you four grandchildren . . . who might give you 16 great-grandchildren. You are in the evolutionary game. However, if you never or rarely have sex (and thus have zero children), that's it for all time. You and your direct lineage are done. Because of this evolutionary ultimatum, the evolved psychology of low-status men responds very differently to the social conditions created by monogamy vs. polygyny (depicted in Figure 8.1). Of course, from a psychological perspective, a man's concern is much more about mates and mating opportunities than about counting children. But this is because, over most of our evolutionary history, more mating and mates for men generally meant more kids.

Now let's look at the impact of marital institutions on the higher-status men in our polygynous society by focusing on Attila. Representing the 75th–80th percentile, Attila is among the monogamously married men with the highest social status in his polygynous community. However, unlike in a monogamous community, Attila is still in the marriage market and will have to choose between investing his time, effort, and resources in his current wife and their children, versus seeking additional wives. If he can just increase his wealth or status a little bit, he can take a second wife. And if he manages a 10-percentile-point leap in social status, he can triple his number of wives. In this situation, Attila will often be motivated to shift his time and energy away from investing in his current wife and her children to instead apply it to obtaining additional wives. By contrast, in the monogamous community, Attila is married to a single wife. However, here the social norms surrounding marriage and sex close off, or at least impede, his pathways to the large evolutionary benefits available in a polygynous society. Faced with this situation, Attila is more likely to settle for smaller, incremental improvements in his status or wealth, and to apply these to investing in his current wife and children. Thus the evolutionary payoffs to status-climbing in polygynous societies are much greater than in monogamous societies, even for higher-status married men. In polygynous societies, the pull to invest in seeking additional wives over investing in one's current wife and her children is just much greater than in monogamous societies.

Importantly, my example assumes that women in this polygynous society are free to choose their husband and that they are picking according to the success of their children *relative* to others in their society. That is, by becoming the second, third, or fourth wife of the richest men in their society, women are doing what's best for themselves and their children. By contrast, women in the monogamous society are prevented from becoming plural wives—even if they want to—and are thus effectively forced to marry lower-status men. Interestingly, because of how monogamous marriage influences social dynamics and cultural evolution, inhibiting female choice—by prohibiting women from freely choosing to marry men who are already married—results in both women and children doing better in the long run (on average). This occurs because of how the social dynamics unleashed by polygyny influence household formation, men's psychology, and husbands' willingness to invest in their wives and children.[18]

The logic I've just sketched for Samu and Attila illustrates how monogamous marriage suppresses male-male reproductive competition and drains the low-status pool of unmarried men, giving these men a stake in the future (e.g., a child, or at least a chance for one). By suppressing the intensity of this competition, monogamous marriage induces shifts that recalibrate men for this new social environment. These shifts likely include on-the-fly responses to the current environment, gradual psychological calibrations that develop as boys grow up, and, through cultural learning, the transmission and accumulation of successful strategies, beliefs, and motivations molded to fit the new institutional environment. Let's start by considering how marriage changes men's favorite hormone.[19]

A Testosterone Suppression System

In males, the testes produce the steroid hormone testosterone in large quantities compared to females (who don't have a dedicated gland). To understand testosterone (T), it's best to step back, start with birds, and then shift to *Homo sapiens*. In birds, testosterone contributes to the development of secondary sex characteristics; but instead of the deep voices, hairy chests, and square jaws seen in humans, male birds variously develop brightly colored plumage, large combs, and fancy wattles (Figure 8.2). Across species, testosterone is also related to mating and courtship displays, including beautiful serenades and athletic dances, as well as to both territorial defense and male-male fights over females. These effects of testosterone appear in many mammals as well, but the cool thing about birds is that many species form enduring pair-bonds with only one other partner per season ("monogamy"), and males even help out in the nest with the offspring—that is, they do paternal investment like fathers in many human societies. Of course, as is the case for 90 percent of mammal species, there are also many bird species that lack both pair-bonding and any male investment in nests, eggs, or chicks. This avian variation allows us to compare the effects of testosterone in species with different patterns of pair-bonding and mating. Do you see where I'm going?

In many monogamous species, such as song sparrows, males try to find one mate each breeding season. Once the eggs arrive, the male will defend the nest and help his mate rear the chicks. Testosterone levels in these males

FIGURE 8.2. A handsome rooster with a bright comb and a large wattle.[20]

respond to the situation and the season. When the mating season is ramping up, he'll have to battle other males to establish a territory, which he needs to attract a mate. In anticipation, his testosterone levels begin rising and continue to increase until his mate begins ovulating, at which point he must guard her 24-7 to keep other males out during this critical period. Once his mate gets pregnant, his testosterone levels drop as he prepares to feed and care for the hatchlings. When this is over, and he no longer has to defend a territory, his testosterone levels drop further. By contrast, in polygynous species such as the red-winged blackbird, whose males fight for large territories in an effort to attract as many mates as possible, male testosterone goes up for the breeding season but then doesn't decline when his mates get pregnant or when his chicks begin arriving. This is not surprising, since males in these polygynous species don't help much in the nest and continue to look for additional mates to form more pair-bonds.

Because you can do experiments on wild birds, we know that in monogamous species certain cues, like seasonal changes in sunlight, drive testosterone changes, and that these hormonal changes influence behavioral shifts. For example, when song sparrows are fitted with special implants that prevent the normal testosterone drop that occurs after a male's mate gets pregnant, males continue fighting and end up doubling the size of their territory relative to those sparrows lacking the implants. The males with implants also became polygynous, securing two or even three mates. In other bird species, testosterone implants increase both male singing and territorial aggression while reducing the birds' efforts to feed their chicks or defend the nest. One suspects they were too busy singing and fighting to worry much about babies. Sound familiar?[21]

In societies with WEIRD monogamy, men are a bit like monogamous birds: getting married and becoming a father lowers a man's testosterone. If he divorces, his T levels typically climb again. The depleting effects of marriage and children on testosterone have been shown in various North American populations, but my favorite study comes from the city of Cebu in the Philippines. In 2005, a team led by the anthropologist Chris Kuzawa measured the testosterone levels of 465 single men in their early 20s. Over the next four years, 208 of these men got married, and 162 of those had children. In 2009, Chris's team again measured the men's T levels. As in the United States, men's testosterone gradually declined with age. But, as Figure 8.3 illustrates, the rate of decline was dependent upon what happened to the men in the intervening years. T levels plummeted among those who both got married and had children, while they declined the least among those who remained single. Notably, the men who were initially highest in testosterone were also the most likely to get married—that is, higher testosterone in 2005 predicted success in the competition for mates in the ensuing four years.[22]

As in birds, this line of research suggests that humans possess a physiological system that regulates men's testosterone, along with other aspects of our psychology, by relying on cues related to mating opportunities, parenting demands, and status competition. When necessary, T levels rise to prepare males to compete for status and mates. But, when it's time to build nests and nurture offspring, T levels decline. Across human societies, fathers with lower testosterone care more for their infants and are better attuned to their

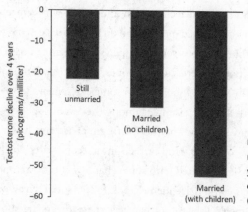

FIGURE 8.3. **Declines in morning testosterone after 4 years for men between the ages of 21.5 and 26.5 years in Cebu (the Philippines).[23]**

cries. WEIRD monogamy norms manipulate these dials by reducing the mating opportunities available to married men and by bringing them into greater contact with their children, both of which lower their testosterone levels.[24]

Aggregating these effects across an entire population, we can begin to see how monogamous norms suppress testosterone at a societal level. By prohibiting higher-status men from monopolizing potential wives, monogamous norms allow many more lower-status men to both get married (pair-bond) and father children. Thus WEIRD marital norms ensure that a higher percentage of men will experience the low-T that attends both monogamous marriage and caring for children. By contrast, in polygynous societies, many more men (40 percent in Figure 8.2) will remain in the "Still Unmarried" category of Figure 8.3 throughout their lives. Thus, in polygynous societies, a higher percentage of men never experience the testosterone declines observed in men from monogamous societies. So, like polygynous birds, unmarried men in polygynous societies retain relatively higher levels of testosterone across their life span.[25]

Interestingly, because polygynous marriage also changes the social world faced by married men, focusing only on marrying off low-status men underestimates monogamy's suppressive effects. To understand why, remember that in polygynous societies married men remain on the marriage market. Consequently, unlike in monogamous societies, men's testosterone doesn't decline with age in polygynous societies. Or if it does, the decline is muted compared to what we see in WEIRD societies. In some cases, men's testosterone may even *go up* with age. For example, among the Swahili-speaking inhabitants of Lamu Island in Kenya, neither getting married nor having children reduces a man's testosterone. However, taking a second wife, which about a quarter of men do, is associated with somewhat *higher* testosterone levels. Here, higher T levels could drive men to look for potential wives, or new wives might elevate men's T levels. Either way, these effects are suppressed under monogamous marriage.[26]

In Tanzania, the impact of different social norms on men's physiology can be seen by comparing Datoga cattle-herders with the nearby Hadza hunter-gatherers. Among the patrilineal Datoga, where about 40 percent of married men have multiple wives, becoming a father has no detectable effect on T levels. For both married and unmarried Datoga men, the only normative constraint on their sex lives is that they absolutely cannot have sex with other men's wives. Further, Datoga men live and sleep in houses with other men, separate from their wives and children. Infants are considered part of the mother's body until weaning, so Datoga men don't handle their babies. In light of such norms, it's not surprising that the testosterone of Datoga fathers doesn't decline. By contrast, among the Hadza, polygynous marriage occurs in only 1 out of 20 men (5 percent), and social norms require fatherly care of infants and children. So, Hadza men's T levels do drop a bit when they have children, and the size of the drop is proportional to the amount of time they spend on childcare.[27]

The key difference between humans and birds is that in our species cultural evolution can generate social norms that exploit these built-in hormonal responses for its own ends. Among groups like the Datoga, the survival of their clans and tribes depended—in part—on the audacity and ferocity of their warriors, and every man was a warrior. By sustaining higher testosterone levels, norms like living separately from wives and children may provide an edge in competition with other clans and tribes. In contrast, Christian monogamy was a particularly potent package for suppressing T levels. Besides limiting men to one wife, the Church's MFP included several other active ingredients. First, it *constrained* men from seeking sex outside of marriage—from visiting prostitutes or having mistresses. To accomplish this, the Church worked to end prostitution and sexual slavery while creating social norms that motivated communities to monitor men's sexual behavior and make violations public. God, of course, was enlisted to monitor and punish the sexual transgressions of both men and women, which fueled the development of Christian notions of sin and guilt. Second, the Church made divorce difficult and remarriage close to impossible, which prevented men from engaging in serial monogamy. In fact, under the Church's program, the only way anyone could legitimately have sex was with one's spouse for procreation.[28]

This contrasts with other monogamous societies, such as Athens or pre-Christian Rome; in these societies, men were limited to one wife but were otherwise not strongly constrained. Not only could men easily divorce, but they could also purchase sex slaves, take foreigners as concubines, and use numerous inexpensive brothels.[29]

The consequence is that WEIRD marriage, which of course was built out of Christian marriage, generates a peculiar endocrinology. It's widely believed by physicians that testosterone "naturally" declines as men age. In the 21st-century United States, these drops are so severe that some middle-aged men are treated medically for low-T. But, as I've explained, across societies possessing more human-typical marriage institutions we don't see these declines as often, and when we do, they aren't nearly as steep as in WEIRD societies. It seems that a WEIRD endocrinology accompanies our WEIRD psychology.[30]

I've spent some time on testosterone to delineate just one biological pathway that institutions have evolved to exploit as a mechanism to influence our behavior, motivations, and decision-making. Here, you're seeing how the Church, through the institution of monogamous marriage, reached down and grabbed men by the testicles. There's little doubt that cultural evolution has found myriad biological pathways into our brains and behavior. Now, let's move from hormones to psychology, and consider how monogamous marriage suppresses men's competitiveness, risk-taking, and revenge-seeking while increasing their impersonal trust and self-regulation.[31]

Trust, Teamwork, and Crime

To explore how monogamous marriage influences psychology, I'll discuss two kinds of evidence. First, because we now know that monogamous marriage suppresses T levels, we'll consider how this hormone affects decision-making, motivation, and teamwork. Second, because monogamous marriage usually increases the availability of potential mates (unmarried women), we'll examine how shifting men's perceptions about the availability of mates influences their patience and decision-making.

What are the impacts of testosterone on our behavior? To prepare individuals for status competition or mating, testosterone operates through a variety of complex biological processes to alter our psychology. In anticipation of status challenges, in contests involving everything from judo and tennis to chess and dominoes, testosterone levels often surge.[32] Studies that experimentally manipulate testosterone show that raising levels can (1) fuel competitive motivation, which can increase aggression; (2) intensify social vigilance for challenges or threats; (3) suppress fear; and (4) heighten people's sensitivity to rewards and inhibit their responsiveness to punishments.[33] Of course, testosterone also increases people's sex drive.

The competitive, zero-sum mind-set favored by testosterone can be costly. In a simple experiment, men were paired with a stranger and given an opportunity to repeatedly press either button A, which slightly increased their own cash payoffs, or button B, which substantially decreased their partner's payoffs. Those interested in earning the most money should have always, or at least mostly, pressed button A, but those most intent on earning more money than their partner (to maximize their *relative* payoffs) would need to use button B (lowering their partner's payoff). When injected with testosterone, men were more likely to spend time pressing button B than they had been when injected with a placebo. The result was that those with boosted testosterone levels tended to beat their partners (opponents?) but earned less total money over the course of the experiment.[34]

Further, we can get a deeper sense of the social consequences of these hormonal effects in an experiment in which participants were placed into two-person groups. Pairs competed against each other in the within-group treatment or competed as a pair against another pair in the between-group treatment. The competition wasn't a wrestling match or tug-of-war but instead a competition for the best scores on the Graduate Record Examination (GRE), a standardized test used in graduate school admissions. In the within-group treatment, participants were entered into a lottery for a prize if they beat *their partner's* test score. In the between-group treatment, participants were entered into the lottery if they and their partner's score beat the other team's.

The results show that those with relatively high testosterone, measured when they arrived at the lab, performed 18 percent better when they had to beat their partner—that is, when facing zero-sum *within-group* competition (Figure 8.4). Meanwhile, those with low testosterone performed 22 percent better during the *between-group* competition. This suggests that if you are facing steep competition between groups, including organizations, companies, nations, or military units, in tasks demanding superior cognitive performance or analytical skills, you should avoid the high-T guys, or suppress their levels with WEIRD marriage norms.[35]

Elevated testosterone levels can also reduce a person's assessment of the trustworthiness of strangers, probably through its effects on their social vigilance and perception of the world as a zero-sum game. In one study, participants were asked to judge the trustworthiness of 75 different strangers based on photographs of their faces. Each participant did this twice, once after getting a dose of testosterone and once after receiving a placebo—of course, people didn't know which shot they got each time. After getting dosed with testosterone, participants judged the same faces as substantially less trustworthy than they did when they received the placebo. Interestingly, those who tended to regard others as more trustworthy in the placebo

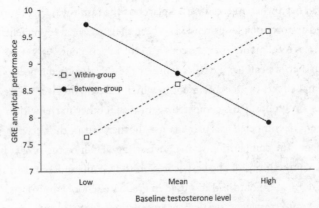

FIGURE 8.4. Performance comparisons for low-T vs. high-T participants in both within-group and between-group competition. Not surprisingly, people with high-T perform well during individual competition within groups. However, when groups compete, those with high-T perform relatively poorly. GRE scores are based only on the analytic subtest of the GRE and were out of 15 possible points.[36]

condition experienced the largest drop in their trustworthiness judgments after receiving a testosterone boost.

Follow-up work using brain scans suggests that testosterone creates this effect on trustworthiness evaluations by suppressing the interconnections between the prefrontal cortex and the amygdala. Uninhibited by the prefrontal cortex, the amygdala drives people's response to untrustworthy faces. Thus, by suppressing testosterone levels, monogamous marriage may be giving men's prefrontal cortices more control, thereby promoting greater self-regulation and self-discipline based on learned standards (such as impersonal norms about trust).[37]

These kinds of experiments confirm that testosterone can and does sometimes influence men's (1) hair-trigger response to challenges, (2) taste for revenge, (3) trust in others, (4) capacity for teamwork, and (5) financial risk-taking. However, it's crucial not to oversimplify the effects of this hormone, which necessarily operates through complex biological interactions involving other hormones and brain chemicals. Moreover, keep in mind that testosterone is not about taking risks, behaving impatiently, acting aggressively, or distrusting people per se. It's about assessing and motivating the most effective actions for climbing the status ladder. It's perfectly plausible that high testosterone could lead individuals—despite their depressed assessments of trustworthiness—to invest with strangers or cooperate on a team if this represents the most promising route to higher status. They may take the risk of being swindled or exploited because there are no less perilous routes up the status mountain. At the societal level, problems arise when the most viable, or only, road to higher status (and mating) demands that status seekers lie, cheat, steal, and kill to get up the ladder.[38]

The problem with laboratory findings like these is that they don't tell us if such effects cash out in the real world. Do they matter?

There's good reason to suspect that they do. Much research has examined the relationship between men's long-term testosterone levels and their real-world behavior. Based on work in WEIRD societies, men with higher testosterone levels are more likely to be arrested, deal in stolen property, fall into debt, and use weapons in a fight. They are also more likely to smoke, abuse drugs, drink heavily, gamble, and engage in dangerous activities. Testosterone is associated with measures of dominance in both teenagers and adults, and there is a weak but persistent relationship between testosterone levels and violent aggression, including domestic violence. Of course, with this kind of real-world evidence, we don't know if higher testosterone levels are causing the behaviors or if the person's experiences are fueling testosterone production, but experimental work like that just described suggests that this is a two-way street. If it's true that higher testosterone levels encourage criminal behavior among lower-status men, and that marriage lowers relative testosterone levels, then does marriage also suppress a man's likelihood of committing crimes? Indeed it does, but before turning to that evidence, let's consider how men's perceptions of sex ratios affect their decision-making.[39]

Many psychological experiments suggest that men monitor the intensity of male-male competition in part by looking at the ratio of competing men to available women in the local environment and recalibrating their patience, risk-taking, and other aspects of their psychology in adaptive and predictable ways. For example, in a delay-discounting decision task similar to those discussed in Chapter 1, men who were experimentally induced to think that the local environment was more sexually competitive—with more men than women—became more willing to take the immediate but smaller payoffs over the delayed but larger payoffs. This and similar experiments suggest that when men perceive greater male-male competition—excess men—they often become less patient and more risk-taking. Of course, like most experiments in psychology, this work was done with WEIRD Americans, so we should worry about whether it generalizes to the species. However, these laboratory findings converge nicely with the real-world effects that "excess men" have on crime rates in China, which we'll examine below. This convergence increases our confidence.[40]

Psychological shifts like these, which affect impulsivity, competitiveness, and self-regulation, probably make individuals more likely to commit crimes, drink to excess, and take illegal drugs. Of course, many nonpsychological factors also influence people's decisions to commit crimes and abuse drugs. Interestingly, while convicted criminals show levels of honesty and cooperation comparable to others from their societies in controlled laboratory experiments, they take bigger risks in seeking higher payoffs in experiments in both Britain and China. In fact, unlike in most populations, where women are less risk-taking than men, female prisoners are slightly more risk-taking than male prisoners. Both prisoners and drug abusers show greater impatience and impulsivity in controlled psychological studies (among WEIRD people) than matched groups who are neither prisoners nor drug users. Taken together, this work suggests that monogamous marriage, by shifting men's psychology in key ways, should lower crime rates.[41]

MONOGAMOUS MARRIAGE REDUCES CRIME

Just like his T levels, when a man gets married in a WEIRD society, his chances of committing a variety of crimes also drop. To start, many studies show that unmarried men are much more likely to commit robbery, murder, and rape than married men. Bachelors are also more likely to gamble, abuse drugs, and drink heavily. These patterns hold even when differences in age, socioeconomic status, employment, and ethnicity are considered. The problem with these studies is that they don't tell us if getting married actually causes men to commit fewer crimes or drink less, or whether criminals and alcoholics are less likely to find marriage partners. Of course, it's possible that the causality goes both ways.

One way around this problem, at least partially, is to follow the same men over the course of their lives and compare their behavior during the married and unmarried periods. In one famous study, 500 boys from a Massachusetts reform school were tracked from age 17 into retirement. The study shows that getting married cuts a man's chances of committing a crime by half, both for property crimes like burglary, theft, and robbery and for violent crimes like assault and battery. Across all crimes, marriage cuts the rate by 35 percent. If guys had a "good" marriage, they were even less likely to commit a crime. Remember, we are comparing individuals *with themselves* during different periods of their lives, so nothing about the person himself explains these effects.[42]

Of course, one worry is that the effects of different life stages might explain the results. Perhaps exuberant young men commit crimes but then grow up, settle down, and get married—so marriage looks like it's causing the decline in crime, but it's just correlated with the "settling down" phase. Conveniently, many of these guys got married and divorced multiple times over their lives, and some became widowers. Strikingly, not only did a man's likelihood of committing a crime *go up* after a divorce—when he became single again—but it also increased after his wife passed away. Numerous other studies support the view that getting married in a monogamous society reduces a man's likelihood of both committing crimes and abusing alcohol or drugs.[43]

What do the effects of WEIRD marriage on crime tell us about the effects of changing a polygynous society into a monogamous one? In polygynous societies, the *math problem* will generally create a larger pool of low-status men, many of whom will never marry or have children. Consequently, they won't experience the psychological shifts, induced by marriage, that reduce their chances of committing a crime. In the absence of this marital prophylaxis, the men in the pool will remain at an increased risk for criminal behavior and other social ills over their entire lives. They will also die younger, for a variety of reasons. So, while the use of reform school boys in the study above may have seemed peculiar, these are precisely the kinds of low-status males who would become trapped in the pool of excess men created by polygynous marriage.[44]

The above inferences follow logically, but how can we be sure that a pool of excess unmarried males in a society will really turn to crime? China's famous one-child policy provides precisely the kind of natural experiment needed to test this reasoning. The one-child policy, which China began to implement in the late 1970s, constrained family size and limited many couples to one child.[45] Because of China's history of patrilineal families, many people possessed a potent cultural preference for having at least one son, to carry on the lineage. Those limited to one child strongly preferred boys. As a result, millions of female fetuses were selectively aborted, and baby girls were orphaned. As this policy was imposed in different provinces at different times, the sex ratio began to gradually shift in favor of males. Between 1988 and 2004, the number of "surplus" men almost doubled, and by 2009 there were 30 million "extra" males.[46]

As the surplus boys became men, arrest rates nearly doubled, and crime rates soared, rising nationally at 13.6 percent per year. Analyzing the data on crime and sex ratios from 1988 to 2004, the economist Lena Edlund and her team showed that as the male-heavy cohorts created by the one-child policy reached maturity in different provinces, crime began to climb and continued climbing as the pool of excess men swelled. Because the policy was implemented in different years in different provinces, the staggered effects across China are clear: in each province, about 18 years after the one-child policy was implemented, the pool of excess males reached maturity and crime rates started going up. Both arrests and crime rates continued to rise in lockstep with the expanding pool of surplus men.[47]

Since men commit most crimes, you'd expect crime to increase simply due to having more men. However, detailed analyses reveal distinct psychological shifts: men born into cohorts with more males relative to females were more likely to commit crimes than men with similar incomes and education who were born into less male-biased cohorts.[48]

Of course, these pools of excess men in China were not created by polygynous marriage. Nevertheless, consistent with both the laboratory evidence above and the effects of WEIRD marriage on men's criminal inclinations, the natural experiment created by China's one-child policy demonstrates that large pools of "excess" unmarried men generate psychological shifts that alter decision-making in ways that result in higher crime rates.[49]

All this suggests that the Church, through its centuries-long struggle to disseminate and enforce its peculiar version of monogamous marriage, *unintentionally* created an environment that gradually domesticated men, making many of us less competitive, impulsive, and risk-prone while at the same time favoring positive-sum perceptions of the world and a greater willingness to team up with strangers. *Ceteris paribus*, this should result in more harmonious organizations, less crime, and fewer social disruptions.[50]

Putting the Pieces Together

Monogamous marriage changes men psychologically, even hormonally, and has downstream effects on societies. Although this form of marriage is neither "natural" nor "normal" for human societies—and runs directly counter to the strong inclinations of high-status or elite men—it nevertheless can give religious groups and societies an advantage in intergroup competition. By suppressing male-male competition and altering family structure, monogamous marriage shifts men's psychology in ways that tend to reduce crime, violence, and zero-sum thinking while promoting broader trust, long-term investments, and steady economic accumulation. Rather than pursuing impulsive or risky behaviors aimed at catapulting themselves up the social ladder, low-status men in monogamous societies have a chance to marry, have children, and invest in the future. High-status men can and will still compete for status, but the currency of that competition can no longer involve the accumulation of wives or concubines. In a monogamous world, zero-sum competition is relatively less important. So, there's greater scope for forming voluntary organizations and teams that then compete at the group level.[51]

With this psychological understanding in the background, consider the reflections of the famed historian of medieval Europe David Herlihy:

> A great social achievement of the early Middle Ages was the imposition of the same rules of sexual and domestic conduct on both rich and poor. The king in his palace, the peasant in his hovel: neither one was exempt. Cheating might have been easier for the mighty, but they could not claim women or slaves as a right. Poor men's chances of gaining a wife and producing progeny were enhanced. It is very likely that the fairer distribution of women across society helped reduce abductions and rapes and levels of violence generally, in the early Middle Ages.[52]

This all occurred long before the earliest sprouts of democracy, representative assemblies, constitutions, and economic growth in Europe, which has led Herlihy and other historians to suggest that it might represent a first step toward social equality, both among men and between the sexes. Whether king or peasant, each man could have only one wife. Of course, European kings did their best to circumvent this rule. Nevertheless, they were increasingly constrained in ways that no respectable Chinese emperor, African king, or Polynesian chief could have ever imagined. Church monogamy also meant that men and women of similar ages usually married as adults, by mutual consent, and potentially without the blessing of their parents. Of course, the greater parity of modern gender roles was a long way off in the Early Middle Ages, but monogamous marriage had started to close the gap.[53]

Some researchers suspect that we develop our mental models for navigating the broader social world based on the family environments we experience growing up. Your family's organization and operation are what you know best, and this can influence how you perceive the rest of the world.

If, for example, your family was relatively more authoritarian and hierarchical, then you may be inclined toward authoritarian organizations later in life. If your family was more egalitarian and democratic, then you might prefer more democratic approaches. This would mean that the spread of monogamous marriage, along with other elements of the Church's MFP, may have created families that were *somewhat* more egalitarian and less authoritarian than those found in most intensive kin-based societies (of course, these wouldn't look particularly egalitarian to modern eyes; it's all relative). When folks began forming towns, guilds, and religious institutions in the 10th and 11th centuries, they would have applied intuitions and insights gained from living in monogamous nuclear families, not from life in, for example, patriarchal clans or segmentary lineages. This may have influenced the kinds of organizations they developed and the laws they preferred.[54]

PART III

New Institutions, New Psychologies

9

Of Commerce and Cooperation

Commerce is a cure for the most destructive prejudices; for it
is almost a general rule that wherever manners are gentle there is
commerce; and wherever there is commerce, manners are gentle.
—Montesquieu (1749), *The Spirit of the Laws*[1]

[Commerce] is a pacific system, operating to cordialise mankind, by
rendering Nations, as well as individuals, useful to each other ... The
invention of commerce ... is the greatest approach toward universal
civilization that has yet been made by any means not immediately
flowing from moral principles.
—Thomas Paine (1792), *Rights of Man*

In the summer of 1994, I spent a few months traveling by dugout canoe
among various remote Matsigenka communities while conducting anthropological fieldwork on how markets shape farming practices. The
Matsigenka, you may recall from Chapter 3, are highly independent slash-
and-burn farmers who traditionally lived in nuclear families or small family
hamlets scattered throughout a region of the Peruvian Amazon. During
this first summer of research, I was repeatedly struck by how these communities, despite their small size, struggled to work together on village projects.
People cooperated easily with their extended families and sometimes with
nearby households, but free-riding prevailed when it came time to build village schools, fix the community's rice processor, or even trim the common grass
field. During the subsequent year, while puzzling over these observations, I
learned about an experiment called the Ultimatum Game. Immediately, I
planned to try it out on the Matsigenka the following summer.[2]

In the Ultimatum Game (UG), two individuals are anonymously paired and must divide a sum of real money—the stake—between them. Say the stake is $100. The first player—the proposer—must make an offer between zero and the full amount ($100) to the second player—the receiver. Suppose the proposer offers $10 out of the $100 to the receiver. The receiver must decide whether to accept or reject this offer. If she accepts, she gets the amount offered ($10 in this example), and the proposer gets the remainder ($90). If the receiver rejects, both players get zero. The interaction is anonymous and one-shot, meaning that the pair will never interact again and won't learn each other's identity.

One fun thing about economic experiments like the UG is that it's possible to use game theory to predict what rational people would do if they only cared about maximizing their own income. This calculation provides a benchmark for what we should expect in a world of rational, self-interested individuals—it's the *Homo economicus* prediction. In the UG, as long as the proposer offers more than zero, receivers face a choice between some cash if they accept, and nothing if they reject. Faced with this simple choice, income-maximizing receivers should always accept non-zero offers. Proposers, realizing the stark choice faced by receivers, should make the smallest positive offer they can. Thus, if we put $100 on the line and limit people to making offers in $10 increments, this theory predicts that proposers should offer receivers only $10 out of the $100.[3]

Would you accept an offer of $10? What's the lowest offer you would accept? As a proposer, what would you offer?

In WEIRD societies, most adults over about age 25 offer half ($50). Offers of less than 40 percent ($40) are frequently rejected. The average offer is usually about 48 percent of the stake. In these populations, following standard game theory by offering $10 (10 percent) is a bad move. In fact, if you are purely selfish but recognize that others are not, you're still stuck offering $50 (50 percent), because if you offer less you'll probably get rejected and end up going home with nothing. Thus unlike the *Homo economicus* prediction, WEIRD people reveal strong inclinations for equal offers in the Ultimatum Game.[4]

In Amazonia, I first conducted the UG among Matsigenka while sitting on the elevated wooden porch of a small abandoned missionary house that was a stone's throw from the Urubamba River. The stakes were 20 Peruvian soles in the local currency, which was what Matsigenka could occasionally earn by working for over two days with a logging or oil company. Most Matsigenka proposers offered 3 soles, or 15 percent of the stake, to the receiver. Several people offered 5 soles (25 percent), and a few offered 10 soles (50 percent). Overall, the mean offer was 26 percent of the 20-sole stake. All of these low offers were immediately accepted, save for one.[5] I'd learned that the Matsigenka were strikingly unlike WEIRD people in the UG.

I hadn't anticipated this result. My WEIRD intuitions had misled me to suspect that the Matsigenka would behave like people in the United States, Europe, and other industrialized societies. When I first heard about the experiment, I'd had a gut-level reaction to the idea of receiving a low offer, so I'd assumed that the Ultimatum Game was probably capturing something innate about human psychology, about our evolved motivations for fairness and our willingness to punish unfairness. However, what was most striking to me was not the statistical results but the interviews I did with the players afterward. Matsigenka receivers didn't see proposers as obligated to "be fair" and to give half the money. Rather, they seemed almost grateful that their anonymous partner decided to give them anything (often 3 soles out of 20). They couldn't understand why someone would reject free money. This, in part, explained why I had so much trouble teaching them the rules of the game. The idea of rejecting any free money seemed so silly that players assumed they were misunderstanding my instructions. Proposers seemed confident that their low offers would be accepted, and some seemed to see themselves as being rather generous by giving 3 or 5 soles. Within their cultural frame, these low offers felt generous.

These interviews contrasted with those I did in Los Angeles after administering an Ultimatum Game that put $160 on the line. It was a sum that was calculated to match the Matsigenka stakes. In this immense urban metropolis, people said they'd feel guilty if they gave less than half.[6] They conveyed the sense that offering half was the "right" thing to do in this situation. The one person who made a low offer (25 percent) deliberated for a long time and was clearly worried about rejection.

In retrospect, having now spent a quarter of a century exploring culture and human nature, my early experimental findings seem obvious. What I was seeing in Matsigenka behavior was merely a reflection of their social norms and lifeways. As we saw in Chapter 3, Matsigenka lack institutions for solving large-scale cooperative dilemmas, establishing command and control, and scaling up their sociopolitical complexity. Instead, they're true individualists. Their internalized motivations are calibrated to navigate the family-level institutions of their societies, so there's no reason to expect them to make equal offers to anonymous others or strangers, or to give up free money to punish locally sensible behaviors by proposers. This is what psychological individualism looks like without the influence of potent impersonal norms, competitive markets, and prosocial religions.[7]

Market Integration and Impersonal Prosociality

In the two decades since my initial work, our team has interviewed and administered a range of similar behavioral experiments to people from 27 diverse societies around the globe (Figure 9.1). Our populations include hunter-gatherers from Tanzania, Indonesia, and Paraguay; herders from Mongolia, Siberia, and Kenya; subsistence farmers from South America and Africa; wage laborers from Accra (Ghana) and Missouri (the United States); and slash-and-burn horticulturalists from New Guinea, Oceania, and Amazonia.

This research derives from two successive phases. Our first phase, which involved Ultimatum Games in 15 societies, tested the idea that exposure to or experience in markets might influence people's decisions in the experiment. Our surprising result was that people from *more* market-integrated societies made *higher* (more equal) offers. Like the Matsigenka, the most

FIGURE 9.1. Mapping all the populations studied by our team of anthropologists and economists using economic games, interviews, and ethnography.[8]

remote and smallest-scale societies not only made much lower offers (with means of about 25 percent), but they also rarely rejected any offers. Thus on both the proposer and receiver sides, WEIRD people as well as those from other industrialized societies were among the *furthest* from the rational benchmarks predicted by economics textbooks.[9]

Alas, since this was the first time anyone ever tried a project like this, our study was far from perfect. For example, we assessed the relative market integration of our societies by quantifying the ethnographic intuitions of our experts during group discussions. This was a bit subjective for my taste, although our assessments turned out to be pretty accurate. To address this and other concerns, we decided to do it all again.

In this second phase, we recruited new populations, added new experiments, and developed more rigorous research protocols. To the Ultimatum Game, we added the Dictator Game and the Third-Party Punishment Game. As you've seen, the Dictator Game is like the Ultimatum Game except that the receiver has no opportunity to reject the proposer's offer, so there's no threat of getting zero due to the receiver's reaction. In the Third-Party Punishment Game, the proposer makes an offer to a passive receiver, as in the Dictator Game. However, there's a third-party enforcer, who is initially given a sum of money equal to half the amount that the proposer and the receiver are dividing up. This third party can pay some of his money to financially punish the proposer at three times his cost if he doesn't like the proposer's offer. For example, if the proposer gives $10 out of the $100 stake to the receiver, the third party can pay $10 out of his $50 allocation to take $30 away from the proposer. In this case, the proposer would go home with $60 ($100 minus $10 minus $30), the receiver with $10, and the third party with $40 ($50 minus $10). In the *Homo economicus* world, because the Third-Party Punishment Game is a one-shot, anonymous interaction, proposers should give nothing to receivers, and third parties should never pay to punish the proposer (what's in it for them?).

To improve our protocols, we (1) fixed the stakes in our experiments at one day's wage in the local economy and (2) assessed market integration by measuring the percentage of household calories that were purchased in the market as opposed to grown, hunted, gathered, or fished by the households themselves.[10]

Across all three of these experiments, people living in more market-integrated communities again made higher offers (closer to 50 percent of the stake). People with little or no market integration offered only about a quarter of the stake. Going from a fully subsistence-oriented population with no market integration (e.g., Hadza hunter-gatherers in Tanzania) to a fully market-integrated community increases offers by 10 to 20 percentile points. Figure 9.2 illustrates this, showing that the more market-integrated a population, as captured by the percentage of calories purchased in the market, the more people offer in the Dictator Game. This experiment is perhaps our cleanest measure of impersonal fairness, since it removes the threat of rejection or punishment. These patterns hold across all three experiments regardless of the effects of income, wealth, community size, education, and other demographic variables.[11]

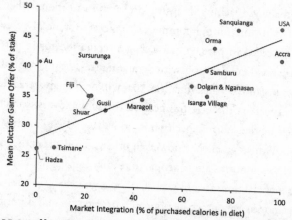

FIGURE 9.2. More market-integrated communities make higher offers in the Dictator Game. Based on data from 336 participants from 34 communities across 16 ethnolinguistic groups in Africa (Samburu, Hadza, Maragoli, Orma, Isanga Village, Accra, and Gusii), New Guinea and Oceania (Fiji, Sursurunga, and Au), South America (Shuar, Sanquianga, and Tsimane'), and Siberia (Dolgan and Nganasan).[12]

Incidentally, of all the variables we analyzed along with market integration, there was only one other that was consistently correlated with higher offers. Can you guess what it might be?

Participants who reported adherence to a world religion, with a Big God and supernatural punishment, offered 6 to 10 percentile points more in both the Dictator Game and the Ultimatum Game. This finding is what inspired the cross-cultural research on religion discussed in Chapter 4.[13]

Why would individuals from more market-integrated communities reveal stronger inclinations toward impersonal fairness in these experiments?

Well-functioning *impersonal* markets, in which strangers freely engage in competitive exchange, demand what I call *market norms*. Market norms establish the standards for judging oneself and others in impersonal transactions and lead to the internalization of motivations for trust, fairness, and cooperation with strangers and anonymous others. These are the social norms usually tapped by economic games, with their salient cues of money and anonymity.[14] In a world lacking intensive kin-based institutions, where people depend on well-functioning commercial markets for nearly everything, individuals succeed in part by cultivating a reputation for impartial fairness, honesty, and cooperation with acquaintances, strangers, and anonymous others because it's these qualities that will help them attract the most customers as well as the best business partners, employees, students, and clients. Such market norms specify how to behave when you don't have a relationship with someone or know each other's family, friends, social status, or caste. Such norms allow people to readily engage in a wide range of mutually beneficial transactions with just about anyone.

Market norms encourage an approach orientation and a positive-sum worldview but demand a sensitivity to the intentions and actions of others. Fairness is met with fairness, trust with trust, and cooperation with cooperation, all judged according to normative standards. Violations of market norms by one's own partners or third parties are met with a willingness to engage in costly norm enforcement. Thus market norms and the impersonal prosociality they encourage are neither unconditional nor altruistic.

Of course, markets also favor a competitive and calculating mind-set—people want to win, but they won't get complete respect unless they win while following the norms and agreed-upon rules. The greatest respect goes to those who succeed by their own talents and hard work while still being fair, honest, and impartial. This is a peculiar standard, since it devalues family connections, personal relationships, tribal parochialism, and clan alliances, which have all been standard over much of human history. In most times and places, in-group loyalty and family honor have trumped impartial fairness.

So far, I've told you only about a sturdy and replicable correlation between market integration and impersonal fairness. This relationship could be due to more fair-minded people moving into more market-integrated communities. The key question is whether greater market integration actually *causes* greater impersonal prosociality. That is, do markets alter people's motivations—via the internalization of market norms—so that they are more prosocial with strangers and anonymous partners?

THE OROMO, MARKETS, AND VOLUNTARY ASSOCIATIONS

Living on the northern slope of Ethiopia's Bale Mountains, the Oromo engage in cattle herding, subsistence farming, and forest gathering. To assess their impersonal prosociality, the economist Devesh Rustagi administered a simple experiment in which individuals were placed into a one-shot cooperative dilemma with an anonymous partner. Participants, after receiving nearly a day's wage in the form of 6 birr bills, could contribute any number of these bills to a "common project" with their partner. Cash contributed to the project by either partner was increased by 50 percent and then split equally between the pair. This meant that each player took home half of the total project money plus whatever they'd kept for themselves. Here, as in the Public Goods Games described earlier, pairs make the most money if both players contribute the maximum—all 6 birr, in this case. Individuals, however, make the most if they contribute nothing and free-ride on the contributions of their partner—this is what *Homo economicus* would do.

Each Oromo participant faced two versions of this game. First, players stated how much they'd contribute—from 0 to 6 birr—to the common project without knowing the amount contributed by their partners. Then each player also committed to how much they'd contribute to the common project for each of the *possible* contributions that their partner could make. In other words, players had to commit to how much they'd contribute if their partner gave 0, 1, 2, 3, 4, 5, or all 6 birr to their joint project.[15]

This approach allowed Devesh to assign participants to categories such as "altruist" or "free rider" and to calculate their propensity to *conditionally cooperate* with their partner. Altruists contributed a lot regardless of how much their partner contributed. As you might guess, altruists were rare—only about 2 percent of Devesh's 734 participants were altruists. By contrast, free riders contributed very little to the common project and were unresponsive to higher cooperative contributions from their partners. These guys comprised about 10 percent of the population. For everyone else (88 percent), Devesh calculated how much their partners' contributions influenced their own contributions. Participants who matched their partners' higher contributions in lockstep got a score of 100—they were perfectly conditionally cooperative. Those whose contributions were unconnected to their partner's contribution got a score of zero. It's also possible to get negative scores, if you tend to give less when your partner gives more. So, this measure of people's propensity for conditional cooperation could theoretically range from −100 to +100.

Across 53 Oromo communities, Figure 9.3 shows that individuals from more market-integrated places were much more conditionally cooperative than those from less market-integrated places. In this study, market integration was measured by how long it took to travel from one's community to one of the four towns in the region that periodically hold "market days." Market days provide the only opportunities for Oromo to sell and buy a wide range of goods, including local products like butter, honey, and bamboo as well as imports like razor blades, candles, and rubber boots. These events attract thousands of people from diverse communities and thus create a dizzying array of transactions. Not surprisingly, the travel time to these towns is correlated with the frequency with which people travel to buy and sell at the markets. The closest communities, with travel times of less than two hours, all had average propensities for conditional cooperation above 60. By contrast, when people had to walk for four or more hours to get to the market, the average propensity for conditional cooperation dropped to less than 20. Overall, for every hour closer to the market, people's propensity for conditional cooperation with an anonymous partner increased by 15.

This research strongly suggests that greater market integration does indeed foster greater impersonal prosociality. Here's why. The geographic location of Oromo clans, and thus their travel time to local markets, is determined by local customs related to patrilineal inheritance, communal ownership, and land use rights that preceded the development of these commercial centers. Because these customs effectively tie individuals to their lands, the relationship between market integration and cooperation can't be due to prosocial Oromo moving closer to the markets. As for the towns, their locations were determined largely by geographic and military concerns that had little to do with the Oromo. Moreover, the relationship between

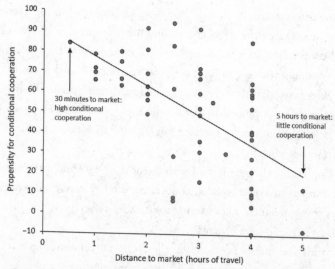

FIGURE 9.3. Oromo from more market-integrated communities were stronger conditional cooperators with anonymous others. Scores for 53 Oromo communities varied from 94 to −9 (734 participants). Notably, for intermediate travel times, between two and four hours, there is a lot of variation among communities, and some remote communities do still reveal high propensities for conditional cooperation. Nevertheless, the broader pattern is clear: people living in more market-integrated communities show greater impersonal prosociality in this one-shot interaction.[16]

market proximity and conditional cooperation held even after Devesh statistically accounted for the effects of a wide range of factors like wealth, inequality, community size, and literacy. The implication is that Oromo who just happened to grow up near market towns more deeply internalized market norms, which manifests in greater impersonal prosociality in these one-shot, anonymous experiments.[17]

Devesh's Oromo study is particularly cool because it allows us to take the next crucial step: it demonstrates that greater impersonal prosociality—internalized market norms—can lay the psychological foundations for constructing more effective voluntary organizations based on formalized agreements and rules.

As part of a large conservation program, these Oromo communities were invited to form voluntary organizations—cooperatives—aimed at limiting deforestation by actively managing logging and grazing. Detailed analyses reveal that the stronger a community's propensity toward conditional cooperation (as assessed in Devesh's experiments), the more likely these communities were to form cooperative associations that created explicit rules to regulate timber extraction and pasturing. Specifically, increasing a community's propensity for conditional cooperation by 20 on our scale raises its likelihood of forming a new cooperative association by 30 to 40 percentile points.[18]

Wait, maybe this was just a big show for the NGO and its representatives? Perhaps market-integrated cooperators are just savvier at extracting money from foreigners. Did forming cooperative associations actually cash out in greater long-term benefits?

It did. The forests surrounding these Oromo communities were assessed every five years to measure local deforestation rates and gauge the effectiveness of forest management. These assessments were based on objective measures, such as the circumference of trees. The data show that both the formation of cooperative associations and the local propensity for conditional cooperation promoted healthier forests. One reason why this occurred is that the stronger people's inclinations toward conditional cooperation, the more time they spent monitoring the common forest and catching free riders who were cutting down young trees or overgrazing common pastures—that is, they engaged in more third-party norm enforcement.[19]

Let's synthesize the key insights from the Oromo in Figure 9.4. This case shows that greater market integration can cause a psychological shift toward greater impersonal prosociality (arrow A). Greater impersonal prosociality (measured as conditional cooperation) fosters the formation of voluntary organizations (arrow B) that develop formal institutions, which often involve explicit rules, written agreements, and mutual monitoring (arrow C). Both these formal institutions (arrow D) and people's motivations for impersonal prosociality (arrow E) contribute to provisioning public goods, which in this case involves forest management. The upshot is that market integration can improve the grassroots provision of public

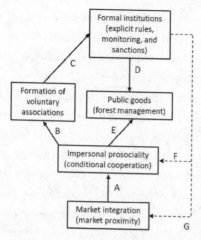

FIGURE 9.4. Greater market integration leads to higher levels of impersonal prosociality and onward to voluntary associations and more effective formal institutions.

goods and the formation of voluntary associations by inculcating social norms that foster impersonal interaction.

Figure 9.4 also illustrates relationships that may exist using dashed lines. Arrow F suggests that growing up in a world with well-functioning formal institutions may nurture greater impersonal prosociality, perhaps by making the rules and standards clear and by suggesting wide agreement. Arrow G proposes that effective formal institutions can improve the functioning of markets, through regulatory agreements or rules, and thereby expand their breadth. These relationships point to a feedback loop in which our psychology coevolves with markets and effective formal institutions.

Surprised? The notion that market integration is associated with greater fairness or cooperation is jarring to many WEIRD people. Aren't people from small-scale societies and rural villages highly prosocial, cooperative, and generous? Don't markets make people self-centered, individualistic, calculating, and competitive?

Yes, to both questions.

To illuminate this seeming contradiction, we must distinguish *interpersonal* prosociality from *impersonal* prosociality. The kindness and generosity found in many small-scale societies and rural villages where I've lived and worked are rooted in intensive kin-based institutions that focus on nurturing and sustaining enduring webs of interpersonal relationships. It's both impressive and beautiful, but this interpersonal prosociality is about relationship-specific kindness, warmth, reciprocity, and—sometimes—unconditional generosity as well as authority and deference. It's focused on the in-group members and their networks. If you're in the group or the network, it can feel like a long and comforting hug.

By contrast, economic experiments typically tap market norms that prescribe fair dealing and honesty with strangers or anonymous others, especially in monetary transactions. This impersonal prosociality is about fairness principles, impartiality, honesty, and conditional cooperation in situations and contexts where interpersonal connections and in-group membership are deemed unnecessary or even irrelevant. In worlds dominated by impersonal contexts, people depend on anonymous markets, insurance, courts, and other impersonal institutions instead of large relational networks and personal ties.[20]

Impersonal markets can thus have dual effects on our social psychology. They simultaneously *reduce* our *interpersonal* prosociality within our in-groups and *increase* our *impersonal* prosociality with acquaintances and strangers.[21] The epigraphs opening this chapter exemplify the frequent observations made by European thinkers from the 12th to the 18th centuries on how commerce seemed to tame people in ways that oiled and honed the interactions among strangers—this is the famous *Doux Commerce* thesis developed by Enlightenment thinkers such as Adam Smith and David Hume. Later, especially after market integration became pervasive in 19th-century Europe, Karl Marx and others began to consider what fully commercialized societies had lost (that nice hug I mentioned), and how the expanding social sphere governed by market norms changed our lives and psychology. The replacement of dense networks of interpersonal relationships and socially embedded exchange with impersonal institutions has sometimes led to alienation, exploitation, and commodification.[22]

Thus, to explain WEIRD psychology, given the impacts of expanding markets on our motivations, we need to know the when, where, and why of *impersonal* exchange in Europe. Once again, a psychological observation turns into a historical question.[23]

"No Hui, No Market Towns"

As I was wandering from store to store in the tiny town of Chol-Chol, I noticed something odd. This was the beginning of my dissertation field research among the Mapuche, an indigenous population that lives in scattered farming homesteads nestled among the rolling hills of southern Chile, in the shadow of the Andes. I'd been shopping for supplies, food, and gifts for my Mapuche hosts when I realized that there were nontrivial price differences between these stores for identical goods. As a cash-strapped graduate student, I pulled out my trusty ethnographer's notebook and started recording the prices. It wasn't long before I'd mapped the shortest walking circuit to purchase each of the items I wanted. Nevertheless, I puzzled over how such small stores, which were so close together, could maintain different prices for the same goods. Shouldn't competition for customers equalize the prices? This wasn't the focus of my research, but the question continued to rattle around in my mind.

Clues to this mystery drifted in slowly over the coming months. I first noticed that town folks always seemed to shop at the same few stores. Some shopped in two or at most three different stores, but no one had optimized a shopping circuit like me. This explained how prices could remain so variable—the competition was limited. But, it also just backed up the question to why people weren't shopping around to get the best prices. Many of these families were poor, and few seemed pressed for time. People seemed happy to chat for hours and were often asking me for rides; I was one of the few people in town with a car. In my free time, I casually inquired as to why people shopped where they did, and specifically asked people why they didn't buy their canned tuna, plastic buckets, or Nescafé (coffee) at the cheapest places.

In retrospect, the answer was obvious. These people had grown up together in the same small town. They all knew one another. While many households were lifelong friends and relatives, other families were considered undesirable, arrogant, or just unfriendly. Beneath an amiable veneer, there were simmering jealousies and long-running grudges, sometimes going back generations. Most of the jealousy seemed linked to money, marriage, or politics. What appeared (to me) to be rather minor differences in income among families sometimes generated powerful envy on one side, and a touch of haughtiness on the other. Occasionally the grudges were political: e.g., their family is rotten because they hadn't (or had) supported the Chilean "savior" (or dictator) Augusto Pinochet 25 years before.

The density of these interpersonal relationships constrained market competition in Chol-Chol. The locals' decisions to purchase everything from bread to firewood couldn't be isolated in a conceptual economic box, the way I had automatically done. Their decisions were *embedded* in bigger and more important enduring relationships. Of course, buying and selling did occur, but this was more *interpersonal* exchange than *impersonal* commerce.[24]

My experience highlights something subtle but interesting. On the one hand, interpersonal relationships facilitate exchange by providing the first and most fundamental basis for the trust required by most types of transactions. Without at least some trust, people won't exchange much at all, for fear of being robbed, exploited, scammed, or even murdered. This means that when exchange is risky and rare, you can increase it by building more and better interpersonal relationships. However, when the web of interpersonal relations becomes too dense, market competition and impersonal commerce get strangled. Exchange still occurs, but it's the slow, embedded kind, as in Chol-Chol.

This suggests that getting impersonal markets up and running requires two things: (1) pruning the dense interpersonal interconnections among buyers and sellers and (2) fostering market norms, which prescribe fair and impartial behavior with acquaintances, strangers, and anonymous others. If you only prune the interpersonal relationships without adding market norms, exchange will actually decline. However, if you only add market norms to a densely interwoven network of interpersonal relationships, nothing happens—interpersonal relationships will continue to dominate exchange. Impersonal markets require both weak interpersonal relationships and potent market norms.

Historically, commerce and trade have long been influenced by interpersonal relationships in opposite ways. Exchange within communities—commerce—has often been limited by excessively entangled interpersonal relationships. If your brother-in-law is one of the two accountants in town, can you really hire the other guy? By contrast, exchange between distant communities—trade—has most commonly been inhibited by a lack of any relationships among the people in each place. Let's look at trade more closely.

WEIRD people tend to think that trade is straightforward: we have wild yams and you have fish; let's swap some yams for some fish. Easy. But, this is misguided. Imagine trying to barter yams for fish in the hunter-gatherer world described by William Buckley in Australia. In this world, other groups were often hostile, and strangers were frequently killed on sight. To conceal their nocturnal locations, bands erected low sod fences around their campfires so they couldn't be spotted from a distance. If I showed up at your campfire with some yams to trade, why wouldn't you just kill me and take them? Or you might have thought we are only offering our toxic yams, which would slowly poison you and your band. Under such conditions, which were probably common over our species' evolutionary history, it's difficult to see how smoothly flowing trade could ever emerge.

Nevertheless, exchange did occur throughout Aboriginal Australia, as red ocher, baskets, mats, quartz, boomerangs, and much more diffused widely through many ethnolinguistic groups, sometimes traveling across the continent. How was this possible?

The key is to realize that trade occurred along chains of interpersonal relationships, threaded together in broad networks that stretched out across hundreds or even thousands of miles. Social ties were forged and reinforced by kin-based institutions that involved social norms governing such things as marriage and communal ceremonies. There were also specialized sets of norms and rituals for building and maintaining long-distance exchange relationships.[25]

What didn't happen easily was impersonal trade—barter or monetary exchange among anonymous strangers. When relationships couldn't be established, groups still sometimes managed to engage in *silent trade*. There are many variants of silent trade, but I'll use the first written description of it, from Herodotus in 440 BCE, to convey the basic setup:

> The Carthaginians tell us that they trade with a race of men who live in a part of Libya beyond the Pillars of Herakles. On reaching this country, they unload their goods, arrange them tidily along the beach, and then, returning to their boats, raise a smoke. Seeing the smoke, the natives come down to the beach, place on the ground a certain quantity of gold in exchange for the goods, and go off again to a distance. The Carthaginians then come ashore and take a look at the gold; and if they think it presents a fair price for their wares, they collect it and go away; if, on the other hand, it seems too little, they go back aboard and wait, and the natives come and add to the gold until they are satisfied.[26]

Such silent bargaining can continue back and forth, but it is usually limited. Of course, there's always a chance that one group will simply steal everything and vanish. Without either personal connections or impersonal trust, this is what human trade looks like. There's no credit, no delayed delivery, no returns, no guarantees, and little bargaining. Nevertheless, silent trade has been observed around the world, in a wide range of societies including those of hunter-gatherers, and deep into antiquity. The existence of both societies that engage in silent trade as well as those without any at all underlines how difficult trade is for our species in the absence of personal relationships or exchange norms.[27]

Historically and ethnographically, when markets for trading between groups did begin to emerge, they developed as periodic events conducted on specific days at established locations—as among the Oromo. In farming societies, markets typically developed in the buffer zones between tribal groups. Behavior in these places was governed by specific norms, which were shared by local populations and often enforced by supernatural punishment. Carrying weapons into the market arena was often taboo, and anyone engaging in violence or theft risked supernatural sanctions. Women, traveling to market to sell their excess harvest, were often accompanied by armed kinsmen for protection. Often, these escorts had to linger at the outskirts of the market arena, and only women were permitted in. Such escorts were necessary because the sacred taboo against violence and theft ended at the market's perimeter. This meant that when merchants crossed the perimeter on their way home, they were sometimes robbed, occasionally by those with whom they'd just traded.[28]

With greater protection for merchants by either state institutions or private security, more impersonal exchange could develop, but this was still limited to situations in which the quality of goods or services could be easily verified, and payments could be made on the spot. This, however, makes exchanges involving *credence goods* challenging. Credence goods are those that buyers can't easily assess for quality. Consider buying a steel sword, which might seem straightforward. But, did the manufacturer add carbon to the iron? If so, how much? Maybe 0.5 percent, which is crappy—or 1.2 percent, which is excellent. How about chromium, to prevent rust, and a combination of cobalt and nickel, to strengthen the blade? Given that you, a merchant in an ancient society, might have to bet your life on your blade's carbon content and tempering, how will you figure this out? Besides the problem of credence goods, trade without trust, honesty, or fairness seriously limits credit, insurance, long-term agreements, and even large shipments (which can't be easily checked for quality).[29]

In ancient and medieval societies outside of Europe, cultural evolution devised a diverse range of ways to address these challenges. We've already seen examples of this in the divine oaths sworn by Mediterranean and Mesopotamian traders while finalizing shipping contracts. Another common, and often complementary, approach to long-distance exchange was for a single, widely scattered clan or ethnic group to handle all aspects of moving goods through a vast trade network.[30] For example, two millennia before the Common Era in Mesopotamia, powerful families governed Assur as it developed into a thriving trading city. Operating like private firms, these large extended families stretched their tentacles across the region by sending their sons and other relatives to reside for decades in the barrios set aside for foreigners in distant cities. Assur's patriarchs ran these operations by dispatching cuneiform instructions and goods like tin, copper, and clothing via mule trains through their extensive networks. Supernatural beliefs likely played a big role as well—the city's eponymous deity was the god of trade.[31]

Three millennia later, vast trade flows across far-flung regions in China were underpinned by sprawling merchant diasporas linked by clan ties, residential connections, and personal relationships. The Hui merchant guild, for example, dominated trade along the Yangtze River and beyond beginning in the 12th century. Calling it a "guild," however, is misleading, because it wasn't like a European guild. It was a kind of super-clan, composed of many patrilineages. Property was corporately owned by the clan or one of the lineages, and rights to use properties and partake in profits was dependent upon both descent and economic contributions. Genealogies were constructed that linked different patrilineages to a common ancestor, and these genealogies provided road maps and Rolodexes to commercial contacts and connections among Hui merchants. Bonds among Hui lineages created the trust necessary for lineages to extend each other credit and capital. Hui businesses were staffed by lineage members and their domestic servants. In this world, the degree of commercialization in different regions *increased* with the elaboration of kin-based ties and the strength of these lineage organizations. The clan provided public goods like charity for poor Hui, care for their elderly, and educational funds for promising Hui scholars, who could get powerful government jobs. The dominance of the Hui merchants led to the ubiquity of the expression "no Hui, no market towns." In highly successful large-scale societies like China, cultural evolution devised a multiplicity of ways to better harness interpersonal relationships, not suppress them.[32]

Of course, state bureaucracies also played a role in the growth of trade. They variously policed markets, established courts, and provided accommodations for foreign merchants. In the courts, the adjudication of disagreements often occurred not between individuals—say, a buyer and a seller—but between clans, tribes, or villages. Such adjudications were frequently not about meting out impartial justice but focused on maintaining harmony and ameliorating bad feelings between clans—judges sought to manage the relationships between kin-groups.[33]

My point is that while many ancient and medieval societies beyond Europe had thriving markets and extensive long-distance trade, they were generally built on webs of interpersonal relationships and kin-based institutions, not on impersonal norms of exchange with broadly applicable principles of fairness and impersonal trust. Hui and Assur merchants represent impressive and sophisticated elaborations of our species' usual approach to trade. The Europeans of medieval Christendom, however, couldn't easily take this well-trodden path to commercialization; the Church had undercut all of the standard tools of intensive kin-based institutions that Hui and Assur patriarchs had deployed to nourish and grow their institutions and networks. Medieval Europeans did try to create family-based trading organizations, but, hampered by the Church's MFP, their efforts were gradually outpaced by voluntary associations (e.g., merchant guilds), impersonal institutions, and market norms.[34]

The Commercial and Urban Revolutions

By 900 CE, the Church had entrenched itself in several regions of western Europe (Figure 7.1), driven out most of its competitors (e.g., Norse and Roman gods), and undermined the once dominant kin-based institutions of these populations. In forging Christendom, the Church tapped people's tribal psychology to create a unified Christian supra-identity that linked people from distant parts of Europe. This was particularly effective because the Church's MFP, with its far-reaching incest taboos, had already largely dissolved people's tribal affiliations and extended kin-based loyalties.

Unshackled from corporate landholdings and ancestral rites, people began to voluntarily join a variety of associations. At first, these seem to have been religious organizations that provided mutual aid, social insurance, and security—replacing several crucial functions of kin-based institutions. Eventually, however, these social tectonics created the first cracks in the rural population dams, leading individuals to begin trickling into newly forming towns and cities in places like northern Italy, France, Germany, Belgium, and England. Residentially and relationally mobile, these individuals joined guilds, monasteries, confraternities, neighborhood clubs, universities, and other associations.[35]

Many of these cities and towns were themselves new voluntary organizations that were actively recruiting artisans, merchants, and, later, lawyers. Soon these burgeoning urban communities began to compete to recruit valuable members by offering better opportunities and more privileges. Citizenship—city membership—often exempted individuals from conscription by local rulers but still obligated them to join in the common defense. Serfs could often gain full citizenship after only one year of residence. Competition among these urban enclaves favored whatever combinations of norms, laws, rights, and administrative organizations attracted the most productive members and generated the most prosperity.[36]

While the urban centers of 11th-century Europe may have superficially looked like puny versions of those in China or the Islamic world, they were actually a newly emerging form of social and political organization, ultimately rooted in, and arising from, a different cultural psychology and family organization. As we've seen in the last two chapters, smaller families with greater residential and relational mobility would have nurtured greater psychological individualism, more analytic thinking, less devotion to tradition, stronger desires to expand one's social network, and greater motivations for equality over relational loyalty. These urbanizing arenas thus created places for more individualistic people to begin to build new relationships and distinct ways of organizing themselves without the binding constraints of family networks, cousin obligations, and tribal loyalties.[37]

The initial trickle of immigrants into urban centers slowly rose to a flood, eventually creating levels of urbanization heretofore unseen in human history. Figure 9.5 plots the percentage of western Europeans living in cities or towns of over 1,000 people. In 800 CE, less than 3 percent of the population were urbanites. During the High Middle Ages, western Europe surged past China's urbanization rate, which remained relatively constant from 1000 to 1800 CE. In the four centuries after 1200 CE, western Europe's urbanization rate doubled, exceeding 13 percent in 1600. Of course, as Figure 9.5 illustrates, these averages conceal much regional variation. In the Netherlands and Belgium, for example, these percentages begin at essentially zero in 900, but then climb to over 30 percent by 1400 CE.[38]

Urbanization was accompanied by the development of administrative assemblies and town councils, with representatives from the communities' guilds and other associations. Some became self-governing, or at least relatively independent of an array of princes, bishops, dukes, and kings. In the 9th and 10th centuries, as the Carolingian Empire was collapsing, the

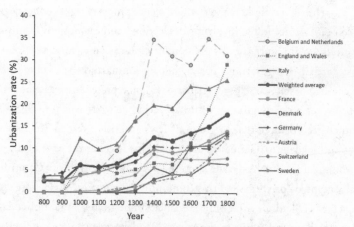

FIGURE 9.5. Urbanization rates in western Europe from 800 to 1800 CE. The thick black line represents the urbanization rate for all of western Europe excluding the Iberian Peninsula. The other lines give the urbanization rates for other regions of interest. Note that the overall urbanization rate includes several regions not shown with individual curves. Urbanization estimates are based on the percentage of the population living in cities or towns with more than 1,000 inhabitants.[39]

first sparks of this eventual blaze of self-government ignited in northern and central Italy, where groups of prominent citizens publicly swore sacred oaths in front of local bishops, who could act as guarantors of these pacts. Governing councils were formed from these groups of sworn members. This didn't happen in southern Italy, which, as we saw in the last chapter, hadn't experienced the MFP at this point in history.[40]

North of the Alps, this urban revolution can be seen in the emergence and rapid diffusion of city charters and town privileges in regions that now include Germany, France, and England. Charters or grants of privileges were initially used to affirm existing customs that had been gestating in successful communities. As in other voluntary associations of the era, membership in towns and cities generally required individuals to take oaths before God in which they pledged to aid their fellow residents and affirmed certain individual rights and obligations. Later, these charters were used in founding new towns, as rulers looked for ways to expand and secure new territories. While some interesting regional variation in these charters existed, what's striking about them is their similarities. They usually granted citizens the right to hold markets, more secure property rights, some degree of self-governance (often involving an election), and exemptions from various tolls, tariffs, and taxes. By 1500, most cities in western Europe were at least partially self-governing. Meanwhile, in China and the Islamic world, no city had developed self-governance based on representative assemblies.[41]

We get an early glimpse of urbanization at work when, in 965 CE, Church records note that "a group of Jews and other traders" had set up shop in Magdeburg (Germany), along the Elbe River at the edge of the old Carolingian Empire. A decade later, the Holy Roman emperor Otto I formally granted "privileges" to this community. Gradually, Magdeburg's approach to civil administration, the regulation of guilds, and criminal laws were forged into what became known as Magdeburg Law.

By 1038 CE, Magdeburg's success had begun to inspire other communities to copy its laws. In the next several centuries, over 80 cities would directly and explicitly copy Magdeburg's charter, laws, and civil institutions. Magdeburg continued to make institutional and legal adjustments, so "daughter cities" always acquired "the Law" in whatever form it took at the time of imitation. In the 13th century, a voluntary religious and military organization called the Teutonic Knights began granting Magdeburg Law to the towns and cities they conquered in Prussia and eastward. With various modifications, these daughter cities typically passed their charters, laws, and formal institutions onto other communities. For example, in Germany, the city of Halle adopted Magdeburg Law; later in the 13th century, Halle's laws and institutions became the model for Środa (a.k.a. Neumarkt) in modern Poland. Środa subsequently passed its charter and laws onto at least 132 other communities.[42]

A surviving set of nine articles from the 12th century gives us a peek at what was going on in medieval Magdeburg. This legislation seems to settle some disputes surrounding various traditions or customs. Specifically, one of the articles affirms that fathers will no longer be liable for murders or assaults committed by their sons provided that six "worthy men" will testify that the father was not present during the killing or injury, or, if he was present, that he didn't participate at all. The law also extended to other relatives.

It was apparently necessary in Magdeburg to make a law that specifically reduced the liability of families for the actions of their violent members. The law seems to mitigate—but not abolish—collective kin-based criminal liability. It appears that self-governing cities were gradually laying down new laws that isolated individuals and their intentions, by demolishing the remnants of their intensive kin-based institutions and their associated intuitions. Recall that such collective liability appeared clearly in the earliest law codes of various European tribal populations, written during the Early Middle Ages, soon after their conversion to Christianity.[43]

Competing with Magdeburg, other cities developed their own charters, laws, and governing institutions. For example, after receiving its initial charter in 1188, Lübeck rose to become the richest city in northern Europe by the mid-14th century, and the mother city for much of the Baltic region, with Lübeck Law diffusing to at least 43 daughter communities.[44] Like Magdeburg and other mother cities, Lübeck also acted as an appeals court when legal questions arose in daughter communities.[45] Creation of a region in the Baltic governed by the same merchant-friendly constitution, administrative procedures, and legal system laid the foundation for a vast trade federation, the Hanseatic League.

Elsewhere in Europe, a parallel process of urbanization was underway. London, for example, received its first charter from William the Conqueror in 1066 and then got an even better deal from Henry I in 1129. Londoners were permitted to elect their sheriffs and control their own courts. The 24 aldermen who governed the city swore an oath to manage affairs in accordance with the charter—a constitutional oath. Here, as in Magdeburg, formal laws were laying various elements of intensive kin-based institutions to rest. Land sales, for example, were partially liberated from traditional inheritance customs. Specifically, under *some conditions*, individuals could sell their land, thereby disinheriting their heirs. The charter also exempted citizens from paying blood money to other families (for murders) and from being compelled to settle legal challenges in trial-by-combat (honor-based morality). Citizens were also spared from a range of tolls and customs duties. As in Germany, London's charter provided a model for other cities, including Lincoln, Northampton, and Norwich.[46]

Of course, emperors, earls, and dukes were not granting urban charters or privileges because they believed in elections, local sovereignty, or individual rights. Rather, there seemed to have been at least three "pulls" and one "shove." First, rulers discovered that freer communities could generate economic prosperity through trade and commerce—they were cash cows that could improve a ruler's finances. Second, growing population centers meant more men, and more men meant larger military forces and greater security. Now, urban charters did often exempt citizens from impressment into the local ruler's armies (for conquest), but at least citizens were responsible for defending their own cities and towns. Third, with the lure of privileges and opportunities, rulers could charter new colonial towns that effectively extended and reinforced their territorial control. Finally, many of the emerging voluntary associations either were primarily military organizations (like the Knights Templar) or included military wings. Merchant guilds, for example, often maintained private security forces to provide protection during long-distance trade. This meant that kings and emperors lacked anything resembling a military monopoly. So, by chartering urban centers and letting them provide for their own defense, rulers found a way to expand their lands, tap new revenue streams, and augment their military power while dealing with the realities of a world increasingly dominated by voluntary associations full of individualistically-minded people.[47] Of course, this would all backfire in the long run for the royals, but it did work for centuries.

The evolution of the social norms, laws, and charters of these urban communities appears to have been influenced by the two crucial forces laid out in Chapter 3: (1) psychological fit and (2) intergroup competition. Individuals were arriving in these urban centers with a proto-WEIRD psychology: they were likely more individualistic, independent, analytic, and self-focused than populations in other complex societies, while also being less devoted to tradition, authority, and conformity. These psychological differences would have shaped the new customs and laws that developed and spread within and across these communities. Greater individualism would have deepened the appeal of laws and practices that endowed individuals with rights, ownership, and responsibilities. Reduced in-group favoritism and less tribalism would have encouraged more equitable treatment of foreigners, as we saw with the laws protecting foreign merchants. Analytical thinking would have fostered the development of abstract or universal principles that could then have been used to develop specific rules, policies, or regulations. Amazingly, the first glimmers of abstract inalienable rights are even perceptible in Magdeburg Law. Analytic thinking and individualism may also have favored the universal applicability of laws to all Christians within a jurisdiction, regardless of their tribe, class, or family. These psychological changes would have influenced the standards of judicial judgments and evidence, resulting in the slow phasing out of trial-by-combat and various other magico-religious ordeals commonly used across history to resolve legal disputes.[48]

Alongside such psychological forces, the evolution of these urban communities over centuries was driven by intergroup competition. Migrants to medieval urban centers, as in the modern world, were likely drawn in search of prosperity, opportunity, and security. The competition among cities and towns for migrants, often shaped by the explicit emulation of the policies and charters of the most prosperous urban centers, would have gradually assembled packages of norms, laws, and formal institutions that fostered economic prosperity and stability in an increasingly individualistic and relationally mobile world. From 1250 to 1650, for example, Bruges, Antwerp, and Amsterdam competed to create business-friendly environments in order to attract foreign merchants. All other things being equal, more successful urban communities would have drawn relatively more migrants, both from the countryside and from competing urban centers. Crucially, remember that these kinds of laws and norms worked particularly well in generating prosperity because they "fit" the emerging psychological patterns of the time—*not* because they were universally good, moral, or effective. A proto-WEIRD psychology first nurtured, and then coevolved with, new economic and political institutions, both formal and informal.[49]

But how, you might wonder, am I able to link the Church's impact on people's social lives and psychology to the rapid growth of urban areas and the formation of participatory governments?

By combining our database on the spread of bishoprics through Europe (Chapter 7) with century-by-century data on the population size and governance of cities from 800 to 1500 CE, Jonathan Schulz asked two questions: Do cities with longer exposure to the Church due to nearby bishoprics (within 100 km [62 mi]) grow faster than less exposed cities? And are cities with longer Church exposure more likely to develop participatory or representative governments? Keeping in mind that the Church arrives in different parts of Europe at different times, a dataset like this is nice because you can compare the same city with itself through time while holding constant both longer-term trends and century-specific shocks like plagues or famines.

Just as we suspected: the longer a city was exposed to the Church, the faster it grew, and the more likely it was to develop participatory governance. In terms of prosperity and size, each additional century of Church exposure meant an additional 1,900 urbanites. After a millennium, that's nearly 20,000 more city dwellers. For political institutions, Figure 9.6 illustrates

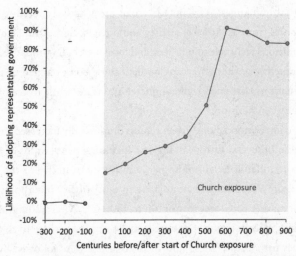

FIGURE 9.6. The likelihood of urban areas adopting any form of representative government from 800 to 1500 CE based on centuries of exposure to the medieval Western Church. The shaded region captures the arrival of the Church. To the left of zero, the unshaded region is the centuries prior to the Church's arrival.[50]

the impact of the Church by looking at the likelihood that a European city develops some form of representative government both before and after the Church arrives. Before the Church arrives, the estimated probability of developing any form of representative government is zero—making pre-Christian Europe just like everywhere else in the world. After the Church arrives, the chances that a city adopts some form of representative government jumps to 15 percent and then increases continuously for the next six centuries, topping out at over 90 percent.[51]

Of course, this analysis can't directly finger the MFP's psychological effects. But, seen in the light of the links between the Church, intensive kinship, and psychology that we saw in the last three chapters, it becomes difficult to imagine that psychological variation didn't play a role.

MARKET INTEGRATION RISES

Medieval European urban communities were increasingly built around a new kind of impersonal commerce and trade, centered in part on contractual exchanges. As I noted, urban areas actively recruited skilled professionals from as far away as they could reach. Successful charters created conditions favorable to markets, and local merchant guilds evolved into town councils or other governing bodies. These bodies aimed to pass laws and regulations that energized commerce and trade while fostering success in intercity competition.[52]

The competition among urban centers dramatically increased the market integration in several European regions, including large swaths of England, Germany, Holland, Belgium, France, and northern Italy. For the German lands, Figure 9.7 shows the cumulative number of city incorporations and grants of market privileges from 1100 to 1500 CE. After 1200, the number of new city incorporations per decade rose from fewer than 10 to about 40 new cities per decade. These new incorporations were followed by a rising number of grants to hold markets. Such market grants had real economic effects. New buildings, for example, tended to be constructed in the years after a city or town received a market grant.[53] This proliferation of urban centers and market grants (think "market days," as among the Oromo) drove ascending rates of market integration for growing urban and peri-urban populations in medieval Europe.

By the 14th century in England, about 1,200 weekly markets were operating, and, according to the economic historian Gary Richardson, "almost everyone was in easy reach of at least one market."[54] In rural areas, most people were within a two-hour walk (4.2 miles or less) from at least one market, and 90 percent of households were within three hours of a market (6 miles or less).

Now, look back at the Oromo data in Figure 9.3. Ninety percent of 14th-century Englishfolk would have been in the upper left quadrant of this plot. This suggests most people would have been conditional cooperators with anonymous others, and, like the Oromo in the most market-integrated communities, they would have been psychologically prepared to forge voluntary associations that make and enforce explicit agreements—contracts—to provide public goods. Unlike medieval Englishfolk, however, the Oromo

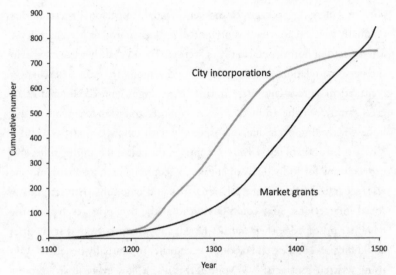

FIGURE 9.7. **Rising numbers of market grants and city incorporations in the German lands from 1100 to 1500 CE. This illustrates both rising urbanization and market integration.**[55]

can't easily move to their local towns, immerse themselves in voluntary associations, or even purchase land near town. Instead, they live enmeshed in patrilineal, polygynous clans. Land is passed from father to son, and arranged marriages build economic and political alliances among clans. As we've seen, life in such kin-based institutions shapes distinct psychological profiles.[56]

In the urban communities of medieval Europe, the success of merchants, traders, and artisans depended—in part—on their reputation for impartial honesty and fairness, and on their industriousness, patience, precision, and punctuality. These reputational systems favored the cultivation of the relevant social standards, attentional biases, and motivations that apply to impersonal transactions. I suspect these changes in both people's psychology and society's reputational standards are an important part of the rapidly rising availability of credit, which helped fuel the commercial revolution.[57]

The emerging packages of market-oriented, impersonal social norms gradually gave rise to what historians call *lex mercatoria*, or Merchant Law. These peculiar norms, and later laws, were strange in that they began to strip the personal relationships out of exchange. Among those in an exchange, contract, or agreement, these norms increasingly ignored differences in class, family, or tribe. Individuals were supposed to be fair, cooperative, and honest with almost anyone, but especially with fellow Christians. Gradually, the diffusion of *lex mercatoria* supplied the cultural framing, rules, and expectations for individuals to engage in economic exchange with anyone else, separated from all the relational ties and emotions that accompany social interactions. Sons could buy bread at the best price, even from the daughter of someone their mother hated, and strangers from distant cities could buy, sell, and extend credit to each other in mutually beneficial ways using written contracts.[58] Of course, this was a slow evolutionary process that, even today, proceeds by baby steps, because certain aspects of human psychology and intensive kin-based institutions tend to push back. Long after the Middle Ages, market norms are still being further stretched to erase differences in religion, race, gender, and sexual preference that continue to influence employment opportunities, salaries, and prison sentences.

However, to understand the diffusion of market norms in medieval Europe, we need to recognize the role played by the newly forming voluntary associations, such as towns and guilds, as well as the more individualistic psychology possessed by their members. On their own, self-interested individuals could exploit the willingness of strangers to extend credit or defer payment. However, to navigate this new social world, individuals were joining guilds, confraternities, charter towns, and a variety of other organizations, as we have seen. Members who violated commercial agreements with strangers jeopardized the reputations of their organizations—who could boot them out. Since all of these organizations were competing, they had important incentives not only to socialize their members but also to enforce rules, punish violators, and make amends with the exploited. Competition among voluntary organizations favored those who most efficiently instilled *lex mercatoria* in their members, since punishing members or compensating victims was costly to the organization.[59]

The most prosperous medieval urban communities would have been those that reaffirmed, bolstered, and backed up these informal norms with effective formal institutions and laws. This process was fostered by the spread of another voluntary association, the university. In the wake of the rediscovery of the Justinian Code of Roman civil law in the 11th century, a group of foreign law students in Bologna formed a corporate group, or *universitas*, focused on studying and learning. Soon, universities began sprouting throughout Europe, reaching Paris and Oxford at the beginning of the 13th century. By 1500 CE, there were over 50 such universities around Christendom, all competing for students and professors. Universities trained lawyers, theologians, and other professionals in writing, logic, and oratory as well as in math, music, and astronomy. This produced a residentially mobile Latin-speaking class who were versed in both Church and civil laws.[60]

Historical analyses reveal that universities spurred economic growth in their hometowns and cities. The creation of university-trained scholars likely contributed to this effect. This new social class was not only literate but increasingly capable of deducing abstract principles from the mishmash of existing customs or laws and then formulating well-structured regulations and policies for their urban communities. Formal laws galvanized and further standardized existing customs related to impersonal commerce and trade.[61]

The early development of commercial and contract law in Europe is important because other complex societies like China didn't substantially develop either until the 19th century, despite being more sophisticated in other forms of law and philosophy. Interestingly, Chinese clans and merchants did write lots of private contracts, and magistrates did apply laws to adjudicate disputes arising from these contracts. However, instead of applying abstract and impersonal principles based on codified rules, magistrates considered a mélange of local customs along with the interpersonal and class relationships involved, offering what amounted to nonbinding arbitration.

That is, they took a more holistic and relational approach to law—because they had a different psychology.[62]

Round Up

As we've seen now with religion, kinship, and markets, institutions can shape our social psychology in important ways. This has operated differently in diverse regions, with exchange-oriented social norms sometimes evolving to foster more smoothly flowing trade between occupational castes or ethno-religious groups. In South Asia, for example, some medieval ports established enduring exchange relationships between local Hindus and Muslim traders on the Indian Ocean. Centuries later, long after the disruption of Islamic trade routes by European powers, trading ports experience less interethnic violence between Hindus and Muslims than nontrading cities. It seems that trade between these groups forged enduring informal institutions, the psychological effects of which persisted long after trade ceased.[63]

These kinds of prosocial effects can be observed today all over the world by examining the relationship between a community's proximity to large rivers or oceans and the attitudes of its inhabitants toward foreigners and immigrants. Large rivers and oceans have long been, and remain, the arteries for much of the world's trade. Living near a port usually means living in an urban center where norms, practices, and beliefs have been shaped by trade and commerce more intensely than elsewhere.

This fact suggests that western Europe had a geographic edge over many parts of the world in developing trade and commerce: this region possesses an unusually large number of natural ports and navigable waterways as well as inland seas in both the north (Baltic) and the south (Mediterranean).[64] Once market norms developed, they could rapidly disseminate along the waterways into the fertile grounds of ports. This geographic preparedness would have catalyzed the process of market integration that I've been describing.

Summarizing our progress: the breakdown of intensive kin-based institutions opened the door to urbanization and the formation of free cities and charter towns, which began developing greater self-governance. Often dominated by merchants, urban growth generated rising levels of market integration and—we can infer—higher levels of impersonal trust, fairness, and cooperation. While these psychological and social changes were occurring, people began to ponder notions of individual rights, personal freedoms, the rule of law, and the protection of private property. These new ideas just fit people's emerging cultural psychology better than many alternatives.

Urbanizing premodern Europe was being transformed from the middle outward, up and down the social strata. The last groups to feel these enduring psychological and social shifts were (1) the most remote subsistence farmers and (2) the highest levels of the aristocracy, who continued to consolidate power for centuries through intensive forms of kinship, long after it had been extirpated from the urban middle classes.

Of course, this wasn't a smooth and continuous transition, even in rapidly growing urban centers. One of the greatest threats to the functioning of voluntary associations was, and remains, intensive kinship. It wasn't uncommon for new organizations, including banks and governments, to be usurped for a time by large, powerful families consolidated by arranged marriages.[65] However, as noted, this is a tough road in the long run because the Church suppressed nearly all the basic tools of intensive kinship. Under these constraints, family businesses struggled to outcompete other organizational forms. At the same time, politically or economically powerful family lineages were simply more likely to die out without polygyny, customary inheritance, remarriage, and adoption. When dominant royal families did die out, urban communities were often able to reforge their formal institutions in ways more appealing to people with a proto-WEIRD psychology.

10

Domesticating the Competition

> But warfare, it can be concluded, is an especially effective means
> of promoting social cohesion in that it provides an occasion upon
> which the members of the society unite and submerge their factional
> differences in the vigorous pursuit of a common purpose.
>
> —anthropologist Robert F. Murphy (1957, p. 1034), ethnographer of the
>   Amazonian Mundurucú

Here's a surprising claim: greater competition among voluntary associations, be they charter towns, universities, guilds, churches, monasteries, or modern firms, can raise people's trust, fairness, and cooperation toward strangers. Historically, the proliferation of voluntary associations in Europe, from the High Middle Ages onward, led to greater and more enduring intergroup competition. This, in turn, has contributed to both increasing and then sustaining higher levels of impersonal prosociality. To understand why, let's first look at how human psychology responds to intergroup competition and then consider the impact of war in Europe over the last millennium.

War, Religion, and Psychology

After decades of rising poverty, civil war erupted in the West African country of Sierra Leone in 1991. War-related violence ravaged the civilian population, mass killings occurred, children were coerced into soldiering, and war crimes piled up. Fighting spread throughout the entire country as villages were targeted by both rebel groups and government forces. Sometimes these armies were scouring regions for enemy enclaves, but other times they were looting peaceful communities, suppressing elections, or stealing alluvial diamonds to buy food and arms. Responding to these threats, many communities formed their own defensive militias, which were built on traditional institutions and chiefly authority. By its end in 2002, the war had taken the lives of over 50,000 civilians, displaced nearly half the population, and left thousands with amputations and other lifelong injuries.[1]

In 2010, a research team led by the economist Alessandra Cassar arrived in Sierra Leone with a battery of simple behavioral experiments designed to assess people's motivations for fairness toward members of their own and other communities. In these experiments, villagers were anonymously paired in a one-off interaction with either a random person from their own village or someone from a distant village. In one experimental task, the Sharing Game, participants were given a choice between (A) 5,000 leones for themselves and 5,000 for the other person or (B) 7,500 leones for themselves and 2,500 for the other person. People could go with an even split (A), or they could increase their own payoff at a cost to the other person (B). Another task offered participants a choice between (A) 5,000 each for themselves and another person or (B) 6,500 for themselves and 8,000 for the other person. In this second task, the Envy Game, people could increase their own payoff by picking option B, but if they did, the other person would get more than they would. The stakes here were significant: 5,000 leones was about one day's wage ($1.25) for an average Sierra Leonean.

This research team, which I later joined, went to Sierra Leone because they wanted to understand how the experience of war might change people. National surveys had suggested that the war had hit families and households to differing degrees, even within the same village. Some families had lost relatives, or had family members who had sustained serious injuries. Others had been displaced because their houses or fields had been destroyed. Some families had experienced both death and displacement.

Building on national-level data, our team interviewed participants about their war exposure. About half had experienced some combination of death, injury, and displacement, while the other half hadn't experienced any of these. I'll refer to the former group as the "most affected" and the latter as the "least affected." Of course, everyone was affected by the war, so our questions about displacement, injury, and death during the war were only meant to capture the war's *relative* impact.

People's war experiences, which had all occurred at least eight years earlier, sharply affected their behavior in our experiments (Figure 10.1). In the Sharing Game, participants who had been least affected by the war picked the egalitarian choice about a third of the time, regardless of the receiver. By contrast, participants who had been most affected by the war were much more egalitarian toward their co-villagers than to those from distant villages. The percentage who split the money with co-villagers in the Sharing Game spiked from a third to nearly 60 percent when participants had been more affected by the war. In the Envy Game, greater war exposure dramatically increased the percentage of egalitarian choices for co-villagers, from 16 percent to 41 percent. That is, people who were hit harder by the war were more inclined to pay a cost of 1,500 leones to keep things even with their fellow villagers. However, with distant villagers the effect reversed: those who were more exposed to the war were half as likely to make the egalitarian choice. Taken together, these and other experiments suggest that war strengthens people's egalitarian motivations, but only toward their in-groups.[2]

Crucially, unlike in many civil wars, most victims in Sierra Leone weren't targeted for their ethnic or religious affiliations, and the country didn't fracture along these lines. Both our analyses and larger national-level studies indicate that much of the violence experienced by ordinary villagers was effectively random. Militias would storm into a community, spraying bullets in all directions, and then torch the most conveniently located houses as villagers either hid or fled. This means that, as in the randomized control trials used to test the effectiveness of new medicines, individuals were

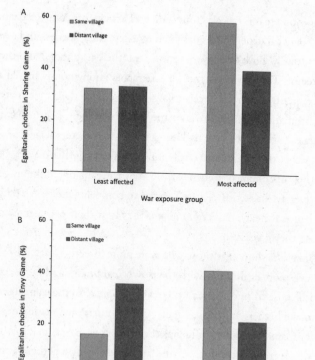

FIGURE 10.1. The effects of war exposure in Sierra Leone for the Sharing Game (A) and the Envy Game (B) when interacting with both co-villagers and people from distant villages.

largely afflicted by, or "dosed with," war-related violence at random. This quasi-randomization allows us to cautiously infer that war is in fact causing the psychological changes captured in our experiments.[3]

Similar patterns emerged when players in a street soccer tournament were studied in Kenema, a regional capital in eastern Sierra Leone that was only 30 km (19 mi) from the rebel headquarters. Researchers studied male soccer players ranging in age from 14 to 31 years who were competing on neighborhood teams in a city tournament. Participants completed a battery of psychological experiments designed to assess their fairness and competitiveness toward both their own teammates (their neighbors) and those on other teams. To measure fairness, participants anonymously played a Dictator Game in which the receiver was either one of their teammates or a player from another team. To measure competitiveness, players were given 10 chances to throw a soccer ball into a basket four meters away. They could pick whether they wanted to (A) compete against another player, who was either their teammate or someone from another team, or (B) simply get paid 500 leones per basket. If players decided to compete (choice A), they'd get 1,500 leones for each basket *but only if* they beat their opponent's score; if they lost, they'd get zero.

The results show that those who were more directly affected by the war were both more egalitarian with their own teammates and more competitive with those from other teams. Greater exposure to the war caused players to make higher (and more equal) offers to their own teammates in the Dictator Game but didn't influence the offers that players made to participants who were not teammates. Similarly, in deciding whether to compete in the ball toss against non-teammates, those least affected by the war eschewed the opportunity, competing less than a quarter of the time, while those most affected by the war competed nearly 75 percent of the time. By contrast, war exposure didn't influence players' decisions to compete against their own teammates. These experimental patterns were mirrored in the soccer games: those least affected by the war received zero foul cards (for rule violations), while those most affected had nearly a 50 percent chance of getting at least one foul card. Here, the experience of war seems to again favor stronger egalitarian motivations for one's in-group as well as greater competitiveness against out-groups.[4]

War's psychological effects also seem to cash out in politics and civil society in Sierra Leone. Based on nationally representative surveys in 2005 and 2007 analyzed by the economists John Bellows and Ted Miguel, people who had been more directly afflicted by the war were more likely to attend community meetings, vote in elections, and join political or social groups. The data further suggest that more war-affected individuals were more likely to join school management committees and probably also more likely to participate in cooperative "road brushing" activities, which help to maintain local roads (a public good). These findings, which converge nicely with the experimental work discussed above, suggest that war experiences fueled people's motivations to join voluntary associations and participate in community governance.[5]

The evidence for war's enduring effects on people's psychology and for its downstream influences on formal institutions are not limited to Sierra Leone. In recent years, a rapidly growing body of research from Nepal, Israel, Uganda, Burundi, Liberia, Central Asia, and the Caucasus reveal similar patterns using a variety of psychological experiments, including Ultimatum and Public Goods Games, as well as an array of survey questions about trust, voting, and participation in social groups. For example: after a decade of civil war in Nepal, communities that were exposed to more war-related violence cooperated more in a Public Goods Game (among community members); they were also more likely to vote and join local groups. In fact, while non-afflicted communities entirely lacked voluntary associations, 70 percent of the war-afflicted communities developed organizations like farming cooperatives, women's coalitions, and youth groups. Here again, war fueled people's motivations to join voluntary associations.[6]

To understand why war evokes these effects on human psychology, let's recall some of the ideas developed in Chapters 2 to 4. With the emergence of cultural evolution in the last two million years, competition among bands, clans, and tribes drove the cultural spread of cooperative social norms that permitted groups to survive both violent conflicts with other groups and natural disasters like floods, earthquakes, droughts, and volcanic eruptions. Among the norms and beliefs favored by this cultural evolutionary process, we've seen examples related to food sharing, communal rituals, and incest taboos. Such norms, along with those concerning mutual aid and communal defense, enmesh individuals in a dense social network that they depend on to survive. Adapting to this ancestral world has left our species with a genetically evolved response to war and other shocks that likely operates in at least three ways. First, shocks spark our interdependence psychology, causing us to invest more heavily in the social ties and communities that we rely on. In the case of war, this depends on who the "us" is that's being attacked. If people perceive that "Ilahita" is being attacked, then they bond more tightly with their fellow villagers and expect others to do the same. For those lacking strong interpersonal networks, shocks will propel them to seek out and invest in new relationships and communities. Second, because social norms have culturally evolved to promote group survival, war and other shocks may psychologically strengthen our commitment to these norms and related beliefs. So, to the degree that social norms prescribe various forms of cooperation, people will become more cooperative along normative lines and more willing to punish deviations from these standards.

These two psychological influences—solidifying interdependent groups and strengthening norms—combine with other aspects of our psychology to create the third effect: wars, earthquakes, and other disasters increase people's religious commitments and ritual participation, resulting in the growth of religious groups. This occurs for a pair of interrelated reasons. First, by strengthening our social norms and related beliefs, wars and other shocks may directly deepen people's faith and related commitments, which can inspire greater engagement in religious groups. Second, by stoking our interdependence psychology, shocks like war motivate people to either further invest in, or join, supportive communities. Because religious groups frequently offer mutual aid and support, this effect tends to increase participation in these groups. Greater investment in such groups often results in better attendance at church or the mosque, which can further strengthen supernatural beliefs (as a side effect). In addition to these effects, religions that promise people life after death and possess repetitive rituals that help individuals manage anxiety may get an especially big boost from the existential threats created by war and other disasters. People will be more attracted to religious groups and less likely to leave them compared to nonreligious communities.

This suggests that some religious groups offer a trifecta: (1) interdependent networks that provide mutual aid, (2) shared commitments to sacred norms, and (3) rituals and supernatural beliefs that help manage existential anxiety and uncertainty. In a world filled with war and other disasters, intergroup competition favors the spread of religious packages that furnish this trifecta because these religions will win in competition with groups lacking these crucial qualities (not because these religions are "true").[7]

Indeed, there's now ample evidence that both natural disasters and war deepen people's religious commitments and ritual participation. By combining global data on the historical intensity of earthquakes, volcanic eruptions, and tropical storms with detailed surveys on religious beliefs from over a quarter of a million individuals in 90 or more countries, the economist Jeanet Bentzen has shown that people living in regions more prone to disasters are more religious, and that specifically they believe more strongly in god as well as heaven, hell, sin, and the devil. For every 1,000 km (621 mi) closer a region is to the core of an earthquake zone, an active volcano, or a storm center, the percentage of people affirming these supernatural beliefs increases by about 10 percentile points. Such effects can be found on every continent and in most major religions.[8]

These psychological effects embed themselves in culturally transmitted beliefs and practices that persist across generations even after people migrate away from disaster-prone areas. When comparing second-generation immigrants who all grew up in the same European country, Jeanet still finds similar patterns: the adult children of immigrants are more religious when their moms came from places that were more exposed to natural disasters.[9]

War, like natural disasters, also increases people's religious commitments. Using the same approach just described to link war and social motivations, my collaborators and I analyzed survey data from Uganda, Sierra Leone, and Tajikistan (Central Asia) to study war's impact on religion. Our analysis shows that those who were more exposed to war were more likely to (1) join religious groups (e.g., churches or mosques), (2) attend rituals, and (3) rank their religious community as their most important group. Our data show not only that war experiences made people more likely to join voluntary organizations in general, but that these voluntary organizations were particularly likely to be religious ones. The effects are big: in both Uganda and Tajikistan, the experience of war doubles or triples the percentage of people participating in religious groups. Now, we don't have data on people's actual religious beliefs, but considering Jeanet's analysis, we suspect that war deepens people's beliefs in heaven, hell, sin, and the devil. However, even if war only increases ritual attendance (which our data do directly support), other research establishes that ritual attendance leads to deeper religious faith.[10]

The data on war and religion further suggest that these effects get stronger—not weaker—in postwar years. Of course, this trend can't continue indefinitely, but our data suggest that people's religious commitments can continue to deepen for at least 12 years after a conflict ends. This could happen for several reasons, but a big one is that when many people all get hit with the same shock at the same time, they will begin preferentially interacting with like-minded others by forming or joining religious organizations. The stronger commitments of those joining these groups will foster greater cooperation and success, which will then attract new members (usually the less committed) who will then acquire the beliefs and norms from those in their new group. This could gradually magnify the enduring psychological effects of shocks on religious faith in the years following a conflict or natural disaster.[11]

Taken together, this research suggests that the experience of war (1) motivates people to invest in their interdependent networks, which could be their clan, tribe, town, or religious community; (2) tightens their adherence to social norms; and (3) deepens their religious commitment. This means that war can create distinct psychological effects, depending upon an individual's group identity, social norms, and religious beliefs. For example, a war shock might bond some people more tightly to their tribe and others to their country; or, it might strengthen adherence to caste norms (which prescribe different attitudes to those from different castes); or, it might galvanize impersonal norms that prescribe fairness toward strangers; and, it might deepen a person's faith in a god that demands a universal morality or in an ancestor spirit who focuses on preserving an ancient patrilineage.

Tajikistan's civil war illustrates these effects. After the collapse of the Soviet Union, political fault lines fractured the collection of clans that compose the Tajik ethnolinguistic group—some Tajik clans supported the government, while others did not. In some communities, by pitting one clan or ethnic group against another, the war sparked simmering suspicions and sometimes conflict between neighbors. In this situation, the psychological impact of war strengthened clan solidarity and traditional kinship norms: those more exposed to the war expressed greater trust in their clan leaders (relative to government officials), stronger support for arranged marriages (a "venerable" clan custom), and more desire to know a merchant personally before conducting any business (relationships over impersonal commerce). The particulars of the political fault lines at the national level (clan vs. clan) influenced how the experience of civil conflict shaped people's psychology within their local communities. It's a good bet that if clans had long since vanished, arranged marriages were considered sinful, and commerce was founded on impersonal principles, then the psychological impacts of war would have been rather different.[12]

As we turn to examine the historical impact of war within Europe, keep the following in mind: psychologically, war tends to tighten our interdependent-network bonds, strengthen our commitments to important social norms, and deepen our religious devotion. These psychological shifts can facilitate the scaling up of human societies by, for example, empowering state-level institutions through greater trust, compliance, or public goods contributions (e.g., road brushing, voting, not taking bribes). However, war can also catalyze fractional differences between ethnic or religious groups within countries and generate a downward spiral in the ability of governments to function effectively. The course favored by societal evolution, when slammed by war shocks, depends on the details of group identity, the existing institutions (clans, chiefdoms, or autonomous cities), the most valued norms (e.g., clan loyalty or impersonal fairness), and specifically how people perceive "who" is on which side of the conflict.[13]

Europeans Made War, and War Made Them WEIRDer

After the collapse of the Carolingian Empire in the ninth century, Europe fragmented into hundreds of independent polities, ranging from the remnants of the old empire and the papal territories to independent cities and feudal lands controlled by warlords who fancied themselves nobles. The average size of these political units was small, something like modern El Salvador. There may not have been any entity that qualified as a "state," except for the Byzantine Empire. This fragmentation energized fierce intergroup competition. As polities do, they started fighting over territory, resources, and honor. At the same time, Viking raiders began sporadically sweeping in from the north to rape and pillage, while powerful Muslim armies pressed northward in Spain, Italy, and Turkey. As explained in Chapter 3, intergroup competition has long been the driving force in societal evolution. However, at the dawn of the High Middle Ages, a new pathway to societal complexity had opened because of the social and psychological impact of the Church's MFP during the Early Middle Ages.[14]

Propelling European societies down this blind alley, wars continued to rage in Europe for a millennium after the Carolingian collapse, until a relative peace developed after World War II. The historical sociologist and political scientist Charles Tilly estimates that between 1500 and 1800, European polities were at war during 80 to 90 percent of all years, and that things may have been even worse during the preceding 500 years. England alone was at war about half of the time from 1100 to 1900. This relentless intergroup conflict had the driving effect on societal evolution discussed in Chapter 3: European societies grew bigger, more powerful, and more complex; if they didn't, they got wiped out or swallowed up. Increasingly effective political and military institutions repeatedly emerged, competed, recombined, and spread at the expense of less effective configurations. Slowly, through this long and unusual selective process, territorial states eventually coalesced, constitutions (charters) were written at the national level, and larger-scale democratic experiments began.[15]

From the beginning, these wars drove rural populations into the protective embrace of towns and cities while fueling the construction of new weapons, castles, and defensive walls. However, in this new social context, endemic war did something more profound and long-lasting: it shocked people's psychology and thereby accelerated cultural evolution along a new pathway, one centered on individuals, voluntary associations, and impersonal interactions.

Of course, endemic warfare is practically business as usual in our species, and Europe certainly wasn't the first region to experience centuries of heart-wrenching conflict. But what was different is that by the 10th century, the Church and the MFP had pushed some populations into a new social and psychological space. Clans, lineages, and tribes had been demolished or at least dramatically weakened. Freed from the constraints and securities of kin-based institutions, people were seeking new voluntary relationships, associations, and communities. Within this social context, the shock of war would have had distinct psychological effects. As I showed above, war would have (1) fueled the formation of new voluntary social groups, while further strengthening existing associations; (2) bolstered the impersonal social norms of such associations; and (3) deepened people's religious commitments. Together, the social and psychological shifts induced by war exposure would have catalyzed the formation of new formal organizations, laws, and governments built to fit a more individualistic and impersonal psychology.

To understand this, let's consider war's psychological impacts on populations living in societies with intensive kin-based institutions. In such communities, the shock of war should tighten people's bonds to their extended kin networks and enduring relationships; deepen their commitments to ancestor gods or tribal deities; and strengthen their adherence to norms about being loyal to one's clan or kindred (nepotism), marrying cousins, and deferring to elders. In Tajikistan, as we saw, the shock of war raised people's trust in clan elders and bolstered support for arranged marriage. In Sierra Leone, war drove the formation of local defense forces built on traditional institutions. In the Sepik, Tuzin observed that warfare tightened both clan loyalties and people's devotion to their age-sets, ritual partners, and the Tambaran. In fact, the entire system may have been bound together by the psychological impacts of war: Ilahita's Tambaran collapsed in the decades after Sepik warfare was quashed by the Australian military.

Consider, too, ancient China. After a millennium of bloody warfare, the number of independent polities had gone from 120, in 1200 BCE, to just one stable state under the Western Han, in 206 BCE. By the end of this scaling-up process, the emperor and his lineage were endowed with the Mandate of Heaven—they were on a divine mission. This meant that they could make laws but were not subject to them. Elites operated as families and clans, not individuals, and were networked by intermarriage. Both power and privilege diffused and descended through the patrilineal tree. Commoners also relied on intensive kinship, although the elite worked to make sure their kin-based institutions never got too strong. Even the famous Confucians, who served as advisor-scholars to early Chinese emperors, originated from elite lineages.[16] Of course, the final contestants in this competition were making the transition from chiefdoms to states by introducing nonrelational institutions to mediate between the elite families and everyone else (Figure 3.3). And, as is so common, these norms either flowed directly out of the military (e.g., merit-based promotion) or were in the service of the military (e.g., conscription and taxes). However, along this highway—bulldozed by war—no town or city decided to endow its citizens with protected rights or draft a written charter establishing a representative assembly to debate local laws. Such ideas probably rarely occurred to anyone. And, even if they did, convincing others to accept them would have been challenging, given the way intensive kin-based institutions structure social incentives and generate psychological motivations favoring clan loyalty, deference to authority, devotion to tradition, and a contextualized, relational morality.[17]

By contrast, because they'd already been under the sway of the Church and the MFP for centuries, the communities that arose from the ashes of the Carolingian Empire followed a different path. The MFP had not only undermined kin-based institutions and favored nuclear families, but it had made it nearly impossible to reconstitute these ancient institutions. Instead, with Christianity's universal morality in the background, individuals joined voluntary associations like charter towns, confraternities, universities, guilds, and religious-military organizations (e.g., the Knights Templar), which often provided members with mutual aid (in case of injury), personal security, and an in-group identity. At the same time, market norms for impersonal exchange were spreading and gradually being inscribed into business contracts, commercial laws, and urban constitutions.

In this new context, by deepening people's commitments to their voluntary associations (including their towns), strengthening their norms of prosociality toward Christian strangers, and bolstering their religious faith, war shocks would have spurred the formation of new impersonal institutions (including those related to government and commerce), encouraged the adoption of laws centered on the individual, and motivated greater contributions to the public good at the level of urban communities and eventually nation-states.

Can we see these impacts of war in Europe over the last millennium in the historical record?

Well, while my lab is still working on ways to detect the historical impact of war on European psychology, we can indeed observe how war influenced the growth of urban areas, the formation of representative assemblies, and the development of self-governing cities. To start, let's consider the impact of local battles and sieges on the subsequent growth of cities. The economists Mark Dincecco and Massimiliano Gaetano Onorato compiled an impressive database of 847 battles and sieges, complete with dates and locations, which they then integrated with estimates of population sizes for cities with over 5,000 people for each century from 900 to 1800 CE. Figure 10.2 shows the distribution of these battles and sieges across time and space in Europe. Dincecco and Onorato asked: If a battle or siege occurred at or near a city during the preceding century, did the affected city grow relatively faster or slower in the next century?

Their analysis suggests that war *accelerated* urban growth. Specifically, exposure to a battle or siege during the preceding century raised the rate of urban growth by at least a quarter. If a city would have grown by 20 percent over a particular century, but a war hit, the city instead grew

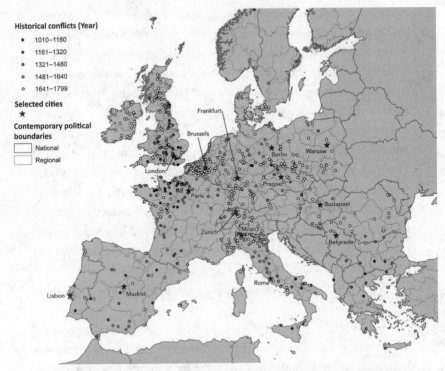

Historical conflicts (Year)
- ● 1010–1160
- ● 1161–1320
- ● 1321–1480
- ○ 1481–1640
- ○ 1641–1799

Selected cities
★

Contemporary political boundaries
☐ National
☐ Regional

FIGURE 10.2. The distribution of battles and sieges in Europe from 1000 to 1800. The darker dots represent battles or sieges earlier in time. I've included contemporary national boundaries for reference along with smaller regions.[18]

by 25 to 30 percent. Of course, prosperous cities might provide attractive targets for marauding armies (more plunder), but the results hold even when a city's prosperity at the beginning of the century is held constant. Since urban growth is closely tied to overall economic productivity, it seems that European wars drove economic prosperity (for those who survived).[19]

This is puzzling. Wars kill people and destroy wealth, buildings, bridges, crops, and much more. Given the gut-wrenching destructiveness of medieval armies, how could war generate urban growth and economic prosperity?[20]

In light of the psychological evidence presented above, European wars potentially did three different things. First, by stoking people's interdependence psychology, war would have solidified the bonds among members of voluntary associations, including the full citizenry of urban centers. It may have also expanded the membership of voluntary associations as people looked to expand their interdependent networks. War couldn't have bonded Europe's clans, tribes, or lineages, because these were mostly gone. Second, war would have strengthened the developing market norms and people's adherence to the city's explicit laws instead of empowering kin-based norms such as "respect your elders." Third, war would have deepened people's Christian faith (unless they were Jewish). This would have primed their sacred oaths, empowered local bishops, and further entrenched the MFP along with Christianity's universalizing morality (which may also have caused trouble for the aforementioned Jews—this morality wasn't all that universal yet).

The wars analyzed thus far only involved battles and sieges within Europe. There was, however, another series of wars involving Europeans during this period outside of Europe—the Crusades. The First Crusade began in 1096, when Pope Urban II called on his Latin Christians to aid their fellow (Orthodox) Christians in the Byzantine Empire and free the Holy Land from the Muslim "onslaught." Inspired by faith and fervor, many lords and knights began raising funds to assemble armies and buy weapons. Soon the nobility and their supporting casts became heavily engaged in these holy wars, which drew in participants from across the social strata. At first, the crusading armies were led by the sons and brothers of kings, but in later Crusades, the kings themselves sometimes took up arms and led. These armies were staffed by earls, sheriffs, dukes, and local landlords, who drafted their vassals and neighbors. Thus, elites and non-elites alike had family members in these wars, many of whom no doubt died or were injured—making them like the "more afflicted" people in our war studies. Based on the research presented above, the Crusades would have had predictable psychological effects.[21]

To assess the impact of the first four Crusades (the fourth ended in 1204), Lisa Blaydes and Christopher Paik compiled a database of elite crusaders, focusing on where they came from. By counting the number from each European polity, they fashioned a measure of "crusader-dosage" that captures the level of engagement in the Crusades for each polity, and presumably the degree of war exposure experienced by the populace at the time. Their analyses show that, in the wake of the Crusades, places that sent more crusaders to the Holy Land later (1) convened more representative assemblies, (2) gave more autonomy to urban areas, and (3) grew faster economically (based on urbanization) compared to polities that were less engaged in the wars. The effects were sizable. For each crusader who mobilized an army and went to war, the number of urban residents in his polity increased by between 1,500 and 3,000 people relative to a similar city without that military mobilization—this represents faster economic growth in urban areas that were more engaged in the Crusades.[22]

Importantly, the political scientists and economic historians who have documented the effects of war in Europe almost entirely ignore the lasting impact of war on psychology and culture. Instead, adhering to the norms of their academic disciplines, they try to connect war directly to economic growth or the formation and strengthening of state institutions. Usually, their explanations are based on war creating certain needs (e.g., better defenses, more revenue, etc.) or changing the costs and benefits of the choices faced by kings, popes, or dukes. Such considerations are often important, but the problem with all of these explanations is that they ignore two things. First, we already know that war affects people's psychology in enduring ways, even if they themselves weren't physically harmed. So, why would we ignore this when explaining long-term changes due to war in medieval Europe or anywhere else? Second, endemic warfare has been common across human societies; yet, as we discussed with reference to China, in most places war didn't push polities or cities toward urbanization, political independence, and representative assemblies or parliaments. War only does these things when it hits populations with a particular cultural psychology and social organization. For example, in the Islamic world, urbanization declined in the wake of the Crusades, and no autonomous cities or representative assemblies popped up. Tellingly, as one historian put it, "true urban autonomies would have been unthinkable" in the Islamic world. That's the point. Psychology, or "thinkability," makes all the difference in how people react to war and in the kinds of formal institutions they build in its wake.[23]

Later, after nation-states began to coalesce, wars would have helped solidify these polities, establish national identities among the populace, and strengthen national-level institutions. One interesting case of this, suggested by Winston Churchill, may be the Hundred Years' War. England and France fought a series of conflicts between 1337 and 1453. Changes in society and technology meant that these battles were fought by professional armies, staffed by men from the lower classes as well as by the highborn. Because the war persisted over more than a century, successive generations of English and French families across the social strata experienced the psychological effects of violent intergroup conflict while fighting for "England" or "France." Thus the Hundred Years' War may have made the English more "English" and the French more "French" in terms of people's social identities. Similarly, the United States went from a loose confederation of 13 independent colonies before the Revolutionary War to a single unified state with a strong federal government after the war—forged in the crucible of the Revolution, we became "Americans" instead of "Virginians" and "Pennsylvanians" (of course, the "we" here hadn't yet expanded to include most of the population).[24]

Along this new pathway, centuries of fierce military competition among diverse European polities drove the evolution of new weapons, strategies, and tactics as well as the military and state institutions that supported war. These institutions included military drill, professional armies, taxation through representative assemblies, state financing via public debt, and even (eventually) mandatory public schooling. Polities that resisted adopting any of these risked losing to the competition. Crucially, these institutions and practices all sprouted and grew in psychological soil that had been heavily fertilized with nascent impersonal norms, rising individual aspirations, and WEIRDer ways of thinking.[25]

Consider this. War is awful, but it may have some psychological effects that can, under the right conditions, promote the growth of cooperative institutions that allow societies to expand and prosper. Can cultural evolution figure out a way to extract the upside effects of this intergroup competition on people's psychology without all the downside—the suffering, destruction, and death?

Taming Intergroup Conflict

Spurred by the arrival of ATMs, phone banking, and new credit-scoring systems, U.S. states began to deregulate their banking sectors in the late 1970s. Prior to this, each new bank had to obtain a charter from its home state. These charters constrained the growth of banks, suppressed the opening of new branches, prevented banks from crossing state lines, and generally limited competition among banks. The new regulations—the "deregulations"— ended local banking monopolies, reduced inefficiencies, and, most important for our story, substantially increased the availability of credit. Credit fueled the creation of new businesses and thereby intensified the competition among firms across the economy, from construction and services to manufacturing and technology.[26]

The way this deregulatory process played out at the state level furnishes a natural experiment that allows us to ask: Does increasing the competition among firms influence people's psychology in ways that parallel those created by the violent forms of intergroup competition discussed above? Could it drive up impersonal trust or cooperation? Regulatory changes in the banking sector were implemented in different states in different years over a few decades based largely on idiosyncratic political factors. That is, they were administered quasi-randomly, at least in relation to a state's trust levels and the intensity of interfirm competition; so, we can think of them as experimental "treatments" that intensified interfirm competition. By comparing the changes in trust levels of states in "treated" (deregulated) vs. "untreated" states over time, we can assess the impact of intergroup competition on impersonal trust.

More specifically, the creation of new firms, sparked by the greater availability of credit generated by deregulation, should have increased interfirm competition broadly across the economy in each state (not just in the banking sector). Under this increased competition, firms that were better at motivating employees to work more cooperatively and efficiently would have stood a better chance of surviving, prospering, and then being copied by other firms. To the degree that the practices, policies, organizational structures, attitudes, and managerial approaches of the more successful firms could be imitated or otherwise acquired (and potentially improved upon), firms across the economy would have—on average—evolved to become more cooperative. However, because growing firms often hire residentially and relationally mobile individuals, greater interfirm competition should strengthen impersonal prosociality, not social embeddedness and *interpersonal* prosociality. As more people spend much of their day in more cooperative environments, governed by impartial norms, they should become generally more cooperative and trusting with anonymous others, even outside of work. Of course, these psychological shifts can reverberate outward across our social webs, as those psychologically affected by intergroup competition interact with and influence others.[27]

This is an interesting story, but is it true? Many believe that all forms of competition turn people into greedy, self-centered connivers. Could cultural evolution really have devised a way to embed a domesticated form of intergroup competition within our economic system? I'm calling this form of intergroup competition (or interfirm competition) "domesticated," because cultural evolution appears to have tamed the "wild" form of intergroup conflict (war), which is often deadly, and built it into modern institutions in ways that can harness its social and psychological effects.

To study whether competition among firms or other voluntary associations could really drive up prosociality, the economists Patrick Francois, Thomas Fujiwara, and Tanguy van Ypersele compiled a database with three key variables. First, they obtained data on the year when each U.S. state deregulated its banking sector. Second, to measure the intensity of interfirm competition, they gathered data on both the entry of new firms and the closure of older firms for each year in each U.S. state. Greater competition should be marked by the entry of more new firms—fresh competitors—and the "death" of older, unsuccessful firms. At the extreme, a monopoly has no competition, so no firms enter or depart. These two measures permit us to confirm whether the banking deregulations did indeed increase inter-firm competition. Third, to measure impersonal trust, they compiled all the available data on responses to the Generalized Trust Question from 1973 to 1994 for most U.S. states (Figure 1.7 maps the GTQ). Recall that the GTQ asks, "Generally speaking, would you say that most people can be trusted or that you can't be too careful in dealing with people?"[28]

Figure 10.3 plots the time trends for changes in the two measures of intergroup competition—firm entries and exits—along with changes in impersonal trust as measured by the percentage of people who are "generally trusting" on the GTQ. Although different states deregulated in different years, we can plot them all together by setting the year of deregulation as "Year 0" and measuring changes in interfirm competition and impersonal trust relative to their values in Year 0. To the right of Year 0 in Figure 10.3, we see how the intensity of competition changed for each year after deregulation. To the left of Year 0, we are looking at the years leading up to deregulation. A −2 on the horizontal axis means two years prior to deregulation, while a 2 indicates two years after deregulation. The vertical axis on the left side gives the increase or decrease in the percentage of people saying "most people can be trusted" *relative* to Year 0. Similarly, the vertical axis on the right side gives the change in the number of firms (per 100 people) entering or exiting the state's economy relative to Year 0.

Strikingly, while prior to deregulation both trust and interfirm competition are stable, intergroup competition seems to step on an escalator as soon as deregulation hits. A few years later, impersonal trust gets on the same escalator. After about a decade, trust levels are over 12 percentile points higher on average in states that deregulated. So, if 50 percent of people in a state thought "most people could be trusted" in the year of deregulation, then after about a decade, 62 percent or more thought so. I've cut the plot off after 10 years, but the data suggest that these upward trends continued for at least another five years. This further suggests that the greater interfirm

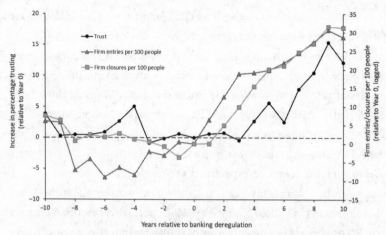

FIGURE 10.3. The relationship between the year of banking deregulation and both interfirm competition and impersonal trust. The horizontal axis plots time before and after the year of banking deregulation (Year 0). The left vertical axis is the change in the percentage of people who think "most people can be trusted" on the GTQ relative to the percentage in Year 0. The right vertical axis is the change in the number of firm entries or closures (per 100 people) relative to that number in Year 0. The firm entry and exit values are logged. The pattern suggests that banking regulation increased the intensity of intergroup competition, which in turn drove up impersonal trust.[29]

competition induced by banking deregulations pushed up people's levels of impersonal trust.[30]

Patrick and his team worried that the apparent effect of banking deregulation on impersonal trust might be idiosyncratic to the United States or specific to the era when most deregulations occurred, the 1980s and 1990s. To address this, the trio analyzed data from Germany that tracked people from 2003 to 2013, a period that ran right through the 2008 economic crash. These data allowed them to trace the impersonal trust of the same individuals as they changed jobs, sometimes moving from one sector or industry of the economy to another. Using data on the competitiveness of 50 different German industries, Patrick's team asked a simple question: What happens to a person's trust when they move from an industry with stronger interfirm competition to one with weaker competition? Remember, we are following the *same individuals through time*.

The results of this analysis reveal that when people move into a more competitive industry, their impersonal trust tends to go up. The results imply that if people move from a hypothetical industry in which three firms divide up the market into one in which four firms divide it up, they will be about 4 percentile points more likely to say "most people can be trusted" on the GTQ. But, when they move into a less competitive industry, their trust goes down (on average). As expected, if they don't move industries or move into a similarly competitive industry, their trust remains about the same. Here, just as in the United States, increasing interfirm competition changes people's psychology by strengthening norms about impersonal prosociality.

Patrick and his team, however, were still not satisfied, so they turned to the economics laboratory, where they could study the impact of raising intergroup competition under controlled experimental conditions. At the Paris School of Economics, they randomly assigned participants—French undergraduates—to either a standard noncompetitive Public Goods Game or to a parallel competitive version of the game. In the standard PGG, participants were teamed with a different anonymous individual for each of 19 rounds. In each round, they were endowed with 10 euros (about $14) and given the opportunity to contribute any portion of this money to a joint project with their partner. Whatever money they contributed to the project was increased by 50 percent (multiplied by 1.5) and then shared equally between the pair. The pair makes the most money when both participants give all 10 euros to the project; but, of course, everyone has a financial incentive to contribute less, and thereby make more money by free-riding on the contributions of their partner. Notably, each anonymous pair played together only once, so it made no rational sense to contribute in the early rounds in hopes of persuading one's partner to give more later.[31]

The competitive version involves the same setup as the PGG above, with paired partners having one opportunity to contribute to a group project before getting randomly re-paired. The key difference was that each team only got to keep the proceeds of their joint contributions to the project if the sum of their contributions *equaled or exceeded* the joint contributions of the pair they were competing with. If you contribute 3 euros and your partner gives 5, that's 8, which grows to 12 in the joint project. In the standard PGG, you'd get 6 euros back from the 12 in the project. However, in the competitive game, you'd only get that 6 euros back from your investment if your competition—the other team—made contributions that tallied to 8 euros or less (before the 50 percent increase). The question is, how do French undergraduates respond to the intergroup competition created by the competitive game?

Figure 10.4 shows the average contributions in each game across the 19 rounds. Without intergroup competition, participants initially contributed only about 3 euros and then their subsequent contributions began sliding toward zero. However, with greater intergroup competition in the competitive game, participants facultatively raised their contributions in round 1 (by 1.6 euros), perhaps anticipating the behavior of others, and then

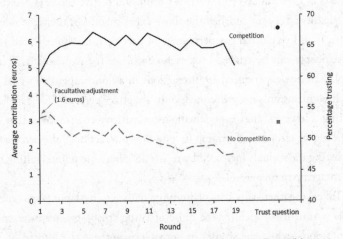

FIGURE 10.4. Average contributions to the group project (a public good) in competitive and noncompetitive versions of the Public Goods Game. The horizontal axis shows the round of the game, and the left vertical axis gives the mean contribution for each round. The percentage of participants at the end of each game who said that "most people can be trusted" in reply to the Generalized Trust Question is plotted on the far right and linked to the right vertical axis.[32]

further increased their contributions over about five rounds before leveling off for the remainder of the game. By the final five rounds of the game, the effect of intergroup competition on cooperation in these one-off interactions had generated a substantial difference: participants in the competitive world were contributing nearly three times as much to the group project (a public good) as those in the world without intergroup competition.[33]

It's not just the French. The impact of intergroup competition in laboratory experiments on cooperation has been observed in a variety of WEIRD populations. Perhaps the most potent way to induce cooperation in PGGs is to combine intergroup competition with opportunities for players to engage in costly punishment. The presence of intergroup competition seems to motivate WEIRD cooperators to immediately "pulverize" (with monetary deductions) anyone who tries free-riding. This quickly brings them into line and effectively drives cooperation up to near its maximum value.[34]

The problem with this earlier work was that we couldn't be totally sure how cooperation in experiments like the Public Goods Game was related to the GTQ. To address this, Patrick's team simply gave the GTQ to their participants after they finished the above experiment. On the right side of Figure 10.4, I've plotted the percentage of participants who reported that "most people can be trusted" for each version of the experiment. When people had just experienced 19 interactions in a noncompetitive world, in which cooperation slowly declined, only about 53 percent were generally trusting. However, after experiencing a competitive environment that induced higher rates of cooperation (in one-shot interactions), the percentage of trusting individuals increased by nearly 15 percentile points, taking the percentage up to 68 percent.[35]

Taken together, this trio of findings nails it. The laboratory experiments permit us to identify the cause of rising trust—greater intergroup competition—while the studies in both Germany and the United States permit us to see these effects at work in real economies and on the broader population.

Do these findings generalize beyond WEIRD people? I suspect that this form of benign intergroup competition is especially well suited to relationally mobile populations with an individualistic psychology and norms for impersonal prosociality. In societies where sociality remains firmly grounded in interpersonal relationships, greater intergroup competition might galvanize clans, family businesses, or Mafia organizations while tightening relationship-based norms instead of those linked to impersonal prosociality. In short, to get the effects shown above for intergroup competition, a population probably needs relatively strong norms for impersonal prosociality relative to norms rooted in intensive kinship or a relational morality. So, it would be a mistake to immediately extend these findings too broadly without considering the cultural-psychological background of the populace.[36]

Nevertheless, this research suggests that nonviolent forms of intergroup competition generate some of the same effects on our psychology as war and can drive cultural evolution in similar ways. There are, of course, important differences. Most benign forms of intergroup competition probably do not deepen people's religious faith or inspire ritual attendance because there is no threat to life and limb.

Remember, we need to conceptually separate *intergroup competition* from *within-group competition*. As we've seen, intergroup competition favors beliefs, practices, customs, motivations, and policies that promote the success of groups in competition with other groups. Thus, intergroup competition often promotes trust, cooperation, and the efficient allocation of pay to employees (e.g., CEOs aren't overpaid). Of course, elevated levels of intergroup competition are also what drive firms to exploit workers in foreign lands and trash the environment. By contrast, within-group competition is the competition among individuals, or small coalitions, that occurs within firms, organizations, or other groups. This form of competition favors the spread of behaviors, beliefs, motivations, practices, etc., that promote the success of individuals within a firm *relative* to others at the same firm. These are practices that benefit some employees at the expense of the firm. When CEOs conspire to get higher salaries for themselves and other executives while playing golf with members of the board of directors, that's within-group competition, and it usually hurts the firm. But, within-group competition is also not entirely unproductive. At moderate levels, it can inspire diligence and productivity.[37]

This means that modern companies, like ancient societies and chiefly institutions, eventually implode in the absence of intergroup competition. Norms and institutions, of course, provide some stability and can inhibit or suppress rampant self-interest for a time. But, eventually individuals and co-alitions within firms or other organizations, especially monopolies, devise ways to exploit the system to benefit themselves. Visionary founders, like great national leaders, might prevent this for a time, but the unfortunate per-sistence of death guarantees that their influence is constrained in the long run.

IN POLITICS, SOCIETY, AND RELIGION

With all this as background, we can now better understand the mod-ern world by recognizing that domesticated forms of intergroup competi-tion have insinuated themselves into WEIRD economic, political, and social systems in several ways. We've just seen how firm-level competition operates in the economic sphere and how this shapes impersonal prosociality. In the political realm, multiparty democracies also harness the power of intergroup competition. All political parties, were they to become the single governing party in a country, would eventually fall into corruption, collusion, and cro-nyism. If this somehow didn't happen over decades, it would certainly hap-pen over generations. However, faced with competitors and well-functioning democratic institutions, political parties must vie for members and votes. As long as individuals can switch their parties or their votes, the competition among parties will tend to spread practices, beliefs, and values that pro-mote a party's success in attracting members and votes. Of course, in no way does this guarantee a healthy political system; but, it at least inhibits the oth-erwise inevitable slide into despotism, polarization, and dysfunction.

Intergroup competition has also embedded itself in society through team sports, religious groups (e.g., churches), and other voluntary associa-tions. Participation in team sports such as ice hockey and soccer provides many children and adolescents with their first experience of intergroup competition, which may have lasting psychological effects. As adults, people emotionally attach themselves to professional or collegiate teams linked to their cities, regions, countries, or favorite universities. The power of this effect became intuitive for me when, as a student at the University of Notre Dame, I'd experience the entire campus rise in exuberance or collapse in sorrow throughout the fall football season, depending on whether our team—the Fightin' Irish—won or lost on a particular Saturday. This shared experience seemed to create a collective sense of meaning and greater solidarity among the student body. While some research does support my intuitions, high-quality studies that effectively isolate the long-term psychological impact of team sports on fans and players are limited.[38]

Like political parties, religious organizations also compete for members, as individuals and families in many societies will readily switch their churches, temples, or even traditions. Some churches grow and spread while others shrink and disappear. In the United States, the centrality of religious freedom and the lack of a state religion may have combined with our porous social safety nets, especially in some states, to fuel over two centuries of intense competition among religious organizations. These patterns suggest that America's unusually high levels of religious devotion, including beliefs in biblical literalism, angels, and hell, is the consequence of intense interchurch competition. Think of contemporary American evangelical churches, which the United States has been exporting across the world since World War II, as the religious equivalent of Walmart or McDonald's.[39]

The differing effects of intergroup vs. within-group competition help us understand why "competition" has both positive and negative connotations. Unregulated and unmonitored, firms facing intense intergroup competition will start violently sabotaging each other while exploiting the powerless. We know this because it has happened repeatedly over many centuries, and continues today. Nevertheless, when properly yoked, moderate levels of nonviolent intergroup competition can strengthen impersonal trust and cooperation. Similarly, extreme forms of within-group competition encourage selfish behavior, envy, and zero-sum thinking. Yet when disciplined by intergroup competition, moderate levels of within-group competition can inspire perseverance and creativity.

When and Why?

To better understand the origins of WEIRD prosociality, we need to examine the emergence of sustained forms of nonviolent intergroup competition, and how and why they became embedded in so many modern Western institutions.

In the wake of the Church's demolition of intensive kinship, people became increasingly individualistic, independent, self-focused, nonconformist, and relationally mobile. They joined voluntary associations that fit their interests, needs, and goals. Guilds, cities, universities, confraternities, churches, and monasteries during the High and Late Middle Ages competed for members—for skilled artisans, savvy lawyers, successful merchants, smart students, prosperous parishioners, and pious monks. Later, states would compete for the best immigrants, intellectuals, craftsmen, engineers, and arms manufacturers. Those dissatisfied with their current organization could move to another group or even start their own association. Successful associations were those that could attract and retain the highest quality and quantity of members.[40]

The intensity of benign intergroup competition in the Middle Ages can be observed in the proliferation of four kinds of competing voluntary associations: cities, monasteries, guilds, and universities. We've already seen the expansion of new urban incorporations in Figure 9.7, and the historical record amply demonstrates the ability of people to favor some European cities over others by voting with their feet. For monasteries, Figure 10.5 shows the broad picture from the 6th to the 15th century. While the number of monasteries had been rising throughout the Early Middle Ages, their proliferation accelerated in the 10th century. In 909, for example, Benedictine monks at Cluny Abbey (France) gained greater independence, reformed their practices, and reorganized their communities. The changes at Cluny, which included stricter monastic discipline, led to the rapid sprouting of new Cluniac communities throughout the 10th and 11th centuries. By this time, the genie was out of the bottle, and new groups of like-minded individuals parted ways with the Cluniacs and struck out on their own, armed

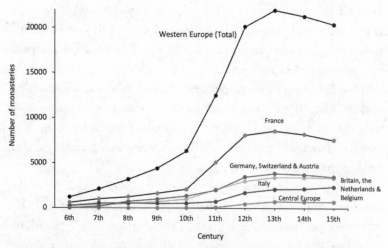

FIGURE 10.5. Growth in the number of monasteries from the 6th century to the 15th century in western Europe as a whole and separately for five different subregions.[41]

with only a shared vision for how to best inspire piety, serve God, and manage a religious community. The best practices of the most successful monasteries were copied and modified by new monasteries. Those with the most effective and popular practices eventually grew into sprawling transnational monastic orders; others floundered and disappeared.[42]

The Cluniacs met their match in 1098, when a pious monk named Robert walked out of a renowned abbey with 20 of his fellow monks. Setting up shop in a remote forest village in eastern France, they started a new religious community built on deep piety, hard work, self-sufficiency, and self-denial. Following their Cluniac forebearers, they set up a hierarchical system that permitted organic growth, as "mother" houses could spawn and nurture "daughter" houses. To organize this, they wrote a charter that made each new abbey independent and largely self-governing, but still unified hierarchically with the rest of the order and subject in some ways to the mother house. Unlike those at Cluny, abbots were democratically elected by their brethren from within their houses. This, the Cistercian Order, spread across Europe, from Bohemia to Ireland, eventually counting 750 houses at its apex in the 15th century. By then, however, the mobile preacher monks of the Dominicans and Franciscans were in ascendency and would eventually outcompete the Cistercians.[43]

Now, if you are thinking, *Monasteries . . . really, who cares about a bunch of monks?* hang on. We'll return to these monks when we discuss the origins of Protestantism, the work ethic, the moral value of manual labor, and technological innovation. Monks are surprisingly important (though if you are a monk, perhaps this isn't so surprising).[44]

Trailing the monasteries by a century or two, the number of guilds also rose dramatically during the High and Late Middle Ages. Figure 10.6A shows the rapid rise in the number of guilds in the British Isles, which occurred largely in the expanding towns and cities of England. These guilds included associations of merchants, clerks, smiths, shepherds, skinners, brewers, and practitioners of many other trades, along with purely religious fraternities. In addition to organizing and regulating groups' shared economic interests, guilds typically provided mutual aid to members, arbitrated disputes, and disciplined antisocial behavior (e.g., theft); they even helped members get into heaven (purportedly). During some eras and in some places, every adult in a town or city was a member of some guild, either directly or through a spouse.

The competition among guilds led to the diffusion of better ways to attract members, foster solidarity, and motivate adherence to guild rules. Guilds likely learned from each other, and recombined different approaches to decision-making, organizational structure, leadership, and punishment. My favorite example involves a motivational technique. Guild members who broke the rules were fined, repeatedly if necessary, and then eventually kicked out if they didn't fall in line. Guilds also managed to harness beliefs about purgatory to both attract members and inspire their compliance with rules. As a privilege of membership, the guild prayed as a community for the souls of deceased members. Prayers from large numbers of people, preferably the virtuous, could reduce a sinner's purgatorial suffering and speed them along to heaven. Such a piece of cultural engineering would have not

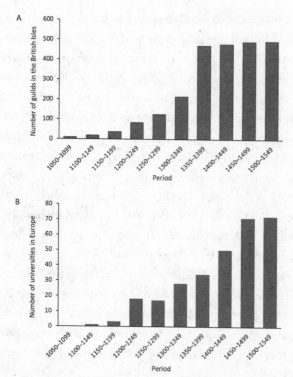

FIGURE 10.6. The top panel (A) shows the number of guilds in the British Isles from 1050 to 1550, while the lower panel (B) displays the number of universities in Europe from 1100 to 1550.[45]

only attracted new members—by providing an HOV lane to heaven—but also equipped the guild with its own supernatural carrot-and-stick policy: "Shape up, or you can suffer in purgatory for a few extra centuries." (If you're skeptical that a person's beliefs about the afterlife can influence their behavior in important ways, please reread Chapter 4.)[46]

Universities also spread rapidly during the Middle Ages, as illustrated in Figure 10.6B. Those in Bologna and Paris provided the two models, from which norms, rules, and policies were adopted, modified, and recombined in creating new universities. As you'll recall, the University of Bologna was founded when students formed an association to hire their own teachers and represent themselves to city officials. In contrast, the University of Paris developed as teachers essentially unionized—forming a guild—in response to the efforts by the bishop and other local religious authorities to interfere in their instruction (professors still hate that). These professors had long insisted on setting their own standards, curricula, syllabi, and examinations, but now they did it as an egalitarian community instead of as individuals. New universities sometimes sprang up when disgruntled students and teachers departed their current university in protest and organized a new institution in a nearby urban center. The University of Bologna gave rise to many such daughter universities in the surrounding Italian communities, though many of these were short-lived. Similarly, through such birth pangs, the University of Oxford delivered its twin in Cambridge in 1209.

A century later, the Church and various ruling elites would begin to charter universities, though these were still largely built on the original models. Papal decisions gave universities, including their student bodies and even professors, a great deal of autonomy and independence. Renowned teachers could move to obtain the best deals, higher pay, job security, and intellectual freedom. Students, too, could select among universities, and as members they were often exempt from local laws (which didn't endear them to the locals).[47]

It's worth noting that both guilds and universities grew rapidly in the 14th century, during a time when the Black Death (bubonic plague) was decimating European populations. The Black Death wiped out 30–60 percent of the population. This suggests that the growth of these voluntary associations didn't reflect population growth but continued despite a population *decline*. This may have occurred in part because the Black Death shocked people's psychology in ways that parallel the effects of war discussed in the last chapter. Such psychological shocks would have strengthened the solidarity of voluntary associations and spurred less connected individuals and nuclear families to seek out the mutual aid, communal support, and the supernatural comforts of Europe's proliferating voluntary associations.

Other societies also developed institutions of higher education, but they had a different psychology behind them. In the Islamic world, for example, madrassas were the most important of these institutions. Each was formed by a charitable endowment for the study of one brand of Islamic law and remained tightly tied to the founder's original vision. Madrassas were also legally regulated, ensuring that nothing inimical to Islam was explored. This means that the great advances delivered by Muslim scientists occurred on the side, when no one was paying attention (which makes these achievements even more impressive). Madrassas, then, unlike their counterparts in medieval Europe, weren't run by an ever-shifting cast of scrappy professors and rebellious students who banded together in self-regulating collectives to demand intellectual freedom, uphold standards, and set curricula.[48]

Overall, the spontaneous formation and proliferation of voluntary organizations capable of self-governance and self-regulation—as illustrated by charter towns, monasteries, guilds, and universities—is one of the hallmarks of European populations in the second millennium. In light of the contemporary psychological evidence, we can infer that the competition among these organizations likely influenced people's motivations, preferences, and social interactions.[49]

DIFFERENT PSYCHOLOGY, DIFFERENT EFFECTS

Western Europe is not unique in harnessing benign forms of intergroup competition. It emerges in many societies and has been harnessed to promote greater sociality.[50] However, the intergroup competition among Europe's guilds, universities, and other associations was different because of its ubiquity as well as how it interacted with people's psychology and institutions. To understand why, remember that people in most places grow up enmeshed in social networks rooted in intensive kinship. They can't easily move their relationships or residences to join new social groups or pledge their lives to them. And even when they can join such associations, their social ties, motivations, moral commitments, and ways of seeing the world still tend to keep them anchored in their inherited, kin-based communities and relational networks. Of course, kin-based groups or inherited communities can benignly compete, but members can't "switch teams" or easily recruit new members if they want to. So, competition among such groups might only further accentuate their divisions, by more tightly binding people to their clans and regulated-relational norms. In this situation, intergroup competition could lower impersonal trust instead of raising it.

To see this, consider how the dismantling of China's collective farms in the early 1980s influenced social life and intergroup competition in the rice belt (Figure 7.5). Once land and businesses could be privately owned or controlled, competition among groups was possible once again. In rural areas, Chinese clans immediately began reconstituting themselves, rejuvenating their communal rituals, repairing their ancestral shrines, and updating their lineage genealogies, which define membership. After a 30-year hiatus, clans soon were competing over land and access to economic opportunities, especially in multiclan villages. The dominant clans in such villages targeted members of the smaller clans, by ostracizing them and sometimes denying them access to fertile fields (which is a big deal if you're a farmer). This led the households of smaller clans to pursue *hui laojia*—a return to one's ancestral village. Leaving their lifelong homes, couples returned, not to the places of their birth, but to villages that their parents, grandparents, or even more distant ancestors had left long ago—villages where *their clan* was dominant.[51]

This clannish behavior paid off. Based on a survey of 366 villages in the mid-1990s, the more a village was dominated by a single clan, the greater the number of private businesses, and the larger the workforce at each business. These effects were big. If the largest clan's share of a village's population increased by 10 percent (say, from 20 to 30 percent), the number of private businesses increased by a third, and the average size of the workforce increased by a quarter. Further, villages with more dominant clans were also better at holding public officials accountable and furnishing public goods such as irrigation works. To understand the implications here, flip things around: communities of mostly unrelated households struggled to open businesses, hire employees, provide public goods, and hold local government officials accountable. This is because, of course, Chinese use "strong ties" and rely on relational embeddedness to find employees, gather information, influence politicians, motivate cooperative labor, and make professional connections.

Unlike people in the MFP-dosed regions of medieval Europe, rural Chinese in the late 20th century didn't spontaneously create myriad voluntary associations of like-minded strangers. Instead, people reaffirmed links to their ancestral homes, strengthened their clan affiliations, and spontaneously re-formed exclusive groups built on the virtues of kin-based loyalty (nepotism). This occurred even though the Chinese government had tried to disband the clans, in part by burning their genealogies, in the 1950s.

Harnessing the Power of Competition

The persistent competition among polities drove the embedding of benign forms of intergroup competition within Europe's economic, political, and social institutions. This accelerated during the latter half of the second millennium, when the most prosperous states were those that "figured out" (consciously or not) how to foster and control healthy competition among voluntary associations. In the economic sphere, guilds slowly gave way to a variety of partnerships and eventually to joint stock companies. In most cases, the entrepreneurs and new associations were well ahead of governments and lawmakers in trying out new ways of sharing risk, transferring ownership, and limiting liability. Stock exchanges, for example, began to take shape in Amsterdam, Antwerp, and London in the 16th and 17th centuries. In London, stock traders were not permitted in the Royal Exchange, due to their poor manners, so they set up shop in a nearby coffeehouse. When their chalkboard lists of disreputable traders no longer sufficed, they created an association of stockbrokers that set professional standards and kicked the untrustworthy types out of the café. A century later, the seed of the New York Stock Exchange would also take root in a coffee shop (and tavern), at the corner of Wall Street and Water Street (coffee shops are like monasteries; they play an unexpectedly influential role in the emergence of the modern world). Stock exchanges permitted companies to find investors and spurred competition among firms for capital investment. New laws and regulations would eventually consolidate the gains of centuries of unintended experimentation by many different associations and societies.[52]

In the political sphere, where the guilds had often dominated, individuals who agreed on policy began forming political parties in 17th-century England. These parties competed to persuade the populace, influence government decisions, and gain greater representation. In the United States, the founding fathers largely despised political parties and consequently made no provision for them in the U.S. Constitution. Nevertheless, political parties spontaneously formed and soon dominated the political scene. Thus, the centrality of political parties to the American system is an interesting case in which the architects of the formal institutions deeply misunderstood how and why their system would eventually function (or fail to function, as is the case in the 21st-century United States).[53]

In the social sphere, the development of team sports and sports leagues placed nonviolent intergroup competition at the center of people's leisure time, where it often became part of their personal identity. Participation in team sports became central to raising children (well, at least boys). After defeating Napoleon at Waterloo, the Duke of Wellington explained that the "battle was won on the playing fields of Eton," by which he meant that the character of British officers was honed on the anvil of sport. Interestingly, cricket, rugby, hockey, soccer (football), American football, and baseball all trace their roots back to preindustrial England. The latter two American sports derive, respectively, from rugby and English folk games, including the children's game of rounders and stoolball. Of course, today, Matsigenka enjoy soccer, Fijians rugby, Japanese baseball, and Indians cricket.[54]

My point is that our modern institutional frameworks incorporate various forms of intergroup competition that drive up people's inclinations to trust and cooperate with strangers and may influence other aspects of our psychology. People learn to work in ad hoc teams, even if those teams are composed of a bunch of strangers. The engine of intergroup competition pushes against the within-group forces of cultural evolution, which often favor self-interest, zero-sum thinking, collusion, and nepotism. Our WEIRD institutional frameworks began developing during the High Middle Ages, as people who were increasingly individualistic, independent, nonconformist, and analytic started assorting themselves into voluntary associations, which in turn began to compete. In the long run, competition among territorial states favored those that developed ways to harness and embed the psychological and economic effects of nonviolent intergroup competition. Of course, no one designed this system, and few even realize how it shapes our psychology or why it often works.

11

Market Mentalities

Whenever commerce is introduced into any country, probity and
punctuality always accompany it . . . Of all the nations in Europe, the
Dutch, the most commercial, are the most faithful to their word.
The English are more so than the Scotch, but much inferior to the
Dutch, and in the remote parts of this country they [are] far less so
than in the commercial parts of it. This is not at all to be imputed
to national character, as some pretend. There is no natural reason
why an Englishman or a Scotchman should not be as punctual in
performing agreements as a Dutchman . . . A dealer is afraid of losing
his character, and is scrupulous in observing every engagement . . .
When the greater part of people are merchants, they always bring
probity and punctuality into fashion, and these, therefore, are the
principal virtues of a commercial nation.

—Adam Smith (1766), "Of the Influence of Commerce on Manners"[1]

They first appeared in 13th-century northern Italy, in cities like Milan,
Modena, and Parma, but quickly diffused to England, Germany, France, and
the Low Countries. In combination with bell towers, they synchronized the
activities of everyone within earshot, telling them when to wake, work, and
eat; they also dictated the commencement of public meetings, court proceedings, and local markets. These, the first mechanical clocks, increasingly took
center stage in late medieval cities around Europe, adorning town halls, market squares, and cathedrals. Like an epidemic disease, mechanical clocks spread
quickly from one urban center to another as towns and cities imitated the

clocks built by their bigger and more successful competitors. Towns explicitly commissioned famous artisans to furnish clocks that were equal to or better than the ones in—variously—Venice, Breslau, Paris, and Pisa. Clocks also infected monasteries and churches, and began dictating to the monks, priests, and parishioners when to labor, dine, and worship. Public clocks became symbols of an orderly urban life and strict religious devotion. By 1450, 20 percent of urban centers with 5,000 or more people had at least one public clock, and by 1600 most churches had a clock.[2]

The spread of public clocks provides a visible historical marker for the emergence of WEIRD time psychology. If you've spent time in Amazonia, Africa, Oceania, or a wide range of other places, you've no doubt noticed the most obvious feature of WEIRD time psychology: an obsession with time thrift. Unlike my Fijian friends, I always feel like time is in short supply. I'm always trying to "save time," "make time," or "find time." All day long, I'm tracking the clock because I need to be on time for my next meeting, appointment, or day-care pickup. By contrast, my Fijian friends and field assistants just can't get into this *clock-time mind-set*, even when I provide both technological aids and direct financial incentives. Early on, when I began managing research projects in the Pacific, I purchased digital watches for all of my research assistants, hoping this might help them be on time for meetings, interviews, and meals. But, this didn't help. They seemed to enjoy wearing the watches, perhaps as a fashion statement, but they almost never thought to actually look at the time. Once, while working on a laptop with a particularly eager research assistant, I looked down at the watch I'd given him to check the hour. I immediately knew the watch was wrong because it disagreed by too much with my own mental clock. His watch turned out to be 25 minutes slow, and we suspected that it had been wrong for weeks.

To measure time thrift, the psychologists Ara Norenzayan and Robert Levine developed a couple of techniques that they applied in 31 cities. In the metropolitan hubs of these cities, their team first discreetly timed people as they walked along major avenues. The idea is that people who are worried about time thrift walk faster. As you might expect, New Yorkers and Londoners blazed along the sidewalks, covering a mile in less than 18 minutes.

Meanwhile, in Jakarta and Singapore, people strolled along at a reasonable pace, taking almost 22 minutes on average to cover a mile. This means that New Yorkers and Londoners were walking at least 30 percent faster than folks in the slower-paced cities. Figure 11.1 shows that urbanites in more individualistic countries tend to walk faster than those in less individualistic countries. This relationship holds even when we statistically control for differences in the size of cities.

To assess time thrift in a second way, the team went to downtown post offices in each city and randomly selected at least eight postal clerks for a stamp purchase. Using a protocol designed to minimize the influence of all factors except for the clerk's pace, they secretly measured the time necessary to complete the transaction. Again, the more individualistic the country, the faster the clerk delivered the stamps. These data suggest that, even when comparing only people working in urban cores, those from more individualistic societies are more worried about time—about running out of it, saving it, or spending it "productively" (whatever that means). Thus, it seems that time thrift is embedded in the individualism complex and pops up in all kinds of ways.[3]

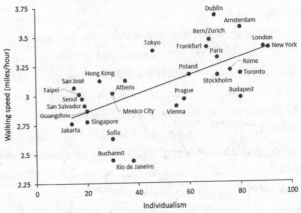

FIGURE 11.1. Relationship between walking speed (miles per hour) and our omnibus measure of individualism (mapped in Figure 1.2) for large cities in 28 countries around the world. Urbanites from more individualistic societies walk faster.[4]

Where does the global variation in time thrift come from?

Much historical evidence, including data on the diffusion of mechanical clocks, suggests that this new time psychology had begun to ferment by the Late Middle Ages, likely from a mélange of individualism, self-focus, and analytic thinking that was brewing in the market towns, monasteries, and free cities of Europe. In these social worlds, achieving personal success and building relationships required individuals to invest in their own attributes and skills while at the same time getting stuff done—stacking up individual achievements. Facing greater impersonal competition, artisans, merchants, monks, and magistrates all aimed to cultivate reputations for punctuality, self-discipline, and precision. The new mechanical clocks didn't initiate the shift toward a clock-time psychology in Europe; rather, they simply marked and catalyzed processes that were already underway. Before the clock, and later alongside it, monks used candles of fixed lengths to time their prayers while teachers, preachers, and builders used hourglasses to fix the lengths of their lectures, sermons, and lunch breaks.

This change in how people thought about time was much broader than simply an obsession with time thrift. Before the High Middle Ages, each "day"—the period from sunrise to sunset—was broken down into 12 hours. However, since the time between sunrise and sunset varies seasonally and geographically, the length of those hours varied. Life was largely organized by natural rhythms—daily, seasonal, and annual—and "the day" was organized by routine tasks. Moreover, there was often little or no distinction between "work time" and "social time," since people socialized all day long while working.

A WEIRDer time psychology increasingly pervaded urban life during the Late Middle Ages and beyond. In the commercial world, merchants began paying workers weekly wages. In this system, "days" were set at a fixed number of hours, which permitted business owners to pay hourly wages for overtime (extra work) or to deduct a certain number of hours based on time lost due to weather or illness. Compensation was also made using piece rates, with workers paid for the quantity of horseshoes, pots, or blankets they produced (for each "piece"). The payment scheme forced artisans to think about efficiency—how many horseshoes can I hammer out in an hour? Markets increasingly opened and closed at specific hours, which heightened competition—all buyers and sellers could interact at the same time. Contracts began including specific dates with penalties, often calculated per day. In the realm of government, town councils began organizing themselves using fixed hours. In 1389, for example, the Nuremberg town council passed a statute that required councilmen to sit together for two hours both before and after lunch (high noon)—based on the sandglass—to discuss business. Late arrivals were fined. In England, courts began ordering defendants and witnesses to appear on specific dates, at particular hours.[5]

The focus on clock time, and the rapid adoption of new time-related technologies, appear to have paid off: European cities that adopted a public clock early—before 1450—grew economically more rapidly than nonadopters during the period from 1500 to 1700. Notably, this prosperity was not immediate but only accrued a few generations later, after these populations had adapted their minds and lifestyles in ways that permitted cities and towns to run like clockwork. Urban centers that installed clocks often later adopted printing presses. Detailed analyses suggest that both innovations subsequently and independently contributed to economic growth. The boost in prosperity induced by having a public clock was roughly equal to that associated with having a university. Interestingly, though, having a university made medieval cities more likely to adopt public clocks.[6]

Now, you might think that adopting a practical technology like a clock or a printing press doesn't require some fancy psychological explanation like the one I'm offering here. Fortunately, history provides a comparative population in the Islamic world. Unlike their immediate neighbors in Christendom, the mosques and cities of the Islamic world seemed immune to the clock epidemic, just as they were to the printing press of the same era. Many Muslims knew of mechanical clocks, so they could have simply hired some Italian clockmakers to fix them up. But, people in these places weren't eager to submit themselves to clock time. Instead, people cared about personal relationships, family ties, and ritual time. Muslims have long had the call to prayer, five times per day, which adds a reliable temporal structure to life (and primes prosociality). As with many other temporal systems, prayer times are based on the sun's position, so they vary seasonally and geographically (as well as with the calculation methods used by different Islamic schools). This means that the periods between calls to prayer throughout the day do not provide a uniform temporal structure—they don't organize the day or people's minds like clock time. Of course, with Christendom's rising prestige, rulers around the world did eventually import European-made mechanical clocks. But, like the ancient water clocks in the Islamic world or in China, these were showpieces and curiosities, not something for craftsmen, merchants, bureaucrats, monks, and inventors to organize their lives around. As I learned from my Fijian friends, clocks only keep you on schedule if you've internalized a devotion to clock time—it's about your mind, not your watch.

The impersonal institutions that developed in Europe, which began employing hourly wages, piece rates, and fines for tardiness, likely motivated people to begin thinking about time and money in similar ways. Today, WEIRD people are always "saving" time, "wasting" time, and "losing" time. Time is always running out, and many of us try to "buy" time. While people in other societies think about time in diverse ways, WEIRD people have long been obsessed with thinking about time and money in the same way. As a contrast, consider this description of time psychology from the Berber-speaking Kabyle farmers in Algeria:

> The profound feelings of dependence and solidarity . . . foster in the Kabyle peasant an attitude of submission and of nonchalant indifference to the passage of time which no one dreams of mastering, using up or saving . . . All the acts of life are free from the limitations of the timetable, even sleep, even work which ignores all obsession with productivity and yields. Haste is seen as a lack of decorum combined with diabolical ambition.[7]

The ethnographer here, Pierre Bourdieu, goes on to note that in this clan-based society, there are no notions of precise mealtimes or exact appointments. The clock is considered the "devil's mill," and upon meeting someone, "the worst discourtesy is to come to the point and express oneself in as few words as possible." Instead of incessantly ticking off minutes and hours, time flows at differing speeds through different experiences, tasks, and events in a ritual cycle. If this sounds exotic, remember, it's you (and especially me), not everyone else. The flavor and texture of time psychology among the Kabyle can be found in societies from around the globe.[8]

Compare Kabyle time to the sense captured in this gem from 1751 in a British colonial city:

Since our Time is reduced to a Standard, and the Bullion of the Day minted out into Hours, the Industrious know how to employ every Piece of Time to a real Advantage in their different Professions: And he that is prodigal of his Hours, is, in Effect, a Squanderer of Money.[9]

Capturing the essence of his own preindustrial society, this colorful quotation comes to us from the inventor, printer, and statesman Ben Franklin in Philadelphia. In giving advice to a young tradesman, Franklin also coined the maxim "Time is money," which has now spread globally and into dozens of languages.[10]

By Franklin's era, pocket watches were diffusing widely, and almost all successful business owners had one. In England, based on the inventories of the property owned by the poor (assessed at their death), nearly 40 percent of people had a pocket watch. In Paris, about a third of wage earners and 70 percent of servants owned a watch. Pocket watches were expensive, which means that many people spent a large fraction of their income to both know the time and impress their friends, customers, and employers. Instead of representing the "devil's mill," as among the Kabyle, a pocket watch in the hands of an artisan signaled that its owner was hardworking, diligent, and punctual.[11]

Broadly, within the context of an increasingly individualistic society, the coevolution of technologies like hourglasses, bells, and watches along with temporal metaphors like "time is money" and cultural practices like hourly pay and piece rates have profoundly shaped how people think about time. New technologies have linearized and digitized time to a degree never seen before, turning it into an ever-draining currency of temporal pennies. By effectively training themselves from a tender age with elements such as wall clocks, hourly chimes, and precise meeting times, people may have internalized the number line that forms the traditional clock face and incorporated this into how they make trade-offs between things now and in the future (time discounting). Whatever the full impact, the roots of these psychological shifts go much deeper into history than the Industrial Revolution and stretch back to at least the 14th century.[12]

How Work Became Virtuous

Accompanying the spread of clock-time psychology in Europe, an expanding middle class began working longer and harder. This *Industrious* Revolution, as the economic historian Jan de Vries calls it, can be tracked back to at least 1650 or so, beyond which the trail of direct evidence peters out. I suspect that this rising industriousness was part of a longer-term trend. People's time psychology was slowly coevolving with a stronger work ethic and greater self-regulation from at least the late Middle Ages through the Industrial Revolution. Clues to these psychological changes can be seen in the spread of mechanical clocks, greater use of the sandglass, rising concerns about punctuality, and the success of the Cistercian Order, with its spiritual emphasis on manual labor, hard work, and self-discipline. And, of course, these concerns and commitments lie at the heart of many Protestant faiths. Ben Franklin was, for example, the son of pious Puritans who lived among Quakers.[13]

One ingenious data source for studying people's changing work habits comes from the Old Bailey, London's Central Criminal Court, which provides a written record of cases from 1748 to 1803. During their court testimony, eyewitnesses often reported what they were doing at the time of a crime. These "spot-checks" provide over 2,000 instantaneous observations that together paint a picture of how Londoners spent their day. The data suggest that the workweek lengthened by 40 percent over the second half of the 18th century. This occurred as people stretched their working time by about 30 minutes per day, stopped taking "Saint Mondays" off (working every day except Sunday), and started working on some of the 46 holy days found on the annual calendar. The upshot was that by the start of the 19th century, people were working about 1,000 hours more per year, or about an extra 19 hours per week.[14]

While the historical evidence on work time makes a powerful case that people were working longer, all the historical data for this era have potential problems. With the Old Bailey evidence, for example, we don't know what factors might have influenced who became a witness in court or how this might have changed over time—perhaps the court slowly developed an informal policy to accept only "reliable people," which biased the witnesses toward people who worked longer hours. To address such concerns, the cognitive scientist Rahul Bhui and I compiled a database of 45,019 observations on how people from different traditional populations around the world use their time. From South America, Africa, and Indonesia, these populations include a variety of farming communities as well as both herders and hunter-gatherers. Like the Old Bailey observations, these data were spot-checks of what people were doing at a particular moment. Here, however, the observations were done by anthropologists, who randomly selected both the individuals observed and the observation times.

When we compare these diverse societies, the data show that men who engaged in more commercial work—like wage labor—spent more of their total day working. The results suggest that going from a fully subsistence-oriented population to a fully commercialized society would result in an increase in work time of 10 to 15 hours every week, raising the workweek from 45 to between 55 and 60 hours, on average. Annually, people worked an additional 500 to 750 hours.[15]

The combination of historical and cross-cultural data suggests that the rise of urbanization (Figure 9.5), impersonal markets (Figure 9.7), and commercial practices involving things like hourly wages probably increased the time that Europeans spent working. One key question is: What motivated people to work longer?

The historical data suggest that although some folks were certainly working to survive, many were working longer hours so that they could buy more stuff from Europe's swelling streams of commercial goods. For the kitchen alone, Londoners could purchase tea, sugar, coffee, pepper, cod, nutmeg, potatoes, and rum. Pocket watches and pendulum clocks appeared in the 16th century and eventually became hot sellers. Literate folks could buy a range of printed books and pamphlets. People wanted all this for the stuff itself, of course, but also because of what it told others about them. In an individualistic world, what you buy tells people about what you can afford as well as what you value. From Bibles to pocket watches, people wanted to tell strangers and neighbors about themselves through their purchases. This, de Vries argues, drove up consumers' desire for diverse goods and their willingness to work longer; stronger demand and more industrious workers drove up both economic production and consumer supply.[16]

So far, the data support the idea that people were gradually working longer hours, but that doesn't tell us if they were working harder or more efficiently. This is a hard question to answer using historical data, but economic historians have devised some clever ways to use certain farm-related tasks to address it. For farming productivity in general, it's difficult to estimate changes in workers' efficiency or motivations over time, because agricultural innovation was ongoing and included novel technologies, improved techniques, and new crops, like potatoes and corn from the New World. However, the preindustrial technique used to thresh grain, which largely involved beating the stalks with a stick to knock the seeds off, didn't change much at all over many centuries. In England, analyses of threshing data suggest that the efficiency of threshers doubled from the 14th to the early 19th century. Because threshing is easy to learn, this change is unlikely to be due to specialization or improved skills. It instead suggests that people were simply working more intensely.[17]

In the countryside, the increasing value placed on hard work and manual labor may have begun within certain segments of the medieval Church and diffused outward. As we saw earlier, the place to start looking is the Cistercian Order. Recall that, in addition to their emphasis on self-discipline, self-denial, and hard work, the Cistercians sought out the simplicity and serenity of remote rural areas. The monks accepted non-literate peasants into their order as lay brothers, and these men took vows of chastity and obedience. The monks also employed a range of servants, laborers, and skilled workers. Small communities, often with shops and artisans, sometimes clustered around the outskirts of monasteries. Together, these members, employees, and other contacts threaded social and economic connections that stretched out into the surrounding communities to create communication lines for the transmission of Cistercian values, habits, practices, and know-how. Figure 11.2 shows the distribution of Cistercian monasteries during the Middle Ages. Ninety percent had been founded by 1300.[18]

To assess whether the Cistercian presence influenced people's work ethic after 1300, we can use contemporary survey data (2008–2010) from over 30,000 people spread around 242 European regions. The survey asked whether "hard work" is an important trait for children to learn. To link this survey measure to the Cistercians, Thomas Anderson, Jeanet Bentzen, and their colleagues calculated the density of Cistercian houses per square kilometer for each region outlined in Figure 11.2. Then, they connected everyone in the survey to the region where they grew up. The results show that the higher the density of Cistercian monasteries in a region during the Middle Ages, the more likely a person from that region today is to say that "hard work" is important for children to learn. This only compares people living within the same modern countries and holds after statistically accounting for various regional and individual differences, including people's education and marital status. The psychological emphasis on "hard work" also manifests in contemporary economic data: regions that experienced a greater Cistercian presence during the Middle Ages are economically more productive in the 21st century and show lower rates of unemployment.[19]

Interestingly, the effect of a historical Cistercian presence in a region

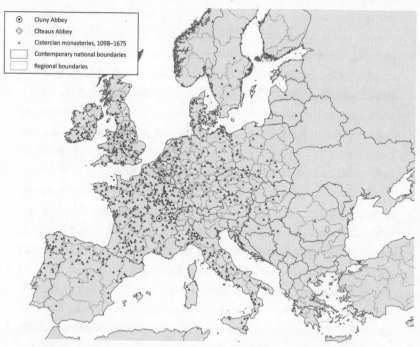

FIGURE 11.2. Distribution of Cistercian monasteries in Europe from the founding of the order at Cîteaux in 1098. Ninety percent of these 734 monasteries were founded before 1300. The map also shows Cluny Abbey, the home of the founder of the Cistercian Order (Chapter 10).[20]

Map legend:
- ⊙ Cluny Abbey
- ✛ Cîteaux Abbey
- ▲ Cistercian monasteries, 1098–1675
- Contemporary national boundaries
- Regional boundaries

operates most strongly on Catholics compared to Protestants. That is, Catholics who grew up in regions that had been historically thick with Cistercians are much more likely to endorse the importance of "hard work" for children compared to Catholics from other regions. This makes sense, since the later diffusion of Protestant communities, whose members also often amplified the value of hard work, would have obscured the earlier influences of the Cistercians.[21]

WAITING FOR PAYDAY

Along with a greater willingness to engage in hard work or difficult tasks, individualism and impersonal markets may also have favored greater self-control and a willingness to delay gratification. In an open market for employees, friends, spouses, and business partners, people want to hire, befriend, marry, and associate with those who can achieve long-term goals, invest now for future payoffs, avoid temptation, and simply show up on time. By contrast, in a world governed by inherited and enduring relationships, people can't just pick whom they want to hire, marry, or work with. They need to consider group loyalty and select partners with whom they have dense social interconnections. This is because it's the embeddedness rather than their partner's or employee's disposition that people rely on.

Research connecting markets and commerce to psychological measures of patience and self-regulation is limited but still suggestive. Consider this study among the BaYaka, a population of African hunter-gatherers in the Congo Basin. Using a simple experiment, the anthropologist Deniz Salali assessed the patience of 164 adults in three different BaYaka communities. Two of these communities were traditional nomadic foraging camps in the forests, 60 km (37 mi) or more from the nearest market town. The third community resided within the town itself. Deniz offered people a choice between receiving either (A) one desirable soup stock cube now, or (B) five such cubes tomorrow. More patient people should be willing to wait a day for the five tasty cubes, while less patient people would tend to take the one immediately.

The BaYaka living in the market town were more patient: 54 percent of the town dwellers were willing to wait for the five cubes, while in the nomadic camps only 18 percent chose to wait. In their analysis, Deniz and her collaborator, Andrea Migliano, show that part of the difference between the town- and forest-dwelling BaYaka arose from differences in people's participation in wage labor. Wage labor often requires individuals to work now and get paid days or weeks later, so this kind of payment scheme is effectively a training regime that demands work now for delayed rewards. And, as with other exchanges in impersonal markets, wage labor also often requires the trust in strangers that accompanies market norms.

In this situation, it's not just that commercial institutions like wage labor create conditions that favor greater time discounting, but it's also

the case that traditional BaYaka institutions disincentivize delaying grat-
ifcation in this situation. Food was, and still is, widely shared in BaYaka
camps, so deciding to wait for the five cubes wouldn't provide the decision-
maker herself with any more tasty soup. Those living in the foraging camps
who decided to wait a day for the five cubes helped only their fellow camp
members, not themselves: when they received the five cubes, sharing norms
required that they be shared with anyone who asked (and people aren't shy
about asking). Thus, camp members really faced a choice between one cube
now or one tomorrow (with extra to give away). Practicing patience in this
institutional environment doesn't pay in ways that will foster the cultivation of deferred gratification *in this context*.[22]

This study alone doesn't nail down an answer to the question of whether
market integration specifically *causes* patience. For one thing, it's possible
that more patient people selectively moved from the forest into the town
because, in town, patience pays off. Second, it's possible that something else
about town life is causing the change besides the market-based norms. Nevertheless, we know that patience, and specifically delay discounting, can be
acquired via cultural learning (Chapter 2), and that it pays off in more income, literacy, and education—greater "success"—once labor markets and
schools arrive on the scene. Together, these facts suggest that both cultural
evolution and individual experience may ratchet up our patience in response
to impersonal institutions, especially markets and schools.[23]

Can we anchor these psychological changes in history? That's a tall order, but maybe we can get some purchase on it.

PATIENCE AND SELF-REGULATION IN HISTORY

The historical record of medieval Europe doesn't provide direct measures of people's patience or self-control that would permit us to observe
changes over time. However, researchers have argued that we can see these
psychological changes in the gradual decline of both interest rates and murder rates. Let's start with interest rates.[24]

Interest rates are heavily influenced by people's willingness to defer
gratification, to discount the future. To see this, consider a choice between

spending $100 tonight on a delicious meal with friends versus investing this money at 10 percent for 30 years. At this interest rate, you'd get $1,745 in 30 years instead of just the $100. The question is whether you are willing to forgo the nice dinner tonight for a big payoff in three decades. If you don't discount the future much, you're more likely to invest the $100 and skip the fancy dinner. But, if 30 years seems too far off to worry about, you'll enjoy the feast. In this situation, the more patient people are, the lower the interest rate can be without the dinner option tempting them. In such populations, we expect the interest rate to decline. By contrast, if people became less patient—more inclined to "eat, drink, and be merry" today (i.e., take the tasty soup cube now)—they'd only forgo immediate payoffs when the future rewards on offer were really big—so, interest rates would go up (or, no one would ever invest). Thus people's willingness to defer gratification is a key contributor to interest rates.

With this in mind, Figure 11.3A shows that interest rates have been dropping in England for nearly a millennium. The earliest estimates of interest rates are in the 10 to 12 percent range. By 1450, they had dropped to just below 5 percent, and by the time England taxied onto the runway of the Industrial Revolution in 1750, interest rates had fallen to below 4 percent (when Londoners were working longer). Rates continued to fall as the Industrial Revolution accelerated, though the decline was modest compared to that observed during the medieval period.[25]

Now, because economists typically assume that psychology is fixed (a big mistake), their default explanations for changes in interest rates typically focus on economic growth or on changes in risk due to political shocks (e.g., the king claims your lands), plagues, or wars (e.g., a different king claims your lands). The rising incomes created by rapid economic growth could lower interest rates because people might—theoretically—spend more profligately now, figuring they can pay it all off later with their higher income. By contrast, in a risky world you could lose your investments when the government confiscates them from you. Or, of course, you might die young in a plague or violent raid. Facing this situation, you consume now so that future events can't steal these pleasures from you.

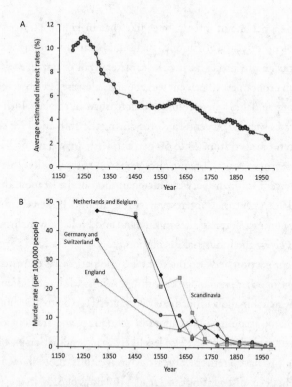

FIGURE 11.3. Indirect measures of patience and self-regulation: (A) estimated interest rates in England from 1150 to 2000, and (B) murder rates in England, Germany, Switzerland, Scandinavia, and the Netherlands and Belgium from 1300 to 1985.[26]

These standard economic explanations, however, don't seem to account for the long-term trends in England. The economic historian Greg Clark argues that some underlying psychological factor like patience must be driving interest rates down. These downward trends continued through periods of uncertainty and instability like the Black Death (1350), the Glorious Revolution (1688), and Britain's many wars against France, Spain, and the Netherlands. Even after 1850, during one of the fastest economic accelerations in history, interest rates kept going down (not up, as some might expect). At least part of this long-term trend probably reflects a psychological change in something like patience or self-control.[27]

While a decline in interest rates like that in Figure 11.3A appears in data from other parts of Europe, such as Holland, we don't see similar trends outside of Europe during the same era. For example, even in complex Asian economies, 10 percent was about the lowest rate observed. In the lower Yangtze delta, where commerce flourished in the late 14th century, interest rates were 50 percent. In Korea during the 18th and 19th centuries, interest rates ranged from 25 to 50 percent, with an average of 37 percent. In 17th-century Osaka, interest rates were comparatively low, between 12 and 15 percent for loans between merchant houses. In Istanbul during the 17th and 18th centuries, interest rates were around 19 percent for private loans. By contrast, interest rates in England and Holland were firmly below 5 percent *before* the Industrial Revolution.[28]

The connection between interest rates and patience is consistent with a wide range of other psychological findings. Adults who, as children, resisted eating the marshmallow immediately (Chapter 1) go on to save more money in their bank accounts, invest more in schooling, and stay out of prison. Those better able to wait were also less likely to have addiction problems and more likely to have a retirement plan. Among adults, those showing greater patience in delay-discounting tasks (e.g., $100 now, or $150 in one year) save more of their income, invest more for the future, and attend school longer. These relationships in the modern world are strongest in Africa, Southeast Asia, and the Middle East, probably because formal institutions play less of a role. Even in remote Amazonian populations, which are just beginning to engage in global markets, those willing to delay gratification in time-discounting tasks go on to attend newly established schools for longer and attain greater literacy. Finally, as noted in Chapter 9, convicted criminals show greater impatience and less self-control than those in demographically matched populations.[29]

However, patience and self-control don't always pay off, and how much they pay off depends on both informal and formal institutions. In Liberia, the economist Chris Blattman and his colleagues conducted a randomized experimental intervention with nearly 1,000 poor men. Some received eight weeks of training that increased their self-control and patience while reducing their impulsivity. These psychological changes resulted in the men committing fewer crimes and saving more money in the short term. However, while this study decisively demonstrates that patience and self-control can be modified culturally, these psychological shifts didn't generally cash out in the long run. The reason was clear: 70 percent of the men reported that their growing nest eggs were stolen, often taken from them by corrupt police during shakedowns. Cultural evolution won't favor the emergence of greater patience in this environment.

Similarly, intensive kinship, through its strong normative obligations to a web of distant relatives, may create pressures that similarly disincentivize the cultivation of self-control or patience. I've seen this frequently in Fiji: an industrious person works hard to save money, but then some distant cousin-brother needs cash for a funeral, wedding, or medical procedure, so the nest egg evaporates. This make sense because intensive kin-based institutions manage risk, retirement, and harmony collectively—through relationships—instead of via individual self-control and secure savings.[30]

The influence of patience and self-control on crime highlighted above points to another long-term statistic that is available well back into the Middle Ages: murder rates. For four different European regions, Figure 11.3B shows that murder rates plummeted from 20–50 per 100,000 people in 1300 CE to less than 2 per 100,000 in 1800, with much of the decline occurring before 1550. Since the massive economic expansion that accelerated after 1800, murder rates have continued to slowly decline in these regions, but this has been relatively gradual compared to the medieval slide. As with interest rates, we aren't directly observing self-control or self-regulation, and murder rates are certainly influenced by many factors besides psychological change. But, crucially, most of these murders were the "barroom brawl" variety in which men (yes, not women) have to suppress their tempers, steel their self-control, and just walk away. Wiping that smug smirk off that asshole's face would feel good now, but what then? Illustrating this, a 13th-century officer of the French Crown defined "homicide" as "when one kills another in the heat of a fight, in which tension turns into insult and insult to fighting, by which one often dies." Indeed, an analysis of homicide records from 13th-century England reveals that 90 percent of cases began as spontaneous acts of aggression in response to insults or quarrels rather than as premeditated acts. In 16th-century Arras (France), 45 percent of murders were committed in or just outside of taverns, while half or more of all violent crimes in Douai (France) and Cologne (Germany) involved booze.[31]

The idea here is that people were adapting psychologically to a world that was transforming from one governed by the external constraints of kinship ties and the incentives generated by family honor to one in which independent shopkeepers, artisans, and merchants held sway, interacting flexibly with myriad strangers in mutually beneficial transactions. In this expanding individualistic world, a reputation for sudden, violent, and undisciplined responses to minor insults or simple misunderstandings didn't pay anymore. Who wants to defend, marry, or do business with a hothead? In an open market of strangers where people are shopping for relationships, you can just find another friend, fiancée, or employee, one with better self-control.[32] In *Traité Genéral du Commerce* (1781), the Dutch lawyer Samuel Ricard makes my case:

> Commerce attaches [men] one to another through mutual
> utility. Through commerce the moral and physical passions are
> superseded by interest ... Commerce has a special character
> which distinguishes it from all other professions. It affects the
> feelings of men so strongly that it makes him who was proud and
> haughty suddenly turn supple, bending and serviceable. Through
> commerce, man learns to deliberate, to be honest, to acquire
> manners, to be prudent and reserved in both talk and action.
> Sensing the necessity to be wise and honest in order to succeed, he
> flees vice, or at least his demeanor exhibits decency and seriousness
> so as not to arouse any adverse judgment on the part of present
> and future acquaintances; he would not dare make a spectacle
> of himself for fear of damaging his credit standing and thus
> society may well avoid a scandal which it might otherwise have
> to deplore.[33]

Tellingly, while murder rates were declining overall, the percentage of victims who were family members of the murderer rose from almost none to over half by the end of the 19th century. Men stopped killing as many strangers and acquaintances in bars over insults and status challenges and instead were more inclined to kill family members. Few stats could more strongly highlight the rise of impersonal prosociality and the concurrent decline of the centrality of kinship.

The gradual diffusion of self-control and patience seems to have spread outward from the urban middle class—the merchants, artisans, professionals, and civil officials—to the laborers and elites. This can be seen in the fact that it was the urban middle class, not the much richer aristocrats, who bought the first government bonds and invested in the early joint stock companies. In the latter half of the 18th century, for example, the stockholders of the East India Company were primarily bankers, government officials, retailers, military personnel, clergymen, and merchants.[34]

Be Yourself: The Origins of WEIRD Personalities

The patterns and dimensions of personality observed among Americans and other WEIRD people are largely believed by psychologists to represent the *human pattern*. I suspect this is wrong. Instead, an evolutionary approach suggests that individuals and populations will—at least partially—adapt or calibrate their dispositions to the stable and enduring niches of the social, economic, and ecological environments they confront over the course of their lives and across generations. Developmentally, we expect children to adapt their personalities to the contours, opportunities, and affordances of the worlds they encounter while growing up. More subtly, we expect cultural evolution to shape personality configurations by favoring different packages of worldviews, motivations, standards, ritualized practices, and routines of life.[35]

To understand the cultural evolution of dispositional traits, and specifically what psychologists define as personality (e.g., extroversion, agreeableness, etc.), let's take a stroll from the origins of farming to the growing commercial cities of medieval Europe. Since the dawn of agriculture about 12,000 years ago, there's been basically one primary occupation open to most people—farmer. With only a male-female division of labor, farm families had to be generalists: sowing, weeding, harrowing, harvesting, reaping, threshing, milling, herding, shearing, and butchering were just some of the basics. People also usually had to build houses, make tools, weave clothing, care for animals, and defend their communities. As societies expanded in size and complexity, broad economic specializations did emerge, but this didn't give individuals a menu of choices. Often, particular clans, kindreds, or local communities cultivated specific skills or know-how, and developed norm-governed relationships with other groups possessing complementary skills.

In the complex chiefdoms of Polynesia, for example, there were clans that variously specialized in farming, fishing, canoe making, and—of course—governing (the chiefs). Whether you were a farmer or a warrior depended on which clan you were born into. As the first cities emerged, occupational specializations and the division of labor expanded, but the structure of knowledge and the manner of recruiting the next generation of specialists didn't change that much. In these communities, individuals couldn't easily pick their preferred occupations. Instead, kin-based institutions dominated, so the occupational choices of individuals were strongly constrained by their families, clans, castes, or ethnic groups. In various places, there were milk-selling clans, merchant families, and sandal-making castes. Instead of finding a niche that fit them and adapting further to better fill it, people had to figure out how to fill whatever niches they were born into. I don't want to exaggerate this, because some movement was sometimes possible, but the options were generally few and the inherited constraints substantial.[36]

In Europe, however, a different world was developing during the Middle Ages. As explained earlier, cities and towns were growing rapidly; impersonal markets were expanding; specialized voluntary associations were selectively recruiting and training members; and diverse occupations were sprouting and proliferating: e.g., clockmaker, lawyer, accountant, printer, gunsmith, and inventor. At the same time, weak kinship ties, greater residential mobility, and an expanding list of rights and privileges in town charters guaranteed individuals substantial freedom to join a growing list of associations, apprenticeships, guilds, and occupations. This social environment meant that individuals had to "sell themselves" based on their personal attributes, specialized abilities, and dispositional virtues, not primarily on their friendships, lineages, or family alliances—though of course the value of relationships and connections fades but never disappears.[37]

In this world, people could increasingly select the occupations or groups that already provided a reasonable fit for their temperaments, preferences, and attributes; then, they could work to further hone their attributes in order to excel in competition against others. A man could make a living as a sociable salesman, conscientious craftsman, scrupulous scribe, or pious priest. Traits got exaggerated or suppressed along the way. Of course, women had dramatically fewer options, but more than in most societies. Remember, they married late, could often pick their husbands, and frequently had paying jobs prior to marriage. Unlike in other societies, women could also skip marriage altogether and instead follow the call of God into Church service. Overall, this gave individuals more latitude to pick the social roles, relationships, and occupations that fit their inherited characteristics. Over time, they could adapt, specialize, and exaggerate their most important traits.[38]

Computer simulations of the process suggest that these social and economic developments would have generated a greater diversity in personal attributes as individuals specialized into different social niches and occupations. Or, to put it differently, the number of distinct personality dimensions would have started rising. Over time, this process would have intensified, because the larger, denser, and more relationally mobile a population, the more individuals can seek out and actually find the relationships and associations that best fit their talents, attributes, inclinations, peculiarities, and preferences.[39]

This approach to personality runs contrary to much work in the discipline of psychology. Personality psychologists have long assumed that certain dispositions are important and universal; and they've sought to reduce personality to certain types or to a small set of dimensions. The most prominent approach argues that humans have five largely independent dimensions of personality: (1) openness to experience ("adventurousness"), (2) conscientiousness ("self-discipline"), (3) extraversion (vs. introversion), (4) agreeableness ("cooperativeness" or "compassion"), and (5) neuroticism ("emotional instability"). These have often been interpreted as capturing the innate structure of human personality. Psychologists call these personality dimensions the "BIG-5," but I'll call them the WEIRD-5.[40]

When psychologists have deployed this approach to personality in non-WEIRD populations, the WEIRD-5 can usually be found, although in places like Hong Kong and Japan, only four of the five dimensions consistently emerge. Unfortunately, most of this cross-cultural work has relied on relationally mobile university students in urban centers. Using such non-representative samples effectively skims off those in each population who are most likely to possess the WEIRD-5 and eliminates much of the institutional, occupational, and demographic variation that we'd expect to be most important for identifying differences in personality across societies. The rough applicability of the WEIRD-5 approach in these settings isn't surprising.[41]

To move forward, rather than this scattershot approach to testing cross-cultural variation, which involves using easily accessible subpopulations that are both homogeneous and nonrepresentative, we need a detailed study of personality from a subsistence-oriented society with few occupations and little contact with global markets.

Fortunately, the anthropologist Mike Gurven and his team shook up the status quo in personality psychology when they delivered just such a study, which landed like a cement block in one of psychology's leading scientific journals. After adapting state-of-the-art psychological tools for use in a non-literate population, Mike's team explored the structure of personality among the Tsimane', a group of farmer-foragers who live in Bolivia's tropical forests. We briefly encountered the Tsimane' in Chapter 9: they were one of the dots in the lower left of Figure 9.2, which shows that they make low offers in the

Dictator Game and aren't integrated into the market economy. Tsimane' essentially have one of two jobs: either you're a husband or you're a wife. Husbands mostly hunt, fish, build houses, and make tools. Wives mostly weave, spin, cook, and care for children. Both spouses pitch in on farming.[42]

The rigorous data collection and in-depth analyses conducted by Mike's team are impressive. They tested over 600 Tsimane', retested the same people, replicated their findings in a fresh sample of 430 couples (where people evaluated their spouses), and checked their findings in a variety of ways.

So, did the Tsimane' reveal the WEIRD-5?

No, not even close. The Tsimane' data reveal only two dimensions of personality. No matter how you slice and dice the data, there's just nothing like the WEIRD-5. Moreover, based on the clusters of characteristics associated with each of the Tsimane''s two personality dimensions, neither matches up nicely with any of the WEIRD-5 dimensions. Mike and his team argue that these dimensions capture the two primary routes to social success among the Tsimane', which can be described roughly as "interpersonal prosociality" and "industriousness." The idea is that if you are Tsimane', you can either focus on working harder on the aforementioned productive activities and skills like hunting and weaving, or you can devote your time and mental efforts to building a richer network of social relationships. Aside from these broad strategies, everyone has to be a generalist. All men, for example, have to learn to craft dugout canoes, track game, and make wooden bows. Extroverts can't become insurance salesmen or cruise directors, while introverts can't become economists or programmers.[43]

With the Tsimane' case under our belt, let's return to the cross-cultural data on personality. I'd suggested that it's not surprising that we perceive the WEIRD-5 emerging across diverse societies, because psychologists have relied almost entirely on urban undergraduates in their cross-cultural studies. However, despite this homogeneity, it's still possible to detect the ongoing cultural evolution of personalities in the cross-cultural data. Recall that among WEIRD people, the five dimensions of personality are usually independent and uncorrelated. This means that knowing someone's score on the "agreeableness" dimension, for example, doesn't tell you about their "extroversion" or "neuroticism."

Now, imagine that the number of social niches available to WEIRD people begins contracting. As the options decline, there may no longer be any niches where people can successfully be both extroverted and neurotic (e.g., movie star) or both introverted and adventurous (e.g., field primatologist). This reduction in the number of social niches will gradually increase the correlations among the existing personality dimensions because the shrinking number of niches and specialists means that everyone has to be more of a generalist, and certain personality combinations just aren't an option. As this process continues, some dimensions will become so correlated that they will effectively collapse into a single new dimension. Eventually, there will be four, three, and finally two personality dimensions.

To test this idea, we can examine the average intercorrelation among the WEIRD-5 personality dimensions across societies. The expectation is that societies with less occupational specialization and fewer social niches will show higher intercorrelations among the WEIRD-5 dimensions. Since the number of social niches available in any population is strongly correlated with occupational specialization and urbanization in the modern world, we should expect places with less urbanization and/or occupational specialization to show greater interdependence (intercorrelation) among their WEIRD-5 dimensions.

Using data from nearly 17,000 people in 55 countries, Aaron Lukaszewski, Mike Gurven, Chris von Rueden, and their colleagues found that the more urbanized a country, or the greater its occupational diversity, the lower the intercorrelations were among the WEIRD-5 dimensions. Figure 11.4 illustrates this using urbanization: people from more rural countries reveal less overall independence among their personality dimensions, which indicates movement toward fewer personality dimensions. This analysis suggests that much of the variation in personality structure among WEIRD societies may arise from differences in urbanization or occupational diversity.[44]

We've already seen how these personality patterns can be anchored

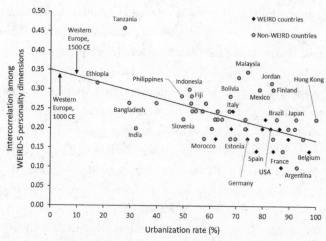

FIGURE 11.4. Relationship between urbanization rates and the intercorrelation of the WEIRD-5 personality dimensions for 55 countries. The urbanization rate is the percentage of people who live in urban areas. The independence of the WEIRD-5 personality dimensions is captured by the average intercorrelation of the five dimensions. The lower this intercorrelation, the more independent the five dimensions. For the historical rates of urbanization in medieval Europe, I've used the percentage of the population living in cities over 10,000 people.[45]

in medieval history, based on the dramatic increases in urbanization (Figure 9.5), market integration (Figure 9.7), and occupational guilds (Figure 10.6). These trends, together with the evidence of the psychological impact of the Church's MFP, suggest that urbanites had an expanding number of social and economic niches they could and did voluntarily enter. For fun, I've marked the approximately comparable urbanization rates for western Europe in Figure 11.4. As you can see, these rates were substantially lower than those found in any of the countries studied at the dawn of the 21st century. This suggests that personality configurations in Europe were probably different in the Middle Ages compared to today, but they had begun evolving in a WEIRD direction.

Of course, we shouldn't take my backward projection in Figure 11.4 too seriously, since we expect modern urbanization rates to capture—in some complex way—the presence of diverse occupations, relational mobility, labor mobility, individualistic motivations, and voluntary associations. For this reason, we don't expect the residents of the urbanized areas in China or the Islamic World during the Middle Ages to have a personality structure anything like the WEIRD-5.

Nevertheless, to the degree that historical urbanization rates roughly capture a world in which individuals could select from a diversity of social niches and occupational specializations, my backward projection might be useful. Imagine sliding back in time along the line in Figure 11.4 toward a more agrarian society with only one main occupation—farmer. At first, the five personality dimensions found in the most urbanized populations become increasingly correlated. And then, they start collapsing into each other. Eventually, if Mike and his collaborators are correct, we'll arrive in a world with something like one or two personality dimensions that correspond to the major strategies for achieving social success based on the local ecology, technology, and set of institutions.

The configuration of our personalities reflects only part of how cultural evolution has shaped this aspect of our psychology. There's perhaps a deeper but subtler impact. As suggested in Chapter 1, intensive kin-based institutions demand that individuals behave in a range of different ways depending on their relationships to other people. Some relationships explicitly call for joking, while others demand quiet submission. By contrast, the world of impersonal markets and relational mobility favors consistency across contexts and relationships as well as the cultivation of unique personal characteristics specialized for diverse niches. For at least a millennium, these cultural evolutionary pressures have fostered a rising degree of dispositionalism. Individuals increasingly sought consistency—to be "themselves"—across contexts and judged others negatively when they failed to show this consistency. Understanding this helps explain why WEIRD people are so much more likely than others to impute the causes of someone's behavior to their personal dispositions over their contexts and relationships (the Fundamental Attribution Error), and why they are so uncomfortable with their own personal inconsistencies (Cognitive Dissonance). Reacting to this culturally constructed worldview, WEIRD people are forever seeking their "true selves" (good luck!). Thus, while they certainly exist across societies and back into history, dispositions in general, and personalities specifically, are just more important in WEIRD societies.[46]

THE ENDOWMENT EFFECT

Traditionally, Hadza hunter-gatherers engaged in no commerce among themselves and little trade with other groups. When necessary, they may have even resorted to silent trade (Chapter 9) with the surrounding agricultural and pastoralist communities. Underlining this pattern, the longtime Hadza ethnographer James Woodburn writes, "Exchange with other Hadza is reprehensible. To barter, to trade or to sell to other Hadza is, even in the 1990s, really not acceptable . . ." Nevertheless, the inexorable expansion of global markets has begun to engulf the Hadza in swarms of curious tourists. How are these impersonal markets influencing Hadza psychology?[47]

In an elegant experiment, the anthropologist-cum-psychologist Coren Apicella and her colleagues examined a phenomenon called the *endowment effect* among the Hadza. Participants were randomly given one of two different-colored lighters, which are useful for starting cooking fires. Then, participants were given an opportunity to exchange their lighter for one of a different color. How often did they make the trade? Because Coren randomly assigned participants to receive one of two different-colored lighters, we'd expect people to trade in their lighters about half of the time—that is, if they are rational and have color preferences.[48]

In WEIRD populations, people rarely trade in this experiment, so the frequency of lighter exchanges would be much lower than 50 percent, and probably about 10 percent. WEIRD people get psychologically attached to stuff they personally own in ways that make them behave in seemingly irrational ways—this emotional attachment is the endowment effect. Something about personally owning a thing seems to make it more valuable. This WEIRD psychological pattern is just as strong in WEIRD kindergarteners as it is in university students, so it's not due to any direct personal experience with buying or selling stuff.[49]

What about the Hadza?

Well, it turns out that it depends on *which* Hadza. In the most remote Hadza camps, where people live as full-time hunter-gatherers and rely very little on trade or markets, Hadza are basically rational actors, trading their lighters about half the time. However, when Coren ran these experiments in the more market-integrated Hadza camps, where people increasingly rely on selling their arrows, bows, and headbands to adventure tourists, participants kept their initial lighters 74 percent of the time.

This is striking: hunter-gatherers with little market integration show no endowment effect, but when part of this population is exposed to impersonal markets, they begin irrationally holding on to their initial endowments. This occurs despite the fact that all Hadza generally share the same kin-based institutions, language, religious beliefs, and other aspects of culture.

Coren got the same results when she replaced the lighters with food, using packages of different kinds of biscuits. The market-integrated Hadza kept their initial biscuits 76 percent of the time, while Hadza living in remote camps kept them only 45 percent of the time. Once again, the Hadza living a traditional lifestyle were basically rational traders, while the market-integrated Hadza revealed a clear endowment effect.

What gives? What's the link between markets and the endowment effect?

This is a good question. I suspect that impersonal markets cultivate an emphasis on personal attributes, unique abilities, and individual ownership. Such markets can also foster conspicuous consumption (like fancy pocket watches), with people using consumer goods to signal their personal qualities. Psychologists have argued that this self-focus leads people to see their own personal property as extensions of themselves, which imbues their stuff with greater value through its connection to the owner's personal identity. Mugs, lighters, and biscuits get better when they are *my* mugs, lighters, and biscuits. This idea has been supported by research comparing the size of the endowment effect between North American and East Asian undergraduates. Not surprisingly, North Americans exhibit a stronger endowment effect than do East Asians. Both groups, of course, are equally market-integrated, but they possess distinct social norms that either elevate the centrality of the individual or suppress it into the collective.[50]

It's important not to see the absence of an endowment effect among the nonmarket Hadza as the "natural condition" of humanity. The Hadza possess their own potent social norms, which promote the widespread sharing of food and other goods in ways not based on direct exchange, partner choice, or reciprocity. For example, they play a gambling game in which players can win each other's arrows, knives, and headbands. If chance favors a particular person and that player manages to accumulate a lot of good stuff, he is under strong social pressure to continue gambling until chance catches up with him and a degree of equality is restored. If he resists, for instance by slipping away to another camp, he'll find himself swamped with endless requests for his bounty of goods. Social norms dictate that he must share, so his store of goods won't last for more than a couple of weeks. In short, among the Hadza, one just can't get too attached to one's stuff, because soon it will be someone else's stuff. Such institutions should suppress any inclination toward an endowment effect.[51]

Given the limited cross-cultural data available, my explanation for the origin of the endowment effect remains only a proposal. The reason we don't know more is that both economists and psychologists studying Western samples have simply assumed for decades that they were measuring a feature of our species' psychology rather than a local cognitive calibration to a society's institutions, languages, and technologies. Like so many other psychological findings, the intensity of the endowment effect ranges from an extreme in WEIRD societies to nonexistent among the traditional Hadza.

Before concluding this chapter, I need to come clean. As with the endowment effect, the ideas presented in this chapter are more speculative than in the preceding chapters, and, while there's much supportive evidence, it is often patchy, and some key insights hinge on single studies. These studies, by pioneers like Mike Gurven and Coren Apicella, are of the highest quality, but they are still only single studies and sometimes involve only one population. In prior chapters, I generally had multiple converging lines of data from different researchers, with large samples from several societies. So, be sure to adjust your confidence accordingly.

It's Big, but How Big?

The big picture in this book is that our minds adapt, often over centuries through cultural evolution, to the institutional and technological worlds we encounter. To understand WEIRD psychology, then, we need to consider the more individualistic world that began developing in parts of Europe during the second millennium of the Common Era. To illustrate some of the relevant psychological patterns created by this process, this chapter has focused on two interrelated packages, one centered around how we think about time, labor, punctuality, and patience, and a second cluster that includes WEIRD personalities, dispositions, and the centrality of the unitary "self." In the High and Late Middle Ages, a growing number of European communities began to adapt how they thought about time and money, along with their feelings about labor, work, and efficiency. With the declining importance of relationships and kin-based institutions, cultivating a personal reputation for hard work, efficiency, self-control, patience, and punctuality became increasingly important. Voluntary organizations such as guilds, monasteries, and towns devised incentives to promote these attributes and inculcate them in members in order to select and define their membership and distinguish themselves from other groups. People increasingly came to believe that God cared about these traits, or at least that possessing them signaled God's favor. This fed into the new Protestant faiths. As cities grew, markets expanded, and voluntary associations proliferated, people increasingly selected the social niches and occupational specializations best suited to their attributes. They then further molded and honed those raw dispositions, talents, and abilities to best fill their chosen niches. The process reformulated the structure of personalities—giving us the WEIRD-5 and cementing the centrality of personal dispositions over contexts and relationships.

Over the course of Parts II and III in this book, we have explored the origins and evolution of some of the major aspects of WEIRD psychology. However, there is every reason to believe that the psychological variation we've seen represents only a thin slice of the total diversity that exists around the world. Moreover, in explaining some of this psychological variation, I've considered the influence and interaction of kin-based institutions, impersonal markets, war, benign intergroup competition, and occupational specialization. These likely capture only a small fraction of the myriad ways that cultural evolution has shaped people's brains and psychology in response to diverse institutions, religions, technologies, ecologies, and languages. All we've done is poke our heads below the surface and look around. This psychological iceberg is clearly big, but we can't tell exactly how big, or how deep into the murky depths it goes.

PART IV

Birthing the Modern World

12

Law, Science, and Religion

I think I can see the whole destiny of America contained in the first Puritan who landed on those shores, as that of the whole human race in the first man.

—Alexis de Tocqueville, *Democracy in America* (1835)[1]

Western law, science, democratic government, and European religions have spread around the globe over the last few centuries. Even in countries without much real democracy or broad political representation, autocratic governments now often put on a big show that involves voting, elections, political parties, and campaigns. In places where the rule of law is weak, there are still written statutes and even inspiring constitutions that look like what you find in the United States, the United Kingdom, Germany, and France. Similarly, whenever I've traveled to remote communities, from Amazonia to the Pacific, I've found small Protestant congregations reading Bibles translated into the local languages. Where did these potent formal institutions and pervasive religions come from?[2]

Many believe that these grand institutions, the bequests of Western civilization, represent the products of reason and the rise of rationality. These institutions—the rationalists argue—are what you get once you strip away Church dogma and apply "reason." This is true even of Protestantism: many believed, and some continue to hold, that (some version of)

Protestantism is what you get if you apply reason to the truths expressed in the Bible and toss away corrupt Church traditions. To the contrary, I would like to suggest a central role for the ongoing psychological changes wrought by cultural evolution during the Middle Ages—by the demolition of Europe's kin-based institutions (Chapters 5–8), the expansion of impersonal markets (Chapter 9), the rise of domesticated forms of intergroup competition (Chapter 10), and the growth of a broad, mobile division of labor in urban centers (Chapter 11). The WEIRDer psychology that was emerging in fragmented communities across Europe, along with the accompanying changes in social norms, made people in these populations more likely to devise, endorse, and adopt particular kinds of ideas, laws, rules, policies, beliefs, practices, and arguments. Many modern ideas about law, government, science, philosophy, art, and religion that would have been "unthinkable," aversive, or nonintuitive to people in most complex societies over most of human history began to "fit" the emerging proto-WEIRD psychology in medieval and Early Modern Europe. In many cases, these new ideas, laws, and policies were filtered and selected by relentless intergroup competition between voluntary associations, including among cities, guilds, universities, monasteries, scientific associations, and eventually territorial states.[3]

Mapping the myriad connections and interactions between these societal developments and people's changing perceptions, motivations, worldviews, and decision biases could easily fill volumes. My goal here, however, is more modest. I want to illustrate how an increasingly WEIRD psychology likely midwifed a few of the quintessentially Western formal institutions that came to dominate the legal, political, scientific, and religious domains of life in the latter half of the second millennium.[4]

To warm up, let's consider four aspects of WEIRD psychology that likely had broad influences on the formal institutions built in Europe during the second millennium of the Common Era.

1. *Analytic thinking*: To better navigate a world of individuals without dense social interconnections, people increasingly thought

about the world more analytically and less holistically/relationally. More analytically oriented thinkers prefer to explain things by assigning individuals, cases, situations, or objects to discrete categories, often associated with specific properties, rather than by focusing on the relationships between individuals, cases, etc. The behavior of individuals or objects can then be analytically explained by their properties or category memberships (e.g., "it's an electron"; "he's an extrovert"). Troubled by contradictions, the more analytically minded seek out higher- or lower-level categories or distinctions to "resolve" them. By contrast, holistically oriented thinkers either don't see contradictions or embrace them. In Europe, analytical approaches gradually came to be thought of as superior to more holistic approaches. That is, they became normatively correct and highly valued.

2. *Internal attributions*: As the key substrates of social life shifted from relationships to individuals, thinkers increasingly highlighted the relevance of individuals' internal attributes. This included stable traits like dispositions, preferences, and personalities as well as mental states like beliefs and intentions. Soon lawyers and theologians even began to imagine that individuals had "rights."

3. *Independence* and *nonconformity*: Spurred by incentives to cultivate their own uniqueness, people's reverence for venerable traditions, ancient wisdom, and wise elders ebbed away. For good evolutionary reasons, humans everywhere tend to conform to peers, defer to their seniors, and follow enduring traditions; but, the incentives of a society with weak kin ties and impersonal markets pushed hard against this, favoring individualism, independence, and nonconformity, not to mention overconfidence and self-promotion.

4. *Impersonal prosociality*: As life was increasingly governed by impersonal norms for dealing with nonrelations or strangers, people came to prefer impartial rules and impersonal laws that applied

to those in their groups or communities (their cities, guilds, monasteries, etc.) independent of social relationships, tribal identity, or social class. Of course, we shouldn't confuse these inchoate inklings with the full-blown liberal principles of rights, equality, or impartiality in the modern world.

These and related aspects of psychology were taking hold in small but influential populations scattered across western Europe by the High Middle Ages. Throughout this book, I've occasionally pointed out the effects of this proto-WEIRD psychology on the creation of new formal institutions, but let's consolidate those ideas here, starting with law and government.

Universal Laws, Conflicting Principles, and Individual Rights

The gradual emergence of a WEIRDer psychology during the High Middle Ages, especially in the Church and free cities, meant that the ideas underpinning Western notions of government and law became "easier to think" and gradually more intuitive. At the same time, the dissolution of intensive kinship and the evaporation of tribal affiliations made it easier to implement laws governing individuals and to develop well-functioning representative assemblies. This change didn't start with fancy intellectuals, philosophers, or theologians positing grand theories of "democracy," the "rule of law," or "human rights." Instead, the ideas formed slowly, piece by piece, as regular Joes with more individualistic psychologies—be they monks, merchants, or artisans—began to form competing voluntary associations. Organizations had to decide how to govern themselves in ways that were both acceptable to current members and capable of attracting new members in competition with other organizations. Through a grinding process of myopic groping—not an intellectual epiphany rooted in some abstract rationality—a growing repertoire of social norms and organizational practices were cobbled together, exscribed into charters, and formulated into written laws. *Lex mercatoria*, for example, evolved into commercial law.

Consider the notion of individual rights or natural rights, which today provides the foundation for important statements like the Universal Declaration of Human Rights, adopted by the UN General Assembly in 1948. As we've already seen, medieval cities and towns competed for members by offering an expanding set of privileges for citizens that were formalized and assembled in urban charters. Urban centers with charters that attracted more members—presumably by offering people what they wanted while at the same time generating economic prosperity—were copied, amended, and recombined. Over time, urban charters increasingly offered legal protections (forms of "due process"), tax exemptions, property rights, mutual insurance, and freedom from conscription (by local rulers). A rising middle class of urbanites pushed rulers by demanding more rights, freedoms, and privileges. Persuaded by rising revenues and greater credit availability, princes, dukes, and other rulers often yielded to these demands.[5]

By 1200, deploying the ideas and concepts already in circulation, Church lawyers—the canonists—began to formally develop the notion of natural rights. These ideas soon infiltrated the universities, which were spreading rapidly during this period (Figure 10.6B). Over the course of centuries, these notions slowly trickled up to state-level governments. For example, in 1628 and 1689, the English Parliament passed the Petition of Right and the Bill of Rights, respectively. Both asserted the rights of individuals and Parliament over the monarch. The Petition of Right anticipates 4 of the 10 amendments in the U.S. Bill of Rights.[6]

We can infer how and why these ideas about individual rights emerged when they did by considering how people's psychology was changing. How would the residentially mobile individuals who were flocking to urban centers in various regions of medieval Europe have thought about law? Freed from the security of kin bonds and compelled to navigate a world of impersonal markets, competing organizations, and growing occupational specializations, they would have increasingly focused on their own attributes, intentions, and dispositions. With a newly analytic orientation, they would have tried to explain and justify rules and laws by referencing people's internal properties, not their relationships or lineages. When necessary, they would have concocted invisible properties like "rights" to organize laws rather than making up laws rationalized by the need to harmonize existing (inherited) relationships.

In contrast to these individual-centered legal developments in medieval Europe, punishments for crimes in China during the same era depended on the relationship between the individuals involved. In general, crimes committed against kin were punished more severely than those against nonrelatives, although elders could commit crimes against junior kin with lesser penalties than vice versa. In fact, even into the 20th century, Chinese fathers could murder their sons and receive only a warning, while a son who harmed his father or older brother faced much stiffer penalties. While such asymmetries can be justified on Confucian principles and by appealing to a deep respect for elders, this doesn't sit well in the WEIRD mind. We can understand it, but it doesn't strike most of us as a good argument in favor of a relational approach to law.[7]

Now let's come at this from the other direction. The Declaration of Independence asserts, "We hold these truths to be self-evident, that all men are created equal, that they are endowed by their creator with certain un-alienable rights, that among these are life, liberty, and the pursuit of happiness." If the idea that people are endowed with such abstract properties makes sense to you, then you are at least a little WEIRD. Claims about "unalienable rights" seem self-evident if one (a) tends to analytically explain or justify things with reference to internal and enduring attributes (not relationships or descent) and (b) prefers impartial rules that apply broadly to *distinct* categories or classes (e.g., "landowner"; "human"). By contrast, from the perspective of most human communities, the notion that each person has inherent rights or privileges disconnected from their social relationships or heritage is not self-evident. And from a scientific perspective, no "rights" have yet been detected hiding in our DNA or elsewhere. This idea sells because it appeals to a particular cultural psychology.[8]

Along with the development of individual rights, the canonists also started hashing out legal notions related to the role of mental states in criminal liability. Roman law as well as other early legal systems had taken some account of people's mental states in assessing criminal liability, usually by distinguishing intentional from accidental killings. But, Western law in the second millennium placed a large and growing emphasis on mental states. The medieval historian Brian Tierney writes,

> The concern with individual intention, individual consent, [and] individual will that characterized twelfth-century culture spilled over into many areas of canon law. In marriage law, by the end of the twelfth century, the simple consent of two parties, without any other formalities, could constitute a valid, sacramental marriage. In contract law, a bare promise could create a binding obligation—it was the intention of the promisor that counted. In criminal law, the degree of guilt and punishment was again related to the intention of the individual defendant, and this led on, as in modern legal systems, to complex considerations about negligence and diminished responsibility, areas of law that we nowadays think of as mediating between the rights of individuals and the maintenance of public order.[9]

In determining a person's criminal culpability, the canonists minutely dissected a perpetrator's beliefs, motives, and intentions. Consider this case: a blacksmith throws a hammer at his assistant and kills him. Medieval lawyers began asking not only if the smith *wanted* to kill his assistant (motive: the dead man had flirted with the blacksmith's wife) but also whether the smith *intended* to kill his assistant and *believed* the hammer would do the job. Does it matter if the blacksmith had intended to kill his assistant next week (using poison) but accidently killed him early with the hammer, thinking he was an intruder breaking in? They decided that the smith's culpability varied depending on which of several distinct mental states existed. In analyzing these mental states, the canonists suggested that criminal liability for murder and battery could be mitigated if people had acted in self-defense or were incapable of understanding what they were doing because they were young, confused, or mentally incapacitated. Unlike their Roman predecessors, whose chief goal was to enforce policies and protect important interests (e.g., property), the canonists were obsessed with the mental state of the accused. This focus on mental states meant that, contrary to laws and customs from early medieval Europe to premodern China, relatives couldn't justifiably share a perpetrator's guilt, responsibility, or punishment if they lacked the mental state necessary for culpability.[10]

These legal developments connect with psychological work discussed in earlier chapters. In addition to studying the impact of intentions on people's judgments of norm-violators in small-scale societies, Clark Barrett's anthropological team also studied how various "mitigating factors" might alter the inferences that people make about a perpetrator's mental state and thereby influence their judgment of culpability for a violent attack such as battery (punching someone in the face). Holding constant both the act itself (the punch) and the outcome (a bloody nose), the team explored five mitigating factors: the perpetrator (1) was acting in self-defense, (2) held an inaccurate belief about the situation, (3) possessed moral commitments distinct from those of the community he'd just arrived in, (4) was insane, or (5) acted out of necessity. In the second condition (inaccurate belief), the perpetrator believed that he was intervening to stop an attack, but in reality the "fighters" were just playing around. For the third condition, involving moral commitments, the perpetrator was from a society where it was considered proper, even respectable, to beat up wimpy-looking young men to toughen them up. In the last condition (necessity), the perpetrator needed to get to a bucket of water to put out a dangerous fire, but in the loud and crowded room he couldn't get to it quickly enough without dispatching an implacable guy in his path.

In all 10 of the populations studied, both self-defense and necessity were important mitigating factors—so, no one totally ignores mental states. But, in some societies, this was the only relevant distinction: perpetrators received no leniency for mistaken beliefs or insanity. At the other extreme, WEIRD people in Los Angeles finely distinguished the perpetrator's "badness" and the punishment he should receive based on all of these mitigating factors. Self-defense and necessity evoked the greatest leniency, respectively, followed by a mistaken belief and then insanity. Interestingly, different moral beliefs actually led WEIRD people to judge the perpetrator more harshly—intentionally punching someone and believing you are doing good seems to be worse than intentionally punching someone but thinking you are doing wrong. Across all 10 populations, the less intensive the kin-based institutions of a society, the more frequently people attended to the nuances of the perpetrator's mental states across our five mitigating factors.[11]

While the primacy of the individual—their rights and mental states—illuminates core trends in the development of the Western legal tradition, something even deeper was going on with law in the High Middle Ages. In his magisterial work *Law and Revolution*, the legal scholar and historian Harold Berman argues that as the 12th-century canonists were studying ancient Roman law—the Justinian Code—they saw something that wasn't really there. Assembled during the sixth century in the Eastern Empire, the Justinian Code is an immense compilation of law running thousands of pages. It includes a dizzying array of statutes, cases, and legal commentaries. Medieval jurists, with their analytical inclinations and Christian-derived moral universalism, naturally assumed that the specific laws and actual decisions were rooted in some set of universal legal principles, categories, or axioms from which all specifics could be derived. Thus, they went about the task of trying to back out general laws and principles from these specific Roman instantiations and cases. However, Berman convincingly argues that Roman legal tradition didn't have such fundamental principles or well-developed legal concepts. He writes,

> Indeed, Roman law from early times was permeated by such concepts as ownership, possession, delict, fraud, theft, and dozens of others. That was its great virtue. However, these concepts were not treated as ideas which pervaded the rules and determined their applicability. They were not considered philosophically. The concepts of Roman law, like its numerous legal rules, were tied to specific types of situations. Roman law consisted of an intricate

network of rules; yet these were not presented as an intellectual system but rather as an elaborate mosaic of practical solutions to specific legal problems. Thus one may say that although there were concepts in Roman law, there was no concept of a concept.[12]

Roman legal scholars had striven for consistency in the application of their laws, not for unifications and syntheses rooted in a set of fundamental principles, axioms, or rights. By contrast, as analytical thinkers from a moralizing religion, the canonists went looking for the universalizing principles.[13]

Since analytical thinkers hate contradictions, much of the development of Western law has been about ferreting out and resolving the contradictions that emerge when one tries to isolate a set of principles and apply them more broadly. The rights of one individual can conflict with the rights of another or the good of the group. If one is more holistically inclined, contradictions are neither especially salient nor bothersome. Since no two real situations are ever precisely identical, always varying in their specific contexts and the personal relationships involved, who's to even say that two legal decisions stand in contradiction? Moreover, in many societies, law is about restoring harmony and maintaining the peace, not, as it is for more analytical thinkers, about defending individual rights or making sure that abstract principles of "justice" are served.[14]

Medieval lawyers thought they were deducing or inferring divine or universal laws—God's laws. They believed that these laws existed (out there, somewhere), so scholars just had to figure them out. This meant that, unlike their predecessors in Germanic or Roman law, medieval rulers were subject to their own laws. The important laws descended from an authority higher than any emperor, king, or prince. This approach, which became increasingly intuitive for Christians with a proto-WEIRD psychology, was crucial to the development of both the constraints on executive power—constitutional government—and notions of the rule of law.[15]

Later, following their brethren in the legal realm, natural philosophers sought laws to explain the physical world. Like the canonists, these scientists believed that there were indeed hidden (divine) laws governing the universe that could be uncovered. As psychological universalists, many believed that if two different models or sets of principles purported to explain some physical phenomenon, they couldn't both be right—the universe is either one way or it's another. As analytical thinkers, they often sought to break complex systems down into their constituent parts—elements, molecules, planets, genes, etc.—and explain their action by reference to internal (and often invisible) properties like mass, charge, gravity, and geometry. As individualists and nonconformists, they would be motivated to show off their genius, creativity, and independence of mind, if only to their friends and peers.

Consider the case of Nicolaus Copernicus, who, in 1514, after receiving his doctorate in canon law, developed a model of the solar system that placed the sun at the center with the planets in orbit—the heliocentric model (published in 1543). To understand Copernicus's contribution, let's consider two background points. First, Islamic astronomers were ahead of their European counterparts until at least the 14th century. In fact, it appears that these scholars, who were working from Ptolemy's ancient model, had figured out most of the major components of Copernicus's model well before he did. In the 13th century, for example, Ibn al-Shatir (a religious timekeeper in Damascus) had produced a mathematical model that was formally identical to that of Copernicus except that it remained earth-centered. But, brilliant as they were, these thinkers never made Copernicus's conceptual breakthrough. Second, while Copernicus got the relative position of the sun correct, he assumed that the planets were in circular orbits. This mistake meant that al-Shatir's model still made better predictions. Nevertheless, the Copernican model was published, faced off against competing models, and inspired subsequent work. Johannes Kepler, building on Copernicus's sun-centered model, explored using elliptical orbits for the planets, and his model solidly beat all prior efforts. Naturally, Kepler believed that he'd discovered some of God's divine laws for the cosmos. So, what was Copernicus's big contribution?[16]

It seems to me that it was his willingness to go out on a limb, bucking fundamental Greek and Christian worldviews by putting the sun at the center and making Earth just another planet. By disregarding authority and challenging the ancient sages, he got the idea out there for others to consider and build on. He also persevered despite the fact that the empirical evidence supporting his model wasn't particularly strong—it's a good thing he was overconfident. Perhaps more important than Copernicus himself, however, was the relative openness of the social world that he lived in. Some scholars criticized his ideas while others lauded them. The Church, for its part, didn't seriously object to his ideas for seven decades, when Galileo pushed the issue. Of course, we don't have psychological data on individual scientists or their communities, but the case nevertheless illustrates how the kinds of psychological differences I've been laying out through this book would have shaped scientific insights, institutions, and discourse.

As Copernicus was banishing Earth from its role at center stage, the impact of a WEIRDer psychology had begun to manifest in a variety of ways. Let's consider two of these. First, with their growing willingness to break with tradition, the intellectuals of the early modern period started to realize that the great ancient sages, like Aristotle, could be wrong; in fact, they were wrong about a great many things. This meant that individuals could discover entirely new knowledge—things no one ever knew. The historian David Wootton argues that the very notion of "discovery" as a conscious activity emerged during this period, marked by the diffusion of words for "discovery" across European languages—variants of "discovery" first appear in 1484 (Portuguese) and 1504 (Italian); then later, in the titles of books, in 1524 (Dutch), 1553 (French), 1554 (Spanish), and 1563 (English).

Second, with an increased focus on mental states, intellectuals began to associate new ideas, concepts, and insights with particular individuals, and to credit the first founders, observers, or inventors whenever possible. Our commonsensical inclination to associate inventions with their inventors has been historically and cross-culturally rare. This shift has been marked by the growth of eponymy in the naming of new lands ("America"), scientific laws ("Boyle's Law"), ways of thinking ("Newtonian"), anatomical parts ("fallopian tubes"), and much more. After about 1600, Europeans even began to relabel ancient insights and inventions based on their purported founders or discoverers. "Pythagoras's theorem," for example, had been called the "Dulcarnon" (a word derived from an Arabic phrase for "two-horned," which described Pythagoras's accompanying diagram). Finally, well before any patent laws, people began adopting the notion that it was wrong to copy and promulgate others' manuscripts, mathematical proofs, or even ideas without giving them credit. People came to think that novel mental states—ideas, concepts, equations, and recipes—were somehow linked to, or "owned" by, the first person to publicly claim them. As intuitive as such ownership might seem to us, it runs counter to customary practices that stretch back into antiquity. The notion that something as immaterial as an idea, song, or concept could be individually owned began to make intuitive sense. Marking this in English, words for "plagiarism" first began to spread in the 16th century, following the introduction in 1598 of the word "plagiary," which derives from the Latin word for kidnapping.[17]

My point: a WEIRDer psychology in some preindustrial European populations favored the development and spread of certain kinds of laws, norms, and principles, including those dealing with both human relations and the physical world. Of course, as both Western law and science began to emerge, they in turn further shaped aspects of WEIRD psychology. Perhaps the easiest place to see the impact of the new legal reforms is in studies of the psychological effects of democratic institutions. Similarly, the influence of science has been considerable. But, as you'll see, scientists may have had their biggest impact on our epistemic norms, by shaping what counts as good evidence or valid reasons.

Representative Governments and Democracy

Elements of participatory and representative governance began diffusing during the High Middle Ages. Elections were increasingly used by voluntary organizations to select leaders and make decisions. We saw, for example, that Cistercian monks in the 11th century began electing their abbots from among the membership. At the same time, representative assemblies formed in some urban communities as guilds and other associations vied for power. Members of these assemblies, rather than representing neighborhoods, often represented guilds or religious organizations within the community. In some cities, the governing councils were simply merchant oligarchies. But elsewhere, the franchise was expanding to include members of a growing number of associations, who increasingly asserted their "right" to representation. Alone, individuals were virtually powerless to assert their rights, but when they banded together in groups with shared interests, they could exert real influence. Since cities, guilds, universities, and monastic orders competed for members, those with the most appealing forms of government tended to grow the fastest and attract the psychologically WEIRDest people.[18]

These social and political changes were supported by early developments in canon law, which laid the foundations for modern corporate law. Canon law asserted that appointed leaders or representatives of corporations (voluntary associations) had to obtain the consent of their membership before taking important actions. This idea evolved into a constitutional principle summarized in the Roman maxim "What concerns everyone ought to be considered and approved by everyone." Medieval European legalists, however, arrived at new principles by unwittingly reinterpreting what they thought they saw in Roman law. The Roman Empire certainly didn't think it needed the consent of the governed—the quotation was context- and case-specific. However, filtered through a proto-WEIRD psychological prism, this maxim starts to sound like common sense, almost a self-evident truth. Since university-trained lawyers were well grounded in canon law, these and other aspects of Church law provided the point of departure for subsequent developments in corporate law and constitutional government throughout Europe and beyond.[19]

The door to formal democratic practices and ideas opened in the High Middle Ages for both social and psychological reasons. Socially, practices like voting or consensus building don't function particularly well when perched atop strong kin-based institutions. To see why, consider this description by the Afghan-born author Tamim Ansary:

But I keep remembering the elections held in Afghanistan after the Taliban had fled the country. Across the nation, people chose delegates to represent them at a national meeting organized by the United States to forge a new democratic government, complete with parliament, constitution, president, and cabinet . . . I met a man who said he had voted in the elections . . . he looked like the traditional rural villagers I had known in my youth, with the standard long shirt, baggy pants, turban, and beard, so I asked him to describe the voting process for me—what was the actual activity?

"Well, sir," he said, "a couple of city men came around with slips of paper and went on and on about how we were supposed to make marks on them, and we listened politely, because they had come a long way and we didn't want to be rude, but we didn't need those city fellows to tell us who our man was. We made the marks they wanted, but we always knew who would be representing us— Agha-i-Sayyaf, of course."

"And how did you settle on Sayyaf?" I asked.

"Settle on him? Sir! What do you mean? His family has lived here since the days of Dost Mohammed Khan and longer . . . Did you know that my sister's husband has a cousin who is married to Sayyaf's sister-in-law? He's one of our own."[20]

The strong in-group loyalty reflected in this passage meant that the only candidate the Afghan men would consider voting for was one of their own, at which point they traced a link to him through a long series of kin ties: *"my sister's husband has a cousin who is married to Sayyaf's sister-in-law."* This influence means that elections are largely determined by the size of the different voting blocs. Bigger clans, tribes, or ethnic groups generally win— sometimes even turning into political parties—and people can't easily switch teams. The dissolution of intensive kinship and tribal organizations in medieval Europe meant that democratic practices had a better shot at working. Similarly, group discussions or debates over new policies aren't very productive if everyone just agrees with the head of their clan or those who share their ethnic markers or religion.[21]

Psychologically, participatory governing practices would have appealed to people in a couple of ways. More individualistic and independent people like to distinguish themselves by expressing their opinions, and often don't mind going against the grain. A group debate or public vote gives individuals a way to set themselves apart from others, to express their uniqueness and sense of personal identity. This contrasts with psychological inclinations that favor peer conformity, deference to elders, shame-avoidance, and respect for traditional authorities. Boldly disagreeing with the group opinion or pointing out the flaws in ancient wisdom has not been a way to impress others in most complex societies.

Relatedly, another aspect of the individualism complex is a preference for choice or control. WEIRD people prefer the things they themselves pick and work harder on tasks they've chosen than on identical tasks assigned by an authority. By contrast, less individualistic populations are not particularly inspired by opportunities to make their own choices or to take control.[22]

These psychological patterns, and specifically people's inclination to buck authority and their desire for choice, influence what researchers call the *democracy premium*. Both laboratory and field experiments suggest that some populations will contribute more to the group and stick more strictly to the group's rules when they have had a say—typically a vote—in decision-making. As usual, laboratory research on this has been based almost exclusively on WEIRD people; however, a couple of recent studies failed to find a democracy premium in Mongolia and China. In rural China, men contributed the most in an experimental Public Goods Game when a "law" was externally imposed on them, not when they voted for it. Psychologically, those with stronger inclinations to defer to authority and less desire for control cooperated more in response to externally imposed laws and less with the results of democratic votes. Only when these psychological tendencies are sufficiently weak in a large fraction of the population does the democracy premium emerge. It's an emergent piece of cultural psychology.[23]

This evidence suggests not only that medieval Europeans would have been more socially and psychologically susceptible to formal democratic institutions, but that democratic institutions would have actually worked better by inspiring those with a proto-WEIRD psychology to contribute more to the group and follow the rules. I also suspect that the changing psychological substrate influenced what people saw as an acceptable source of legitimacy in government. Like most sovereigns over the course of human history, medieval European rulers had found their source of legitimacy in some combination of divine mandates and the specialness of their lineage. Gradually, however, especially after 1500, individuals began to see "the people" or "the governed" as a potential source of legitimacy—not gods, descent, or some mix of these. This argument, which connects intensive kin-based institutions through psychology to democratic institutions, hinges on contemporary research, much of it done in university laboratories. Is there a way to make these connections in the real world and link them back into history?

We can tackle this in three ways. First, in the modern world, if we look at the adult children of immigrants to Europe—as we did with impersonal trust, individualism, and conformity in Chapter 7—we find that individuals whose origins can be traced to societies with more intensive kinship engage in less political activity: they vote less, sign fewer petitions, support fewer boycotts, and attend fewer demonstrations. Remember, although their parents migrated from other countries, these individuals all grew up in the same European countries. Despite that, individuals with cultural backgrounds involving less intensive kinship are more engaged politically, an effect that holds even after the influence of age, sex, religion, income, employment status, and any feelings of discrimination (among many other factors) are statistically held constant. These findings suggest that intensive kinship—operating through cultural transmission—psychologically inhibits participatory governance, political pluralism, and the quality of democratic institutions. Similarly, if we again zoom in on Italy, we find that the higher the rate of cousin marriage in an Italian province during the 20th century, the lower the voter turnout in the 21st century.[24]

Second, recall from Chapter 9 that the longer a city was exposed to the Church's Marriage and Family Program through proximity to a bishopric, the more likely that city was to develop a representative form of government (Figure 9.6). So, exposure to the MFP did indeed cash out in more participatory governance and less autocracy. Tellingly, the probability of adopting participatory or representative forms of government in the Islamic world or in China during the same era was zero—it was "unthinkable."[25]

Finally, when comparing countries, we see similar relationships between intensive kinship and democracy. Countries with more intensive kinship have governments deemed less democratic in international rankings. In fact, knowing the historical rate of cousin marriage in a country allows us to account for about half of the total variation in the quality of national-level democratic institutions (Figure 12.1). When intensive kin-based institutions persist, national-level democratic institutions flounder.[26]

Taken together, these lines of evidence support the notion that the Church, by dissolving intensive kinship and shifting people's psychology, opened the way for the slow expansion of political pluralism and modern democracy.[27]

To be clear, this is not one-way causation. Psychology, norms, and formal institutions interact in a kind of feedback loop. The emergence of particular psychological patterns within a population can prepare the way for new formal institutions, including laws, democracy, and representative governments; at the same time, the creation of new formal institutions— fitted to a population's psychology and social norms—can then catalyze further psychological shifts. To see this, let's consider the long-term psychological effects of adopting formal democratic institutions during the preindustrial era.

Beginning in the 13th century, the region that became modern Switzerland was developing a kaleidoscope of towns and cities. Some of these urban areas began adopting forms of participatory governance, while others remained under the autocratic rule of hereditary nobles. This patchy mixture of democracy and autocracy continued until Napoleon conquered the

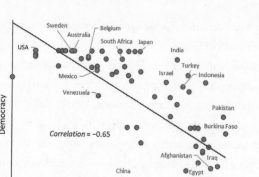

FIGURE 12.1. The relationship between the prevalence of cousin marriage and the quality of national-level democratic institutions. Countries with more cousin marriage have weaker democracies.[28]

region, in 1803, and granted all communities the right to self-government, at which point democracy prevailed.

Spotting this natural experiment, the economists Marcella Veronesi and Devesh Rustagi administered a two-person Public Goods Game to 262 people drawn from 174 communities around Switzerland. This one-shot experiment was the same one that Devesh had deployed among the Oromo in Ethiopia to study market integration (Chapter 9). In this experiment, individuals are asked how much they will contribute for each of the possible amounts that their partner might contribute (if their partner goes first), and these decisions are binding. This method allows researchers to assess people's inclinations for conditional cooperation with strangers by assigning each participant a score from −100 to 100 based on how positively or negatively they respond to others' contributions. The average score for this Swiss sample is 65. To assess when different Swiss communities first established democratic or participatory formal institutions, the economics duo dug into the historical data. Since all Swiss communities became democratic in some way after Napoleon's arrival, they calculated how long each community had been under some form of democratic or participatory governance prior to 1803 CE.

The analysis shows that people from Swiss communities with a longer history of participatory governance are more conditionally cooperative with strangers today. In fact, for each additional century of exposure to democratic government, a contemporary person's inclination for conditional cooperation increases by nearly nine points. Since the average is 65, nine points is a big effect. Expressed differently, comparing communities that had participatory governance before Napoleon arrived with those who only developed it after, the results show that individuals from the "pre-Napoleon democracies" (scoring 83) are roughly twice as conditionally cooperative as those from "post-Napoleon democracies" (scoring only 42).

Of course, maybe there's something special about the communities that adopted democratic forms of government early, something that both caused the precocious political developments and explains the contemporary psychological differences. This isn't a true experiment, because we didn't get to randomly assign "democracy" to some communities but not others.

To tackle this concern, Marcella and Devesh took advantage of a random political shock. In 1218, Duke Berthold suddenly died without heirs, bringing the Zähringen dynasty to an abrupt, peaceful, and unexpected end. The cities and towns within the former Zähringen realm were freed to develop their own forms of governance, and many developed participatory or representative institutions. Meanwhile, the other surrounding dynasties didn't suddenly end, so their communities had to wait for later opportunities, and some had to wait for Napoleon. The duke's death without heirs provides the randomness we need. Knowing about this historical shock allows us to "pull out"—with some statistical razzle-dazzle—just the variation in historical democratic governance that we know is effectively random and see if it alone can explain contemporary conditional cooperation with strangers.

Sure enough, the analysis confirms that each additional century of democratic governance causes the modern Swiss to increase their conditional cooperation by nearly nine percentile points, roughly the same as in the full analysis above. It seems that formal democratic institutions do indeed make their populations more conditionally cooperative, at least in Switzerland.[29]

My point: an increasingly WEIRD psychology fostered the development of more democratic and participatory forms of governance, and, once established, these formal institutions pushed WEIRD psychology further along, at least in some dimensions, perhaps by further reducing the value of extended families and dense relational networks while encouraging impersonal commerce and greater competition among voluntary associations.[30]

The WEIRDest Religion

Protestantism is a family of religious faiths that place individuals' personal commitments and their relationship with the divine at the core of spiritual life. Fancy rituals, immense cathedrals, big sacrifices, and ordained priests typically play little role and may be openly condemned. Individuals, through the power of their own choices, build a personal relationship directly with God, in part by reading and pondering holy scripture on their own or in small groups. To connect with God, adherents needn't defer to their ancestors, great sages, a religious hierarchy, or Church traditions. In principle, the only thing Protestants defer to is scripture. In many denominations, anyone can become a religious leader and no special training is required. These leaders are formally equal with their congregations, though of course their prestige may permit certain privileges. Salvation—a contingent afterlife—is generally achieved based on people's own internal mental states—their faith. Rituals and good deeds play little or no role. Intentions and beliefs, or what's in a person's heart, are most important. Thinking about murder, theft, or adultery is often a sin in and of itself. Leading denominations also emphasize that all people have a calling—a freely chosen occupation or vocation—that uniquely fits their special attributes and endowments. Working hard to successfully pursue one's calling with diligence, patience, and self-discipline is doing God's work. Sometimes this helps individuals get to heaven, but other times it just publicly marks them as one of the chosen.[31]

Ring any bells? I'm hoping this description resonates with the psychological patterns we've been stacking up and explaining throughout this book: individualism, independence, nonrelational morality, impersonal prosociality (equality of strangers), nonconformity, resistance to tradition, guilt over shame, hard work, self-regulation, the centrality of mental states in moral judgments, and the molding of one's disposition to a chosen occupation.

What Protestantism did in the 16th century was to sacralize the psychological complex that had been percolating in Europe during the centuries leading up to the Reformation. The case I've made is that many populations had already developed an individualistic psychology that embodied—if only in inchoate forms—the psychological core of the 16th-century religious movements that made up Protestantism. Martin Luther himself was an Augustinian *monk* employed at a *university* in the *charter town* of Wittenberg (that's three voluntary associations). Protestant faiths spread so rapidly, in part, because their core religious values and ways of seeing the world meshed with the era's proto-WEIRD psychology. Of course, there were lots of political and economic reasons why various kings, dukes, and princes leapt into this bandwagon—e.g., the Church owned tons of land that these rulers could confiscate. But, rulers got away with this in part because Protestant faiths resonated deeply with important swaths of the populace. In other words, the processes I've been describing throughout this book—the emergence of nuclear families, impersonal markets, and competing voluntary associations—had tilled the psychological fields of Europe for the seeds of the Reformation.[32]

Of course, the Protestant Reformation wasn't a bolt from the blue, nor is it best understood as a single movement or event. Instead, it represents a cultural evolutionary process in which like-minded individuals were developing diverse religious organizations, each with its own supernatural beliefs, rituals, and practices. Some of these religious packages fit better with the emerging psychological patterns than those found within the mainline Roman Catholic Church. Many harbingers of the Reformation had appeared during the Middle Ages. For example, observers going back to at least Max Weber have noticed the similarity between Protestantism and the Cistercian Order (1089). Later, in the 14th century, John Wycliffe in England argued that Christians should read the scripture for themselves rather than relying on popes and priests. As Luther would do over a century later, he translated the Bible into the local language—Middle English. Like Luther and his contemporaries, Wycliffe revered Augustine and inveighed against both the papal hierarchy and indulgences. Though they were snuffed out before taking root, religious movements like Wycliffe's were more compatible with the proto-WEIRD psychology developing in many European populations than were their Catholic competitors. By understanding that Protestantism was in part a response to the changing psychological landscape, we can understand not only why it emerged and spread but also why it tended to be so individualistic, disciplined, egalitarian, self-focused, faith-oriented, and mentalistic.[33]

In contrast to many Protestant sects, the Church itself was—perhaps ironically—built on a patriarchal (Roman) family model. Authority is vertical and strict, as in a patrilineage. Religious elders, who came to be called "father" or "papa" (pope), possessed privileged access to divine truths and special powers, including the power to grant (channel) God's forgiveness. Endowed with wisdom and holiness, Church leaders should be revered and obeyed. Only through the Church, and its specialized rites and elite practitioners, can an average person find a path to God and the afterlife. There are no unmediated personal relationships with God.[34]

Of course, faced with competition from various Protestant denominations, the Church evolved over time in ways that made it more compatible with WEIRD psychology, especially in certain corners like the Jesuit Order. These reforms, however, could only go so far, since the Church undermines its eternal authority every time it changes the rules for admission to heaven. Prior to the Reformation, without much competition for adherents, the Church hadn't been adapting to the changing psychology of the faithful.

Is Protestantism, like democratic governance, also a two-way psychological street? Did the institutions and beliefs developed by these proliferating religious communities foster subsequent psychological changes?

Did Protestantism—or at least some Protestant denominations—catalyze downstream effects on people's psychology in ways that fueled economic prosperity?

Yes, probably, although as you'll see, it's complicated. In the Prelude, you saw how the Protestant belief that each Christian should read the Bible for themselves drove the spread of literacy and formal schooling, first across Europe, and then around the globe. By driving widespread literacy, Protestantism thickened people's corpus callosa, sharpened their verbal memories, and eroded their facial recognition abilities. But, how else did Protestantism shape people's minds?[35]

BOOSTER SHOTS

Protestantism acts like a booster shot for many of the WEIRD psychological patterns we've been examining throughout this book. In Chapter 6 we examined, at the national level, the influence of kinship intensity and exposure to the Western Church on many psychological measures. These same analyses also revealed that over and above the impact of kinship intensity or Church dosage, countries with Protestant majorities show even higher individualism (Figures 1.2 and 6.4), greater impersonal trust (Figures 1.7 and 6.6), and a stronger emphasis on creativity compared to majority Catholic countries. On average, people in Protestant countries gave more anonymous blood donations, and their diplomats at the United Nations accumulated even fewer unpaid parking tickets. Comparing just individuals from the same regions within Europe (Chapter 7), those who identified themselves as Protestants (compared to Catholics) showed greater individualism-independence, less conformity-obedience, and more impersonal trust and fairness toward strangers. Here, the "booster shots" of Protestantism are over and above the historical influence of the Church.[36]

Other analyses using different datasets further underscore and extend these findings. Comparing thousands of individuals within 32 countries, the economist Benito Arruñada finds that Protestants are (1) less tied to their families, (2) less tolerant of tax fraud, and (3) more trusting of strangers than are demographically and economically similar Catholics in the same countries. Protestants are also less willing to lie in court to save a friend who was driving recklessly in the Passenger's Dilemma (Figure 1.6). This suggests that, relative to Catholics, European Protestants show an even stronger nonrelational morality and greater impersonal prosociality.[37]

Filling in this picture further, psychological research led by Adam Cohen compares the importance of mental states for Protestants, Catholics, and Jews in the United States. Consider this vignette, which was administered to participants at the University of Pennsylvania:

> Mr. K. is a 1992 graduate of the University of Pennsylvania. He is very involved with his job at a marketing research firm. Mr. K. was eager to graduate college and start working so that he would not be dependent on his parents anymore because, to tell the truth, Mr. K. has never liked his parents very much. In his heart, Mr. K. finds them to be too involved in his life and they have very different personalities and goals from him.

You then learn that Mr. K. either (A) largely ignores his parents, forgetting to call or visit on their birthdays, or (B) pretends to like them by calling, visiting, and sending nice birthday gifts.

Does Mr. K. have a good character? Is it better to "fake it" and just go through the motions of honoring one's parents, even if you don't personally like them, or should you remain true to your feelings (or change your feelings)?

Protestants differed from Jews at Penn. On average, Jews felt that Mr. K. had a good character when he behaved in nice ways toward his parents. When his feelings and actions matched and he treated his parents poorly, they rated him as having a bad character. Protestants, by contrast, thought that Mr. K. was just a bad character; they rated him pretty much the same—poorly—independent of his actions. What mattered to Protestants was Mr. K.'s mental state—he was apparently feeling the "wrong" way about his parents.

Similar results emerge if you have Jews and Protestants judging a man who considered having an affair with an attractive coworker—pondering it a lot—but eventually deciding against it. The Jews tended to let him off lightly, focusing on what he actually did. Protestants, by contrast, were much tougher on the man, despite his steely self-control. Notably, American Jews and Protestants didn't differ on how they judged the man if he went ahead with the affair; they only differed when his actions didn't match his mental states. President Jimmy Carter, a southern Baptist from Georgia, crystallized the Protestant sentiment aptly when he said in an interview, "I've looked on a lot of women with lust. I've committed adultery in my heart many times." By contrast, many non-Protestants maintain that it's not adultery if it remains only a mental state.[38]

Comparing American Protestants and Catholics reveals somewhat smaller differences, but it still appears that Protestants are more focused than Catholics on people's internal states, beliefs, feelings, and dispositions. In one battery of studies, Cohen and his collaborators showed that Protestants are more inclined than Catholics to make the Fundamental Attribution Error—that tendency of WEIRD people to focus on others' internal dispositions over obvious contextual factors when judging them. Cohen's team makes the case, through a series of experiments, that this effect is driven by how Protestants think about the independence of the soul. Unlike Catholics, who have their Church, priests, sacraments (e.g., Confession and Penance), communities, and the prayers of their families and friends to help their souls enter the kingdom of heaven, Protestants stand alone, naked and solitary before a judgmental God.

Okay, but what about Max Weber's hypothesis, which linked Protestantism, via its effect on psychology, to the origins of capitalism? Do Protestants—or some Protestant sects (e.g., Calvinists)—show a stronger work ethic, greater thrift, and more patience, as suggested by the famous German sociologist?

SACRED WORK, FORBIDDEN SEX, AND SUICIDE

Establishing a firm causal connection between Protestantism and psychological outcomes such as a stronger work ethic has proven tricky for several reasons. First, we've learned of religious movements in Europe prior to the Reformation that probably created similar psychological effects. Monastic movements like the Cistercians, who emphasized the purifying power of work, were bubbling up in Europe for five centuries prior to the Reformation. As we saw, "Cistercian-treated" Catholics look "Protestant" in their work ethic, which means that if you want to isolate the impact of Protestantism, you need to account for the Cistercians. Second, the Church's ongoing competition with Protestantism may have narrowed the difference between Protestants and Catholics, at least locally wherever the competition was fierce. For example, forged in the fires of the Counter-Reformation, the Jesuit Order strongly promoted schooling, literacy, self-discipline, and industry in a manner that parallels many Protestant faiths. Recent evidence suggests that the Jesuits—at least where they had full control—created long-term psychological legacies that seem even more "Protestant" than those of the Cistercians. Third, clear findings may also be blurred by other ethnic and religious groups who have independently developed strong work ethics of their own—both cultural Jews and Han Chinese provide ready examples. Finally, there's a case to be made that some aspects of Puritan psychology broke free from their religious moorings and infused themselves more broadly into the foundations of American culture and psychology— as Alexis de Tocqueville noted in the opening epigraph, even nonreligious Americans (like me) seem a bit "Protestant."[39]

Despite these challenges, a growing body of work supports the notion that Protestant beliefs and practices foster hard work, patience, and diligence. Let's start with the big picture. Globally, if we compare countries, the higher the percentage of Protestants in a country, the more patient people are in the delay-discounting task mapped in Figure 1.4. This effect gets even bigger if one uses the percentage of Protestants in 1900 instead of the contemporary values.[40]

The problem with this research, like most that connects Protestantism to either psychological measures like delay discounting or to actual behavior like working hours, is that people today can switch religions or drop out entirely. So, we can't tell if more patient people like Protestantism or if maybe higher incomes cause people to both become more patient and adopt Protestantism. Both could cause the observed correlations. Fortunately, there's a natural experiment created by the complex politics of the Holy Roman Empire in the 16th century that suggests, at least tentatively, that Protestantism does indeed foster a stronger work ethic. At the Peace of Augsburg in 1555, which ended the war between the emperor Charles V and the rebellious Lutheran princes, it was decided that each local ruler within the empire could individually decide if their populace would be Catholic or Protestant. These local rulers made their decisions for a variety of idiosyncratic reasons, including personal religious convictions and the necessities of regional politics. Eventually, Germans would be able to freely pick their religions, but by then the die was cast, and most people simply stuck with the faith that had been selected by the local ruler who happened to be in charge after the Peace of Augsburg. Today, the impact of these princely decisions still explains much of the variation in Protestant and Catholic affiliations across German counties (Figure P.2 for variation in 1871).

You can see the natural experimental setup here if you think of the 16th-century rulers' decisions as imposing a Protestant or Catholic "treatment" on different populations throughout the empire—some populations got the "Protestant treatment," while others got the "Catholic treatment." Knowing the decisions of the rulers allows us to extract and study only the variation in contemporary religion—Catholic vs. Protestant—that was caused by the rulers' decisions. Combining this with data on people's contemporary work time, detailed analyses reveal that those populations "treated" with Protestantism now work longer hours compared to those treated with Catholicism. Specifically, Protestantism induces Germans to work approximately three to four more hours per week on average. This effect holds independent of people's age, sex, education, marital status, and number of children, among other factors. The upshot is that while Protestants don't receive higher wages than Catholics (once differences in education are accounted for), they do end up making higher incomes because they work longer hours and tend to pick jobs, like starting businesses, that permit them to work more. This is consistent with other work showing that being unemployed reduces the sense of well-being in Protestants more than it does in Catholics; presumably, Protestants' occupations tend to be more central to their sense of self or proximity to God.[41]

Complementing this real-world evidence, laboratory work by psychologists has begun to probe some of the ways that Protestant beliefs may increase self-regulation and cause people to work harder. After committing a sin, Catholics who experience guilt can set things right by confessing their sin to a priest and doing Penance. Having completed their Penance, Catholics are forgiven and can merge back on the fast track to heaven (or so they think). For Protestants, in contrast, there's no straightforward route from sin to confession, penance, and forgiveness. Instead, doing something sinful—which includes things like thinking about forbidden sex—seems to evoke a compensatory response that involves doing more "good stuff." Since many Protestants see their occupations as divine callings, or simply see productive work as purifying, their compensatory response is often to work harder.

Exploring this in the laboratory, Emily Kim and her colleagues first used a clever technique to induce a sample of Protestant, Catholic, and Jewish men to think about sex with their sisters, and then reminded some of the men of eternal salvation using a word-unscrambling task. Finally, they had the men work on various projects. When Protestants were induced to think about sibling incest, they worked harder and more creatively on the projects. This effect was especially strong after they were reminded of salvation. By contrast, the guilt experienced by Jews or Catholics—if anything—deflated their efforts on these projects. Now, this effect could be due to either the fact that Protestants more strongly perceive incestuous thoughts as wrong or because they have no easy way to wash those sins away.

This research suggests that, by modifying Catholic beliefs, some forms of Protestantism may have stumbled onto an ingenious way to harness men's cravings for forbidden sex to motivate them to work harder, longer, and more creatively. Protestants can boil off their guilt through productive work, by heeding their calling. If this preliminary research holds up, it represents a fascinating means through which religious beliefs have evolved to tap a deep reservoir of creative energy.

Whatever the source of people's motivations, the Protestant work ethic can be observed in the real world in a variety of ways, including in voting patterns. Using a natural experiment in Switzerland, researchers have demonstrated that a history of Protestantism influences how citizens vote on national referendums. Switzerland has a substantial degree of direct democracy, so there are voting records on many specific laws. The results show that Protestants tend to vote against statutes that would limit work time, such as those that mandate more vacation, lower the official retirement age, and shorten the workweek. Protestants want to work—it's a sacred value.[42]

What about the role of Protestantism in the massive economic expansion that occurred in Europe after 1500, and particularly in the economic takeoff known as the Industrial Revolution? Before addressing this question, I must emphasize that the psychological changes I've been describing had fully prepared the way for individualizing religions built on the centrality of mental states, personal faith, and individual intentions. If Charles V had executed Luther immediately at the Diet of Worms in 1521 (snuffing out the Protestant Reformation), something like Protestantism would have soon sprung up to take its place. I can suggest this with some confidence because, even prior to Luther, Protestant-like movements were already popping up. For example, a movement called the Brethren of the Common Life had diffused throughout many cities and towns in the Netherlands and into Germany during the 14th century. Like the later Protestant movements, the Brethren preached the value of manual labor and encouraged individuals to develop their own personal relationship with God. Of course, as part of this, it was thought that people should learn to read scripture for themselves. Unlike Protestantism, the Brethren managed to get a stamp of approval from a local bishop, so they were officially inside the Church. Before Luther stepped on the stage in 1517, the Brethren had spread literacy and probably fueled urban growth in many Dutch and some German cities. The key here is to realize that Protestantism was a set of thematically related religious movements that were coalescing in diverse ways around the psychological patterns that had developed in several European populations.[43]

With this point underlined, the spread of Protestantism (or particular versions of it) likely did change people's psychology, preferences, and behaviors in ways that propelled economic growth and political change. After 1500, the more Protestant regions of Europe grew economically more quickly than the Catholic regions, even though many of the Catholic regions were initially richer. After 1800, Protestant faiths probably had their biggest impact on income and economic growth. By instilling thrift, patience, and an internalized work ethic while at the same time requiring literacy and encouraging schooling, Protestantism had psychologically prepared the rural populace to participate in and fuel the Industrial Revolution. Evidence from the 19th century during the German Industrial Revolution shows that compared to Catholicism, early Protestantism fostered higher literacy rates, greater incomes, and more engagement in manufacturing and service industries (vs. agriculture).[44]

Politically, Protestantism probably encouraged the formation of democratic and representative governments, first in Europe and then around the globe. This occurred (and continues to occur) for several interrelated reasons. First, unlike the hierarchical Church, Protestantism requires communities to develop their own self-governing religious organizations using democratic principles. Going all the way back to the early Protestant reforms under Ulrich Zwingli, Swiss towns and villages were encouraged to use majority votes to make local decisions. This gives Protestants experience in creating self-governing organizations and implementing democratic principles. In the 19th and 20th centuries, Protestant missionaries encouraged the formation of political action groups and NGOs throughout the world. Second, as I've explained, Protestantism promoted literacy, schooling, and the printing press. These tend to strengthen the middle class, foster economic productivity, and permit freer speech. Finally, the booster shot to WEIRD psychology provided by Protestantism makes impartial laws, personal independence, and freedom of expression even more psychologically appealing and socially necessary. Globally, non-European countries that have historically experienced more intensive missionary activity from Protestants became more democratic by the second half of the 20th century.[45]

Besides encouraging literacy, schooling, democracy, and economic growth, Protestantism has another important effect. It can open people up to suicide. The journey to God in these most individualistic of faiths is ultimately a solo act that can leave people feeling isolated and alone. Max Weber noted that Protestantism can induce "a feeling of unprecedented loneliness." Other observers have long suspected that at least some forms of Protestantism, with their emphasis on self-reliance and personal responsibility, might increase people's chances of committing suicide relative to Catholicism. This is a long-running debate that stretches back to at least the late 19th century, when the French sociologist Émile Durkheim highlighted the question.

Today, better datasets have permitted researchers to shed new light on this old question. In particular, the economists we met back in the Prelude, Sascha Becker and Ludger Woessmann, assembled the earliest available statistical data on suicide from 305 counties in 19th-century Prussia. They first established that counties with higher percentages of Protestants in the 19th century had higher suicide rates. All-Protestant counties had on average nearly 15 more suicides annually (per 100,000 people) than did all-Catholic counties. The average suicide rate for a county was 13 per 100,000, so 15 more deaths is a big effect. This relationship remains even after statistically removing other important factors such as literacy, household size, urbanization, and the extent of the manufacturing/services sector.

Then, as they did with literacy, Becker and Woessmann used a county's distance from the epicenter of the German Reformation to create a natural experiment: counties closer to Wittenberg received higher "dosages" of Protestantism. They then used historical data to look at suicide rates after those counties "baked" for a few centuries. Here, the effect was even stronger: counties that happened to receive a bigger historical dosage of Lutheranism had much higher suicide rates. For every 100 km (62 mi) closer to Wittenberg, the percentage of Protestants in a county increased by 7 to 9 percentile points in the 19th century. And, for every increase of 20 percentile points in the share of Protestants (vs. Catholics) in a county, the suicide rate went up by 4 to 5 people per 100,000. Other studies suggest that these results apply to Switzerland and probably much of Europe. Overall, the data suggest that Protestantism can leave people feeling forlorn and thereby increase their chances of committing suicide.[46]

To be clear, in the account I'm developing here, the emergence of Protestantism is both a *consequence* and a *cause* of people's changing psychology. As a cluster of faiths, Protestantism represents the religious coalescence of the proto-WEIRD ways of thinking and feeling that had been culturally evolving in many urban centers during the Middle Ages. Yet by wrapping these values, motivations, and worldviews together, giving them God's blessing, and linking them to a contingent afterlife, some Protestant faiths created powerful cultural recombinations that not only produced even WEIRDer psychologies but also contributed to economic growth, the effectiveness of democratic institutions, and higher suicide rates.

Dark Matter or Enlightenment?

In the 17th and 18th centuries, a complex of interrelated ideas about constitutional governments, liberty, impartial law, natural rights, progress, rationality, and science had begun to consolidate in the minds of leading European intellectuals such as John Locke, David Hume, Voltaire, Montesquieu, Thomas Paine, and Adam Smith. This flotsam of WEIRD ideas had been accumulating for centuries, pushed along by the swelling river of psychological dark matter—individualism, dispositionalism, analytic thinking and impersonal prosociality—that I've been analyzing throughout this book. This psychological dark matter—invisible and hard to detect like physical dark matter—has long been manifesting in the charters and constitutions of free cities, monastic orders, and universities, as well as in canon law. Enlightenment thinkers drew from and recombined these ideas and concepts using minds equipped with a proto-WEIRD psychology. Both Locke and Rousseau, for example, saw society as built on a social contract between individuals in which the government's authority derived from the consent of the governed. That is, they began to understand society as a voluntary association—specifically, as a corporation. Centuries earlier, canon law had stipulated that a corporation's leaders needed the consent of its members to take actions that would affect those members. Further, because of the central role of impersonal markets and merchants, contract law based on the norms of *lex mercatoria* had been developed to an unprecedented degree in medieval Europe. The very idea that a person can act freely, independently of their clans, kindreds, or lineages, to make socially isolated agreements (contracts) presupposes an unusually individualistic world of impersonal exchange.[47]

Like their intellectual forebearers in the Church, Enlightenment thinkers also constructed their political and scientific theories by assigning properties to individuals or objects—they were analytic thinkers. In particular, Enlightenment political theories assigned individuals natural rights, such as Locke's "life, liberty, and property," and built from there. We saw that this approach was already in practical use in the independent cities of the 12th century, albeit in a less grandiose form, and then was refurbished into philosophical constructs when imported into canon law. In the 14th century, natural rights were made even more respectable—philosophically speaking—by Franciscan monks like William of Ockham (you probably know his famous razor). By contrast, most non-Western political theories bestowed political power and economic privileges based on lineage ties, genealogical descent, or divine commands, not individual rights. But, the WEIRDer your psychology, the less inclined you'll be to focus on relational ties, and the more motivated you'll be to start making up invisible properties, assigning them to individuals, and using them to justify universally applicable laws.[48]

The bottom line is that the Enlightenment thinkers didn't suddenly crack the combination on Pandora's box and take out the snuff box of reason and the rum bottle of rationality from which the modern world was then conceived. Instead, they were part of a long, cumulative cultural evolutionary process that had been shaping how European populations perceived, thought, reasoned, and related to each other stretching back into Late Antiquity. They were just the intellectuals and writers on the scene when WEIRDer ways of thinking finally trickled up to some of the last holdouts in Europe, the nobility.

13

Escape Velocity

Nothing is more usual, among states which have made some advances
in commerce, than to look on the progress of their neighbours with
a suspicious eye, to consider all trading states as their rivals, and
to suppose that it is impossible for any of them to flourish, but at
their expense . . . But I go farther, and observe, that where an open
communication is preserved among nations, it is impossible but
the domestic industry of every one must receive an increase from
the improvements of the others. Compare the situation of Great
Britain at present, with what it was two centuries ago. All the arts
both of agriculture and manufactures were then extremely rude
and imperfect. Every improvement, which we have since made,
has arisen from our imitation of foreigners; and we ought so far
to esteem it happy, that they had previously made advances in
arts and ingenuity. But this intercourse is still upheld to our great
advantage: Notwithstanding the advanced state of our manufactures,
we daily adopt, in every art, the inventions and improvements of
our neighbours. The commodity is first imported from abroad,
to our great discontent, while we imagine that it drains us of our
money: Afterwards, the art itself is gradually imported, to our visible
advantage . . . had they not first instructed us, we should have been at
present barbarians; and did they not still continue their instructions,
the arts must fall into a state of languor, and lose that emulation and
novelty which contribute so much to their advancement.

—David Hume (1777), at the dawn of the British Industrial Revolution[1]

In the latter half of the 18th century, the Industrial Revolution erupted out of the English Midlands, and an economic tsunami began to swell. This wave of economic change, which in many ways continues to crash across the globe today, pushed the average British income from $3,430 in 1800 (the same as in 21st-century Kenya) to over $8,000 in 1900 and $32,543 in 2000 (Figure 13.1A). Swept along by Britain's surge, other western European populations along with the United States soon became full participants in this upwelling. Greater prosperity led to other changes, including rising life expectancies, declining infant mortality, and the virtual disappearance of famines. The average British life expectancy rose from 39 years in 1800 to 46 years a century later, and to 78 years in 2000 (Figure 13.1B). Today, as in much of western Europe, newborns can expect to live for over eight decades.[2]

That's not the half of it. Cities were lit up for the first time at night using gas lamps, and eventually people's homes glowed with the illumination of electrified wire loops. People turned black rocks (coal) into steam power for rapid travel by land and water. Later, harnessing a yellow-black sludge that bubbled up from the ground (petroleum), travel became even faster, easier, and safer until people were jetting through the sky at 30,000 feet in aluminum tubes while nibbling on honey-roasted peanuts. People also figured out how to send their voices through metal wires and eventually through the air on invisible waves. Medical detectives mapped deaths to isolate public health threats, like cholera from contaminated water pumps, and physicians figured out how to use weakened or dead pathogens to immunize babies against the deadly plagues that had decimated urban communities around the globe for eons.

The economic, political, and military power this revolution gave Europeans energized the spread of global commerce and fueled the diffusion of European laws, schools, religions, and political institutions. Of course, along with this global expansion came conquests, atrocities, and disasters, including genocide, subjugation, dislocation, oppression, slavery, and environmental devastation. Nevertheless, whether one prefers to focus on the economic and technological triumphs or the conquests and atrocities,

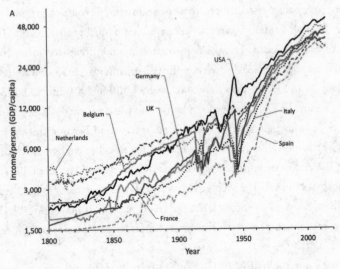

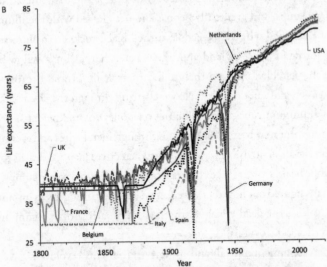

FIGURE 13.1. (A) Income per person (Gross Domestic Product per capita) from 1800 to 2018 and (B) average life expectancy (in years) from 1800 to 2018 in eight European countries. Income is in international dollars, fixed at 2011 prices and adjusted for purchasing power differences across space and time.[3]

the question remains the same: How and why did this innovation-driven economic and military expansion explode out of Europe after 1500?[4]

Recall my space aliens from Chapter 1 who were surveying the earth from their orbital perch around 1000 CE. Or consider the earthly view from Toledo, Spain, through the eyes of the Muslim scholar Said ibn Ahmad in 1068. Said divided the world into two main groups: those who had contributed to science and learning—the "civilized"—and the "barbarians" who had not. For Said, civilized peoples included Indians, Jews, Egyptians, Persians, Greeks, and Romans (by which he meant Byzantines). He subdivided the barbarians into an upper crust, including the Chinese and the Turks (impressive fighters), and the rest, consisting of the "black barbarians" to the south (sub-Saharan Africans) and the "white barbarians" to the north (Europeans). Crystallizing a widely shared view among Muslim scholars of the era, Said evaluated the English and Dutch of the 11th century as follows:

> The other peoples of this group who have not cultivated the
> sciences are more like beasts than like men. For those of them who
> live furthest to the north, between the last of the seven climates
> and the limits of the inhabited world, the excessive distance of the
> sun in relation to the zenith line makes the air cold and the sky
> cloudy. Their temperaments are therefore frigid, their humors raw,
> their bellies gross, their color pale, their hair long and lank. Thus
> they lack keenness of understanding and clarity of intelligence
> and are overcome by ignorance and apathy, lack of discernment, and
> stupidity . . .[5]

Said's northerners probably wouldn't have impressed my alien anthropologists, either. Few would have guessed that before the new millennium was over, these barbarians, along with their cultural descendants in North America, would have conquered much of the world, lit up the earth at night, vanquished most plagues, learned to fly, split the atom, walked on the moon, built machines that learn, and begun tinkering with the informational code underlying life.

If the alien anthropologists had returned in 1500, Europe would have looked more urbanized, with many impressive cathedrals and numerous castles. In northern Italian cities like Venice, Genoa, Milan, Florence, and Bologna, the Renaissance would have been in full swing. Britain, however, wouldn't yet have stood out as the obvious birthplace of the Industrial Revolution. Muslim observers had begun to notice that something was afoot in Europe a century or so earlier. With some astonishment, the famed historian Ibn Khaldûn remarked, in about 1377, "We have heard of late that in the lands of the Franks, that is, in the country of Rome and its dependencies on the northern shore of the Mediterranean Sea, the philosophic sciences are thriving, their works reviving, their sessions of study increasing, their assemblies comprehensive, their exponents numerous, and their students abundant." The aliens might have also noted the passage of some modest-looking ships sailing from the Iberian Peninsula across the Atlantic Ocean and around the southern tip of Africa.[6]

While this would have been curious, much of the action was still elsewhere. Over in Turkey, the Ottoman Empire was expanding rapidly around the middle of the 15th century, after having crushed the last remnants of the "civilized" Byzantine Empire in Constantinople (now Istanbul). The Ottoman emperor, Suleiman the Magnificent, would soon begin expanding into Hungary, Serbia, Slovakia, and Croatia. In China, having explored the coasts of India and Africa in a fleet of majestic sailing ships that dwarfed the later vessels of Christopher Columbus and Vasco da Gama, the Ming Dynasty had restored both the Grand Canal and the Great Wall, built the Forbidden City, and assembled an immense army and vast harem.

The bottom line is that for much of the first half of the second millennium, Europe remained a relative backwater, at least as judged by the other leading powers of the era. However, as Ibn Khaldûn's prescient puzzlement suggests, observers were beginning to notice that something was afoot among the "northern barbarians" by the middle of the millennium.

Much ink has been spilled trying to explain why the Industrial Revolution occurred at all, and, given that it did occur, why it began in Europe instead of anywhere else. During the first half of the second millennium, the leading candidates for the source of this earth-shaking economic transformation would have been China, India, and the Islamic world, not Europe. Proposed explanations for "Why Europe?" emphasize the development of representative governments, the rise of impersonal commerce, the discovery of the Americas, the availability of English coal, the length of European coastlines, the brilliance of Enlightenment thinkers, the intensity of European warfare, the price of British labor, and the development of a culture of science. I suspect that all of these factors may have played some role, even if minor in some cases; but, what's missing is an understanding of the psychological differences that began developing in some European populations in the wake of the Church's dissolution of Europe's kin-based institutions. These psychological changes fostered, and were then reinforced by, the subsequent development of impersonal markets, competing voluntary associations, new religious faiths, representative governance, and science. My effort here is not so much to reject existing explanations but to lay some deeper social and psychological footings in the shifting sands that most explanations of the Industrial Revolution are built on.[7]

Before proceeding, let me underline a key point: none of these other explanations for the Industrial Revolution can account for the psychological variation and change I've documented in the last 12 chapters. So even if these other explanations are partially right, they've failed to notice the mastodon in the courtyard. It's no longer tenable to continue pretending that all populations are psychologically indistinguishable or that cultural evolution doesn't systematically modify how people think, feel, and perceive.

While there are many theories about the causes of the Industrial Revolution, there's actually broad agreement that to explain the acceleration of economic growth since the mid-18th century, we need to explain the acceleration of technological innovation. So, whether your explanation is based on the fortuitous emergence of representative governments during the Glorious Revolution or on the high price of English labor, it must somehow cash out in rising and sustained rates of innovation after 1750 or so. To understand the origins of innovation, we need to return to our study of human nature.

As we've seen, the secret of our species' success lies not in our raw intellect or reasoning powers but in our capacity to learn from those around us and then diffuse what we learned outward, through our social networks, and down to future generations. Over time, because we learn selectively from others and integrate insights from diverse individuals and populations, the process of cultural evolution can give rise to an ever-growing and -improving repertoire of tools, skills, techniques, goals, motivations, beliefs, rules, and norms. This body of cultural know-how is maintained collectively in the minds and practices of a community or network. To understand innovation, the key questions to ask are: What determines the rate of cumulative cultural evolution? What factors cause this adaptive information, including technological prowess, to accumulate more rapidly?[8]

Many assume that *innovation*—the successful diffusion and implementation of an improvement—depends mostly on *invention*, the creation of a single improvement by a person or team for the first time. Many also assume that inventions require the involvement of particularly smart individuals—geniuses—who have lots of free time and strong material incentives (big payoffs). These elements, of course, can play a role. But, research in cultural evolution suggests that there are two much more important factors. First, the larger the population of engaged minds, the faster the rate of cumulative cultural evolution. That is, the larger the network of people learning or doing something, the more opportunities there will be for individuals to produce improvements, whether through fortuitous inspirations, lucky mistakes, careful experiments, or some combination. Second, the greater the interconnectedness among individuals—among learners and their teachers over generations—the faster the rate of cumulative cultural evolution. Put differently, the greater the diversity of teachers, experts, and others that learners have access to, the more selective they can be in whom they learn from and what they learn. A well-connected learner can "invent" new things simply by copying skills, practices, or ideas from different experts and then recombining these, intentionally or accidentally. Innovation can emerge even in the absence of conscious invention—a process that was probably the primary driver of cumulative cultural evolution over much of our species' evolutionary history.[9]

If this feels off, it's probably because you've been seduced by the "myth of the heroic inventor," as historians of technology call it. This WEIRD folk model of how innovation works exalts singular acts of invention by geniuses (it's attractive to individualists). However, four facts drawn from the history of technological development undermine it. First, complex innovations almost always arise from the accumulation of small additions or modifications, so even the most important contributors make only incremental additions. This is why so many blockbuster innovations were developed independently by multiple people at the same time—the key ideas were already out there, scattered among the minds of others, and someone was going to put them together eventually.[10] Second, most innovations are really just novel recombinations of existing ideas, techniques, or approaches; a tool is taken from one domain and applied in another. Third, lucky mistakes, fortunate misunderstandings, and serendipitous insights play a central role in invention and often represent the only difference between famous inventors and anonymous tinkerers. Finally, necessity is certainly *not* the mother of invention. Over the course of human history, people often ignored life-saving inventions for years, sometimes only realizing how much they needed an invention long after its arrival (e.g., penicillin, nitrous oxide, the wheel). Although plagues, marauders, famines, and droughts have persistently provided humanity with plentiful existential incentives to innovate, Mother Necessity has rarely nurtured human ingenuity to create the crucial inventions. Instead, people have mostly suffered, died, or fled instead of inventing their way out of crises.[11]

To illustrate these points, consider five important innovations:

1. *Printing press (1440–1450 CE)*: Johannes Gutenberg recombined a number of tools, techniques, and components that had been circulating around Europe for decades. In particular, he combined the existing screw presses used for cheese and wine with block

printing techniques and movable metal type. For this last crucial idea, Gutenberg combined his knowledge of soft metals, acquired from his father (who worked in the Mainz mint), with the idea of movable type (which he may have learned about from a traveling apprentice whose Dutch master had experimented with movable wooden type). Of course, the rapid diffusion of Gutenberg's press was driven by its complementarity with new religious commitments to scriptural literacy.[12]

2. *Steam engine (1769)*: While working on a repair job, the instrument maker James Watt figured out how to improve the efficiency of a Newcomen steam engine by adding a separate condenser for the steam. In 1712, this early steam engine had been developed by the ironmonger and Baptist elder Thomas Newcomen. Newcomen had recombined insights from air pumps with the idea of using a piston, which he likely found in a book about pressure cookers (published in 1687) by the French Huguenot Denis Papin. Improving this recombination, one of Newcomen's breakthroughs came when a soldered crack in his engine's boiler did indeed "break through," spraying cool water into the steam chamber. This caused the pressure to plunge, which pulled the piston downward so hard that it broke the engine. The power of the sudden vacuum created by the accidental injection of cool water directly into the steam was unmistakable. While Newcomen's engine opened a new era, both Denis Papin and the British military engineer Thomas Savery had come up with steam power at about the same time.[13]

3. *Spinning mule (1779)*: Samuel Crompton's invention is called a "mule" because it so obviously combines Richard Arkwright's water frame (1769) with James Hargreaves's spinning jenny (1764). Hargreaves got the idea for his jenny when he saw a single-thread wheel loom accidentally flip over onto the floor. Both the wheel and the spindle continued to rotate, but the spindle was upright, which suggested the possibility of using multiple spindles

in an upright position. Despite not having a patent, Hargreaves went public with his invention, which opened the door to Crompton's recombination. The spinning mule rapidly transformed the manufacture of cotton textiles from a cottage industry into a factory enterprise.[14]

4. *Vulcanized rubber (1844–1845)*: Charles Goodyear developed the process employed to produce the rubber now used in tires—vulcanization. Goodyear's key breakthrough occurred when he accidentally brought some sulfur-treated latex gum into contact with a hot stove. Goodyear noticed that the substance charred and hardened instead of melting. He'd gotten the idea of treating gum with sulfur in 1839 from Nathaniel Hayward, who, while working with a German chemist, had found that treating latex gum with sulfur removed its annoying stickiness. Europeans hadn't been aware of the useful properties of latex gums until two French naturalists noticed that indigenous Amazonians were using latex to make boots, hoods, tents, containers, and much more. However, unlike the Amazonians, when Europeans bumbled across latex's properties, factories immediately sprang up in Britain, France, and the United States to make erasers, rubber boots, and raincoats.[15]

5. *Incandescent light bulb (1879)*: Thomas Edison and his Menlo Park team "invented" the incandescent light bulb by improving on a line of nearly two dozen bulbs patented between 1841 and 1878 by inventors from Scotland, Belgium, France, and Russia. In Britain, Joseph Swan received a patent for a similar bulb in the same year as Edison. This cumulative process can be traced to Ben Franklin, who, while visiting his native Boston in 1743, saw a Scot named Archibald Spencer demonstrate the effect of static electricity in a public lecture. Franklin purchased Spencer's equipment and introduced this phenomenon to three of his associates in Philadelphia. In 1761, one of these associates, Ebenezer Kinnersley, demonstrated that heated wires can give off light—incandescence.[16]

My point is that innovation is driven by the recombination of ideas, insights, and technologies, along with a healthy dose of serendipity and unintended consequences. As a result, any institutions, norms, beliefs, or psychological inclinations that increase the flow of ideas among diverse minds or open up more opportunities for fortune to show us the way will energize innovation.

Of course, getting the ideas to meet is one thing, but in the case of technology, an inventor has to physically make it. Since no one has all the skills or know-how to do everything that goes into any complex invention, we need to think about the division of labor, or what should be thought of as a society's division of information. As most societies scaled up over human history and the pool of cultural knowledge expanded, different groups began to specialize in certain skills, creating experts like blacksmiths, sandal makers, weavers, farmers, and warriors. Blacksmiths could exchange their plows and horseshoes for sandals, rope, wheat, and protection. In this world, with a complex division of labor, cumulative cultural evolution and innovation still depend on the size and interconnectedness of populations, but now people with different skills, knowledge, and expertise need to be able to find each other, develop trust, and then work together. Illustrating this for steam power, James Watt famously wrote to his partner John Roebuck that "my principal hindrance in erecting engines is always smith-work." Watt depended on the skills and expertise of several skilled artisans, including ironmasters like John Wilkinson, whose technique for boring cannon barrels proved essential to making the cylinders used in Watt's engines.[17]

The upshot is that cumulative cultural evolution—including innovation—is fundamentally a social and cultural process that turns societies into *collective brains*. Human societies vary in their innovativeness due in large part to the differences in the fluidity with which information diffuses through a population of engaged minds and across generations as well as to how willing individuals are to try novel practices or adopt new beliefs, concepts, and tools.[18]

Now, applying our understanding of the collective brain to Europe over the last millennium, the social and psychological changes I've high-lighted can account for not only the dramatic, innovation-driven accelera-tion in economic growth that began in the latter half of the 18th century (Figure 13.1) but also the more moderate patterns of economic expansion prior to industrialization. In Chapter 9, we saw that urbanization—a proxy for economic prosperity—had been climbing in much of western Europe since 900 CE. Consistent with this, historical data show that both Holland and England had experienced a long-term rise in income since at least the 13th and 16th centuries, respectively. Thus, while the Industrial Revolution does indeed mark a striking acceleration, it was in fact part of a long-term trend that stretches back many centuries.[19]

Much of the economic growth prior to the 17th century probably de-rived from expanding commerce and trade—the "Commercial Revolution" of the 13th century—which was anchored in rising levels of impersonal trust, fairness, and honesty that developed along with market norms and competition among voluntary associations. However, some of this early growth also arose from innovation, including many technological devel-opments. Early in the Middle Ages, agricultural production was gradually improved by the water mill (sixth century, Roman origin), heavy plow (sev-enth century, Slavic origin), crop rotation (eighth century), and both the horseshoe and the harness (ninth century, probably from China). Water mills were deployed to mechanize the production of beer (861, northwest France), hemp (990, southeast France), cloth (962, northern Italy; Switzer-land), iron (probably 1025, southern Germany), oil (1100, southeast France), mustard (1250, southeast France), poppies (1251, northwest France), paper (1276, northern Italy), and steel (1384, Belgium). In the Late Middle Ages, as we've seen, both the mechanical clock and the printing press diffused widely and generated economic growth in the cities that adopted them early. The social and psychological shifts I've described help explain why Europeans developed an openness to new ideas, technologies, and practices from anywhere and everywhere. The more ideas they absorbed, the more recombinations emerged and the faster innovation chugged along.[20]

Why were these populations becoming so innovative?[21]

Wiring Up the Collective Brain

The growth of Europe's collective brain was nourished by the coevolution of the psychological changes and institutional developments that I've documented throughout this book. Psychological developments such as greater impersonal trust, less conformity, broader literacy, and greater independence would have opened the flow of ideas, beliefs, values, and practices among individuals and communities within Europe. At the same time, the proliferation of voluntary associations and rising urbanization, especially the growth of free cities, would have expanded the collective brain by bringing diverse individuals together and aligning their interests. In fact, four voluntary associations—charter cities, monasteries, apprenticeships, and universities—all contributed to broadening the flow of knowledge and technology around Europe. At an individual level, people's desire to come up with new ideas and improved techniques—to uniquely distinguish themselves—would have interacted synergistically with rising levels of patience, time thrift, analytic thinking, overconfidence, and positive-sum thinking (optimism). When viewed in the context of these social, psychological, and institutional changes, which accumulated gradually over a millennium, Europe's technological and economic acceleration seems a lot less puzzling.[22]

Our story begins with the Church's demolition of Europe's intensive kin-based institutions. Breaking kin-groups down into nuclear families would have had complex effects on the collective brain. Young learners in isolated nuclear families are stuck learning from Mom and Dad for lots of important skills, abilities, motivations, and techniques—anything that requires close contact, extended observation, or patient instruction. By contrast, kin-based institutions like clans or kindreds provide a richer set of teachers and more opportunities for learning. An aspiring teenage weaver in a clan, for example, could potentially learn weaving techniques from her cousins, great-aunts, and father's brothers' wives, as well as from her mother. Of course, since intensive kin-groups foster greater conformity and obedience, her more experienced relatives might not be particularly open to new techniques or novel recombinations, especially radical ones. Consequently, learners won't be as inclined to seek out novelty or violate tradition in order to highlight their uniqueness or individuality.

Nevertheless, while large kin-groups beat nuclear families in size and interconnectedness by tying more people together, nuclear families have the potential to be part of even larger collective brains if they can build broad-ranging relationships or join voluntary groups that connect them with a sprawling network of experts. Moreover, unconstrained by the bonds of kinship, learners can potentially select particularly knowledgeable or skilled teachers from this broader network. To see why this is important, consider the difference between learning a crop rotation strategy from the best person in your extended family (a paternal uncle, say) or the best person in your town (the rich farmer with the big house). Your uncle probably had access to the same agricultural know-how as your father, though perhaps he was more attentive than your father or incorporated a few insights of his own. By contrast, the most successful farmer in the community may very well have cultural know-how that your father's family never acquired, and you may be able to combine insights from him with those from your own family to produce an even better set of routines or practices.[23]

To see the power of interconnectedness, consider a simple experiment that Michael Muthukrishna and I did with 100 undergraduates. We created "transmission chains" in which successive groups of participants individually faced a challenging task over 10 rounds, or "generations." In the first generation, naïve participants entered the laboratory and were given the task but no instructions: against the clock, they had to figure out how to use a notoriously difficult image-editing program to reproduce a complex geometrical figure. When their time expired, each participant was asked to write down any instructions or tips for those in the next generation—their "students." Crucially, participants were randomly split into two treatments, one in which they received instructions from only one person in the prior generation (the one-to-one treatment) and another in which they could look at the instructions of up to five individuals from the prior generation (the five-to-one treatment). The one-to-one treatment creates a single cultural lineage—like parent-to-child transmission in a nuclear family—while the five-to-one treatment allows information to spread broadly through each generation, like a voluntary association. After the first generation, each new group of participants received the original target image, the image or images produced by their model(s) in the prior generation, and the appropriate tips and instructions.[24]

The results are stark. Over 10 generations, the average performance of individuals in the five-to-one treatment improved dramatically, going from an average score of just over 20 percent in generation 1 to over 85 percent in generation 10 (100 percent would be a perfect replication of the target). By contrast, those in the one-to-one treatment showed no systematic improvement over the generations. In generation 10, the *least* skilled person in the five-to-one group was superior to the *most* skilled person in the one-to-one treatment.

Michael and I also wondered if participants in the five-to-one treatment simply picked the best teacher in the prior generation and copied them, or if they picked up tips and techniques from multiple teachers. Our detailed analysis shows that, although participants were most influenced by the most skilled among their models, learners picked up stuff from almost all of their teachers. On average, the only teacher that students entirely ignored was the least skilled. By combining techniques and insights from multiple teachers, participants came up with what amounted to "new inventions" that arose by recombining elements learned from different teachers.

If a traveler suddenly arrived on the scene and met the people in generation 10 in both the one-to-one and five-to-one treatments, he might infer that those in the five-to-one treatment were smarter than those in the one-to-one treatment. Of course, the differences in our experiment arose from the differences in the social network structure that we imposed, and in how that structure influenced each group's interconnectedness across generations, not from differences in individual intelligence. But, those in the five-to-one treatment still looked smarter.[25]

Historically, this is important, because going well back into the Middle Ages, we see that one of the unusual features of social and economic life among Europeans was the employment of nonrelatives (and nonslaves) as household servants and farmhands (Chapter 5). For a few years, before getting married or setting out on one's own, many tweens, teenagers, and young adults were farmed out to other households, often to richer and more successful households, as helpers. Such "life-cycle servants" are peculiar to Europe after the dissolution of intensive kinship.[26]

This custom meant that young people frequently received opportunities to see how richer and more successful households operated, just before setting off on their own. When newly married couples set up their own households—which they often did because the Church promoted neolocal residence—they could put into practice any tips, techniques, preferences, or motivations they had picked up during their time in this second household. These culturally-transmitted tidbits could have included anything from the use of crop rotation and horse collars to family planning or the centrality of self-restraint in household disputes.

The need for newly married couples to set up their own independent households may also have encouraged experimentation. Within their respective domains (plowing, cooking, sewing, etc.), men and women became their own bosses at younger ages. Instead of waiting until their grandfathers, fathers, and older brothers all died before they took charge, men found themselves at the head of their own small household in their mid-20s (on average). Younger people are less risk-averse and less tied to tradition, so any institutions that favor putting younger people in charge will be more dynamic. This would have sped up experimentation and innovation.[27]

MONKS AND JOURNEYMEN

Beyond the organization of households and farms, the spread of monasteries, apprenticeships (often regulated by guilds), urban centers, universities, and impersonal markets all played a role in accelerating innovation in artisanal skills, technical know-how, and the industrial arts. The earliest effects probably arose when monasteries developed into transnational franchises and diffused into every corner of Christendom (Figure 10.5). Monasteries carried with them the latest crops, agricultural techniques, production methods, and industries. They introduced techniques for beer brewing, beekeeping, and cattle breeding into widely disparate regions. Monks, for example, developed salmon fisheries in Ireland, cheese-making in Parma, and irrigation in Lombardy.

The Cistercian Order, in particular, built a sprawling network of monastery-factories that deployed the latest techniques for grinding wheat, casting iron, tanning hides, fulling cloth, and cultivating grapes. Most Cistercian monasteries had a water mill, and some had four or five such mills for different jobs. In France's Champagne region, for example, the Cistercians were the leading iron producers from roughly 1250 to 1700. The motherhouse in Burgundy planted vineyards, which produced one of the world's most famous vintages, and houses in Germany devised ways to cultivate vines on terraced hillsides. At mandatory annual meetings, hundreds of Cistercian abbots shared their best technical, industrial, and agricultural practices with the entire order. This essentially threaded Europe's collective brain with Cistercian nerves, pulsing the latest technical advances out to even the most remote monasteries (mapped in Figure 11.2). With their strict devotion to an austere life, monks freely dispensed their know-how, strategies, and skills to local communities.[28]

Meanwhile, in the growing urban centers of the Middle Ages, apprenticeship institutions emerged that opened the door to residentially-mobile artisans and craftsmen. Unlike other societies, these more impersonal institutions became the central foci for the transmission of technical skills and craft know-how across generations. The most skilled masters attracted numerous apprentices, and these apprentices paid for their training in various ways, including through direct payments to their masters and via their labor during extended internships. Guilds sometimes regulated this process, usually aiming to ensure that both masters and apprentices lived up to their obligations under guild rules.[29]

Unsurprisingly, masters often wanted to train their own sons or other relatives instead of strangers. However, compared to the strongly lineal transmission of similar know-how in places like China and India, European masters seeded their skills much more broadly across the population, thereby fueling more recombination and faster cumulative cultural evolution. Hard data are not plentiful, but one database of medieval guilds from the Netherlands shows that four out of five apprentices were not sons of their master. Later, in 17th-century London, the percentage of artisans trained by nonrelatives ranged from 72 to 93 percent. By contrast, in India and China, the rates were likely flipped, with almost all skilled artisans having been trained by a relative or close family tie. Even today in China, new workers and non-kin are prevented from learning the most important craft skills; proprietary techniques remain confined to particular lineages.[30]

Besides permitting apprentices from diverse families to access the top masters (as in the five-to-one experimental treatment above), these institutions would have spurred rapid innovation in several other ways. First, an extended period of training developed between apprentice and master: the *journeyman* stage. After completing an apprenticeship, a newly minted journeyman, as the name implies, relocated to work at another shop under a different master, often in another town or city. This allowed recently trained individuals to observe how another expert did things. In addition, at the shops of respected masters, several journeymen from different cities and shops often came together. This meant the knowledge of multiple masters could be pooled, recombined, and honed by a team of journeymen and apprentices. Drawing on this diversity, journeymen who became masters could develop their own signature approaches, which they would have wanted to do because they were individualists who sought to impress others with their uniqueness. As noted, Gutenberg may have gotten the idea of movable type from a former traveling apprentice.[31]

Second, because cities and guilds were engaged in intergroup competition, highly skilled masters were a hot commodity and could be recruited to move their shops between cities. Unlike in most places and times, people weren't bound by intensive kin ties and obligations to particular locales, so many masters did move. By 1742 in Vienna, for example, more than three-quarters of the 4,000 masters had been born elsewhere. They came from the entirety of the German-speaking world but primarily from a core region that ran from the Danube to the Upper Rhine. In England, which had greater mobility than anywhere else, lads flocked to London from around Europe for apprenticeships, including one James Watt, who apprenticed there as an instrument maker. Third, being independent and mobile, artisans of all kinds tended to cluster in towns and cities, and often on the same street and block. This would have created competition, incentivized improvements, and produced more opportunities to learn from each other. By contrast, in China, where craft techniques and skills were transmitted within clans, artisans remained dispersed and rooted in their rural homelands.[32]

Of course, countries, cities, and even skilled masters wanted to keep valuable know-how secret. Narrow self-interest favors secrecy, while the collective brain thrives on openness and the flow of information. Unlike other societies, however, Europe's family structure, residential mobility, intergroup competition, and impersonal markets pushed hard against secrecy. Masters were continually poached by ambitious cities, and journeymen sought out the best opportunities. Laws to stymie information flow were unpopular and difficult to enforce, allowing industrial espionage to flourish. Some guilds even began to develop explicit norms about the sharing of know-how within the guild. For example, master shipbuilders in Holland exchanged their secrets and insights at mandatory annual meetings. This sharing was probably motivated by a combination of prizes for excellence—giving the clever prestige—and informal punishments for the stingy, if they refused to share.[33]

BIGGER CITIES, BETTER BRAINS

The more numerous and the more abundant the civilization (population) in a city, the more luxurious is the life of its inhabitants in comparison with that (of the inhabitants) of a lesser city.
—the Muslim historian Ibn Khaldûn, *The Muqaddimah* (1377, Chapter 4)

At a larger scale, the proliferation and growth of cities and towns expanded Europe's collective brain. On the eve of the first millennium, rural folk began flowing into urban centers in several regions of Europe, especially in a band running from northern Italy through Switzerland and Germany into the Low Countries and eventually to London. City incorporations proliferated, and the number of people living in cities of over 10,000 rose 20-fold, from about 700,000 in 800 CE to nearly 16 million people in 1800. During the same millennium, the urban population in the Islamic world didn't even double and China's remained flat.[34]

Urban centers, and especially urban clusters, expand the collective brain by bringing people, ideas, and technologies together. The mass action of cities, particularly when propelled by individualists seeking out mutually beneficial relationships, creates innovations as ideas meet, recombine, and make baby ideas. Cities also allow people with different skills and areas of expertise to encounter one another, discover complementary interests, and collaborate. Suppose I'm James Watt and my new design for a steam engine demands a precision-bored cylinder. I'd best live in a place where I can both find out that such precision work is possible and also actually be able to locate someone to do the job. The bigger and more fluid the city or urban cluster, the better.[35]

To illustrate the power of the metropolis, Figure 13.2 plots the size of the working-age population in contemporary U.S. cities against their annual innovation rates, captured here using the total number of patent applications in 2002. Knowing the population of a city allows us to explain 70 percent of the variation among U.S. cities in innovation. The size of this relationship, which I've plotted on log scales, tells us that cities have synergy. For each 10-fold increase in population size (e.g., from 10,000 to 100,000 people), there's 13 times more innovation. If all cities did was concentrate individuals, we'd expect a 10-fold increase in population size to create a proportional increase in inventions. Instead, we get a 13-fold increase. Here, I've used patent applications for 2002, but the same strong relationship holds back to 1975, where our dataset runs out.[36]

The data come from the contemporary United States, so you might worry that this relationship didn't hold in the past. However, analyses of preindustrial innovation rates in England also show that larger populations and denser urban areas dominated innovation and technical improvement,

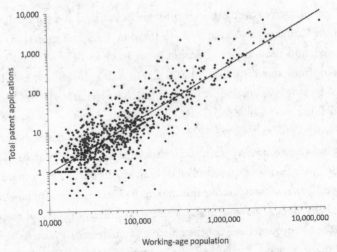

FIGURE 13.2. More populous cities generate more inventions, captured as patent applications in 2002. This is based on data from 800 U.S. urban areas. The correlation shown on the plot is 0.84.[37]

including in patent data. In fact, the synergistic effects of cities were probably even stronger in the era before airplanes, telephones, and the internet.[38]

Urban areas of Christendom were growing and becoming more interconnected. One way to capture this is to imagine how many other minds a person in a city could—in principle—access in order to learn from or collaborate with. To get at this, we assume each person can access everyone in their own city, and then we weight the populations of other cities by the cost of traveling to them. So, if you live in a populous city that is tightly connected to surrounding cities by cheap transportation, you are part of a larger collective brain—even if you yourself don't travel. We can then average this for each modern European country each century. Figure 13.3 shows the change in urban interconnectedness from 1200 to 1850. The first thing to notice is that, except for a decline in the wake of the Black Death in the 14th century, urban interconnectedness has been rising throughout Europe since 1200. However, interconnectedness rose faster in some regions than in others. In particular, the Netherlands accelerated early, around 1400, and Britain accelerated dramatically after about 1600.

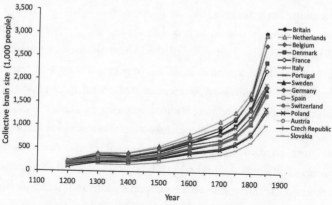

FIGURE 13.3. Growth of the collective brain in Europe from 1200 to 1850. The collective brain here is measured as the size and interconnectedness among urban areas in Europe. Here, we first assume that each person can interact with the entire population of their home city. In addition, we assume that each person can interact with, or at least learn from, those in other cities, but that the ability to do so is dependent on the cost of travel between city pairs. So, we divide the populations of other European cities by the cost of travel between city pairs, and add this to the population of the home city in order to yield overall interconnectedness scores. We then aggregate and average the interconnectedness to the country level. Urbanites get more interconnected as their home cities grow, nearby cities expand, and travel costs decline.[39]

The impact of Europe's expanding collective brain manifested in rising economic productivity. For instance, by the 12th century Europeans had developed the spinning wheel for making woolen clothing. This invention, which represents the first known application of belt-driven power, doubled or even tripled the productivity of wool spinners. Later, under the guilds, weaving efficiency increased by 300 percent between about 1300 and 1600 in the high-quality woolen industry. In the manufacture of gilded books, productivity increased by 750 percent during the 16th century. In London, the price of watches dropped by about 75 percent between 1685 and 1810, suggesting substantial improvements in manufacturing efficiency. Of course, some of these productivity gains were probably due to individuals working longer and harder (Chapter 11), but numerous specific inventions and technological modifications point to an important role for innovation.[40]

The point I'm making is that the dissolution of intensive kinship not only spurred urbanization in Europe but altered the psychology of these new urbanites in ways that distinguished them from other populations around the world. Greater individualism, impersonal trust, and relational mobility meant that individuals were more likely to seek out and develop relationships with people who were not tied into their social networks. Impersonal norms about fairness, honesty, and cooperation provided a framework for such interactions, and formal contracts poured the concrete to backstop agreements of all kinds. All of these psychological and social changes would have increased the interconnectedness of populations and fueled greater innovation. So far, we've considered the innovation-inducing impacts of monasteries, apprenticeships, and cities. Let's move on to two other voluntary associations: universities and knowledge societies.

KNOWLEDGE SOCIETIES AND PROTESTANTS

Universities, which, as we've seen, began spreading at the end of the 12th century, also helped innervate Europe's collective brain. Although they didn't have a big influence on technical training or engineering until late in our story, universities contributed to innovation by facilitating the circulation of educated individuals and books around Europe while also encouraging the speedy adoption of mechanical clocks and printing presses. Universities created a class of highly literate and mobile intellectuals and professionals who accepted positions as lawyers, doctors, administrators, professors, and notaries in urban communities throughout Christendom. They also provided homes and some autonomy for intellectuals of many stripes—including Isaac Newton and Daniel Bernoulli—which created competition among the growing number of wealthy aristocrats who, after their own university education, wanted to surround themselves with leading thinkers and eventually scientists.[41]

By the 16th century, a mobile community of individualistic and analytically-oriented thinkers had begun to form a loose web called the *Republic of Letters* that networked much of western and central Europe. Members of this virtual community sent one another handwritten letters often carried on the wings of commerce or by postal services, which were both public and private. Intellectuals penned letters about their ideas to friends and colleagues as well as to other correspondents around Europe. Upon reaching key nodes, important communications were often translated (if necessary), hand-copied, and sent out to other network members in a kind of starburst pattern. This not only linked thinkers in France, Britain, Holland, Germany, and northern Italy but also networked far-flung intellectuals like the mathematician Marino Ghetaldi in Croatia, who constructed the first parabolic mirror, and Jan Brożek in Krakow, who showed mathematically that the hexagonal honeycombs used by bees represent the most efficient solution to storing honey. Both scientists had spent time at a nodal university (Padua) at the core of the Republic, and Ghetaldi became pen pals with Galileo. Crucially, these axonal connections defied political boundaries: British intellectuals, for example, continued to interact with their Dutch counterparts through three wars, and French thinkers learned about Newton's contributions in his *Principia* (1687) despite incessant wars between Britain and France throughout this era.[42]

At the same time, while the Republic continued to communicate via handwritten letters, the quartet of the printing press, the paper mill, literacy, and Protestantism was supporting a symphony of books, pamphlets, technical manuals, magazines, and eventually both scholarly journals and public libraries that further networked the collective brain.[43]

At local and regional levels, the Republic seeded and nurtured a variety of philosophical and scientific associations across Europe. These knowledge societies met periodically, often at salons or in coffeehouses, to discuss the latest developments in politics, science, philosophy, and technology. Many societies had small libraries and most held lectures, either monthly or quarterly. These voluntary associations were crucial because they connected local intellectuals with a broader class of engineers, entrepreneurs, artisans, and tinkerers. The Birmingham Lunar Society, for example, fostered interactions between scientists like Benjamin Franklin and Joseph Black (who discovered latent heat), mechanics like James Watt and John Whitehurst (hydraulics), and entrepreneurs like Matthew Boulton and John Roebuck.

If you're an inventor like James Watt, trying to troubleshoot a broken New-comen steam engine owned by the University of Glasgow, it's nice to be able to chat with Joseph Black about thermodynamics and then access Boulton's staff of smiths and artisans. Illustrating the proliferation of knowledge soci-eties from 1600 to 1800, Figure 13.4 shows that the number of knowledge societies, and specifically those focused on science and technology, grew es-pecially rapidly after 1750.[44]

Making the case for the importance of the Republic of Letters and these proliferating knowledge societies, the renowned economic historian Joel Mokyr notes how communities evolved a set of social norms about freely sharing knowledge. The origins of these norms are best understood in light of the increasingly WEIRD psychology that had been evolving across Europe. Because the main focus of these voluntary associations was to share new ideas and findings, the prestige of members was derived from their con-tributions of original insights or new discoveries. There were reputational incentives for members to get their new ideas "out there" as soon as possible, so they could be recorded and credited in the minds of others. Norms also required members to respond to critics within the community, where con-tributions were judged by peers—acknowledged experts whose authority derived from their own contributions. This led to the development of norms

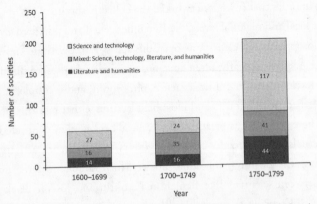

FIGURE 13.4. **The growth of knowledge societies in Europe between 1600 and 1800.**[45]

that praised the public sharing of knowledge and sanctioned those who kept secrets, fabricated evidence, or stole ideas from others.[46]

Along with knowledge sharing, new epistemic norms were also developing. Epistemic norms set cultural standards for what counts as "good" evidence and a "sound" argument. Although research on this question is limited, some work suggests that epistemic norms vary in important ways across societies and through history. For example, in many populations, even today, the experience that one has during a dream can "count" as evidence and provide justifications for one's actions. A mother who treats her child with a broth made from the seeds of a plant that she dreamed about can be judged as having acted wisely, as long as the child gets better. Elsewhere, as in many WEIRD populations, that mother would be judged poorly no matter how the child fared. Similarly, populations vary in the weight they give ancient sages and the advice of elders. Most complex societies have weighted ancient sages quite heavily. In Europe, however, as it slowly dawned on folks like Copernicus that the ancients had been wrong about many aspects of the natural world, from medicine to astronomy, it mattered less and less whether one's new findings or latest proposals confirmed or denied the views of the sages. Individuals and groups who relied on better epistemic standards—which themselves were debated—got the answer right more frequently, and the competition for prestige in this social world drove the honing of these epistemic norms.

The norms of knowledge societies evolved into the institution of WEIRD science. During the mid-17th century, for example, an informal association of physicians and natural philosophers (i.e., scientists) had been meeting around London. In 1660, this "invisible college" was formalized into the Royal Society by an official charter from King Charles II, making it the first national scientific association. A few years later, the group started publishing the world's second scientific journal, the *Philosophical Transactions of the Royal Society*, a publication that's alive and well today. At its inception, the journal conducted peer reviews of submitted articles and carefully date-stamped submissions to ensure priority for new contributions.[47]

Recent analyses confirm that knowledge societies did indeed spur innovation both before and during the Industrial Revolution. Using British patent data from 1752 to 1852, the economist James Dowey shows that the larger the number of knowledge societies in a region at the beginning of a decade, the more patents people in that area received in the ensuing 10 years. This holds even if you only compare the same region with itself in different decades or if you only compare different regions but keep the decade constant. It also holds if you only look at patents that had big impacts—i.e., those that fed into later innovations. The effects of these knowledge societies on innovation were over and above those created by rising urbanization, population density, literacy, and the stock of existing knowledge—all of which also contributed to higher innovation rates.[48]

The problem with this analysis is that patents might be a bad measure of innovation, especially during this early epoch, since we know that many famous inventors never patented their inventions. To address the problem, Dowey looked at the innovations featured at the first world's fair, the Great Exhibition in London in 1851. From British inventors, roughly 6,400 innovations were selected for exhibition from roughly 8,200 entries. Of those 6,400 exhibitions, about 30 percent received prizes based on their utility and novelty. Analyses of both the exhibits selected and the prizewinners show the centrality of Britain's knowledge societies. The greater the number of society members in a region, the more exhibitions from that region appeared at the fair, and the more likely those exhibitions were to win prizes. Specifically, for every 750 additional society members in a region, the number of exhibits and prizes from a region increased by nearly 50 percent.[49]

But, why did some regions have more knowledge societies than others?

Recall that once Protestantism broke the Church's monopoly in the 16th century, a variety of religious faiths sprouted and began competing for members. Although most Protestant faiths strongly promoted universal literacy, many remained hostile to science, innovation, and notions of progress. A few Protestant faiths, however, embraced science, technological improvement, and entrepreneurship in different ways, often as a means of doing God's work. Dowey's analyses suggest that several Protestant faiths, which were later grouped as Unitarians, encouraged the formation of knowledge societies. Regions infused with Unitarian congregations were nearly four times more likely to develop a knowledge society than were other regions. This meant that Unitarian regions typically developed a knowledge society nearly a half century (46 years) before regions without Unitarians. Over time, the social and economic success of these Protestant sects spurred competitive emulation by other faiths—so most people became more open to science. This suggests that, in Britain, Unitarianism fostered the creation of knowledge societies, and knowledge societies propelled innovation.[50]

In France, innovation can also be linked to knowledge societies, urban interconnectedness, and certain forms of Protestantism. As in England, French cities with knowledge societies before 1750 grew economically faster until at least 1850. Here, we can look deeper by using subscriptions to the Enlightenment's most famous publication, Denis Diderot's *Encyclopédie*, as a measure of urban interconnectedness. In addition to essays by leading thinkers on government, religion, and philosophy, the *Encyclopédie* diffused material on new technologies and the industrial arts to thousands of subscribers from the urban middle class in 118 French cities. Detailed analyses show that the more subscriptions a French city had (per capita) to the *Encyclopédie,* the more innovations (exhibitions) from that city appeared at the 1851 Great Exhibition, and the more that city prospered during the century after 1750. That is, cities that were more plugged into Europe's collective brain innovated and grew more than less connected cities. The relationship between economic growth and urban interconnectedness appears both before and after the French Revolution, but not before 1750, so we aren't seeing an association between preexisting stocks of human know-how, affluence, or infrastructure.[51]

Why did some French cities network themselves into Europe's collective brain more effectively than other cities?

As with England's Unitarians, one important factor was probably the diffusion of a brand of Calvinist Protestantism that created the widely dispersed community of Huguenots. In comparing them to French Catholics, observers around 1700 described the Huguenots as "sober," "industrious," and determined to learn to read, write, and do arithmetic. It was also noted that they were "active in trade" and had a "real spirit" for it. A half century later, another writer observed the Huguenots' "frugality," "zeal for their work," "old-time thrift," opposition to "luxury and idleness," and capacity for "grasping all new ideas." He suggested that the Huguenots' "great fear of the judgment of God" drove them to focus on economic achievement. These observations converge with the contemporary studies of the impacts of Protestant faiths on people's psychology that I discussed in the last chapter. Such psychological inclinations would have made the Huguenots keenly interested in the *Encyclopédie*.

Sure enough, French cities with more Huguenots in the 17th and 18th centuries purchased more subscriptions to the *Encyclopédie* and subsequently prospered economically compared to other communities, probably at least partly through greater innovation.[52] But, the Huguenots faced rising levels of persecution from the French state during this same period, and tens of thousands fled to places like Britain, Denmark, Switzerland, and the Dutch Republic. Many innovators and entrepreneurs were lost to France's competitors in the process. We encountered one of them above, Denis Papin, whose book about pressure cookers probably supplied key insights for Newcomen's steam engine. If France hadn't oppressed its religious minorities, the steam engine might have been invented there.[53]

Nevertheless, Protestant faiths like Calvinism still created competition for the Church and thus drove key changes. Responding to the Protestants' push for education and practical knowledge, the Jesuits promoted schooling, craft skills, and scientific thinking. Many famous intellectuals of the French Enlightenment, including Voltaire, Descartes, Diderot, and Condorcet, were educated in Jesuit schools, and many Jesuit priests became important scientists.

Let's zoom out. To illustrate the growing network connections in Europe's collective brain, I've been focusing on the flow of ideas and know-how within Christendom. Crucially, however, the social and psychological changes wrought by the Church's MFP also led Europeans to absorb ideas, practices, and products from around the world more rapidly than societies that were more respectful of ancestors, devoted to tradition, and inclined to conform. Important ideas and know-how related to gunpowder, windmills, papermaking, printing presses, shipbuilding, and navigation were acquired often via circuitous routes, from prosperous societies in China, India, and the Islamic world. During the High Middle Ages, for example, returning crusaders probably brought the idea of wind power back with them from the Middle East. But, when Europeans developed this idea, their mills were mounted horizontally, which is more efficient, instead of vertically, as in Persia. Beyond their original use in grinding grain, European communities gradually deployed windmills for a growing list of jobs, including throwing silk, extracting oil, and manufacturing gunpowder. Later, Europeans dumped their awkward roman numerals (I, II, III, etc.) for more user-friendly arabic numerals (1, 2, 3, etc.), including a symbol for zero that had originated in India. After 1500, when Europeans opened global trade routes and subjugated vast overseas empires, the products, technologies, and practices from other distant societies flooded in, further energizing science, innovation, and production: latex, quinine, fertilizer (guano), potatoes, sugar, coffee, and the cotton gin (inspired by the Indian charka), just to highlight a few. Europeans of the early modern period no doubt thought that they were superior to these other peoples, but this didn't stop them from readily assimilating the useful ideas, crops, technologies, and practices they encountered. In many cases, the products or technologies that poured into Europe's collective brain were rapidly modified and recombined to create new innovations.[54]

In closing this section, let me return to a central point: the competition among cities, states, religions, universities, and other voluntary associations helped keep Europe's collective brain humming. Kings and other elites, in Europe and throughout history, have tended to crack down on anyone with a disruptive new idea, technique, or invention that might shake up the existing power structure. In Europe, this problem was mitigated by a combination of political disunity—there were many competing states—and the relative cultural unity nurtured by the transnational networks woven by a variety of voluntary associations, including the Church, universities, guilds, and the Republic of Letters. This combination afforded innovators, intellectuals, and skilled artisans options that their counterparts elsewhere in the world usually lacked. Rebellious minds—whether individuals or entire groups—could escape oppression by moving to another patron, university, city, country, or continent. Every time a king, guild, university, or religious community cracked down on some economically productive individuals or innovative groups, it lost in competition to its more tolerant and open counterparts. Among Britain's North American colonies, Philadelphia prospered and grew in part because it offered a degree of religious freedom and tolerance unavailable in competing cities. This intergroup competition favored social norms, cultural beliefs, and formal institutions that promoted tolerance, impartiality, and liberty. Later, in the 19th and 20th centuries, an openness to immigrants helps explain both the overall innovativeness and rapid economic growth of the United States as well as differences among counties and states. U.S. counties that took in more immigrants—even when compelled to by circumstances—were subsequently more innovative, educated, and prosperous.[55]

More Inventive?

Although the primary thrusters that accelerated innovation during the Industrial Revolution were fueled by the expanding size and interconnectedness of Europe's collective brain, there were also changes that probably made individuals—even in isolation—more likely to invent stuff. To understand this, we need to consider both how certain proto-WEIRD psychological traits would have contributed to individual inventiveness and how the new economic and social conditions would have further bolstered these traits in an autocatalytic interaction. First, recall some of the psychological traits we've already discussed: patience, hard work, and analytical thinking. Following Edison's observation that invention (or "genius") is 1 percent inspiration and 99 percent perspiration, it seems likely that as individuals became more industrious and patient, their chances of producing a successful invention would have risen. Moreover, the ongoing shift toward greater analytical thinking may have spurred innovation in several ways, including through a greater interest in experimentation, more faith in the existence of universal laws, and stronger inclinations to classify and categorize the world in context-free ways (into, e.g., species, elements, diseases, etc.).[56]

Beyond these aspects of psychology, the rising inclination toward positive-sum thinking would have had important consequences for inventiveness. The idea is that people became increasingly inclined to see social and economic interactions in the world, especially with strangers, as having the potential to be win-win. This is important because, as many anthropologists (as well as David Hume, in the opening epigraph) have observed, agricultural populations tend to perceive the world as zero-sum. This means that if some individuals get more—a better harvest or a beautiful child—it comes at a cost for everyone else, which leads to envy, anger, and strong social pressures for redistribution. Individuals who see the world as zero-sum are unlikely to waste time working to improve a tool, technology, or process because they implicitly believe that any productivity gains they might achieve will be at the expense of someone else (this, of course, is sometimes the case in the short run) and others will think badly of them. In addition, since those who see the world as zero-sum tend to think that others will envy their success, they may conceal their improvements and productivity, which closes off the collective brain. This suggests that as individuals become more inclined to see the world in positive-sum terms, they become more inclined to pursue technological improvements.[57]

A general inclination to see the world in positive-sum terms may open the psychological door to the diffusion of beliefs about "human progress." Historians have long argued that these cultural commitments played a role in both the Industrial and Scientific Revolutions, not to mention the Enlightenment. A belief in human progress and technological advancement, which was often grounded in religious faith, seems to have driven the work of many innovators and scientists leading up to the Industrial Revolution. Demonstrating this in an analysis of nearly 1,500 British inventors from 1547 to 1851, the economic historian Anton Howes argues that invention was spurred by the diffusion of an "improving mentality," which was primarily transmitted from prestigious mentors to those under their tutelage. In keeping with the structure created by Europe's unusual apprenticeship system, these spreading networks would have permitted an "improving mentality" to diffuse widely along tracks that had been greased by a general psychological inclination toward positive-sum thinking. The idea here is that notions of progress and improvement appeal more strongly to someone who views the world through a positive-sum lens.[58]

Catalyzing these slowly evolving psychological shifts, the improving economic and social conditions would have permitted a rising number of individuals to more effectively adapt their minds—over ontogeny—to the new institutions, norms, and values they confronted. The new conditions included improved nutrition (more calories, protein, etc.) and shrinking families, leading to less sibling competition and greater parental investment in each child. Like other species, humans seem to have genetically evolved a system that responds adaptively to early life cues that are used, in a sense, to predict how much an individual should invest in physical growth and mental skills for the long term. If life will be nasty, brutish, and short, there's less incentive to invest. In humans, this means that young children, infants, and even fetuses seem to sense their environment (e.g., "I'm always hungry and cold") and then apply either more or less self-control toward acquiring the locally valued attributes and skills. Specifically, greater affluence cues the young to invest more in molding their minds to fit the social norms and aspirations of their communities, including those that promote climbing the status ladder. For example, in a military aristocracy where personal honor and lineage are everything, cues of affluence would have led boys to psychologically invest in internalizing their family's notions of honor, deepening their clan loyalty, tracking the alliances of competitors, and developing hair-trigger aggressive responses to any slights to their honor. By contrast, in the urban centers of Early Modern Europe, with their emphasis on schooling and impersonal markets, the valued psychological attributes would have involved a positive-sum worldview, greater trust in strangers, sharpened punctuality, more analytic thinking, and superior reading skills (e.g., the Huguenots). In either case, the cognitive changes associated with these adaptive responses would have made people "smarter" in the sense that they were better cognitively adapted to the culturally-constructed worlds that they needed to navigate.

Evidence from the modern world confirms that improved food availability and nutrition during gestation, infancy, and early childhood fosters the development of valued cognitive abilities and social motivations. Shocks like famines and food shortages, if they occur before about age five, inhibit the development of self-control, positive-sum thinking, and the acquisition of mental skills related to abstract problem-solving and pattern recognition. Early-life deprivations may also suppress the internalization of costly social norms, such as those related to impersonal trust and cooperation. In the modern world, this results in long-term effects that lower people's educational attainment and income as adults.[59]

Historically, agricultural productivity in premodern Europe had been on the rise for centuries prior to the Industrial Revolution for both technological and psychological reasons. After 1500, however, contact with diverse populations around the world led to the sudden infusion of valuable new crops, especially from the Americas. Most notably, staples like potatoes, corn (maize), and sweet potatoes arrived, along with valuable nutritional sources like tomatoes, chili peppers, and peanuts. Europeans assimilated potatoes and corn—cornerstones of the conquered Incan and Aztec Empires, respectively—into their own food system. Analyses suggest that the potato alone accelerated the growth of European cities by at least 25 percent between 1700 and 1900. Importantly, these new crops not only improved the quantity and quality of food overall, they also helped eliminate famines in Europe. These changes to nutrition and food availability would have accelerated both the psychological changes I've been describing and the rates of innovation. Interestingly, improvements in the food supply and population health were precocious in England during the run-up to the Industrial Revolution.[60]

The effects of nutritional deficiencies or shocks on cognitive and social skills may also have been mitigated by the introduction of government-run social safety nets. When harvests fail or parents lose their jobs, children can suffer deprivations that impact their mental abilities as adults. In the wake of the Protestant Reformation, European governments began to replace the existing patchwork of social safety nets, much of it run by the Church, with their own secular safety nets. In Britain, this began in earnest under Queen Elizabeth, with the Old Poor Law of 1601. This early system, which endured until 1834, charged each parish with the obligation to care for the poor and the legal right to fund this effort through local taxes. At any given time, 5–15 percent of Britons were supported directly by the Old Poor Law. Such broader and stronger safety nets would have sharpened the population's cognitive and social skills on average. These psychological effects, along with the greater independence from families and churches that such insurance gives individuals, help explain why stronger safety nets promote more innovation, both in preindustrial England and in the modern world.[61]

As malnutrition and food shortages declined, both formal schools and the social norms surrounding literacy could exert an even stronger influence on cognitive development in preindustrial Europe. As we saw in the Prelude, Protestantism drove the early diffusion of literacy and schooling across Europe and put pressure on the Church to develop its own educational options. Martin Luther put the burden for educating the youth on government, and the schools that subsequently developed in Germany became a model for other countries. In Puritan New England during the 1630s, for example, the local government opened public schools and a college (Harvard) to train ministers, most of whom would serve Unitarian congregations. However, even before formal schools opened, Puritan parents looked for ways to teach their children to read, write, and do arithmetic. Protestants also believed that girls needed schooling, which led to more educated and literate mothers. As noted in the Prelude, maternal literacy has especially large effects on child health and cognitive development.[62]

Taken together, there's good reason to suspect that individuals in many preindustrial European communities were cultivating psychological traits that would have made them more inventive, which would have further fueled the collective brain.

Psychology and Innovation in the Modern World

The assembly of the innovation engine that propelled the Industrial Revolution becomes easier to see once we recognize how the psychology of premodern Europeans had been quietly evolving in the background for at least eight centuries. Of course, there are many economic and geographic factors that matter too, but if there's a secret ingredient in the recipe for Europe's collective brain, it's the psychological package of individualism, analytic orientation, positive-sum thinking, and impersonal prosociality that had been simmering for centuries. The relationship between psychology and innovation can still be seen today. Using data on patents to assess innovation rates, Figure 13.5 shows that more individualistic countries are much more innovative. This relationship holds even when the influence of differences in formal schooling, latitude, legal protections, religious denominations, and the percentage of the population that is of European descent is statistically held constant, or if you only compare countries on the same continent. It also holds if you only look at high-impact innovations—patents

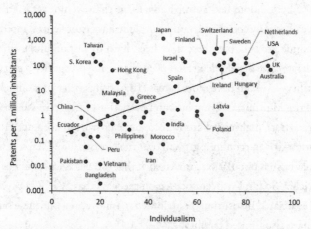

FIGURE 13.5. **Innovation rates and psychological individualism.** Innovation here is measured using patents per million people in 2009, and individualism is captured using the omnibus measure mapped in Figure 1.2.[63]

cited by other later patents—instead of all patents. Of course, in this one analysis, we can't be sure that the individualism complex is causally responsible for the differences in innovation seen across countries. Nevertheless, this is certainly the kind of relationship we'd expect in light of all the evidence linking WEIRD psychology to the expansion of the collective brain and greater innovativeness.[64]

Such data suggest that the social and psychological differences among populations—quite independent of formal institutions and governments—generate large differences in innovation rates. And, at least by the mid-18th century, innovation has been the primary driver of economic growth, prosperity, and longevity. Thus, by understanding how cultural evolution has shaped the basic institutions of family and marriage, and how this in turn drove social and psychological changes, we can more clearly illuminate the origins of the modern world, including the wealth and poverty of nations.

Escaping the Trap

In sustaining rising incomes over the long haul—after 1800—the populations of Christendom had another advantage that I've not yet highlighted. Historically, many societies around the globe have experienced rapid bursts of economic growth, but these have been hard to sustain and even harder to accelerate. The big challenge has been that rising prosperity results in rising fertility—women have more babies. This creates what economic historians call the Malthusian Trap: human populations can expand at geometric rates (very fast), making it hard for economic growth to keep up. However, innovation-driven economic growth over the last two, or perhaps more, centuries has beaten population growth such that the average person has gotten much richer. So far, I've been focused on the ways that WEIRD psychology and its associated institutions contributed to innovation, but these same elements have also limited fertility.

Many of preindustrial Europe's unusual norms related to marriage and the family would have lowered women's fertility and reduced population growth. First, based on contemporary research, both the imposition of monogamous marriage and the ending of arranged marriages would have lowered the total number of babies a woman had in her lifetime. This happens because these norms raise the age at which women marry (shrinking the window for pregnancies) and increase their power within the marriage, both of which reduce women's fertility. Second, the MFP favored neolocal residence and generated high rates of mobility for young people (they were no longer tied down by kin obligations). In general, anything that separates a woman from her blood or affinal relatives lowers her fertility, because she has less support in childcare and will experience less pressure from nosy relatives to get pregnant. Third, unlike other complex societies, many European women never married or had children—the Church created a way for women to escape marriage pressure by entering the sisterhood (the nunnery). Finally, formal schooling for girls—promoted by Protestantism—generally lowers fertility. This happens for several reasons, but one is simply that schooling allows women to avoid early marriage to finish their education. Now, European populations did grow in response to economic prosperity after 1500, but kin-based institutions and marriage norms constrained that expansion and shifted it into cities (via migration). In short, the demolition of kin-based institutions in Europe helped spring the Malthusian Trap by fueling innovation while simultaneously suppressing fertility.[65]

To close, let's summarize this chapter on a Post-it. To explain the innovation-driven economic expansion of the last few centuries, I've argued that the social changes and psychological shifts sparked by the Church's dismantling of intensive kinship opened the flow of information through an ever-broadening social network that wired together diverse minds across Christendom. In laying this out, I highlighted seven contributors to Europe's collective brain: (1) apprenticeship institutions, (2) urbanization and impersonal markets, (3) transregional monastic orders, (4) universities, (5) the Republic of Letters, (6) knowledge societies (along with their publications like the *Encyclopédie*), and (7) new religious faiths that not only promoted literacy and schooling but also made industriousness, scientific insight, and pragmatic achievement sacred. These institutions and organizations, along with a set of psychological shifts that made individuals more inventive but less fecund, drove innovation while holding population growth in check, eventually generating unparalleled economic prosperity.

14

The Dark Matter of History

Humans are an intensely cultural species. For over a million years, the products of cumulative cultural evolution—our complex technologies, languages, and institutions—have driven our genetic evolution, shaping not only our digestive systems, teeth, feet, and shoulders but also our brains and psychology. The centrality of cultural change meant that, generation after generation, young learners had to adapt and calibrate their minds and bodies to an ever-shifting landscape of sharing norms, food taboos, gender roles, technical demands (e.g., projectile weapons and underwater foraging), and grammatical conventions. At the same time, cultural evolution has favored an arsenal of mind hacks, including rituals, socialization practices (e.g., bedtime stories), and games, that mold people's psychology in ways that allow them to more effectively navigate their culturally-constructed worlds. The consequence of this culture-gene coevolutionary process is that to understand people's psychology we have to consider not only our genetic inheritance but also how our minds have adapted ontogenetically and culturally to the local technologies and institutions—present or even a few generations past. Thus, we should expect a rich array of diverse cultural psychologies to go along with disparate societies. The cultural evolution of psychology is the dark matter that flows behind the scenes throughout history.

To build up an understanding of the interaction between institutions and psychology, I began by drilling down to focus on our species' oldest and most fundamental institutions—those related to kinship and religion. Given their anchoring in our species' evolved psychology, it's not surprising that kin-based institutions culturally evolved as the primary way that mobile hunter-gatherers organize themselves and stretch out their cooperative networks. However, after the origins of sedentary agriculture, the need to control territory in the face of fierce intergroup competition drove the intensification of kin-based institutions, leading to the norm clusters that organize clans, cousin marriage, corporate ownership, patrilocal residence, segmentary lineages, and ancestor worship. As societies scaled up, the most successful political institutions remained heavily entwined with kinship. Even after the emergence of premodern states, with their military forces and tax-collecting bureaucracies, kin-based institutions still dominated life among both the elite and the lower strata. All of this means that some of the contemporary psychological variation we observe can be traced, through a variety of pathways, back to the ecological, climatic, and biogeographic factors that influenced the emergence of kin-based institutions and states.

Alongside kinship, both religions and rituals have also been culturally evolving over eons to harness aspects of our species' evolved psychology in ways that expand the social sphere and foster cooperation in larger groups. However, the emergence of diverse universalizing religions with the development of cosmopolitan empires provided new opportunities for cultural evolution to "experiment with" a variety of divine prescriptions and prohibitions related to marriage and the family. Some universalizing faiths endorsed marriage to close relatives (Zoroastrianism), while other faiths forbade previously common unions, such as those between cousins or affines. Similarly, some religions permitted men to marry as many wives as they wanted to (or could), while others limited them to only four and required equality among the wives (Islam). By the outset of the first millennia of the Common Era, the Roman Empire was a bubbling cauldron of religious competition that included the old Roman state religion, Judaism, Zoroastrianism, Mithraism, a potpourri of Christian faiths, and a panoply of local religions. From this cauldron, one strain of Christianity stumbled upon a peculiar set of taboos, prohibitions, and prescriptions regarding marriage and the family that eventually crystallized into the Church's Marriage and Family Program.

These prohibitions and prescriptions, which were infused into Christianizing populations under the Western Church over many centuries (arrow A in Figure 14.1), altered people's social lives (arrow B) and psychology (arrow C) by demolishing intensive kin-based organizations. These changes would have favored a psychology that was more individualistic, analytically-oriented, guilt-ridden, and intention-focused (in judging others) but less bound by tradition, elder authority, and general conformity. The elimination of polygynous marriage and the tightening of constraints on male sexuality may also have inhibited male status-seeking and competition, which would have suppressed zero-sum thinking, impatience, and risk-seeking.

The social and psychological changes driven by the breakdown of intensive kinship opened the door to rising urbanization, expanding impersonal markets (arrows D and E), and competing voluntary associations like charter towns, guilds, and universities. By facilitating and enforcing impersonal interactions in various ways, urban centers and commercial markets further stimulated impersonal prosociality and impartial rule-following while incentivizing personal attributes like patience, positive-sum thinking, self-regulation, and time thrift (arrows F and G). By producing a growing division of labor, within which an expanding class of individuals could select their occupations and social niches, these new social environments may have fostered more differentiated personality profiles—expanding eventually into the WEIRD-5—and strengthened people's inclinations to think in dispositional ways about other individuals and groups.

The quiet fermentation of these psychological and social changes influenced the formation of governments, laws, religious faiths, and economic

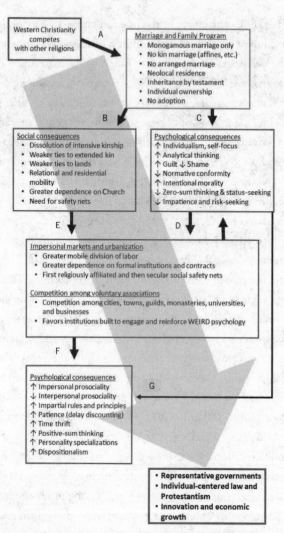

FIGURE 14.1. Outline of the main processes described in this book.

institutions in the latter half of the Middle Ages and beyond. Creating laws, for example, that focus on individuals and their properties ("rights") just makes sense if one lives in communities with weak family ties, substantial relational mobility, and a developing individualistic psychology that parses the world in dispositional ways ("she's trustworthy"). By contrast, if one lives in a community where relational ties are central and people are primarily judged by their social and family connections, building law and government around individual rights doesn't seem like common sense. It doesn't "fit" people's psychological inclinations.

In the last chapter, I examined how cultural evolution—in the wake of the transformation of European kinship and rising urbanization— expanded Christendom's collective brain and altered key aspects of people's psychology in ways that would have catalyzed innovation, suppressed fertility, and propelled economic growth. We saw how these ongoing social and psychological changes gradually opened the flow of ideas, beliefs, practices, and techniques within a sprawling network of interconnected minds, each of which was motivated to produce new insights and challenge old assumptions. This occurred in myriad ways, including through the diffusion of literacy (due to Protestantism), the proliferation of scientific societies, and the accelerating flow of artisans, scholars, and merchants through far-flung European cities and towns. This expanding collective brain sparked the Enlightenment, drove the Industrial Revolution, and continues to propel economic growth around the globe.

Now, with this summary in mind, let's return to the three core questions that I posed back in Chapter 1:

1. *How can we explain global psychological variation, and specifically the variation highlighted throughout this book (Table 1.1)?*
   Answer: To explain psychological variation broadly, we need to examine how history has unfolded in different ways in different places and consider the coevolution of people's minds with different institutions, technologies, and languages. Targeting the psychological patterns highlighted in Table 1.1, I focused on the evolution of institutions related to (1) intensive kinship, (2) impersonal markets and urbanization, (3) competition among voluntary associations, and (4) complex divisions of labor with substantial individual mobility.

2. *Why are WEIRD societies particularly unusual, so often occupying the extreme ends of global distributions of psychology and behavior?* Answer: The sect of Christianity that evolved into the Roman Catholic Church stumbled onto a collection of marriage and family policies that demolished Europe's intensive kin-based institutions. This grassroots transformation of social life propelled these populations down a previously inaccessible pathway of societal evolution and opened the door to the rise of voluntary associations, impersonal markets, free cities, and so on.

3. *What role did these differences play in the Industrial Revolution and in the global expansion of Europe during the last few centuries?* Answer: By the High Middle Ages, the social and psychological shifts induced by the Church had made some European communities susceptible to notions of individual rights, personal accountability, abstract principles, universal laws, and the centrality of mental states. This fertilized the psychological soil for the growth of representative governments, constitutional legitimacy, and individualistic religious faiths as well as the rise of Western law and science. These changes accelerated the ongoing social and psychological transformations that energized innovation and economic growth.

Guns, Germs, and Other Factors

By 1000 CE, at the beginning of Europe's transformation, the world was already highly economically unequal and likely quite psychologically diverse. Propelled by the early development of food production, the most prosperous and urbanized societies were all in Eurasia—in the Middle East, India, and China. Highlighting this pattern in his Pulitzer Prize–winning book *Guns, Germs, and Steel,* Jared Diamond argues that Eurasia, and particularly the Middle East, got a big head start in the formation of complex societies because these regions ended up with many of the world's most productive crops and best mammalian candidates for domestication. Eurasia got the wild ancestors of wheat, barley, millet, oats, and rice, along with cows, horses, pigs, goats, sheep, water buffaloes, and camels. Meanwhile, the Americas ended up with few wild plants or animals that were both easy to domesticate and productive. Corn, the major staple in the New World, required numerous genetic changes from its wild version to yield a productive crop—so it was a long road. For domesticated animals, the Americas ended up with llamas, guinea pigs, and turkeys—which gave them no general-purpose work animals like oxen, horses, water buffaloes, or donkeys to pull plows, carry heavy burdens, and crank mills. In Australia, the candidate crops and domesticated animals were even fewer than in the Americas.[1]

Accentuating these inequalities in fauna and flora, Eurasia's complex societies also developed more rapidly due to an east-west geographic orientation. This fostered the rapid development and diffusion of new crops, agricultural knowledge, domesticated animals, and technological know-how. As discussed in Chapter 3, this geographic orientation would have further fueled the intensive competition among societies that drives up political and economic complexity.

Taken together, the elements of Diamond's elegant argument nicely explain why we'd expect the largest and most powerful societies to emerge first in Eurasia, as opposed to the Americas, Australia, Africa, New Guinea, or Oceania, and it even points to where we'd expect to find them: the "lucky latitudes" that run through China, India, the Middle East, and the Mediterranean.[2]

Diamond's argument explains much of the global-level inequality that we observe in the world of 1000 CE. Subsequent analyses, further testing his ideas, have confirmed that biogeographic factors like the availability of domesticates, irrigation potential, and the orientation of continental axes are associated with the development of intensive agriculture, which in turn midwifed the early formation of states. With their head starts on people in other regions, these populations subsequently developed larger societies, political hierarchies, complex economies, urban centers, and sophisticated technologies.[3]

However, the strong positive relationship between these head starts and later economic prosperity weakens after 1200 or so, as European populations that experienced neither precocious states nor early agriculture took off economically. In fact, the leading economies during this takeoff were in some of the places where agriculture and states arrived relatively late within the Eurasian context: England, Scotland, and the Netherlands. In the last two centuries, these regions, along with British-descent societies like the United States, saw economic growth the likes of which had never been seen before in human history (Figure 13.1).[4]

My account picks up the story of global inequality where Diamond's explanation falls off—circa 1000—and places the coevolution of institutions and psychology at center stage. In a deep historical sense, Diamond's approach effectively accounts for why, at the opening of the second millennium, Said ibn Ahmad could see his civilization, and a few others, as superior to both the northern and southern "barbarians." Ancient Middle Eastern and Mediterranean societies, with origins that trace back to the earliest agriculture on earth, had bequeathed an immense cultural inheritance to Said's Islamic world that sustained its dominance well into the 16th century. Diamond's biogeographic approach, however, doesn't help us account for why the Industrial Revolution began in England, or why the Scottish Enlightenment first began to glow in Edinburgh and Glasgow. Only by considering the social and psychological changes induced by the Church's reorganization of the family can we understand Europe's peculiar pathway and the resulting patterns of global inequality that have developed in the last few centuries.[5]

However, recognizing the cultural and psychological impact created by a long history of societal complexity helps us to understand why some societies, like Japan, South Korea, and China, have been able to adapt relatively rapidly to the economic configurations and global opportunities created by WEIRD societies. Two factors are likely important. First, these societies had all experienced long histories of agriculture and state-level governments that had fostered the evolution of cultural values, customs, and norms encouraging formal education, industriousness, and a willingness to defer gratification. These are, in a sense, preexisting cultural adaptations that happened to dovetail nicely with the new institutions acquired from WEIRD societies. Second, their more powerful top-down orientations permitted these societies to rapidly adopt and implement key kin-based institutions copied from WEIRD societies. Japan, for example, began copying WEIRD civil institutions in the 1880s during the Meiji Restoration, including prohibitions on polygynous marriage. Similarly, as noted earlier, the Chinese Communist government initiated a program in the 1950s to abolish clans, polygyny, arranged marriages, unions between close relatives, and purely patrilineal inheritance (i.e., daughters had to receive an equal inheritance). In South Korea, the government passed a Western-style civil code in 1957 that required the consent of both grooms and brides to marry, prohibited polygynous marriage, and forbade marriage to relatives out to third cousins, through both blood and marriage. Since then, a variety of amendments have shifted South Korean society even further away from patriarchal intensive kinship. In 1991, inheritance finally became bilateral, so sons and daughters now inherit equally. In all three of these Asian societies, the European Marriage Pattern that had come to dominate medieval Europe under the Catholic Church was implemented rapidly from the top down.[6]

The big difference here, compared to preindustrial Europe, is that these 19th- and 20th-century Asian societies could also copy and adapt working versions of representative governments, Western legal codes, universities, scientific research programs, and modern business organizations in ways that permitted them to plug directly into the global economy. Modern formal institutions are now to a degree available "off the shelf," though their performance depends on the cultural psychology of the populace.[7]

My approach may also illuminate why populations with particularly long histories of agriculture, like those in Egypt, Iran, and Iraq, haven't fully integrated with the modern formal political and economic institutions that first arose in Europe. These societies have maintained quite intensive forms of kinship, probably for religious reasons. Islam, due largely to its divinely sanctioned inheritance customs (daughters must inherit half of what sons inherit), likely drove the diffusion of, or at least helped sustain, an otherwise rare endogamous marriage custom in which daughters marry their father's brother's sons. Specifically, as agricultural and pastoral societies adopted Islam, the need to sustain family landholdings against the possible loss of land each time a daughter married out (and into another clan) favors marrying within clans to avoid the continual depletion of wealth—land is the primary form of wealth in many such societies. This custom encourages particularly intensive forms of kinship, which as I've shown favor certain ways of thinking and feeling along with particular formal institutions (e.g., not democracy).[8]

AFFLUENCE AND PSYCHOLOGY

Many WEIRD people have a set of folk beliefs that lead them to assume that any observed psychological differences among populations are due to economic differences—differences in people's income, wealth, and material security. There is some truth to this intuition. Psychological shifts can emerge facultatively (on the fly) when individuals face sudden scarcity; or, changes may develop when infants and children psychologically and physiologically calibrate, while growing up, to more plentiful or less uncertain environments—I noted such effects when examining the influence of social safety nets on innovation (Chapter 13). They can also arise as people adaptively learn the most successful strategies, motivations, and worldviews from those in their communities or social networks—different psychological inclinations, approaches, and abilities will be more or less successful in more impoverished, constrained, or uncertain situations.[9]

However, there's little reason to suspect that rising wealth tindered the original sparks that ignited the modern world. In European Christendom, rising income and material security were, at least at first, a consequence—not a cause—of changing kin-based institutions and shifting psychological patterns. To see this, consider four points. First, the ordering of historical changes suggests that wealth, income, and material security (stability)—hereinafter glossed as "affluence"—can't be the first movers, since they follow both the institutional and psychological patterns I've outlined. Specifically, based on court records, kinship terminologies, Church histories, and other data sources, changes in European kinship long preceded rising affluence. Similarly, judging from literary sources, personal mobility, and legal writings, the first psychological shifts in individualism and independence arose before any substantial increases in affluence. Second, as I've frequently noted, many of the analyses of psychological variation presented throughout this book statistically hold constant the impacts of wealth, income, and even people's subjective experience of material security. Sometimes these affluence measures do show some independent relationships to people's psychological traits, but often they don't show any effects at all. When the effects of affluence do appear, they are typically small compared to the factors I've emphasized: religion, kin-based organizations, impersonal markets, and intergroup competition.[10]

To see this more clearly, let's consider a third point: the predicted patterns of psychological variation appear in both elite and poor populations. In all stratified societies, the elite are well-fed, rich, and usually feel secure (at least relative to the poor)—so, they all should show the psychological effects of affluence. Concretely, think of the UN diplomats, corporate managers, or high-level executives studied in Chapter 6. All are materially comfortable, yet their propensity for (1) impersonal honesty (parking illegally, see Figure 6.11), (2) universal morality (lying in court to protect their reckless buddies, see Figure 6.7), and (3) nepotism (hiring relatives into executive positions) varies immensely and can be explained by our measures of kinship intensity and Church exposure. In fact, we saw just as much psychological variation among these well-off elites as we did in both the nationally representative surveys and undergraduate samples. This suggests that affluence plays little role in shaping these global psychological differences.[11]

These patterns are further underlined by considering who drove the Industrial Revolution. The elites of Early Modern Europe held most of the wealth. Wealth buys armies, and armies buy security. If it was affluence that drove a WEIRDer psychology, then it should have been Europe's aristocrats who fueled the entrepreneurial engines of the Industrial Revolution. Instead, as we have seen, it was the urbanizing individualists, artisans, and clergy in the middle class who invested in the first joint stock companies and invented the printing press, steam engine, and spinning mule. The elites, by contrast, just got themselves repeatedly into debt by spending on personal extravagance instead of investing their wealth and saving for the long run. This is precisely the opposite of what an affluence-driven approach predicts.[12]

At the other end of the affluence spectrum, we again see substantial psychological variation. Recall the differences in impersonal prosociality observed in and among the hunter-gatherers, herders, and subsistence farmers from around the world. Many of these populations live on less than two dollars per day. Famines, hurricanes, droughts, injuries, and diseases are real threats to everyone's life and family. Yet not only did researchers uncover substantial psychological variation among these populations, but the most important factors that explained people's motivations for treating strangers fairly related to market integration and religion. These relationships remained strong even after we statistically held constant the small and inconsistent influences of affluence.[13]

This brings us to our fourth point. While some researchers have sought to argue that rising wealth and greater material security can directly shift some aspects of people's psychology—such as patience or trust—many aspects of psychology that I've described here have never been associated with affluence. For example, no one has explained or shown that greater wealth causes people to think more analytically, emphasize intentions in making moral judgments, or experience guilt over shame.

The bottom line is that rising wealth, income, and material security are part of the story and likely do have some effects; but, they were neither the initial sparks nor the most important drivers of psychological change over the last 15 centuries.

DO GENES CONTRIBUTE TO GLOBAL PSYCHOLOGICAL DIVERSITY?

To explain the origins of WEIRD psychology and the Industrial Revolution, I've argued that people's psychology shifted through adaptive cultural and developmental processes but not substantially through natural selection acting on genes. This is a good bet, given what we now know about how cultural learning, institutions, rituals, and technologies shape our psychology, brains (e.g., literacy), and hormones (e.g., monogamous marriage) without tinkering with our genes.[14]

It is possible, however, that the cultural and economic developments I've described also created selection pressures on genes favoring some of the same psychological differences. It's important to confront this possibility head-on, for a couple of reasons. First, as noted above, the products of cultural evolution have shaped our species' genetic evolution well back into the Stone Age. And in more recent millennia, the agricultural revolution and animal domestication have further altered the human genome in myriad ways, including favoring genes that permit people to more efficiently process both milk and alcohol. So, the notion that culture can influence our genome is now well established. Second, both our evolved tribal psychology and WEIRD inclinations toward dispositional explanations of behavior predispose us to see innate or essential differences where none exist. This explanatory bias has led some researchers to assume that any observed or inferred psychological differences among populations are due to genetic differences. The durability of this bias makes it all the more important to be crystal clear about the evidence.[15]

Overall, the many lines of research explored in this book suggest that cultural processes have dominated the formation of the psychological diversity that is apparent around the globe as well as within Europe, China, and India. Although natural selection acting on genes may have sluggishly responded to the world created by the religious beliefs, institutions, and economic changes I've described, there are a number of reasons to think that genes probably contribute little to contemporary variation. And, if they do, they may be pushing in the opposite direction to that typically presumed.

At the broadest level, cultural evolutionary processes are fast and powerful relative to natural selection acting on genes. This means that over periods of centuries (as is the case here), cultural adaptation will tend to dominate genetic adaptation, though in the longer run—over many millennia—genetic evolution can have larger effects and, in many cases, push things further than culture alone could. Moreover, by adaptively "fitting" people—psychologically—to their institutional environments, cultural evolution will often (but not always) deplete the strength of natural selection acting to address the same adaptive challenges. As I mentioned, the classic example of this is the evolution of genetic variants over thousands of years that permit adults to break down the lactose in milk. The selection for these genetic variants began with the cultural diffusion of animal herding (cows, goats, etc.). Both genetic and cultural evolution responded. In some populations, people developed cheese- and yogurt-making techniques that allowed adults to access the nutritional bounty in milk without possessing any special genes. Only in other populations, where those practices never evolved culturally, did genetic variants spread that permitted adults to process lactose.[16]

More recently, the power of cultural over genetic evolution can be strikingly seen in research on the genetic and cultural contributions to educational attainment during the 20th century. In European-descent populations, researchers have identified roughly 120 genes that are associated with schooling outcomes. Genes can potentially influence educational attainment in many ways, including by influencing people's willingness to sit still, pay attention, use birth control, avoid drugs, and do homework, as well as by contributing to their raw cognitive abilities. Interestingly, studies in both the United States and Iceland reveal that natural selection has reduced the frequency of these genes, resulting in a drop of 1.5 months of total schooling per generation. That is, genes that make people less likely to continue their schooling have increased in frequency in these populations. This genetically induced push against schooling, however, was rolled over by cultural evolution, which was speeding in the opposite direction. Over the same period, culture drove up people's educational attainment by 25.5 months (and IQ by 6 to 8 points) per generation. Over the entire 20th century, culture has raised Americans' educational attainment by 9 to 11 years, while natural selection has lowered it by less than 8 months.[17]

Now, in the historical account I've developed, the adaptive processes created by both cultural and genetic evolution might have—in principle—been pushing in the same direction. As long as social and economic success remained positively linked to survival and reproduction, both genetic and cultural evolution would have favored a WEIRDer psychology. However, there are good reasons to suspect this was not the case and that natural selection faced tremendous headwinds compared to cultural evolution. Much of the institutional and psychological action emerged in the urbanizing areas of Europe, in the charter towns and free cities I've highlighted. This is where the residentially mobile individuals clustered, guilds sprouted, impersonal markets flourished, urban charters blossomed, and universities bore fruit.

Given this distribution, here's the rub: urban areas in Europe were genetic death traps, a situation known as the "urban graveyard effect." Before the modern era, European urban dwellers died from infectious diseases (and probably wars) much more frequently than their rural counterparts, and their life expectancy at birth was up to 50 percent lower. Any psychological or behavioral inclinations derived from genes that might have caused an individual to want to live in a city *would have been selected against*. For example, if some folks had a genetic predisposition to trust strangers or think analytically, and this attracted them to the opportunities of urban life, natural selection would have quickly snuffed out these genes, or at least lowered their frequencies.[18]

Instead, European cities and towns survived and grew only through a constant inflow of rural immigrants. To sustain their populations, this inflow was so large that at any given time 30 percent of the populace had to have been born elsewhere. To actually grow, say, by 10 percent per decade, towns and cities required an inflow of twice this. This graveyard effect, combined with a near-constant flux of immigrants from the hinterlands, makes it hard to imagine much of a role for genetic evolution in creating WEIRD psychology—if anything, natural selection would have been *operating against* a psychology adapted to dense populations, impersonal markets, individualism, specialized occupational niches, and anonymous interactions.[19]

I've also argued that some of the key cultural evolutionary action occurred in monastic houses, like those of the Cistercian Order. Of course, from natural selection's point of view, monasteries are also genetic graveyards. Even if we assume that monastic vows of chastity were frequently violated (with women), monks were still having fewer children than they would have if they'd not joined this particular voluntary association.

Unlike natural selection acting on genes, the selective processes of cultural evolution would have been much less impacted by the graveyard effect. Most urban immigrants were young, single, and childless. They joined voluntary associations, like guilds, where they were enculturated and socialized by successful peers and prestigious elders. Once in, they could establish a firmer foothold by marrying into the native population. Those who died were readily replaced by eager new arrivals from rural areas who learned from the most successful survivors. Unlike genetic offspring, cultural learners don't rely on acquiring anything from their genetic parents but instead can selectively draw their "cultural parents" from among the survivors who achieve prestige and prosperity.

Cities have survived and prospered because culture has been winning over genes. The cultural evolutionary processes I've described forged efficient governing institutions while threading together a vast collective brain that ultimately improved public health by creating innovations like vaccination, water treatment, sanitation, and germ theory. Only in the last century has the mortality component of the graveyard effect vanished, or at least gone into remission, and many cities are now healthier than the countryside. Urbanites, however, still have fewer children than their rural counterparts.

Overall, the urban graveyard effect suggests that, if anything, there may have been selection against any genes favorable to a WEIRDer psychology. Culture may have had to wrestle its way upstream against a slower and weaker genetic opponent.

Globalization and Its Discontents

Does it matter that individuals and populations vary in how they perceive, think, feel, reason, and make moral judgments? Does it matter that these differences were produced by cultural evolution and that this changing psychological landscape influenced the character of our governments, laws, religions, and commerce?

Indeed it does. This view changes our understanding of who we are and where our most cherished institutions, beliefs, and values came from. The much-heralded ideals of Western civilization, like human rights, liberty, representative democracy, and science, aren't monuments to pure reason or logic, as so many assume. People didn't suddenly become rational during the Enlightenment of the 17th and 18th centuries, and then invent the modern world. Instead, these institutions represent cumulative cultural products—born from a particular cultural psychology—that trace their origins back over centuries, through a cascade of causal chains involving wars, markets, and monks, to a peculiar package of incest taboos, marriage prohibitions, and family prescriptions (the MFP) that developed in a radical religious sect—Western Christianity. The Christian leaders who repeatedly beefed up, implemented, and enforced the MFP at ecumenical councils over centuries revealed no long-term instrumental vision for how they'd create a new kind of world, though they no doubt had some nonreligious motives in addition to a genuine desire to serve a powerful supernatural being who—they believed—was deeply concerned about people's sex lives. Nevertheless, the unintended success of the MFP in restructuring medieval European populations directed societal evolution down a new pathway.

After 1500, European societies began expanding around the globe, often with devastating consequences, especially for those outside of Eurasia or from less complex societies. In the modern world, what we call "globalization" is merely the continuation of the processes I've described from Late Antiquity. Impersonal institutions like representative governments, universities, and social safety nets, which all evolved in Europe (before the Enlightenment), have been exported and transplanted into numerous populations. Often, especially in formerly non-state societies, the newly transplanted institutions created a misfit with people's cultural psychology, leading to poorly functioning governments, economies, and civil societies. And then, all too often, this led to rising poverty, corruption, and malnutrition as well as to civil wars between clans, tribes, and ethnic groups. Many policy analysts can't recognize these misfits because they implicitly assume psychological unity, or they figure that people's psychology will rapidly shift to accommodate the new formal institutions. But, unless people's kin-based institutions and religions are rewired from the grass roots, populations get stuck between "lower-level" institutions like clans or segmentary lineages, pushing them in one set of psychological directions, and "higher-level" institutions like democratic governments or impersonal organizations, pulling them in others: Am I loyal to my kinfolk over everything, or do I follow impersonal rules about impartial justice? Do I hire my brother-in-law or the best person for the job?

This approach helps us understand why "development" (i.e., the adoption of WEIRD institutions) has been slower and more agonizing in some parts of the world than in others. The more dependent a population was, or remains, on kin-based and related institutions, the more painful and difficult is the process of integrating with the impersonal institutions of politics, economics, and society that developed in Europe over the second millennium. Rising participation in these impersonal institutions often means that the webs of social relationships, which had once ensconced, bound, and protected people, gradually dissolve under the acid of urbanization, global markets, secular safety nets, and individualistic notions of success and security. Besides economic dislocation, people face the loss of meaning they derive from being a nexus in a broad network of relational connections that stretches both back in time to their ancestors and ahead to their descendants. The nature of "the self" transforms through this social and economic reorganization.

Of course, the process of European domination, colonialism, and now globalization is complex, and I'm not highlighting the very real and pervasive horrors of slavery, racism, plunder, and genocide. There are plenty of books on those subjects. Here, my point is that because human psychology adapts culturally, over generations, large-scale social transformations like those associated with globalization will necessarily create mismatches between people's cultural psychology and new institutions or practices, thereby shocking their sense of meaning and personal identity. This can happen even in the absence of the aforementioned horrors and can continue long after they've ended.

Unfortunately, the social sciences and standard approaches to policy are poorly equipped to understand or deal with the institutional-psychological mismatches that arise from globalization. This is because, not only is little attention given to the psychological variation among populations, but there's almost no effort to explain how these differences arise. Psychologists, for example, largely assume (often implicitly) that they are studying the genetically evolved hardware of a computational machine, akin to a desktop computer, and leave it to the anthropologists and sociologists to describe the software—the cultural content—that is downloaded into our psychological hardware. It turns out, however, that our brains and cognition evolved genetically to be self-programmable to a substantial degree and stand primed from birth to adapt their computational processing to the social, economic, and ecological environments they face. This means you can't truly understand psychology without considering how the minds of populations have been shaped by cultural evolution. As we've seen in many studies, but most strikingly in those involving the children of immigrants to places like the United States and Europe, people's psychology is influenced not only by the communities they grew up in but also by the ghosts of past institutions— by the worlds faced by their ancestors around which rich systems of beliefs, customs, rituals, and identities were built. The result is that textbooks that now purport to be about "Psychology" or "Social Psychology" need to be retitled something like "The Cultural Psychology of Late 20th-Century Americans." Tellingly, the primary way that culture enters the discipline of psychology is as an explanation for why people in places like Japan and Korea are psychologically different from Americans. If you want to learn about Japanese or Korean psychology, you need to go to textbooks on cultural psychology. Psychologists treat Americans, and WEIRD people more generally, as a culture-free population; it's "culture" that makes everyone else appear deviant. Hopefully, it's now clear that we are the WEIRD ones.

Similarly, the discipline of economics remains saddled with a way of thinking that has little place for culturally-evolved differences in motivations or preferences, let alone differences in perception, attention, emotion, morality, judgment, and reasoning. People's preferences and motivations are taken as fixed. Even when thinking about something as straightforward as people's beliefs, the standard approach in economics is to assume that these beliefs reflect their empirical reality. Cultural evolution, however, need not create a correspondence between reality and people's beliefs. In Africa, for example, there's little doubt that people's actions are strongly influenced by widespread beliefs in, and concerns about, witchcraft. Yet despite a laser-like focus on understanding why African economic growth has been sluggish, there's almost no research in economics on witchcraft in Africa or anywhere else—most economists won't even entertain this possibility. Of course, inclinations to believe in supernatural beings are common: about half of Americans believe in ghosts, while a similar fraction of Icelanders accept the existence of elves. The key is to figure out how and why certain kinds of beliefs evolve and persist in different ways in different places. Far from being inconsequential, certain kinds of supernatural beliefs and rituals have fueled the success of large-scale, politically complex societies.[20]

One challenge created by all of this psychological diversity, especially given the peculiarity of WEIRD psychology, is that we generally see and understand the world through our own cultural models and local intuitions. When policymakers, politicians, and military strategists infer how people in other societies will understand their actions, judge their behavior, and respond, they tend to assume perceptions, motivations, and judgments similar to their own. However, policies—even when implemented perfectly—can have one effect in London or Zurich and very different effects in Baghdad or Mogadishu, because the people in each of these places are psychologically distinct.

Instead of ignoring psychological variation, policy analysts need to consider both how to tailor their efforts to particular populations and how new policies might alter people's psychology in the long run. Consider, for example, the psychological impact of permitting polygamy or cousin marriage in communities where people find it normative, such as in particular countries, religious communities, or immigrant enclaves. What impact will laws have that reduce competition among firms such that a few giant companies dominate the marketplace? Should competing voluntary associations or market integration in rural regions be encouraged or discouraged? Such decisions not only have economic effects, they also have psychological and social implications over the long haul—they change people's brains. Even if the immediate economic effects are small or positive, it's worth contemplating the psychological changes that may ensue and create knock-on political and social effects.

In closing, there's little doubt that our psychology will continue to evolve in the future, both culturally and, over millennia, genetically. In many societies, new technologies are augmenting our memories, shaping our cognitive abilities, and rearranging our personal relationships and marriage patterns. At the same time, greater gender equality and rising levels of education are reorganizing and shrinking our families. Robots and artificial intelligence are increasingly doing our manual work and many of our most laborious cognitive tasks. Online commerce and tighter security in financial transactions may be reducing our need for impeccable reputations and dissolving our internalized motivations to trust and cooperate with strangers. Facing this new world, there seems little doubt that our minds will continue to adapt and change. We'll think, feel, perceive, and moralize differently in the future, and we'll struggle to comprehend the mentality of those who lived back at the dawn of the third millennium.

Milestones in the Marriage
and Family Program

EXPANDED VERSION OF TABLE 5.2. MILESTONES IN THE MARRIAGE AND FAMILY PROGRAM: 300 TO 2000 CE

Year	Prohibitions and Declarations on Marriage from the Church and Secular Rulers
305–6	Synod of Elvira (Granada, Spain) decrees that any man who takes the sister of his dead wife as his new wife (sororate marriage) should abstain from Communion for five years. Those marrying their daughters-in-law should abstain from Communion until near death.
315	Synod of Neocaesarea (Turkey) forbids marrying the wife of one's brother (levirate marriage) and possibly also sororate marriage.
325	Council of Nicaea (Turkey) prohibits marrying the sister of one's dead wife as well as Jews, pagans, and heretics.
339	The Roman Emperor Constantius II prohibits uncle-niece marriages, in accordance with Christian sentiment, and imposes the death penalty on violators.

(continued)

EXPANDED VERSION OF TABLE 5.2. MILESTONES IN THE MARRIAGE AND FAMILY PROGRAM: 300 TO 2000 CE (*cont.*)

Year	Prohibitions and Declarations on Marriage from the Church and Secular Rulers
355	The Roman Emperor Constantius II prohibits levirate marriage.
374	Basilius of Caesarea argues against sororate marriage in a letter to Diodor von Tarsus.
384/7	The Christian Roman Emperor Theodosius reaffirms prohibitions against sororate and levirate marriages and bans first cousin marriage. In 409, the Western emperor Honorius softens the law by allowing dispensations. It is not clear how long this persisted in the West. The dissolving Western Empire makes continued enforcement unlikely.
396	The Eastern Roman Emperor Arcadius, also a Christian, again prohibits first cousin marriage, but without the harsh penalties. In 400 or 404, however, he changes his mind and makes cousin marriage legal in the Eastern Empire.
Around 400	The pope, in letters to the Gallic bishops, argues that sororate marriage is forbidden for Christians and calls for penalties and the annulment of such marriages.
402	Roman Synod under Pope Innocent I forbids marriage to the sister of a man's deceased wife.
506	Synod of Agde (France, Visigoth Kingdom) prohibits first and second cousin marriage, and marriage to a brother's widow, wife's sister, stepmother, uncle's widow, uncle's daughter, or any kinswoman. These are defined as incest.
517	Synod of Epaone (France or Switzerland, Burgundian kingdom) decrees that unions with first and second cousins are incestuous and henceforth forbidden, although existing unions are not dissolved. The synod also forbids marriage to stepmothers, widows of brothers, sisters-in-law, and aunts by marriage. Many subsequent synods in the area of what would become the Carolingian Empire refer to this synod for incest regulations.
530	The Eastern Roman (Byzantine) Emperor Justinian prohibits marriage between a godfather and his godchild as well as between a man and his adopted child.
527/31	Second Synod of Toledo (Spain) prescribes excommunication for all engaged in incestuous marriages. The number of years of excommunication should equal the number of years of the marriage. This is affirmed by synods in 535, 692, and 743.
533	Synod of Orleans (France) forbids marriage with a stepmother.
535	Synod of Clermont (France) repeats the legislation of the Synods of Epaone and Agde.
535	The Byzantine Emperor Justinian increases punishment for levirate and sororate marriage to confiscation of property, a prohibition on holding administrative positions, exile, and, for lower-status people, whipping.

EXPANDED VERSION OF TABLE 5.2. MILESTONES IN THE MARRIAGE AND FAMILY PROGRAM: 300 TO 2000 CE (cont.)

Year	Prohibitions and Declarations on Marriage from the Church and Secular Rulers
538	First documented letter between a Frankish king and the pope is about incest (marriage to the wife of one's deceased brother). While the pope disapproves, he leaves the decision about the extent of Penance to the bishops.
538	Third Synod of Orleans (France) prohibits marriage to one's stepmother, stepdaughter, brother's widow, wife's sister, first and second cousin, and uncle's widow.
541	Fourth Synod of Orleans (France) renews the canon of the Third Synod of Orleans.
546	Synod of Lerida (Spain) re-enforces proscriptions of the Synod of Toledo but decreases punishments.
567	Second Synod of Tours (France) forbids marriage to one's niece, cousin, or wife's sister and confirms the canons of Orleans, Epaone, and Auvergne.
567/73	Synod of Paris (France) prohibits marriage to one's brother's widow, stepmother, uncle's widow, wife's sister, daughter-in-law, aunt, stepdaughter, and stepdaughter's daughter.
583	Third Synod of Lyons (France) renews canons against incest.
585	Second Synod of Macon (France) renews canons against incest with stronger condemnations than earlier synods.
585/92	The Synod of Auxerre (France) forbids marriage to stepmothers, stepdaughters, brothers' widows, wives' sisters, cousins, or uncles' widows.
589	Reccared I, the Visigothic King (Spain), decrees the dissolution of incestuous marriages, punishing offenders with exile and the transfer of their property to their children.
596	The Frankish King Childbert II decrees the death penalty for marriage to one's stepmother but leaves the punishment of other incest violations to the bishops. If the convicted resists the Church's punishment, his property should be seized and redistributed to relatives.
600	Pope Gregory I, in a letter to the Anglo-Saxon mission (see the text), prohibits marriage to first cousins (for Anglo-Saxons) and closer kin (e.g., uncle-niece unions) as well as levirate marriage. Incest now is defined as including relations with close affinal and spiritual kin (the children of one's godparents).
615	Fifth Synod of Paris (France) renews the legislation of the Synods of Orleans, Epaone, Auvergne, and Auxerre.
627	Synod of Clichy implements the same punishment and enforcement procedures that were decreed by Childbert II in 596. A systematic collection of incest legislation is compiled around this time and becomes part of the *Collectio vetus Gallica*, the oldest collection of canons from Gaul.

(continued)

EXPANDED VERSION OF TABLE 5.2. MILESTONES IN THE MARRIAGE
AND FAMILY PROGRAM: 300 TO 2000 CE *(cont.)*

Year	Prohibitions and Declarations on Marriage from the Church and Secular Rulers
643	Lombard laws of Rothari forbid marriage to one's stepmother, stepdaughter, or sister-in-law.
673	Synod of Hertford (England) forbids incest (without specifying the extent) and decrees that one man can only marry one woman and no man shall leave his wife except because of infidelity. If he does leave her, he cannot remarry.
690	Bishop Theodore of Canterbury's (England) widely distributed penitentials forbid sororate, levirate, and first cousin marriages, including to affines, but do not demand that cousin marriages be dissolved.
692	At the Synod of Trullo (Turkey), the Eastern Church finally forbids marriage to one's first cousins and corresponding affinal kin. This prohibits a father and a son marrying a mother and a daughter or two sisters, and two brothers marrying a mother and a daughter or two sisters.
716	Pope Gregory II, in a legation to Bavaria, prohibits marriage up to first cousins. The penalty is excommunication.
721	Roman Synod (Italy) prohibits marriage to one's brother's wife, niece, grandchild, stepmother, stepdaughter, cousins, and all kinfolk, including anyone married to a blood relative. It also prohibits marriage to one's godmother. In 726, Pope Gregory II specifies that for missionary purposes the prohibitions are up to first cousins, but for others the prohibitions include all known relatives. His successor, Gregory III, clarifies this prohibition such that marriages of third cousins are allowed, but marriages to all affinal kin within the prohibited circle are not. The decisions of this council are widely disseminated.
723/4	The Lombard King Liutprand (Italy) prohibits marriage with one's stepmother, stepdaughter, sister-in-law, and widows of cousins.
725	Roman Synod threats anathema against those who marry their godmothers.
741	Pope Zacharias forbids the marriage of a godfather with his godchild or the godchild's mother.
741	Under the Byzantine Emperor Leo III, the prohibitions in the Eastern Church are increased to include marriage of second cousins and, slightly later, second cousins once removed. The penalty for cousin marriage becomes whipping.
743	Roman Synod under Pope Zacharias orders Christians to refrain from marrying cousins, nieces, and other kinfolk. Such incest is punishable by excommunication and, if necessary, anathema.
744	Synod of Soissons (France) forbids marriage with relatives.

EXPANDED VERSION OF TABLE 5.2. MILESTONES IN THE MARRIAGE AND FAMILY PROGRAM: 300 TO 2000 CE *(cont.)*

Year	Prohibitions and Declarations on Marriage from the Church and Secular Rulers
753	Synod of Metz (France) prohibits marriage to stepmothers, stepdaughters, wives' sisters, nieces, granddaughters, cousins, and aunts. Offenders will be fined. Offenders unable to pay the fine will be sent to prison if they are free; if not, they will be beaten. The synod also prohibits (1) marriage of a father to the godmother of his child, (2) marriage of a child to his godmother, and (3) marriage of a confirmed person to the person who presented him for Confirmation (a Catholic rite of passage).
755	The Synod of Verneuil (France), convened under the Frankish King Pepin, commands that marriages be performed publicly.
756	Synod of Verbier (France) prohibits the marriage of third cousins and closer and decrees existing marriages between second cousins are to be ended. Those married to third cousins need only do Penance.
756/7	Synod of Aschheim (Germany) forbids incestuous marriages.
757	Synod of Compiègne (France) rules that existing marriages of second cousins or closer must be nullified. The Frankish King, Pepin, threatens secular punishments for any who disagree.
786	Papal legates in England forbid incestuous marriages with relatives and kin (without specifying the extent).
796	Synod of Friuli (Italy) directs attention to prenuptial investigations into potentially incestuous marriages and prohibits clandestine unions. The synod prescribes a waiting time before marriage during which neighbors and elders can reveal whether blood relations exist that would prohibit marriage. It also stipulates that although infidelity by the wife is a legitimate reason for divorce, remarriage is impossible as long as both spouses live. Charlemagne puts his secular authority behind these rulings in 802.
802	Charlemagne's capitulary insists that nobody should attempt to marry until the bishops and priests, together with the elders, have investigated the blood relations of the prospective spouses.
813	Synod of Arles (France) reaffirms the prohibitions of previous synods.
813	Synod of Mainz (Germany) forbids marriage between third cousins or closer and marriage to one's godchild or godchild's mother or to the mother of the child that one offered for Confirmation. The latter restrictions are also confirmed by Pope Nicholas I in 860 in his reply to the Bulgarians.
874	Synod of Douci (France) urges subjects to refrain from marrying third cousins. To strengthen the ruling, the synod makes the children of such incestuous unions ineligible for succession to an estate.

(continued)

EXPANDED VERSION OF TABLE 5.2. MILESTONES IN THE MARRIAGE AND FAMILY PROGRAM: 300 TO 2000 CE (cont.)

Year	Prohibitions and Declarations on Marriage from the Church and Secular Rulers
909	Synod of Trosle (France) clarifies and affirms the Synod of Douci, deeming that children born in an incestuous marriage are ineligible to inherit property or titles.
922	Synod of Koblenz (Germany) reaffirms the provisions of the Synod of Mainz in 813.
927	Synod of Trier (Germany) decrees a Penance of nine years for marriage between in-laws and blood relatives.
948	Synod of Ingelheim (Germany) prohibits marriage with all kin as far back as memory goes.
997	The Patriarch of Constantinople, Tomos of Sisinnios, forbids affinal marriages: (1) two brothers with two (female) cousins, (2) two (male) cousins with two sisters, (3) an uncle and his nephew with two sisters, or (4) two brothers with an aunt and her niece.
1003	At the Synod of Diedenhofen (Germany), the Emperor Heinrich II substantially widens the ban on incest to include sixth cousins, forbidding marriage between people who share one of their 128 great-great-great-great-great-grandparents.
Around 1014	In England, Wulfstan, Archbishop of York drafts law codes for the rulers Æthelred and Cnut that contain prohibitions against incest up to fourth cousins. The punishment for incest is enslavement.
1023	Synod of Seligenstadt (Germany) likewise forbids cousin marriage to sixth cousins. Bishop Burchard of Worms's *Decretum* also extends the definition of incestuous marriage to include sixth cousins.
1032	Synod of Bourges (France) forbids cousin marriage, though the precise extent is unclear.
1046	Peter Damian, an influential Benedictine monk and later cardinal, argues in favor of a ban up to and including sixth cousins.
1047	Synod of Tulujas (France) forbids cousin marriage.
1049	Synod of Rheims (France) forbids cousin marriage.
1059	At the Synod of Rome, Pope Nicholas II forbids marriage to sixth cousins or as far back as relatives can be traced. His successor, Pope Alexander II, likewise decrees that marriages to sixth cousins or closer relatives are forbidden. The Kingdom of Dalmatia gets a temporary dispensation, forbidding marriages only out to fourth cousins.
1060	Synod of Tours (France) reiterates the provisions of the 1059 Synod of Rome.
1063	Synod of Rome forbids marriages up to sixth cousins.
1072	Synod of Rouen (France) forbids non-Christian marriages and decrees that the priest must inquire about the relationship of those about to get married.

EXPANDED VERSION OF TABLE 5.2. MILESTONES IN THE MARRIAGE AND FAMILY PROGRAM: 300 TO 2000 CE (cont.)

Year	Prohibitions and Declarations on Marriage from the Church and Secular Rulers
1075	Synod of London forbids marriages up to sixth cousins, including affinal kin.
1094	*Decretum* of Ivo of Chartres: marriages of up to sixth cousins are forbidden.
1101	In Ireland, the Synod of Cashel introduces the incest prohibitions of the Roman Catholic Church.
1102	Synod of London nullifies existing marriages between sixth cousins (and closer) and decrees that third parties who knew of marriages among relatives are implicated in the crime of incest.
1123	The First Lateran Council (Italy) condemns unions between blood relatives (without specifying the relatedness). It declares that those who contracted incestuous marriages will be deprived of their hereditary rights.
1125	Synod of London repeats the provisions of the 1075 Synod of London, extending the incest ban out to include sixth cousins.
1139	Second Lateran Council (Italy) condemns unions between blood relatives (without specifying the degree).
1140	*Decretum* of Gratian: marriages of up to sixth cousins are forbidden.
1142	In Peter Lombard's *Books of Sentences*, marriage up to and including sixth cousins is forbidden.
1166	Synod in Constantinople (Turkey) reinforces the earlier Eastern Church's prohibition on cousin marriages (second cousins once removed and closer), and tightens enforcement.
1174	Synod of London forbids clandestine unions, presumably to facilitate the policing of incestuous marriages.
1176	The Bishop of Paris, Odo, helps introduce "the bans of marriage"—that is, the public notice of impending marriages in front of the congregation.
1200	Synod of London requires the publication of the "bans of marriage," and decrees that marriages be conducted publicly. Kin marriages are forbidden (but the degree of kinship is not specified).
1215	Fourth Lateran Council (Italy) decreases the marriage prohibitions to third cousins and all closer blood relatives and in-laws. They also formalize and integrate prior rulings into a constitution of canons. This brought prenuptial investigation and marriage bans into formal legislation.
1917	Pope Benedict XV loosens restrictions, prohibiting only marriage to second cousins and all closer blood and affinal relatives.
1983	Pope John Paul II further loosens incest restrictions, allowing second cousins and more distant relatives to marry.

This table draws primarily on Ubl (2008) and the *Dictionary of Christian Antiquities* (Smith and Cheetham, 1875 [vol. I]). Additional sources include Goody (1983; 1990; 2000), Gavin (2004), Sheehan (1996), Addis (2015), Brundage (1987), Ekelund et al. (1996), and Smith (1972).

APPENDIX B

Additional Plots

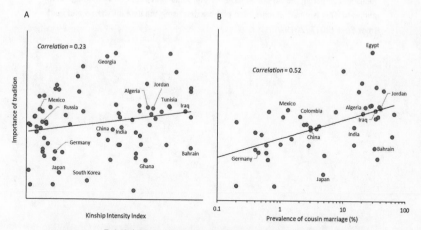

FIGURE B.1. Relationship between the importance of tradition and the (A) Kinship Intensity Index (96 countries) and (B) prevalence of cousin marriage (56 countries). Tradition is a country average based on responses to this question: How similar are you to the person described by this statement: "Tradition is important to her/him. She/he tries to follow the customs handed down by her/his religion or her/his family" (1–7 scale). Cousin marriage is plotted on a logarithmic scale.

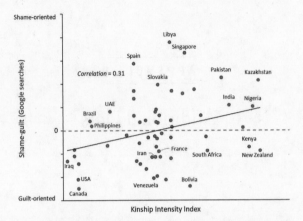

FIGURE B.2. Relationship between the frequency of searches for "shame" vs. "guilt" on Google and the Kinship Intensity Index (KII). The dashed line represents the zero line; countries above the line search more often for "shame" than "guilt." Those below the dashed line search for "guilt" more than "shame." The plot statistically removes the variation among the nine languages used, allowing us to focus on comparing the 56 countries. Note that Enke didn't use cousin marriage in his analyses. This is a partial regression plot created using the data on shame and guilt from Enke (2017, 2019).

The Psychological Impacts of Relational and Residential Mobility

As you enter the psychological laboratory, an experimenter greets you and leads you into a small room. The experimenter explains that you will be helping them test out a new questionnaire, and that you've been selected to be the "reviewer." Your job is to review the questionnaires just completed by two other participants, who are in nearby testing rooms. Based on these questionnaires, you need to pick one of the two to be your partner in a collaborative task that will occur in the second half of the session. In the questionnaire, the other participants have responded to a series of scenarios. In each scenario, the main character faces a dilemma in which they can either split their time to help both a friend and a stranger equally or put all their time into helping only the friend. The questionnaire then asks respondents who they liked more, the egalitarian who splits her time between the friend and the stranger, or the loyal friend, who only helped her friend. One of your potential partners always preferred the egalitarian helper. The other always liked the loyal friend. Now, the question is, who do you want to work with?

Did your family move residences while you were a child?

Among WEIRD college students, those who had *never moved* residences preferred the person who always picked the loyal friend over the egalitarian helper 90 percent of the time. If they'd moved once in their lives, the percentage dropped to 75 percent. When participants had moved two or three times while growing up, their preference for the person who always picked the "loyal friend" dropped even further, down to 62 percent of the time. Those who had moved as a child also said that they "liked" both the egalitarian helper and the person who always picked the egalitarian helper more (Lun, Oishi, and Tenney, 2012; Oishi, Kesebir, Miao, Talhelm, Endo, Uchida, Shibanai, and Norasakkunkit, 2013; Oishi, Schug, Yuki, and Axt, 2015; Oishi and Talhelm, 2012).

Experiments like this suggest that the experiences associated with residential moves strengthen people's preferences for egalitarianism and improve how they treat strangers. Something about these experiences seems to flatten the in-group vs. out-group distinction and shift people away from relying too heavily on their long-enduring social networks.

Some of these psychological effects are probably developmental, arising as children experience the need to form new relationships after a residential move. However, psychologists can also obtain some of these effects *facultatively*: in one experiment (Oishi and Talhelm, 2012), participants were randomly assigned to imagine themselves in a place that they would like to either visit temporarily or settle in permanently. Then, after this mental experience, participants were asked to write about how they feel. Getting people to think about these different situations primed mind-sets that subtly shifted their preferences. Priming residential stability caused participants to prefer loyal friends just a bit more than egalitarian individuals, while priming residential mobility—temporary visits—reversed things, creating a slight preference for egalitarians over loyal friends. These mental reminders (primes) also increase people's motivations to expand their social networks—to establish and nourish new relationships. Overall, this research suggests that residential mobility causes people to seek out new relationships and to prefer egalitarians. Priming results are always a worry, since they often don't replicate. I offer this research here to suggest that along with developmental effects, changes in residence may also create facultative impacts.

Physically moving residences obviously creates a need to build new relationships. That is, it gives rise to the potential for what psychologists refer to as *relational mobility*, which covers all the factors that constrain or promote the formation of new relationships or the dissolution of old ones. Being enmeshed in a patrilineal clan, for example, not only reduces people's geographic mobility, by tying them to communally owned ancestral lands, but also inhibits people's relational mobility through the binding obligations and responsibilities one acquires toward fellow clan members (Oishi, Schug, Yuki, and Axt, 2015; Yuki, Sato, Takemura, and Oishi, 2013).

Socially and psychologically, research suggests that greater residential and relational mobility leads people not only to make less of a distinction between in-groups and out-groups but also to form larger social networks, favor new experiences, prefer novelty, and perhaps even think more creatively (Hango, 2006; Li et al., 2016; Mann, 1972; Oishi, 2010; Oishi et al., 2015; Oishi and Talhelm, 2012; Park and Peterson, 2010).

Further, studies comparing societies with lower relational mobility, such as Japan, to those with higher mobility, such as the United States, reveal how mobility influences people's social networks. Both Americans and Japanese prefer to hang around those with backgrounds, goals, personalities, values, and interests similar to their own. However, even among people's closest friends, only Americans actually seem to have connected with—rather than just quietly preferred—individuals who are noticeably like themselves along these dimensions. This pattern emerges because, unlike most Japanese, Americans are relatively unconstrained in seeking out and forming new relationships. By contrast, the relational immobility of societies like Japan constrains individuals from freely forming voluntary associations with people who share their interests, goals, and other characteristics.

This research, done with both Japanese and Americans, suggests that any factors that increase individuals' geographic or relational mobility can tilt their psychology in particular ways. The medieval Church, by demolishing Europe's kin-based and tribal institutions, would have increased both residential and relational mobility. Socially, in the absence of the norms that typically govern kin-based organizations, individuals and nuclear families would have been freer to develop new, non-kin-based relationships and to independently migrate because they would have been less constrained by larger family obligations, responsibilities, and joint property holdings. The result would have been greater relational mobility. Similarly, with the loss of kin-based social safety nets and the need to find unrelated marriage partners, individuals would have had more incentives to move and fewer to stay put, resulting in greater residential mobility. Indeed, in the modern world people who value family ties less are more willing to move geographically. In fact, even the adult children of immigrants whose parents came from a country with stronger family ties are less likely to move geographically than are the children of immigrants who came from countries with weaker family ties. In medieval and Early Modern Europe, the weakening of kin ties likely contributed to the substantial flow of migrants from rural to urban areas—to rising urbanization (Alesina et al., 2015; Alesina and Giuliano, 2013, 2015; Dincecco and Onorato, 2018; Kleinschmidt, 2000; Winter, 2013).

Broadly, kin-based institutions manipulate our psychology in several different ways, and I suspect that the contributions made by relational or residential mobility to the global variation we saw in the last chapter were relatively modest. However, the effects of relational mobility are important, because they develop quickly, both facultatively and developmentally. This contrasts with culturally-evolved values, beliefs, worldviews, motivations, and parenting strategies, which may take decades or centuries to take shape.

The rapid psychological effects of mobility are particularly relevant when thinking about how rural immigrants to the charter towns, free cities, monasteries, and universities of medieval Europe would have responded before cultural evolution had time to construct special social norms for impersonal exchange or the full psychological package that forms the individualism complex. Based on the above research, migrants to charter towns and free cities would have been psychologically more inclined toward (1) having an egalitarian view of strangers vs. friends and family members, and (2) building broader social networks with like-minded others.

NOTES

Prelude: Your Brain Has Been Modified

1. Dehaene, 2009; Dehaene et al., 2010; Dehaene et al., 2015; Szwed et al., 2012; Ventura et al., 2013. The label "*Letterbox*" is from Dehaene, 2009.

2. Illiterate people in modern societies may still possess a slight right-side bias in face processing (Dehaene et al., 2015). However, this bias may not emerge in people raised in societies devoid of written scripts—that is, in most societies throughout human history. In modern societies, illiterates still adapt to a world filled with written words and letters even if they don't eventually become proficient readers.

3. Coltheart, 2014; Dehaene, 2014; Dehaene et al., 2015; Henrich, 2016; Kolinsky et al., 2011; Ventura et al., 2013. Constrained by human neurogeography, the location of the *Letterbox* varies only slightly for writing systems as diverse as those used for English, Hebrew, Chinese, and Japanese.

4. Another improved cognitive skill that many readers share is the ability to discriminate mirror images, such as "ʃ" from "ʅ". The sharpening of this ability depends on the particular script that people learned. Latin-based scripts require readers to

distinguish lateral mirror images, such as *d* from *b* or *p* from *q*. This script-specific specialization extends beyond letters to other shapes and objects. These readers can readily distinguish symbols that are not letters—">" from "<"—but they are slower at identifying when two mirror images actually represent the same object. This deficit is odd because, like other primates, humans are innately inclined to ignore the differences between lateral mirror images; consequently, most of the world's ancient writing systems don't require mirror-image distinctions. Learning Latin-based scripts (used in all western European languages) compels learners to overcome a natural inclination in our attention system (Kolinsky et al., 2011). For a general discussion of the cognitive impact of literacy, see Huettig and Mishra, 2014.

This innate human deficit is far from obvious to those who develop new scripts for unwritten languages. For example, the elegant Cree syllabary, designed by the Methodist missionary James Evans in the 1830s, involves mostly mirror-image symbols. As an English reader, James no doubt failed to recognize the inherent challenges associated with learning to distinguish mirror images (Berry and Bennett, 1995). This new script spread widely through Cree-speaking populations until written English eventually pushed it out.

5. There is a debate about subliminal priming (Kouider and Dehaene, 2007).

6. Henrich, 2016, Chapter 14.

7. Becker and Woessmann, 2009, 2010; Buringh and Van Zanden, 2009.

8. Data from Buringh and Van Zanden, 2009.

9. To be theologically correct, purgatory exists out of time, so Catholics aren't supposed to think of this as a "reduced sentence." However, indulgences often released souls from specific amounts of time in purgatory and more expensive indulgences purchased even speedier releases (Dohrn-van Rossum, 1996).

10. Dittmar and Seabold, 2016; McGrath, 2007. More broadly, an intense competition developed across Europe among diverse Protestant sects and a reforming Catholic Church (Pettegree, 2015). This competition was most acute in the free cities and charter towns, especially in those where a competitive printing press industry was developing.

11. McGrath, 2007. In Chapter 12, I'll discuss several religious movements prior to the Reformation that had pushed biblical literacy, especially in the Netherlands, where the Brethren of the Common Life developed within the Church (Akçomak, Webbink, and ter Weel, 2016). This meant that Dutch Catholics were likely relatively literate compared to populations elsewhere on the eve of the Reformation.

12. Becker and Woessmann, 2009.

13. Becker and Woessmann, 2009, 2010; McGrath, 2007.

14. Unfortunately, the 1816 census lacks specific information on literacy, so that finding couldn't be checked (Becker and Woessmann, 2010).

15. The relationship between Protestantism and literacy in 19th-century Prussia is more persuasive than similar correlations across countries because there are many

more differences between countries (in such factors as history, institutions, culture, and climate) that might account for the relationship. Prussia was comparatively homogeneous.

16. Commonly used in economics, this statistical razzle-dazzle is called an instrumental variable regression (Becker and Woessmann, 2009). See Cantoni (2012) on the centrality of Wittenberg for the spread of Protestantism, and Dittmar and Seabold (2016) for the importance of the printing press and the relevance of Mainz.

17. Becker and Woessmann, 2009.

18. Interestingly, the "extra literacy" induced by Protestantism explains the higher incomes and lower reliance on farming found in more Protestant counties after the Industrial Revolution arrives (Becker and Woessmann, 2009).

19. Boppart, Falkinger, and Grossmann, 2014. The leaders of the Reformation in Zurich and Geneva were Ulrich Zwingli and John Calvin, respectively. For work in China, see Bai and Kung, 2015; Chen, Wang, and Yan, 2014.

20. Becker, Hornung, and Woessmann, 2011; Becker and Woessmann, 2009; Boppart et al., 2014. Many people suspect that the development of Gutenberg's press must have played a role in the spread of literacy. Indeed, the printing press did catalyze the diffusion of both literacy and Protestantism in Europe (Cantoni, 2012; Dittmar and Seabold, 2016; Pettegree, 2015; Rubin, 2014). However, the printing press isn't a strong catalyst outside of Europe. After the arrival of European printing presses, literacy doesn't begin rising in non-European cities around the globe. Widespread literacy also never developed in China and Korea, which had previously developed their own presses and publishing industries (Briggs and Burke, 2009). These comparisons suggest that, in the beginning, cheaply printed books didn't create readers. Instead, numerous motivated readers provided an untapped market for cheap books and pamphlets. Without Protestantism to create the demand, printing presses had few customers. Tellingly, the two books most printed on Gutenberg's new presses were, of course, the Bible, which remains the most printed book of all time, and Thomas à Kempis's *The Imitation of Christ*, which is devoted to religious teachings on living a pious life. Finally, 1,500 years before Martin Luther, new religious prescriptions among Jews after the destruction of the Second Temple led to widespread male literacy and eventually to the adoption of urban occupations. Here, as with the Protestant case, idiosyncratic religious beliefs about the need for all males to read the Torah drove literacy, though in this case there were no printing presses in sight (Botticini and Eckstein, 2005, 2007, 2012).

21. Gallego and Woodberry, 2010; Nunn, 2014. During the first half of the 20th century in Africa, over 90 percent of formal schooling was provided by Christian missionaries. In the 1940s, on the eve of decolonialization, 97 percent of students in Nigeria and Ghana were attending missionary schools. The analyses by Gallego and Woodberry include statistical controls for population density,

the strength of the rule of law, and geographic proximity to oceans, rivers, and national capitals. Interestingly, researchers have long noted that former British colonies in Africa have higher literacy rates than other European colonies. However, the "British advantage" vanishes when the effects of competition among Protestants and Catholics are considered. Nunn (2014) arrives at similar conclusions, and also controls for the influence of early explorers, railroads, agricultural suitability, and slave trade intensity. Nunn's analysis indicates that the impact of early missionaries operates through both entire ethnic groups and local communities. The ethnic group is three times more important than the local community in channeling missionary influences on education. For similar work in China and India, see Bai and Kung, 2015; Chen et al., 2014; Mantovanelli, 2014.

22. Nunn (2014) provides evidence indicating that the impact of Protestant missionaries, unlike their Catholic counterparts, operates through the inculcation and transmission of religious values related to education.

23. Becker and Woessmann, 2008. This indicates that Protestantism caused more girls to be enrolled in school relative to Catholicism. The impact of Protestantism was relatively small, only increasing the fraction of girls enrolled in school by 3–5 percent. But, that is impressive in this context, since by 1816 girls already represented nearly half of all Prussian students (47 percent). For research in India and Africa, see Mantovanelli, 2014; Nunn, 2014. These effects can be inferred in other ways. In South America, the effect of Jesuit missions among the Guarani raised everyone's literacy, but the Jesuits had a particularly large impact on female literacy (Caicedo, 2017).

Regarding the effect of literate mothers on their babies, see Bus, Van Ijzendoorn, and Pellegrini, 1995; Kalb and van Ours, 2014; LeVine et al., 2012; Mar, Tackett, and Moore, 2010; Niklas, Cohrssen, and Tayler, 2016; Price, 2010; Smith-Greenaway, 2013. I've two concerns with this research. First, most of it (but not all) ignores the potential role of genes: parents with genes that incline them toward reading, verbal fluency, etc., influence their children by passing these genes on to them. This may cause both adults and children to read more and develop certain cognitive abilities independent of what parents themselves actually do. Second, it's not clear how much of these cognitive benefits persist into adulthood (Harris, 1998; Plomin et al., 2016).

24. Becker, Pfaff, and Rubin, 2016.

25. Becker et al., 2016; C. Young, 2009. Note that one analysis using urbanization as a measure of economic growth indicates that (1) Protestantism didn't spur urban growth relative to Catholicism within the Holy Roman Empire until the 19th century, and (2) the effects of Protestantism on literacy occurred principally outside of urban areas (Cantoni, 2015). Remember, however, that most people lived in rural areas in this preindustrial world. In urban areas, the potential positive effects of Protestantism may have been mitigated by the Counter-Reformation

and the actions of monastic orders like the Jesuits. On the influence of literacy and related cognitive skills on economic growth after 1800, see Cantoni, 2015; Hanushek and Woessmann, 2012.

26. Becker et al., 2016. These findings address Weber's (1958) hypothesis regarding Protestantism and Capitalism. In broadest terms, the profusion of research in the last decade strongly suggests that Weber was on the right track, although he seems to have underemphasized the importance of literacy and social networks while overemphasizing the "work ethic"—see Chapter 12.

27. McGrath, 2007.

28. Henrich, 2016.

29. If public officials needed to be literate for practical reasons, then the elevated literacy rate would have expanded the fraction of the populace who could enter public service.

30. Henrich, Heine, and Norenzayan, 2010a, 2010b.

31. It's also possible that high levels of literacy combined with cheap novels (thanks to the printing press) may have made a growing number of readers more capable of feeling the pain of others—more empathic. The idea is that by reading fiction people get to practice putting themselves into the shoes of others and seeing the world from another's perspective. Consistent with this, several studies in Western societies show that people who read more fiction tend to be more compassionate and better at reading others' emotions (Mar, Oatley, and Peterson, 2009; Mar and Rain, 2015; Mar et al., 2006). However, there remains a question as to whether reading fiction does indeed increase empathy (Bal and Veltkamp, 2013; Kidd and Castano, 2013; Panero et al., 2016)—perhaps, instead, more empathic people are more inclined to read fiction. Establishing this causal connection is important, as stronger compassionate inclinations are linked to greater prosociality, more charitable giving, and less violence. Rising empathy, possibly driven by rising rates of literacy and plentiful books, may help explain the dramatic decline in violence observed in England and Europe since the 16th century (Clark, 2007a; Pinker, 2011). This is plausible given the research suggesting that empathy can be increased through training (van Berkhout and Malouff, 2016).

1. WEIRD Psychology

1. Acemoglu and Robinson, 2012; Clark, 2007a; Diamond, 1997; Hibbs and Olsson, 2004; Landes, 1998; Mokyr, 2002; Morris, 2010.

2. Altrocchi and Altrocchi, 1995; Ma and Schoeneman, 1997. The "Personal attributes, abilities, and aspirations" variable in Figure 1.1A combines Ma and Schoeneman's variables "personal attributes" and "self-worth." The "Roles and relationships" variable in Figure 1.1B covers a somewhat broader range of possible answers than the "Roles and relationships" variable in Figure 1.1A.

3. Ma and Schoeneman, 1997.

4. Heine, 2016; Henrich, Heine, and Norenzayan, 2010a. When thinking about these self-concepts (i.e., responses to "I am____" or "Who am I" questions), a common mistake is to assume that a focus on personal attributes, achievements, and interests is at odds with group membership or sociality (Yuki and Takemura, 2014). This is not the case. The key difference has to do with the nature of the relationships between individuals and their groups. Maasai, Samburu, and Cook Islanders are embedded in complex sets of inherited family structures that involve a wide range of social norms endowing every person with a rich set of obligations, responsibilities, and privileges vis-à-vis others in their groups. By contrast, WEIRD people seek out and voluntarily join groups of strangers that fit their personal interests, goals, principles, and aspirations. Knowing that a person is a member of one of these groups, whether it's "sea kayakers" or "Republicans," tells us about the person's interests and values. Often, group memberships are more about principles or activities than the specific relationships involved. This is especially true when membership in voluntary groups changes. When I respond with "I am . . . a scientist," my answer probably doesn't make you think of me and all my scientist buddies hanging out or helping each other when we get injured; instead (hopefully?), it conveys my commitment to understanding the world through open inquiry governed by reason and evidence. It's a group, but really it's about me.

5. The scale I'm describing is often thought of as running from "individualism" to "collectivism" (Hofstede, 2003; Tönnies, 2011; Triandis, 1994, 1995). It captures a spectrum that has been recognized in one form or another for at least a century. For an entertaining discussion, see Dan Hruschka's piece at evolution-institute .org/article/infections-institutions-and-life-histories-searching-for-the-origins-of -ind. Note that I'm avoiding the term "collectivism" here because it carries too much confusing semantic baggage.

6. Heine, 2016; Hofstede, 2003; Triandis, 1989, 1994, 1995.

7. Of course, the institutions that create regulated-relational societies vary immensely, as do the psychologies of the people in these societies. Many people in China, for example, are strongly achievement-oriented, though this motivation pattern seems to arise from a desire to comply with the expectations of one's family rather than from internalized standards. Nevertheless, this achievement orientation makes China less like many traditional communities and, at least outwardly, more like WEIRD societies. Similarly, Japan's traditional kin-based community institutions seem to have infused themselves into the WEIRD social, political, and economic formal institutions adopted from Europe and the United States after the Meiji Restoration in the late 19th century and again after World War II. This institutional synthesis has given Japan a unique social psychology, distinct not only from WEIRD societies but also from populations in South Korea and China, with which it's often mistakenly lumped together with psychologically (Hamilton and Sanders, 1992; Herrmann-Pillath, 2010).

8. In shopping for relationships in an individualistic world, people tend to (1) promote their personal attributes while (2) remaining as consistent as possible across different social contexts so as to best advertise just how deep their "special" attributes run. What is perceived as relatively constant about individuals are their attributes, not their relationships, since neighbors, employers, and friends can all change over time. The in-group vs. out-group distinction is fundamentally different here because it doesn't usually partition off one's inherited network of personal relationships from everyone else. Instead, in-groups are often based on social categories that are believed to mark underlying individual attributes, ranging from principles and beliefs to preferences and interests ("Liberals" or "Catholics"). In this world, people change religions, political parties, names, countries, cities, sports teams, genders, and spouses.

9. Hofstede, 2003.

10. There are other important dimensions of global psychological variation (Gelfand et al., 2011; Hofstede, 2003; Triandis, 1994).

11. Acemoglu, Akcigit, and Celik, 2013; Gorodnichenko and Roland, 2011; Talhelm et al., 2014).

12. Hruschka et al., 2014; Hruschka and Henrich, 2013a, 2013b.

13. Some critics will ignore these points and pretend I never made them.

14. Campbell et al., 1996; Church et al., 2006; English and Chen, 2011; Heine, 2016; Heine and Buchtel, 2009; Kanagawa, Cross, and Markus, 2001. Unfortunately, too much of this research is focused on East Asian and American undergraduates.

15. Suh, 2002.

16. Campbell et al., 1996; Diener and Diener, 1995; Falk et al., 2009; Heine and Buchtel, 2009; Heine and Lehman, 1999. This evidence is limited because (1) psychologists mostly study WEIRD populations and (2) when they study non-WEIRD people, it has been mostly East Asian undergraduates. See Ethan Watters (2010) for a discussion of clinical psychology and psychiatry from a cross-cultural perspective.

17. Foster, 1967; Heine, 2016; McNeill, 1991; Nisbett, 2003. The process of psychologically adapting to the social incentives of these different worlds can be seen in our brains. For example, recent work in neuroscience reveals that people who think of themselves as independent agents have larger orbital frontal cortices than do those who think of themselves as interdependent nodes in relational networks (Kitayama et al., 2017).

18. Wallbott and Scherer, 1995. This result relies on classifying the experiences reported based on the descriptions provided by the participants and not on using the emotion labels given by the participants. WEIRD people, especially Americans, are notoriously confused about the difference between "guilt" and "shame" (Fessler, 2004).

19. Fessler, 2004; Martens, Tracy, and Shariff, 2012; Sznycer et al., 2016, 2018; Tracy and Matsumoto, 2008; Wallbott and Scherer, 1995; Wong and Tsai, 2007.

20. Benedict, 1946; Elison, 2005; Fessler, 2007; Levy, 1973; Scheff, 1988; Tracy and Matsumoto, 2008; Vaish, Carpenter, and Tomasello, 2011; Wong and Tsai, 2007.

21. In societies with strict class divisions or castes, those at the low end of the social spectrum can feel shame just by being in the presence of higher-ups—because the higher-ups look down on low-status people.

22. Similarly, WEIRD people may feel guilty for not helping a friend move or for not visiting her in the hospital, and this guilt can motivate them to approach the person and attempt to repair and preserve the relationship. However, few of these behaviors are governed by obligatory social norms closely monitored by tight-knit networks.

23. Milgram, 1963. If the academic discipline of psychology had developed elsewhere— say, in Hong Kong or Fiji—I suspect that "conformity" would have seemed obvious and would thus have been uninteresting.

24. Bond and Smith, 1996. Thanks to Damian Murray for the data.

25. Asch, 1956; Bond and Smith, 1996. The conformity effect size in the figure gives the difference in the average number of errors made between the treatment and control scaled by the standard deviation. So, an effect size of 1 means that the treatment average is one standard deviation higher than the control average.

26. Bond and Smith (1996) conducted an extensive analysis using the full dataset (whereas I collapsed all the WEIRD countries together for plotting). They show that not only are Hofstede's individualism measures correlated with conformity, but so are two other measures of individualism (Schwartz and Bilsky, 1990; Trompenaars and Hampden-Turner, 1998).

27. To see how conformity affects real life, consider left-handedness. In WEIRD societies today, about 10–16 percent of adults are left-handed. Outside the WEIRD world, from Asia to Africa, the frequency of left-handers is often below 6 percent and occasionally falls to below 1 percent. In China it's 0.23 percent, and among traditional Zulu communities in Africa it is close to zero (Coren, 1992; Kushner, 2013; Laland, 2008; Schaller and Murray, 2008).

28. Replotted from Dohmen et al. (2015). Thanks to Anke Becker and the authors for providing this data to me ahead of publication.

29. Dohmen et al., 2015. Their measure of patience combines the temporal-discounting measure I described using hypothetical monetary amounts with a survey question about people's willingness to give up things now for the future. This survey package was assembled and calibrated based on its ability to predict actual laboratory temporal-discounting measures that involved choices with real money (Falk et al., 2016). Notably, the sums of money used in these choices were calibrated so that the amounts were matched on buying power at the country level.

30. More patient countries also experienced more rapid economic growth, both in the short term since World War II and in the longer run, since the acceleration of

economic growth after 1820. These relationships hold after statistically removing the effect of a wide range of other factors, including latitude, rainfall, temperature, European colonization, and impersonal trust (more on trust below).

31. These measures are also related to executive function (Casey et al., 2011; A. Diamond, 2012; A. Diamond and Lee, 2011; A. Diamond and Ling, 2016; Duckworth and Kern, 2011; Mischel, Shoda, and Rodriguez, 1989; Mischel et al., 2011; Strömbäck, 2017).

32. Chabris et al., 2008; Dohmen et al., 2015; Duckworth and Seligman, 2005; Falk et al., 2016; Kirby et al., 2002; Mischel et al., 1989; Moffitt et al., 2011. Among eighth graders, for example, the less they discounted the future (picked the delayed choice, B) in the fall of the school year, the higher their grades and achievement test scores were at the end of that year. In fact, although both matter, patience was more important than IQ in predicting scholastic achievement. Notably, recent work has confirmed the ability of the marshmallow test to predict later scholastic achievement (Watts, Duncan, and Quan, 2018). However, this work appears to challenge the results by including a broad range of control variables. These controls capture many of the avenues through which culture shapes people's patience, including the social context experienced by the child, the home environment, and the participant's parents' patience. In short, it's easy to weaken the relationship between measures of patience and later academic performance by statistically removing all the factors that create variation in patience in the first place.

33. Fisman and Miguel, 2007. Interestingly, diplomats from countries who received more U.S. aid tended to get fewer tickets. The corruption index used in this paper combines all the major international corruption indices and then takes the first principal component. All the indices are highly correlated.

34. When the behavior of individuals, rather than of whole delegations, was tracked, it turned out that diplomats became more likely to get parking tickets the longer they spent at the UN, prior to the start of enforcement. In the absence of any threat of penalties, self-interest slowly corroded the cultural standards they arrived with, especially when they came from less corrupt countries. Similarly, the NYPD's enforcement action was decisive in 2002 but was particularly effective on diplomats from less corrupt countries.

35. Gächter and Schulz, 2016. There's no reason to expect that income differences or stake size affect these findings—see the supplemental materials of Gächter and Schulz (2016). Notably, the amount of money across countries was set to deliver equal purchasing power in each place.

36. Adapted from Gächter and Schulz (2016).

37. Trompenaars and Hampden-Turner, 1998. Thanks to Dan Hruschka for the data (Hruschka and Henrich, 2013b).

38. Trompenaars and Hampden-Turner, 1998.

39. This map combines data from Algan and Cahuc (2013) and two surveys, the World Values Survey (Inglehart et al., 2014) and the Afrobarometer (www .afrobarometer.org).

40. Algan and Cahuc, 2010, 2013.

41. Johnson and Mislin, 2012. For another large-scale study establishing this relationship, see Fehr et al. (2002). For work linking the GTQ to laboratory economic experiments measuring cooperation and fairness, see Francois, Fujiwara, and van Ypersele, 2011; Herrmann, Thöni, and Gächter, 2008; Peysakhovich and Rand, 2016.

42. The impressive generalized trust levels in China (see Figure 1.7) represent, at least in part, a powerful set of regulated-relational institutions, and not the impersonal prosociality of WEIRD people. We can understand this difference by looking at studies of trust among American and Chinese managers attending business school (Chua, Ingram, and Morris, 2008; Chua, Morris, and Ingram, 2009, 2010; Peng, 2004). Unlike their American counterparts, Chinese managers developed trusting professional relationships preferentially with others who were embedded in their broader social networks and who were linked to them through multiple ties. These important business relationships, which establish a foundation for trust in commercial transactions, are also deeply personal relationships. Moreover, economic dependence between business associates implies that a personal relationship exists, and often this connection simulates a familial relationship, like that between brothers or fathers and sons. There's even a special Mandarin word for this network of business-relevant personal relationships—*guanxi*. Not surprisingly, Chinese also typically have more actual relatives in their professional networks. In contrast, when American managers have connections to the close associates of particular colleagues, this doesn't influence their trust assessments of these colleagues. That is, possessing redundant social pathways to a particular colleague doesn't cause Americans to trust that colleague more. Similarly, economic dependence on a business associate makes a personal relationship between Americans less likely, not more likely, as in China. WEIRD friendships are supposed to be "pure" and should ideally be free of such "messy" dependencies. Studies like this suggest that Chinese business and commerce, despite adopting the formal structures and outward appearance of WEIRD models, remain founded on, and organized by, regulated-relational networks. With this in mind, we can go back to the global surveys and look at responses to other trust-related questions. In China, only 11 percent of the population said yes when asked, "Do you trust people whom you meet for the first time?" Meanwhile, in the United States, the UK, France, and Germany, one-third to one-half said yes. Similarly, only 9 percent of Chinese said they'd trust a person of a different nationality. By contrast, 52 percent of Germans said they'd trust such a person, and the number increased to over 65 percent in the United States and Australia (Greif and Tabellini, 2010). The key to trust in

China is building personal relationships in dense networks that informally create economic and social interdependence.

43. Thoni, 2017.

44. Alesina and Giuliano, 2010, 2013; Algan and Cahuc, 2010, 2013; Falk et al., 2018; Herrmann et al., 2008; Hruschka and Henrich, 2013b.

45. Barrett et al., 2016.

46. This finding doesn't reflect a lack of ability to infer others' mental states or intentions. In Yasawa, my collaborators and I have done numerous experiments on mentalizing abilities—thinking about others' beliefs, intentions, and motivations—over many years (McNamara et al., 2019a, 2019b). It turns out that Yasawans are skilled at mentalizing and their language has an adequate vocabulary for discussing mental states. Nevertheless, they are disinclined to openly discuss other people's mental states and, as shown in this experiment, often don't use them in making moral judgments of strangers. They focus on outcomes and consequences, not inferred mental states. Interestingly, in our poisoning scenario—wherein an actor either intentionally or accidentally pours something toxic into his village's water source, poisoning his neighbor and almost killing him—both the Himba herders in Namibia and the Hadza hunter-gatherers in Tanzania along with the Yasawans also ignored the actor's intentions in making moral judgments.

47. Hamilton and Sanders, 1992; Robbins, Shepard, and Rochat, 2017. Complementing this, recent work in cultural neuroscience comparing Japanese and American children is beginning to show how inferring the mental states of others is underpinned by somewhat different patterns of brain activation in these groups (Kobayashi, Glover, and Temple, 2007).

48. Curtin et al., 2019; Gluckman, 1972a, 1972b.

49. For research on the Mapuche, see Faron, 1968; Henrich and Smith, 2004; Stuchlik, 1976.

50. Miyamoto, Nisbett, and Masuda, 2006; Nisbett, 2003; Nisbett et al., 2001.

51. The yourmorals.org website, where people take psychological tests for fun, likely doesn't attract a random or even representative sample of any country. This concern has been partially addressed using a compilation of other datasets, based on both triads and other tasks. Among undergraduates, the most holistic thinkers run from Middle Eastern Arabs to Chinese and eastern European participants (Varnum et al., 2008) and finally to Brits and Americans. Thanks to Ara Norenzayan for supplying me with data on Middle Eastern Arabs. And, as with the trust question, northern Italians are more analytic than southern Italians (Knight and Nisbett, 2007).

52. Thanks to Thomas Talhelm for providing this data from yourmorals.org (Talhelm, Graham, and Haidt, 1999).

53. Chua, Boland, and Nisbett, 2005; Goh and Park, 2009; Goh et al., 2007; Goh et al., 2010; Masuda and Nisbett, 2001; Masuda et al., 2008; Miyamoto et al., 2006. Cultural neuroscientists, by administering these kinds of Triad Tasks to participants

in a functional MRI scanner, have revealed different executive control strategies in the brains of East Asians and Euro-Americans (Gutchesset et al., 2010).

54. Falk et al., 2009; Heine, 2016; Nisbett, 2003.

55. Falk et al., 2018; Henrich, Heine, and Norenzayan, 2010a, 2010b; Nielsen et al., 2017; Rad et al., 2018.

2. Making a Cultural Species

1. Barwick, 1984; Flannery, 2002; Gat, 2015; Morgan, 1852; Smyth, 1878. I'm drawing on Buckley's accounts as reported by both Morgan and Langhorne. I've also enriched this with information from Flannery, Barwick, Gat, and Smyth on the region and populations.

2. Sometimes this operated as "sister exchange," in which a man swapped his sister for the sister of a man in another clan. Other times, girls were married off to nourish alliances between clans and tribes. Buckley wisely avoided the competition over women, though he does appear to have had two wives and a daughter during his Aboriginal life.

3. On multiple occasions, Buckley describes the ceremonial consumption of human flesh. In at least some cases, the justification seems to be to imbibe the strength of one's enemies.

4. Chudek and Henrich, 2011; Chudek, Muthukrishna, and Henrich, 2015; Chudek et al., 2013; Henrich, 2016; Henrich and Broesch, 2011; Henrich and Gil-White, 2001; Laland, 2004; Rendell et al., 2011. The technical jargon for "who-cues" is "model-based cues." Another adaptive learning strategy is called "conformist transmission." Consistent with theoretical predictions about the evolution of conformist transmission (Nakahashi, Wakano, and Henrich, 2012; Perreault, Moya, and Boyd, 2012), ample evidence indicates that people tend to use the frequency of cultural traits around them in deciding whether to adopt a practice or belief (Muthukrishna, Morgan, and Henrich, 2016).

5. Broesch, Henrich, and Barrett, 2014; Henrich, 2016, Chapters 4–5; Medin and Atran, 2004; Sperber, 1996. Humans also possess evolved psychological abilities that support our cultural learning in important domains by supplying background assumptions, organizational building blocks, and ready inferences. For example, in learning about animals and plants, young children and adults from diverse societies are primed to think in terms of immutable, hierarchically related categories. If we are told about a tiger that was spotted near a lake at night, we automatically infer that "nocturnal hunting by water" is likely a feature of all tigers and not merely a fleeting oddity of this one particular tiger. Moreover, children and adults readily extend this inference, though less confidently, to species that seem like tigers, such as lions. This specialized cognitive system helps explain both how small-scale societies like the Wathaurung accumulate and maintain such vast storehouses of knowledge about plants and animals as well as why people often struggle to apprehend the mutability of species. Alongside these specializations

for learning about plants and animals (Atran and Medin, 2008; Atran, Medin, and Ross, 2005; Medin and Atran, 1999; Wertz 2019), humans also have other psychological abilities that facilitate learning in several other important domains (e.g., Hirschfeld and Gelman, 1994; Moya and Boyd 2015).

6. Bauer et al., 2018; Moya, Boyd, and Henrich, 2015; Schaller, Conway, and Tanchuk, 2002.

7. Giuliano and Nunn, 2017; Henrich, 2016; Hoppitt and Laland, 2013; Morgan et al., 2012; Muthukrishna, Morgan, and Henrich, 2016.

8. Berns et al., 2010; Engelmann et al., 2012; Garvert et al., 2015; Henrich, 2016, Chapter 14; Little et al., 2008; Little et al., 2011; Losin, Dapretto, and Iacoboni, 2010; Morgan and Laland, 2012; Zaki, Schirmer, and Mitchell, 2011. There's much debate about the function of the medial prefrontal cortex—see Euston et al. (2012) and Grossman et al. (2013) for recent reviews.

9. Henrich, 2016.

10. Jones, 2007.

11. See Henrich et al. (2015) for a review of the relevant analytical models and computer simulations. For laboratory experiments on cultural evolution, see Derex and Boyd, 2016; Derex, Godelle, and Raymond, 2014; Derex et al., 2013; Kempe and Mesoudi, 2014; Muthukrishna et al., 2013.

12. Garfield and Hewlett, 2016; Hewlett and Cavalli-Sforza, 1986; Hewlett et al., 2011; Salali et al., 2016; Terashima and Hewlett, 2015. Supporting the claim that boys copy prestigious hunters, the famed ethnographer Barry Hewlett reports that boys pay special attention to *metuma*, the great elephant hunters (thanks to Barry, for the proper grammar).

13. Even subtler than poisons are the ingenious food-processing protocols that have allowed small-scale societies to access a wide variety of staple plant foods. In the Andes, culinary practices incorporate special kinds of clays to neutralize the toxins that wild potatoes evolved to protect themselves from fungi, bacteria, and mammals. In California, hunter-gatherers evolved a broad array of techniques for leaching the tannins from acorns, which were often their primary food source. In these cases and many more, individuals who dropped the labor-intensive steps or relied on their innate taste cues as a guide risked poisoning themselves and their children, if not immediately, then slowly through an accretion of toxins over decades. In a world of cumulative cultural evolution, there are big costs to not relying on cultural learning and to not copying with sufficient accuracy (Henrich, 2016, Chapters 3 and 7; Johns, 1986; Mann, 2012).

14. Henrich, 2016; Horner and Whiten, 2005.

15. Here, we are using the diversity of contemporary foraging societies combined with archaeological, ecological, and genetic data to glean insights into the lifeways of Paleolithic peoples. I am not suggesting that any modern population is "primitive" or "static" in any sense or somehow solely representative of societies before the origins of agriculture. A cultural evolutionary approach avoids such

outdated misunderstandings. Nevertheless, because ethnographically and historically known hunter-gatherers often used many of the same tools and technologies to hunt and gather many of the same species as did Paleolithic peoples, detailed studies can provide many important insights when used in conjunction with archaeological, linguistic, and genetic evidence (Flannery and Marcus, 2012). Ancient DNA, for example, suggests that Paleolithic populations likely had social organizations not too different from those of contemporary foragers (Sikora et al., 2017).

16. Bhui, Chudek, and Henrich, 2019a; Henrich and Henrich, 2014.

17. Lewis, 2008; Schapera, 1930.

18. Henrich (2016) provides a discussion of how such taboos can remain stable. Disproving the effect of taboo violations on hunting is unlikely, since the norm package includes incentives against reporting any "tests" of the taboo, intentional or accidental. Taboo violators risk getting sanctioned no matter why they broke the taboo.

19. Gurven, 2004. Food taboos themselves are quite diverse, variously prohibiting people with certain relationships to the hunter (or the hunter himself) from eating certain parts of an animal or prohibiting entire classes of people from eating particular parts or entire species. In Buckley's region, the uninitiated men of some tribes were tabooed from eating female animals and all porcupines. It seems that cultural evolution was somehow always aiming at the same target, but jury-rigged a variety of institutional contraptions to get there (Barnes, 1996; Flannery and Marcus, 2012; Gould, 1967; Hamilton, 1987; Henrich, 2016, Chapter 9; Lewis, 2008; Smyth, 1878).

20. Henrich, 2016. Note, I am using the older, and still more common, orthography for "Ju/'hoansi." For the newer orthography, check out: en.wikipedia.org/wiki /Jul'hoan_language.

21. Bailey, Hill, and Walker, 2014; Chapais, 2009; Lee, 1979, 1986; Marshall, 1959; Walker and Bailey, 2014. In 1964, men had a total of 36 different names, while women had 32 (Lee, 1986; Marshall, 1959).

22. Other supporting social norms further solidify these kin-based links. In some hunter-gatherer societies, for example, norms specify that a father has the right to name his children and should name them after one of his parents or close relatives. Tapping a well-established piece of psychology, this ancient naming custom invites the father's relatives to treat new babies like their older namesakes. This effectively pulls new arrivals closer to their paternal side, and helps reduce the asymmetry created by the powerful maternal-child bonds common to all primates (Henrich, 2016, Chapter 9). Some primate species show a limited ability to detect their fathers; this is weak compared to their ability to locate their maternal relatives (Chapais, 2009; Henrich, 2016).

23. Dyble et al., 2018; Hamilton, 1987; Henrich, 2016; Wiessner, 2002.

24. Hill et al., 2011.

25. Henrich, 2016, Chapter 9.

26. Fessler and Navarrete, 2004; Lieberman, 2007; Lieberman, Fessler, and Smith, 2011; Lieberman, Tooby, and Cosmides, 2003. In principle, these taboos apply to third cousins, though the Ju/'hoansi were sometimes a bit fuzzy on who their third cousins were. Notably, young Ju/'hoansi adults couldn't easily marry their cousins, because their first marriages were arranged by their parents. On changing marriage norms among the Ju/'hoansi, see Wiessner, 2009.

27. Lee, 1986; Marshall, 1959, 1976. Alongside these incest prohibitions, Ju/'hoansi also have certain marriage preferences. For example, if a married man dies, his wife will ideally marry his brother—levirate marriage. Since the Ju/'hoansi permit polygynous marriage, they can marry even if the living brother is already married. These affines don't have to marry, but it would be considered good if they did. Similarly, if a man's wife dies, he should consider marrying her sister, unless she's already married. It's also considered nice if, after a band sends one of its sons or daughters off to live in a different band, the receiving band sends a replacement back at some later point. This vague preference solidified into strongly enforced "sister exchange" norms in other societies. Finally, Ju/'hoansi will tolerate it if, on their second or later marriage, people marry non-kin, like those of another tribe or ethnolinguistic group; but this is somewhat frowned upon.

28. Durkheim, 1995; Henrich, 2016, Chapter 9; Whitehouse and Lanman, 2014. Biesele was quoted in Wade, 2009, endnote 107.

29. Alcorta and Sosis, 2005; Alcorta, Sosis, and Finkel, 2008; Henrich, 2016; Lang et al., 2017; Launay, Tarr, and Dunbar, 2016; Mogan, Fischer, and Bulbulia, 2017; Tarr, Launay, and Dunbar, 2014, 2016; Tarr et al., 2015; Watson-Jones and Legare, 2016; Wen, Herrmann, and Legare, 2015.

30. Carpenter, Uebel, and Tomasello, 2011; Chartrand and Bargh, 1999; Henrich and Gil-White, 2001; Over et al., 2013.

31. Bastiaansen, Thioux, and Keysers, 2009; Brass, Ruby, and Spengler, 2009; Heyes, 2013; Laland, 2017; van Baaren et al., 2009. In adapting our behavior, synchronous movement activates our opioid system, creating a surge of endorphins that raise our pain tolerance. The endorphins released by physical exertion, like hours of dancing, contribute to these effects.

32. Marshall, 1999, p. 90.

33. Hamann et al., 2011.

34. Some rituals offer ways to insert individuals into the kinship system or to create more binding ties within the kinship network (Lynch, 1986). Sometimes called "fictive kinship" (Hruschka, 2010), rituals can establish "blood brothers" (and sometimes "blood sisters") or ritual parents (think "godparents"). Among Ache hunter-gatherers in Paraguay, ritual bonds that link adults and children create lifelong relationships that interconnect individuals and bands in ways that foster

cooperation, promote security, and increase the flow of new ideas among groups (Hill et al., 2014).

35. Flannery and Marcus, 2012; Henrich, 2016, Chapter 10.

36. Henrich, 2016; Reich, 2018.

37. Henrich, 2016, Chapter 11. As part of this coevolutionary process, we have also evolved to be especially good at spotting norm violations and identifying norm-violators (Cummins, 1996a, 1996b; Engelmann, Herrmann, and Tomasello, 2012; Engelmann et al., 2013; Fiddick, Cosmides, and Tooby, 2000; Nunez and Harris, 1998). For more on why humans evolved to internalize norms, see Ensminger and Henrich, 2014; Gavrilets and Richerson, 2017. For empirical work on norm internalization, see Rand, 2016; Rand, Peysakhovich et al., 2014; Yamagishi et al., 2016; 2017). Internalized norms can be especially valuable in making decisions that trade off long-term costs like losing one's good reputation against short-term benefits. This is because people, like all animals, struggle to properly discount future payoffs against immediate rewards. This process also selects against reactive forms of aggression (Wrangham, 2019).

38. This lays an evolutionary foundation for what psychologists call "fusion" (Bowles, Choi, and Hopfensitz, 2004; Swann and Buhrmester, 2015; Swann et al., 2012; Van Cleve and Akçay, 2014; Whitehouse et al., 2014).

39. Baron and Dunham, 2015; Buttelmann et al., 2013; Dunham, Baron, and Banaji, 2008; Henrich, 2016; Kinzler and Dautel, 2012; Moya, 2013; Moya et al., 2015; Shutts, Banaji, and Spelke, 2010; Shutts, Kinzler, and DeJesus, 2013; Shutts et al., 2009.

40. Frankenhuis and de Weerth, 2013; McCullough et al., 2013; Mittal et al., 2015; Nettle, Frankenhuis, and Rickard, 2013. Mothers may even pass certain calibrations down to their children epigenetically, through modifications to their DNA expression machinery or through other biological mechanisms (Wang, Liu, and Sun, 2017).

41. Alcorta and Sosis, 2005; Henrich and Boyd, 2016.

42. Henrich, 2016.

3. Clans, States, and Why You Can't Get Here from There

1. Ferrero, 1967.

2. The basic point here is similar to that developed in Fukuyama, 2011.

3. Forge, 1972.

4. Tuzin, 1976, 2001. Even for sneak attacks, where numbers were less important, raiders knew that they'd eventually face the vengeance of a larger and thus deadlier foe.

5. Ilahita proper was about 1,500 people. The value of 2,500 people comes from considering the hamlets that huddled in Ilahita's protective shadow (Tuzin, 1976, 2001).

6. The ideal marital arrangement was sister exchange—meaning that men of different clans or subclans agreed to swap their sister for a wife.

7. Durkheim (1933) has long made this distinction, between "organic" and "mechanical" solidarity.

8. Buhrmester et al., 2015; Whitehouse, 1995; Whitehouse, 1996; Whitehouse and Lanman, 2014. Whitehouse (1996) coined the term "rites of terror."

9. Image by Beth Curtin (thanks!).

10. Tuzin, 1976, 2001.

11. The Tambaran gods also punished people for breaking truces with surrounding communities. Punishing truce-breakers would have addressed a prickly asymmetry between defense and offense in Ilahita. While community defense was everyone's responsibility, offensive raids could be initiated independently by any clan for their own reasons (which typically involved vengeance). Tuzin suggests that Ilahita's clans were disinclined to act unilaterally because of the threat of supernatural punishment.

12. Tuzin, 2001, p. 83.

13. Grossmann et al., 2008; Tuzin, 1976, 2001.

14. For an overview of this approach, see Henrich, 2004, 2016; Richerson et al., 2016.

15. Bowles, 2006; Choi and Bowles, 2007; Keeley, 1997; Mathew and Boyd, 2011; Richerson et al., 2016; Soltis, Boyd, and Richerson, 1995; Turchin, 2015; Wrangham and Glowacki, 2012.

16. Differential migration has been observed in both the rates of switching groups at the boundaries of small-scale tribal populations (Knauft, 1985; Tuzin, 1976, 2001) and in migration patterns among nations in the modern world (Connor, Cohn, and Gonzalez-Barrera, 2013). See Boyd and Richerson (2009) for a theoretical model.

17. Boyd, 2001; Boyd and Richerson, 2002, p. 79; Harrison, 1987; Roscoe, 1989; Tuzin, 1976, p. 79; Wiessner and Tumu, 1998.

18. Smaldino, Schank, and McElreath, 2013. A common confusion involves arguing that because groups may have only rarely encountered each other on the ground, intergroup competition was unimportant. Groups can compete to survive without actually encountering each other.

19. Richerson and Boyd (2005). For a review of the work on religion and fertility, see Blume, 2009; Norenzayan, 2013.

20. What comes next always depends on what came before, and modifications are usually small and gradual. In the Sepik, for example, Tuzin's reconstruction suggests that the dual ritual-group system found in the Tambaran probably emerged from an earlier marriage-group system in which the marriage elements slowly fell away and were replaced by ritual components. Similarly, based on research in Australia where such systems are common, the complex eight-tier system probably arose when communities with two different four-tier systems met and began to negotiate ways to intermarry. Likewise, the four-tier system probably emerged when two

groups met who each had their own two-tier system. Regarding adoption, one in five children in Ilahita was adopted (as in much of the Pacific). This helped sustain an ongoing and healthy competition among ritual groups and thereby diminished the hold of descent and co-residence (Tuzin, 1976, 2001). On matrilineal societies, see Ember, Ember, and Pasternack, 1974; Jones, 2011.

21. Acemoglu and Robinson, 2012; Diamond, 1997, 2005. There's nothing unilineal, stagist, or progressive about this cultural evolutionary approach.

22. Baksh, 1984; Davis, 2002 (1); Johnson, 2003, 1978. Also see Rosengren and Shepard cited in Johnson, 2003.

23. Johnson, 2003.

24. Johnson, 2003; Snell, 1964.

25. Camino, 1977.

26. Baksh, 1984; Johnson, 2003, 1978. Note that, although some of the ways in which Matsigenka explain behavior parallels the patterns found in WEIRD populations, they don't look for, or demand, explanations to the same degree as found in WEIRD populations.

27. Ferrero, 1967; Johnson, 2003, pp. 34, 135. Similarly, ethnographers have observed how at "beer feasts" Matsigenka use aggressive joking to publicly shame recalcitrant norm-violators. The targets of these attacks don't turn red, slump, shrink away, or even respond angrily; instead, they just stoically take it. Johnson argues that guilt plays an important role among the Matsigenka, as it does among WEIRD people. However, by comparison, he argues that guilt among the Matsigenka is understated, and that those who experience it are less anxiety-ridden (Johnson, 2003, p. 132).

28. Johnson, 2003, p. 168, observes, "The Matsigenka lack a sense of belonging to any group larger than the hamlet."

29. Gardner, 2013; Henrich and Henrich, 2007; Johnson, 2003; Johnson and Earle, 2000.

30. Richerson, Boyd, and Bettinger, 2001.

31. Bowles, 2011; Bowles and Choi, 2013; Matranga, 2017.

32. As noted in Chapter 2, there's good reason to suspect that intergroup competition also drove up societal complexity and competitiveness in the Paleolithic era. But, the emergence of agriculture had a big impact on cultural evolution because of its potential to sustain larger and denser populations. However, prior to food production, there had always been special geographical locations where residents could access vast animal herds or rich marine foods. Such areas may have seen increases in population size and complexity. Food production was special because the technical and ecological know-how were portable, at least along latitudinal lines and ecological contours, which held out the potential for transforming vast swaths of territory that would otherwise have sustained only thinly scattered populations of hunter-gatherers. Instead, a network of villages, towns, and eventually cities could form (Ashraf and Michalopoulos, 2015; Diamond, 1997).

33. Bowles, 2011; Diamond, 1997; Matranga, 2017. The expansion of farmers into territories once occupied by hunter-gatherers is well documented in Asia, Africa, and the Americas. Models that purport to explain farming as a rational response to climatic changes ignore the collective-action problems associated with storage and agriculture as well as the threat of intergroup predation (Matranga, 2017). Why store or plant if you can just raid and steal?

34. Godelier, 1986; Hill et al., 2011. The ancient Greeks may have had similar views on the hereditary contribution of mothers to their children (Zimmer, 2018).

35. If these alliances and conflicts sound fanciful, they're not. Whether it's Amazonian tribes, Viking sagas, or royal houses in Europe, China, or the Islamic world, more closely related individuals tend to form coalitions against less closely related individuals. Throughout history, brothers teamed up to kill half-brothers, and stepmothers abused their stepchildren in favor of their own children (Alvard, 2009; Daly and Wilson, 1998; Dunbar, Clark, and Hurst, 1995; Fukuyama, 2011; Miller, 2009; Palmstierna et al., 2017).

36. Murdock, 1949. People don't need to know the genealogy; they just need to know what kinship terms their parents or grandparents used for each other.

37. Alvard, 2003; Alvard, 2011; Chapais, 2008; Ember et al., 1974; Murdock, 1949; Walker and Bailey, 2014; Walker et al., 2013.

38. Usually, clan membership is inherited from one's father, but there are often other ways into patrilineal clans, including through rituals and adoption (Murdock, 1949).

39. Gluckman, 1972a, 1972b. Based on his experience in Ilahita, Tuzin argues that the greatest impact of the Euro-Australian court system, which was imposed in Papua New Guinea in 1975, involved a shift from a clan-based to an individual-centered notion of responsibility (Tuzin, 2001, pp. 49–50).

40. Fox, 1967; Walker, 2014; Walker and Bailey, 2014; Walker and Hill, 2014.

41. Abrahams, 1973; Chapais, 2009; Fox, 1967. If the wife dies, norms about sororate marriage specify that the surviving husband should marry one of the dead wife's unmarried sisters or cousin-sisters.

42. Toren, 1990.

43. Baker, 1979; Lindstrom, 1990; Toren, 1990; Weiner, 2013.

44. Jones, 2011; Murphy, 1957; Walker, 2014.

45. Intensive kin-based institutions affect how communities break down. When hunter-gatherer communities with extensive kinship systems break apart, individuals or nuclear families make independent decisions about which subgroup to stick with. By contrast, when clan-based communities fission, they typically fracture along lineage lines, as in the Sepik. This maximizes the kin ties within each new group, making the new, smaller, communities even more tightly bound by blood (Walker and Hill, 2014).

46. Fortes, 1953; Kelly, 1985; Murdock, 1949; Sahlins, 1961; Strassmann and Kurapati, 2016. Complementing these prescribed alliances, norms also specify a

gradation of the violent means that can be used against more distant groups and calibrate a clan's willingness to pursue peace. In some places, for example, men can only use their fists in conflicts with closely related clans. However, as the genealogical distance grows, the appropriate weapons escalate to clubs and then arrows. Finally, when facing other tribes, poisoned arrows become the weapon of choice.

47. Adapted from Moscona, Nunn, and Robinson, 2017.

48. Kelly, 1985; Sahlins, 1961; Vansina, 1990.

49. Moscona et al., 2017. One problem with the analysis of trust here is that it's not clear how much of the effect is due to having clans of any sort as opposed to having the full set of segmentary lineage institutions.

50. Ahmed, 2013; Grosjean, 2011; Nisbett and Cohen, 1996. The impact of segmentary lineages on murder rates in the United States holds even after statistically controlling for all the factors that usually explain crime rates.

51. Bernardi, 1952, 1985; Berntsen, 1976; Eisenstadt, 2016; Lienard, 2016; Ritter, 1980. While traveling, initiated members can always find hospitality in the homes of their age-set peers.

52. Bernardi, 1985; Berntsen, 1976; de Wolf, 1980; Fosbrooke, 1956.

53. Many egalitarian societies have what anthropologists call "big men," who act as leaders (Henrich, Chudek, and Boyd, 2015; Sahlins, 1963). Piggybacking on our prestige psychology (Cheng, Tracy, and Henrich, 2010; Cheng et al., 2013), these successful individuals assemble large followings or coalitions that are then parlayed into substantial influence on community decisions. Using their political influence, they can often accomplish cooperative feats, like building a spirit house, organizing a war party, or throwing an immense feast. The issue with big men is that they can't pass their accumulated influence and authority down to the next generation. When big men die, there's often a mad scramble for political power and many years may pass without an effective leader (Godelier, 1986; Heizer, 1978; Johnson, 2003; Lee, 1979; Paine, 1971; Sturtevant, 1978).

54. Earle, 1997; Flannery and Marcus, 2012; Johnson and Earle, 2000; Kirch, 1984; Toren, 1990.

55. Flannery and Marcus, 2012; Harrison, 1987, 1990; Roscoe, 1989.

56. Avatip's largest clan also controlled one of four hereditary ritual offices called Simbuks, which were passed to sons or younger brothers. Officeholders were in charge of performing certain rituals, which related to everything from headhunting to yam growing. Although the functions of these offices were confined to the ritual sphere, Simbuks were believed to possess powerful sorcery that could be used to kill and were themselves immune to local forms of Avatip sorcery. They also tended to intermarry only with the families of other Simbuks. It's not hard to imagine how Simbuks could be turned into chiefs, and eventually into an elite class.

57. Some prefer to call these "ranked societies" (Flannery and Marcus, 2012).

58. Chiefdoms can exist without a chief, but not without ranked kin-based segments of society.

59. Diamond, 1997; Earle, 1997; Flannery and Marcus, 2012; Johnson and Earle, 2000; Marcus and Flannery, 2004. Because of the competing elite lineages within a single chiefly clan, most chiefdoms contain an inherent instability that is mitigated by the threat of war (Chacon et al., 2015). Eventually, the chief has only daughters, or twin boys, or an incompetent oldest son who contrasts with a much beloved and respected second son.

60. Carneiro, 1967; Fukuyama, 2011; Goldman, 1970; Kirch, 1984, 2010. Through this process, a division of labor often develops in which different clans and villages specialize in different activities. Highly ranked clans provide priests, while other clans supply warriors. Clans living near rivers or oceans might provide canoes or fish to the elites in tribute. These hereditary occupations, which can become castes, provide some of the benefits of economic specialization and create a sense of mutual interdependence within chiefdoms (Goldman, 1970; Henrich and Boyd, 2008). See Chapter 12.

61. Stratification can emerge in a variety of ways, but one straightforward way is for a single intermarrying community like Avatip to conquer and subordinate surrounding ethnic groups with whom they don't intermarry. This would set up the entire Avatip community as an upper stratum who exacts tribute from the vanquished.

62. Marcus, 2008; Redmond and Spencer, 2012; Spencer, 2010; Turchin, 2015; Turchin et al., 2017.

63. Earle, 1997; Flannery, 2009; Flannery and Marcus, 2012; Marcus, 2008; Redmond and Spencer, 2012; Spencer and Redmond, 2001.

64. Bondarenko, 2014; Bondarenko and Korotayev, 2003; Fried, 1970. Here's what I mean by "somewhat meritocratic": in the Western Zhou (China), over half of all bureaucratic appointments were not based on kinship. In the Inca Empire, the staffing of the state institutions only went beyond members of the 12 elite clans after the empire expanded (Chacon et al., 2015).

65. Eisenstadt, 2016; Flannery, 2009; Gluckman, 1940.

66. Bondarenko, 2014; Bondarenko and Korotayev, 2003; Kirch, 1984, 2010. Statistically, as societies scale up to chiefdoms, kin-based institutions intensify. However, the transition to state usually causes a decline in this intensity. Note, I follow Kirch (2010) here in considering the existence of "states" in Hawaii in the 18th century. Others have argued that Hawaiian polities were particularly complex chiefdoms until the 19th century (e.g., Johnson and Earle, 2000). However, as I explained, the boundaries between "chiefdoms" and "states" are fuzzy because they depend on drawing arbitrary lines based on the accumulation of society-wide institutions that defy kin-based and relational forms of organization.

67. Berman, 1983.

68. Carneiro, 1970, 1988; Johnson and Earle, 2000; Richerson et al., 2016.

69. Diamond, 1997; Diamond, 2005; Flannery and Marcus, 2012; Morris, 2014; Turchin, 2005, 2010, 2015; Turchin et al., 2013.

4. The Gods Are Watching. Behave!

1. Shariff and Norenzayan, 2007. Note, the unscrambling task was actually slightly more complicated and involved dropping a word that didn't fit. I'm simplifying.

2. This is Study 2 (Shariff and Norenzayan, 2007). The effects in Study 1 are even larger. You might worry that participants noticed the God-primes in the unscrambling task and wanted to please the researchers. This is unlikely for two reasons. First, because of how the task was conducted, participants believed that the experimenters couldn't figure out how much money they gave. Second, when asked if they noticed anything unusual about the words in the unscrambling task, almost no one mentioned anything about religion or God. Yet people's actual behavior says otherwise—their unconscious mental processes noticed something in the sentence task and they reacted accordingly.

3. Shariff et al., 2016.

4. Thanks to Azim Shariff for supplying the data for this plot (Shariff and Norenzayan, 2007). Note, the underlying sample sizes are small and thus not always estimated with great certainty. However, the broad patterns are consistent with other studies (Everett, Haque, and Rand, 2016; Rand, Dreber et al., 2014).

5. Duhaime, 2015.

6. The impact of the call to prayer on Muslims has also been confirmed in the laboratory, where exposure to the call reduced cheating on a math test from 47 to 32 percent (Aveyard, 2014).

7. Edelman, 2009; Malhotra, 2010. Technically, the data only shows when people purchased pornography online. I'm assuming they then watched it.

8. Henrich, 2009; Sperber et al., 2010.

9. Gervais, 2011; Gervais and Henrich, 2010; McNamara et al., 2019a; Norenzayan, Gervais, and Trzesniewski, 2012; Willard, Cingl, and Norenzayan, 2020; Willard and Norenzayan, 2013.

10. Chudek et al., 2017; Willard et al., 2019. It's commonly claimed that the ancient Chinese, or those in "the East" more generally, lacked mind-body dualism. This position, however, is belied by both qualitative and quantitative historical evidence (Goldin, 2015; Slingerland and Chudek, 2011; Slingerland et al., 2018).

11. Atran and Norenzayan, 2004; Boyer, 2001, 2003. Many supernatural beliefs that we could hold—in principle—never develop in any society. There don't appear to be, for example, any instances of gods who have only minds in the winter and only bodies in the summer.

12. A parallel logic applies to rituals (Legare and Souza, 2012, 2014).

13. Barnes, 2010; Boehm, 2008; Murdock, 1934, p. 185; Radcliffe-Brown, 1964, p. 152; Willard and Norenzayan, 2013; Wright, 2009.

14. Murdock, 1934, p. 253; Radcliffe-Brown, 1964, p. 168; Wright, 2009. Sometimes there was contingency: Andaman Islanders reported that if someone drowned,

the individual would live on underwater as a sea spirit; otherwise, the ghosts of the dead were destined to haunt the forests. The contingent connections between socially meaningful actions in life and the quality of a person's afterlife were just not there.

15. Lee, 2003; Marshall, 1962. In being more like people, the gods of the smallest-scale societies are sometimes morally concerned, often about local domains such as sharing within the clan (Purzycki et al., 2019; Singh and Henrich, 2019).

16. Blume, 2009; Norenzayan et al., 2016a, 2016b; Strassmann et al., 2012. There's also reason to think that the gods should evolve to favor the rapid reproduction of adherents while tabooing any form of nonreproductive sexual activity (e.g., oral sex, condoms, same-sex interactions, etc.). Unlike the treatment of strangers or avoidance of adultery, we don't expect intergroup competition to spread divine concerns about instinctually easy behaviors; the gods, for example, don't need to command mothers to love their babies or men to think more frequently about sex.

17. Mark Collard also sometimes participated in these early meetings. Later, the anthropologist Ben Purzycki and religious studies scholar Martin Lang played central roles in guiding our cross-cultural research.

18. Lang et al., 2019; Purzycki et al., 2016; Purzycki et al., 2017.

19. We also assessed people's beliefs about their gods' willingness to reward the faithful and found that it had no impact on their biases against strangers. Some might find this puzzling, given the obsession with God's sweetness in modern variants of Christianity. But, it's not hard to see why this makes sense. First, relying on punishment means that a god doesn't have to do much—people fear the punishment and behave themselves. Rewards are a different story. To sustain a behavior by rewarding, you must be constantly giving people goodies—the rewards. This requires more activity from the gods, which is problematic if they don't actually exist. Second, psychological research suggests that people respond more strongly to loss, or threats of loss, than to potential gains—sticks beat carrots. Other research on cheating reveals similar patterns: Christians who report believing in a more loving God were more likely to cheat on a math test than those who reported believing in a punishing God. This is not to say that divine rewards have no role, but merely to show why cultural evolution should focus primarily on punishment, perhaps reserving rewards for extraordinary behavior by rare individuals (Norenzayan et al., 2016a, 2016b; Shariff and Norenzayan, 2011).

20. Data from Purzycki et al., 2016.

21. Lang et al., 2019. Unlike in the priming studies above, here we've only shown correlations between our monitoring-and-punishing indices and allocations in the two experiments. Showing such correlations doesn't definitively demonstrate that people's supernatural beliefs influenced their economic decisions. It's possible, for example, that more fair-minded people are more attracted to beliefs in punishing gods. However, the detailed analyses behind our findings make it difficult

to explain these relationships as due to anything other than supernatural beliefs causing people to behave more prosocially. Our analyses show that our findings can't be due to differences among our study communities or to either educational or economic factors.

22. We also conducted priming experiments in our cross-cultural study. Such experiments are difficult in remote field sites where people have little formal education and often need to concentrate to understand the experiments. Having to concentrate probably depletes the impact of primes. Despite this, we did observe some priming effects that sharply contrast the impact of Big Gods and local gods. However, we sometimes didn't see any impact of the primes. This leaves the interpretation unclear, since we can't tell if these reminders don't affect people or if something about the experimental situations meant that the primes didn't get through (Lang et al., 2019).

23. Work building on the priming studies discussed at the beginning of this chapter reveals the centrality of supernatural punishment. In two experiments (Yilmaz and Bahçekapili, 2016), Turkish Muslims were assigned to one of three groups and primed with (1) supernatural punishment, (2) nonpunishing religiosity, or (3) neutral (nonreligious) reminders. The first study used a modified version of the unscrambling task developed by Azim and Ara, while the second study used selected passages from the Koran. After the tasks, participants rate how likely they'd be to donate to charity, give blood, etc. Compared to a neutral prime, Muslims reminded of a punishing god elevated their prosocial inclinations by between 60 and 100 percent. Those reminded of the neutral or merciful elements of religion raised their prosocial inclinations only by 20 to 50 percent.

24. Atran, 2002; Diamond, 1997; Munson et al., 2014; Rubin, 2017; Smith, 1917; Wright, 2009. Smith gives the number of 18 for prominent followers of Akbar's Divine Faith.

25. Norenzayan et al., 2016a, 2016b. For a simple experiment showing the capacity for religion to inspire harm, see Bushman (2007).

26. Handy, 1941; Hogbin, 1934; Lindstrom, 1990; Williamson, 1937. To examine this, the psychologist Rita McNamara and I studied villagers on Fiji's Yasawa Island. Yasawans possess a syncretic mix of religious beliefs that include both the Christian God and their traditional ancestor gods. While playing the Random Allocation Game, we unconsciously primed participants with (1) Jesus, (2) ancestor gods, or (3) flowers. We found that those primed with the ancestor gods shifted to allocate more to a local community member over a distant stranger—that is, they increased their favoritism toward fellow clan members. This makes perfect sense, since the ancestor gods in this population are concerned only about the local community (McNamara and Henrich, 2018). Also see Hadnes and Schumacher, 2012.

27. Whitehouse et al. (2019) partially supports the view presented herein by showing that belief in moralizing gods can inhibit the collapse of more complex societies

after they scale up. The authors, however, attempt to argue that their data doesn't support the view that moralizing gods facilitated the scaling-up process—only the stabilization of complex societies. Unfortunately, their analyses contain serious errors. For example, the authors transform a large amount of missing data (60 percent of the data is missing) for various societies and centuries into evidence for the absence of moralizing gods. That is, they make the classic error of explicitly assuming an absence of evidence represents evidence of absence (no moralizing gods). When this missing data is handled properly, their major claims do not hold (Beheim et al., 2019). For how a statistics textbook deals with this data, see McElreath (2020). There are also important concerns about the quality of the data used by Whitehouse et al. (Slingerland et al., 2019).

28. Diamond, 1997; Goldman, 1958; Watts et al., 2015. The 40 percent comes from Watts et al., but it's not scaled to rate per unit time. Instead, it's a 40 percent chance between linguistic splits in the Austronesian tree. The average number of splits between the proto-Austronesian population and the terminal populations is 15.9. Based on an expansion duration of 5,000 years, we get an average of about 315 years between splits.

29. Hogbin, 1934, p. 263; Turner, 1859; Williamson, 1937, p. 251; Wright, 2009, p. 57.

30. Goldman, 1955, 1970; Kelekna, 1998; Kirch, 1984, 2010; Wright, 2009. Tongan chiefs had to sacrifice their own children, although these were typically children of their secondary wives.

31. Williamson, 1937; Wright, 2009, pp. 55–56.

32. Handy, 1927, p. 78.

33. Aubet, 2013; Collins, 1994; Leick, 1991; Wright, 2009. There were also gods of adultery and thievery in Polynesia (Williamson, 1937, p. 19).

34. For an overview of ancient Mesopotamian gods, see oracc.museum.upenn.edu /amgg/listofdeities. In Babylon, one hymn to Shamash is explicit that merchants can't cheat on their weights and measures; this sentiment is later echoed in the Old Testament, Proverbs 11:1: "false balance is an abomination to the LORD, but a just weight is his delight" (Aubet, 2013).

35. Aubet, 2013; Leick, 1991; Rauh, 1993.

36. Mikalson, 2010. The gods were also thought to take more seriously the sacrifices and prayers of honorable people over those of the less worthy (Rives, 2006).

37. Mikalson, 2010; Norenzayan et al., 2016a, 2016b. Silver begins his *Economic Structures of Antiquity* (1995, p. 5) with the central role of the gods in economic exchange: "The economic role of the gods found important expression in their function as protectors of honest business practices." The gods not only punished oath breakers themselves but also those who failed to report underhanded business practices and deceitful sales techniques. This helps solve what's called the "second-order free rider problem."

38. Rives, 2006, pp. 50–52, 105–131.

39. Rauh, 1993. The Pausanias quotation is from Kemezis and Maher (2015, p. 317).
40. McNeill, 1991; O'Grady, 2013; Rives, 2006. Several universalizing religions developed the notion of a "man-god," a manifestation of the divine who could provide a powerful role model for aspirants (e.g., Jesus, Gautama Buddha, etc.). Scholars have long disputed the idea that Buddha is a god; however, recent research focused on how people on the ground actually think and talk about Buddha shows that he's a god (Purzycki and Holland, 2019). For my purposes, this is what matters.
41. Gier and Kjellberg, 2004; Harper, 2013; McCleary, 2007; McNeill, 1991. The two different approaches to moral universalism are interesting because in one case God is the source of morality, and in the other case the gods are subject to the moral laws of the universe.
42. Barro and McCleary, 2003; McCleary and Barro, 2006. These authors also use an instrumental variable approach to estimate the effects of afterlife beliefs on economic growth. Thanks to Robert Barro and Rachel McCleary for providing their data. Also see Tu, Bulte, and Tan, 2011.
43. Assessing the net effect of any particular package of religious beliefs and practices on a population's economic productivity is tricky. While belief in a contingent afterlife seems to stimulate economic growth, presumably by motivating hard work and broader social connections, ritual participation may itself create a drag on productivity, as religious people invest larger amounts of time and money in noneconomic activities. However, as I discuss below, rituals are probably crucial for instilling the faith, meaning that without rituals, beliefs in a contingent afterlife won't spread or remain common (Willard and Cingl, 2017). This suggests that intergroup competition will tend to favor ritual forms that deliver the most "bang for the buck"—those packages that most efficiently generate faithful and disciplined disciples with the least input of ritual and devotional time. This also suggests that in places where people's time is economically most productive, the number of hours devoted to rituals and devotions will tend to decline.
44. Shariff and Rhemtulla, 2012. These findings are further supported by analyses of global surveys linking both a stronger belief in god and in hell/heaven with people finding less justification for cheating on taxes, avoiding fares on public transportation, buying stolen property, and skirting 11 other such public goods (Atkinson and Bourrat, 2011). I suspect that the notion of heaven is probably psychologically quite attractive compared to hell, for obvious reasons. So when intergroup competition wanes, belief in hell naturally declines, while notions of heaven stay common. When intergroup competition intensifies, notions of hell spread because they, in combination with beliefs about heaven, favor greater success in intergroup competition—Big Gods need big sticks. For other relevant analyses linking crime and religiosity, see Baier and Wright, 2001; Kerley et al., 2011; Stark and Hirschi, 1969.
45. Alquist, Ainsworth, and Baumeister, 2013; Baumeister, Masicampo, and Dewall, 2009; Genschow, Rigoni, and Brass, 2017; Martin, Rigoni, and Vohs, 2017;

Protzko, Ouimette, and Schooler, 2016; Rigoni et al., 2012; Shariff et al., 2014; Srinivasan et al., 2016; Stillman and Baumeister, 2010; Vohs and Schooler, 2008. While tantalizing, this work needs further scrutiny. Some efforts at replication have failed (Giner-Sorolla, Embley, and Johnson, 2017; Post and Zwaan, 2014). Moreover, while research with children on the link between self-control and free will broadly confirms these patterns among Americans, the same patterns don't emerge among children from Singapore, China, or Peru (Chernyak et al., 2013; Kushnir, 2018; Wente et al., 2016; Wente et al., 2020). In many non-WEIRD populations, free will may foster a psychology that allows people to overcome their own desires in favor of complying with social norms (instead of personal standards) or deferring to the in-group.

46. Inglehart and Baker, 2000; Rai and Holyoak, 2013; Young and Durwin, 2013. This is often called "moral realism" instead of "moral universalism." I've relabeled it to avoid importing unwanted philosophical baggage. I'm interested in what people actually believe and how it influences their behavior.

47. Atkinson and Whitehouse, 2011; Norenzayan et al., 2016a; Whitehouse, 2000, 2004. Whitehouse (1995) pioneered the distinction between "imagistic" and "doctrinal" rituals. Norenzayan et al. (2016a) integrated this observation into a broader cultural evolutionary approach to religion. Through the creation of sacred texts, the evolution of writing systems plays an important role here.

48. Henrich, 2009, 2016; Kraft-Todd et al., 2018; Lanman and Buhrmester, 2017; Tenney et al., 2011; Wildman and Sosis, 2011; Willard, Henrich, and Norenzayan, 2016; Xygalatas et al., 2013; Singh and Henrich, 2019b.

49. Religious architecture such as cathedrals, temples, or tombs may also tap our reliance on CREDs, since it's hard to imagine why a community would spend so much of its wealth on a giant cathedral, instead of on roads, bridges, canals, mills, and reservoirs, if they didn't truly believe.

50. Lanman, 2012; Willard and Cingl, 2017.

51. Baumeister, Bauer, and Lloyd, 2010; Carter et al., 2011; McCullough and Willoughby, 2009; Wood, 2017. As with so much psychological research, these findings come primarily from WEIRD people. However, global measures of patience combined with data on religion suggest these effects probably generalize beyond WEIRD populations (Dohmen et al., 2015; Falk et al., 2018).

52. Aubet, 2013; Ekelund et al., 1996; Ginges, Hansen, and Norenzayan, 2009; Guiso, Sapienza, and Zingales, 2009; Hawk, 2015; Jha, 2013; Johnson and Koyama, 2017; Lewer and Van den Berg, 2007; Rauh, 1993; Watson-Jones and Legare, 2016; Wen et al., 2015.

53. Over 75 percent of the world's population in 2010 reported adherence to Christianity (31.5 percent), Islam (23.2 percent), Hinduism (15 percent), or Buddhism (7.1 percent). Non–world religions capture only 5.9 percent of the global population. The biggest competition for world religions comes not from traditional

religions but from those classified as "Unaffiliated." Unfortunately, this category doesn't tell us much, since it is dominated by people in China (where "religion" has long been a politically sensitive issue) and includes true atheists in Europe and North America. It seems that some of the world's major religions are now spreading rapidly in China: www.pewforum.org/2012/12/18/global-religious -landscape-exec.

5. WEIRD Families

1. I'm referring here to American kinship (Schneider and Homans, 1955), although the basic patterns apply fairly broadly across WEIRD populations. For a discussion of English kinship, see Strathern, 1992. For a discussion of kinship and states, see Fukuyama, 2011; Murdock, 1949.

2. I'm drawing here on the extended version of the Ethnographic Atlas called the Database of Places, Language, Culture, and Environment, at D-PLACE.org (Kirby et al., 2016). Mainstream cultural anthropologists have long criticized the Atlas. To address these concerns, my lab examined the relationships between the data in the Atlas and corresponding data in 21st-century surveys. If the Atlas is "tabulated nonsense," as some anthropologists have claimed (Leach, 1964, p. 299), we shouldn't find any relationships between the data in each source. However, our analyses—spearheaded by the economist Anke Becker—reveal a striking degree of persistence in cultural practices across time, with the data from the Atlas predicting survey responses of members of the same ethnic group a century later (Bahrami-Rad, Becker, and Henrich, 2017). Of course, this is not to say that there aren't important criticisms of the Atlas or that we do not need to build something better. But, the summary dismissal of the Atlas found in cultural anthropology and surrounding fields reflects a lack of scientific training, an aversion to quantification, and statistical illiteracy.

3. Figure 5.1 probably underestimates just how unusual WEIRD kinship is for several reasons. First, I've not included some key traits, like the existence of clans or distinctive kinship terminologies, which would further isolate WEIRD populations. Second, even when practices like bilateral descent "look" superficially similar to what we see in other groups, such analyses still miss the degree to which non-WEIRD communities remain enmeshed in kin-based institutions that are essential to their personal security, economic prosperity, marriage prospects, and social identity. For example, both WEIRD people and Ju/'hoansi hunter-gatherers track descent bilaterally. Unlike WEIRD people, however, Ju/'hoansi think about their world in terms of kin relations and possess ways to incorporate strangers into their relational networks. Otherwise, without seating a new arrival within their kinship network, they wouldn't know how to behave toward such a person. Third, after 1500, Catholic missions spread around the globe and immediately began trying to impose Catholic marriage on anyone they could find, which

meant working to suppress practices like polygyny and cousin marriage. In some cases, the missionaries had altered family structures before the anthropologists arrived to start writing stuff down. For example, the Pueblo Tewa of the American Southwest likely possessed a patrilineal clan-based organization prior to missionization, which began in the 17th century (Murdock, 1949). By the time researchers documented this group's kinship organization in detail around 1900, Tewa kinship had been molded to conform to match WEIRD patterns, despite the fact that the Tewa retained many of their traditional religious beliefs. Finally, the coding of these kinship traits is necessarily crude; for example, the ancient Egyptians are coded as "monogamous." However, while monogamous marriage was imposed on the lower strata in ancient Egypt, elite men continued to practice polygyny (Scheidel, 2009a, 2009b).

4. These data were compiled by Jonathan Schulz by augmenting the data compiled by Alan Bittles and colleagues (Bittles, 1998; Bittles and Black, 2010).

5. Bittles, 1998, 2001; Bittles and Black, 2010. See Baker (1979) on Chinese kinship.

6. Ember, 1967; Hoff and Sen, 2016; Shenk, Towner, Voss, and Alam, 2016.

7. Berman, 1983; Fukuyama, 2011; Gluckman, 2006; Greif, 2006a, 2006c; Greif and Tabellini, 2010; Marshall, 1959.

8. The estimate of 85–90 percent of Christians tracing their cultural lineage back to the Western Church comes from a Pew survey (www.pewforum.org/2011/12 /19/global-christianity-exec) and from Wikipedia (en.wikipedia.org/wiki/List _of_Christian_denominations_by_number_of_members#Catholic_Church _%E2%80%93_1.285_billion).

9. Mitterauer and Chapple, 2010. In India, China, and Persia, missionaries from the Nestorian and Oriental Churches had to compete with other universalizing religions, sophisticated philosophical visions, and savvy salvation cults. These ancient differences may parallel the relative success of modern Christian missions in converting Africans from their traditional belief systems to Christianity compared to converting Africans who have already been inoculated with Islam (Kudo, 2014).

10. Goody, 1983; Mitterauer and Chapple, 2010; Ubl, 2008. I'm following the lead of anthropologists like Jack Goody, economists like Avner Greif, and historians like Michael Mitterauer and Karl Ubl.

11. Amorim et al., 2018; Anderson, 1956; Ausenda, 1999; Berman, 1983; Burguiere et al., 1996; Charles-Edwards, 1972; Goody, 1983; Greif, 2006a, 2006c; Greif and Tabellini, 2010; Heather, 1999; Herlihy, 1985; Karras, 1990; Loyn, 1974, 1991; Mitterauer and Chapple, 2010; Ross, 1985; Tabellini, 2010.

12. Anderson, 1956.

13. Early European law codes are particularly informative because they typically regulate relationships between kin-groups, often specifying in detail how many shillings one kin-group needed to pay another kin-group for murders, injuries, or property damage. Usually, the fine was the same regardless of whether it was intentional or

accidental. In the case of murder, including involuntary manslaughter, members of one kin-group had to pay blood money, called *wergild*, to another kin-group even if they weren't personally involved. Kin-based responsibilities, including vengeance, were clear: in Spain, it was legal to avenge the death of a relative if the avenger shared a great-great-grandfather with the original victim (third cousins). Such laws regarding compensation are not unusual and can be found across diverse societies in the 20th century, from New Guinea to Africa (Berman, 1983; Diamond, 2012b; Glick, 1979; Gluckman, 1972a, 1972b; Goody, 1983; Greif, 2006a, 2006c; Grierson, 1903; Kroeber, 1925; Curtin et al., 2019).

14. Anderson, 1956; Berman, 1983; Charles-Edwards, 1972; Goody, 1983; Greif, 2006a, 2006c; Heather, 1999; Herlihy, 1985; Karras, 1990; Mitterauer and Chapple, 2010; Ross, 1985. In the literature, secondary wives are often called "concubines." Because of the different usages of the term "concubine," I will use the term "secondary wife."

15. Brundage, 1987; Burguiere et al., 1996; Goody, 1990; Shaw and Saller, 1984. Shaw and Saller provide evidence that rates of cousin marriage among aristocrats were low in most Roman regions during the early empire. They suggest that powerful families may have benefited more from connecting to wealthy families just entering the empire. I've not been able to locate quantitative data on cousin marriage for the lower classes.

16. Following what became a standard protocol, the monks encouraged the newly converted king to view himself as a divinely ordained protector and to develop a written code of laws. They likely sought to influence what got codified into written law.

17. Berman, 1983; Brundage, 1987; Goody, 1983; Higham, 1997; Ross, 1985. There is debate on the authenticity of Gregory's letter (his "Book of Replies"). The best scholarship on this comes from Karl Ubl, which supports the letter's authenticity (D'Avray, 2012; Ubl, 2008). If you are reading this endnote, you may be curious about how Gregory replied to Augustine's question about receiving Communion after a sex dream. I read Gregory's reply as saying, "no Communion until the dreamer is cleansed, and the fires of temptation doused." But, you can read a translation of Gregory's reply for yourself in *Bede's Ecclesiastical History of England* (Chapter 27), at www.gutenberg.org/files/38326/38326-h/38326-h.html#toc71.

18. Brundage, 1987; Goody, 1983; Ross, 1985.

19. Brundage, 1987; Harper, 2013. For "prostitute" in Latin, see Brundage, 1987, p. 25.

20. Lynch, 1986.

21. Goody, 1969; Silk, 1987. For pre-Christian adoption practices among European tribes, see Lynch, 1986, p. 180.

22. Chapais, 2009; Fox, 1967; Goody, 1996; Korotayev, 2000, 2004.

23. Studying these incest taboos led the Medieval historian David Herlihy to write, "No other society is known to have applied the incest taboo with such extreme rigor" (Herlihy, 1990, p. 1).

24. See Appendix A for sourcing.

25. Technically, this was "excommunication," but the impact here was substantially different from that in the later medieval Church (Smith and Cheetham, 1880).

26. These prohibitions on marrying affines endured for over a millennium. In the UK, for example, only in the early 20th century did Parliament undo the impact of canon law, with the Deceased Wife's Sister's Marriage Act of 1907 and the Deceased Brother's Widow's Marriage Act of 1921. Nowadays, in the UK at least, you can marry your wife's sister or husband's brother, but only if your spouse dies—still no polygamous marriage. This law was the outcome of a long political campaign and a growing number of illegal marriages to relatives (Kuper, 2010)—especially the sisters of dead wives—in the 18th and 19th centuries by both traditional elites and the expanding entrepreneurial class of industrialists and intellectuals (e.g., Mathew Bolton).

27. Goody, 1983; Mitterauer, 2015; Schulz et al., 2019; Smith and Cheetham, 1880; Ubl, 2008. Affinal links were created not just by marriage but also by sex—so technically, you couldn't marry anyone your father, brother, or sister had sex with.

28. The exception to this pattern is the Christian Roman emperors who had experimented, unsuccessfully, with imposing the death penalty for incest.

29. Ekelund et al., 1996; Smith, 1972.

30. Ausenda, 1999; Heather, 1999; Miller, 2009. The Lombard case was based on the kinship circle that Pope Gregory had set out for the Anglo-Saxons a century earlier. The new pope, however, stoutly refused. He argued that this had been a special circumstance involving a "rude people" who had only recently come to Christianity; the Church was easing them into a Christian lifestyle. By contrast, the Lombards lived in Italy and had been Christians for centuries, though they had to be converted from Arian to Catholic Christianity. Other evidence comes from letters complaining about continuing customary marriage practices. For example, in 874, Pope John VII wrote to the king of Mercia (England) to complain about men marrying their kin (Goody, 1983, p. 162).

31. Ekelund et al., 1996; Miller, 2009. In Iceland, after the Fourth Lateran Council reduced the constraints on cousin marriage, cousins could marry with a payment of one-tenth of their property.

32. Anderson, 1956; Mitterauer and Chapple, 2010; Schulz, 2019.

33. Anderson, 1956, p. 29.

34. Mitterauer, 2011, 2015.

35. Harper, 2013; Mitterauer, 2011, 2015; Smith and Cheetham, 1880.

36. Mitterauer, 2011, 2015.

37. Korotayev, 2004; Mitterauer, 2011, 2015; Smith and Cheetham, 1880; www .iranicaonline.org/articles/marriage-next-of-kin. The Old Testament is explicit on the topic: "If brothers dwell together, and one of them dies and has no son, the wife of the dead man shall not be married outside the family to a stranger. Her husband's brother shall go in to her and take her as his wife and perform

the duty of a husband's brother to her" (Deuteronomy 25:5–10). His brotherly "duty" was to inseminate her in order to carry on her dead husband's name—to continue his lineage. Similarly, in the New Testament, the Sadducees use Moses's endorsement of levirate marriage in an effort to undermine Jesus's notion of the afterlife by asking him who would be a woman's husband in the resurrection, her original husband or one of his brothers that she subsequently married after each of them successively died (in the story, her first husband had six brothers). Jesus could have responded by challenging the premise, which was based on levirate marriage, or by proposing polyandry (this would have been my move). Instead, Jesus accepts levirate marriage, and instead claims that there's no marriage in the resurrection—we'll be like the angels in heaven. In medieval Egypt, both Jews and Coptic Christians engaged in extensive cousin marriage (Goody, 1983, p. 82).

38. Technically, the Orthodox ban extended to seventh-degree relatives by the Roman method, which tabooed a woman from marrying her third cousin's father but not her third cousin (Ubl, 2008).

39. Key figures in the Church of Late Antiquity did comment on both the social and health impacts of marriage to close kin. St. Augustine wrote, "To the patriarchs of antiquity, it was a matter of religious duty to ensure that the bonds of kinship should not gradually become so weakened by the succession of the generations that they ceased to be bonds of kinship at all. And so they sought to reinforce such bonds by means of the marriage tie before kinship became too remote, thereby calling kinship back, so to speak, as it fled ... Who would doubt, however, that the state of things at the present time is more virtuous, now that marriage between cousins is prohibited? And this is not only because of the multiplication of kinship bonds just discussed: it is not merely because, if one person cannot stand in a dual relationship when this can be divided between two persons, the number of family ties is thereby increased" (Augustine, 1998, pp. 665–66). St. Ambrose, mentor to Augustine, comments on the harmful health effects found among the children of close relatives (Ambrose, 1881). But, this feels like post hoc rationalization of his preferred policies, since his observations cannot justify the extension of incest taboos to distant affines, stepsiblings, and godparents. In the case of levirate marriage or marriage to one's stepmother (after one's father's death), a lost bond is simply automatically replaced. Even more to the point, however, no one picked up on these comments in justifying Church policies as they were actually implemented. Ambrose himself references divine law—not offspring health—in aiming to dissuade a patriarch from marrying his son to his half-sister's daughter (Ambrose, 1881, pp. 351–54).

On the contemporary health consequences of marriage among relatives, see Bittles and Black, 2010. For work on the social and health costs of polygynous marriage, see Barbieri et al., 2016; Henrich, Boyd, and Richerson, 2012; Kong et al., 2012.

Of course, Christianity does provide solid scriptural grounds for pushing against tight family bonds. For example, Jesus says, in Matthew 12:47–50 (New

International Version), "Someone told him [Jesus], 'Your mother and brothers are standing outside, wanting to speak to you.' He replied to him, 'Who is my mother, and who are my brothers?' Pointing to his disciples, he said, 'Here are my mother and my brothers. For whoever does the will of my Father in heaven is my brother and sister and mother." Jesus also says, according to Matthew 10:35–36, "For I have come to turn a man against his father, a daughter against her mother, a daughter-in-law against her mother-in-law—man's enemies will be the members of his own household." Notably, however, these biblical verses didn't lead Coptic, Nestorian, or Syrian Christianity to adopt anything like the MFP.

40. From this point of view, the motivations of Church leaders aren't paramount. Church leaders, just like the leaders of the Isis cult or Nestorian Christianity, may have developed their beliefs, prohibitions, and prescriptions based on deep religious convictions; or, some may have been playing political games for their own enrichment. It doesn't matter. What does matter is how these beliefs and norms cashed out in the long run, in competition with other religions and institutions. Of course, the fact that some policies tended to fill the pews, swell the coffers, and expand the bishops' lands while other policies did not likely shaped the formation of the MFP. But, while such tactical thinking no doubt played a role, there's no reason to think that anyone did, or even could have, foreseen the MFP's long-term consequences. The MFP evolved and spread because it "worked." I'm parting ways with Jack Goody (1983) here. Goody seems to argue that because the Church's policies made the Church rich, then they must have been intentionally constructed to accomplish that end. However, much work on cultural evolution reveals how complex institutions can be and often are assembled without anyone understanding how or why they work (Henrich, 2016). The key is to step back and see the Church as one religious group among many who were all unconsciously "experimenting" with different religious packages.

41. Mitterauer, 2011, 2015. This calculation assumes a stable population in which all couples have two children, with half males and half females. It also assumes people always marry nonrelatives. For cousins, this means the number of cousins is 2^{2n}, where n is the type of cousin. For sixth cousins, $2^{2\cdot6}$ yields 4,096 people. Half of these are opposite-sex individuals. To obtain 2,730, I added the first through fifth cousins to this number. These cousins have an equal number of parents (aunts and uncles of various genealogical distances), so the total doubles when we add them.

42. Goody, 1969, 1983.

43. Goody, 1983; MacFarlane, 1978. In the early law codes of the Visigoths, for example, adoption was forbidden. The code did make legal provisions for fosterage, but this doesn't get the job done since it doesn't include a transfer of kinship ties, personal identity, ritual duties, or inheritance rights—foster children remained connected to their genetic parents' kin-groups.

44. Ausenda, 1999; Ekelund et al., 1996; Goody, 1983; Heather, 1999; Herlihy, 1985; Mitterauer and Chapple, 2010; Ross, 1985.

45. Goody, 1983; Smith, 1972.

46. Ekelund et al., 1996.

47. Brown, 2012.

48. Brown, 2012.

49. Ausenda, 1999; Ekelund et al., 1996, locs 137, 258; Goody, 1983, pp. 105, 124. Both the Visigoth King Wamba and Emperor Charlemagne realized what was happening and took steps to curtail it.

50. Berman, 1983; Goody, 1983; Greif, 2006a, 2006b, 2006c; Heather, 1999; Mitterauer and Chapple, 2010. On the Franks, see Goody, 1983, p. 118. The Church may have copied this strategy from Roman emperors, who were bequeathed immense sums by their friends and supporters (Shaw and Saller, 1984).

51. Ekelund et al., 1996; Goody, 1983, pp. 127, 131; Heldring, Robinson, and Vollmer, 2018.

52. This is an inference based on anthropological understandings of what creates and sustains tribal groups (Henrich, 2016; McElreath, Boyd, and Richerson, 2003) along with the fact that tribes existed during the Early Middle Ages but were gone from many regions of Europe by the High Middle Ages.

53. D'Avray, 2012; Ekelund et al., 1996; Mitterauer and Chapple, 2010; Smith and Cheetham, 1880; Ubl, 2008.

54. Ekelund et al., 1996; Heather, 1999; Mitterauer and Chapple, 2010. The supplemental materials of Schulz et al. (2018) summarize the research on this: psyarxiv .com/d6qhu.

55. This map combines information from multiple sources (Hajnal, 1965; Macucal, 2013; Shepherd, 1926; Speake, 1987; the Editors of the Encyclopaedia Britannica, 2018). For the Celtic Church, I used the diffusion of papal bishopric from Schulz et al., 2018. In Italy, see Ramseyer, 2006; Schulz, 2019; Wickham, 1981. For the Carolingian Empire, pre-Christian Germany, and eastward, see Menke, 1880; Schulz et al., 2018; Shepherd, 1926.

56. Hajnal, 1982; Herlihy, 1985; Mitterauer and Chapple, 2010; Toubert, 1996.

57. Berman, 1983; Ember, 1967; Greif and Tabellini, 2010; Mitterauer and Chapple, 2010; Silverman and Maxwell, 1978.

58. Higham, 1997; Mitterauer and Chapple, 2010. It's also plausible that the particular intensive kin-based institutions possessed by the Anglo-Saxons and other Germanic tribes already included some MFP kinship norms, such as bilateral descent and individual ownership (Lancaster, 2015; MacFarlane, 1978). So, the Church would have had less work to do.

59. Brundage, 1987; Charles-Edwards, 1972; Clark, 2007a; Goody, 1983; Greif, 2006; Greif and Tabellini, 2010; Herlihy, 1985; Laslett, 1984; Laslett and Wall, 1972; MacFarlane, 1978; Mitterauer and Chapple, 2010; Toubert, 1996. Regions that were ecologically unsuited to manorial agriculture were spared the strong, early dosing of the MFP.

60. Baker, 1979; Goody, 1990; Lynch, 2003. In Europe, the most successful households were nuclear, neolocal, and independent; in China, they were extended, patrilocal, and interdependent.

61. The age of marriage, of course, fluctuates for a variety of reasons. This doesn't change the fact that northwestern Europe increasingly displayed a pattern that was historically and cross-culturally distinct (Van Zanden and De Moor, 2010).

62. Lee and Feng, 2009; Van Zanden and De Moor, 2010.

63. MacFarlane, 1978; Silverman and Maxwell, 1978; Lynch, 2003. Two other elements associated with this patterning are: (1) inheritance by testament: property was no longer transmitted across generations automatically, according to customary norms (instead, individuals increasingly decided who inherits what; and, significantly, default rules favored spouses and children over siblings and uncles); and (2) retirement: a life stage develops in which people lose their leadership roles and economic centrality during a period prior to death; this contrasts with most societies, where the elderly remain economically and socially central unless they become cognitively impaired.

64. Mitterauer and Chapple, 2010. Even within the region broadly dominated by the Church and the European Marriage Pattern, one can still find remote pockets where traditional kin-based institutions have endured. For example, in the coastal marshes of Friesland on the North Sea, lineage organizations and blood revenge persisted for centuries after they had disappeared from the surrounding regions of France and Germany.

65. To this day, Christian religious traditions in rural Finland, Russia, the Balkans, and the Baltics reflect ancient ancestor worship. Serbian Christians in the western Balkans, for example, celebrate the feast of the patron "saint" of the household, which is regarded as one of the most solemn feast days on their Christian calendar. Unlike all other feast days, it's celebrated at the home of the senior patriarch. Sons inherit their household saint from their fathers, and wives get the saint of their husbands—though people are prohibited from marrying someone who shares the same household saint (i.e., clan exogamy). At the ritual, a list of forefathers (ancestors) is read aloud, and sometimes animals are sacrificed to those ancestors (Mitterauer and Chapple, 2010). This is ancestor worship thinly veiled in Christian garb.

66. Bartlett, 1993; Cantoni and Yuchtman, 2014; Greif, 2006a, 2006c; Herlihy, 1985; Kleinschmidt, 2000; Lilley, 2002; Lopez, 1976; MacFarlane, 1978.

67. Kleinschmidt, 2000, p. 25.; Lynch, 2003.

68. Herlihy, 1985; Ross, 1985.

69. Andersen et al., 2012; Bartlett, 1993; Berman, 1983; Ekelund et al., 1996; Kleinschmidt, 2000; Mokyr, 2002; Woods, 2012.

6. Psychological Differences, Families, and the Church

1. Bahrami-Rad et al., 2017.

2. This map combines data from the Ethnographic Atlas with the current distribu-

tion of ethnolinguistic groups around the world (Schulz et al., 2019). To infer KII values for all ethnolinguistic groups, we first calculated them for the thousand or so in the Atlas. Then, using linguistic phylogenies, we assigned KIIs to all other populations using the most closely related group from the Atlas. With this, we aggregated up to the country level for the cross-national analyses or linked them directly to individuals in global surveys for individual-level analyses. The language map comes from www.worldgeodatasets.com.

3. Both Benjamin Enke and my team created versions of the Kinship Intensity Index (Enke, 2017, 2019; Schulz et al., 2019). Because these indexes ended up pretty similar, and give similar results, I'm going to ignore the small differences in how they were constructed and conflate them in the main text. The fact that these two different indexes yield converging results only strengthens the case.

4. Readers familiar with evolutionary biology might suspect that groups with higher relatedness should be more cooperative. This is true, but the amount of relatedness found in these populations is so tiny that it cannot explain much actual, real-world cooperation. We are comparing tiny amounts of genetic relatedness to very tiny amounts.

5. Data from Gelfand et al., 2011. I've not included Israel in this analysis because it's not clear how to assign a KII value. I could link some of the subpopulations in Israel to a KII value via their language, Hebrew, but this language had been dead for thousands of years before its revival in the mid-19th century.

6. The correlations on the plots are Spearman correlations. To understand why cousin marriage has nonlinear effects, realize that each marriage builds a relationship between two families. The first marriage between two families creates a bond. A second marriage can strengthen this bond, but it's not as important as the first marriage. For this reason, more cousin marriage has diminishing marginal returns on social tightness.

7. Data from Bond and Smith, 1996; Murray, Trudeau, and Schaller, 2011. See Gelfand et al. (2011) for a relationship between tightness and conformity. Note, if you use the effect size for each experiment (Figure 1.3) instead of the error percentages, the results are equally strong. I've used the error rates because they are easier to understand.

8. If you use data from a subset of well-studied populations from the Ethnographic Atlas (the Standard Cross-Cultural Sample) that has information on the inculcation of obedience, you find the same relationship (Enke, 2017, 2019).

9. Elison, 2005; Fessler, 2004; Wallbott and Scherer, 1995.

10. Enke, 2017, 2019; Jaffe et al., 2014; Stephens-Davidowitz, 2018; Wong and Tsai, 2007.

11. Enke, 2017; Schulz et al., 2019. There are also strong relationships between our two measures of kinship intensity and the subjective value of family ties within the nuclear family (Alesina and Giuliano, 2015).

12. Ahmed, 2013, pp. 21–23; Hilton, 2001.

13. In the Sepik region of New Guinea (Chapter 4), Ilahita's villagers presumed that strangers were "sorcerers and thieves" and would "scarcely think to visit them in their dens," and this continued decades after warfare ended. If visiting strangers requested accommodations while visiting Ilahita, they were quartered on roofed platforms, without walls, so they could be watched (Tuzin, 1976, pp. 22–23).

14. Enke, 2017; Schulz et al., 2018. The trust data come from the World Values Survey (Inglehart et al., 2014).

15. Enke, 2017, 2019. Kinship intensity can also explain the variation in trust mapped in Figure 1.7 using the Generalized Trust Question. However, this relationship is weaker. As noted in Chapter 1, detailed analyses reveal that in some countries, like China, people say "most people can be trusted" when they respond to the Generalized Trust Question, but then also say that you cannot trust foreigners, adherents of other religions, or those you've just met for the first time. This shows that, while the GTQ does indeed measure impersonal trust in Europe and the United States, it doesn't always capture it elsewhere. It's a WEIRD question (Chua et al., 2008, 2009; Enke, 2017; Greif and Tabellini, 2015; Schulz et al., 2019). See the supplemental materials and links in Schulz et al. (2019) for a discussion.

16. Enke, 2017; Schulz et al., 2019.

17. The Passenger's Dilemma data are from Schulz et al., 2019; Trompenaars and Hampden-Turner, 1998.

18. Enke, 2017; Haidt, 2012; Haidt and Graham, 2007.

19. Enke, 2017, 2019. Regarding the analysis of immigrants, we should worry that what's driving the results is something about the home countries of these immigrants that just happens to be correlated with intensive kinship. To deal with this, Benjamin statistically removed the effects of things like people's schooling and the GDP per capita of the immigrant's country of origin, as well as a host of geographic factors like temperature, distance from the equator, agricultural fertility, and malaria prevalence. The results hold. Some might further worry that European colonization or settlement might be driving the results, but they even hold when he statistically removed the influence of the percentage of people of European descent in the home country and compared only individuals from countries colonized by the same European power. Finally, we might worry that these results on morality arise simply from the differences in trust discussed above; however, Benjamin's analyses suggest that intensive kinship influences morality over and above its impact on generalized trust (Enke, 2017, 2019). Benjamin also provides additional analyses of the MFQ dimensions in Enke, 2019.

20. Bowles, 2004; Henrich and Henrich, 2007.

21. Bowles and Gintis, 2002; Fehr and Gächter, 2000, 2002; Herrmann et al., 2008.

22. Herrmann et al., 2008; Schulz et al., 2019. Herrmann et al. increased contributions to the group project by 40 percent, not 50 percent. I'm simplifying.

23. Schulz et al., 2019.

24. Schulz et al., 2019.

25. Schulz et al., 2019.

26. Gächter, Renner, and Sefton, 2008.

27. Gächter and Herrmann, 2009; Herrmann et al., 2008.

28. Enke (2017, 2019) performed this analysis using his KII measure. Economists call these two types of punishment "altruistic punishment" and "antisocial punishment." The terms are too value-laden. Depending on the institutions of a society, so-called antisocial punishment can maintain the social order, while altruistic punishment could spark cycles of violence. Each represents an adaptive psychological calibration to a certain social structure (Bhui et al., 2019a; Henrich and Henrich, 2014).

29. The differences in third-party norm enforcement vs. revenge also emerged when Benjamin analyzed survey questions from the Global Preferences Survey (Chapter 1). The results, based on data from tens of thousands of individuals from 75 countries, show that individuals from populations with less intensive kin-based institutions—lower KII values—were more willing to punish "someone who treats others unfairly," and rather disinclined to seek revenge (Enke, 2017, 2019). Further, focusing only on the 2,430 first-generation immigrants from 147 countries in the GPS, the results show that individuals from countries with more intensive kinship express stronger inclinations toward revenge relative to third-party norm enforcement. This holds even when we only compare immigrants from different places who are currently living in the same country and when we statistically account for other factors such as the person's age, gender, household income, and formal schooling (Enke, 2017, 2019).

30. Barrett et al., 2016; Gluckman, 1972a, 1972b, 2006; Harper, 2013; Moore, 1972.

31. Barrett et al., 2016; Curtin et al., 2019. Thanks to Clark Barrett, Alyssa Crittenden, Alex Bolyanatz, Martin Kanovsky, Geoff Kushnick, Anne Pisor, and Brook Scelza for supplying the information about their field sites necessary to construct the Contemporary Kinship Intensity Index.

32. Curtin et al., 2019; Gluckman, 1972a, 1972b. Based on work by my team in Yasawa, there's no reason to suspect that these differences in the role of intentionality are due to differences in people's cognitive ability to infer the mental states of others. Such mentalizing abilities are central to many important tasks in humans, ranging from cultural learning to conversations. Instead, it appears that people don't always attend to others' mental states, especially when forming certain kinds of moral or reputational judgments of third parties (McNamara et al., 2019a, 2019b).

33. Berman, 1983; Drew, 1991, 2010a, 2010b; Gurevich, 1995; Harper, 2013.

34. Varnum et al., 2010.

35. Schulz et al., 2018.

36. Barry, Child, and Bacon, 1959; Berry, 1966; Liebenberg, 1990; Witkin and Berry, 1975; Witkin et al., 1977. Several different experiments on field independence tell broadly the same story. For variation in field independence based on the embedded-figures task, see Kuhnen et al., 2001. This kinship terminology is called the "Eskimo System" (Murdock, 1949).

37. Diamond, 1997; Enke, 2017; Hibbs and Olsson, 2004.

38. Assigning these years is tricky for a couple of reasons. The two most important ones are that modern borders don't respect different historical events, and it's often hard to know precisely when incorporation into the Church began (papal bulls don't announce it). Parts of Germany, for example, were incorporated as early as 734 CE, but other parts entered much later, in the 12th century. These are important concerns; but put a pin in them for now, because in the next chapter we'll vaporize these problems by drilling down to study the regional impacts of bishoprics within European countries.

39. Putterman and Weil, 2010; Schulz et al., 2019.

40. We didn't create Church dosages running all the way to 2000 CE for two reasons. First, the Church's MFP restrictions eased a bit after the Fourth Lateran Council in 1215 and further with Protestantism in the 16th century, so the strongest dosages were really administered from roughly 500 to 1200 CE. Second, to figure out church dosages for the rest of the world, we had to account for the massive emigration out of Europe that occurred after 1500 and for the African slave trade, among other large population movements. For this, we needed to use Putterman and Weil's migration matrix.

41. Schulz et al., 2019.

42. De Jong, 1998; Enke, 2017; Schulz et al., 2018; Ubl, 2008.

43. Schulz et al., 2019.

7. Europe and Asia

1. Schulz et al., 2019.

2. We are using only rates of first cousin marriages in these analyses because the second cousin marriages are missing from the Vatican archives due to the powers granted to the bishop of Sicily.

3. Because we have data from only 68 regions spread across four countries, only three of our four psychological dimensions hold up well when we compare regions within countries and ignore the differences between countries (Schulz et al., 2019).

4. This relationship is quite sturdy. When we statistically account for educational differences among provinces as well as differences in agricultural productivity, climate, coastal proximity, precipitation, and much more, the relationship holds or gets stronger. This relationship even holds if we only compare provinces within Italy's 20 local regions, which mitigates concerns that we are capturing broad

north-south differences. Note that blood donations are always low when cousin marriage rates are relatively high. However, when cousin marriage is rare, the donation rates are not uniformly high but instead highly variable. This underlines the point that, while dissolving intensive kinship opens the door to impersonal prosociality, it doesn't make a population walk through.

5. Schulz et al. (2019) re-analyzed data from Guiso, Sapienza, and Zingales, 2004.

6. Akbari, Bahrami-Rad, and Kimbrough, 2016; Schulz, 2019; Schulz et al., 2018.

7. Schulz et al., 2019. Also see Enke, 2017, 2019.

8. Alesina and Giuliano, 2010; Alesina et al., 2015; Enke, 2017; Fernández and Fogli, 2009; Giuliano, 2007. Cousin marriage can stoutly resist assimilation, at least in the short term. Among migrants to WEIRD societies such as Britain and Belgium, marriage to close relatives actually increases in the second generation, compared to the home country. In Britain, one study shows that cousin marriages were 76 percent of all marriages for second-generation Pakistani Brits, while in Pakistan comparable rates were under 50 percent. In Belgium, first-generation migrants from Morocco and Turkey also had higher rates of cousin marriage compared to their counterparts back home, though by the second generation, rates were only a little higher than those found in the home country. This is not surprising: when marriage to close relatives is normative and religiously permitted, a variety of economic, social, demographic, and ecological factors jointly sustain its prevalence (Reniers, 2001; Shaw, 2001).

9. Bray, 1984; Greif and Tabellini, 2015; Talhelm et al., 2014.

10. Greif and Tabellini, 2010, 2015; Mitterauer and Chapple, 2010. Then, in 1949, the new Communist government disbanded the clans, invalidated their rules, and redistributed their property. Since 1979 there has been a resurgence of clans in China (see Chapter 10).

11. Of course, this isn't a purely environmental factor, because the ecological effects are dependent upon farmers possessing (1) the technical know-how for paddy rice agriculture and (2) the appropriate varieties of domesticated rice. Fortunately, these elements spread quickly compared to kin-based institutions.

12. Henrich, 2014; Talhelm et al., 2014.

13. Adapted from Talhelm et al., 2014.

14. Thanks to Avner Greif (Greif and Tabellini, 2010, 2015) and Thomas Talhelm for supplying their data.

15. Kitayama et al., 2009; Talhelm et al., 2014. The −0.5mm for the Japanese participants was not distinguishable from zero using conventional confidence measures. Note that the circles of the sociogram are measured by their diameter.

16. The comparison with American undergraduates is based on these references (Knight and Nisbett, 2007; Varnum et al., 2008) and a personal communication with Thomas Talhelm (August 31, 2015, via email), who has administered the Triad Task used in China to undergraduates at the University of Virginia.

17. Talhelm, 2015; Talhelm et al., 2014.

18. They did an instrumental variable regression with rice suitability as their instrument (Talhelm et al., 2014).

19. Talhelm et al., 2014, has received some critiques (Ruan, Xie, and Zhang, 2015; Zhou, Alysandratos, and Naef, 2017), which, while interesting, don't seriously jeopardize my use of these findings within the broader context of this book. The patterns presented here are further confirmed by Liu et al., 2019.

20. Buggle, 2017.

21. However, while I suspect that this ecological variation played some role, remember that many other social, economic, and ecological conditions besides those associated with paddy rice or irrigation favor intensive kinship. Often, the primary driver of intensive kinship derives from warfare between communities, as we saw in Ilahita.

22. Baker, 1979. Also following the Church's MFP, China initiated land reforms that sought to break down and redistribute the corporate holdings of patrilineal clans (Greif and Tabellini, 2015). The 1980 law set the minimum age for women to marry at 20 years ("The marriage law of the people's Republic of China [1980]," 1984). Of course, there are important differences between the medieval Church and China in the 20th century. For example, divorce in modern China is by mutual consent, women are equal under the law, and children receive full rights regardless of whether their parents were married. Interestingly, the Ming Dynasty had previously tried banning cousin marriage, but it didn't take (Fêng, 1967).

23. Hango, 2006; Li, Hamamura, and Adams, 2016; Lun, Oishi, and Tenney, 2012; Mann, 1972; Oishi and Talhelm, 2012; Oishi et al., 2013; Oishi et al., 2015; Park and Peterson, 2010; Sato et al., 2008; Su and Oishi, 2010; Yuki et al., 2013. The relevant window for moving seems to be between 5 and 18 years of age. For a cross-national study of relational mobility and its psychological correlates in 39 countries, see Thomson et al. (2018).

8. WEIRD Monogamy

1. Motolinía, 1973.

2. Toribio wrote extensively about the customs and beliefs of those he aimed to convert and used his influence to protect and defend indigenous peoples when and where he could. Though he was a critic of the Spanish government's approach to the indigenous population, he never veered from his commitment to spreading Christianity, and apparently baptized over 400,000 people in his lifetime. Toribio was considered a moderate voice for indigenous peoples, often in contrast to the ardent bishop of Chiapas, Bartolomé de las Casas.

3. Jankowiak, 2008, pp. 172–73.

4. Jankowiak, 2008, p. 165. Also see Jankowiak, Sudakov, and Wilreker, 2005.

5. "Peculiar" is the term used by the historian Walter Scheidel (2009) in characterizing monogamous marriage in the ancient world.

6. Henrich, 2016; Muller, Wrangham, and Pilbeam, 2017; Pilbeam and Lieberman, 2017. On polyandry, see Starkweather and Hames, 2012. By "group-living" I'm excluding primates like gibbons.

7. Buss, 2007.

8. Henrich, Boyd, and Richerson, 2012; Hewlett and Winn, 2014. You might think that women should prefer polyandry, one wife with multiple husbands. However, unlike men with multiple wives, women face a rather different evolutionary calculus, which has shaped their evolved inclinations, emotions, and motivations. A polyandrous woman cannot reproduce "in parallel" like a man, by impregnating multiple husbands during the same period—so, no advantage there. Moreover, as a mammal, she's stuck with the two biggest jobs, pregnancy and nursing, which she simply can't farm out to extra husbands. Even worse, having sex with multiple husbands can generate confusion about paternity, which can result in less fatherly investment and more sexual jealousy among the husbands. Finally, once she hits menopause, continuing to add virile young husbands as she ages does her no good at all, at least from a reproductive perspective (though it could be fun). So, extra husbands are rarely worth the trouble, and certainly can't accelerate a woman's reproduction in the same way that additional wives can for a man. This evolutionary reasoning means that natural selection has shaped women's inclinations in ways that make them wary of polyandrous arrangements, and men's inclinations in ways that make the practice downright aversive (usually, but not always!). Taken together, our evolved psychological tendencies will suppress or inhibit the spread and popularity of polyandrous marriage norms, though under certain conditions, cultural evolution has forged creative solutions to these psychological obstacles and generated moderate levels of polyandrous marriage (Levine and Silk, 1997).

9. Henrich, Boyd, and Richerson, 2012; Levine and Silk, 1997. This tends to occur in economic situations where (1) households benefit from the labor of multiple husbands and (2) brothers can collectively marry the same woman, mitigating concerns about paternity.

10. Henrich, Boyd, and Richerson, 2012; Hewlett, 1996, 2000; Marlowe, 2003, 2004.

11. The 10 percent of monogamous hunter-gatherers is somewhat deceiving, since most do not actually taboo either polygynous or polyandrous marriage. Instead, they live under a combination of ecological conditions and egalitarian institutions that mute the economic inequality among men such that even the highest-status guys can't attract more than one wife. From the women's point of view, the available men are all sufficiently similar that becoming the second wife of a married man never looks like a better deal than becoming the first wife of an

unmarried man. In some cases, these ecological conditions have demanded social norms that actively flatten inequalities through institutions like broad food sharing. Groups like this end up with only monogamous marriages, de facto. Notably, some of these "monogamous" groups had social norms that permitted husbands to "loan" their wives to other men for a night or two. The services provided by a loaned wife included cooking but extended to sex. So, clearly, the norms in these societies were rather different from those governing WEIRD monogamy.

12. Betzig, 1982, 1993; Henrich, Boyd, and Richerson, 2012; Scheidel, 2008, 2009. Note, labeling societies as having a "polyandrous" marriage system means that polyandrous marriages occur at low to moderate rates, and it's important to realize that these occur alongside both polygynous and monogamous marriages.

13. Bergreen, 2007; Betzig, 1982, 1986, 1993; Motolinía, 1973; Scheidel, 2008, 2009a, 2009b. It is often argued that noble marriages and harems were formed purely to build political alliances. While there's no doubt that political marriages were part of the story, many details point to the centrality of sex and reproduction. First, as noted in the main text, elite wives were often set off in a special category (the "alliance" category), but the elite men also built harems of lower-class women. Second, government bureaucracies were charged with running beauty contests to pick the emperor's wives or concubines. If it's all about political connections, why is beauty relevant? Third, there were often entire institutions focused on the sexuality of these wives and concubines. For example, in China, court ladies monitored the menstruation cycles of the harem, which was guarded by eunuchs.

14. When I first encountered collections of examples like these—harem sizes—I immediately worried that they represented cherry-picked cases that might highlight the extremes or excesses of complex societies (or the prejudices of Western observers). However, a deeper dive into the anthropological and historical records suggests these cases were probably closer to the average for highly stratified societies than to the extremes.

Even more strikingly, recent analyses of genetic data from around the world suggest that rising levels of polygyny were so common in the last 10,000 years that they left a heel print on our Y chromosomes—that's the DNA carried only by males. Using the rich information embedded in both Y chromosomes and mitochondrial DNA (which is inherited only from the mother), geneticists have estimated the number of mothers vs. the number of fathers going well back into our evolutionary history. In a purely monogamous world, we'd expect the ratio of the number of mothers to fathers to be something close to one. Before agriculture, the data show that there was a pretty constant ratio of roughly two to four mothers for every father. However, a few thousand years after agriculture began, while the number of mothers was rapidly increasing as populations expanded, the number of fathers plummeted. That is, the number of fathers dropped, while the overall population was rising! At the peak of this climb, there were over 16 mothers for each father.

This genetic patterning is most consistent with a combination of high levels of polygyny and ferocious intergroup competition. Expanding agricultural clans, segmentary lineages, and chiefdoms either killed or enslaved all the men in the societies they conquered and took all the fertile females as wives, concubines, or sex slaves (Heyer et al., 2012; Karmin et al., 2015; Zeng, Aw, and Feldman, 2018). Consistent with this, dips in the number of fathers appear earliest in regions where agriculture first began, in the Middle East (e.g., Mesopotamia), as well as in both South and East Asia. Europe, where agriculture arrived later, reveals the deepest dip, hitting its nadir between 5,000 and 6,000 years ago. The Andean populations, where agriculture began relatively late, don't show the dip until 2,000 to 3,000 years ago.

15. Henrich, Boyd, and Richerson, 2012; Scheidel, 2009a, 2009b. On the Indian Supreme Court, see www.ibtimes.co.uk/india-bans-polygamy-muslims-not -fundamental-right-islam-1487356.

16. This is my version of Craig Jones's coinage, "polygamy's math problem." Polyandry doesn't have a math problem.

17. Fenske, 2015; Field et al., 2016; Marlowe, 2000, 2003, 2005, 2010. Unlike in modern African societies, we are assuming the population is not growing.

18. Henrich, Boyd, and Richerson, 2012. This applies to state-level societies but not necessarily to smaller-scale societies.

19. See the supplemental materials of Henrich, Boyd, and Richerson, 2012.

20. The rooster image was adapted from one taken by Muhammad Mahdi Karim, found at commons.wikimedia.org/w/index.php?curid=5507626.

21. Beletsky et al., 1995; Wingfield, 1984; Wingfield et al., 1990; Wingfield, Lynn, and Soma, 2001. Similarly, polygynous birds implanted with an androgen suppressor tend to hang out at the nest and care for the chicks.

22. Gettler et al., 2011. For a recent review, see Grebe et al., 2019.

23. These data are from Gettler et al. (2011). Afternoon T levels tell the same story. Readers might wonder why the Cebu population has monogamous marriage, given that they are non-WEIRD. The answer is the MFP. In 1521 CE, the explorer Ferdinand Magellan arrived in Cebu. His chronicler recorded extensive polygyny, writing that men can "have as many wives as they wish, but there is always a chief one" (Pigfetta, 2012, loc. 2322). Magellan and his priestly team immediately began preaching Christianity and complaining about the polygyny (Pigfetta, 2012, Chapter 25). Following Magellan, Catholic missions began arriving in the Philippines during the 16th century. Cebu had nearly five centuries of exposure to the MFP before Kuzawa and his team arrived to measure men's testosterone.

24. Alvergne, Faurie, and Raymond, 2009; Booth et al., 2006; Burnham et al., 2003;

Fleming et al., 2002; Gettler et al., 2011; Gray, 2003; Gray and Campbell, 2006; Gray et al., 2002; Mazur and Booth, 1998; Mazur and Michalek, 1998; Storey et al., 2000.

25. Beletsky et al., 1995.

26. Gray, 2003; Gray and Campbell, 2006; Gray et al., 2002; Muller et al., 2009. Note, WEIRD men tend to have quite high absolute testosterone levels, probably because they are generally well fed and live in low-pathogen environments. It's widely thought that what matters is relative, not absolute, testosterone levels, suggesting that our endocrine systems calibrate to certain levels (Wingfield et al., 1990).

27. Muller et al., 2009.

28. Sellen, Borgerhoff Mulder, and Sieff, 2000.

29. Betzig, 1992; Harper, 2013.

30. Ellison et al., 2002.

31. Henrich, 2016, Chapter 14.

32. These hormonal relationships are complex, and depend heavily on the individuals' subjective assessments of the situation (Salvador, 2005; Salvador and Costa, 2009).

33. For reviews of testosterone and status, see Booth et al., 2006; Eisenegger, Haushofer, and Fehr, 2011; Mazur and Booth, 1998. Testosterone may also improve motor control and coordination (Booth et al., 2006; Mazur and Booth, 1998). For research on social vigilance and fear reduction, see van Honk et al., 2001; van Honk et al., 2005. For changes in sensitivity to gains and losses, see van Honk et al., 2004.

34. Kouri et al., 1995; Pope, Kouri, and Hudson, 2000. These experiments involve small samples, so caution is warranted.

35. This experiment involved both men and women, matched in same-sex pairs (Mehta, Wuehrmann, and Josephs, 2009). The effects are much stronger in men but also appear in women. High-testosterone individuals in Figure 8.4 are those with levels one standard deviation or more above the mean, while those with low testosterone levels are one standard deviation or more below the mean. The data were conditioned and standardized separately for men and women before it was combined on the plot. Unfortunately, the sample size in this experiment is small (60 individuals).

36. Data from Mehta, Wuehrmann, and Josephs, 2009.

37. Bos, Terburg, and van Honk, 2010. This study involved only women. However, there's good reason to suspect that these psychological effects apply to men as well (Bos et al., 2010; Hermans, Putman, and van Honk, 2006; van Honk, Terburg, and Bos, 2011). For the follow-up work on the connection to the amygdala, see Bos et al., 2012.

38. Mehta and Josephs, 2010; Storey et al., 2000. By driving status-seeking behavior, higher testosterone can also drive men to take greater financial risks, at least under

some conditions (Apicella, Dreber, and Mollerstrom, 2014). However, as I've emphasized, there's no simple and direct relationship between testosterone and risky behavior per se, and efforts to confirm this link have been mixed (Apicella, Carré, and Dreber, 2015). Another approach is to simply dose men with testosterone and have them make financial choices. In a setup that resembled real life, young men were administered either testosterone or a placebo, and then had a series of opportunities to invest money in pairs of stocks. The men who had their testosterone artificially elevated increased their investment in the riskier stocks—those with larger price swings—by 46 percent compared to the placebo group (Cueva et al., 2015).

39. Booth, Johnson, and Granger, 1999; Booth et al., 2006; Mazur and Booth, 1998; Soler, Vinayak, and Quadagno, 2000. Men with testosterone levels more than one standard deviation above the mean are 28 percent more likely to engage in crime than are men one standard deviation below the mean.

40. Ackerman, Maner, and Carpenter, 2016. Polygynous marriage dramatically steepens the inequality in mating opportunities available to "winners" and "losers." Research on the effects of such winner-take-all environments converges with the findings in this chapter (Becker and Huselid, 1992; Bothner, Kang, and Stuart E., 2007; Frick and Humphreys, 2011; Taylor, 2003).

41. Arantes et al., 2013; Block and Gerety, 1995; Blondel, Lohéac, and Rinaudo, 2007; Cohn, Fehr, and Marechal, 2014; Hanoch, Gummerum, and Rolison, 2012; Khadjavi and Lange, 2013; Pratt and Cullen, 2000; Reynolds, 2006; Wichary, Pachur, and Li, 2015.

42. Henrich, Boyd, and Richerson, 2012; Sampson and Laub, 1993; Sampson, Laub, and Wimer, 2006.

43. Duncan, Wilkerson, and England, 2006; Farrington and West, 1995; Horney, Osgood, and Marshall, 1995.

44. Jin et al., 2010.

45. The actual policy is more complex than simply one child per couple. For example, the policy was amended to permit rural couples to have a second child if their first child was a girl. Whatever these complexities, the bottom line is that the pressure to have boys shifted the sex ratio.

46. Edlund et al., 2007, 2013.

47. The emergence of a psychological shift in surplus men underlines the power of these effects in two ways. First, under the one-child policy, families typically had one male heir at most to carry on the lineage, continue family traditions, and care for aging parents. In light of strongly held values, this situation would have motivated parents and grandparents to do everything in their power to guarantee the health, marriage, and prosperity of their only boy. Second, this all occurred during China's massive economic expansion, so jobs and opportunities abounded. However, even though many males were going to do economically much better than their fathers, they faced tougher competition to find mates. Both of these trends

should have operated to reduce men's likelihood of committing a crime (Edlund et al., 2007, 2013).

48. The effect of surplus men on crime, created here by the one-child policy, is independent of the wealth of provinces, employment rates, educational levels, inequality, migration, police, welfare expenditures, and the age structure of the population. Not surprisingly, unmarried men in the surplus pool, or what researchers in this field call "forced bachelors," are more likely to engage in the commercial sex trade and get sexually transmitted diseases (Liu, Li, and Feldman, 2012).

49. Anthropologists in the mid-20th century had already made the link between higher rates of polygynous marriage and higher crime rates (Bacon, Child, and Barry, 1963; Burton and Whiting, 1961).

50. Monogamous marriage also influences paternal investment, intrahousehold conflict, and the organization of families in ways that improve the health and safety of infants and children relative to polygynous marriage (Henrich, Boyd, and Richerson, 2012).

51. These societal-level benefits are likely most relevant in complex, stratified human societies with intercommunity trade, standing armies, well-developed commerce, and highly skilled occupations. Under these conditions, normative monogamy will promote success in intergroup competition and will spread among societies. It is important to emphasize that normative monogamous marriage isn't always favored by intergroup competition (Henrich, Boyd, and Richerson, 2012). In some circumstances, intergroup competition may favor polygynous marriage (Fleisher and Holloway, 2004; Sahlins, 1961; White, 1988).

52. Herlihy, 1985.

53. Despite actively and energetically promoting the Church's incest taboos, both Merovingian and Carolingian rulers were polygynous. Charlemagne had 10 known primary and secondary wives.

54. Herlihy, 1995; Todd, 1985.

9. Of Commerce and Cooperation

1. For the Montesquieu and Paine quotations, see Hirschman, 1982.

2. Henrich, 1997; Henrich and Henrich, 2007.

3. For an introduction to behavioral economics, see Camerer (2003). The game-theoretical analysis also assumes that individuals believe that everyone else is a rational selfish maximizer, too.

4. These patterns arise from nonstudent adults in WEIRD societies (Ensminger and Henrich, 2014; Henrich et al., 2004). Most experiments, however, have been done among university students, who make lower offers and are generally less prosocial (Bellemare, Kröeger, and Van Soest, 2008).

5. Interestingly, the only person who rejected a low offer was actually not a current resident of the community but a relative who was visiting from Cusco (Henrich, 2000; Henrich and Smith, 2004).

6. Henrich, 2000; Henrich and Smith, 2004.

7. Henrich and Henrich, 2007; Johnson, 2003; Johnson and Earle, 2000.

8. Ensminger and Henrich, 2014; Henrich et al., 2004; 2005.

9. Henrich et al., 2004; Henrich et al., 2005.

10. Ensminger and Henrich, 2014; Henrich, Ensminger et al., 2010.

11. In addition to replicating the effect of market integration from Phase I, Phase II also replicated the same unusual patterns of results from particular populations using our revised protocols and new experiments. In New Guinea, for example, we found communities who both made offers over 50 percent and sometimes rejected those offers (Bolyanatz, 2014; Tracer, 2003, 2004; Tracer, Mueller, and Morse, 2014).

12. Adapted from Henrich, Ensminger et al., 2010. The regression line on this figure is fitted to all of these data points except the two New Guinea populations. In New Guinea, it appears that our experiments tapped social norms about the treatment of other community members, not impersonal fairness (Bolyanatz, 2014; Ensminger and Henrich, 2014; Tracer, 2004; Tracer et al., 2014). All published analyses include the New Guinea populations (Ensminger and Henrich, 2014; Henrich et al., 2006; Henrich, Ensminger et al., 2010; Henrich, McElreath et al., 2006), but I'm removing them here because I'm focused specifically on impersonal fairness.

13. Ensminger and Henrich, 2014; Henrich, Ensminger et al., 2010. Our world religion variable does not explain the variation in offers in the TPG. We think we know why: see the supplemental materials of Henrich, Ensminger et al. (2010) and Laurin et al., 2012.

14. Ensminger and Henrich, 2014; Henrich, 2016.

15. Kosfeld and Rustagi, 2015; Rustagi, Engel, and Kosfeld, 2010. When players made their decisions, they knew they'd be paid for one of the two, either the simultaneous contribution or the sequential conditional version. This gave them an incentive to take both seriously.

16. Data are drawn from Rustagi et al., 2010.

17. Of course, it's still possible that something about the towns besides their markets increased people's conditional cooperation. In pondering this, consider two additional facts. First, the primary reason that people go to town is to attend market days. So, even if it's somehow not the specific activity of commerce itself that's doing the psychological work here, it's still the market days that are attracting people to the towns. Second, the effect of markets on conditional cooperation still holds if you use people's frequency of market trips instead of their market proximity. Other similar studies from Uganda (Voors et al., 2012) and China (Tu and Bulte, 2010) converge on the same basic insight about market integration and impersonal prosociality. However, one piece of counterevidence on the effect of markets comes from Siziba and Bulte (2012). In two African countries, external interventions increased the market access in randomly selected communities.

Then, two years after the initial implementation, researchers found that impersonal trust hadn't increased. There are several possible reasons for this result, but a simple explanation is that it may take more than two years for markets to drive cultural evolution in new directions. It's also possible that these markets remained organized by interpersonal exchange, not impersonal exchange.

18. I'm drawing these numbers from the instrumental variable regression in Rustagi et al., 2010.

19. Rustagi, Engel, and Kosfeld, 2010.

20. Priming experiments done with American undergraduates show that markets can increase impersonal prosociality—trust, in this case. In an experimental task, researchers primed some participants using a word-unscrambling task that contained several items related to commerce, exchange, or trade. Other participants did a word-unscramble that didn't contain market-related words. Then, both groups played a simple trust game. Participants primed with markets were more trusting in the experiment than those not reminded of markets (Al-Ubaydli et al., 2013).

21. Researchers have explored the psychological impact of reminding people of "money" using priming techniques. Money can act as a prime for "market norms." Among other aspects of psychology, this work examines the effect of "cash primes" on interpersonal prosociality. As expected, reminders of money make people less interpersonally prosocial, reducing helping, generosity, empathy, and sociability (Vohs, 2015; Vohs, Mead, and Goode, 2006, 2008).

22. Bowles, 1998; Fourcade and Healy, 2007; Hirschman, 1982.

23. Hirschman, 1982. The 12th-century historian William of Malmesbury (1125) wrote, "Englishmen and Frenchmen, having a more civilized way of life, dwell in cities and are familiar with trade and commerce" (Lilley, 2002, p. 78). Research that purports to contradict the *Doux Commerce* thesis isn't applicable to the more nuanced approach I'm taking here (Falk and Szech, 2013).

24. Plattner, 1989.

25. On exchange in Aboriginal Australia generally, see McBryde, 1984; McCarthy, 1939; Smyth, 1878; Stanner, 1934. For discussions of trade and markets, see Cassady, 1974; Grierson, 1903; Hawk, 2015.

26. Probably based on accounts from the Carthaginian explorer Hanno, this quotation comes from *The History of Herodotus* (Book IV), at classics.mit.edu /Herodotus/history.3.iii.html.

27. Grierson, 1903; Hawk, 2015; Woodburn, 1982, 1998. One problem with archaeological work arguing for trade is that it's usually based on the movement of materials, which can also move through raiding and theft.

28. Cassady, 1974; Grierson, 1903.

29. See Plattner (1989) for a discussion of large apple shipments. Credence goods are everywhere, and in the absence of internalized market norms or interpersonal relationships, markets for these goods would flounder. Consider buying fresh

buffalo milk in the informal markets of Delhi and Uttar Pradesh. To study these markets, Devesh Rustagi and his collaborator Markus Kroll first purchased a liter of milk from many independent sellers at several markets and had the samples tested for their water content. Strikingly, all the samples had been diluted with water. However, the amount of added water varied from a low of 4 percent to a high of 37 percent, with an average dilution of 18 percent—so about one-fifth of each liter of milk was added water. Then, to verify that milk is a credence good, Devesh and Markus conducted a contest among milk sellers—experts on milk dilution—in which participants were paid handsomely for accurately predicting how much water had been added to various samples. Their results were clear: no one could accurately assess if water had been added, at least for volumes under about 40 percent. The sellers couldn't even get the rank ordering of dilution approximately correct. So, milk is indeed a strong credence good (unless you happen to have modern laboratory facilities at your disposal). Finally, the research duo measured the impartial honesty of 72 milk sellers using the Impersonal Honesty Game, where people are paid according to their reported rolls of a six-sided die. Not surprisingly, milk sellers who misreported their rolls more frequently also diluted their milk by a higher percentage—confirming that the dice game measures precisely the kind of behavior that we are interested in. For every six misreports out of 40 total die rolls, milk sellers increased their dilution by 3 percentile points. Interestingly, there were only two characteristics of the milk sellers that were consistently associated with their impartial honesty, as captured by the dilution of their milk: ritual attendance and caste membership. Sellers who attended rituals more frequently, diluted their milk less. By contrast, members of the clan-based herding caste were more likely to dilute their milk (Kröll and Rustagi, 2018).

30. Greif, 2006b, 2006c; Greif and Tabellini, 2010, 2015.

31. Aubet, 2013; Hawk, 2015. For another example, see Greif's work on the Maghribi merchants of the 11th century in the Mediterranean (Greif, 1989, 1993, 2006c).

32. Ma, 2004 (p. 269), 2007.

33. Berman, 1983; Greif, 2003, 2006a, 2006b, 2006c; Greif and Tabellini, 2010, 2015; Hawk, 2015; Ma, 2004; Weber, 1978. Interestingly, in many places, laws and judicial procedures were extensions of religious beliefs and practices.

34. Faure, 1996; Greif, 2006b, 2006c; Ma, 2004; Rowe, 2002. In the less clannish and more individualistic regions of China (for example, the north), merchant organizations or guilds were based on residential origin instead of clans, but the underlying patterns were similar. Beyond this, the historical and anthropological record also reveals lots of group-specific exchange norms, which governed transactions of certain goods and services between prescribed groups such as castes or occupational clans.

35. Berman, 1983; Greif, 2006b, 2006c; Lynch, 2003; Mitterauer and Chapple, 2010; Moore, 2000; Pirenne, 1952.

36. Bartlett, 1993; Berman, 1983; Lilley, 2002; Pirenne, 1952; Stephenson, 1933.

37. Bosker, Buringh, and Van Zanden, 2013; Stasavage, 2016; Weber, 1958a.

38. Buringh and Van Zanden, 2009; Cantoni and Yuchtman, 2014; Greif, 2006b, 2006c; Greif and Tabellini, 2010; Lopez, 1976. It would take a few more centuries for Europe to pass the Islamic world (Bosker et al., 2013). However, there's some dispute about the precise magnitude of these estimates for urbanization. Some have argued that the urbanization rates for China are low due to the sprawling peri-urban areas, which were denser than in Europe (Ma, 2004). This doesn't affect the substance of my point. The crucial qualitative pattern holds even if the precise estimates are variable.

39. Data from Bairoch, Batou, and Chevre, 1988. Also see Buringh and Van Zanden, 2009; Cantoni and Yuchtman, 2014; Lynch, 2003. I'm counting all settlements over 1,000 people as "urban" here in an effort to capture the process at its earliest stages.

40. Guiso, Sapienza, and Zingales, 2016; Lynch, 2003.

41. Bartlett, 1993; Berman, 1983; Bosker et al., 2013; Greif and Tabellini, 2015; Lilley, 2002; Stasavage, 2016.

42. Bartlett, 1993; Berman, 1983; Lilley, 2002; Stephenson, 1933. See Stephenson, 1933, p. 25, for quotation.

43. Bartlett, 1993; Berman, 1983; Grierson, 1903; Stephenson, 1933.

44. Berman, 1983.

45. Bartlett, 1993.

46. Stephenson, 1933. Along the contested border with Wales, William the Conqueror's cousin William FitzOsbern began to set up shop as the new earl of Hereford. The new earl granted a charter to Hereford based on the Law of Breteuil, which itself was based on a charter from his home back in Normandy (France). The new Law of Hereford soon began diffusing throughout Wales and over to Ireland, creating dozens of "daughter" and "granddaughter" communities.

47. Bartlett, 1993; Berman, 1983; Greif, 2008; Lilley, 2002; Stephenson, 1933; Lynch, 2003.

48. Berman, 1983, p. 379; Stephenson, 1933.

49. Gelderblom, 2013.

50. Schulz, 2019. One worry is that the Church might have decided to place its bishoprics in places that appeared to have a bright future. However, the Church's goal was to spread everywhere, and consequently it opportunistically spread wherever it could. Jonathan's analyses account for factors that Church leaders might have used in making their decisions, such as a region's initial level of prosperity (in 500 CE), the presence of Roman roads, and a host of ecological and agricultural variables.

51. Data from Schulz, 2019.

52. Berman, 1983; Cantoni and Yuchtman, 2014; Stephenson, 1933. It has commonly been assumed that medieval guilds had strong monopolistic control and created protectionist tariffs. However, based on a quantitative analysis of the available

evidence on laws and charters in England, Richardson (2004) argues that the monopolistic impact of medieval guilds has been greatly overestimated. Crucially, while guilds could sometimes control production within their hometowns, their products still had to compete with those of similar guilds in other towns. For an alternative view, see Ogilvie, 2019.

53. Bosker et al., 2013; Cantoni and Yuchtman, 2014.

54. Adapted from Cantoni and Yuchtman, 2014.

55. Richardson, 2004.

56. Gibson, 2002; Kosfeld and Rustagi, 2015; Richardson, 2004; Rustagi et al., 2010. Single young men, who are numerous in this polygynous society, do often migrate to towns for employment, but they tend to remain socially and psychologically attached to their kin-based networks back home.

57. Berman, 1983; Clark, 2007a; Lopez, 1976.

58. Benson, 1989; Berman, 1983; Gelderblom, 2013. The economic historian Avner Greif describes long-distance trading as follows: "In such exchanges, a trader's decision to transact is independent of his partner's personal reputation. It is made without knowledge of that partner's past conduct, or the expectation of future trade with him, or the ability to report misconduct to future trading partners" (Greif, 2006c, pp. 221–22).

59. Gelderblom, 2013; Greif, 2002, 2003, 2006b, 2006c.

60. Berman, 1983; Cantoni and Yuchtman, 2014; Greif, 2003, 2006b, 2006c.

61. Cantoni and Yuchtman, 2014; Gelderblom, 2013; Jacob, 2010, pp. 11–12.

62. Benson, 1989; Berman, 1983; Gelderblom, 2013; Greif and Tabellini, 2015; Ma, 2007. On banking, see Rubin, 2017.

63. Jha, 2013.

64. Ahmed, 2009; Durante, 2010; Gelderblom, 2013; Greif and Tabellini, 2015; Guiso et al., 2016; Jha, 2013; Nunn and Wantchekon, 2011. Nunn and Wantchekon (2011) point out that proximity to oceans and rivers is associated with impersonal trust on every inhabited continent except Africa. This relationship probably doesn't emerge in Africa due to a combination of (1) Africa's lack of natural ports and navigable waterways (Sowell, 1998) and (2) the long-term effects of the slave trade—between 1500 and roughly 1800, proximity to the ocean in Africa meant a greater threat of enslavement. Meanwhile, in medieval Europe, historians observe that commercial ties "stimulated a welcoming attitude toward foreign traders and targeted efforts to adapt local institutions to their business needs" (Gelderblom, 2013, p. 4). For evidence on the effects of historical institutions and events on psychology, see Dell, 2010; Grosjean, 2011; Nunn, 2007, 2009; Nunn and Wantchekon, 2011.

65. This can be seen in the northern half of Italy, where free city-states first emerged from the ruins of the Carolingian Empire in the late ninth century. With ready access to Mediterranean trade, new inventions, and foreign institutions, these communities sped ahead of the rest of Europe in commerce, economic prosper-

ity, and the formation of new institutional forms. However, in some cases the voluntary associations were formed by powerful patrilineages that swore pacts to work together, rather than by individuals or nuclear families deciding to join. This may have laid the foundations for the later pushback by powerful Italian families (Guiso et al., 2016; Jacob, 2010). The lingering effects of kin-based institutions can be seen during the commercial revolution, when intensive kin-based institutions took over Tuscan merchant banks (Padgett and Powell, 2012). However, these merchant banks, unlike their Hui counterparts in China, lasted only a century before they were beaten out by more competitive organizations. Even after the Industrial Revolution, the entrepreneurial class of England sought to consolidate power through cousin marriage (Kuper, 2010).

10. Domesticating the Competition

1. Bellows and Miguel, 2006, 2009.
2. Bauer et al., 2014. These studies make extensive efforts to demonstrate that greater war exposure is essentially random, so there's little reason to worry that certain psychological patterns or motivations led individuals or their families into war. In the accounts of rebel attacks on villages, as noted, soldiers would typically enter the community and start firing at random, torching houses that happened to be in their path. The only exception to this seems to be community leaders, who were specifically targeted.
3. Of course, it's possible that violence was nonrandom in some hidden way, which is why true experiments are better than natural experiments. These issues are discussed by Bauer et al., 2016, 2014.
4. Cecchi, Leuveld, and Voors, 2016. In and of itself, this study didn't clearly demonstrate a causal relationship between war and decision-making. However, in light of the several lines of converging evidence for Sierra Leone, I'm using causal language here.
5. Bellows and Miguel, 2006, 2009.
6. Annan et al., 2011; Bauer et al., 2014, 2016; Bellows and Miguel, 2006, 2009; Blattman, 2009; Buhrmester et al., 2015; Cassar, Grosjean, and Whitt, 2013; Gilligan, Pasquale, and Samii, 2014; Voors et al., 2012; Whitehouse et al., 2014. Some of this work suggests that war may have its biggest psychological impact on children, adolescents, and young adults. In 2008, only six months after the Russian military bombed South Ossetia, our team studied Georgian schoolchildren using the same experimental games later deployed in Sierra Leone. Our experiments show that the attack had shifted the social behavior of Georgian children as young as six in ways similar to those seen among adults in Sierra Leone. Taken together, our findings in Georgia and Sierra Leone, where many of our adult participants had been children during the war, suggest that war has its biggest impact on people's psychology during a window that opens in middle childhood and extends into the early 20s (Bauer et al., 2014).

7. Bauer et al., 2014; Henrich, 2016; Henrich, Bauer et al., 2019; Lang, Kratky et al., 2015; Sosis and Handwerker, 2011.

8. These numbers and results derive from Bentzen (2013), but also see Bentzen (2019) for similar supportive analyses using a large sample and other additional data. Bentzen (2019) suggests the results may not hold strongly for Buddhists.

9. The results are further strengthened by studies of the effects of individual earthquakes on religious beliefs (Sibley and Bulbulia, 2012). For research linking tropical storms and earthquakes to social motivations, see Castillo and Carter, 2011; Rao et al., 2011; Vardy and Atkinson, 2019.

10. Henrich et al., 2019.

11. Henrich et al., 2019. The impact of war may also increase over time as people reflect on their experiences—exegetic reflection (Newson, Buhrmester, and Whitehouse, 2016).

12. Cassar et al., 2013; Henrich et al., 2019. Notably, within communities riven by violence, those more exposed to war distrusted their fellow villagers (those outside their clans) more than unknown strangers even a decade after the conflict. Thanks to Alessandra Cassar and Pauline Grosjean for helpful background information.

13. Cohen, 1984; Collier, 2007; Morris, 2014; Tilly, 1993; Turchin, 2015.

14. Dincecco and Onorato, 2016, 2018; Pirenne, 1952; Scheidel, 2019.

15. Dincecco and Onorato, 2016, 2018; MacFarlane, 2014; Tilly, 1993. Given recent findings for the impact of royal marriages on rates of conflict in Europe after 1500 (Benzell and Cooke, 2016), it's possible that the Church's constraints on marrying kinfolk, including affines, increased the frequency of conflict in the Early and High Middle Ages. Notably, after the Fourth Lateran Council and especially after the rise of Protestantism, these constraints were weakened.

16. I'm ignoring the short-lived Qin dynasty—thus the word "stable."

17. Fukuyama, 2011; Hui, 2005; Levenson and Schurmann, 1971; Morris, 2014.

18. Data from Dincecco and Onorato, 2016.

19. Dincecco and Onorato, 2016, 2018. These authors conducted a wide range of analyses that mitigate worries that this approach might not really be capturing the causal effects of war.

20. Martines, 2013.

21. To accomplish this, they sold some of their lands or used them as collateral on big loans, though eventually sovereigns figured out how to levy taxes (Blaydes and Paik, 2016). The need for elites to sell their lands—free and clear (often to merchants)—helped push along the Church's campaign against communal ownership (inheritance customs) and their preferred policies for individual ownership.

22. Blaydes and Paik, 2016. Ideally, we would have data on the mobilization of both elites and non-elites for war, so here the data on mobilization of elites stands in as a proxy for overall mobilization. After the Crusades, the volume of trade in Europe notably picked up, and cities like Flanders and Bruges became hubs for spices, silk,

porcelain, and other luxury goods that the crusaders encountered while traveling. The Crusades may also have consolidated people's understanding of "Europe" or "Christendom" as a cultural entity.

23. Blaydes and Paik, 2016; Bosker et al., 2013; Cahen, 1970; Dincecco and Onorato, 2016, 2018; Fried, Ettinger et al., 1994; Hoffman, 2015; Stasavage, 2016. The quotation is from Cahen (1970). There were politically autonomous territories that were effectively single cities in the Muslim world; but, these were ruled by emirs, not representative assemblies or parliaments (Bosker et al., 2013).

24. Churchill, 2015. The impact of war on the creation of progressive tax policies (Scheve and Stasavage, 2010) is likely a consequence of how war alters our psychology.

25. Aghion et al., 2018; Hoffman, 2015; McNeill, 1982; Stasavage, 2011, 2016.

26. Kroszner and Strahan, 1999. In 1994, this state-level process resulted in the Riegle-Neal Interstate Banking and Branching Efficiency Act, which eliminated restrictions on branching in all U.S. states.

27. Nelson and Winter, 1985; Richerson et al., 2016. It's well established that firms copy each other (Davis and Greve, 1997; Shenkar, 2010). Experiments show how prosocial behavior can diffuse through social networks (Fowler and Christakis, 2010).

28. Francois et al., 2011, 2018.

29. Thanks to Patrick Francois and Thomas Fujiwara for supplying their data (Francois et al., 2011, 2018).

30. Francois et al., 2011, 2018.

31. There is every reason to believe that humans are well calibrated to low-frequency and even one-shot interactions, based on what is known about our ancestral environments (Chudek, Zhao, and Henrich, 2013; Fehr and Henrich, 2003; Henrich, 2016).

32. Thanks to Patrick Francois and Thomas Fujiwara for providing their data (Francois et al., 2011).

33. The findings from Patrick's team are not due to increases in income generated by intergroup competition (Francois et al., 2011). In fact, based on their analyses, increases in income don't cause increases in trust (Francois, Fujiwara, and van Ypersele, 2018).

34. Bornstein and Benyossef, 1994; Bornstein, Budescu, and Zamir, 1997; Bornstein, Gneezy, and Nagel, 2002; Puurtinen and Mappes, 2009; Sääksvuori, Mappes, and Puurtinen, 2011.

35. Francois et al., 2011; Peysakhovich and Rand, 2016.

36. Muthukrishna et al., 2017.

37. Shleifer, 2004. Of course, CEO salaries are affected by many processes (Murphy, 2013; Murphy and Zabojnik, 2004).

38. Greenwood, Kanters, and Casper, 2006; Newson et al., 2016; Wann, 2006; Wann and Polk, 2007.

39. Finke and Stark, 2005; Norris and Inglehart, 2012.

40. Berman, 1983; Cantoni and Yuchtman, 2014; de la Croix, Doepke, and Mokyr, 2018; De Moor, 2008; Ekelund et al., 1996; Epstein, 1998; Gelderblom, 2013; Greif, 2006c; Greif and Tabellini, 2015; Kleinschmidt, 2000; Lynch, 2003; McNeill, 1982; Mokyr, 2013; Serafinelli and Tabellini, 2017; Van Zanden, 2009a, 2009b.

41. Van Zanden, 2009a, 2009b, Table 2.

42. Andersen et al., 2017; Mokyr, 2002; Van Zanden, 2009.

43. Andersen et al., 2017; Donkin, 1978; Herbermann et al., 1908; Mokyr, 2002; Woods, 2012. Also, en.wikipedia.org/wiki/Cistercians. Regarding the decline of the Cistercians: there are suggestions that the Cistercians, and especially the lay brothers, may have begun dipping too frequently into the copious amounts of wine they produced (Gimpel, 1976). Just as with urbanization and markets, the growth of monasteries accelerated in the High Middle Ages. However, the rapid growth of the Cistercians in the 10th to the 12th century was not urban at all but rural. The Cistercians preferred undeveloped land and often ended up in remote swamps. Thus these new monasteries are not merely an effect that "goes along" with urbanization and commerce. Instead, the proliferation of all these voluntary associations is driven by the same cause: the social and psychological changes wrought by the Church. Notably, while the spread of many monasteries was not associated with the growth of cities, it was most dramatic in regions that had long been under the Western Church, where the grassroots changes in the organization of the family had already occurred.

44. Weber, 1958b. Alongside monasteries, competition also occurred among parish churches. Residentially and relationally mobile, medieval Europeans apparently moved to parish churches they preferred (Ekelund et al., 1996).

45. The guild data are from the Database of English Guilds compiled by Gary Richardson ("Database English Guilds," 2016). The university data are from Verger (1991).

46. Richardson, 2004, 2005; Richardson and McBride, 2009. Religion played a central role in guild life (Ogilvie, 2019).

47. Berman, 1983; Cantoni and Yuchtman, 2014; Huff, 1993; Van Zanden, 2009; Verger, 1991; Woods, 2012.

48. Berman, 1983; Huff, 1993; Verger, 1991. Medieval Europeans appear to have acquired, recombined, and reinterpreted some of the key constituents of the university—as an institution—from Islamic and ultimately Central Asian societies (Beckwith, 2012). Like their counterparts in the Islamic world, the universities of premodern China never developed the independence of those in Europe (Hayhoe, 1989).

49. Lynch, 2003.

50. Alvard, 2011; Barnes, 1996; Tuzin, 1976, 2001. Ilahita's Tambaran, for example, prescribed competitions among the ritual groups in the form of yam-growing contests. Throughout this region, farmers had long competed to see who could

grow the biggest and longest yam, which typically weighed hundreds of pounds. In Ilahita, this yam-growing competition was turned into a team sport, but one that occurred among the ritual groups, not among the clans. The work was carried out in teams, and the competitive experience probably nurtured greater solidarity among members of the ritual groups. Because the members of these groups came from different clans, the team competition should have effectively tightened the interpersonal bonds among clans, strengthening Ilahita as a whole.

51. Greif and Tabellini, 2015; Liangqun and Murphy, 2006; Peng, 2004.

52. Goetzmann and Rouwenhorst, 2005; Stringham, 2015.

53. Christmas, 2014; Hofstadter, 1969. New religious associations erupted all over Europe during the 16th century. Wars were fought, monasteries were destroyed, and internal strife festered in communities with diverse religious faiths. However, in 1682, the Quaker William Penn obtained a grant from the English king to set up a colony in Pennsylvania. As a Quaker, he could have set up a theocratic state, as some Puritans had in New England. Instead, he wrote a charter of liberties for his new colony that, among other basic rights, guaranteed religious freedom. Philadelphia soon swelled with new arrivals—Quakers, Jews, Catholics, Huguenots, Amish, and Lutherans (a skilled bunch)—and flourished economically, outcompeting its less tolerant North American rivals.

54. Harris, 1998, p. 190; MacFarlane, 2014; www.baseball-reference.com/bullpen /origins_of_baseball.

11. Market Mentalities

1. Quoted in Smith, 1997, p. 17.

2. Boerner and Severgnini, 2015; Cipolla, 1977; Dohrn-van Rossum, 1996; Thompson, 1967.

3. Levine, 2008; Levine and Norenzayan, 1999. Ara and Bob also measured time thrift in a third way. They randomly picked 15 downtown banks in each city and compared the time on the bank's public clock to standard ("correct") time. This allowed them to calculate an average clock-deviance measure for each city. The idea here is that if people are more psychologically attuned to clock time, and more worried about each minute, they will set their clocks more accurately and correct them more frequently. In Zurich and Vienna, the clocks were off by 25 seconds or less on average. In Athens and Jakarta, the deviations were 2.5 to 3.5 minutes on average. In linking these differences to other aspects of psychology, my re-analysis reveals that more individualistic populations showed less clock deviance—consistent with time-thrift concerns—but we also found that "tighter" societies (with greater concerns for norm compliance) showed less clock deviance. Psychological tightness is increased by many factors, including historical kinship intensity (Chapter 7), as well as by environmental shocks and wars. So, the links to psychological and historical variation here are complex.

4. Levine and Norenzayan, 1999.

5. Cipolla, 1977; Dohrn-van Rossum, 1996; Kleinschmidt, 2000; Richardson, 2004, pp. 19–20. In the schools that spread in the wake of the Reformation (1517, see the Prelude), the start and end of the day were often marked by bells, which were tied to mechanical clocks. Teachers and tutors would flip sandglasses when they commenced instruction. A more precise view of time also appears in the written recipes for production. At the beginning of the 12th century, the recipe for the gold mixture used to illustrate book manuscripts mentions that the ore must be ground in a mill for "two to three hours." By the 15th century, time specifications are more common and increasingly precise. A recipe for gunpowder, for example, specifies that the sulfur, saltpeter, and ammonium chloride should be stirred over a fire for half an hour (Dohrn-van Rossum, 1996, pp. 307–308).

6. Boerner and Severgnini, 2015; Dohrn-van Rossum, 1996.

7. Thompson, 1967, pp. 58–59. For work on how people in different societies think about time, see Boroditsky, 2011.

8. Bourdieu, 1990, p. 222; Hallowell, 1937; Levine, 2008; Thompson, 1967, pp. 58–59; nobaproject.com/modules/time-and-culture.

9. www.franklinpapers.org/franklin/framedVolumes.jsp.

10. Smith, 2015.

11. de Vries, 1994, 2008; Glennie and Thrift, 1996; Thompson, 1967.

12. Alonso, 2013; Cooperrider, Marghetis, and Núñez, 2017; Dehaene et al., 2008; Droit-Volet, 2013; Glennie and Thrift, 1996; Han and Takahashi, 2012; Takahashi, 2005; Takahashi et al., 2009. Weber (1958b) noted the importance of clock time in his discussion of Protestantism and capitalism.

13. de Vries, 1994, 2008; Doepke and Zilibotti, 2008; Voth, 1998.

14. de Vries, 2008; Voth, 1998.

15. Bhui and Henrich, 2019. We found no relationship between commercial work and total work time for women in these small-scale societies, though we did find that women worked longer than men.

16. de Vries, 1994, 2008; Glennie and Thrift, 1996; Henrich, 1997; Pettegree, 2015; Sahlins, 1998; Thompson, 1967.

17. Clark, 1987. Similar patterns emerge for reaping in England (Clark, 1987) and France (Grantham, 1993). One alternative possibility is that people were better fed over time, due in part to the massive increases in calories available from new crops like corn and potatoes (Nunn and Qian, 2011).

18. Andersen et al., 2017; Donkin, 1978; Gimpel, 1976; Woods, 2012.

19. Andersen et al., 2017. I wanted to verify a few things about Andersen et al.'s analysis, so my lab team obtained the data. To it we added detailed data on the locations of monasteries for several non-Cistercian Orders, including the Cluniac, Dominican, and Franciscan Orders. This permitted us to compare the "Cistercian effects" with those created by non-Cistercian monasteries. When we statistically controlled for the presence of non-Cistercian monasteries, the impact

of the Cistercians actually intensified a bit. Moreover, though the non-Cistercian monks did create small positive effects on people's beliefs about hard work, these were tiny compared to the Cistercians and could only be distinguished from zero when we focused solely on Catholics. In this case, the Cistercian effect was 23 times larger than the non-Cistercian monastic effect. Second, we used an Albers equal-area conic projection for Europe instead of the Robinson projection used by Andersen et al. This gives a more accurate estimate of the land area of each region. Overall, our re-analysis confirms Andersen et al.'s findings. Thanks to Cammie Curtin for her work on this.

20. Data are drawn from Donkin, 1978. Thanks to Jeanet Bentzen for sharing her team's data.

21. The effects of market-thinking on work effort have also been explored by unconsciously priming people with impersonal "commerce." Priming people with money, and specifically cash, is an easy way to stoke up our commercial psychology and study its effects. The basic setup in money-priming experiments goes like this: Participants are randomly assigned to either (1) a money-priming condition in which they handle some cash, see images of cash, or unscramble phrases involving money, or (2) a control condition in which they do something quite similar to the experimental condition but without any monetary or market cues. Then, participants are given a difficult task to complete, and the researchers assess how long they persist, how efficiently they work, and how well they perform overall. Importantly, people are not paid for their performance in these tasks, but just reminded of money in some conditions. The results are generally consistent: when undergraduates from countries as diverse as the United States, India, Italy, and Turkey were primed with cash, they worked longer, harder, and faster on the subsequent tasks compared to those in the nonmoney (control) conditions. Not surprisingly, they also performed better overall on these tasks. The same results have been obtained using young children, which suggests that these cultural effects run deep (Gasiorowska et al., 2016; Vohs, 2015; Vohs et al., 2006, 2008).

22. Salali and Migliano, 2015. Deniz also found that the Bantu farmers living in the same town waited for the 5 cubes about 58 percent of the time, making them a bit more patient than the town-dwelling hunter-gatherers, the BaYaka. This also supports the notion that farming, especially certain kinds of farming, may fertilize the psychological ground for some kinds of institutions—like banks and savings accounts—by favoring a greater ability to defer gratification (Galor and Özak, 2016).

23. Godoy et al., 2004; Reyes-Garcia et al., 2007; Salali and Migliano, 2015; Tucker, 2012. Another study reports an increase in patience among immigrants to the United States from the former Soviet bloc. The longer that immigrants were in contact with WEIRD culture, the more patient they became, even after they returned home (Klochko, 2006).

24. Clark, 2007a; Elias, 1981; Pinker, 2011.

25. Clark, 2007a. There's a lot going on behind the scenes here, because these interest rates are only indirect estimates (Clark, 1987, 2007a). In a preindustrial agricultural economy with little inflation, where almost all productive wealth involves land, interest rates can be estimated from average returns on land or from rent charges on land. For example, if lands could be sold for $1,000 and can produce $100 per year—say, in commercial crops—then the estimated interest rate is 10 percent. Similarly, a rent charge is like a loan: I give you $100 and you put your lands up as collateral and promise to pay me $1 per year, forever. Under this deal, the annual interest rate is estimated to be 1 percent. For a useful discussion, see faculty.econ.ucdavis.edu/faculty/gclark/ecn110a/readings/chapter9.pdf.

26. Clark, 2007a; Eisner, 2001, 2003. To examine how these calculations were made, see Clark, 1987, 2007a. I averaged the estimates for interest rates based on both land returns and rent charges, and smoothed the curves by using a running average of seven estimates.

27. Clark, 2007a; Dohmen et al., 2015. Clark suggests that these psychological changes are likely due to genetic changes, but he leaves open the possibility that it's culture (Clark, 2007b). To the contrary, several converging lines of evidence suggest that cultural evolution is playing the driving role here. I deal with the possible influence of culture on genes in the last chapter.

28. Clark, 2007a; Rubin, 2017; Van Zanden, 2009. The interest rate data run to 2001, but due to the running average, the ending year on the plot is 1974.

29. Arantes et al., 2013; Block and Gerety, 1995; Blondel et al., 2007; Casey et al., 2011; Cohn et al., 2014; Dohmen et al., 2015; Godoy et al., 2004; Hanoch et al., 2012; Khadjavi and Lange, 2013; Mischel et al., 1989; Pratt and Cullen, 2000; Reyes-García et al., 2007; Reynolds, 2006; Wichary et al., 2015.

30. Blattman, Jamison, and Sheridan, 2016; Squires, 2016.

31. Eisner, 2001, 2003.

32. Eisner, 2001, 2003; Elias, 1981; Lopez, 1976, p. 124.

33. Hirschman, 1982, p. 1465.

34. Some might argue that this shift in patience and self-control was driven by a change in people's life history strategies. If this were true, we would expect the elite to already possess low rates of violence, since they were all well fed. This was not the case. The elite, in fact, continued dueling into the 19th century and, as noted, didn't make long-term financial investments. By contrast, both the decline in violence and the long-term investments came from the urban middle class: the artisans, merchants, bankers, lawyers, officials, and accountants (Appiah, 2010; Doepke and Zilibotti, 2008; Pinker, 2011).

35. Heine and Buchtel, 2009; Smaldino, 2019.

36. Barth, 1965; Carneiro, 1987; Hallpike, 1968; Henrich and Boyd, 2008; Moll-Murata, 2008; Prak and Van Zanden, 2013; Roy, 2013. In 18th-century India, one of several similar ethnographic descriptions reads, ". . . Indians do not follow that general and superficial method of education by which children are treated as

if they were all intended for the same condition, and for discharging the same duties; but those of each cast are from their infancy formed for what they are to be during their whole lives" (Roy, 2013, p. 74). Meanwhile, in late Imperial China, urban occupations remained associated with particular regional or clan origins (Moll-Murata, 2013; Winter, 2013).

37. de la Croix et al., 2018; Lopez, 1976; Mokyr, 2002.
38. MacFarlane, 1978; Van Zanden and De Moor, 2010; Winter, 2013.
39. Smaldino et al., 2019.
40. There are debates among psychologists about the nature of personality and its origins, so I'm characterizing a common but not universal view (Heine, 2016; Ross and Nisbett, 1991). One study of nonstudent adults failed to identify the WEIRD-5 personality configuration in samples from Ghana, Kenya, Sri Lanka, Yunnan, Laos, Vietnam, the Philippines, Colombia, Macedonia, Serbia, and Georgia (Laajaj et al., 2019). However, the same paper did find the WEIRD-5 when using highly biased online samples from the same countries. Such divergent findings underline my point from the main text. The online participants were young, highly educated, and literate in German, Dutch, English, or Spanish—the survey was only available in those languages. The sample was further biased by the fact that online survey takers participated out of an interest in learning about themselves and their personalities—which is a WEIRD cultural trait associated with individualism and built by the very processes I'm describing. When researchers selectively sample from populations with full access to diverse social niches and occupations, they can recover the WEIRD-5. For interesting work on the geographic variation in personality, see Obschonka et al., 2018; Rentfrow et al., 2017.
41. Heine and Buchtel, 2009; Schmitt et al., 2007.
42. Gurven et al., 2013; Gurven et al., 2009. Two common critiques to the work by Gurven and his collaborators are: (1) WEIRD-5 traits are highly genetically heritable, and (2) nonhuman animals reveal the WEIRD-5 personality structure. The first point represents a general failure to recognize that many purely culturally acquired skills, like basketball and TV watching, are also highly genetically heritable (Hatemi et al., 2015; Plomin, Defries, and McLearn, 2000; Plomin et al., 2016). Of course, genes create myriad influences through many indirect paths, but the existence of those paths depends on institutions, ecology, and many other factors. With regard to nonhumans, I've yet to see persuasive evidence of the WEIRD-5 in animals that can't be explained by the use of human coders from urbanized and occupationally diverse societies (Weiss et al., 2012). Of course, this doesn't imply that animals lack dispositional traits of various kinds, like novelty-seeking and gregariousness. This phenomenon of observer-projected personalities applies to people, too. In a study among the Ache forager-horticulturalists in Paraguay, when the Ache themselves did the usual personality inventory, the WEIRD-5 didn't emerge. However, when the anthropologist who had worked

closely with the Ache for 30 years rated them using the same inventory, the WEIRD-5 emerged in full (Bailey et al., 2013).

43. Gurven et al., 2013. Notably, in discussing the challenges of their work, Gurven's team notes how Tsimane' participants struggled with the "dispositional" terminology used in the standard personality inventory. Tsimane' apparently just don't think about cross-contextual characteristics the way that WEIRD people do. Consequently, when you give them the identical personality inventory a year later, their answers are less consistent than those of typical WEIRD participants—but that could be because the people themselves don't value consistency across time and context as much as WEIRD people.

44. Lukaszewski et al., 2017. Note that most WEIRD societies are below the line in Figure 11.4—look at the black diamonds. This suggests that something, over and above the current levels of urbanization and occupational diversity, may be pushing down the interdependence among personality dimensions. One possibility is simply that these particularly WEIRD places have a longer history of widespread urbanization, relational mobility, and occupational choice—so cultural evolution has had more time to mold personality configurations in these populations. Interestingly, the correlations among some pairs of personality dimensions rise more rapidly with declining urbanization than do those between other dimensions. As urbanization declines, the dimensions of agreeableness, conscientiousness, and openness seem to collapse into each other more rapidly than do those for extroversion and neuroticism. These results are particularly striking because—as I noted— these studies didn't randomly sample adults around each country. Instead, most of these samples were urban-dwelling undergraduates. If we instead randomly sampled adults from these countries, I suspect that the results would be even more dramatic.

45. Thanks to Mike Gurven for providing the data (Lukaszewski et al., 2017). Here, for medieval Europe, I'm calculating urbanization rates based on the percentage of the population in cities over 10,000 people (instead of over 1,000 people as in Figure 9.5) to improve comparability with contemporary estimates of urbanization rates.

46. Choi, Nisbett, and Norenzayan, 1999; Morris and Peng, 1994.

47. Marlowe, 2010; Woodburn, 1982, 1998, p. 54, 2016.

48. Apicella, Azevedo et al., 2014.

49. Apicella, Azevedo et al., 2014; Plott and Zeiler, 2007.

50. Harbaugh, Krause, and Vesterlund, 2001; Maddux et al., 2010; Morewedge and Giblin, 2015.

51. Smith et al., 2018; Woodburn, 1998.

12. Law, Science, and Religion

1. Tocqueville, 1835, p. 279.

2. Rockmore et al., 2017.

3. Pinker, 2018.

4. For examples, see MacFarlane, 1978, 2014; McCloskey, 2007; Tierney, 1997.

5. Bartlett, 1993; Berman, 1983; Lilley, 2002; Stephenson, 1933; Tierney, 1997.

6. Tierney, 1997, p. 76.

7. Boswell, 1988; Burguiere and Klapisch-Zuber, 1996; Gellhorn, 1987; Greif and Tabellini, 2015; Lape, 2002; Slingerland, 2008, 2014. Similarly, the kinfolk of Chinese officials received penalties depending on the official's rank and the closeness of the perpetrator's relationship to him. Of course, these biases still emerge in WEIRD societies today, but it's not part of the formal law, and few find it acceptable. Like Chinese fathers, both Roman and Greek fathers in the ancient world had broad authority to kill their children, abandon them, or sometimes sell them into slavery (Boswell, 1988; Burguiere and Klapisch-Zuber, 1996; Lape, 2002). For an insiders' take on thinking and reasoning in China during the early 20th century, see Yutang, 1936.

8. Of course, the founding fathers struggled with some glaring inconsistencies, including their participation in the institution of slavery. But, this contradiction bothered them and many other analytical thinkers, which is crucial. They knew it would eventually have to be resolved, either by ending slavery or by concluding that slaves were a different kind of creation and thus not subject to the self-evident assertion about unalienable rights. Less analytic thinkers are just not so bothered by category contradictions (Buchtel and Norenzayan, 2008; Ji, Nisbett, and Su, 2001; Nisbett, 2003).

9. Tierney, 1997, p. 56.

10. Berman, 1983; Tierney, 1997. Berman (1983, p. 195) writes, "As God rules through law, so ecclesiastical and secular authorities, ordained by him, declare legal principles and impose appropriate sanctions and remedies for their violation. They cannot look directly into men's souls, as God can, but they can find ways to approximate his judgment."

11. Barrett et al., 2016; Curtin et al., 2019.

12. Berman, 1983, p. 150.

13. Berman, 1983, Chapters 3 and 4; Tierney, 1997. Berman writes, "On the one hand, the Romans did not use cases in order to illustrate principles or to test them by going back a step, so to speak, in order to see their applications. On the other hand, they reduced their cases to bare holdings, without treating them in their fullness..." (Berman, 1983, p. 139).

14. Nisbett, 2003; Yutang, 1936. To see what I mean, consider the famous magistrate and the Mob dilemma: "An unidentified member of an ethnic group is known to be responsible for a murder that occurred in a town . . . Because the town has a history of severe ethnic conflict and rioting, the town's Police Chief and Judge know that if they do not immediately identify and punish a culprit, the townspeople will start anti-ethnic rioting that will cause great damage to property owned by members of the ethnic group, and a considerable number of serious injuries and deaths in the ethnic population . . . The Police Chief and Judge are faced with a

dilemma. They can falsely accuse, convict, and imprison Mr. Smith, an innocent member of the ethnic group, in order to prevent the riots. Or they can continue hunting for the guilty man, thereby allowing the anti-ethnic riots to occur, and do the best they can to combat the riots until the guilty man is apprehended . . . The Police Chief and Judge decide to falsely accuse, convict, and imprison Mr. Smith, the innocent member of the ethnic group, in order to prevent the riots. They do so, thereby preventing the riots and preventing a considerable number of ethnic group deaths and serious injuries" (Doris and Plakias, 1998, p. 324). What do you think of the Police Chief and the Judge?

Americans were much more likely to judge the Police Chief and Judge harshly for convicting an innocent man. In China, peace and harmony overrode individual rights and justice in the minds of many. Differences like these flow directly from our intuitions about the prominence of the individual, the importance of his or her rights, and the centrality of impartial rules over a more particularistic morality (Doris and Plakias, 1998).

15. Berman, 1983; Fukuyama, 2011. As voluntary associations emerged and spread, both the Church and secular rulers began to work out new laws to deal with these collectives. With the early spread of bishoprics and monasteries across western Europe, the Church took the lead in the late 11th and 12th centuries by developing a branch of canon law dealing with voluntary associations—legally "corporations." Putting those new university-trained lawyers to work, the Church developed an integrated body of law for dealing with religious fraternities, student bodies, monasteries, parish churches, and almshouses. The lawyers had to figure out questions such as: Could these entities own property, inherit land, make contracts, break contracts, commit crimes, and be punished? If so, how would such situations relate to individual members or the corporate leadership? Further, was the corporation responsible for the actions of its members, for their crimes and debts? To address these issues, the Church developed and defined a new understanding of the "corporation."

These new laws were informed by several sources, especially Roman law. However, the canonists rejected Roman precedents in several important ways. For example, canon law rejected the Roman notion that voluntary associations could gain legal standing only by royal decree. Instead, any group, through their voluntary commitments (often taken in sacred oaths), could constitute a corporation and gain legal standing—or what is called a "legal personality." Canon law also stipulated that corporations could make new laws for members and punish law-breakers. This was a good move, since towns and cities were already doing this (Berman, 1983).

16. Barker and Goldstein, 2001; Huff, 1993. Some suggest that Aristarchus of Samos also proposed a heliocentric version of the solar system, in the third century BCE.

17. Wootton, 2015.

18. Blaydes and Paik, 2016; Dilcher, 1997; Isaacs and Prak, 1996; Serafinelli and Tabellini, 2017; Stasavage, 2011. Admittedly, this was complicated by the effects of merchant guilds on economic performance and the practical challenges of geography (Stasavage, 2011, 2014, 2016).

19. Berman, 1983.

20. Ansary, 2010, p. 352.

21. Ansary, 2010, p. 352; Ben-Bassat and Dahan, 2012.

22. Heine, 2016; Henrich, Heine, and Norenzayan, 2010a. In contrast to American parents, research in Vanuatu shows that adults think that children who are better conformists are "smarter" (Clegg, Wen, and Legare, 2017; Wen, Clegg, and Legare, 2017).

23. Campos-Ortiz et al., 2013; Dal Bó, Foster, and Putterman, 2010; Iyengar and De-Voe, 2003; Iyengar, Lepper, and Ross, 1999; Vollan et al., 2017.

24. Schulz, 2019.

25. Bosker et al., 2013; Cahen, 1970, p. 520; Schulz, 2019; Van Zanden, Buringh, and Bosker, 2012.

26. Schulz, 2019; Woodley and Bell, 2012.

27. Schulz, 2019.

28. Thanks to Jonathan Schulz for this data.

29. Rustagi and Veronesi, 2017. A similar pattern appears in northern Italy. There, the cities most influenced by the MFP—with a bishopric—were more likely to construct formal self-governing institutions, which usually had some participatory character. However, beyond this, achieving self-governance seems to have created long-term psychological effects on citizens. At the turn of the second millennium, Italian cities that had managed to achieve self-governance during the Middle Ages not only possessed more nonprofit organizations per 1,000 people—more voluntary associations—but also had adult populations that were more likely to donate their organs to strangers—stronger impersonal prosociality. Children from these historically free cities also cheated less on national mathematics examinations—greater impersonal honesty (Guiso et al., 2016).

30. Bosker et al., 2013; Guiso et al., 2016; Van Zanden et al., 2012.

31. Durant, 2014; MacCulloch, 2005; McGrath, 2007; Weber, 1958b.

32. The seeds of Protestantism germinated all over Europe, particularly where the Church had transformed people's psychology. But, sometimes these seedlings were stamped out by a powerful bishop or an absolutist state, often in alliance with each other. In France, for example, the Huguenots (reformed Calvinists) sprung up in many places, especially in the south and west, accounting for as much as 10 percent of the population. Sadly, relentless persecution by the Crown all but eliminated French Protestantism by the death of Louis XV in 1774 (Hornung, 2014; Scoville, 1953; Squicciarini and Voigtländer, 2015).

33. Andersen et al., 2017; Baumol, 1990; Kieser, 1987; Pettegree, 2015; Weber, 1958. Reformation ideas diffused exactly where you'd expect them to: 50 of the 65 free cities in the Holy Roman Empire adopted Protestant ideas. In these places,

reformers had to convince councils of guildsmen, merchants, and other citizens. This is not to suggest that Protestantism could have spread simply by winning the war of ideas. The Church might have choked Protestantism in its crib, as it had with other competitors, if it hadn't been for the invading Ottoman Turks (Iyigun, 2008). Thus the binding effects created by war with Islam (Chapter 10), or the threat of it, may have allowed Protestantism to survive those precarious early years when it was weak and vulnerable.

34. Burguiere and Klapisch-Zuber, 1996.

35. Becker et al., 2016.

36. Similar effects emerge even when the quality of formal institutions is used to explain psychological variation. Protestantism stands out over and above the impact of government effectiveness (Hruschka and Henrich, 2013b).

37. Algan and Cahuc, 2014; Arruñada, 2010; Guiso, Sapienza, and Zingales, 2003.

38. Cohen, 2015; Cohen and Hill, 2007; Cohen and Rozin, 2001; Li et al., 2012. For related work see Sanchez-Burks, 2002, 2005; Uhlmann and Sanchez-Burks, 2014. Jimmy Carter was quoted in the epigraph of Cohen and Rozin (2001), based on an interview in *Playboy* magazine.

39. Baumol, 1990; Caicedo, 2017; Kieser, 1987; Tocqueville, 1835; Uhlmann et al., 2010; Uhlmann and Sanchez-Burks, 2014. The Jesuit missions had many of the same psychological and economic effects as Protestantism, including when compared head-to-head with other monastic orders like the Franciscans (Caicedo, 2017).

40. Ashkanasy et al., 2004; Casey et al., 2011; Dohmen et al., 2015.

41. Spenkuch, 2017; Van Hoorn and Maseland, 2013. Also see Becker and Woessmann, 2009; Nunziata and Rocco, 2014; Schaltegger and Torgler, 2010.

42. Basten and Betz, 2013. Swiss Protestants also tend to vote against laws that would favor greater redistribution, such as unemployment insurance, disability insurance, and capital gains taxes.

43. Akçomak et al., 2016.

44. Becker et al., 2016; Becker and Woessmann, 2009; Cantoni, 2015; Cavalcanti, Parente, and Zhao, 2007; de Pleijt, 2016; C. Young, 2009. Interestingly though, Protestantism probably didn't have noteworthy effects on the growth of European cities in the centuries following 1517, since urban areas had long been on the vanguard of cultivating values, practices, and motivations related to hard work, punctuality (clock diffusion), impersonal trust, creativity, independence, individualism, and literacy. Plus, some cities had already been influenced by the Brethren of the Common Life and related movements, so a booster shot from Protestantism would have been superfluous.

Protestantism also had some important effects on economic growth by freeing up large amounts of land and shutting down educational pathways that led into the Church. When rulers turned Protestant, they seized the lands held by monasteries and other Church-related organizations. Sometimes these lands were sold off, which put more wealth into the hands of the gentry or entrepreneurial class (Heldring et al., 2018). Or rulers used the lands for administrative centers and palaces (Cantoni, Dittmar, and Yuchtman, 2018).

45. MacCulloch, 2005; McGrath, 2007; Woodberry, 2012. Of course, despite the broad psychological currents, many Protestant movements quickly became oppressive and authoritarian as they tried to establish a new orthodoxy. However, the psychological genie was out of the bottle.

46. Becker and Woessmann, 2016; Torgler and Schaltegger, 2014. Additional analyses further suggest that the suicide-inducing effects of Protestantism can be suppressed by frequently attending church. In Protestant regions where people regularly attend Sunday rituals, suicide rates are comparable to those among Catholics. Moreover, those who attend rituals more frequently consider suicide to be less acceptable or justifiable. Notably, today, the beliefs of Protestants and Catholics in Europe are converging, so the labels are becoming less meaningful.

47. Israel, 2010; Pinker, 2018.

48. Davies, 2004; Israel, 2010; Lape, 2002; Tierney, 1997.

13. Escape Velocity

1. Hume, 1987, p. 34.

2. Pinker, 2018, www.gapminder.org/data.

3. Data from www.gapminder.org/data.

4. The answer can't be that Early Modern Europeans were "evil." First, tyrannical emperors gripped with the thirst for conquest and subjugation have been commonplace throughout human history (Hoffman, 2015; Keeley, 1997; McNeill, 1982, 1991; Pinker, 2011). This wasn't new. Second, even if "evilness" had emerged in Europe, such an explanation just backs the question up to why European societies evolved this unfortunate trait in the first place and how it resulted in Europe's immense economic and military power.

5. Lewis, 2001, p. 52.

6. Khaldûn, 1377.

7. Acemoglu, Johnson, and Robinson, 2005; Acemoglu and Robinson, 2012; Allen, 2009; Hoffman, 2015; Landes, 1998; Mitterauer and Chapple, 2010; Mokyr, 2016; Pinker, 2018; Robinson, 2011; Sowell, 1998.

8. Boyd, Richerson, and Henrich, 2011; Henrich, 2016; Muthukrishna and Henrich, 2016.

9. Creanza, Kolodny, and Feldman, 2017; Henrich, 2004, 2016; Kolodny, Creanza, and Feldman, 2015; Muthukrishna and Henrich, 2016. In mathematical models and laboratory experiments, populations can be "too" interconnected, leading to lower rates of innovation because diverse approaches don't develop independently (Derex and Boyd, 2016). While it's possible to confirm this theoretical

finding in laboratory experiments, I've not seen any evidence that it's relevant in the real world. Real human populations naturally fragment and fracture due to the evolutionary dynamics of language, tribalism, political collapse, and ethnicity (McElreath et al., 2003). The problem that we humans have always faced is getting together and sustaining large-scale cooperation (Boyd, 2017; Turchin, 2015), not breaking ourselves down into fractured and parochial local groups.

10. Basalla, 1988; Henrich, 2009; Mokyr, 1990. This has become somewhat less true since about the mid-19th century, with the development of top-down science, but it was certainly still true prior to 1800 (Mokyr, 2002).

11. Akcigit, Kerr, and Nicholas, 2013; Basalla, 1988; Diamond, 1997, 1999; Hargadon, 2003; Meyers, 2007; Miu, Gulley, Laland, and Rendell, 2018; Mokyr, 1990, 2002; Muthukrishna and Henrich, 2016; Sneader, 2005; Williams, 1987. For an example of the myth in action, in perky prose, see Pinker (1997, p. 209).

12. Briggs and Burke, 2009; Burke, 2012; Cipolla, 1994; Diamond, 1999; Dittmar and Seabold, 2016; Pettegree, 2015; Rubin, 2014. Gutenberg was also lucky that European scripts contain only a few dozen characters unlike the thousands in Chinese, and a thriving paper industry had already developed in Europe based on Chinese papermaking techniques that were transmitted to Europe via the Islamic world. European papermaking combined the Chinese-Islamic techniques with water mills to mechanize production. Prior to Gutenberg, movable type had been cast in bronze in 14th-century Korea, apparently an improvement on the baked-clay molds developed in 11th-century China.

13. Basalla, 1988; Mokyr, 2002, 2011, 2016; Rolt and Allen, 1977; Wootton, 2015). After tracing the many components of the steam engine back in time, the historian Joseph Needham concluded, "No single man was the 'father of the steam-engine'; no single civilization either" (1964, p. 50). But, somehow all those pieces came together in 18th-century Britain.

14. Baines, 1835; Mokyr, 2002.

15. Goodyear, 1853; Nunn and Qian, 2010; Saccomandi and Ogden, 2014. Mayan societies had developed a vulcanization process at least 200 years before Columbus (Hosler, Burkett, and Tarkanian, 1999). In a case of possible double invention, a Brit named Thomas Hancock received a patent for a similar vulcanization process eight weeks before Goodyear, though some evidence suggests that he may have reverse-engineered the process using samples that trace back to Goodyear.

16. Blake-Coleman, 1992; Conot, 1979; Diamond, 1997; Hargadon, 2003.

17. Henrich, 2016; Meisenzahl and Mokyr, 2012; Mokyr, 2002; Muthukrishna and Henrich, 2016.

18. Allen, 1983; Nuvolari, 2004; Sasson and Greif, 2011.

19. Economic historians have long argued that Europe was stuck at zero growth—in a Malthusian Trap—until about 1800 (Clark, 2007a; Galor and Moav, 2002). However, a growing body of evidence suggests that some populations exited the

trap more gradually, with positive growth extending back into the Middle Ages (Fouquet and Broadberry, 2015; Humphries and Weisdorf, 2017; Van Zanden, 2009a).

20. Algan and Cahuc, 2010, 2014; Basalla, 1988; Cantoni and Yuchtman, 2014; Cipolla, 1994; Gelderblom, 2013; Gimpel, 1976; Guiso et al., 2004; Guiso, Sapienza, and Zingales, 2008; Karlan, Ratan, and Zinman, 2014; Lopez, 1976; Mokyr, 1990, 2002; White, 1962.

21. By the 18th century, crucial innovations were bubbling up almost constantly: Fahrenheit's thermometer (1709), Harrison's sea clock to measure longitude (1736), Roebuck's process for making sulfuric acid (1746), Whitney's cotton gin (1793), Jenner's smallpox vaccine (1798), and Medhurst's air compressor (1799), to name just a few headliners.

22. Andersen et al., 2017; Buringh and Van Zanden, 2009; Cantoni and Yuchtman, 2014; Mokyr, 2016; Wootton, 2015.

23. Coy, 1989; de la Croix et al., 2018; Henrich, 2009.

24. Muthukrishna et al., 2013. There is now a large experimental literature on this effect (Derex et al., 2013, 2014; Kempe and Mesoudi, 2014).

25. There is a simple way in which cumulative cultural evolution does indeed make individuals "smarter"—i.e., more likely to invent something new (Henrich, 2016; Muthukrishna and Henrich, 2016). Most new ideas and inventions, whether they are industrial machines, scientific theories, or artistic styles, represent recombinations from an existing stock of ideas, approaches, tools, and ways of thinking. As this cultural stock of ideas and tools grows, the number of possible new recombinations skyrockets. The wheels on the first carts, for example, would eventually be re-deployed with other elements for pottery, waterpower, wind power, pulleys, and gears. Not only do individuals from societies with larger cultural stocks have more tools and concepts to work with—wheels, springs, pulleys, levers, elastic energy, steam power, nuclear fusion, etc.—but they even have more concepts to think with. Mechanical clocks shaped how people thought about the universe, steam engines shaped how they thought about digestion, and digital computers continue to shape how we think about thinking (brains). The larger the stock of tools, concepts, and metaphors that people have access to, the more likely they are to create or bumble across something new and useful.

26. Laslett, 1977; Laslett and Wall, 1972; MacFarlane, 1978; Mitterauer and Chapple, 2010; Mitterauer and Sieder, 1982; Lynch, 2003.

27. Acemoglu et al., 2013; De Moor and Van Zanden, 2010; Falk et al., 2018; Hajnal, 1982; Laslett, 1977; Laslett and Wall, 1972; Mitterauer and Sieder, 1982.

28. Donkin, 1978; Gimpel, 1976; Mokyr, 1990; Woods, 2012.

29. de la Croix et al., 2018; Epstein, 1998; Van Zanden, 2009a, 2009b.

30. Coy, 1989; de la Croix et al., 2018; Epstein, 1998, 2013; Moll-Murata, 2013; Ogilvie, 2019; Prak and Van Zanden, 2013; Roy, 2013; Van Zanden, 2009a, 2009b.

31. Ogilvie, 2019. As part of apprenticeship institutions, social norms often made traveling a "moral and social obligation" during the medieval period. Later, guilds increasingly enforced this traveling requirement. Guilds sometimes facilitated this process in several ways, including by giving journeymen official credentials that were recognized within their regions and by developing reciprocal agreements among guilds and masters (de la Croix et al., 2018).

32. de la Croix et al., 2018; Epstein, 1998; Leunig et al., 2011. In 18th-century France, over 80 percent of journeymen had been born somewhere other than the town or city where they were currently working. Some argue that craftsmen were more concentrated in European cities than in Chinese cities due to differences in the nature of war (de la Croix et al., 2018)—this relates to my discussion of war in Chapter 10.

33. Cipolla, 1994; de la Croix et al., 2018; Epstein, 1998; Leunig et al., 2011.

34. Bosker et al., 2013.

35. Meisenzahl and Mokyr, 2012; Mokyr, 1995, 2002, 2011, 2013.

36. Bettencourt, 2013; Bettencourt, Lobo, and Strumsky, 2007; Gomez-Lievano, Patterson-Lomba, and Hausmann, 2017; Pan et al., 2013.

37. Thanks to Andrés Gómez for these data. The patent data are "fractionated" between cities if a patent included more than one inventor. So, if a patent has three inventors, each of their home cities gets one-third of a patent. Three data points were left off the plot for cities of 10,000 people or fewer.

38. Bettencourt, Lobo, Helbing et al., 2007; Carlino, Chatterjee, and Hunt, 2007; Collard et al., 2012; Dowey, 2017; Henrich, 2016; Kline and Boyd, 2010; Lind and Lindenfors, 2010; Lobo et al., 2013; Mokyr, 1995; Simon and Sullivan, 1989; Squicciarini and Voigtländer, 2015; van Schaik et al., 2003. The fact that these patterns extend back into the preindustrial world isn't surprising, since the underlying cultural evolutionary principles applied here can also explain the differences in technological complexity among traditional farming populations around the world. There is, however, a lively debate about the influence of population size and interconnectedness among hunter-gatherers on technology (Henrich et al., 2016).

39. Thanks to Noel Johnson and Mark Koyama for supplying these data (Johnson and Koyama, 2017).

40. Epstein, 1998; Gimpel, 1976; Kelly and Ó Gráda, 2016; Mokyr, 1990; Van Zanden, 2009a, 2009b.

41. Cantoni and Yuchtman, 2014; Mokyr, 2016.

42. Inkster, 1990; Mokyr, 2016. Also see en.wikipedia.org/wiki/Marino_Ghetaldi and en.wikipedia.org/wiki/Jan_Bro%C5%BCek. Naturally, the pulsing of this informational network quickened as it catalyzed the creation of new transportation and communication technologies. The development of canals, locks, stagecoaches, and eventually railroads dramatically thickened the nerves in the

collective brain. In Britain, for example, the stagecoach from London to Edinburgh took 10 to 12 days in 1750, but by 1836 the trip took less than two days (45.5 hours, to be precise), at which point the stagecoach met its match when it collided with the steam locomotive. Similarly, in France, the travel times between many cities were halved between 1765 and 1785 (Daunton, 1995; Mokyr, 2011).

43. Dowey, 2017; Mokyr, 2002, 2011, 2016; Pettegree, 2015. The first known reference to the Republic of Letters is dated 1417 in Italy, but things don't seem to crank up for a few centuries, at least based on current historical evidence. In 1697, the Reverend Thomas Bray called for the establishment of 400 lending libraries throughout Britain. He argued that by making knowledge more accessible, the libraries would "raise a Noble Spirit of Emulation in those Learned Societies and would excite more of the members thereof to exert themselves in being serviceable to the world" (quoted in Mokyr, 2011, p. 299).

44. Dowey, 2017; Mokyr, 2011, 2016.

45. Figure adapted from Mokyr, 2011. www.references.net/societies/1600_1699 .html.

46. Mokyr, 2016.

47. Mokyr, 2011, 2016.

48. Dowey, 2017.

49. Dowey, 2017; Inkster, 1990; Simon and Sullivan, 1989. The presence of public libraries and Masonic lodges—which each likely diffused knowledge in their own ways—may also have had some influence, although their effect is harder to distinguish from all the other factors. In 1717, Freemasons founded their first Great Lodge in London, and the organization proliferated from there. By 1767, there were 440 such lodges in England—206 in London and 234 in the provinces. By 1800, Freemasons counted many "leading men of science" among their 50,000 members.

50. Dowey, 2017; Jacob, 2000; Merton, 1938; Mokyr, 2016. For research linking the density of engineers to innovation, see Maloney and Caicedo, 2017.

51. Squicciarini and Voigtländer, 2015. I'm referring to the quarto edition of the *Encyclopédie* in the main text. Though the earliest version of the *Encyclopédie* went mostly to a small number of wealthy foreigners, the quarto edition (1777–79) was more affordable. Greater innovativeness also appears to have nourished human growth, literally: between 1819 and 1826, French soldiers from provinces with more *Encyclopédie* subscribers were taller than conscripts from less well-subscribed provinces. This means they were better fed and healthier as children, which suggests that this innovation-induced prosperity was likely felt broadly across social classes. Interestingly, though the *Encyclopédie* was more famous, it was actually a French makeover of the *Cyclopadeia*, first published in London in 1728 (Mokyr, 2011, 2016). Here again, we see the power of imitation. Finally, the results using

the *Encyclopédie* can be confirmed using another important publication: the *Descriptions des arts et métiers* is a multivolume collection of 116 folios and supplements published by the Parisian Royal Academy of Sciences between 1761 and 1788. These volumes covered the industrial arts, ranging from metallurgy and milling to mining and weaving. French cities in which more people purchased copies of the *Descriptions* experienced faster economic growth during the century after 1750.

All of these findings for France, for the knowledge societies and subscriptions to both *Descriptions* and the *Encyclopédie*, hold independent of the cities' initial prosperity, average literacy rates, and geographic locations as well as whether they possessed universities or printing presses, among other factors. Crucially, none of these three interconnectedness measures—membership in knowledge societies or subscriptions to the *Encyclopédie* or *Descriptions*—are associated with economic growth prior to their creation. For example, *Encyclopédie* subscriptions cannot account for economic prosperity or the height of soldiers prior to 1750. This is important, because one might worry that knowledge societies and literary material merely spread to already prosperous places or tracked longer-running historical trends. These analyses suggest that, rather than capturing something historically deep about these different parts of France, we are seeing the effects of how different cities plugged themselves into Europe's collective brain.

52. Quoted in Scoville, 1953, pp. 443–44; Squicciarini and Voigtla, 2015. Huguenots in 18th-century France had to practice in secret. But, we know that they persisted: once Napoleon instituted religious freedom, they suddenly reappeared—and, across cities, their post-Napoleon population sizes were highly correlated with their pre-1700 population sizes. It's worth noting that Calvinists eliminated so many annual Catholic holidays that they would have worked 15–20 percent more than Catholics.

53. Hornung, 2014; Inkster, 1990.

54. Basalla, 1988; Cipolla, 1994; Hoffman, 2015; McNeill, 1982; Mokyr, 2011, 2016; Seife, 2000. Medieval European physicians adopted medical ideas and practices from Muhammad ibn Zakariya al-Razi, a Persian who wrote about experimental approaches (treatment vs. control), the symptomology of smallpox vs. measles, and techniques for distilling alcohol (from the Arabic *al-kuhl*). Eventually, Europeans began using algebra (from the Arabic *al-jabr*), as developed by Muḥammad ibn Mūsā al-Khwārizmī and other Muslim polymaths in Persia. Similarly, forged by a proto-WEIRD psychology, the European university was likely a recombination of institutional elements drawn from Islamic, and ultimately Central Asian, societies (Beckwith, 2012).

55. Bosker et al., 2013; McNeill, 1982; Sequeira, Nunn, and Qian, 2017; Serafinelli and Tabellini, 2017; Stasavage, 2011, 2016. Alternatively, even if the rebel him-

self couldn't escape his country, his books often could. After Galileo's final book was banned by the Church, he published it in Holland, outside of the Church's jurisdiction. Copies nevertheless made their way back to Rome, and the edition promptly sold out.

56. Ji, Zhang, and Guo, 2008; Nisbett, 2003. Of course, more holistic thinkers are more prepared to appreciate complex interactions than are the more analytically inclined. But, this might discourage individuals from devising simple experiments aimed at isolating a single factor from the real world's tangled web of causality. Analytical thinking also creates blind spots. For example, experiments suggest that analytical thinkers tend to expect that stock prices will follow their current trends, going either up or down, instead of anticipating reversals or cycles.

57. Foster, 1965; Henrich, 2009.

58. Howes, 2017; Mokyr, 2011, 2016. Interestingly, Howes's study of British innovators suggests that many inventors had little or no specialized training in the domains in which they innovated (e.g., Newcomen and Watt). Instead, they often brought fresh eyes to an old problem, technique, or technology and were either self-taught or collaborated with people who possessed the requisite skills or know-how. What innovators shared was tenacity, an "improving mentality," social connections with other innovators (often via a knowledge society), and usually a bit of luck.

People's industriousness may have been bolstered by new beverages: sugar mixed into caffeinated drinks—tea and coffee. These products only began arriving in Europe in large quantities after 1500, when overseas trade began to dramatically expand. The consumption of sugar, for example, rose 20-fold between 1663 and 1775. By the 18th century, sugary caffeinated beverages were not only becoming part of the daily consumption of the urban middle class, but they were also spreading into the working class. We know from his famous diary that Samuel Pepys was savoring coffee by 1660. The ability of these beverages to deliver quick energy—glucose and caffeine—may have provided innovators, industrialists, and laborers, as well as those engaged in intellectual exchanges at cafés (as opposed to taverns), with an extra edge in self-control, mental acuity, and productivity. While sugar, coffee, and tea had long been used elsewhere, no one had previously adopted the practice of mixing sugar into caffeinated drinks (Hersh and Voth, 2009; Nunn and Qian, 2010). Psychologists have linked the ingestion of glucose to greater self-control, though the mechanism is a matter of debate (Beedie and Lane, 2012; Gailliot and Baumeister, 2007; Inzlicht and Schmeichel, 2012; Sanders et al., 2012). The anthropologist Sidney Mintz (1986, p. 85) suggested that sugar helped create the industrial working class, writing that "by provisioning, sating—and, indeed, drugging—farm and factory workers, [sugar] sharply reduced the overall cost of creating and reproducing the metropolitan proletariat."

59. Almond and Currie, 2011; Baumard, 2018; Clark, 2007a; Flynn, 2007, 2012; Frankenhuis and de Weerth, 2013; Hanushek and Woessmann, 2012; Haushofer and Fehr, 2014; Hersh and Voth, 2009; Hoddinott et al., 2011; Jaffee et al., 2001; Kelly, Mokyr, and Gráda, 2014; LeVine et al., 2012; McNeill, 1999; Muthukrishna and Henrich, 2016; Nisbet, 2009; Nisbett et al., 2012; Nores and Barnett, 2010; Nunn and Qian, 2011; Rindermann and Thompson, 2011; Whaley et al., 2003. Health and cognitive abilities may also have been improved by lower rates of inbreeding.

60. Kelly et al., 2014.

61. Greif and Iyigun, 2012, 2013; Iyigun, Nunn, and Qian, 2017; Muthukrishna and Henrich, 2016.

62. Davis, 2014; LeVine et al., 2012; Nisbett, 2009; Nisbett et al., 2012; Nores and Barnett, 2010; Whaley et al., 2003.

63. Gorodnichenko and Roland, 2016. We used only the 2009 innovation data from the Economist Intelligence Unit and the individualism data from Hofstede's website.

64. Gorodnichenko and Roland, 2011, 2016. The same pattern emerges if you compare companies around the world instead of countries. Among firms, those based in individualistic countries tend to hire younger CEOs. This occurs presumably because such populations are less inclined to defer to their elders. Firms with younger CEOs are not only more innovative but are also especially likely to create high-impact innovations (Acemoglu et al., 2013; Acemoglu, Akcigit, and Celik, 2016). These are two references to the same paper, but the earlier version contains valuable analyses for my point here that were dropped from the later version.

These effects can also be found in the economics laboratory using American students. In one experiment, university students were asked to brainstorm creative ideas for saving a failing restaurant business. Based on a random flip of the coin, half of the participants were unconsciously primed to think about themselves and their own uniqueness—individualism—while the other half were primed to think about their relationship and similarities to others—relationalism. Those primed with individualism came up with more ideas in total and more unique ideas than those primed with relational thinking. Individualism fosters creativity, even among highly individualistic Americans (Goncalo and Staw, 2006).

65. Clark, 2007a; De Moor and Van Zanden, 2010; Lee and Feng, 2009; Mitterauer and Sieder, 1982; Newson, 2009; Newson et al., 2007; Van Zanden, 2009a.

14. The Dark Matter of History

1. Chanda and Putterman, 2007; Diamond, 1997; Hibbs and Olsson, 2004; Morris, 2010. I've left out the differences in the evolution of resistance to infectious diseases.

This becomes very relevant when Eurasians begin expanding and clash with populations in the Americas and Australia.

2. Diamond, 1997; Kremer, 1993; Morris, 2010; Turchin, 2015; Turchin et al., 2013. The phrase "lucky latitudes" comes from Morris.

3. Chanda and Putterman, 2007; Hibbs and Olsson, 2004; Putterman, 2008; Putterman and Weil, 2010.

4. One way to see what was going on is to trace the strength of the relationship between intensive kinship and economic prosperity back in time. Starting in the modern world, populations with more intensive kinship or strong family ties show lower rates of economic prosperity. However, tracking this correlation back in time reveals that it shrinks and nearly vanishes during the period 1000–1500 CE (Enke, 2017, 2019). In light of the analyses in Chapters 6 and 7, which connect the Church to the dissolution of kinship, it seems likely that the Church effectively broke the otherwise strong links between biogeographic factors and food production, on the one hand, and early state formation and economic prosperity, on the other hand.

5. Hibbs and Olsson, 2004; Olsson and Paik, 2016; Putterman, Bockstette, and Chanda, 2001; Putterman and Weil, 2010.

6. Baker, 1979; Greif and Tabellini, 2015; Henrich et al., 2012; Wha-Sook, 1995.

7. Bentzen, Kaarsen, and Wingender, 2016; Buggle, 2017; Chanda and Putterman, 2007; Galor and Özak, 2016; Hamilton and Sanders, 1992; Putterman and Weil, 2010; Sowell, 1998. The case I've made for the origins of WEIRD psychology and the rise of European societies in the second millennium is broadly consistent with views ranging from those of the great sociologist Max Weber to my fine colleagues Daron Acemoglu and James Robinson, who wrote *Why Nations Fail*. With Weber, my account shares a central role for religion and the nature of European cities, as well as a recognition that culture and institutions can shape basic aspects of people's psychology. In a sense, I'm updating Weber in light of our modern understanding of cultural and genetic evolution as well as newly available historical, psychological, and economic data. Daron and James, on the other hand, argue for the centrality of "political institutions" in creating prosperous states in the modern world. By "institutions" they mean some combination of formal organizations and laws (constitutional checks on the executive) as well as "informal institutions," which are the social norms, expectations, and related practices that shape how formal institutions operate on the ground. Their "institutions" are a blend of what I've called "formal institutions" and "culture" (social norms, etc.). As you've seen throughout this book, I think both formal and informal political institutions are important. However, I also argue that we need to consider how these "higher-level" political-economic institutions interface with both "lower-level" institutions, such as those related to kinship, marriage, and religion, and people's cultural psychology. Only by considering the most fundamental of institutions can we

explain why the "pluralistic" political institutions that Daron and James place so much importance on first emerged in western Europe. The approach taken by Daron and James, like many economists, eschews the idea that psychology evolves culturally and that important psychological differences exist and persist. Based on my nine years as a professor of economics, I suspect this is because such variation doesn't fit easily into the theoretical frameworks or worldviews of their disciplinary tradition—i.e., the culture and informal institutional rules of economics (Acemoglu, Johnson, and Robinson, 2002; Acemoglu and Robinson, 2012; Weber, 1958a, 1958b, 1978). Thanks to Dan Smail for prompting me to look more closely at Weber.

8. Korotayev, 2000, 2004; Schulz, 2019.

9. Baumard, 2018; Hruschka et al., 2014; Hruschka and Henrich, 2013b; Mullainathan and Shafir, 2013.

10. Goody, 1983; Greif, 2006; Greif and Tabellini, 2010; MacFarlane, 1978; Mitterauer and Chapple, 2010; Mitterauer and Sieder, 1982; Serafinelli and Tabellini, 2017.

11. Some researchers have argued that much psychological variation can be explained by differences in "slow" vs. "fast" life histories strategies (Baumard, 2018), which are often evoked based on the early environments experienced by children. This is interesting work, and may play some role, but serious concerns persist, both theoretical (Baldini, 2015; Barbaro et al., 2016) and empirical (Purzycki, Ross et al., 2017).

12. Doepke and Zilibotti, 2008; Jacob, 2013.

13. Ensminger and Henrich, 2014; Henrich, Ensminger et al., 2010; Henrich et al., 2004; Lang et al., 2019.

14. Henrich, 2016.

15. Clark, 2007a; Wade, 2014.

16. Durham, 1991; Henrich, 2016.

17. Beauchamp, 2016; Flynn, 2007; Kong et al., 2017; Nisbett, 2009; Okbay et al., 2016. The numerical estimates come from Beauchamp.

18. Dincecco and Onorato, 2018; Ogilvie, 2019; Winter, 2013. Of course, one could argue that at some point the countryside came under the sway of the impersonal markets, voluntary associations, and new laws that might have created genetic selection pressures for a WEIRDer psychology in the rural areas that didn't suffer from the graveyard effect. This is certainly possible, but three factors mitigate its relevance: (1) this would have only become important centuries later in our story, (2) the urban graveyards would have still lured away the WEIRDest among those in the countryside, and (3) the more that rural social networks came to resemble urban ones, the more susceptible these areas would have been to infectious diseases—the same networks that foster innovation and commerce among strangers also open the door to the transmission of pathogens.

19. Dincecco and Onorato, 2018; Winter, 2013.
20. Gershman, 2015; Nunn and De La Sierra, 2017. For the ghost statistic, see www .economist.com/graphic-detail/2018/10/31/pagan-beliefs-persist-in-the-new -world. For the elves, www.theatlantic.com/international/archive/2013/10/why -so-many-icelanders-still-believe-in-invisible-elves/280783.

BIBLIOGRAPHY

Abrahams, R. (1973). Some aspects of levirate. In J. Goody (ed.), *The Character of Kinship*. Cambridge: Cambridge University Press.

Acemoglu, D., Akcigit, U., and Celik, M. A. (2013). Young, restless and creative: Openness to disruption and creative innovations. Working Paper No. 19894, National Bureau of Economic Research. www.nber.org/papers/w19894.

Acemoglu, D., Akcigit, U., and Celik, M. A. (2016). Young, restless and creative: Openness to disruption and creative innovations. Working paper, static1.squarespace .com/static/57fa873e8419c230ca01eb5f/t/5935737a8419c282eb2c1756 /1496675232862/CreativeInnovation_170605_fin.pdf.

Acemoglu, D., Johnson, S., and Robinson, J. (2005). The rise of Europe: Atlantic trade, institutional change, and economic growth. *American Economic Review* 95 (3), 546–79.

Acemoglu, D., Johnson, S., and Robinson, J. A. (2002). Reversal of fortune: Geography and institutions in the making of the modern world income distribution. *Quarterly Journal of Economics* 117 (4), 1231–94.

Acemoglu, D., and Robinson, J. (2012). *Why Nations Fail: The Origins of Power, Prosperity, and Poverty*. New York: Random House Digital.

Ackerman, J. M., Maner, J. K., and Carpenter, S. M. (2016). Going all in: Unfavorable sex ratios attenuate choice diversification. *Psychological Science* 27 (6), 799–809.

Addis, W. E. (2015). *A Catholic Dictionary*. Aeterna Press.

Aghion, P., Jaravel, X., Persson, T., and Rouzet, D. (2019). Education and military rivalry. *Journal of the European Economic Association* 17 (2), 376–412.

Ahmed, A. M. (2009). Are religious people more prosocial? A quasi-experimental study with madrasah pupils in a rural community in India. *Journal for the Scientific Study of Religion* 48 (2), 368–74.

Ahmed, A. S. (2013). *The Thistle and the Drone: How America's War on Terror Became a Global War on Tribal Islam*. Washington, DC: Brookings Institution Press.

Akbari, M., Bahrami-Rad, D., and Kimbrough, E. O. (2017). Kinship, fractionalization and corruption. *Journal of Economic Behavior and Organization* 166, 493–528.

Akcigit, U., Kerr, W. R., and Nicholas, T. (2013). The mechanics of endogenous innovation and growth: Evidence from historical U.S. patents. Working paper, siepr .stanford.edu/system/files/shared/1311.

Akçomak, S., Webbink, D., and ter Weel, B. (2016). Why did the Netherlands develop so early? The legacy of the brethren of the common life. *The Economic Journal* 126 (593), 821–60.

Alcorta, C. S., and Sosis, R. (2005). Ritual, emotion, and sacred symbols: The evolution of religion as an adaptive complex. *Human Nature* 16 (4), 323–59.

Alcorta, C. S., Sosis, R., and Finkel, D. (2008). Ritual harmony: Toward an evolutionary theory of music. *Behavioral and Brain Sciences* 31 (5), 576–77.

Alesina, A. F., Algan, Y., Cahuc, P., and Giuliano, P. (2015). Family values and the regulation of labor. *Journal of the European Economic Association* 13 (4), 599–630.

Alesina, A. F., and Giuliano, P. (2010). The power of the family. *Journal of Economic Growth* 15 (2), 93–125.

Alesina, A. F., and Giuliano, P. (2013). Family ties. In Philippe Aghion and Steven N. Durlauf (eds.), *Handbook of Economic Growth* 2A (pp. 177–215). Oxford, UK: North Holland/Elsevier.

Alesina, A. F., and Giuliano, P. (2015). Culture and institutions. *Journal of Economic Literature* 53 (4), 898–944.

Algan, Y., and Cahuc, P. (2010). Inherited trust and growth. *American Economic Review* 100 (5), 2060–92.

Algan, Y., and Cahuc, P. (2013). Trust and growth. *Annual Review of Economics* 5 (1), 521–49.

Algan, Y., and Cahuc, P. (2014). Trust, growth, and well-being: New evidence and policy implications. In Philippe Aghion and Steven N. Durlauf (eds.), *Handbook of Economic Growth* 2A (pp. 49–120). Oxford: North Holland/Elsevier.

Allen, R. C. (1983). Collective invention. *Journal of Economic Behavior and Organization* 4 (1), 1–24.

Allen, R. C. (2009). *The British Industrial Revolution in Global Perspective*. Cambridge: Cambridge University Press.

Almond, D., and Currie, J. (2011). Killing me softly: The fetal origins hypothesis. *Journal of Economic Perspectives* 25 (3), 153–72.

Alonso, S. (2013). Temporal discounting and number representation. *Journal of Behavioral Finance* 14 (3), 240–51.

Alquist, J. L., Ainsworth, S. E., and Baumeister, R. F. (2013). Determined to conform: Disbelief in free will increases conformity. *Journal of Experimental Social Psychology* 49 (1), 80–86.

Altrocchi, J., and Altrocchi, L. (1995). Polyfaceted psychological acculturation in Cook Islanders. *Journal of Cross-Cultural Psychology* 26 (4), 426–40.

Al-Ubaydli, O., Houser, D., Nye, J., Paganelli, M. P., and Pan, X. S. (2013). The causal effect of market participation on trust: An experimental investigation using randomized control. *PLoS One* 8 (3), e55968.

Alvard, M. (2011). Genetic and cultural kinship among the Lamaleran whale hunters. *Human Nature* 22 (1–2), 89–107.

Alvard, M. S. (2003). Kinship, lineage, and an evolutionary perspective on cooperative hunting groups in Indonesia. *Human Nature* 14 (2), 129–63.

Alvard, M. S. (2009). Kinship and cooperation. *Human Nature* 20 (4), 394–416.

Alvergne, A., Faurie, C., and Raymond, M. (2009). Variation in testosterone levels and male reproductive effort: Insight from a polygynous human population. *Hormones and Behavior* 56 (5), 491–97.

Ambrose. (1881). *The Letters of Saint Ambrose, Bishop of Milan*. London; Oxford: James Parker.

Amorim, C. E. G., Vai, S., Posth, C., Modi, A., Koncz, I., Hakenbeck, S., . . . Veeramah, K. R. (2018). Understanding 6th-century barbarian social organization and migration through paleogenomics. *Nature Communications* 9 (1), 3547.

Andersen, T. B., Bentzen, J., Dalgaard, C.-J., and Sharp, P. (2017). Pre-Reformation roots of the Protestant ethic. *The Economic Journal* 127 (604), 1756–93.

Anderson, R. T. (1956). *Changing Kinship in Europe*. Berkeley: University of California Press.

Annan, J., Blattman, C., Mazurana, D., and Carlson, K. (2011). Civil war, reintegration, and gender in northern Uganda. *Journal of Conflict Resolution* 55 (6), 877–908.

Ansary, T. (2010). *Destiny Disrupted: A History of the World Through Islamic Eyes*. New York: PublicAffairs.

Apicella, C. L., Azevedo, E. M., Christakis, N. A., and Fowler, J. H. (2014). Evolutionary origins of the endowment effect: Evidence from hunter-gatherers. *American Economic Review* 104 (6), 1793–805.

Apicella, C. L., Carre, J. M., Dreber, A. (2015). Testosterone and economic risk taking: A review. *Adaptive Human Behavior and Physiology* 1 (3), 358–85.

Apicella, C. L., Dreber, A., and Mollerstrom, J. (2014). Salivary testosterone change following monetary wins and losses predicts future financial risk-taking. *Psychoneuroendocrinology* 39, 58–64.

Appiah, A. (2010). *The Honor Code: How Moral Revolutions Happen* (1st ed.). New York: W. W. Norton.

Arantes, J., Berg, M. E., Lawlor, D., and Grace, R. C. (2013). Offenders have higher delay-discounting rates than non-offenders after controlling for differences in drug and alcohol abuse. *Legal and Criminological Psychology* 18 (2), 240–53.

Arruñada, B. (2010). Protestants and Catholics: Similar work ethic, different social ethic. *The Economic Journal* 120 (547), 890–918.

Asch, S. E. (1956). Studies of independence and conformity: A minority of one against a unanimous majority. *Psychological Monographs* 70 (9), 1–70.

Ashkanasy, N., Gupta, V., Mayfield, M. S., and Trevor-Roberts, E. (2004). Future orientation. In R. J. House, P. J. Hanges, M. Javidan, P. W. Dorfman, and V. Gupta (eds.), *Culture, Leadership, and Organizations: The GLOBE Study of 62 Societies* (pp. 282–342). Thousand Oaks, CA: SAGE Publications.

Ashraf, Q., and Michalopoulos, S. (2015). Climatic fluctuations and the diffusion of agriculture. *Review of Economics and Statistics* 97 (3), 589–609.

Atkinson, Q. D., and Bourrat, P. (2011). Beliefs about God, the afterlife and morality support the role of supernatural policing in human cooperation. *Evolution and Human Behavior* 32 (1), 41–49.

Atkinson, Q. D., and Whitehouse, H. (2011). The cultural morphospace of ritual form. *Evolution and Human Behavior* 32 (1), 50–62.

Atran, S. (2002). *In Gods We Trust: The Evolutionary Landscape of Religion*. New York: Oxford University Press.

Atran, S., and Medin, D. L. (2008). *The Native Mind and the Cultural Construction of Nature*. Cambridge, MA: MIT Press.

Atran, S., Medin, D. L., and Ross, N. (2005). The cultural mind: Environmental decision making and cultural modeling within and across populations. *Psychological Review* 112 (4), 744–76.

Atran, S., and Norenzayan, A. (2004). Religion's evolutionary landscape: Counterintuition, commitment, compassion, communion. *Behavioral and Brain Sciences* 27 (6), 713–70.

Aubet, M. E. (2013). *Commerce and Colonization in the Ancient Near East*. Cambridge: Cambridge University Press.

Augustine (1998). *The City of God Against the Pagans*. Cambridge: Cambridge University Press.

Ausenda, G. (1999). Kinship and marriage among the Visigoths. In P. Heather (ed.), *The Visigoths from the Migration Period to the Seventh Century: An Ethnographic Perspective* (pp. 129–68). Woodbridge, UK: Boydell Press.

Aveyard, M. E. (2014). A call to honesty: Extending religious priming of moral behavior to Middle Eastern Muslims. *PLoS One* 9 (7), e99447.

Bacon, M. K., Child, I. L., and Barry, H. (1963). A cross-cultural study of correlates of crime. *Journal of Abnormal and Social Psychology* 66 (4), 291–300.

Bahrami-Rad, D., Becker, A., and Henrich, J. (2017). Tabulated nonsense? Testing the validity of the Ethnographic Atlas and the persistence of culture. Working paper.

Bai, Y., and Kung, J. K. S. (2015). Diffusing knowledge while spreading God's message: Protestantism and economic prosperity in China, 1840–1920. *Journal of the European Economic Association* 13 (4), 669–98.

Baier, C. J., and Wright, B. R. E. (2001). "If you love me, keep my commandments": A meta-analysis of the effect of religion on crime. *Journal of Research in Crime and Delinquency* 38 (1), 3–21.

Bailey, D. H., Hill, K. R., and Walker, R. S. (2014). Fitness consequences of spousal relatedness in 46 small-scale societies. *Biology Letters* 10 (5), 20140160.

Bailey, D. H., Walker, R. S., Blomquist, G. E., Hill, K. R., Hurtado, A. M., and Geary, D. C. (2013). Heritability and fitness correlates of personality in the Ache, a natural-fertility population in Paraguay. *PLoS One* 8 (3), e59325.

Baines, E. (1835). *History of the Cotton Manufacture in Great Britain*. London: H. Fisher, R. Fisher, and P. Jackson.

Bairoch, P., Batou, J., and Chèvre, P. (1988). *La population des villes Europeennes de 800 à 1850: Banque de données et analyse sommaire des résultats*. Geneva, Switzerland: Librairie Droz.

Baker, H. D. R. (1979). *Chinese Family and Kinship*. New York: Columbia University Press.

Baksh, M. (1984). Cultural ecology and change of the Machiguenga Indians of the Peruvian Amazon. Dissertation, University of California, Los Angeles.

Bal, P. M., and Veltkamp, M. (2013). How does fiction reading influence empathy? An experimental investigation on the role of emotional transportation. *PLoS One* 8 (1), e55341.

Baldini, R. (2015). Harsh environments and "fast" human life histories: What does the theory say? Preprint. www.biorxiv.org/content/10.1101/014647v2.full.pdf.

Barbaro, N., Boutwell, B. B., Barnes, J. C., and Shackelford, T. K. (2017). Genetic confounding of the relationship between father absence and age at menarche. *Evolution and Human Behavior* 38 (3), 357–65.

Barbieri, C., Hübner, A., Macholdt, E., Ni, S., Lippold, S., Schröder, R., . . . Pakendorf, B. (2016). Refining the Y chromosome phylogeny with southern African sequences. *Human Genetics* 135 (5), 541–53.

Barker, P., and Goldstein, B. R. (2001). Theological foundations of Kepler's astronomy. *Osiris* 16 (1), 88–113.

Barnes, M. H. (2010). *Stages of Thought: The Co-evolution of Religious Thought and Science*. New York: Oxford University Press.

Barnes, R. H. (1996). *Sea Hunters of Indonesia: Fishers and Weavers of Lamalera*. Oxford: Clarendon Press.

Baron, A. S., and Dunham, Y. (2015). Representing "us" and "them": Building blocks of intergroup cognition. *Journal of Cognition and Development* 16 (5), 780–801.

Barrett, H. C., Bolyanatz, A., Crittenden, A. N., Fessler, D. M. T., Fitzpatrick, S., Gurven, M., . . . Laurence, S. (2016). Small-scale societies exhibit fundamental variation in the role of intentions in moral judgment. *Proceedings of the National Academy of Sciences* 113 (17), 4688–93.

Barro, R. J., and McCleary, R. M. (2003). Religion and economic growth across countries. *American Sociological Review* 68 (5), 760.

Barry, H., Child, I. L., and Bacon, M. K. (1959). Relation of child training to subsistence economy. *American Anthropologist* 61 (1), 51–63.

Barth, F. (1965). *Political Leadership Among Swat Pathans*. Toronto: Oxford University Press.

Bartlett, R. (1993). *The Making of Europe: Conquest, Colonization and Cultural Change, 950–1350* (1st ed.). London: Allen Lane.

Barwick, D. E. (1984). Mapping the past: An atlas of Victorian clans 1835–1904. In I. McBryde (ed.), *Aboriginal History* (Vol. 8, pp. 100–131). Canberra: Australian National University Press.

Basalla, G. (1988). *The Evolution of Technology*. Cambridge Studies in the History of Science. Cambridge: Cambridge University Press.

Basten, C., and Betz, F. (2013). Beyond work ethic: Religion, individual, and political preferences. *American Economic Journal: Economic Policy* 5 (3), 67–91.

Bastiaansen, J. A. C. J., Thioux, M., and Keysers, C. (2009). Evidence for mirror systems in emotions. *Philosophical Transactions of the Royal Society B: Biological Sciences* 364 (1528), 2391–404.

Bauer, M., Blattman, C., Chytilová, J., Henrich, J., Miguel, E., and Mitts, T. (2016). Can war foster cooperation? *Journal of Economic Perspectives* 30 (3), 249–74.

Bauer, M., Cahlíková, J., Chytilová, J., and Želinský, T. (2018). Social contagion of ethnic hostility. *Proceedings of the National Academy of Sciences* 115 (19), 4881–86.

Bauer, M., Cassar, A., Chytilová, J., and Henrich, J. (2014). War's enduring effects on the development of egalitarian motivations and in-group biases. *Psychological Science* 25, 47–57.

Baumard, N. (2018). Psychological origins of the Industrial Revolution. *Behavioral and Brain Sciences*, 42, E189.

Baumeister, R. F., Bauer, I. M., and Lloyd, S. A. (2010). Choice, free will, and religion. *Psychology of Religion and Spirituality* 2 (2), 67–82.

Baumeister, R. F., Masicampo, E. J., and Dewall, C. N. (2009). Prosocial benefits of feeling free: Disbelief in free will increases aggression and reduces helpfulness. *Personality and Social Psychology Bulletin* 35 (2), 260–68.

Baumol, W. J. (1990). Entrepreneurship: Productive, unproductive, and destructive. *Journal of Political Economy* 98 (5), 891–921.

Beauchamp, J. P. (2016). Genetic evidence for natural selection in humans in the contemporary United States. *Proceedings of the National Academy of Sciences* 113 (28), 7774–79.

Becker, B. E., and Huselid, M. A. (1992). The incentive effects of tournament compensation systems. *Administrative Science Quarterly* 37 (2), 336–50.

Becker, S. O., Hornung, E., and Woessmann, L. (2011). Education and catch-up in the Industrial Revolution. *American Economic Journal: Macroeconomics* 3 (3), 92–126.

Becker, S. O., Pfaff, S., and Rubin, J. (2016). Causes and consequences of the Protestant Reformation. *Explorations in Economic History* 62, 1–25.

Becker, S. O., and Woessmann, L. (2008). Luther and the girls: Religious denomination and the female education gap in nineteenth-century Prussia. *Scandinavian Journal of Economics* 110 (4), 777–805.

Becker, S. O., and Woessmann, L. (2009). Was Weber wrong? A human capital theory of Protestant economic history. *Quarterly Journal of Economics* 124 (2), 531–96.

Becker, S. O., and Woessmann, L. (2010). The effect of Protestantism on education before the industrialization: Evidence from 1816 Prussia. *Economics Letters* 107 (2), 224–28.

Becker, S. O., and Woessmann, L. (2016). Social cohesion, religious beliefs, and the effect of Protestantism on suicide. *Review of Economics and Statistics* 98 (2), 209–25.

Beckwith, C. L. (2012). *Warriors of the Cloisters: The Central Asian Origins of Science in the Medieval World.* Princeton, NJ: Princeton University Press.

Beedie, C. J., and Lane, A. M. (2012). The role of glucose in self-control: Another look at the evidence and an alternative conceptualization. *Personality and Social Psychology Review* 16 (2), 143–53.

Beheim, B., Atkinson, Q., Bulbulia, J., Gervais, W. M., Gray, R., Henrich, J., Lang, M., ... Willard., A. (2019). Treatment of missing data determines conclusions regarding moralizing gods. https://psyarxiv.com/jwa2n/.

Beletsky, L. D., Gori, D. F., Freeman, S., and Wingfield, J. C. (1995). Testosterone and polygyny in birds. *Current Ornithology* 12, 1–41.

Bellemare, C., Kröeger, S., and Van Soest, A. (2008). Measuring inequity aversion in a heterogeneous population using experimental decisions and subjective probabilities. *Econometrica* 76 (4), 815–39.

Bellows, J., and Miguel, E. (2006). War and institutions: New evidence from Sierra Leone. *American Economic Review* 96 (2), 394–99.

Bellows, J., and Miguel, E. (2009). War and local collective action in Sierra Leone. *Journal of Public Economics* 93 (11–12), 1144–57.

Bellwood, P. (2001). Early agriculturalist population diasporas? Farming, languages, and genes. *Annual Review of Anthropology*, 30, 181–207.

Ben-Bassat, A., and Dahan, M. (2012). Social identity and voting behavior. *Public Choice* 151 (1–2), 193–214.

Benedict, R. (1946). *The Chrysanthemum and the Sword: Patterns of Japanese Culture.* Boston: Houghton Mifflin.

Benson, B. L. (1989). The spontaneous evolution of commercial law. *Southern Economic Journal* 55 (3), 644–61.

Bentzen, J. S. (2013). Origins of religiousness: The role of natural disasters. Working paper, ssrn.com/abstract=2221859.

Bentzen, J. S. (2019). Acts of God? Religiosity and natural disasters across subnational world districts. *The Economic Journal* 129 (622), 2295–321.

Bentzen, J. S., Kaarsen, N., and Wingender, A. M. (2017). Irrigation and autocracy. *Journal of the European Economic Association* 15 (1), 1–53.

Benzell, S. G., and Cooke, K. (2016). A network of thrones: Kinship and conflict in Europe, 1495–1918, 1–5. Working paper, kmcooke.weebly.com/uploads/3/0/9/4 /30942717/royals_benzellcooke.pdf.

Bergreen, L. (2007). *Marco Polo: From Venice to Xanadu* (1st ed.). New York: Alfred A. Knopf.

Berman, H. J. (1983). *Law and Revolution: The Formation of the Western Legal Tradition*. Cambridge, MA: Harvard University Press.

Bernardi, B. (1952). The age-system of the Nilo-Hamitic peoples: A critical evaluation. *Africa: Journal of the International African Institute* 22 (4), 316–32.

Bernardi, B. (1985). *Age Class Systems: Social Institutions and Polities Based on Age*. Cambridge: Cambridge University Press.

Berns, G. S., Capra, C. M., Moore, S., and Noussair, C. (2010). Neural mechanisms of the influence of popularity on adolescent ratings of music. *NeuroImage* 49 (3), 2687–96.

Berntsen, J. L. (1976). The Maasai and their neighbors: Variables of interaction. *African Economic History* 2, 1–11.

Berry, J. W. (1966). Temne and Eskimo perceptual skills. *International Journal of Psychology* 1 (3), 207–229.

Berry, J. W., and Bennett, J. A. (1995). Syllabic literacy and cognitive performance among the Cree and Ojibwe people of northern Canada. In I. Taylor and D. R. Olson (eds.), *Scripts and Literacy: Reading and Learning to Read Alphabets, Syllabaries and Characters* (pp. 341–57). Norwell, MA: Kluwer.

Bettencourt, L. M. A. (2013). The origins of scaling in cities. *Science* 340 (6139), 1438–41.

Bettencourt, L. M. A., Lobo, J., and Strumsky, D. (2007). Invention in the city: Increasing returns to patenting as a scaling function of metropolitan size. *Research Policy* 36 (1), 107–120.

Bettencourt, L. M., Lobo, J., Helbing, D., Kühnert, C., and West, G. B. (2007). Growth, innovation, scaling, and the pace of life in cities. *Proceedings of the National Academy of Sciences* 104 (17), 7301–7306.

Betzig, L. L. (1982). Despotism and differential reproduction: A cross-cultural correlation of conflict asymmetry, hierarchy, and degree of polygyny. *Ethology and Sociobiology* 3 (4), 209–221.

Betzig, L. L. (1986). *Despotism and Differential Reproduction: A Darwinian View of History*. Piscataway, NJ: Aldine Transaction.

Betzig, L. L. (1992). Roman polygyny. *Ethology and Sociobiology* 13 (5–6), 309–349.

Betzig, L. L. (1993). Sex, succession, and stratification in the first six civillizations. In L. Ellis (ed.), *Social Stratification and Socioeconomic Inequity* (Vol. 1). Westport, CT: Praeger.

Bhui, R., Chudek, M., and Henrich, J. (2019a). How exploitation launched human cooperation. *Behavioral Ecology and Sociobiology* 73 (6), 78.

Bhui, R., Chudek, M., and Henrich, J. (2019b). Work time and market integration in the original affluent society. *Proceedings of the National Academy of Sciences* 116 (44), 22100–22105.

Bittles, A. H. (1998). Empirical estimates of the global prevalence of consanguineous marriage in contemporary societies. Working paper. researchrepository.murdoch .edu.au/id/eprint/13494/1/empirical_estimates.pdf.

Bittles, A. H. (2001). A background summary of consanguineous marriage. Working paper, consang.net/index.php/Summary.

Bittles, A. H., and Black, M. L. (2010). Consanguinity, human evolution, and complex diseases. *Proceedings of the National Academy of Sciences* 107 (Suppl. 1), 1779–86.

Blake-Coleman, B. C. (1992). *Copper Wire and Electrical Conductors: The Shaping of a Technology*. Philadelphia: Harwood Academic.

Blattman, C. (2009). From violence to voting: War and political participation in Uganda. *American Political Science Review* 103, 231–47.

Blattman, C., Jamison, J. C., and Sheridan, M. (2016). Reducing crime and violence: Experimental evidence on adult noncognitive investments in Liberia. Working paper, www.nber.org/papers/w21204.

Blaydes, L., and Paik, C. (2016). The impact of Holy Land crusades on state formation: War mobilization, trade integration and political development in medieval Europe. *International Organization* 70 (3), 551–86.

Block, M. K., and Gerety, V. E. (1995). Some experimental-evidence on differences between student and prisoner reactions to monetary penalties and risk. *Journal of Legal Studies* 24 (1), 123–38.

Blondel, S., Lohéac, Y., and Rinaudo, S. (2007). Rationality and drug use: An experimental approach. *Journal of Health Economics* 26 (3), 643–58.

Blume, M. (2009). The reproductive benefits of religious affiliation. In E. Voland and W. Schiefenhovel (eds.), *The Biological Evolution of Religious Mind and Behavior* (pp. 117–26). Berlin: Springer-Verlag.

Bockstette, V., Chanda, A., and Putterman, L. G. (2002). States and markets: The advantage of an early start. *Journal of Economic Growth,* 7, 347–69.

Boehm, C. (2008). A biocultural evolutionary exploration of supernatural sanctioning. In J. A. Bulbulia, R. Sosis, E. Harris, R. Genet, C. Genet, and K. Wyman (eds.), *Evolution of Religion* (pp. 143–52). Santa Margarita, CA: Collins Foundation Press.

Boerner, L., and Severgnini, B. (2015). Time for growth. Working paper, ssrn.com /abstract=2652782.

Bolyanatz, A. H. (2014). Economic experimental game results from the Sursurunga of New Ireland, Papua New Guinea. In J. Ensminger and J. Henrich (eds.), *Experimenting with Social Norms: Fairness and Punishment in Cross-Cultural Perspective* (pp. 275–308). New York: Russell Sage Foundation.

Bond, R., and Smith, P. B. (1996). Culture and conformity: A meta-analysis of studies using Asch's (1952b, 1956) line judgment task. *Psychological Bulletin* 119 (1), 111–37.

Bondarenko, D. M. (2014). On the nature and features of the (early) state: An anthropological reanalysis. *Zeitschrift für Ethnologie* 139 (2), 215–32.

Bondarenko, D. M., and Korotayev, A. V. (2003). "Early state" in cross-cultural perspective: A statistical reanalysis of Henri J. M. Claessen's database. *Cross-Cultural Research* 37 (1), 105–132.

Booth, A., Granger, D. A., Mazur, A., and Kivlighan, K. T. (2006). Testosterone and social behavior. *Social Forces* 85 (1), 167–91.

Booth, A., Johnson, D. R., and Granger, D. A. (1999). Testosterone and men's health. *Journal of Behavioral Medicine* 22 (1), 1–19.

Boppart, T., Falkinger, J., and Grossmann, V. (2014). Protestantism and education: Reading (the Bible) and other skills. *Economic Inquiry* 52 (2), 874–95.

Bornstein, G., and Benyossef, M. (1994). Cooperation in inter-group and single-group social dilemmas. *Journal of Experimental Social Psychology* 30, 52–67.

Bornstein, G., Budescu, D., and Zamir, S. (1997). Cooperation in intergroup, N- person, and two-person games of chicken. *Journal of Conflict Resolution* 41 (3), 384–406.

Bornstein, G., Gneezy, U., and Nagel, R. (2002). The effect of intergroup competition on group coordination: An experimental study. *Games and Economic Behavior* 41 (1), 1–25.

Boroditsky, L. (2011). How languages construct time. In S. Dehaene & E. Brannon (eds.), *Space, Time and Number in the Brain: Searching for the Foundations of Mathematical Thought* (pp. 333–41). Cambridge, MA: Elsevier Academic Press.

Bos, P. A., Hermans, E. J., Ramsey, N. F., and van Honk, J. (2012). The neural mechanisms by which testosterone acts on interpersonal trust. *NeuroImage* 61 (3), 730–37.

Bos, P. A., Terburg, D., and van Honk, J. (2010). Testosterone decreases trust in socially naive humans. *Proceedings of the National Academy of Sciences* 107 (22), 9991–95.

Bosker, M., Buringh, E., and van Zanden, J. L. (2013). From Baghdad to London, unraveling urban development in Europe, North Africa and the Middle East, 800–1800. *Review of Economics and Statistics* 95 (4), 1418–37.

Boswell, J. (1988). *The Kindness of Strangers: The Abandonment of Children in Western Europe from Late Antiquity to the Renaiassance*. New York: Pantheon Books.

Bothner, M. S., Kang, J., and Stuart E., T. (2007). Competitive crowding and risk taking in a tournament: Evidence from NASCAR racing. *Administrative Science Quarterly* 52 (2), 208–247.

Botticini, M., and Eckstein, Z. (2005). Jewish occupational selection: Education, restrictions, or minorities? *Journal of Economic History* 65 (4), 922–48.

Botticini, M., and Eckstein, Z. (2007). From farmers to merchants, conversions and diaspora: Human capital and Jewish history. *Journal of the European Economic Association* 5 (5), 885–926.

Botticini, M., and Eckstein, Z. (2012). *The Chosen Few: How Education Shaped Jewish History, 70–1492*. Princeton Economic History of the Western World. Princeton, NJ: Princeton University.

Bourdieu, P. (1990). Time perspectives of the Kabyle. In J. Hassard (ed.), *The Sociology of Time* (pp. 219–37). London: Palgrave Macmillan.

Bowles, S. (1998). Endogenous preferences: The cultural consequences of markets and other economic institutions. *Journal of Economic Literature* 36 (1), 75–111.

Bowles, S. (2004). *Microeconomics: Behavior, Institutions, and Evolution*. Princeton, NJ: Princeton University Press.

Bowles, S. (2006). Group competition, reproductive leveling, and the evolution of human altruism. *Science* 314 (5805), 1569–72.

Bowles, S. (2011). Cultivation of cereals by the first farmers was not more productive than foraging. *Proceedings of the National Academy of Sciences* 108 (12), 4760–65.

Bowles, S., and Choi, J. K. (2013). Coevolution of farming and private property during the early Holocene. *Proceedings of the National Academy of Sciences* 110 (22), 8830–35.

Bowles, S., Choi, J. K., and Hopfensitz, A. (2004). The coevolution of individual behaviors and group level institutions. *Journal of Theoretical Biology* 223 (2), 135–47.

Bowles, S., and Gintis, H. (2002). Behavioural science: Homo reciprocans. *Nature* 415 (6868), 125–28.

Boyd, D. (2001). Life without pigs: Recent subsistence changes among the Irakia Awa, Papua New Guinea. *Human Ecology* 29 (3), 259–81.

Boyd, R. (2017). *A Different Kind of Animal: How Culture Formed Our Species*. Princeton, NJ: Princeton University Press.

Boyd, R., and Richerson, P. J. (2002). Group beneficial norms can spread rapidly in a structured population. *Journal of Theoretical Biology* 215, 287–96.

Boyd, R., and Richerson, P. J. (2009). Culture and the evolution of human cooperation. *Philosophical Transactions of the Royal Society B: Biological Sciences* 364 (1533), 3281–88.

Boyd, R., Richerson, P. J., and Henrich, J. (2011). The cultural niche: Why social learning is essential for human adaptation. *Proceedings of the National Academy of Sciences* 108 (2), 10918–25.

Boyer, P. (2001). *Religion Explained: The Evolutionary Origins of Religious Thought*. New York: Basic Books.

Boyer, P. (2003). Religious thought and behaviour as by-products of brain function. *Trends in Cognitive Sciences* 7 (3), 119–24.

Brass, M., Ruby, P., and Spengler, S. (2009). Inhibition of imitative behaviour and social cognition. *Philosophical Transactions of the Royal Society B: Biological Sciences* 364 (1528), 2359–67.

Bray, F. (1984). *The Rice Economies: Technology and Development in Asian Societies*. Berkeley: University of California Press.

Briggs, A., and Burke, P. (2009). *A Social History of the Media: From Gutenberg to the Internet* (3rd ed.). Cambridge, UK: Polity Press.

Broesch, J., Barrett, H. C., and Henrich, J. (2014). Adaptive content biases in learning about animals across the lifecourse. *Human Nature* 25 (2), 181–99.

Brown, P. (2012). *Through the Eye of a Needle: Wealth, the Fall of Rome, and the Making of Christianity in the West, 350–550 AD*. Princeton, NJ: Princeton University Press.

Brundage, J. A. (1987). *Law, Sex, and Christian Society in Medieval Europe*. Chicago: University of Chicago Press.

Buchtel, E. E., and Norenzayan, A. (2008). Which should you use, intuition or logic? Cultural differences in injunctive norms about reasoning. *Asian Journal of Social Psychology* 11 (4), 264–73.

Buggle, J. C. (2017). Irrigation, collectivism and long-run technological divergence. Working paper, www.unil.ch/de/files/live/sites/de/files/wo.

Buhrmester, M. D., Fraser, W. T., Lanman, J. A., Whitehouse, H., and Swann, W. B. (2015). When terror hits home: Identity fused Americans who saw Boston bombing victims as "family" provided aid. *Self and Identity* 14 (3), 253–70.

Burguiere, A., Klapisch-Zuber, C., Segalen, M., and Zonabend, F. (1996). *A History of the Family: Distant Worlds, Ancient Worlds*. Cambridge, MA: Belknap Press of Harvard University Press.

Buringh, E., and Van Zanden, J. L. (2009). Charting the "rise of the West": Manuscripts and printed books in Europe, a long-term perspective from the sixth through eighteenth centuries. *Journal of Economic History* 69 (2), 409–445.

Burke, J. (2012). *Connections*. New York: Simon & Schuster.

Burnham, T. C., Chapman, J. F., Gray, P. B., McIntyre, M. H., Lipson, S. F., and Ellison, P. T. (2003). Men in committed, romantic relationships have lower testosterone. *Hormones and Behavior* 44 (2), 119–22.

Burton, R., and Whiting, J. (1961). The absent father and cross-sex identity. *Merrill-Palmer Quarterly* 7 (2), 85–95.

Bus, A. G., Van Ijzendoorn, M. H., and Pellegrini, A. D. (1995). Joint book reading makes for success in learning to read: A meta-analysis on intergenerational transmission of literacy. *Review of Educational Research* 65 (1), 1–21.

Bushman, B. J., Ridge, R. D., Das, E., Key, C. W., and Busath, G. L. (2007). When God sanctions killing: Effect of scriptural violence on aggression. *Psychological Science* 18 (3), 204–207.

Buss, D. (2007). *Evolutionary psychology: The New Science of the Mind* (3rd ed.). Boston: Allyn and Bacon.

Buttelmann, D., Zmyj, N., Daum, M. M., and Carpenter, M. (2013). Selective imitation of in-group over out-group members in 14-month-old infants. *Child Development* 84 (2), 422–28.

Cahen, C. (1970). Economy, society, institutions. In P. M. Holt, A. K. S. Lambton, and B. Lewis (eds.), *Islamic Society* (pp. 511–38). Cambridge: Cambridge University Press.

Caicedo, F. V. (2017). The mission: Human capital transmission, economic persistence and culture in South America. Working paper, econ2017.sites.olt.ubc.ca/files/2018/01/Th.

Camerer, C. (2003). *Behavioral Game Theory: Experiments on Strategic Interaction*. Princeton, NJ: Princeton University Press.

Camino, A. (1977). Trueque, correrías e intercambios entre los Quechuas Andinos y los Piro y Machiguenga de la montaña Peruana. *Amazonía Peruana* 1 (2), 123–40.

Campbell, J. D., Trapnell, P. D., Heine, S. J., Katz, I. M., Lavallee, L. F., and Lehman, D. R. (1996). Self-concept clarity: Measurement, personality correlates, and cultural boundaries. *Journal of Personality and Social Psychology* 70 (1), 141–56.

Campos-Ortiz, F., Putterman, L. G., Ahn, T. K., Balafoutas, L., Batsaikhan, M., and Sutter, M. Security of property as a public good: Institutions, socio-political environment and experimental behavior in five countries (November 27, 2012). CESifo Working Paper Series No. 4003. ssrn.com/abstract=2181356.

Cantoni, D. (2012). Adopting a new religion: The case of Protestantism in 16th century Germany. *The Economic Journal* 122 (560), 502–531.

Cantoni, D. (2015). The economic effects of the Protestant Reformation: Testing the Weber hypothesis in the German lands. *Journal of the European Economic Association* 13 (4), 561–98.

Cantoni, D., Dittmar, J., and Yuchtman, N. (2018). Religious competition and reallocation: The political economy of secularization in the Protestant Reformation. *Quarterly Journal of Economics* 133 (4), 2037–2096, doi.org/10.1093/qje/qjy011.

Cantoni, D., and Yuchtman, N. (2014). Medieval universities, legal institutions, and the commercial revolution. *Quarterly Journal of Economics* 129 (2), 823–87.

Carlino, G. A., Chatterjee, S., and Hunt, R. M. (2007). Urban density and the rate of invention. *Journal of Urban Economics* 61 (3), 389–419.

Carneiro, R. (1967). On the relationship between size of population and complexity of social organization. *Southwestern Journal of Anthropology* 23 (3), 234–43.

Carneiro, R. (1987). The evolution of complexity in human societies and its mathematical expression. *International Journal of Comparative Sociology* 28 (3), 111–28.

Carneiro, R. L. (1970). A theory of the origin of the state. *Science* 169 (3947), 733–38.

Carneiro, R. L. (1988). The circumscription theory: Challenge and response. *American Behavioral Scientist* 31 (4), 497–511.

Carpenter, M., Uebel, J., and Tomasello, M. (2013). Being mimicked increases prosocial behavior in 18-month-old infants. Child Development 84 (5), 1511–18.

Carter, E. C., McCullough, M. E., Kim-Spoon, J., Corrales, C., and Blake, A. (2011). Religious people discount the future less. *Evolution and Human Behavior* 33 (3), 224–31.

Casey, B. J., Somerville, L. H., Gotlib, I. H., Ayduk, O., Franklin, N. T., Askren, M. K., . . . Shoda, Y. (2011). Behavioral and neural correlates of delay of gratification 40 years later. *Proceedings of the National Academy of Sciences* 108 (36), 14998–15003.

Cassady, R. (1974). *Exchange by Private Treaty. Studies in Marketing.* Austin, TX: Bureau of Business Research.

Cassar, A., Grosjean, P., and Whitt, S. (2013). Legacies of violence: Trust and market development. *Journal of Economic Growth* 18 (3), 285–318.

Castillo, M., and Carter, M. (2011). Behavioral responses to natural disasters. Working paper, ices.gmu.edu/wp-content/uploads/2011/07/Beh.

Cavalcanti, T. V., Parente, S. L., and Zhao, R. (2007). Religion in macroeconomics: A quantitative analysis of Weber's thesis. *Economic Theory* 32 (1), 105–123.

Cecchi, F., Leuveld, K., and Voors, M. (2016). Conflict exposure and competitiveness: Experimental evidence from the football field in Sierra Leone. *Economic Development and Cultural Change* 64 (3), 405–435.

Chabris, C. F., Laibson, D., Morris, C. L., Schuldt, J. P., and Taubinsky, D. (2008). Individual laboratory-measured discount rates predict field behavior. *Journal of Risk and Uncertainty* 37 (2–3), 237–69.

Chacon, Y., Willer, D., Emanuelson, P., and Chacon, R. (2015). From chiefdom to state: The contribution of social structural dynamics. *Social Evolution and History* 14 (2), 27–45.

Chanda, A., and Putterman, L. (2007). Early starts, reversals and catch-up in the process of economic development. *Scandinavian Journal of Economics* 109 (2), 387–413.

Chapais, B. (2009). *Primeval Kinship: How Pair-Bonding Gave Birth to Human Society.* Cambridge, MA: Harvard University Press.

Charles-Edwards, T. M. (1972). Kinship, status and the origins of the hide. *Past and Present* 56 (1), 3–33.

Chartrand, T. L., and Bargh, J. A. (1999). The chameleon effect: The perception-behavior link and social interaction. *Journal of Personality and Social Psychology* 76 (6), 893–910.

Chen, Y., Wang, H., and Yan, S. (2014). The long-term effects of Protestant activities in China. Working paper, ssrn.com/abstract=2186818.

Cheng, J. T., Tracy, J., Foulsham, T., and Kingstone, A. (2013). Dual paths to power: Evidence that dominance and prestige are distinct yet viable avenue to social status. *Journal of Personality and Social Psychology* 104, 103–125.

Cheng, J. T., Tracy, J. L., and Henrich, J. (2010). Pride, personality, and the evolutionary foundations of human social status. *Evolution and Human Behavior* 31 (5), 334–47.

Chernyak, N., Kushnir, T., Sullivan, K. M., and Wang, Q. (2013). A comparison of American and Nepalese children's concepts of freedom of choice and social constraint. *Cognitive Science* 37 (7), 1343–55.

Choi, I., Nisbett, R. E., and Norenzayan, A. (1999). Causal attribution across cultures: Variation and universality. *Psychological Bulletin* 125 (1), 47–63.

Choi, J. K., and Bowles, S. (2007). The coevolution of parochial altruism and war. *Science* 318 (5850), 636–40.

Christmas, B. S. (2014). *Washington's Nightmare: A Brief History of American Political Parties.* Self-published.

Chua, H. F., Boland, J. E., and Nisbett, R. E. (2005). Cultural variation in eye movements during scene perception. *Proceedings of the National Academy of Sciences* 102 (35), 12629–33.

Chua, R. Y. J., Ingram, P., and Morris, M. W. (2008). From the head and the heart: Locating cognition- and affect-based trust in managers' professional networks. *Academy of Management Journal* 51 (3), 436–52.

Chua, R. Y. J., Morris, M. W., and Ingram, P. (2009). Guanxi vs networking: Distinctive configurations of affect- and cognition-based trust in the networks of Chinese vs American managers. *Journal of International Business Studies* 40 (3), 490–508.

Chua, R. Y. J., Morris, M. W., and Ingram, P. (2010). Embeddedness and new idea discussion in professional networks: The mediating role of affect-based trust. *Journal of Creative Behavior* 44 (2), 85–104.

Chudek, M., Brosseau-Liard, P. E., Birch, S., and Henrich, J. (2013). Culture-gene coevolutionary theory and children's selective social learning. In M. R. Banaji and S. A. Gelman (eds.), *Navigating the Social World: What Infants, Children, and Other Species Can Teach Us* (p. 181). New York: Oxford University Press.

Chudek, M., and Henrich, J. (2011). Culture-gene coevolution, norm-psychology and the emergence of human prosociality. *Trends in Cognitive Sciences* 15 (5), 218–26.

Chudek, M., McNamara, R. A., Birch, S., Bloom, P., and Henrich, J. (2017). Do minds switch bodies? Dualist interpretations across ages and societies. *Religion, Brain and Behavior* 8 (4), 354–68.

Chudek, M., Muthukrishna, M., and Henrich, J. (2015). Cultural evolution. In D. M. Buss (ed.), *The Handbook of Evolutionary Psychology* (2nd ed., Vol. 2). Hoboken, NJ: John Wiley and Sons.

Chudek, M., Zhao, W., and Henrich, J. (2013). Culture-gene coevolution, large-scale cooperation and the shaping of human social psychology. In R. Joyce, K. Sterelny, and B. Calcott (eds.), *Signaling, Commitment, and Emotion*. Cambridge, MA: MIT Press.

Church, A. T., Katigbak, M. S., Del Prado, A. M., Ortiz, F. A., Mastor, K. A., Harumi, Y., . . . Cabrera, H. F. (2006). Implicit theories and self-perceptions of traitedness across cultures: Toward integration of cultural and trait psychology perspectives. *Journal of Cross-Cultural Psychology* 37 (6), 694–716.

Churchill, W. (2015). *A History of the English-Speaking Peoples: The Birth of Britain* (Vol. 1). New York: Bloomsbury.

Cipolla, C. M. (1977). *Clocks and Culture, 1300–1700*. New York: W. W. Norton.

Cipolla, C. M. (1994). *Before the Industrial Revolution: European Society and Economy, 1000–1700*. New York: W. W. Norton.

Clark, G. (1987). Productivity growth without technical change in European agriculture before 1850. *Journal of Economic History* 47 (2), 419–32.

Clark, G. (2007a). *A Farewell to Alms: A Brief Economic History of the World*. The Princeton Economic History of the Western World. Princeton, NJ: Princeton University Press.

Clark, G. (2007b). Genetically capitalist? The Malthusian era, institutions and the formation of modern preferences. Working paper, faculty.econ.ucdavis.edu/faculty/gclark/papers/Capitalism%20Genes.pdf.

Clegg, J. M., Wen, N. J., and Legare, C. H. (2017). Is non-conformity WEIRD? Cultural variation in adults' beliefs about children's competency and conformity. *Journal of Experimental Psychology: General* 146 (3), 428–41.

Cohen, A. B. (2015). Religion's profound influences on psychology: Morality, intergroup relations, self-construal, and enculturation. *Current Directions in Psychological Science* 24 (1), 77–82.

Cohen, A. B., and Hill, P. C. (2007). Religion as culture: Religious individualism and collectivism among American Catholics, Jews, and Protestants. *Journal of Personality* 75 (4), 709–742.

Cohen, A. B., and Rozin, P. (2001). Religion and the morality of mentality. *Journal of Personality and Social Psychology* 81 (4), 697–710.

Cohen, R. (1984). Warfare and state formation: Wars make states and states make wars. In R. B. Ferguson (ed.), *Warfare Culture and Environment* (pp. 329–58). Cambridge, MA: Academic Press.

Cohn, A., Fehr, E., and Marechal, M. A. (2014). Business culture and dishonesty in the banking industry. *Nature* 516 (7529), 86–89.

Collard, M., Ruttle, A., Buchanan, B., and O'Brien, M. J. (2012). Risk of resource failure and toolkit variation in small-scale farmers and herders. *PLoS One* 7 (7), e40975.

Collier, P. (2007). *The Bottom Billion: Why the Poorest Countries Are Failing and What Can Be Done About It.* New York: Oxford University Press.

Collins, P. (1994). The Sumerian goddess Inanna (3400–2200 BC). *Papers from the Institute of Archaeology,* 5, 103–118.

Coltheart, M. (2014). The neuronal recycling hypothesis for reading and the question of reading universals. *Mind and Language* 29 (3), 255–69.

Connor, P., Cohn, D., and Gonzalez-Barrera, A. (2013). *Changing patterns of global migration and remittances: More migrants in the U.S. and other wealthy countries; more money to middle-income countries.* PEW Research Center: Social and Demographic Trends. www.pewsocialtrends.org/wp-content/uploads/sites/3/2013/12/global-migration-final_12-2013.pdf.

Conot, R. E. (1979). *A Streak of Luck* (1st ed.). New York: Seaview Books/Simon & Schuster.

Cooperrider, K., Marghetis, T., and Núñez, R. (2017). Where does the ordered line come from? Evidence from a culture of Papua New Guinea. *Psychological Science* 28 (5), 599–608.

Coren, S. (1992). *The Left-Hander Syndrome: The Causes and Consquences of Left-Handedness.* New York: Free Press.

Coy, M. W. (ed.). (1989). *Apprenticeship: From Theory to Method and Back Again.* J. C. Nash (ed.), SUNY Series in the Anthropology of Work. Albany: State University of New York Press.

Creanza, N., Kolodny, O., and Feldman, M. W. (2017). Greater than the sum of its parts? Modelling population contact and interaction of cultural repertoires. *Journal of the Royal Society Interface* 14 (130), 1–11.

Cueva, C., Roberts, R. E., Spencer, T., Rani, N., Tempest, M., Tobler, P. N., Herbert, J., and Rustichini, A. (2015). Cortisol and testosterone increase financial risk taking and may destabilize markets. *Scientific Reports* 5, 1–16.

Cummins, D. D. (1996a). Evidence for the innateness of deontic reasoning. *Mind and Language* 11 (2), 160–90.

Cummins, D. D. (1996b). Evidence of deontic reasoning in 3- and 4-year-old children. *Memory and Cognition* 24 (6), 823–29.

Curtin, C., Barrett, H. C., Bolyanatz, A., Crittenden, A. N., Fessler, D. M. T., Fitzpatrick, S., . . . Henrich, J. (2019). When mental states don't matter: Kinship intensity and intentionality in moral judgement. henrich.fas.harvard.edu/files/henrich/files/kinship-intentionality-main-text.pdf.

D'Avray, D. (2012). Review article: Kinship and religion in the early Middle Ages. *Early Medieval Europe* 20 (2), 195–212.

Dal Bó, P., Foster, A., and Putterman, L. (2010). Institutions and behavior: Experimental evidence on the effects of democracy. *American Economic Review* 100 (5), 2205–2229.

Daly, M., and Wilson, M. (1998). *The Truth About Cinderella*. London: Weidenfeld and Nicolson.

Database English Guilds. (2016). DataverseNL. hdl.handle.net/10411/10100.

Daunton, M. J. (1995). *Progress and Poverty: An Economic and Social History of Britain, 1700–1850*. New York: Oxford University Press.

Davies, J. K. (2004). Athenian citizenship: The descent group and the alternatives. *The Classical Journal* 73 (2), 105–121.

Davis, G. F., and Greve, H. R. (1997). Corporate elite networks and governance changes in the 1980s. *American Journal of Sociology* 103 (1), 1–37.

Davis, H. E. (2014). Variable education exposure and cognitive task performance among the Tsimane' forager-horticulturalists. Dissertation, University of New Mexico.

Davis, P. M. (2002). *Los machiguengas aprenden a leer: Breve historia de la educación bilingüe y el desarrollo comunal entre los machiguengas del bajo Urubamba* (1). Lima: Fondo Editorial de la Pontificia Universidad Católica del Perú.

De Jong, M. (1998). An unsolved riddle: Early medieval incest legislation. In I. Wood (ed.), *Franks and Alamanni in the Merovingian Period: An Ethnographic Perspective* (pp. 107–140). Woodbridge, UK: Boydell & Brewer.

de la Croix, D., Doepke, M., and Mokyr, J. (2018). Clans, guilds, and markets: Apprenticeship institutions and growth in the pre-industrial economy. *Quarterly Journal of Economics* 133 (1), 735–75.

De Moor, T. (2008). The silent revolution: A new perspective on the emergence of commons, guilds, and other forms of corporate collective action in Western Europe. *International Review of Social History* 53 (S16), 179.

De Moor, T., and Van Zanden, J. L. (2010). Girl power: The European marriage pattern and labour markets in the North Sea region in the late medieval and early modern period. *Economic History Review* 63 (1), 1–33.

de Pleijt, A. M. (2016). Accounting for the "little divergence": What drove economic growth in pre-industrial Europe, 1300–1800? *European Review of Economic History* 20 (4), 387–409.

de Vries, J. (1994). The industrial revolution and the industrious revolution. *Journal of Economic History* 54 (2), 249–70.

de Vries, J. (2008). *The Industrious Revolution: Consumer Behavior and the Household Economy, 1650 to the Present.* Cambridge: Cambridge University Press.

de Wolf, J. J. (1980). The diffusion of age-group organization in East Africa: A reconsideration. *Africa* 50 (3), 305–310.

Dehaene, S. (2009). *Reading in the Brain: The Science and Evolution of a Human Invention.* New York: Viking.

Dehaene, S. (2014). Reading in the brain revised and extended: Response to comments. *Mind and Language* 29 (3), 320–35.

Dehaene, S., Cohen, L., Morais, J., and Kolinsky, R. (2015). Illiterate to literate: Behavioural and cerebral changes induced by reading acquisition. *Nature Reviews: Neuroscience* 16 (4), 234–44.

Dehaene, S., Izard, V., Spelke, E., and Pica, P. (2008). Log or linear? Distinct intuitions of the number scale in Western and Amazonian indigene cultures. *Science* 320 (5880), 1217–20.

Dehaene, S., Pegado, F., Braga, L. W., Ventura, P., Nunes Filho, G., Jobert, A., Dehaene-Lambertz, G., Kolinsky, R., Morais, J., Cohen, L. (2010). How learning to read changes the cortical networks for vision and language. *Science* 330 (6009), 1359–64.

Dell, M. (2010). The persistent effects of Peru's mining mita. *Econometrica* 78 (6), 1863–1903.

Derex, M., Beugin, M. P., Godelle, B., and Raymond, M. (2013). Experimental evidence for the influence of group size on cultural complexity. *Nature* 503 (7476), 389–91.

Derex, M., and Boyd, R. (2016). Partial connectivity increases cultural accumulation within groups. *Proceedings of the National Academy of Sciences* 113 (11), 2982–87.

Derex, M., Godelle, B., and Raymond, M. (2014). How does competition affect the transmission of information? *Evolution and Human Behavior* 35 (2), 89–95.

Diamond, A. (2012). Activities and programs that improve children's executive functions. *Current Directions in Psychological Science* 21 (5), 335–41.

Diamond, A., and Lee, K. (2011). Interventions shown to aid executive function development in children 4 to 12 years old. *Science* 333 (6045), 959–64.

Diamond, A., and Ling, D. S. (2016). Conclusions about interventions, programs, and approaches for improving executive functions that appear justified and those that, despite much hype, do not. *Developmental Cognitive Neuroscience* 18, 34–48.

Diamond, J. (1999). Invention is the mother of necessity. *The New York Times Magazine*, 142–44 (April 18).

Diamond, J. M. (1997). *Guns, Germs, and Steel: The Fates of Human Societies*. New York: W. W. Norton.

Diamond, J. M. (2005). *Collapse: How Societies Choose to Fail or Succeed*. New York: Viking.

Diamond, J. M. (2012). *The World Until Yesterday: What Can We Learn from Traditional Societies?* New York: Viking.

Diener, E., and Diener, M. (1995). Cross-cultural correlates of life satisfaction and self-esteem. *Journal of Personality and Social Psychology* 68 (4), 653–63.

Dilcher, G. (1997). The urban belt and the emerging modern state. In *Resistance, Representation, and Community* (pp. 217–55). Oxford: Clarendon Press.

Dincecco, M., and Onorato, M. G. (2016). Military conflict and the rise of urban Europe. *Journal of Economic Growth* 21 (3), 259–82.

Dincecco, M., and Onorato, M. G. (2018). *From Warfare to Wealth: The Military Origins of Urban Prosperity in Europe*. New York: Cambridge University Press.

Dittmar, J. E., and Seabold, S. (2016). Media, markets, and radical ideas: Evidence from the Protestant Reformation. Working paper, www.jeremiahdittmar.com/files/dittmar_seabold_print_religion.pdf.

Doepke, M., and Zilibotti, F. (2008). Occupational choice and the spirit of capitalism. *Quarterly Journal of Economics* 123 (2), 747–93.

Dohmen, T., Enke, B., Falk, A., Huffman, D., and Sunde, U. (2018). Patience and comparative development. Working paper, www.iame.uni-bonn.de/people/thomas-dohmen/patience-and-comparative-development-paper.

Dohrn-van Rossum, G. (1996). *History of the Hour: Clocks and Modern Temporal Orders*. Translated by Thomas Dunlap. Chicago: University of Chicago Press.

Dollinger, P. (1970). *The German Hansa*. Translated and edited by D. S. Ault and S. H. Steinberg. London: Macmillan.

Donkin, R. A. (1978). *The Cistercians: Studies in the Geography of Medieval England and Wales*. Toronto: Pontifical Institute of Mediaeval Studies.

Doris, J. M., and Plakias, A. (2008). How to argue about disagreement: Evaluative diversity and moral realism. In W. Sinnott-Armstrong (ed.), *Moral Psychology*, Vol. 2. *The Cognitive Science of Morality: Intuition and Diveristy* (pp. 303–331). Cambridge, MA: MIT Press.

Dowey, J. (2017). Mind over matter: Access to knowledge and the British industrial revolution. Dissertation, London School of Economics and Political Science.

Drew, K. F. (trans.). (1991). *The Laws of the Salian Franks*. Philadelphia: University of Pennsylvania Press.

Drew, K. F. (trans.). (2010a). *The Burgundian Code*. Philadelphia: University of Pennsylvania Press.

Drew, K. F. (trans.). (2010b). *The Lombard Laws*. Philadelphia: University of Pennsylvania Press.

Droit-Volet, S. (2013). Time perception in children: A neurodevelopmental approach. *Neuropsychologia* 51 (2), 220–34.

Duckworth, A. L., and Kern, M. L. (2011). A meta-analysis of the convergent validity of self-control measures. *Journal of Research in Personality* 45 (3), 259–68.

Duckworth, A. L., and Seligman, M. E. P. (2005). Self-discipline outdoes IQ in predicting academic performance of adolescents. *Psychological Science* 16 (12), 939–44.

Duhaime, E. P. (2015). Is the call to prayer a call to cooperate? A field experiment on the impact of religious salience on prosocial behavior. *Judgment and Decision Making* 10 (6), 593–96.

Dunbar, R. I. M., Clark, A., and Hurst, N. L. (1995). Conflict and cooperation among the Vikings: Contingent behavioral decisions. *Ethology and Sociobiology* 16 (3), 233–46.

Duncan, G. J., Wilkerson, B., and England, P. (2006). Cleaning up their act: The effects of marriage and cohabitation on licit and illicit drug use. *Demography* 43 (4), 691–710.

Dunham, Y., Baron, A. S., and Banaji, M. R. (2008). The development of implicit intergroup cognition. *Trends in Cognitive Sciences* 12 (7), 248–53.

Durant, W. (2011). *The Reformation: The Story of Civilization*. New York: Simon and Schuster.

Durante, R. (2010). Risk, cooperation and the economic origins of social trust: An empirical investigation. Working paper, ssrn.com/abstract=1576774.

Durham, W. H. (1991). *Coevolution: Genes, Culture, and Human Diversity*. Stanford, CA: Stanford University Press.

Durkheim, E. (1933). *The Division of Labor in Society*. Translated by George Simpson. Glencoe, IL: Free Press.

Durkheim, E. (1995). *The Elementary Forms of Religious Life*. Translated by Karen E. Fields. New York: Free Press.

Dyble, M., Gardner, A., Vinicius, L., and Migliano, A. B. (2018). Inclusive fitness for in-laws. *Biology Letters* 14 (10), 1–3.

Earle, T. (1997). *How Chiefs Come to Power*. Stanford, CA: Stanford University Press.

Edelman, B. (2009). Red light states: Who buys online adult entertainment? *Journal of Economic Perspectives* 23 (1), 209–220.

The Editors of the Encyclopedia Britannica. (2018). Sicily. In *Encyclopedia Britannica Online*. Encyclopedia Britannica.

Edlund, L., Li, H., Yi, J., and Zhang, J. (2007). Sex ratios and crime: Evidence from China's one-child policy. *IZA Discussion Paper* No. 3214, pp. 1–51.

Edlund, L., Li, H., Yi, J., and Zhang, J. (2013). Sex ratios and crime: Evidence from China. *Review of Economics and Statistics* 95 (5), 1520–34.

Eisenegger, C., Haushofer, J., and Fehr, E. (2011). The role of testosterone in social interaction. *Trends in Cognitive Sciences* 15 (11), 263–71.

Eisenstadt, S. N. (2016). African age groups: A comparative study. *Africa* 23 (2), 100–113.

Eisner, M. (2001). Modernization, self-control and lethal violence: The long-term dynamics of European homicide rates in theoretical perspective. *British Journal of Criminology* 41 (4), 618–38.

Eisner, M. (2003). Long-term historical trends in violent crime. *Crime and Justice* 30, 83–142.

Ekelund, R. B., Hebert, R., Tollison, R. D., Anderson, G. M., and Davidson, A. B. (1996). *Sacred Trust: The Medieval Church as an Economic Firm.* New York: Oxford University Press.

Elias, N. (2000. *The Civilizing Process.* Hoboken, NJ: Blackwell Publishing.

Elison, J. (2005). Shame and guilt: A hundred years of apples and oranges. *New Ideas in Psychology* 23 (1), 5–32.

Ellison, P. T., Bribiescas, R. G., Bentley, G. R., Campbell, B. C., Lipson, S. F., Panter-Brick, C., and Hill, K. (2002). Population variation in age-related decline in male salivary testosterone. *Human Reproduction* 17 (12), 3251–53.

Ember, C. R., Ember, M., and Pasternack, B. (1974). On the development of unilineal descent. *Journal of Anthropological Research* 30 (2), 69–94.

Ember, M. (1967). The emergence of neolocal residence. *Transactions of the New York Academy of Sciences* 30 (2), 291–302.

Engelmann, J. B., Moore, S., Capra, C. M., and Berns, G. S. (2012). Differential neurobiological effects of expert advice on risky choice in adolescents and adults. *Social Cognitive and Affective Neuroscience* 7 (5), 557–67.

Engelmann, J. M., Herrmann, E., and Tomasello, M. (2012). Five-year-olds, but not chimpanzees, attempt to manage their reputations. *PLoS One* 7 (10), e48433.

Engelmann, J. M., Over, H., Herrmann, E., and Tomasello, M. (2013). Young children care more about their reputation with ingroup members and potential reciprocators. *Developmental Science* 16 (6), 952–58.

English, T., and Chen, S. (2011). Self-concept consistency and culture: The differential impact of two forms of consistency. *Personality and Social Psychology Bulletin* 37 (6), 838–49.

Enke, B. (2017). Kinship systems, cooperation and the evolution of culture. Working paper, www.nber.org/papers/w23499.

Enke, B. (2019). Kinship, cooperation, and the evolution of moral systems. *Quarterly Journal of Economics* 134 (2), 953–1019.

Ensminger, J., and Henrich, J. (Eds). (2014). *Experimenting with Social Norms: Fairness and Punishment in Cross-Cultural Perspective.* New York: Russell Sage Foundation.

Epstein, S. R. (1998). Craft guilds, apprenticeship, and technological change in pre-industrial Europe. *Journal of Economic History* 58 (3), 684–713.

Epstein, S. R. (2013). Transferring technical knowledge and innovating in Europe, c. 1200–1800. In M. Prak and J. L. van Zanden (eds.), *Technology, Skills and the Pre-Modern Economy in the East and the West* (pp. 25–68). Boston: Brill.

Euston, D. R., Gruber, A. J., and McNaughton, B. L. (2012). The role of medial prefrontal cortex in memory and decision making. *Neuron* 76 (6), 1057–70.

Everett, J. A. C., Haque, O. S., and Rand, D. G. (2016). How good is the Samaritan, and why? An experimental investigation of the extent and nature of religious prosociality using economic games. *Social Psychological and Personality Science 7* (3), 248–55.

Ewert, U. C., and Selzer, S. (2016). *Institutions of Hanseatic Trade: Studies on the Political Economy of a Medieval Network*. Frankfurt: Peter Lang.

Falk, A., Becker, A., Dohmen, T., Enke, B., Huffman, D., and Sunde, U. (2018). Global evidence on economic preferences. *Quarterly Journal of Economics* 91 (1), 335–41.

Falk, A., Becker, A., Dohmen, T., Huffman, D., and Sunde, U. (2016). The preference survey module: A validated instrument for measuring risk, time, and social preferences. Working paper, ssrn.com/abstract=2725035.

Falk, A., and Szech, N. (2013). Morals and markets. *Science* 340 (6133), 707–711.

Falk, C. F., Heine, S. J., Yuki, M., and Takemura, K. (2009). Why do Westerners self-enhance more than East Asians? *European Journal of Personality* 23 (3), 183–203.

Faron, L. C. (1968). *The Mapuche Indians of Chile*. Prospect Heights, IL: Waveland Press.

Farrington, D. P., and West, D. J. (1995). Effects of marriage, separation, and children on offending by adult males. *Current Perspectives on Aging and the Life Cycle* 4, 249–81.

Faure, D. (1996). The lineage as business company: Patronage versus law in the development of Chinese business. In R. A. Brown (ed.), *Chinese Business Enterprise* (pp. 82–121). London: Routledge.

Fehr, E., Fischbacher, U., von Rosenblatt, B., Schupp, J., and Wagner, G. G. (2002). A nation-wide laboratory: Examining trust and trustworthiness by integrating behavioral experiments into representative surveys. CEPR Discussion Papers 122 (141), 519–42.

Fehr, E., and Gächter, S. (2000). Cooperation and punishment in public goods experiments. *American Economic Review* 90 (4), 980–95.

Fehr, E., and Gächter, S. (2002). Altruistic punishment in humans. *Nature* 415 (6868), 137–40.

Fehr, E., and Henrich, J. (2003). Is strong reciprocity a maladaption? In P. Hammerstein (ed.), *Genetic and Cultural Evolution of Cooperation* (pp. 55–82). Cambridge, MA: MIT Press.

Fêng, H. (1967). *The Chinese Kinship System*. Cambridge, MA: Harvard University Press.

Fenske, J. (2015). African polygamy: Past and present. *Journal of Development Economics* 117, 58–73.

Fernández, R., and Fogli, A. (2009). Culture: An empirical investigation of beliefs, work, and fertility. *American Economic Journal: Macroeconomics* 1 (1), 146–77.

Ferrero, A. (1967). *Los Machiguengas: Tribu Selvática del Sur-Oriente Peruano*. Villava-Pamplona, Spain: Editorial OPE.

Fessler, D. M. T. (2004). Shame in two cultures: Implications for evolutionary approaches. *Journal of Cognition and Culture* 4 (2), 207–262.

Fessler, D. M. T. (2007). From appeasement to conformity: Evolutionary and cultural perspective on shame, competition, and cooperation. In J. Tracy, R. Robins, and J. P. Tangney (eds.), *The Self-Conscious Emotion: Theory and Research*. New York: Guilford Press.

Fessler, D. M. T., and Navarrete, C. D. (2004). Third-party attitudes toward sibling incest: Evidence for Westermarck's hypotheses. *Evolution and Human Behavior* 25 (5), 277–94.

Fiddick, L., Cosmides, L., and Tooby, J. (2000). No interpretation without representation: The role of domain-specific representations and inferences in the Wason selection task. *Cognition* 77 (1), 1–79.

Field, E., Molitor, V., Schoonbroodt, A., and Tertilt, M. (2016). Gender gaps in completed fertility. *Journal of Demographic Economics* 82 (2), 167–206.

Finke, R., and Stark, R. (2005). *The Churching of America, 1776–2005: Winners and Losers in Our Religious Economy*. New Brunswick, NJ: Rutgers University Press.

Fisman, R., and Miguel, E. (2007). Corruption, norms, and legal enforcement: Evidence from diplomatic parking tickets. *Journal of Political Economy* 115 (6), 1020–1048.

Flannery, K., and Marcus, J. (2012). *The Creation of Inequality: How Our Prehistoric Ancestors Set the Stage for Monarchy, Slavery, and Empire*. Cambridge, MA: Harvard University Press.

Flannery, K. V. (2009). Process and agency in early state formation. *Cambridge Archaeological Journal* 9 (1), 3–21.

Flannery, T. (2002). *The Life and Adventures of William Buckley: Thirty-Two Years a Wanderer Amongst the Aborigines of the Then Unexplored Country Round Port Philip, Now the Province of Victoria*. Melbourne: Text Publishing.

Fleisher, M. L., and Holloway, G. J. (2004). The problem with boys: Bridewealth accumulation, sibling gender, and the propensity to participate in cattle raiding among the Kuria of Tanzania. *Current Anthropology* 45 (2), 284–88.

Fleming, A. S., Corter, C., Stallings, J., and Steiner, M. (2002). Testosterone and prolactin are associated with emotional responses to infant cries in new fathers. *Hormones and Behavior* 42 (4), 399–413.

Flynn, J. R. (2007). *What Is Intelligence? Beyond the Flynn Effect*. Cambridge: Cambridge University Press.

Flynn, J. R. (2012). *Are We Getting Smarter? Rising IQ in the Twenty-First Century*. Cambridge: Cambridge University Press.

Forge, A. (1972). Normative factors in the settlement size of Neolithic cultivators (New Guinea). In P. Ucko, R. Tringham, and G. Dimbelby (eds.), *Man, Settlement and Urbanisation* (pp. 363–76). London: Duckworth.

Fortes, M. (1953). The structure of unilineal descent groups. *American Anthropologist* 55 (1), 17–41.

Fosbrooke, H. A. (1956). The Masai age-group system as a guide to tribal chronology. *African Studies* 15 (4), 188–206.

Foster, G. M. (1965). Peasant society and the image of limited good. *American Anthropologist* 67 (2), 293–315.

Foster, G. M. (1967). *Tzintzuntzan: Mexican Peasants in a Changing World*. Boston: Little, Brown.

Fouquet, R., and Broadberry, S. (2015). Seven centuries of economic growth and decline. *Journal of Economic Perspectives* 29 (4), 227–44.

Fourcade, M., and Healy, K. (2007). Moral views of market society. *Annual Review of Sociology* 33, 285–311.

Fowler, J. H., and Christakis, N. A. (2010). Cooperative behavior cascades in human social networks. *Proceedings of the National Academy of Sciences* 107 (12), 5334–38.

Fox, R. (1967). *Kinship and Marriage: An Anthropological Perspective.* Pelican Anthropology Library. Harmondsworth, UK: Penguin.

Francois, P., Fujiwara, T., and van Ypersele, T. (2011). Competition builds trust. Working paper, thred.devecon.org/papers/2010/2010-011_Fran.

Francois, P., Fujiwara, T., and van Ypersele, T. (2018). The origins of human prosociality: Cultural group selection in the workplace and the laboratory. *Science Advances* 4 (9), eaat2201.

Frankenhuis, W. E., and de Weerth, C., (2013). Does early-life exposure to stress shape or impair cognition? *Current Directions in Psychological Science* 22 (5), 407–412.

Frick, B., and Humphreys, B. R. (2011). Prize structure and performance: Evidence from NASCAR. Working paper, core.ac.uk/download/pdf/6243659.pdf.

Fried, L. P., Ettinger, W. H., Lind, B., Newman, A. B., and Gardin, J. (1994). Physical disability in older adults: A physiological approach. *Journal of Clinical Epidemiology* 47 (7), 747–60.

Fried, M. H. (1970). On the evolution of social stratification and the state. In E. O. Laumann, P. M. Siegel, and R. W. Hodge (eds.), *The Logic of Social Hierarchies* (pp. 684–95). Chicago: Markham.

Fukuyama, F. (2011). *The Origins of Political Order: From Prehuman Times to the French Revolution* (1st ed.). New York: Farrar, Straus and Giroux.

Gächter, S., and Herrmann, B. (2009). Reciprocity, culture and human cooperation: Previous insights and a new cross-cultural experiment. *Philosophical Transactions of the Royal Society B: Biological Sciences* 364 (1518), 791–806.

Gächter, S., Renner, E., and Sefton, M. (2008). The long-run benefits of punishment. *Science* 322 (5907), 1510.

Gächter, S., and Schulz, J. F. (2016). Intrinsic honesty and the prevalence of rule violations across societies. *Nature* 531 (7595), 496–99.

Gailliot, M. T., and Baumeister, R. F. (2007). The physiology of willpower: Linking blood glucose to self-control. *Personality and Social Psychology Review* 11 (4), 303–327.

Gallego, F. A., and Woodberry, R. (2010). Christian missionaries and education in former African colonies: How competition mattered. *Journal of African Economies* 19 (3), 294–329.

Galor, O., and Moav, O. (2002). Natural selection and the origin of economic growth. *Quarterly Journal of Economics* 117 (4), 1133–91.

Galor, O., and Özak, Ö. (2016). The agricultural origins of time preference. *American Economic Review* 106 (10), 3064–3103.

Gardner, P. M. (2013). South Indian foragers' conflict management in comparative perspective. In D. P. Fry (ed.), *War, Peace, and Human Nature: The Convergence of Evolutionary and Cultural Views* (pp. 297–314). New York: Oxford University Press.

Garvert, M. M., Moutoussis, M., Kurth-Nelson, Z., Behrens, T. E. J., and Dolan, R. J. (2015). Learning-induced plasticity in medial prefrontal cortex predicts preference malleability. *Neuron* 85 (2), 418–28.

Gasiorowska, A., Chaplin, L. N., Zaleskiewicz, T., Wygrab, S., and Vohs, K. D. (2016). Money cues increase agency and decrease prosociality among children: Early signs of market-mode behaviors. *Psychological Science* 27 (3), 331–44.

Gat, A. (2015). Proving communal warfare among hunter-gatherers: The quasi-Rousseauan error. *Evolutionary Anthropology: Issues, News, and Reviews* 24 (3), 111–26.

Gavrilets, S., and Richerson, P. J. (2017). Collective action and the evolution of social norm internalization. *Proceedings of the National Academy of Sciences* 114 (23), 6068–6073.

Geertz, C. (1974). "From the native's point of view": On the nature of anthropological understanding. *Bulletin of the American Academy of Arts and Sciences* 28 (1), 26–45.

Gelderblom, O. (2013). *Cities of Commerce: The Institutional Foundations of International Trade in the Low Countries, 1250–1650.* The Princeton Economic History of the Western World. Princeton, NJ: Princeton University Press.

Gelfand, M. J., Raver, J. L., Nishii, L., Leslie, L. M., Lun, J., Lim, B. C., . . . Yamaguchi, S. (2011). Differences between tight and loose cultures: A 33-nation study. *Science* 332 (6033), 1100–1104.

Gellhorn, W. (1987). China's quest for legal modernity. *Journal of Chinese Law* 1 (1), 1–22.

Genschow, O., Rigoni, D., and Brass, M. (2017). Belief in free will affects causal attributions when judging others' behavior. *Proceedings of the National Academy of Sciences* 114 (38), 10071–10076.

Gershman, B. (2015). Witchcraft beliefs and the erosion of social capital: Evidence from Sub-Saharan Africa and beyond. *Journal of Development Economics* 120, 182–208.

Gervais, W. M. (2011). Finding the faithless: Perceived atheist prevalence reduces antiatheist prejudice. *Personality and Social Psychology Bulletin* 37 (4), 543–56.

Gervais, W. M., and Henrich, J. (2010). The Zeus problem: Why representational content biases cannot explain faith in gods. *Journal of Cognition and Culture* 10 (3), 383–89.

Gettler, L. T., McDade, T. W., Feranil, A. B., and Kuzawa, C. W. (2011). Longitudinal evidence that fatherhood decreases testosterone in human males. *Proceedings of the National Academy of Sciences* 108 (39), 16194–99.

Gibson, M. A. (2002). Development and demographic change: The reproductive ecology of a rural Ethiopian Oromo population. Dissertation, University College London.

Gier, N. F., and Kjellberg, P. (2004). Buddhism and the freedom of the will: Pali and Mahayanist responses. In J. K. Campbell, M. O'Rourke, and D. Shier (eds.), *Freedom and Determinism* (pp. 277–304). Cambridge, MA: MIT Press.

Gilligan, M. J., Pasquale, B. J., and Samii, C. (2014). Civil war and social cohesion: Lab-in-the-field evidence from Nepal. *American Journal of Political Science* 58 (3), 604–619.

Gimpel, J. (1976). *The Medieval Machine: The Industrial Revolution of the Middle Ages*. New York: Holt, Rinehart and Winston.

Giner-Sorolla, R., Embley, J., and Johnson, L. (2017). Replication of Vohs and Schooler (2008, PS, study 1), osf.io/i29mh.

Ginges, J., Hansen, I., and Norenzayan, A. (2009). Religion and support for suicide attacks. *Psychological Science* 20 (2), 224–30.

Giuliano, P. (2007). Living arrangements in Western Europe: Does cultural origin matter? *Journal of the European Economic Association* 5 (5), 927–52.

Giuliano, P., and Nunn, N. (2017). Understanding cultural persistence and change. NBER working paper 23617, 1–51.

Glennie, P., and Thrift, N. (1996). Reworking E. P. Thompson's "Time, Work-discipline and Industrial Capitalism." *Time and Society* 5 (3), 275–99.

Glick, T. F. (1979). *Islamic and Christian Spain in the Early Middle Ages*. Princeton, NJ: Princeton University Press.

Gluckman, M. (1940). The kingdom of the Zulu of South Africa. In M. Fortes and E. E. Evans-Pritchard (eds.), *African Political Systems* (pp. 25–55). New York: Oxford University Press.

Gluckman, M. (1972a). *The Allocation of Responsibility*. Manchester, UK: Manchester University Press.

Gluckman, M. (1972b). *The Ideas in Barotse Jurisprudence*. Manchester, UK: Manchester University Press.

Gluckman, M. (2006). *Politics, Law, and Ritual in Tribal Society*. Piscataway, NJ: Aldine Transaction.

Godelier, M. (1986). *The Making of Great Men: Male Domination and Power Among the New Guinea Baruya*. Cambridge: Cambridge University Press.

Godoy, R., Byron, E., Reyes-García, V., Leonard, W. R., Patel, K., Apaza, L., Eddy Pérez, E., Vadez, V., and Wilkie, D. (2004). Patience in a foraging-horticultural society: A test of competing hypotheses. *Journal of Anthropological Research* 60 (2), 179–202.

Goetzmann, W. N., and Rouwenhorst, K. G. (2005). *The Origins of Value: The Financial Innovations That Created Modern Capital Markets*. New York: Oxford University Press.

Goh, J. O., Chee, M. W., Tan, J. C., Venkatraman, V., Hebrank, A., Leshikar, E. D., Jenkins, L., Sutton, B. P., Gutchess, A. H., and Park, D. C. (2007). Age and culture modulate object processing and object-scene binding in the ventral visual area. *Cognitive Affective and Behavioral Neuroscience* 7 (1), 44–52.

Goh, J. O., and Park, D. C. (2009). Culture sculpts the perceptual brain. *Cultural Neuroscience: Cultural Influences on Brain Function* 178, 95–111.

Goh, J. O. S., Leshikar, E. D., Sutton, B. P., Tan, J. C., Sim, S. K. Y., Hebrank, A. C., and Park, D. C. (2010). Culture differences in neural processing of faces and houses in the ventral visual cortex. *Social Cognitive and Affective Neuroscience* 5 (2–3), 227–35.

Goldin, P. (2015). The consciousness of the dead as a philosophical problem in ancient China. In R. King (ed.), *The Good Life and Conceptions of Life in Early China and Greek Antiquity* (pp. 59–92). Berlin: De Gruyter.

Goldman, I. (1955). Status rivalry and cultural evolution in Polynesia. *American Anthropologist* 57 (4), 680–97.

Goldman, I. (1958). Social stratification and cultural evolution in Polynesia. *Ethnohistory* 5 (3), 242–49.

Goldman, I. (1970). *Ancient Polynesian Society*. Chicago: University of Chicago Press.

Gomez-Lievano, A., Patterson-Lomba, O., and Hausmann, R. (2017). Explaining the prevalence, scaling and variance of urban phenomena. *Nature Human Behaviour* 1 (1), No. 12.

Goncalo, J. A., and Staw, B. M. (2006). Individualism–collectivism and group creativity. *Organizational Behavior and Human Decision Processes* 100 (1), 96–109.

Goody, J. (1969). Adoption in cross-cultural perspective. *Comparative Studies in Society and History* 11 (1), 55–78.

Goody, J. (1983). *The Development of the Family and Marriage in Europe: Past and Present Publications*. Cambridge: Cambridge University Press.

Goody, J. (1990). *The Oriental, the Ancient and the Primitive: Systems of Marriage and the Family in the Pre-Industrial Societies of Eurasia*. Cambridge: Cambridge University Press.

Goody, J. (1996). Comparing family systems in Europe and Asia: Are there different sets of rules? *Population and Development Review* 22 (1), 1–20.

Goodyear, C. (1853). *Gum-Elastic and Its Varieties, with a Detailed Account of Its Applications and Uses and of the Discovery of Vulcanization* (Vol. 1). New Haven, CT: Privately published by the author.

Gorodnichenko, Y., and Roland, G. (2011). Individualism, innovation, and long-run growth. *Proceedings of the National Academy of Sciences* 108 (4), 1–4.

Gorodnichenko, Y., and Roland, G. (2016). Culture, institutions, and the wealth of nations. *Review of Economics and Statistics* 99 (3), 402–416.

Gould, R. A. (1967). Notes on hunting, butchering, and sharing of game among the Ngatatjara and their neighbors in the West Australian Desert. *Kroeber Anthropological Society Papers* 36, 41–66.

Grantham, G. W. (1993). Divisions of labor: Agricultural productivity and occupational specialization in preindustrial France. *Economic History Review* 46 (3), 478–502.

Gray, P. B. (2003). Marriage, parenting, and testosterone variation among Kenyan Swahili men. *American Journal of Physical Anthropology* 122 (3), 279–86.

Gray, P. B., and Campbell, B. C. (2006). Testosterone and marriage among Ariaal men of northern Kenya. *American Journal of Physical Anthropology* 48 (5), 94–95.

Gray, P. B., Kahlenberg, S. M., Barrett, E. S., Lipson, S. F., and Ellison, P. T. (2002). Marriage and fatherhood are associated with lower testosterone in males. *Evolution and Human Behavior* 23 (3), 193–201.

Grebe, N. M., Sarafin, R. E., Strenth, C. R., and Zilioli, S. (2019). Pair-bonding, Fatherhood, and the Role of Testosterone: A Meta-Analytic Review. *Neuroscience and Biobehavioral Reviews* 98, 221–33.

Greenwood, P. B., Kanters, M. A., and Casper, J. M. (2006). Sport fan team identification formation in mid-level professional sport. *European Sport Management Quarterly* 6 (3), 253–65.

Greif, A. (1989). Reputation and coalitions in medieval trade: Evidence on the Maghribi traders. *Journal of Economic History* 49 (4), 857–82.

Greif, A. (1993). Contract enforceability and economic institutions in early trade: The Maghribi traders' coalition. *American Economic Review* 83 (3), 525–48.

Greif, A. (2002). Institutions and impersonal exchange: From communal to individual responsibility. *Journal of Institutional and Theoretical Economics* 158 (1), 168–204.

Greif, A. (2003). On the history of the institutional foundations of impersonal exchange. *Journal of Economic History* 63 (2), 555.

Greif, A. (2006a). Family structure, institutions, and growth: The origins and implications of Western corporations. *American Economic Review* 96 (2), 308–312.

Greif, A. (2006b). History lessons: The birth of impersonal exchange: The community responsibility system and impartial justice. *Journal of Economic Perspectives* 20 (2), 221–36.

Greif, A. (2006c). *Institutions and the Path to the Modern Economy: Lessons from Medieval Trade*. Political Economy of Institutions and Decisions. Cambridge: Cambridge University Press.

Greif, A. (2008). Coercion and exchange: How did markets evolve? Working paper, ssrn.com/abstract=1304204.

Greif, A., and Iyigun, M. (2013). Social organizations, violence, and modern growth. *American Economic Review* 103 (3), 534–38.

Greif, A., and Tabellini, G. (2010). Cultural and Institutional Bifurcation: China and Europe Compared. *American Economic Review* 100 (2), 135–40.

Greif, A., and Tabellini, G. (2015). The clan and the city: Sustaining cooperation in China and Europe. *Journal of Comparative Economics* 45, 1–35.

Grierson, P. J. H. (1903). *The Silent Trade: A Contribution to the Early History of Human Intercourse*. Edinburgh: W. Green.

Grosjean, P. (2011). The institutional legacy of the Ottoman Empire: Islamic rule and financial development in South Eastern Europe. *Journal of Comparative Economics* 39 (1), 1–16.

Grosjean, P. (2014). A history of violence: The culture of honor and homicide in the U.S. South. *Journal of the European Economic Association* 12 (5), 1285–1316.

Grossmann, I., Na, J., Varnum, M., Kitayama, S., and Nisbett, R. (2008). Not smarter, but wiser: Dialectical reasoning across lifespan. *International Journal of Psychology* 43 (3–4), 239–40.

Grossmann, T. (2013). The role of medial prefrontal cortex in early social cognition. *Frontiers in Human Neuroscience* 7, 1–6.

Guiso, B. L., Sapienza, P., and Zingales, L. (2004). The role of social capital in financial development. *American Economic Review* 94 (3), 526–56.

Guiso, L., Sapienza, P., and Zingales, L. (2003). People's opium? Religion and economic attitudes. *Journal of Monetary Economics* 50 (1), 225–82.

Guiso, L., Sapienza, P., and Zingales, L. (2008). Trusting the stock market. *Journal of Finance* 63 (6), 2557–2600.

Guiso, L., Sapienza, P., and Zingales, L. (2009). Cultural biases in economic exchange? *Quarterly Journal of Economics* 124 (3), 1095–1131.

Guiso, L., Sapienza, P., and Zingales, L. (2016). Long-term persistence. *Journal of the European Economic Association* 14 (6), 1401–1436.

Gurevich, A. (1995). *The Origins of European Individualism*. The Making of Europe. Oxford: Wiley-Blackwell.

Gurven, M. (2004). To give and to give not: The behavioral ecology of human food transfers. *Behavioral and Brain Sciences* 27 (4), 543–83.

Gurven, M., von Rueden, C., Massenkoff, M., Kaplan, H., and Lero Vie, M. (2013). How universal is the Big Five? Testing the five-factor model of personality variation among forager-farmers in the Bolivian Amazon. *Journal of Personality and Social Psychology* 104 (2), 354–70.

Gurven, M., Winking, J., Kaplan, H., von Rueden, C., and McAllister, L. (2009). A bioeconomic approach to marriage and the sexual division of labor. *Human Nature* 20 (2), 151–83.

Gutchess, A. H., Hedden, T., Ketay, S., Aron, A., and Gabrieli, J. D. E. (2010). Neural differences in the processing of semantic relationships across cultures. *Social Cognitive and Affective Neuroscience* 5 (2–3), 254–63.

Hadnes, M., and Schumacher, H. (2012). The gods are watching: An experimental study of religion and traditional belief in Burkina Faso. *Journal for the Scientific Study of Religion* 51 (4), 689–704.

Haidt, J. (2012). *The Righteous Mind: Why Good People Are Divided by Politics and Religion*. New York: Pantheon Books.

Haidt, J., and Graham, J. (2007). When morality opposes justice: Conservatives have moral intuitions that liberals may not recognize. *Social Justice Research* 20 (1), 98–116.

Hajnal, J. (1965). European marriage patterns in perspective. In D. V. Glass and D. E. C. Eversley (eds.), *Population in History: Essays in Historical Demography* (pp. 101–143). Chicago: Aldine.

Hajnal, J. (1982). Two kinds of preindustrial household formation system. *Population and Development Review* 8 (3), 449–94.

Hallowell, A. I. (1937). Temporal orientation in Western civilization and in a pre-literate society. *American Anthropologist* 39 (4), 647–70.

Hallpike, A. C. R. (1968). The status of craftsmen among the Konso of south-west Ethiopia. *Africa* 38 (3), 258–69.

Hamann, K., Warneken, F., Greenberg, J. R., and Tomasello, M. (2011). Collaboration encourages equal sharing in children but not in chimpanzees. *Nature* 476 (7360), 328–31.

Hamilton, A. (1987). Dual social system: Technology, labour and women's secret rites in the eastern Western Desert of Australia. In W. H. Edwards (ed.), *In Traditional Aboriginal Society: A Reader* (pp. 34–52). Melbourne: Macmillan.

Hamilton, V. L., and Sanders, J. (1992). *Everyday Justice: Responsibility and the Individual in Japan and the United States*. New Haven, CT: Yale University Press.

Han, R., and Takahashi, T. (2012). Psychophysics of time perception and valuation in temporal discounting of gain and loss. *Physica A: Statistical Mechanics and Its Applications* 391 (24), 6568–76.

Handy, E. S. C. (1927). *Polynesian Religion*. Honolulu: Bernice P. Bishop Museum.

Handy, E. S. C. (1941). Perspectives in Polynesian religion. In *Polynesian Anthropological Studies* (Vol. 49, pp. 121–39). New Plymouth, NZ: Thomas Avery and Sons.

Hango, D. W. (2006). The long-term effect of childhood residential mobility on educational attainment. *Sociological Quarterly* 47 (4), 631–34.

Hanoch, Y., Gummerum, M., and Rolison, J. (2012). Second-to-fourth digit ratio and impulsivity: A comparison between offenders and nonoffenders. *PLoS One* 7 (10), e47140.

Hanushek, E. A., and Woessmann, L. (2012). Do better schools lead to more growth? Cognitive skills, economic outcomes, and causation. *Journal of Economic Growth* 17 (4), 267–321.

Harbaugh, W. T., Krause, K., and Vesterlund, L. (2001). Are adults better behaved than children? Age, experience, and the endowment effect. *Economics Letters* 70 (2), 175–81.

Hargadon, A. (2003). *How Breakthroughs Happen: The Surprising Truth About How Companies Innovate*. Boston, MA: Harvard Business School Press.

Harper, K. (2013). *From Shame to Sin: The Christian Transformation of Sexual Morality in Late Antiquity*. Cambridge, MA: Harvard University Press.

Harreld, D. J. (2015). *A Companion to the Hanseatic League*. Brill's Companions to European History. Leiden: Brill.

Harris, J. R. (1998). *The Nurture Assumption: Why Children Turn Out the Way They Do*. New York: Touchstone.

Harrison, S. (1987). Cultural efflorescence and political evolution on the Sepik River. *American Ethnologist* 14 (3), 491–507.

Harrison, S. (1990). *Stealing People's Names: History and Politics in a Sepik River Cosmology*. Cambridge Studies in Social and Cultural Anthropology. Cambridge: Cambridge University Press.

Hatemi, P. K., Smith, K., Alford, J. R., Martin, N. G., and Hibbing, J. R. (2015). The genetic and environmental foundations of political, psychological, social, and economic behaviors: A panel study of twins and families. *Twin Research and Human Genetics* 18 (3), 243–55.

Haushofer, J., and Fehr, E. (2014). On the psychology of poverty. *Science* 344 (6186), 862–67.

Hawk, B. (2015). *Law and Commerce in Pre-industrial Societies*. Leiden; Boston: Koninklijke Brill.

Hayhoe, R. (1989). China's universities and Western academic models. *Higher Education* 18 (1), 49–85.

Heather, P. J. (1999). *The Visigoths from the Migration Period to the Seventh Century: An Ethnographic Perspective*. Studies in Historical Archaeoethnology. Woodbridge, UK: Boydell Press.

Heine, S. J. (2016). *Cultural Psychology* (3rd ed.). New York: W. W. Norton.

Heine, S. J., and Buchtel, E. E. (2009). Personality: The universal and the culturally specific. *Annual Review of Psychology* 60, 369–94.

Heine, S. J., and Lehman, D. (1999). Culture, self-discrepancies, and self-satisfaction. *Personality and Social Psychology Bulletin* 25 (8), 915–25.

Heizer, R. (1978). *Handbook of North American Indians: California* (W. Sturtevant, ed.) (Vol. 8). Washington, DC: Smithsonian Institution.

Heldring, L., Robinson, J. A., and Vollmer, S. (2018). The long-run impact of the dissolution of the English monasteries. Working paper, pdfs.semanticscholar.org/af39/4d1fe6ebf414.

Henrich, J. (1997). Market incorporation, agricultural change, and sustainability among the Machiguenga Indians of the Peruvian Amazon. *Human Ecology* 25 (2), 319–51.

Henrich, J. (2000). Does culture matter in economic behavior? Ultimatum Game bargaining among the Machiguenga of the Peruvian Amazon. *American Economic Review* 90 (4), 973–80.

Henrich, J. (2004a). Cultural group selection, coevolutionary processes and large-scale cooperation. *Journal of Economic Behavior and Organization* 53 (1), 3–35.

Henrich, J. (2004b). Demography and cultural evolution: Why adaptive cultural processes produced maladaptive losses in Tasmania. *American Antiquity* 69 (2), 197–214.

Henrich, J. (2009a). The evolution of costly displays, cooperation and religion. *Evolution and Human Behavior* 30 (4), 244–60.

Henrich, J. (2009b). The evolution of innovation-enhancing institutions. In S. J. Shennan and M. J. O'Brien (eds.), *Innovation in Cultural Systems: Contributions in Evolutionary Anthropology* (pp. 99–120). Cambridge, MA: MIT Press.

Henrich, J. (2014). Rice, psychology, and innovation. *Science* 344 (6184), 593–94.

Henrich, J. (2015). Culture and social behavior. *Current Opinion in Behavioral Sciences* 3, 84–89.

Henrich, J. (2016). *The Secret of Our Success: How Culture Is Driving Human Evolution, Domesticating Our Species, and Making Us Smarter.* Princeton, NJ: Princeton University Press.

Henrich, J., Bauer, M., Cassar, A., Chytilová, J., and Purzycki, B. G. (2019). War increases religiosity. *Nature Human Behaviour* 3 (2), 129–35.

Henrich, J., and Boyd, R. (2008). Division of labor, economic specialization, and the evolution of social stratification. *Current Anthropology* 49 (4), 715–24.

Henrich, J., and Boyd, R. (2016). How evolved psychological mechanisms empower cultural group selection. *Behavioral and Brain Sciences* 39, e40.

Henrich, J., Boyd, R., Bowles, S., Camerer, C., Fehr, E., and Gintis, H. (2004). *Foundations of Human Sociality: Economic Experiments and Ethnographic Evidence from Fifteen Small-Scale Societies.* New York: Oxford University Press.

Henrich, J., Boyd, R., Bowles, S., Camerer, C., Fehr, E., Gintis, H., . . . Tracer, D. (2005). "Economic man" in cross-cultural perspective: Behavioral experiments in 15 small-scale societies. *Behavioral and Brain Sciences* 28 (6), 795–815; discussion, 815–55.

Henrich, J., Boyd, R., Derex, M., Kline, M. A., Mesoudi, A., Muthukrishna, M., Powell, A., Shennan, S., and Thomas, M. G. (2016). Appendix to Understanding Cumulative Cultural Evolution: A Reply to Vaesen, Collard, et al., ssrn.com/abstract =2798257.

Henrich, J., Boyd, R., and Richerson, P. J. (2012). The puzzle of monogamous marriage. *Philosophical Transactions of the Royal Society B: Biological Sciences* 367 (1589), 657–69.

Henrich, J., and Broesch, J. (2011). On the nature of cultural transmission networks: Evidence from Fijian villages for adaptive learning biases. *Philosophical Transactions of the Royal Society B: Biological Sciences* 366 (1567), 1139–48.

Henrich, J., Chudek, M., and Boyd, R. (2015). The big man mechanism: How prestige fosters cooperation and creates prosocial leaders. *Philosophical Transactions of the Royal Society B: Biological Sciences* 370 (1683), 20150013.

Henrich, J., Ensminger, J., McElreath, R., Barr, A., Barrett, C., Bolyanatz, A., . . . Ziker, J. (2010). Market, religion, community size and the evolution of fairness and punishment. *Science* 327, 1480–84.

Henrich, J., and Gil-White, F. J. (2001). The evolution of prestige: Freely conferred deference as a mechanism for enhancing the benefits of cultural transmission. *Evolution and Human Behavior* 22 (3), 165–96.

Henrich, J., Heine, S. J., and Norenzayan, A. (2010a). Most people are not WEIRD. *Nature* 466 (7302), 29.

Henrich, J., Heine, S. J., and Norenzayan, A. (2010b). The WEIRDest people in the world? *Behavioral and Brain Sciences* 33 (2–3), 61–83.

Henrich, J., and Henrich, N. (2014). Fairness without punishment: Behavioral experiments in the Yasawa Island, Fiji. In J. Ensminger and J. Henrich (eds.), *Experiment-*

ing with Social Norms: Fairness and Punishment in Cross-Cultural Perspective. New York: Russell Sage Foundation.

Henrich, J., McElreath, R., Barr, A., Ensminger, J., Barrett, C., Bolyanatz, A., . . . Ziker, J. (2006). Costly punishment across human societies. *Science* 312 (5781), 1767–70.

Henrich, J., and Smith, N. (2004). Comparative experimental evidence from Machiguenga, Mapuche, and American populations. In J. Henrich, R. Boyd, S. Bowles, H. Gintis, E. Fehr, and C. Camerer (eds.), *Foundations of Human Sociality: Economic Experiments and Ethnographic Evidence from Fifteen Small-Scale Societies* (pp. 125–67). New York: Oxford University Press.

Henrich, N., and Henrich, J. (2007). *Why Humans Cooperate: A Cultural and Evolutionary Explanation.* New York: Oxford University Press.

Herbermann, C. G., Pace, E. A., Pallen, C. B., Shahan, T. J., and Wynne, J. J. (eds.). (1908). Cistercians. In *The Catholic Encyclopedia.* New York: Robert Appleton.

Herlihy, D. (1985). *Medieval Households.* Studies in Cultural History. Cambridge, MA: Harvard University Press.

Herlihy, D. (1990). Making sense of incest: Women and the Marriage Rules of the Early Middle Ages. *Studies in Medieval Culture* 28, 1–16.

Herlihy, D. (1995). Biology and history: The triumph of monogamy. *Journal of Interdisciplinary History* 25 (4), 571–83.

Hermans, E. J., Putman, P., and van Honk, J. (2006). Testosterone administration reduces empathetic behavior: A facial mimicry study. *Psychoneuroendocrinology* 31 (7), 859–66.

Herrmann, B., Thöni, C., and Gächter, S. (2008). Antisocial punishment across societies. *Science* 319 (5868), 1362–67.

Herrmann-Pillath, C. (2010). Social capital, Chinese style: Individualism, relational collectivism and the cultural embeddedness of the institutions-performance link. *China Economic Journal* 2 (3), 325–50.

Hersh, J., and Voth, H.-J. (2009). Sweet diversity: Colonial goods and the rise of European living standards after 1492. Working paper, ssrn.com/abstract=1462015.

Hewlett, B. S. (1996). Cultural diversity among African Pygmies. In S. Kent (ed.), *Cultural Diversity Among Twentieth-Century Foragers: An African Perspective* (pp. 215–44). Cambridge: Cambridge University Press.

Hewlett, B. S. (2000). Culture, history, and sex: Anthropological contributions to conceptualizing father involvement. *Marriage and Family Review* 29 (2–3), 59–73.

Hewlett, B. S., and Cavalli-Sforza, L. L. (1986). Cultural transmission among Aka pygmies. *American Anthropologist* 88 (4), 922–34.

Hewlett, B. S., Fouts, H. N., Boyette, A. H., and Hewlett, B. L. (2011). Social learning among Congo Basin hunter-gatherers. *Philosophical Transactions of the Royal Society B: Biological Sciences* 366 (1567), 1168–78.

Hewlett, B. S., and Winn, S. (2014). Allomaternal nursing in humans. *Current Anthropology* 55 (2), 200–229.

Heyer, E., Chaix, R., Pavard, S., and Austerlitz, F. (2012). Sex-specific demographic behaviours that shape human genomic variation. *Molecular Ecology* 21 (3), 597–612.

Heyes, C. (2013). What can imitation do for cooperation? In K. Sterelny, R. Joyce, B. Calcott, and B. Fraser (eds.), *Cooperation and Its Evolution* (pp. 313–32). Cambridge, MA: MIT Press.

Hibbs, D. A., and Olsson, O. (2004). Geography, biogeography, and why some countries are rich and others are poor. *Proceedings of the National Academy of Sciences* 101 (10), 3715–20.

Higham, N. J. (1997). *The Convert Kings: Power and Religious Affiliation in Early Anglo-Saxon England*. Manchester, UK: Manchester University Press.

Hill, K. R., Walker, R. S., Božičević, M., Eder, J., Headland, T., Hewlett, B., Hurtado, A. M., Marlowe, F., Wiessner, P., and Wood, B. (2011). Co-residence patterns in hunter-gatherer societies show unique human social structure. *Science* 331 (6022), 1286–89.

Hill, K. R., Wood, B., Baggio, J., Hurtado, A. M., and Boyd, R. (2014). Hunter-gatherer inter-band interaction rates: Implications for cumulative culture. *PLoS One* 9 (7), e102806.

Hilton, I. (2001). Letter from Pakistan: Pashtun code. *The New Yorker* (December 3).

Hirschfeld, L. A., and Gelman, S. A. (1994). *Mapping the Mind: Domain Specificity in Cognition and Culture*. Cambridge: Cambridge University Press.

Hirschman, A. O. (1982). Rival interpretations of market society: Civilizing, destructive or feeble? *Journal of Economic Literature* 20 (4), 1463–84.

Hoddinott, J., Maluccio, J., Behrman, J. R., Martorell, R., Melgar, P., Quisumbing, A. R., Ramirez-Zea, M., Stein, A. D., and Yount, K. M. (2011). The consequences of early childhood growth failure over the life course. IFPRI Discussion Paper No. 1073. Washington, DC: International Food Policy Research Institute.

Hoff, K., and Sen, A. (2016). The kin-system as a poverty trap? In S. Bowles, S. N. Durlauf, and K. Hoff (eds.), *Poverty Traps* (pp. 95–115). Princeton, NJ: Princeton University Press.

Hoffman, P. T. (2015). *Why Did Europe Conquer the World?* Princeton, NJ: Princeton University Press.

Hofstadter, R. (1969). *The Idea of a Party System: The Rise of Legitimate Opposition in the United States, 1780–1840*. Berkeley: University of California Press.

Hofstede, G. H. (2003). *Culture's Consequences: Comparing Values, Behaviors, Institutions and Organizations Across Nations* (2nd ed.). Thousand Oaks, CA: Sage Publications.

Hogbin, H. I. (1934). *Law and Order in Polynesia: A Study of Primitive Legal Institutions*. London: Christophers.

Hoppitt, W., and Laland, K. N. (2013). *Social Learning: An Introduction to Mechanisms, Methods, and Models*. Princeton, NJ: Princeton University Press.

Horner, V., and Whiten, A. (2005). Causal knowledge and imitation/emulation switching in chimpanzees (*Pan troglodytes*) and children (*Homo sapiens*). *Animal Cognition* 8 (3), 164–81.

Horney, J., Osgood, D. W., and Marshall, I. H. (1995). Criminal careers in the short-term: Intra-individual variability in crime and its relation to local life circumstances. *American Sociological Review* 60 (5), 655–73.

Hornung, E. (2014). Immigration and the diffusion of technology: The Huguenot diaspora in Prussia. *American Economic Review* 104 (1), 84–122.

Hosler, D., Burkett, S. L., and Tarkanian, M. J. (1999). Prehistoric polymers: Rubber processing in ancient Mesoamerica. *Science* 284 (5422), 1988–91.

Howes, A. (2017). The relevance of skills to innovation during the British Industrial Revolution, 1651–1851. Working paper, www.eh.net/eha/wp-content/uploads/2016/08/H.

Hruschka, D. J. (2010). *Friendship: Development, Ecology, and Evolution of a Relationship.* Berkeley: University of California Press.

Hruschka, D. J., Efferson, C., Jiang, T., Falletta-Cowden, A., Sigurdsson, S., McNamara, R., Sands, M., Munira, S., Slingerland, E., and Henrich, J. (2014). Impartial institutions, pathogen stress and the expanding social network. *Human Nature* 25 (4), 567–79.

Hruschka, D. J., and Henrich, J. (2013a). Economic and evolutionary hypotheses for cross-population variation in parochialism. *Frontiers in Human Neuroscience* 7, 559.

Hruschka, D. J., and Henrich, J. (2013b). Institutions, parasites and the persistence of in-group preferences. *PLoS One* 8 (5), e63642.

Huettig, F., and Mishra, R. K. (2014). How literacy acquisition affects the illiterate mind: A critical examination of theories and evidence. *Linguistics and Language Compass* 8 (10), 401–427.

Huff, T. E. (1993). *The Rise of Early Modern Science: Islam, China, and the West.* Cambridge: Cambridge University Press.

Hui, V. T. (2005). *War and State Formation in Ancient China and Early Modern Europe.* Cambridge: Cambridge University Press.

Hume, D. (1987). *Essays: Moral, Political, and Literary.* Indianapolis: Liberty Fund.

Humphries, J., and Weisdorf, J. (2017). Unreal wages? Real income and economic growth in England, 1260–1850. *The Economic Journal* 129 (623), 2867–87.

Inglehart, R., and Baker, W. E. (2000). Modernization, cultural change, and the persistence of traditional values. *American Sociological Review* 65 (1), 19–51.

Inglehart, R., Haerpfer, C., Moreno, A., Welzel, C., Kizilova, K., Diez-Medrano, J., . . . et al. (eds.). (2014). World Values Survey: All Rounds—Country-Pooled Datafile Version: www.worldvaluessurvey.org/WVSDocumentationWVL.jsp. Madrid: JD Systems Institute.

Inkster, I. (1990). Mental capital: Transfers of knowledge and technique in eighteenth century Europe. *Journal of European Economic History* 19 (2), 403–441.

Inzlicht, M., and Schmeichel, B. J. (2012). What is ego depletion? Toward a mechanistic revision of the resource model of self-control. *Perspectives on Psychological Science* 7 (5), 450–63.

Isaacs, A. K., and Prak, M. (1996). Cities, bourgeoisies, and states. In R. Wolfgang (ed.), *Power, Elites and State Building* (pp. 207–234). New York: Oxford University Press.

Israel, J. (2010). *A Revolution of the Mind: Radical Enlightenment and the Intellectual Origins of Modern Democracy*. Princeton, NJ: Princeton University Press.

Iyengar, S. S., and DeVoe, S. E. (2003). Rethinking the value of choice: Considering cultural mediators of intrinsic motivation. *Nebraska Symposium on Motivation* 49, 129–74.

Iyengar, S. S., Lepper, M. R., and Ross, L. (1999). Independence from whom? Interdependence with whom? Cultural perspectives on ingroups versus outgroups. In D. A. Prentice and D. T. Miller (eds.), *Cultural Divides: Understanding and Overcoming Group Conflict* (pp. 273–301). New York: Russell Sage Foundation.

Iyigun, M. (2008). Luther and Suleyman. *Quarterly Journal of Economics* 123 (4), 1465–1494.

Iyigun, M., Nunn, N., and Qian, N. (2017). The long-run effect of agricultural productivity and conflict, 1400–1900. NBER working paper, www.nber.org/papers/w24066.

Jacob, M. (2010). Long-term persistence: The free and imperial city experience in Germany. Working paper, ssrn.com/abstract=1616973.

Jacob, M. C. (2000). Commerce, industry, and the laws of Newtonian science: Weber revisited and revised. *Canadian Journal of History* 35 (2), 275–92.

Jacob, M. C. (2013). *The First Knowledge Economy: Human Capital and the European Economy, 1750–1850*. Cambridge: Cambridge University Press.

Jaffe, K., Florez, A., Gomes, C. M., Rodriguez, D., and Achury, C. (2014). On the biological and cultural evolution of shame: Using internet search tools to weight values in many cultures. Working paper, arxiv.org/abs/1401.1100.

Jaffee, S., Caspi, A., Moffitt, T. E., Belsky, J., and Silva, P. (2001). Why are children born to teen mothers at risk for adverse outcomes in young adulthood? Results from a 20-year longitudinal study. *Development and Psychopathology* 13 (2), 377–97.

Jankowiak, W. (2008). Co-wives, husband, and the Mormon polygynous family. *Ethnology* 47 (3), 163–80.

Jankowiak, W., Sudakov, M., and Wilreker, B. C. (2005). Co-wife conflict and cooperation. *Ethnology* 44 (1), 81–98.

Jha, S. (2013). Trade, institutions and ethnic tolerance: Evidence from South Asia. *American Political Science Review* 107 (4), 806–32.

Ji, L. J., Nisbett, R. E., and Su, Y. (2001). Culture, change, and prediction. *Psychological Science* 12 (6), 450–56.

Ji, L. J., Zhang, Z. Y., and Guo, T. Y. (2008). To buy or to sell: Cultural differences in stock market decisions based on price trends. *Journal of Behavioral Decision Making* 21 (4), 399–413.

Jin, L. E. I., Elwert, F., Freese, J., and Christakis, N. A. (2010). Maturity may affect longevity in men. *Demography* 47 (3), 579–86.

Johns, T. (1986). Detoxification function of geophagy and domestication of the potato. *Journal of Chemical Ecology* 12 (3), 635–46.

Johnson, A. (2003). *Families of the Forest: Matsigenka Indians of the Peruvian Amazon.* Berkeley: University of California Press.

Johnson, A. W., and Earle, T. (2000). *The Evolution of Human Societies: From Foraging Group to Agrarian State.* Stanford, CA: Stanford University Press.

Johnson, N. D., and Koyama, M. (2017). Jewish communities and city growth in preindustrial Europe. *Journal of Development Economics* 127, 339–54.

Johnson, N. D., and Mislin, A. (2012). How much should we trust the World Values Survey trust question? *Economics Letters* 116 (2), 210–12.

Johnson, O. R. (1978). Interpersonal relations and domestic authority among the Machiguenga of the Peruvian Amazon. Dissertation, Columbia University.

Jones, D. (2011). The matrilocal tribe: An organization of demic expansion. *Human Nature* 22 (1–2), 177–200.

Jones, D. E. (2007). *Poison Arrows: North American Indian Hunting and Warfare.* Austin: University of Texas Press.

Kalb, G., and van Ours, J. C. (2014). Reading to young children: A head-start in life? *Economics of Education Review* 40, 1–24.

Kanagawa, C., Cross, S. E., and Markus, H. R. (2001). "Who am I?": The cultural psychology of the conceptual self. *Personality and Social Psychology Bulletin* 27, 90–103.

Karlan, D., Ratan, A. L., and Zinman, J. (2014). Savings by and for the poor: A research review and agenda. *Review of Income and Wealth* 60 (1), 36–78.

Karmin, M., Saag, L., Vicente, M., Sayres, M. A. W., Järve, M., Talas, U. G., . . . Pagani, L. (2015). A recent bottleneck of Y chromosome diversity coincides with a global change in culture. *Genome Research* 25 (4), 459–66.

Karras, R. M. (1990). Concubinage and slavery in the Viking age. *Scandinavian Studies* 62 (2), 141–62.

Keeley, L. (1997). *War Before Civilization.* New York: Oxford University Press.

Kelekna, P. (1998). War and theocracy. In E. M. Redmond (ed.), *Chiefdoms and Chieftaincy in the Americas* (pp. 164–88). Gainesville: University of Florida Press.

Kelly, M., Mokyr, J., and Gráda, C. Ó. (2014). Precocious Albion: A new interpretation of the British industrial revolution. *Annual Review of Economics* 6 (1), 363–89.

Kelly, M., and Ó Gráda, C. (2016). Adam Smith, watch prices, and the Industrial Revolution. *Quarterly Journal of Economics* 131 (4), 1727–52.

Kelly, R. C. (1985). *The Nuer Conquest: The Structure and Development of an Expansionist System.* Ann Arbor, MI: University of Michigan Press.

Kemezis, A. M., and Maher, M. (2015). *Urban Dreams and Realities in Antiquity.* Leiden: Brill.

Kempe, M., and Mesoudi, A. (2014). An experimental demonstration of the effect of group size on cultural accumulation. *Evolution and Human Behavior* 35 (4), 285–90.

Kerley, K. R., Copes, H., Tewksbury, R., and Dabney, D. A. (2011). Examining the relationship between religiosity and self-control as predictors of prison deviance. *International Journal of Offender Therapy and Comparative Criminology* 55 (8), 1251–71.

Khadjavi, M., and Lange, A. (2013). Prisoners and their dilemma. *Journal of Economic Behavior and Organization* 92, 163–75.

Khaldûn, I. (2015). *The Muqaddimah: An Introduction to History.* (F. Rosenthal, ed.). Princeton, NJ: Princeton University Press.

Kidd, D. C., and Castano, E. (2013). Reading literary fiction improves theory of mind. *Science* 342 (6156), 377–80.

Kieser, A. (1987). From asceticism to administration of wealth: Medieval monasteries and the pitfalls of rationalization. *Organization Studies* 8 (2), 103–123.

Kinzler, K. D., and Dautel, J. B. (2012). Children's essentialist reasoning about language and race. *Developmental Science* 15 (1), 131–38.

Kirby, K. N., Godoy, R., Reyes-García, V., Byron, E., Apaza, L., Leonard, W., Pérez, E., Vadez, V., and Wilkie, D. (2002). Correlates of delay-discount rates: Evidence from Tsimane' Amerindians of the Bolivian rain forest. *Journal of Economic Psychology* 23 (3), 291–316.

Kirby, K. R., Gray, R. D., Greenhill, S. J., Jordan, F. M., Gomes-Ng, S., Bibiko, H.-J., . . . Gavin, M. C. (2016). D-PLACE: A Global Database of Cultural, Linguistic and Environmental Diversity. *PLoS One* 11 (7), 1–14.

Kirch, P. V. (1984). *The Evolution of the Polynesian Chiefdoms.* New Studies in Archaeology. Cambridge: Cambridge University Press.

Kirch, P. V. (2010). *How Chiefs Became Kings: Divine Kingship and the Rise of Archaic States in Ancient Hawai'i.* Berkeley: University of California Press.

Kitayama, S., Park, H., Sevincer, A. T., Karasawa, M., and Uskul, A. K. (2009). A cultural task analysis of implicit independence: Comparing North America, Western Europe, and East Asia. *Journal of Personality and Social Psychology* 97, 236–55.

Kitayama, S., Yanagisawa, K., Ito, A., Ueda, R., Uchida, Y., and Abe, N. (2017). Reduced orbitofrontal cortical volume is associated with interdependent self-construal. *Proceedings of the National Academy of Sciences* 114 (30), 7969–74.

Kleinschmidt, H. (2000). *Understanding the Middle Ages.* Woodbridge, UK: Boydell Press.

Kline, M. A., and Boyd, R. (2010). Population size predicts technological complexity in Oceania. *Proceedings of the Royal Society B: Biological Sciences* 277 (1693), 2559–64.

Klochko, M. A. (2006). Time preference and learning versus selection: A case study of Ukrainian students. *Rationality and Society* 18 (3), 305–331.

Knauft, B. M. (1985). Good company and violence: Sorcery and social action in a lowland New Guinea society. *Journal for the Scientific Study of Religion* 26 (1), 126–28.

Knight, N., and Nisbett, R. E. (2007). Culture, class and cognition: Evidence from Italy. *Journal of Cognition and Culture* 7 (3), 283–91.

Kobayashi, C., Glover, G. H., and Temple, E. (2007). Cultural and linguistic effects on neural bases of "theory of mind" in American and Japanese children. *Brain Research* 1164, 95–107.

Kolinsky, R., Verhaeghe, A., Fernandes, T., Mengarda, E. J., Grimm-Cabral, L., and Morais, J. (2011). Enantiomorphy through the looking glass: Literacy effects on mirror-image discrimination. *Journal of Experimental Psychology: General* 140 (2), 210–38.

Kolodny, O., Creanza, N., and Feldman, M. W. (2015). Evolution in leaps: The punctuated accumulation and loss of cultural innovations. *Proceedings of the National Academy of Sciences* 112 (49), e6762–e6769.

Kong, A., Frigge, M. L., Masson, G., Besenbacher, S., Sulem, P., Magnusson, G., . . . Stefansson, K. (2012). Rate of de novo mutations and the importance of father's age to disease risk. *Nature* 488 (7412), 471–75.

Kong, A., Frigge, M. L., Thorleifsson, G., Stefansson, H., Young, A. I., Zink, F., . . . Stefansson, K. (2017). Selection against variants in the genome associated with educational attainment. *Proceedings of the National Academy of Sciences* 114 (5), e727–e732.

Korotayev, A. (2000). Parallel-cousin (FBD) marriage, Islamization, and Arabization. *Ethnology* 39 (4), 395–407.

Korotayev, A. (2004). *World Religions and Social Evolution*. New York: Edwin Mellen.

Kosfeld, M., and Rustagi, D. (2015). Leader punishment and cooperation in groups: Experimental field evidence from commons management in Ethiopia. *American Economic Review* 105 (2), 747–83.

Kouider, S., and Dehaene, S. (2007). Levels of processing during non-conscious perception: A critical review of visual masking. *Philosophical Transactions of the Royal Society B: Biological Sciences* 362 (1481), 857–75.

Kouri, E. M., Lukas, S. E., Pope, H. G., and Oliva, P. S. (1995). Increased aggressive responding in male volunteers following the administration of gradually increasing doses of testosterone cypionate. *Drug and Alcohol Dependence* 40 (1), 73–79.

Kraft-Todd, G. T., Bollinger, B., Gillingham, K., Lamp, S., and Rand, D. G. (2018). Credibility-enhancing displays promote the provision of non-normative public goods. *Nature* 563 (7730), 245–48.

Kremer, M. (1993). Population growth and technological change: One Million B.C. to 1990. *Quarterly Journal of Economics* 108 (3), 681–716.

Kroeber, A. L. (1925). *Handbook of the Indians of California*. United States Bureau of American Ethnology. Washington, DC: Government Printing Office.

Kröll, M., and Rustagi, D. (2018). Reputation, dishonesty, and cheating in informal milk markets in India. Working paper, ssrn.com/abstract=2982365.

Kroszner, R. S., and Strahan, P. E. (1999). What drives deregulation? Economics and politics of the relaxation of bank branching restrictions. *Quarterly Journal of Economics* 114 (4), 1437–67.

Kudo, Y. (2014). Religion and polygamy: Evidence from the Livingstonia Mission in Malawi. IDE Discussion Papers, ideas.repec.org/p/jet/dpaper/dpaper477.htm.

Kuhnen, U., Hannover, B., Roeder, U., Shah, A. A., Schubert, B., Upmeyer, A., and Zakaria, S. (2001). Cross-cultural variations in identifying embedded figures: Comparisons from the United States, Germany, Russia, and Malaysia. *Journal of Cross-Cultural Psychology* 32 (3), 365–71.

Kuper, A. (2010). *Incest and Influence.* Cambridge, MA: Harvard University Press.

Kushner, H. I. (2013). Why are there (almost) no left-handers in China? *Endeavour* 37 (2), 71–81.

Kushnir, T. (2018). The developmental and cultural psychology of free will. *Philosophy Compass* 13 (11), e12529.

Laajaj, R., Macours, K., Alejandro, D., Hernandez, P., Arias, O., Gosling, S., Potter, J., Rubio-Codina, M., and Vakis, R. (2019). Challenges to capture the big five personality traits in non-WEIRD populations. *Science Advances* 5 (7), eaaw5226.

Laland, K. N. (2004). Social learning strategies. *Learning and Behavior* 32 (1), 4–14.

Laland, K. N. (2008). Exploring gene-culture interactions: Insights from handedness, sexual selection and niche-construction case studies. *Philosophical Transactions of the Royal Society B: Biological Sciences* 363 (1509), 3577–89.

Laland, K. N. (2017). *Darwin's Unfinished Symphony: How Culture Made the Human Mind.* Princeton, NJ: Princeton University Press.

Lancaster, L. (2015). Kinship in Anglo-Saxon society—I. *British Journal of Sociology* 9 (3), 230–50.

Landes, D. S. (1998). *The Wealth and Poverty of Nations: Why Some Are So Rich and Some So Poor.* New York: W. W. Norton.

Lang, M., Bahna, V., Shaver, J. H., Reddish, P., and Xygalatas, D. (2017). Sync to link: Endorphin-mediated synchrony effects on cooperation. *Biological Psychology* 127, 191–97.

Lang, M., Kratky, J., Shaver, J. H., Jerotijevic, D., and Xygalatas, D. (2015). Effects of anxiety on spontaneous ritualized behavior. *Current Biology* 25 (14), 1892–97.

Lang, M., Purzycki, B. G., Apicella, C. L., Atkinson, Q. D., Bolyanatz, A., Cohen, E., . . . Lang, M. (2019). Moralizing gods, impartiality and religious parochialism across 15 societies. *Proceedings of the Royal Society B: Biological Sciences* 286, 1–10.

Lanman, J. A. (2012). The importance of religious displays for belief acquisition and secularization. *Journal of Contemporary Religion* 27 (1), 49–65.

Lanman, J. A., and Buhrmester, M. D. (2017). Religious actions speak louder than words: Exposure to credibility-enhancing displays predicts theism. *Religion, Brain & Behavior* 7 (1), 3–16.

Lape, S. (2002). Solon and the institution of the "democratic" family form. *The Classical Journal* 98 (2), 117–39.

Laslett, P. (1977). *Family Life and Illicit Love in Earlier Generations: Essays in Historical Sociology.* Cambridge: Cambridge University Press.

Laslett, P. (1984). *The World We Have Lost: Further Explored* (3rd ed.). New York: Scribner.

Laslett, P., and Wall, R. (1972). *Household and Family in Past Time*. Cambridge: University Press.

Launay, J., Tarr, B., and Dunbar, R. I. M. (2016). Synchrony as an adaptive mechanism for large-scale human social bonding. *Ethology* 122 (10), 779–89.

Laurin, K., Shariff, A. F., Henrich, J., and Kay, A. C. (2012). Outsourcing punishment to God: Beliefs in divine control reduce earthly punishment. *Proceedings of Royal Society B: Biological Sciences* 279 (1741), 3272–81.

Leach, E. (1964). Reply to Raoul Naroll's "On Ethnic Unit Classification." *Current Anthropology* 5 (4), 283–312.

Lee, J. Z., and Feng, W. (2009). *One Quarter of Humanity*. Cambridge, MA: Harvard University Press.

Lee, R. B. (1979). *The !Kung San: Men, Women, and Work in a Foraging Society*. Cambridge: Cambridge University Press.

Lee, R. B. (1986). !Kung kin terms, the name relationship and the process of discovery. In M. Biesele, R. Gordon, and R. B. Lee (eds.), *The Past and Future of !Kung Ethnography: Essays in Honor of Lorna Marshall* (pp. 77–102). Hamburg: Helmut Buske.

Lee, R. B. (2003). *The Dobe Ju/'hoansi*. Belmont, CA: Wadsworth/Thomson Learning.

Legare, C. H., and Souza, A. L. (2012). Evaluating ritual efficacy: Evidence from the supernatural. *Cognition* 124 (1), 1–15.

Legare, C. H., and Souza, A. L. (2014). Searching for control: Priming randomness increases the evaluation of ritual efficacy. *Cognitive Science* 38 (1), 152–61.

Leick, G. (2002). *A Dictionary of Ancient Near Eastern Mythology*. London: Routledge.

Leunig, T., Minns, C., and Wallis, P. (2011). Networks in the premodern economy: The market for London apprenticeships, 1600–1749. *Journal of Economic History* 71 (2), 413–43.

Levenson, J. R., and Schurmann, F. (1971). *China: An Interpretive History: From the Beginnings to the Fall of Han*. Berkeley: University of California Press.

Levine, N. E., and Silk, J. B. (1997). Why polyandry fails: Sources of instability in polyandrous marriages. *Current Anthropology* 38 (3), 375–98.

LeVine, R. A., LeVine, S., Schnell-Anzola, B., Rowe, M. L., and Dexter, E. (2012). *Literacy and Mothering: How Women's Schooling Changes the Lives of the World's Children*. New York: Oxford University Press.

Levine, R. N. (2008). *A Geography of Time: On Tempo, Culture, and the Pace of Life*. New York: Basic Books.

Levine, R. V., and Norenzayan, A. (1999). The pace of life in 31 countries. *Journal of Cross-Cultural Psychology* 30 (2), 178–205.

Levy, R. I. (1973). *Tahitians: Mind and Experience in the Society Islands*. Chicago: University of Chicago Press.

Lewer, J. J., and Van den Berg, H. (2007). Religion and international trade: Does the sharing of a religious culture facilitate the formation of trade networks? *American Journal of Economics and Sociology* 66 (4), 765–94.

Lewis, B. (2001). *The Muslim Discovery of Europe.* New York: W. W. Norton.

Lewis, J. (2008). Ekila: Blood, bodies, and egalitarian societies. *Journal of the Royal Anthropological Institute* 14 (2), 297–315.

Li, L. M. W., Hamamura, T., and Adams, G. (2016). Relational mobility increases social (but not other) risk propensity. *Journal of Behavioral Decision Making* 29 (5), 481–88.

Li, Y. J., Johnson, K. A., Cohen, A. B., Williams, M. J., Knowles, E. D., and Chen, Z. (2012). Fundamental(ist) attribution error: Protestants are dispositionally focused. *Journal of Personality and Social Psychology* 102 (2), 281–90.

Liangqun, L., and Murphy, R. (2006). Lineage networks, land conflicts and rural migration in late socialist China. *Journal of Peasant Studies* 33 (4), 612–45.

Liebenberg, L. (1990). *The Art of Tracking: The Origin of Science.* Cape Town: David Philip.

Lieberman, D. (2007). Inbreeding, incest, and the incest taboo: The state of knowledge at the turn of the century. *Evolution and Human Behavior* 28 (3), 211–13.

Lieberman, D., Fessler, D. M. T., and Smith, A. (2011). The relationship between familial resemblance and sexual attraction: An update on Westermarck, Freud, and the incest taboo. *Personality and Social Psychology Bulletin* 37 (9), 1229–32.

Lieberman, D., Tooby, J., and Cosmides, L. (2003). Does morality have a biological basis? An empirical test of the factors governing moral sentiments relating to incest. *Proceedings of the Royal Society B: Biological Sciences* 270 (1517), 819–26.

Lienard, P. (2016). Age grouping and social complexity. *Current Anthropology* 57 (13), S105–S117.

Lilley, K. D. (2002). *Urban Life in the Middle Ages, 1000–1450.* European Culture and Society. New York: Palgrave.

Lind, J., and Lindenfors, P. (2010). The number of cultural traits is correlated with female group size but not with male group size in chimpanzee communities. *PLoS One* 5 (3), e9241.

Lindstrom, L. (1990). Big men as ancestors: Inspiration and copyrights on Tanna (Vanuatu). *Ethnology* 29 (4), 313–26.

Little, A. C., Burriss, R. P., Jones, B. C., DeBruine, L. M., and Caldwell, C. A. (2008). Social influence in human face preference: Men and women are influenced more for long-term than short-term attractiveness decisions. *Evolution and Human Behavior* 29 (2), 140–46.

Little, A. C., Jones, B. C., Debruine, L. M., and Caldwell, C. A. (2011). Social learning and human mate preferences: A potential mechanism for generating and maintaining between-population diversity in attraction. *Philosophical Transactions of the Royal Society B: Biological Sciences* 366 (1563), 366–75.

Liu, H. J., Li, S. Z., and Feldman, M. W. (2012). Forced bachelors, migration and HIV transmission risk in the context of China's gender imbalance: A meta-analysis. *AIDS Care* 24 (12), 1487–95.

Liu, S. S., Morris, M. W., Talhelm, T., and Yang, Q. (2019). Ingroup vigilance in collectivistic cultures. *Proceedings of the National Academy of Sciences* 116 (29), 14538–46.

Lobo, J., Bettencourt, L. M. A., Strumsky, D., and West, G. B. (2013). Urban scaling and the production function for cities. *PLoS One* 8 (3), e58407.

Lopez, R. S. (1976). *The Commercial Revolution of the Middle Ages, 950–1350*. Cambridge: Cambridge University Press.

Losin, E. A. R., Dapretto, M., and Iacoboni, M. (2010). Culture and neuroscience: Additive or synergistic? *Social Cognitive and Affective Neuroscience* 5 (2–3), 148–58.

Loyn, H. R. (1974). Kinship in Anglo-Saxon England. *Anglo-Saxon England* 3, 3326–30.

Loyn, H. R. (1991). *Anglo-Saxon England and the Norman Conquest*. London: Longman.

Lukaszewski, A. W., Gurven, M., von Rueden, C. R., and Schmitt, D. P. (2017). What explains personality covariation? A test of the socioecological complexity hypothesis. *Social Psychological and Personality Science* 8 (8), 943–52.

Lun, J., Oishi, S., and Tenney, E. R. (2012). Residential mobility moderates preferences for egalitarian versus loyal helpers. *Journal of Experimental Social Psychology* 48 (1), 291–97.

Lynch, J. H. (1986). *Godparents and Kinship in Early Medieval Europe*. Princeton, NJ: Princeton University Press.

Lynch, K. A. (2003). *Individuals, Families, and Communities in Europe, 1200–1800: The Urban Foundations of Western Society*. Cambridge: Cambridge University Press.

Ma, D. (2004). Growth, institutions and knowledge: A review and reflection on the historiography of 18th–20th century China. *Australian Economic History Review* 44 (3), 259–77.

Ma, D. (2007). Law and economic growth: The case of traditional China. Working paper, www.iisg.nl/hpw/papers/law-ma.pdf.

Ma, V., and Schoeneman, T. J. (1997). Individualism versus collectivism: A comparison of Kenyan and American self-concepts. *Basic and Applied Social Psychology* 19 (2), 261–73.

MacCulloch, D. (2005). *The Reformation*. New York: Penguin Books.

MacFarlane, A. (1978). *The Origins of English Individualism: The Family, Property and Social Transition*. Oxford: Blackwell.

MacFarlane, A. (2014). *Invention of the Modern World*. Les Brouzils, France: Odd Volumes of the Fortnightly Review.

Macucal. (2013). Desarrollo de la reconquista desde 914 hasta 1492 [map]. Wikimedia Commons, the Free Media Repository.

Maddux, W. W., Yang, H., Falk, C., Adam, H., Adair, W., Endo, Y., Carmon, Z., and Heine, S. J. (2010). For whom is parting with possessions more painful? Cultural differences in the endowment effect. *Psychological Science* 21 (12), 1910–17.

Malhotra, D. (2010). (When) are religious people nicer? Religious salience and the "Sunday effect" on pro-social behavior. *Judgment and Decision Making* 5 (2), 138–43.

Maloney, W. F., and Caicedo, F. V. (2017). Engineering growth: Innovative capacity and development in the Americas. Working paper, ssrn.com/abstract=2932756.

Mann, C. C. (2012). *1493: Uncovering the New World Columbus Created.* New York: Vintage Books.

Mann, P. A. (1972). Residential mobility as an adaptive experience. *Journal of Consulting and Clinical Psychology* 39 (1), 37–42.

Mantovanelli, F. (2014). The Protestant legacy: Missions and literacy in India. Working paper, ssrn.com/abstract=2413170.

Mar, R. A., Oatley, K., Hirsh, J., dela Paz, J., and Peterson, J. B. (2006). Bookworms versus nerds: Exposure to fiction versus non-fiction, divergent associations with social ability, and the simulation of fictional social worlds. *Journal of Research in Personality* 40 (5), 694–712.

Mar, R. A., Oatley, K., and Peterson, J. B. (2009). Exploring the link between reading fiction and empathy: Ruling out individual differences and examining outcomes. *Communications* 34 (4), 407–428.

Mar, R. A., and Rain, M. (2015). Narrative fiction and expository nonfiction differentially predict verbal ability. *Scientific Studies of Reading* 19 (6), 419–33.

Mar, R. A., Tackett, J. L., and Moore, C. (2010). Exposure to media and theory-of-mind development in preschoolers. *Cognitive Development* 25 (1), 69–78.

Marcus, J. (2008). The archaeological evidence for social evolution. *Annual Review of Anthropology* 37 (1), 251–66.

Marcus, J., and Flannery, K. V. (2004). The coevolution of ritual and society: New C-14 dates from ancient Mexico. *Proceedings of the National Academy of Sciences* 101 (52), 18257–61.

Marlowe, F. W. (2000). Paternal investment and the human mating system. *Behavioural Processes* 51 (1–3), 45–61.

Marlowe, F. W. (2003). The mating system of foragers in the standard cross-cultural sample. *Cross-Cultural Research* 37 (3), 282–306.

Marlowe, F. W. (2004). Marital residence among foragers. *Current Anthropology* 45 (2), 277–84.

Marlowe, F. W. (2005). Hunter-gatherers and human evolution. *Evolutionary Anthropology* 14 (2), 54–67.

Marlowe, F. W. (2010). *The Hadza: Hunter-Gatherers of Tanzania*. M. Borgerhoff Mulder and Joe Henrich (eds.), Origins of Human Behavior and Culture. Berkeley: University of California Press.

The marriage law of the People's Republic of China (1980). (1984). *Pacific Affairs* 57 (2), 266–69.

Marshall, L. (1959). Marriage among !Kung Bushmen. *Africa* 29 (4), 335–65.

Marshall, L. (1962). !Kung Bushman religious beliefs. *Africa* 32 (3), 221–52.

Marshall, L. (1976). *The !Kung of Nyae Nyae*. Cambridge, MA: Harvard University Press.

Marshall, L. (1999). *Nyae Nyae !Kung Beliefs and Rites*. Cambridge, MA: Harvard University Press.

Martens, J. P., Tracy, J. L., and Shariff, A. F. (2012). Status signals: Adaptive benefits of displaying and observing the nonverbal expressions of pride and shame. *Cognition and Emotion* 26 (3), 390–406.

Martin, N. D., Rigoni, D., and Vohs, K. D. (2017). Free will beliefs predict attitudes toward unethical behavior and criminal punishment. *Proceedings of the National Academy of Sciences* 114 (28), 7325–30.

Martines, L. (2013). *Furies: War in Europe, 1450–1700*. New York: Bloomsbury.

Masuda, T., Ellsworth, P. C., Mesquita, B., Leu, J., Tanida, S., and Van de Veerdonk, E. (2008). Placing the face in context: Cultural differences in the perception of facial emotion. *Journal of Personality and Social Psychology* 94 (3), 365–81.

Masuda, T., and Nisbett, R. E. (2001). Attending holistically versus analytically: Comparing the context sensitivity of Japanese and Americans. *Journal of Personality and Social Psychology* 81, 922–34.

Mathew, S., and Boyd, R. (2011). Punishment sustains large-scale cooperation in prestate warfare. *Proceedings of the National Academy of Sciences* 108 (28), 11375–80.

Matranga, A. (2017). The ant and the grasshopper: Seasonality and the invention of agriculture. Working paper, mpra.ub.uni-muenchen.de/76626.

Mazur, A., and Booth, A. (1998). Testosterone and dominance in men. *Behavioral and Brain Sciences* 21 (3), 353–63.

Mazur, A., and Michalek, J. (1998). Marriage, divorce, and male testosterone. *Social Forces* 77 (1), 315–30.

McBryde, I. (1984). Exchange in south eastern Australia: An ethnohistorical perspective. *Aboriginal History* 8 (2), 132–53.

McCarthy, F. D. (1939). "Trade" in aboriginal Australia, and "trade" relationships with Torres Strait, New Guinea and Malaya. *Oceania* 10 (1), 80–104.

McCleary, R. M. (2007). Salvation, damnation, and economic incentives. *Journal of Contemporary Religion* 22 (1), 49–74.

McCleary, R. M., and Barro, R. J. (2006). Religion and economy. *Journal of Economic Perspectives* 20 (2), 49–72.

McCloskey, D. N. (2007). *The Bourgeois Virtues: Ethics for an Age of Commerce*. Chicago: University of Chicago Press.

McCullough, M. E., Pedersen, E. J., Schroder, J. M., Tabak, B. A., and Carver, C. S. (2013). Harsh childhood environmental characteristics predict exploitation and retaliation in humans. *Proceedings of the Royal Society B: Biological Sciences* 280 (1750), 1–7.

McCullough, M. E., and Willoughby, B. L. B. (2009). Religion, self-regulation, and self-control: Associations, explanations, and implications. *Psychological Bulletin* 135 (1), 69–93.

McElreath, R., Boyd, R., and Richerson, P. J. (2003). Shared norms and the evolution of ethnic markers. *Current Anthropology* 44 (1), 122–29.

McElreath, R. (2020). *Statistical Rethinking: A Bayesian Course with Examples in R and STAN.* Chapman & Hall/CRC Texts in Statistical Science. CRC Press.

McGrath, A. E. (2007). *Christianity's Dangerous Idea: The Protestant Revolution—A History from the Sixteenth Century to the Twenty-First* (1st ed.). New York: HarperOne.

McNamara, R. A., and Henrich, J. (2018). Jesus vs. the ancestors: How specific religious beliefs shape prosociality on Yasawa Island, Fiji. *Religion, Brain & Behavior* 8 (2), 185–204.

McNamara, R. A., Willard, A. K., Norenzayan, A., and Henrich, J. Thinking about thoughts when the mind is unknowable: Mental state reasoning through false belief and empathy across societies. (In preparation.)

McNamara, R. A., Willard, A. K., Norenzayan, A., and Henrich, J. (2019b). Weighing outcome vs. intent across societies: How cultural models of mind shape moral reasoning. *Cognition* 182, 95–108.

McNeill, W. H. (1982). *Pursuit of Power: Technology, Armed Force, and Society Since A.D. 1000.* Chicago: University of Chicago Press.

McNeill, W. H. (1991). *The Rise of the West: A History of the Human Community: With a Retrospective Essay.* Chicago: University of Chicago Press.

McNeill, W. H. (1999). How the potato changed the world's history. *Social Research* 66 (1), 67–83.

Medin, D. L., and Atran, S. (1999). *Folkbiology.* Cambridge, MA: MIT Press.

Medin, D. L., and Atran, S. (2004). The native mind: Biological categorization and reasoning in development and across cultures. *Psychological Review* 111 (4), 960–83.

Mehta, P. H., and Josephs, R. A. (2010). Testosterone and cortisol jointly regulate dominance: Evidence for a dual-hormone hypothesis. *Hormones and Behavior* 58 (5), 898–906.

Mehta, P. H., Wuehrmann, E. V., and Josephs, R. A. (2009). When are low testosterone levels advantageous? The moderating role of individual versus intergroup competition. *Hormones and Behavior* 56 (1), 158–62.

Meisenzahl, R., and Mokyr, J. (2012). The rate and direction of invention in the British Industrial Revolution: Incentives and institutions. In J. Lerner and S. Stern (eds.), *The Rate and Direction of Inventive Activity Revisited* (pp. 443–79). Chicago: University of Chicago Press.

Menke, T. (1880). Europe according to its ecclesiastical circumstances in the Middle Ages. In *Hand Atlas for the History of the Middle Ages and Later* (3rd ed.). Gotha, Germany: Justus Perthes.

Merton, R. K. (1938). Science, technology and society in seventeenth century England. *Osiris* 4, 360–632.

Meyers, M. A. (2007). *Happy Accidents: Serendipity in Modern Medical Breakthroughs.* New York: Arcade.

Mikalson, J. D. (2010). *Ancient Greek Religion.* Hoboken, NJ: Wiley-Blackwell.

Milgram, S. (1963). Behavioral study of obedience. *Journal of Abnormal and Social Psychology* 67 (4), 371–78.

Miller, W. I. (2009). *Bloodtaking and Peacemaking: Feud, Law, and Society in Saga Iceland.* Chicago: University of Chicago Press.

Mintz, S. W. (1986). *Sweetness and Power: The Place of Sugar in Modern History.* New York: Penguin.

Mischel, W., Ayduk, O., Berman, M. G., Casey, B. J., Gotlib, I. H., Jonides, J., . . . Shoda, Y. (2011). "Willpower" over the life span: Decomposing self-regulation. *Social Cognitive and Affective Neuroscience* 6 (2), 252–56.

Mischel, W., Shoda, Y., and Rodriguez, M. L. (1989). Delay of gratification in children. *Science* 244 (4907), 933–38.

Mittal, C., Griskevicius, V., Simpson, J. A., Sung, S. Y., and Young, E. S. (2015). Cognitive adaptations to stressful environments: When childhood adversity enhances adult executive function. *Journal of Personality and Social Psychology* 109 (4), 604–621.

Mitterauer, M. (2011). Kontrastierende heiratsregeln: Traditionen des Orients und Europas im interkulturellen Vergleic. *Historische Sozialkunde* 41 (2), 4–16.

Mitterauer, M. (2015). Heiratsmuster im interkulturellen Vergleich: Von der Goody-These zum Korotayev-Modell. In T. Kolnberger, N. Franz, and P. Péporté (eds.), *Populations, Connections, Droits Fondamentaux: Mélanges pour Jean-Paul Lehners* (pp. 37–60). Berlin: Mandelbaum Verlag.

Mitterauer, M., and Chapple, G. (2010). *Why Europe? The Medieval Origins of Its Special Path.* Chicago: University of Chicago Press.

Mitterauer, M., and Sieder, R. (1982). *The European Family: Patriarchy to Partnership from the Middle Ages to the Present.* Hoboken, NJ: Blackwell.

Miu, E., Gulley, N., Laland, K. N., and Rendell, L. (2018). Innovation and cumulative culture through tweaks and leaps in online programming contests. *Nature Communications* 9 (1), 1–8.

Miyamoto, Y., Nisbett, R. E., and Masuda, T. (2006). Culture and the physical environment: Holistic versus analytic perceptual affordances. *Psychological Science* 17 (2), 113–19.

Moffitt, T. E., Arseneault, L., Belsky, D., Dickson, N., Hancox, R. J., Harrington, H., . . . Caspi, A. (2011). A gradient of childhood self-control predicts health, wealth, and public safety. *Proceedings of the National Academy of Sciences* 108 (7), 2693–98.

Mogan, R., Fischer, R., and Bulbulia, J. A. (2017). To be in synchrony or not? A meta-analysis of synchrony's effects on behavior, perception, cognition and affect. *Journal of Experimental Social Psychology* 72, 13–20.

Mokyr, J. (1990). *The Lever of Riches*. New York: Oxford University Press.

Mokyr, J. (1995). Urbanization, technological progress, and economic history. In H. Giersch (ed.), *Urban Agglomeration and Economic Growth* (pp. 51–54). Berlin and Heidelberg: Springer.

Mokyr, J. (2002). *The Gifts of Athena: Historical Origins of the Knowledge Economy*. Princeton, NJ: Princeton University Press.

Mokyr, J. (2011). The intellectual origins of modern economic growth. *Economic History Review* 64 (2), 357–84.

Mokyr, J. (2013). Cultural entrepreneurs and the origins of modern economic growth. *Scandinavian Economic History Review* 61 (1), 1–33.

Mokyr, J. (2016). *A Culture of Growth: The Origins of the Modern Economy*. Princeton, NJ: Princeton University Press.

Moll-Murata, C. (2008). Chinese guilds from the seventeenth to the twentieth centuries: An overview. *International Review of Social History* 53 (Suppl. 16), 213–47.

Moll-Murata, C. (2013). Guilds and appenticeship in China and Europe: The Jingdezhen and European ceramics industries. In M. Prak and J. L. van Zanden (eds.), *Technology, Skills and the Pre-Modern Economy in the East and the West* (pp. 225–58). Leiden: Brill.

Moore, R. I. (2000). *The First European Revolution: c. 970–1215. The Making of Europe*. Malden, MA: Blackwell.

Moore, S. F. (1972). Legal liability and evolutionary interpretation: Some aspects of strict liability, self-help and collective responsibility. In M. Gluckman (ed.), *The Allocation of Responsibility* (pp. 88–93). Manchester, UK: Manchester University Press.

Morewedge, C. K., and Giblin, C. E. (2015). Explanations of the endowment effect: An integrative review. *Trends in Cognitive Sciences* 19 (6), 339–48.

Morgan, J. (1852). *The Life and Adventures of William Buckley: Thirty-Two Years a Wanderer Amongst the Aborigines of Then Unexplored Country Round Port Phillip, Now the Province of Victoria*. Hobart, Tasmania: A. Macdougall.

Morgan, T. J. H., and Laland, K. (2012). The biological bases of conformity. *Frontiers in Neuroscience* 6 (87), 1–7.

Morgan, T. J. H., Rendell, L. E., Ehn, M., Hoppitt, W., and Laland, K. N. (2012). The evolutionary basis of human social learning. *Proceedings of the Royal Society B: Biological Sciences* 279 (1729), 653–62.

Morris, I. (2010). *Why the West Rules—for Now: The Patterns of History, and What They Reveal About the Future*. New York: Farrar, Straus and Giroux.

Morris, I. (2014). *War, What Is It Good For? The Role of Conflict in Civilisation, from Primates to Robots*. London: Profile Books.

Morris, M. W., and Peng, K. (1994). Culture and cause: American and Chinese attributions for social and physical events. *Journal of Personality and Social Psychology* 67 (6), 949–71.

Moscona, J., Nunn, N., and Robinson, J. A. (2017). Keeping it in the family: Lineage organizations and the scope of trust in Sub-Saharan Africa. *American Economic Review* 107 (5), 565–71.

Motolinía, T. (1973). *Motolinía's History of the Indians of New Spain*. Westport, CT: Greenwood Press.

Moya, C. (2013). Evolved priors for ethnolinguistic categorization: A case study from the Quechua-Aymara boundary in the Peruvian Altiplano. *Evolution and Human Behavior* 34 (4), 265–72.

Moya, C., and Boyd, R. (2015). Different selection pressures give rise to distinct ethnic phenomena. *Human Nature* 26, 1–27.

Moya, C., Boyd, R., and Henrich, J. (2015). Reasoning about cultural and genetic transmission: Developmental and cross-cultural evidence from Peru, Fiji, and the United States on how people make inferences about trait transmission. *Topics in Cognitive Science* 7 (4), 595–610.

Mullainathan, S., and Shafir, E. (2013). *Scarcity: Why Having Too Little Means So Much*. New York: Henry Holt.

Muller, M., Wrangham, R., and Pilbeam, D. (2017). *Chimpanzees and human evolution*. Cambridge, MA: Harvard University Press.

Muller, M. N., Marlowe, F. W., Bugumba, R., and Ellison, P. T. (2009). Testosterone and paternal care in East African foragers and pastoralists. *Proceedings of the Royal Society B: Biological Sciences* 276 (1655), 347–54.

Munson, J., Amati, V., Collard, M., and Macri, M. J. (2014). Classic Maya bloodletting and the cultural evolution of religious rituals: Quantifying patterns of variation in hieroglyphic texts. *PLoS One* 9 (9), e107982.

Murdock, G. P. (1934). *Our Primitive Contemporaries*. New York: Macmillan.

Murdock, G. P. (1949). *Social Structure*. New York: Macmillan.

Murphy, K. J. (2013). Executive compensation: Where we are, and how we got there. In G. M. Constantinides, M. Harris, and R. M. Stulz (eds.), *Handbook of the Economics of Finance* (Vol. 2). Amsterdam: Elsevier B.V.

Murphy, K. J., and Zabojnik, J. (2004). CEO pay and appointments: A market-based explanation for recent trends. *American Economic Review* 94 (2), 192–96.

Murphy, R. F. (1957). Intergroup hostility and social cohesion. *American Anthropologist* 59 (6), 1018–1035.

Murray, D. R., Trudeau, R., and Schaller, M. (2011). On the origins of cultural differences in conformity: Four tests of the pathogen prevalence hypothesis. *Personality and Social Psychology Bulletin* 37 (3), 318–29.

Muthukrishna, M., Francois, P., Pourahmadi, S., and Henrich, J. (2017). Corrupting cooperation and how anti-corruption strategies may backfire. *Nature Human Behaviour* 1 (7), 1–5.

Muthukrishna, M., and Henrich, J. (2016). Innovation in the collective brain. *Philosophical Transactions of the Royal Society B: Biological Sciences* 371 (1690), 1–14.

Muthukrishna, M., Morgan, T. J. H., and Henrich, J. (2016). The when and who of social learning and conformist transmission. *Evolution and Human Behavior* 37 (1), 10–20.

Muthukrishna, M., Shulman, B. W. B. W., Vasilescu, V., and Henrich, J. (2013). Sociality influences cultural complexity. *Proceedings of the Royal Society B: Biological Sciences* 281 (1774), 20132511.

Nakahashi, W., Wakano, J. Y., and Henrich, J. (2012). Adaptive social learning strategies in temporally and spatially varying environments. *Human Nature* 23 (4), 386–418.

Needham, J. (1964). The pre-natal history of the steam engine. *Transactions of the Newcomen Society* 35 (1), 3–58.

Nelson, R. R., and Winter, S. G. (1985). *Evolutionary Theory of Economic Change.* Cambridge, MA: Harvard University Press.

Nettle, D., Frankenhuis, W. E., and Rickard, I. J. (2013). The evolution of predictive adaptive responses in human life history The evolution of predictive adaptive responses in human life history. *Proceedings of the Royal Society B: Biological Sciences* 280, 20131343.

Newson, L. (2009). Why do people become modern? A Darwinian explanation. *Population and Development Review* 35 (1), 117–58.

Newson, L., Postmes, T., Lea, S. E. G., Webley, P., Richerson, P. J., and McElreath, R. (2007). Influences on communication about reproduction: The cultural evolution of low fertility. *Evolution and Human Behavior* 28 (3), 199–210.

Newson, M., Buhrmester, M., and Whitehouse, H. (2016). Explaining lifelong loyalty: The role of identity fusion and self-shaping group events. *PLoS One* 11 (8), 1–13.

Nicolle, D., Embleton, G. A., and Embleton, S. (2014). *Forces of the Hanseatic League: 13th–15th centuries.* Men-at-Arms 494. Oxford: Osprey.

Nielsen, M., Haun, D., Kärtner, J., and Legare, C. H. (2017). The persistent sampling bias in developmental psychology: A call to action. *Journal of Experimental Child Psychology* 162, 31–38.

Niklas, F., Cohrssen, C., and Tayler, C. (2016). The sooner, the better: Early reading to children. *SAGE Open* 6 (4), 1–11.

Nisbet, R. E. (2003). *The Geography of Thought: How Asians and Westerners Think Differently . . . and Why.* New York: Free Press.

Nisbet, R. E. (2009). *Intelligence and How to Get It: Why Schools and Cultures Count.* New York: W. W. Norton.

Nisbett, R. E., Aronson, J., Blair, C., Dickens, W., Flynn, J., Halpern, D. F., and Turkheimer, E. (2012). Intelligence: New findings and theoretical developments. *American Psychologist* 67 (2), 130–59.

Nisbett, R. E., and Cohen, D. (1996). *Culture of Honor: The Psychology of Violence in the South.* Boulder, CO: Westview Press.

Nisbett, R. E., Peng, K., Choi, I., and Norenzayan, A. (2001). Culture and systems of thought: Holistic versus analytic cognition. *Psychological Review* 108, 291–310.

Norenzayan, A. (2013). *Big Gods: How Religion Transformed Cooperation and Conflict.* Princeton, NJ: Princeton University Press.

Norenzayan, A., Gervais, W. M., and Trzesniewski, K. H. (2012). Mentalizing deficits constrain belief in a personal god. *PloS One* 7 (5), e36880.

Norenzayan, A., Shariff, A. F., Gervais, W. M., Willard, A. K., McNamara, R. A., Slingerland, E., and Henrich, J. (2016a). Parochial prosocial religions: Historical and contemporary evidence for a cultural evolutionary process. *Behavioral and Brain Sciences* 39, E29.

Norenzayan, A., Shariff, A. F., Gervais, W. M., Willard, A. K., McNamara, R. A., Slingerland, E., and Henrich, J. (2016b). The cultural evolution of prosocial religions. *Behavioral and Brain Sciences* 39, E1.

Nores, M., and Barnett, W. S. (2010). Benefits of early childhood interventions across the world: (Under) investing in the very young. *Economics of Education Review* 29 (2), 271–82.

Norris, P., and Inglehart, R. (2012). *Sacred and Secular: Religion and Politics Worldwide.* Cambridge: Cambridge University Press.

Nunez, M., and Harris, P. L. (1998). Psychological and deontic concepts: Separate domains or intimate connection? *Mind and Language* 13 (2), 153–70.

Nunn, N. (2007). Relationship-specificity, incomplete contracts, and the pattern of trade. *Quarterly Journal of Economics* 122 (2), 569–600.

Nunn, N. (2009). The importance of history for economic development. *Annual Review of Economics* 1 (1), 65–92.

Nunn, N. (2014). Gender and missionary influence in colonial Africa. In E. Akyeampong, R. Bates, N. Nunn, and J. Robinson (eds.), *Africa's Development in Historical Perspective* (pp. 489–512). Cambridge: Cambridge University Press.

Nunn, N., and De La Sierra, R. S. (2017). Why being wrong can be right: Magical warfare technologies and the persistence of false beliefs. *American Economic Review* 107 (5), 582–87.

Nunn, N., and Qian, N. (2010). The Columbian exchange: A history of disease, food, and ideas. *World Crops* 24 (2), 163–88.

Nunn, N., and Qian, N. (2011). The potato's contribution to population and urbanization: Evidence from a historical experiment. *Quarterly Journal of Economics* 126 (2), 593–650.

Nunn, N., and Wantchekon, L. (2011). The slave trade and the origins of mistrust in Africa. *American Economic Review* 101 (7), 3221–52.

Nunziata, L., and Rocco, L. (2014). The Protestant ethic and entrepreneurship: Evidence from religious minorities from the former Holy Roman Empire. *MPRA* Working paper, mpra.ub.uni-muenchen.de/53566.

Nuvolari, A. (2004). Collective invention during the British Industrial Revolution: the case of the Cornish pumping engine. *Cambridge Journal of Economics* 28 (3), 347–63.

O'Grady, S. (2013). *And Man Created God: A History of the World at the Time of Jesus.* New York: St. Martin's Press.

Obschonka, M., Stuetzer, M., Rentfrow, P. J., Shaw-Taylor, L., Satchell, M., Silbereisen, R. K., Potter, J., and Gosling, S. D. (2018). In the shadow of coal: How large-scale industries contributed to present-day regional differences in personality and well-being. *Journal of Personality and Social Psychology* 115 (5), 903–927.

Ockenfels, A., and Weinmann, J. (1999). Types and patterns: An experimental east-west-German comparison of cooperation and solidarity. *Journal of Public Economics* 71 (2), 275–87.

Ogilvie, S. (2019). *The European Guilds.* Princeton, NJ: Princeton University Press.

Oishi, S. (2010). The psychology of residential mobility: Implications for the self, social relationships, and well-being. *Perspectives on Psychological Science* 5 (1), 5–21.

Oishi, S., Kesebir, S., Miao, F. F., Talhelm, T., Endo, Y., Uchida, Y., Shibanai, Y., and Norasakkunkit, V. (2013). Residential mobility increases motivation to expand social network: But why? *Journal of Experimental Social Psychology* 49 (2), 217–23.

Oishi, S., Schug, J., Yuki, M., and Axt, J. (2015). The psychology of residential and relational mobilities. In M. J. Gelfand, C. Chiu, and Y. Hong (eds.), *Handbook of Advances in Culture and Psychology* (Vol. 5, pp. 221–72). New York: Oxford University Press.

Oishi, S., and Talhelm, T. (2012). Residential mobility: What psychological research reveals. *Current Directions in Psychological Science* 21 (6), 425–30.

Okbay, A., Beauchamp, J. P., Fontana, M. A., Lee, J. J., Pers, T. H., Rietveld, C. A., . . . Benjamin, D. J. (2016). Genome-wide association study identifies 74 loci associated with educational attainment. *Nature* 533 (7604), 539–42.

Olsson, O., and Paik, C. (2016). Long-run cultural divergence: Evidence from the Neolithic Revolution. *Journal of Development Economics* 122, 197–213.

Over, H., Carpenter, M., Spears, R., and Gattis, M. (2013). Children selectively trust individuals who have imitated them. *Social Development* 22 (2), 215–24.

Padgett, J. F., and Powell, W. W. (2012). *The Emergence of Organizations and Markets.* Princeton, NJ: Princeton University Press.

Paine, R. (1971). Animals as capital: Comparisons among northern nomadic herders and hunters. *Anthropological Quarterly* 44 (3), 157–72.

Palmstierna, M., Frangou, A., Wallette, A., and Dunbar, R. (2017). Family counts: Deciding when to murder among the Icelandic Vikings. *Evolution and Human Behavior* 38 (2), 175–80.

Pan, W., Ghoshal, G., Krumme, C., Cebrian, M., and Pentland, A. (2013). Urban characteristics attributable to density-driven tie formation. *Nature Communications* 4, 1961.

Panero, M. E., Weisberg, D. S., Black, J., Goldstein, T. R., Barnes, J. L., Brownell, H., and Winner, E. (2016). Does reading a single passage of literary fiction really improve theory of mind? An attempt at replication. *Journal of Personality and Social Psychology* 111 (5), e46–e54.

Park, N., and Peterson, C. (2010). Does it matter where we live? The urban psychology of character strengths. *The American Psychologist* 65 (6), 535–47.

Peng, Y. S. (2004). Kinship networks and entrepreneurs in China's transitional economy. *American Journal of Sociology* 109 (5), 1045–1074.

Perreault, C., Moya, C., and Boyd, R. (2012). A Bayesian approach to the evolution of social learning. *Evolution and Human Behavior* 33 (5), 449–59.

Pettegree, A. (2015). *Brand Luther: 1517, Printing, and the Making of the Reformation*. New York: Penguin Press.

Peysakhovich, A., and Rand, D. G. (2016). Habits of virtue: Creating norms of cooperation and defection in the laboratory. *Management Science* 62 (3), 631–47.

Pigfetta, A. (2012). *Magellan's Voyage: A Narrative Account of the First Circumnavigation*. New York: Dover.

Pilbeam, D., and Lieberman, D. E. (2017). Reconstructing the last common ancestor to chimpanzees and humans. In M. N. Muller, R. W. Wrangham, and D. Pilbeam (eds.), *Chimpanzees and Human Evolution* (pp. 22–141). Cambridge, MA: Harvard University Press.

Pinker, S. (1997). *How the Mind Works*. New York: W. W. Norton.

Pinker, S. (2011). *The Better Angels of Our Nature: Why Violence Has Declined*. New York: Viking.

Pinker, S. (2018). *Enlightenment Now: The Case for Reason, Science, Humanism, and Progress*. New York: Viking.

Pirenne, H. (1952). *Medieval Cities*. Princeton, NJ: Princeton University Press.

Plattner, S. (1989). Economic behavior in markets. In S. Plattner (ed.), *Economic Anthropology* (pp. 209–221). Stanford, CA: Stanford University Press.

Plomin, R., DeFries, J. C., Knopik, V. S., and Neiderhiser, J. M. (2016). Top 10 replicated findings from behavioral genetics. *Perspectives in Psychological Science* 11 (1), 3–23.

Plomin, R., DeFries, J., McClearn, G. E., and McGuffin, P. (2001). *Behavioral Genetics* (4th ed.). New York: Worth.

Plott, C. R., and Zeiler, K. (2007). Exchange asymmetries incorrectly interpreted as evidence of endowment effect theory and prospect theory? *American Economic Review* 97 (4), 1449–66.

Pope, H. G., Kouri, E. M., and Hudson, J. I. (2000). Effects of supraphysiologic doses of testosterone on mood and aggression in normal men: A randomized controlled trial. *Archives of General Psychiatry* 57 (2), 133–40.

Post, L., and Zwaan, R. (2014). What is the value of believing in free will? Two replication studies. osf.io/mnwgb.

Prak, M., and Van Zanden, J. L. (eds.). (2013). *Technology, Skills and the Pre-Modern Economy in the East and the West*. Leiden: Brill.

Pratt, T. C., and Cullen, F. T. (2000). The empirical status of Gottfredson and Hirschi's general theory of crime: A meta-analysis. *Criminology* 38 (3), 931–64.

Price, J. (2010). The effect of parental time investments: Evidence from natural within-family variation. NBER working paper, www.uvic.ca/socialsciences/economics /assets/docs/pastdept-4/price_parental_time.pdf.

Protzko, J., Ouimette, B., and Schooler, J. (2016). Believing there is no free will corrupts intuitive cooperation. *Cognition* 151, 6–9.

Purzycki, B. G., Apicella, C. L., Atkinson, Q. D., Cohen, E., McNamara, R. A., Willard, A. K., Xygalatas, D., Norenzayan, A., and Henrich, J. (2016). Moralistic gods, supernatural punishment and the expansion of human sociality. *Nature* 530 (7590), 327–30.

Purzycki, B. G., Henrich, J., Apicella, C. L., Atkinson, Q. D., Baimel, A., Cohen, E., . . . Norenzayan, A. (2017). The evolution of religion and morality: A synthesis of ethnographic and experimental evidence from eight societies. *Religion, Brain & Behavior* 8 (2), 101–132.

Purzycki, B. G., and Holland, E. C. (2019). Buddha as a God: An empirical assessment. *Method and Theory in the Study of Religion* 31, 347–75.

Purzycki, B. G., Ross, C. T., Apicella, C. L., Atkinson, Q. D., Cohen, E., McNamara, R. A., . . . Henrich, J. (2018). Material security, life history, and moralistic religions: A cross-cultural examination. *PLoS One* 13 (3), e0193856.

Purzycki, B. G., Willard, A. K., Klocová, E. K., Apicella, C., Atkinson, Q., Bolyanatz, A., . . . Ross, C. T. (2019). *The moralization bias of gods' minds: A cross-cultural test*.

Putterman, L. (2008). Agriculture, diffusion and development: Ripple effects of the Neolithic revolution. *Economica* 75 (300), 729–48.

Putterman, L., and Weil, D. N. (2010). Post-1500 population flows and the long-run determinants of economic growth and inequality. *Quarterly Journal of Economics* 125 (4), 1627–82.

Puurtinen, M., and Mappes, T. (2009). Between-group competition and human cooperation. *Proceedings of the Royal Society B: Biological Sciences* 276 (1655), 355–60.

Rad, M. S., Martingano, A. J., and Ginges, J. (2018). Toward a psychology of *Homo sapiens*: Making psychological science more representative of the human population. *Proceedings of the National Academy of Sciences* 115 (45), 11401–11405.

Radcliffe-Brown, A. R. (1964). *The Andaman Islanders*. Glencoe, IL: Free Press.

Rai, T. S., and Holyoak, K. J. (2013). Exposure to moral relativism compromises moral behavior. *Journal of Experimental Social Psychology* 49 (6), 995–1001.

Ramseyer, V. (2006). *The Transformation of a Religious Landscape: Medieval Southern Italy, 850–1150*. Ithaca, NY: Cornell University Press.

Rand, D. G. (2016). Cooperation, fast and slow: Meta-analytic evidence for a theory of social heuristics and self-interested deliberation. *Psychological Science* 27 (9), 1192–1206.

Rand, D. G., Dreber, A., Haque, O. S., Kane, R. J., Nowak, M.A., and Coakley, S. (2014). Religious motivations for cooperation: An experimental investigation using explicit primes. *Religion, Brain & Behavior* 4 (1), 31–48.

Rand, D. G., Peysakhovich, A., Kraft-Todd, G. T., Newman, G. E., Wurzbacher, O., Nowak, M. A., and Greene, J. D. (2014). Social heuristics shape intuitive cooperation. *Nature Communications* 5, 3677.

Rao, L.-L., Han, R., Ren, X.-P., Bai, X.-W., Zheng, R., Liu, H., . . . Li, S. (2011). Disadvantage and prosocial behavior: The effects of the Wenchuan earthquake. *Evolution and Human Behavior* 32 (1), 63–69.

Rauh, N. K. (1993). *The Sacred Bonds of Commerce: Religion, Economy, and Trade Society at Hellenistic Roman Delos, 166–87 B.C.* Leiden: Brill.

Redmond, E. M., and Spencer, C. S. (2012). Chiefdoms at the threshold: The competitive origins of the primary state. *Journal of Anthropological Archaeology* 31 (1), 22–37.

Reich, D. (2018). *Who We Are and How We Got Here: Ancient DNA and the New Science of the Human Past.* New York: Oxford University Press.

Rendell, L., Fogarty, L., Hoppitt, W. J. E., Morgan, T. J. H., Webster, M. M., and Laland, K. N. (2011). Cognitive culture: Theoretical and empirical insights into social learning strategies. *Trends in Cognitive Sciences* 15 (2), 68–76.

Rentfrow, P. J., Gosling, S. D., Potter, J., Rentfrow, P. J., Gosling, S. D., and Potter, J. (2017). A theory of the emergence, persistence, and expression of geographic variation in psychological characteristics. *Perspectives on Psychological Science* 3 (5), 339–69.

Reyes-García, V., Godoy, R., Huanca, T., Leonard, W., McDade, T., Tanner, S., and Vadez, V. (2007). The origins of monetary income inequality: Patience, human capital, and division of labor. *Evolution and Human Behavior* 28 (1), 37–47.

Reynolds, B. (2006). A review of delay-discounting research with humans: Relations to drug use and gambling. *Behavioural Pharmacology* 17 (8), 651–67.

Richardson, G. (2004). Guilds, laws, and markets for manufactured merchandise in late-medieval England. *Explorations in Economic History* 41 (1), 1–25.

Richardson, G. (2005). Craft guilds and Christianity in late-medieval England: A rational-choice analysis. *Rationality and Society* 17 (2), 139–89.

Richardson, G., and McBride, M. (2009). Religion, longevity, and cooperation: The case of the craft guild. *Journal of Economic Behavior and Organization* 71 (2), 172–86.

Richerson, P. J., Baldini, R., Bell, A., Demps, K., Frost, K., Hillis, V., . . . Zefferman, M. R. (2016). Cultural group selection plays an essential role in explaining human cooperation: A sketch of the evidence. *Behavioral and Brain Sciences* 39, 1–68.

Richerson, P. J., and Boyd, R. (2005). *Not by Genes Alone: How Culture Transformed Human Evolution.* Chicago: University of Chicago Press.

Richerson, P. J., Boyd, R., and Bettinger, R. L. (2001). Was agriculture impossible during the Pleistocene but mandatory during the Holocene? A climate change hypothesis. *American Antiquity* 66 (3), 387–411.

Rigoni, D., Kuhn, S., Gaudino, G., Sartori, G., and Brass, M. (2012). Reducing self-control by weakening belief in free will. *Consciousness and Cognition* 21 (3), 1482–90.

Rindermann, H., and Thompson, J. (2011). Cognitive capitalism: The effect of cognitive ability on wealth, as mediated through scientific achievement and economic freedom. *Psychological Science* 22 (6), 754–63.

Ritter, M. L. (1980). The conditions favoring age-set organization. *Journal of Anthropological Research* 36 (1), 87–104.

Rives, J. B. (2006). *Religion in the Roman Empire*. Hoboken, NJ: Wiley-Blackwell.

Robbins, E., Shepard, J., and Rochat, P. (2017). Variations in judgments of intentional action and moral evaluation across eight cultures. *Cognition* 164, 22–30.

Robinson, J. A., and Acemoglu, D. (2011). Why nations fail: The origins of power, prosperity and poverty. PowerPoint presentation. Morishima Lecture, London School of Economics, June 6. www.lse.ac.uk/assets/richmedia/channels/publicLecturesAnd Events/slides/20110608_1830_whyNationsFail_sl.pdf.

Rockmore, D. N., Fang, C., Foti, N. J., Ginsburg, T., and Krakauer, D. C. (2017). The cultural evolution of national constitutions. *Journal of the Association for Information Science and Technology* 69 (3), 483–94.

Rolt, L. T. C., and Allen, J. S. (1977). *The Steam Engine of Thomas Newcomen*. New York: Science History.

Roscoe, P. B. (1989). The pig and the long yam: The expansion of a Sepik cultural complex. *Ethnology* 28 (3), 219–31.

Ross, L., and Nisbett, R. E. (1991). *The Person and the Situation: Perspectives of Social Psychology*. Philadelphia: Temple University Press.

Ross, M. C. (1985). Concubinage in Anglo-Saxon England. *Past and Present* 108, 3–34.

Rowe, W. T. (2002). Stability and social change. In J. K. Fairbank and D. Twitchett (eds.), *The Cambridge History of China* (Vol. 9, pp. 473–562). Cambridge: Cambridge University Press.

Roy, T. (2013). Appenticeship and Industrialization in India, 1600–1930. In M. Prak and J. L. van Zanden (eds.), *Technology, Skills and the Pre-Modern Economy in the East and the West* (pp. 69–92). Leiden: Brill.

Ruan, J., Xie, Z., and Zhang, X. (2015). Does rice farming shape individualism and innovation? *Food Policy* 56, 51–58.

Rubin, J. (2014). Printing and Protestants: An empirical test of the role of printing in the Reformation. *Review of Economics and Statistics* 96 (2), 270–86.

Rubin, J. (2017). *Rulers, Religion, and Riches: Why the West Got Rich and the Middle East Did Not*. Cambridge: Cambridge University Press.

Rustagi, D., Engel, S., and Kosfeld, M. (2010a). Conditional cooperation and costly monitoring explain success in forest commons management. *Science* 330 (6006), 961–65.

Rustagi, D., and Veronesi, M. (2017). Waiting for Napoleon? Democracy and norms of reciprocity across social groups. Working paper, www.brown.edu/academics /economics/sites/br.

Sääksvuori, L., Mappes, T., and Puurtinen, M. (2011). Costly punishment prevails in intergroup conflict. *Proceedings of the Royal Society B: Biological Sciences* 278 (1723), 3428–36.

Saccomandi, G., and Ogden, R. W. (2014). *Mechanics and Thermomechanics of Rubberlike Solids*. Vienna: Springer.

Sahlins, M. (1998). The original affluent society. In J. Gowdy (ed.), *Limited Wants, Unlimited Means: A Reader on Hunter-Gatherer Economics and the Environment* (pp. 5–41). Washington, DC: Island Press/The Center for Resource Economics.

Sahlins, M. D. (1961). The segmentary lineage: An organization of predatory expansion. *American Anthropologist* 63 (2), 322–45.

Sahlins, M. D. (1963). Poor man, rich man, big-man, chief: Political types in Melanesia and Polynesia. *Comparative Studies in Society and History* 5 (3), 285–303.

Salali, G. D., Chaudhary, N., Thompson, J., Grace, O. M., van der Burgt, X. M., Dyble, M., . . . Migliano, A. B. (2016). Knowledge-sharing networks in hunter-gatherers and the evolution of cumulative culture. *Current Biology* 26 (18), 2516–21.

Salali, G. D., and Migliano, A. B. (2015). Future discounting in Congo Basin hunter-gatherers declines with socio-economic transitions. *PLoS One* 10 (9), 1–10.

Salvador, A. (2005). Coping with competitive situations in humans. *Neuroscience and Biobehavioral Reviews* 29, 195–205.

Salvador, A., and Costa, R. (2009). Coping with competition: Neuroendocrine responses and cognitive variables. *Neuroscience and Biobehavioral Reviews* 33 (2), 160–70.

Sampson, R. J., and Laub, J. H. (1993). *Crime in the Making: Pathways and Turning Points Through Life*. Cambridge, MA: Harvard University Press.

Sampson, R., Laub, J., and Wimer, C. (2006). Does marriage reduce crime? A counterfactual approach to within-individual causal effects. *Criminology* 44 (3), 465–509.

Sanchez-Burks, J. (2002). Protestant relational ideology and (in)attention to relational cues in work settings. *Journal of Personality and Social Psychology* 83 (4), 919–29.

Sanchez-Burks, J. (2005). Protestant relational ideology: The cognitive underpinnings and organizational implications of an American anomaly. *Research in Organizational Behavior* 26, 265–305.

Sanders, M. A., Shirk, S. D., Burgin, C. J., and Martin, L. L. (2012). The gargle effect: Rinsing the mouth with glucose enhances self-control. *Psychological Science* 23 (12), 1470–72.

Sasson, D., and Greif, A. (2011). Risk, institutions and growth: Why England and not China? *IZA Discussion Papers* 5598, 1–51.

Sato, K., Yuki, M., Takemura, K., Schug, J., and Oishi, S. (2008). The "openness" of a society determines the relationship between self-esteem and subjective well-being (1): A cross-societal comparison. *International Journal of Psychology* 43 (3–4), 652.

Schaller, M., Conway, L. G. I., and Tanchuk, T. L. (2002). Selective pressures on the once and future contents of ethnic stereotypes: Effects of the communicability of traits. *Journal of Personality and Social Psychology* 82 (6), 861–77.

Schaller, M., and Murray, D. R. (2008). Pathogens, personality, and culture: Disease prevalence predicts worldwide variability in sociosexuality, extraversion, and openness to experience. *Journal of Personality and Social Psychology* 95 (1), 212–21.

Schaltegger, C. A., and Torgler, B. (2010). Work ethic, Protestantism, and human capital. *Economics Letters* 107 (2), 99–101.

Schapera, I. (1930). *The Khoisan Peoples of South Africa*. London: Routledge.

Scheff, T. J. (1988). Shame and conformity: The deference-emotion system. *American Sociological Review* 53 (3), 395–406.

Scheidel, W. (2008). Monogamy and polygyny in Greece, Rome and world history. Working paper, ssrn.com/abstract=1214729.

Scheidel, W. (2009a). A peculiar institution? Greco-Roman monogamy in global context. *History of the Family* 14 (3), 280–91.

Scheidel, W. (2009b). Sex and empire: A Darwinian perspective. In I. Morris and W. Scheidel (eds.), *The Dynamics of Ancient Empires: State Power from Assyria to Byzantium* (pp. 255–324). New York: Oxford University Press.

Scheidel, W. (2019). *Escape from Rome: The Failure of Empire and the Road to Prosperity*. Princeton, NJ: Princeton University Press.

Scheve, K., and Stasavage, D. (2010). The conscription of wealth: Mass warfare and the demand for progressive taxation. *International Organization* 64 (4), 529–61.

Schmitt, D. P., Allik, J., McCrae, R. R., and Benet-Martinez, V. (2007). The geographic distribution of big five personality traits: Patterns and profiles of human self-description across 56 nations. *Journal of Cross-Cultural Psychology* 38 (2), 173–212.

Schneider, D. M., and Homans, G. C. (1955). Kinship terminology and the American kinship system. *American Anthropologist* 57 (6), 1194–1208.

Schulz, J. (2019). Kin networks and institutional development. Working paper, ssrn.com/sol3/papers.cfm?abstract_id=2877828.

Schulz, J. F., Barahmi-Rad, D., Beauchamp, J., and Henrich, J. (2018). The origins of WEIRD psychology. June 22. https://psyarxiv.com/d6qhu/.

Schulz, J. F., Bahrami-Rad, D., Beauchamp, J. P., and Henrich, J. (2019). Global psychological variation, intensive kinship and the Church. *Science* 366 (707), 1–12.

Schwartz, S. H., and Bilsky, W. (1990). Toward a theory of the universal content and structure of values: Extensions and cross-cultural replications. *Journal of Personality and Social Psychology* 58 (5), 878–91.

Scoville, W. C. (1953). The Huguenots in the French economy, 1650–1750. *Quarterly Journal of Economics* 67 (3), 423–44.

Seife, C. (2000). *Zero: The Biography of a Dangerous Idea*. London: Souvenir Press.

Sellen, D. W., Borgerhoff Mulder, M., and Sieff, D. F. (2000). Fertility, offspring quality, and wealth in Datoga pastoralists. In L. Cronk, N. Chagnon, and W. Irons (eds.), *Adaptation and Human Behavior: An Anthropological Perspective* (pp. 91–114). New York: Aldine de Gruyter.

Sequeira, S., Nunn, N., and Qian, N. (2020). Immigrants and the making of America. *Review of Economic Studies*, 87 (1), 382–419.

Serafinelli, M., and Tabellini, G. (2017). Creativity over time and space. Working paper, ssrn.com/abstract=3070203.

Shariff, A. F., Greene, J. D., Karremans, J. C., Luguri, J. B., Clark, C. J., Schooler, J. W., Baumeister, R. F., Vohs, K. D. (2014). Free will and punishment: A mechanistic view of human nature reduces retribution. *Psychological Science* 25 (8), 1563–70.

Shariff, A. F., and Norenzayan, A. (2007). God is watching you: Priming God concepts increases prosocial behavior in an anonymous economic game. *Psychological Science* 18 (9), 803–809.

Shariff, A. F., and Norenzayan, A. (2011). Mean gods make good people: Different views of God predict cheating behavior. *International Journal for the Psychology of Religion* 21 (2), 85–96.

Shariff, A. F., and Rhemtulla, M. (2012). Divergent effects of beliefs in heaven and hell on national crime rates. *PLoS One* 7 (6), e39048.

Shariff, A. F., Willard, A. K., Andersen, T., and Norenzayan, A. (2016). Religious priming: A meta-analysis with a focus on prosociality. *Personality and Social Psychology Review* 20 (1), 27–48.

Shaw, B. D., and Saller, R. P. (1984). Close-kin marriage in Roman society? *Man* 19 (3), 432–44.

Shenk, M. K., Towner, M. C., Voss, E. A., and Alam, N. (2016). Consanguineous marriage, kinship ecology, and market transition. *Current Anthropology* 57 (13), S167–S180.

Shenkar, O. (2010). *Copycats: How Smart Companies Use Imitation to Gain a Strategic Edge*. Cambridge, MA: Harvard Business Press.

Shepherd, W. R. (1926). The Carolingian and Byzantine Empires and the Califate About 814 [map]. In W. R. Shepherd (ed.), *Historical Atlas* (pp. 54–55). New York: Henry Holt.

Shleifer, A. (2004). Does competition destroy ethical behavior? *American Economic Review* 94 (2), 414–18.

Shrivastava, S. (ed.). (2004). *Medical Device Materials: Proceedings from the Materials and Processes for Medical Devices Conference* (Sept. 8–10, 2003). Materials Park, OH: ASM International.

Shutts, K., Banaji, M. R., and Spelke, E. S. (2010). Social categories guide young children's preferences for novel objects. *Developmental Science* 13 (4), 599–610.

Shutts, K., Kinzler, K. D., and DeJesus, J. M. (2013). Understanding infants' and children's social learning about foods: Previous research and new prospects. *Developmental Psychology* 49 (3), 419–25.

Shutts, K., Kinzler, K. D., Mckee, C. B., and Spelke, E. S. (2009). Social information guides infants' selection of foods. *Journal of Cognition and Development* 10 (1–2), 1–17.

Sibley, C. G., and Bulbulia, J. (2012). Faith after an earthquake: A longitudinal study of religion and perceived health before and after the 2011 Christchurch New Zealand earthquake. *PLoS One 7* (12), e49648.

Sikora, M., Seguin-Orlando, A., Sousa, V. C., Albrechtsen, A., Ko, A., Rasmussen, S, . . . Willerslev, E. (2017). Ancient genomes show social and reproductive behavior of early Upper Paleolithic foragers. *Science* 358 (6363), 659–62.

Silk, J. B. (1987). Adoption among the Inuit. *Ethos* 15 (3), 320–30.

Silver, M. (1995). *Economic Structures of Antiquity*. London: Westport Press.

Silverman, P., and Maxwell, R. J. (1978). How do I respect thee? Let me count the ways: Deference towards elderly men and women. *Behavior Science Research* 13 (2), 91–108.

Simon, J. L., and Sullivan, R. J. (1989). Population size, knowledge stock, and other determinants of agricultural publication and patenting: England, 1541–1850. *Explorations in Economic History* 26 (1), 21–44.

Singh, M., and Henrich, J. (2019). Self-denial by shamans promotes perceptions of religious credibility. Preprint. https://doi.org/10.31234/osf.io/kvtqp.

Singh, M., Kaptchuck, T., and Henrich, J. (2019). Small gods, rituals, and cooperation: The Mentawai crocodile spirit *Sikaoinan*. Preprint. https://doi.org/10.31235/osf.io/npkdy.

Siziba, S., and Bulte, E., (2012). Does market participation promote generalized trust? Experimental evidence from Southern Africa. *Economic Letters* 117 (1), 156–60.

Slingerland, E. (2008). *What Science Offers the Humanities: Integrating Body and Culture*. Cambridge: Cambridge University Press.

Slingerland, E. (2014). *Trying Not to Try: The Art and Science of Spontaneity*. New York: Crown.

Slingerland, E., and Chudek, M. (2011). The prevalence of mind-body dualism in early China. *Cognitive Science* 35 (5), 997–1007.

Slingerland, E., Monroe, M. W., Sullivan, B., Walsh, R. F., Veidlinger, D., Noseworthy, W., . . . Spicer, R. Historians respond to Whitehouse *et al.* (2019), "Complex societies precede moralizing gods throughout world history." *Journal of Cognitive Historiography* 5 (1–2), 124–41.

Slingerland, E., Nichols, R., Nielbo, K., and Logan, C. (2018). The distant reading of religious texts: A "big data" approach to mind-body concepts in early China. *Journal of the American Academy of Religion* 85 (4), 985–1016.

Smaldino, P., Lukaszewski, A., von Rueden, C., and Gurven, M. (2019). Niche diversity can explain cross-cultural differences in personality structure. *Nature Human Behaviour*, 3, 1276–83.

Smaldino, P. E., Schank, J. C., and McElreath, R. (2013). Increased costs of cooperation help cooperators in the long run. *American Naturalist* 181 (4), 451–63.

Smith, A. (1997). Lecture on the influence of commerce on manners. In D. B. Klein (ed.), *Reputation: Studies in the Voluntary Elicitation of Good Conduct* (pp. 17–20). Ann Arbor: University of Michigan Press.

Smith, C. E. (1972). *Papal Enforcement of Some Medieval Marriage Laws.* Port Washington, NY: Kennikat Press.

Smith, D. N. (2015). Profit maxims: Capitalism and the common sense of time and money. *Current Perspectives in Social Theory* 33, 29–74.

Smith, K., Larroucau, T., Mabulla, I. A., and Apicella, C. L. (2018). Hunter-gatherers maintain assortativity in cooperation despite high-levels of residential change and mixing. *Current Biology* 28 (19), P3152–P3157.E4.

Smith, V. A. (1917). *Akkar, the Great Mogul, 1542–1605.* Oxford: Clarendon Press.

Smith, W., and Cheetham, S. (1880). *A Dictionary of Christian Antiquities.* London: John Murray.

Smith-Greenaway, E. (2013). Maternal reading skills and child mortality in Nigeria: A reassessment of why education matters. *Demography* 50 (5), 1551–61.

Smyth, R. B. (1878). *The Aborigines of Victoria.* Melbourne: J. Ferres.

Sneader, W. (2005). *Drug Discovery: A History.* Chichester, UK: Wiley.

Snell, W. W. (1964). *Kinship Relations in Machiguenga.* Dallas, TX: SIL International.

Soler, H., Vinayak, P., and Quadagno, D. (2000). Biosocial aspects of domestic violence. *Psychoneuroendocrinology* 25 (7), 721–39.

Soltis, J., Boyd, R., and Richerson, P. (1995). Can group-functional behaviors evolve by cultural group selection? *Current Anthropology* 36 (13), 473–94.

Sosis, R., and Handwerker, W. P. (2011). Psalms and coping with uncertainty: Religious Israeli women's responses to the 2006 Lebanon War. *American Anthropologist* 113 (1), 40–55.

Sowell, T. (1998). *Conquests and Cultures: An International History.* New York: Basic Books.

Speake, G. (ed.). (1987). Monks and missions. In *Atlas of the Christian Church* (pp. 44–45). New York: Facts on File.

Spencer, C. S. (2010). Territorial expansion and primary state formation. *Proceedings of the National Academy of Sciences* 107 (16), 7119–26.

Spencer, C. S., and Redmond, E. M. (2001). Multilevel selection and political evolution in the Valley of Oaxaca, 500–100 B.C. *Journal of Anthropological Archaeology* 20 (2), 195–229.

Spenkuch, J. L. (2017). Religion and work: Micro evidence from contemporary Germany. *Journal of Economic Behavior and Organization* 135, 193–214.

Sperber, D. (1996). *Explaining Culture: A Naturalistic Approach.* Oxford; Cambridge, MA: Blackwell.

Sperber, D., Clement, F., Heintz, C., Mascaro, O., Mercier, H., Origgi, G., and Wilson, D. (2010). Epistemic vigilance. *Mind and Language* 25 (4), 359–93.

Squicciarini, M. P., and Voigtländer, N. (2015). Human capital and industrialization: Evidence from the age of the Enlightenment. *Quarterly Journal of Economics* 130 (4), 1825–83.

Squires, M. (2017). Kinship taxation as a constraint to microenterprise growth: Experimental evidence from Kenya. Working paper. uvic.ca/socialsciences/economics/assets/docs/seminars/Squires%20Kinship%20Taxation.pdf.

Srinivasan, M., Dunham, Y., Hicks, C. M., and Barner, D. (2016). Do attitudes toward societal structure predict beliefs about free will and achievement? Evidence from the Indian caste system. *Developmental Science* 19 (1), 109–125.

Stanner, W. E. H. (1934). Ceremonial economics of the Mulluk Mulluk and Madngella Tribes of the Daly River, North Australia: A preliminary paper. *Oceania* 4 (4), 458–71.

Stark, R., and Hirschi, T. (1969). Hellfire and delinquency. *Social Problems* 17 (2), 202–213.

Starkweather, K. E., and Hames, R. (2012). A survey of non-classical polyandry. *Human Nature* 23 (2), 149–72.

Stasavage, D. (2011). *States of Credit: Size, Power, and the Development of European Polities.* Princeton, NJ: Princeton University Press.

Stasavage, D. (2014). Was Weber right? The role of urban autonomy in Europe's rise. *American Political Science Review* 108 (2), 337–54.

Stasavage, D. (2016). Representation and consent: Why they arose in Europe and not elsewhere. *Annual Review of Political Science* 19 (1), 145–62.

Stephens-Davidowitz, S. (2018). *Everybody Lies: Big Data, New Data, and What the Internet Can Tell Us About Who We Really Are.* New York: Dey Street Books.

Stephenson, C. (1933). *Borough and Town: A Study of Urban Origins in England.* Monographs of the Mediaeval Academy of America. Cambridge, MA: Mediaeval Academy of America.

Stillman, T. F., and Baumeister, R. F. (2010). Guilty, free, and wise: Determinism and psychopathy diminish learning from negative emotions. *Journal of Experimental Social Psychology* 46 (6), 951–60.

Storey, A. E., Walsh, C. J., Quiton, R. L., and Wynne-Edwards, K. (2000). Hormonal correlates of paternal responsiveness in new and expectant fathers. *Evolution and Human Behavior* 21 (2), 79–95.

Strassmann, B. I., and Kurapati, N. T. (2016). What explains patrilineal cooperation? *Current Anthropology* 57 (Suppl. 13), S118–S130.

Strassmann, B. I., Kurapati, N. T., Hug, B. F., Burke, E. E., Gillespie, B. W., Karafet, T. M., and Hammer, M. F. (2012). Religion as a means to assure paternity. *Proceedings of the National Academy of Sciences* 109 (25), 9781–85.

Strathern, M. (1992). *After Nature: English Kinship in the Late Twentieth Century.* Lewis Henry Morgan Lectures. Cambridge: Cambridge University Press.

Stringham, E. (2015). On the origins of stock markets. In C. J. Coyne and P. J. Boettke (eds.), *The Oxford Handbook of Austrian Economics* (pp. 1–20). New York: Oxford University Press.

Strömbäck, C., Lind, T., Skagerlund, K., Västfjäll, D., and Tinghög, G. (2017). Does self-control predict financial behavior and financial well-being? *Journal of Behavioral and Experimental Finance* 14, 30–38.

Stuchlik, M. (1976). *Life on a Half Share: Mechanisms of Social Recruitment Among the Mapuche of Southern Chile.* London: C. Hurst.

Sturtevant, W. C. (1978). *Handbook of North American Indians: Arctic.* Washington, DC: Smithsonian Institution.

Su, J. C., and Oishi, S. (2010). Culture and self-enhancement. A social relation analysis. Unpublished manuscript.

Suh, E. M. (2002). Culture, identity consistency, and subjective well-being. *Journal of Personality and Social Psychology* 83 (6), 1378–91.

Swann, W. B., and Buhrmester, M. D. (2015). Identity fusion. *Current Directions in Psychological Science* 24 (1), 52–57.

Swann, W. B., Jetten, J., Gómez, A., Whitehouse, H., and Bastian, B. (2012). When group membership gets personal: A theory of identity fusion. *Psychological Review* 119 (3), 441–56.

Sznycer, D., Tooby, J., Cosmides, L., Porat, R., Shalvi, S., and Halperin, E. (2016). Shame closely tracks the threat of devaluation by others, even across cultures. *Proceedings of the National Academy of Sciences* 113 (10), 201514699.

Sznycer, D., Xygalatas, D., Agey, E., Alami, S., An, X.-F., Ananyeva, K. I., . . . Tooby, J. (2018). Cross-cultural invariances in the architecture of shame. *Proceedings of the National Academy of Sciences* 115 (39), 201805016.

Szwed, M., Vinckier, F., Cohen, L., and Dehaene, S. (2012). Towards a universal neurobiological architecture for learning to read. *Behavioral and Brain Sciences* 35 (5), 308–309.

Tabellini, G. (2010). Culture and institutions: Economic development in the regions of Europe. *Journal of the European Economic Association* 8 (4), 677–716.

Takahashi, T. (2005). Loss of self-control in intertemporal choice may be attributable to logarithmic time-perception. *Medical Hypotheses* 65 (4), 691–93.

Takahashi, T., Hadzibeganovic, T., Cannas, S. A., Makino, T., Fukui, H., and Kitayama, S. (2009). Cultural neuroeconomics of intertemporal choice. *Neuroendocrinology Letters* 30 (2), 185–91.

Talhelm, T. (2015). The rice theory of culture. Dissertation, Department of Psychology, University of Virginia.

Talhelm, T., Graham, J., and Haidt, J. The budding collectivism revolution. Working paper.

Talhelm, T., Zhang, X., Oishi, S., Shimin, C., Duan, D., Lan, X., and Kitayama, S. (2014). Large-scale psychological differences within China explained by rice versus wheat agriculture. *Science* 344 (6184), 603–608.

Tarr, B., Launay, J., Cohen, E., and Dunbar, R. (2015). Synchrony and exertion during dance independently raise pain threshold and encourage social bonding. *Biology Letters* 11 (10), 1–4.

Tarr, B., Launay, J., and Dunbar, R. I. M. (2014). Music and social bonding: "Self-other" merging and neurohormonal mechanisms. *Frontiers in Psychology* 5, 1096.

Tarr, B., Launay, J., and Dunbar, R. I. M. (2016). Silent disco: Dancing in synchrony leads to elevated pain thresholds and social closeness. *Evolution and Human Behavior* 37 (5), 343–49.

Taylor, J. (2003). Risk-taking behavior in mutual fund tournaments. *Journal of Economic Behavior and Organization* 50 (3), 373–83.

Tenney, E. R., Small, J. E., Kondrad, R. L., Jaswal, V. K., and Spellman, B. A. (2011). Accuracy, confidence, and calibration: How young children and adults assess credibility. *Developmental Psychology* 47 (4), 1065–1077.

Terashima, H., and Hewlett, B. S. (2016). *Social Learning and Innovation in Contemporary Hunter-Gatherers: Evolutionary and Ethnographic Perspectives.* Replacement of Neanderthals by Modern Humans Series. Tokyo: Springer.

Thompson, E. P. (1967). Time, work-discipline, and industrial capitalism. *Past and Present* 38 (1), 56–97.

Thomson, R., Yuki, M., Talhelm, T., Schug, J., Kito, M., Ayanian, A. H., . . . Visserman, M. L. (2018). Relational mobility predicts social behaviors in 39 countries and is tied to historical farming and threat. *Proceedings of the National Academy of Sciences* 115 (29), 7521–26.

Thoni, C. (2017). Trust and cooperation: Survey evidence and behavioral experiments. In P. Van Lange, B. Rockenbach, and M. Yamagishi (eds.), *Trust in Social Dilemmas* (pp. 155–72). New York: Oxford University Press.

Tierney, B. (1997). *The Idea of Natural Rights.* Atlanta: Scholars Press for Emory University.

Tilly, C. (1993). *Coercion, Capital and European States, AD 990–1992.* Hoboken, NJ: Wiley.

Tocqueville, A. de (1835; 1969). *Democracy in America.* Garden City, NY: Doubleday.

Todd, E. (1985). *Explanation of Ideology: Family Structure and Social System.* Hoboken, NJ: Blackwell.

Tönnies, F. (2011). *Community and Society.* New York: Dover.

Toren, C. (1990). *Making Sense of Hierarchy.* London: Athlone Press.

Torgler, B., and Schaltegger, C. (2014). Suicide and religion: New evidence on the differences between Protestantism and Catholicism. *Journal for the Scientific Study of Religion* 53 (2), 316–40.

Toubert, P. (1996). The Carolingian moment. In A. Burguiere, C. Klapisch-Zuber, M. Segalen, and F. Zonabend (eds.), *A History of the Family* (pp. 379–406). Cambridge, MA: Belknap Press of Harvard University Press.

Tracer, D. P. (2003). Selfishness and fairness in economic and evolutionary perspective: An experimental economic study in Papua New Guinea. *Current Anthropology* 44 (3), 432–38.

Tracer, D. P. (2004). Market integration, reciprocity, and fairness in rural Papua New Guinea: Results from two-village Ultimatum Game experiments. In J. Henrich, R. Boyd, S. Bowles, C. Camerer, E. Fehr, and H. Gintis (eds.), *Foundations of Human Sociality: Economic Experiments and Ethnographic Evidence from Fifteen Small-Scale Societies* (pp. 232–59). New York: Oxford University Press.

Tracer, D. P., Mueller, I., and Morse, J. (2014). Cruel to be kind: Effects of sanctions and third-party enforcers on generosity in Papua New Guinea. In J. Ensminger and J. Henrich (eds.), *Experimenting with Social Norms: Fairness and Punishment in Cross-Cultural Perspective* (pp. 177–96). New York: Russell Sage Foundation.

Tracy, J. L., and Matsumoto, D. (2008). The spontaneous expression of pride and shame: Evidence for biologically innate nonverbal displays. *Proceedings of the National Academy of Sciences* 105 (33), 11655–60.

Triandis, H. C. (1989). The self and social-behavior in differing cultural contexts. *Psychological Review* 96 (3), 506–520.

Triandis, H. C. (1994). *Culture and Social Behavior*. New York: McGraw-Hill.

Triandis, H. C. (1995). *Individualism and Collectivism. New Directions in Social Psychology*. Boulder, CO: Westview Press.

Trompenaars, A., and Hampden-Turner, C. (1998). *Riding the Waves of Culture: Understanding Cultural Diversity in Global Business*. New York: McGraw-Hill.

Tu, Q., and Bulte, E. (2010). Trust, market participation and economic outcomes: Evidence from rural China. *World Development* 38 (8), 1179–90.

Tu, Q., Bulte, E., and Tan, S. (2011). Religiosity and economic performance: Micro-econometric evidence from Tibetan area. *China Economic Review* 22 (1), 55–63.

Tucker, B. (2012). Do risk and time experimental choices represent individual strategies for coping with poverty or conformity to social norms? *Current Anthropology* 53 (2), 149–80.

Turchin, P. (2005). *War and Peace and War: The Life Cycles of Imperial Nations*. New York: Pi Press/Pearson.

Turchin, P. (2010). Warfare and the evolution of social complexity: A multilevel-selection approach. *Structure and Dynamics* 4 (3), 1–37.

Turchin, P. (2015). *Ultrasociety: How 10,000 Years of War Made Humans the Greatest Cooperators on Earth*. Chaplin, CT: Beresta Books.

Turchin, P., Currie, T. E., Turner, E. A. L., and Gavrilets, S. (2013). War, space, and the evolution of Old World complex societies. *Proceedings of the National Academy of Sciences* 110 (41), 16384–89.

Turchin, P., Currie, T. E., Whitehouse, H., Francois, P., Feeney, K., Mullins, D., ... Spencer, C. (2017). Quantitative historical analyses uncover a single dimension of complexity that structures global variation in human social organization. *Proceedings of the National Academy of Sciences* 115 (2), e144–e151.

Turner, G. (1859). *Nineteen Years in Polynesia: Missionary Life, Travels, and Researches in the Islands of the Pacific*. London: John Snow, Paternoster Row.

Tuzin, D. (1976). *The Ilahita Arapesh: Dimensions of Unity*. Berkeley: University of California Press.

Tuzin, D. (2001). *Social Complexity in the Making: A Case Study Among the Arapesh of New Guinea*. London: Routledge.

Ubl, K. (2008). *Inzestverbot und Gesetzgebung. Die Konstruktion eines Verbrechens, 300–1100*. Berlin: Walter de Gruyter.

Uhlmann, E. L., Poehlman, T. A., Tannenbaum, D., and Bargh, J. A. (2010). Implicit Puritanism in American moral cognition. *Journal of Experimental Social Psychology* 47 (2), 312–20.

Uhlmann, E. L., and Sanchez-Burks, J. (2014). The implicit legacy of American Protestantism. *Journal of Cross-Cultural Psychology* 45 (6), 992–1006.

Vaish, A., Carpenter, M., and Tomasello, M. (2011). Young children's responses to guilt displays. *Developmental Psychology* 47 (5), 1248–62.

van Baaren, R., Janssen, L., Chartrand, T. L., and Dijksterhuis, A. (2009). Where is the love? The social aspects of mimicry. *Philosophical Transactions of the Royal Society B: Biological Sciences* 364 (1528), 2381–89.

van Berkhout, E. T., and Malouff, J. M. (2016). The efficacy of empathy training: A meta-analysis of randomized controlled trials. *Journal of Counseling Psychology* 63 (1), 32–41.

Van Cleve, J., and Akçay, E. (2014). Pathways to social evolution: Reciprocity, relatedness, and synergy. *Evolution* 68 (8), 2245–58.

van Honk, J., Peper, J. S., and Schutter, D. J. L. G. (2005). Testosterone reduces unconscious fear but not consciously experienced anxiety: Implications for the disorders of fear and anxiety. *Biological Psychiatry* 58 (3), 218–25.

van Honk, J., Schutter, D. J. L. G., Hermans, E. J., Putman, P., Tuiten, A., and Koppeschaar, H. (2004). Testosterone shifts the balance between sensitivity for punishment and reward in healthy young women. *Psychoneuroendocrinology* 29 (7), 937–43.

van Honk, J., Terburg, D., and Bos, P. A. (2011). Further notes on testosterone as a social hormone. *Trends in Cognitive Sciences* 15 (7), 291–92.

van Honk, J., Tuiten, A., Hermans, E., Putman, P., Koppeschaar, H., Thijssen, J., Verbaten, R., and van Doornen, L. (2001). A single administration of testosterone induces cardiac accelerative responses to angry faces in healthy young women. *Behavioral Neuroscience* 115 (1), 238–42.

Van Hoorn, A., and Maseland, R. (2013). Does a Protestant work ethic exist? Evidence from the well-being effect of unemployment. *Journal of Economic Behavior and Organization* 91, 1–12.

van Schaik, C. P., Ancrenaz, M., Borgen, G., Galdikas, B., Knott, C. D., Singleton, I., Suzuki, A., Utami, S. S., and Merrill, M. (2003). Orangutan cultures and the evolution of material culture. *Science* 299 (5603), 102–105.

Van Zanden, J. L. (2009a). *The Long Road to the Industrial Revolution: The European Economy in a Global Perspective, 1000–1800, Vol. 1.* Leiden: Brill.

Van Zanden, J. L. (2009b). The skill premium and the "great divergence." *European Review of Economic History* 13 (1), 121–53.

Van Zanden, J. L., Buringh, E., and Bosker, M. (2012). The rise and decline of European parliaments, 1188–1789. *Economic History Review* 65 (3), 835–61.

Van Zanden, J. L., and De Moor, T. (2010). Girl power: The European marriage pattern and labour markets in the North Sea region in the late medieval and early modern period. *Economic History Review* 63 (1), 1–33.

Vansina, J. (1990). *Paths in the Rainforests: Towards a History of Political Tradition in Equatorial Africa.* Madison: University of Wisconsin Press.

Vardy, T., and Atkinson, Q. D. (2019). Property damage and exposure to other people in distress differentially predict prosocial behavior after a natural disaster. *Psychological Science* 30 (4), 563–75.

Varnum, M. E. W., Grossmann, I., Katunar, D., Nisbett, R. E., and Kitayama, S. (2008). Holism in a European context: Differences in cognitive style between central and east Europeans and Westerners. *Journal of Cognition and Culture* 8 (3), 321–33.

Varnum, M. E. W., Grossmann, I., Kitayama, S., and Nisbett, R. E. (2010). The origin of cultural differences in cognition: The social orientation hypothesis. *Current Directions in Psychological Science* 19 (1), 9–13.

Ventura, P., Fernandes, T., Cohen, L., Morais, J., Kolinsky, R., and Dehaene, S. (2013). Literacy acquisition reduces the influence of automatic holistic processing of faces and houses. *Neuroscience Letters* 554, 105–109.

Verger, J. (1991). Patterns. In H. de Ridder-Symoens (ed.), *A History of the University in Europe: Volume 1, Universities in the Middle Ages* (pp. 35–68). Cambridge: Cambridge University Press.

Vohs, K. D. (2015). Money priming can change people's thoughts, feelings, motivations, and behaviors: An update on 10 years of experiments. *Journal of Experimental Psychology: General* 144 (4), 1–8.

Vohs, K. D., Mead, N. L., and Goode, M. R. (2006). The psychological consequences of money. *Science* 314 (5802), 1154–56.

Vohs, K. D., Mead, N. L., and Goode, M. R. (2008). Merely activating the concept of money changes personal and interpersonal behavior. *Current Directions in Psychological Science* 17 (3), 208–212.

Vohs, K. D., and Schooler, J. W. (2008). The value of believing in free will: Encouraging a belief in determinism increases cheating. *Psychological Science* 19 (1), 49–54.

Vollan, B., Landmann, A., Zhou, Y., Hu, B., and Herrmann-Pillath, C. (2017). Cooperation and authoritarian values: An experimental study in China. *European Economic Review* 93, 90–105.

Voors, M. J., Nillesen, E. E. M., Verwimp, P., Bulte, E. H., Lensink, R., and Van Soest, D. P. (2012). Violent conflict and behavior: A field experiment in Burundi. *American Economic Review* 102 (2), 941–64.

Voth, H. J. (1998). Time and work in eighteenth-century London. *Journal of Economic History* 58 (1), 29–58.

Wade, N. (2009). *The Faith Instinct: How Religion Evolved and Why It Endures*. New York: Penguin Press.

Wade, N. J. (2014). *A Troublesome Inheritance: Genes, Race, and Human History*. New York: Penguin Press.

Walker, R. S. (2014). Amazonian horticulturalists live in larger, more related groups than hunter-gatherers. *Evolution and Human Behavior* 35 (5), 384–88.

Walker, R. S., and Bailey, D. H. (2014). Marrying kin in small-scale societies. *American Journal of Human Biology* 26 (3), 384–88.

Walker, R. S., Beckerman, S., Flinn, M. V., Gurven, M., von Rueden, C. R., Kramer, K. L., . . . Hill, K. R. (2013). Living with kin in lowland horticultural societies. *Current Anthropology* 54 (1), 96–103.

Walker, R. S., and Hill, K. R. (2014). Causes, consequences, and kin bias of human group fissions. *Human Nature* 25 (4), 465–75.

Wallbott, H. G., and Scherer, K. R. (1995). Cultural determinants in experiencing shame and guilt. In J. P. Tangney and K. W. Fischer (eds.), *Self-Conscious Emotions: The Psychology of Shame, Guilt, Embarrassment, and Pride* (pp. 465–87). New York: Guilford Press.

Wang, Y., Liu, H., and Sun, Z. (2017). Lamarck rises from his grave: Parental environment-induced epigenetic inheritance in model organisms and humans. *Biological Reviews of the Cambridge Philosophical Society* 92 (4), 2084–2111.

Wann, D. L. (2006). Understanding the positive social psychological benefits of sport team identification: The team identification-social psychological health model. *Group Dynamics* 10 (4), 272–96.

Wann, D. L., and Polk, J. (2007). The positive relationship between sport team identification and belief in the trustworthiness of others. *North American Journal of Psychology* 9 (2), 251–56.

Watson-Jones, R. E., and Legare, C. H. (2016). The social functions of group rituals. *Current Directions in Psychological Science* 25 (1), 42–46.

Watters, E. (2010). *Crazy Like Us: The Globalization of the American Psyche*. New York: Free Press.

Watts, J., Greenhill, S. J., Atkinson, Q. D., Currie, T. E., Bulbulia, J., and Gray, R. D. (2015). Broad supernatural punishment but not moralizing high gods precede the evolution of political complexity in Austronesia. *Proceedings of the Royal Society B: Biological Sciences* 282 (1804), 20142556.

Watts, T. W., Duncan, G. J., and Quan, H. (2018). Revisiting the marshmallow test: A conceptual replication investigating links between early delay of gratification and later outcomes. *Psychological Science* 29 (7), 1159–77.

Weber, M. (1958a). *The City*. New York: Free Press.

Weber, M. (1958b). *The Protestant Ethic and the Spirit of Capitalism*. New York: Scribner.

Weber, M. (1978). *Economy and Society*. Berkeley: University of California Press.

Weiner, M. S. (2013). *The Rule of the Clan: What an Ancient Form of Social Organization Reveals About the Future of Individual Freedom*. New York: Farrar, Straus and Giroux.

Weiss, A., Inoue-Murayama, M., King, J. E., Adams, M. J., and Matsuzawa, T. (2012). All too human? Chimpanzee and orang-utan personalities are not anthropomorphic projections. *Animal Behaviour* 83 (6), 1355–65.

Wen, N. J., Clegg, J. M., and Legare, C. H. (2017). Smart conformists: Children and adolescents associate conformity with intelligence across cultures. *Child Development* 90 (3), 746–58.

Wen, N. J., Herrmann, P. A., and Legare, C. H. (2015). Ritual increases children's affiliation with in-group members. *Evolution and Human Behavior* 37 (1), 54–60.

Wente, A. O., Bridgers, S., Zhao, X., Seiver, E., Zhu, L., and Gopnik, A. (2016). How universal are free will beliefs? Cultural differences in Chinese and U.S. 4- and 6-year-olds. *Child Development* 87 (3), 666–76.

Wente, A., Zhao, X., Gopnik, A., Kang, C., and Kushnir, T. (2020). The developmental and cultural origins of our beliefs about self-control. In A. Mele (ed.), *Surrounding Self-Control*. New York: Oxford University Press.

Wertz, A. E. (2019). How plants shape the mind. *Trends in Cognitive Sciences* 23 (7), 528–31.

Wha-Sook, L. (1995). Marriage and divorce regulation and recognition in Korea. *Family Law Quarterly* 29 (3), 603.

Whaley, S. E., Sigman, M., Neumann, C., Bwibo, N., Guthrie, D., Weiss, R. E., Alber, S., and Murphy, S. P. (2003). The impact of dietary intervention on the cognitive development of Kenyan school children. *The Journal of Nutrition* 133 (11), 3965–71.

White, D. R. (1988). Rethinking polygyny: Co-wives, codes, and cultural systems. *Current Anthropology* 29 (4), 529–44.

White, L. (1962). *Medieval Technology and Social Change*. New York: Oxford University Press.

Whitehouse, H. (1995). *Inside the Cult: Religious Innovation and Transmission in Papua New Guinea*. Oxford Studies in Social and Cultural Anthropology. Oxford: Clarendon Press.

Whitehouse, H. (1996). Rites of terror: Emotion, metaphor and memory in Melanesian initiation cults. *Journal of the Royal Anthropological Institute* 2 (4), 703–715.

Whitehouse, H. (2000). *Arguments and Icons: Divergent Modes of Religiosity*. New York: Oxford University Press.

Whitehouse, H. (2004). *Modes of Religiosity: A Cognitive Theory of Religious Transmission*. Lanham, MD: Altamira Press.

Whitehouse, H., and Lanman, J. A. (2014). The ties that bind us: Ritual, fusion, and identification. *Current Anthropology* 55 (6), 674–95.

Whitehouse, H., McQuinn, B., Buhrmester, M., and Swann, W. B. (2014). Brothers in arms: Libyan revolutionaries bond like family. *Proceedings of the National Academy of Sciences* 111 (50), 17783–85.

Whitehouse, H., François, P., Savage, P. E., Currie, T. E., Feeney, K. C., Cioni, E., Purcell, R., . . . Turchin, P. (2019). Complex societies precede moralizing gods throughout world history. *Nature* 568, 226–29.

Wichary, S., Pachur, T., and Li, M. (2015). Risk-taking tendencies in prisoners and nonprisoners: Does gender matter? *Journal of Behavioral Decision Making* 28 (5), 504–514.

Wickham, C. (1981). *Early Medieval Italy: Central Power and Local Society, 400–1000*. Ann Arbor: University of Michigan Press.

Wiessner, P. (2002). Hunting, healing, and hxaro exchange: A long-term perspective on !Kung (Ju/'hoansi) large-game hunting. *Evolution and Human Behavior* 23 (6), 407–436.

Wiessner, P. (2009). Parent-offspring conflict in marriage. In S. Shennan (ed.), *Pattern and Process in Cultural Evolution* (pp. 251–63). Berkeley: University of California Press.

Wiessner, P., and Tumu, A. (1998). *Historical Vines*. (W. Merrill and I. Karp, eds.) Smithsonian Series in Ethnographic Inquiry. Washington, DC: Smithsonian Institution.

Wildman, W. J., and Sosis, R. (2011). Stability of groups with costly beliefs and practices. *Journal of Artificial Societies and Social Simulation* 14 (3), 1–25.

Willard, A. K., and Cingl, L. (2017). Testing theories of secularization and religious belief in the Czech Republic and Slovakia. *Evolution and Human Behavior* 38 (5), 604–615.

Willard, A. K., Cingl, L., and Norenzayan, A. (2019). Cognitive biases and religious belief: A path model replication in the Czech Republic and Slovakia with a focus on anthropomorphism. *Social Psychological and Personality Science* 11 (2), 97–106 journals.sagepub.com/doi/10.1177/1948550619841629.

Willard, A. K., Henrich, J., and Norenzayan, A. (2016). The role of memory, belief, and familiarity in the transmission of counterintuitive content. *Human Nature* 27 (3), 221–43.

Willard, A. K., and Norenzayan, A. (2013). Cognitive biases explain religious belief, paranormal belief, and belief in life's purpose. *Cognition* 129 (2), 379–91.

Williams, T. I. (1987). *The History of Invention*. New York: Facts on File.

Williamson, R. W. (1937). *Religion and Social Organization in Central Polynesia*. Cambridge: Cambridge University Press.

Wingfield, J. C. (1984). Androgens and mating systems: Testosterone-induces polygyny in normally monogamous birds. *The Auk* 101 (4), 665–71.

Wingfield, J. C., Hegner, R. E., Dufty, Jr., A. M., Ball, G. F., Dufty, A. M., and Ball, G. F. (1990). The "challenge hypothesis": Theoretical implications for patterns of testosterone secretion, mating systems, and breeding strategies. *The American Naturalist* 136 (6), 829–46.

Wingfield, J. C., Lynn, S. E., and Soma, K. K. (2001). Avoiding the "costs" of testosterone: Ecological bases of hormone-behavior interactions. *Brain, Behavior and Evolution* 57 (5), 239–51.

Winter, A. (2013). Population and migration: European and Chinese experiences compared. In P. Clark (ed.), *The Oxford Handbook of Cities in World History* (pp. 403–20). New York: Oxford University Press.

Witkin, H. A., and Berry, J. J. W. (1975). Psychological differentiation in cross-cultural perspective. *Journal of Cross-Cultural Psychology* 6 (1), 5–78.

Witkin, H. A., Moore, C. A., Goodenough, D., and Cox, P. W. (1977). Field-dependent and field-independent cognitive styles and their educational implications. *Review of Educational Research* 47 (1), 1–64.

Wong, Y., and Tsai, J. (2007). Cultural models of shame and guilt. In J. L. Tracy, R. W. Robins, and J. P. Tangney (eds.), *The Self-Conscious Emotion: Theory and Research* (pp. 209–223). New York: Guilford Press.

Wood, C. (2017). Ritual and the logic of self-regulation. *Religion, Brain & Behavior* 7 (3), 266–75.

Woodberry, R. D. (2012). The missionary roots of liberal democracy. *American Political Science Review* 106 (2), 244–74.

Woodburn, J. (1982). Egalitarian societies. *Man* 17 (3), 431–51.

Woodburn, J. (1998). Sharing is not a form of exchange: An analysis of property-sharing in immediate return hunter-gatherer societies. In C. M. Hann (ed.), *Property Relations: Renewing the Anthropological Tradition* (pp. 48–63). Cambridge: Cambridge University Press.

Woodburn, J. (2016). Silent trade with outsiders: Hunter-gatherers' perspectives. *Journal of Ethnographic Theory* 6 (2), 473–96.

Woodley, M. A., and Bell, E. (2012). Consanguinity as a major predictor of levels of democracy: A study of 70 nations. *Journal of Cross-Cultural Psychology* 44 (2), 263–80.

Woods, T. E. (2012). *How the Catholic Church Built Western Civilization*. Washington, DC: Regnery History.

Wootton, D. (2015). *The Invention of Science: A New History of the Scientific Revolution*. London: Penguin.

Worm, W. (1950). *The Hanseatic League*. Economic Coooperation Administration–Office of the Special Representative Information Division, Editorial Research and Analysis Section.

Wrangham, R. (2019). *The Goodness Paradox: How Evolution Made Us Both More and Less Violent*. London: Profile Books.

Wrangham, R. W., and Glowacki, L. (2012). Intergroup aggression in chimpanzees and war in nomadic hunter-gatherers: Evaluating the chimpanzee model. *Human Nature* 23 (1), 5–29.

Wright, R. (2009). *The Evolution of God*. Boston: Little, Brown.

Xygalatas, D., Mitkidis, P., Fischer, R., Reddish, P., Skewes, J., Geertz, A. W., Roepstorff, A., and Bulbulia, J. (2013). Extreme rituals promote prosociality. *Psychological Science* 24 (8), 1602–1605.

Yamagishi, T., Matsumoto, Y., Kiyonari, T., Takagishi, H., Li, Y., Kanai, R., and Sakagami, M. (2017). Response time in economic games reflects different types of decision conflict for prosocial and proself individuals. *Proceedings of the National Academy of Sciences* 114 (24), 6394–99.

Yamagishi, T., Takagishi, H., Fermin, A. D. R., Kanai, R., Li, Y., and Matsumoto, Y. (2016). Cortical thickness of the dorsolateral prefrontal cortex predicts strategic choices in economic games. *Proceedings of the National Academy of Sciences* 113 (20), 5582–87.

Yilmaz, O., and Bahçekapili, H. G. (2016). Supernatural and secular monitors promote human cooperation only if they remind of punishment. *Evolution and Human Behavior* 37 (1), 79–84.

Young, C. (2009). Religion and economic growth in Western Europe: 1500–2000. Working paper, citation.allacademic.com/meta/p_mla_apa_research_citation/3/0/9/0/6/pages309064/p309064-1.php.

Young, L., and Durwin, A. J. (2013). Moral realism as moral motivation: The impact of meta-ethics on everyday. *Journal of Experimental Social Psychology* 49 (2), 302–306.

Young, R. W. (2009). The ontogeny of throwing and striking. *Human Ontogenetics* 3 (1), 19–31.

Yuki, M., Sato, K., Takemura, K., and Oishi, S. (2013). Social ecology moderates the association between self-esteem and happiness. *Journal of Experimental Social Psychology* 49 (4), 741–46.

Yuki, M., and Takemura, K. (2014). Intergroup comparison and intragroup relationships: Group processes in the cultures of individualism and collectivism. In M. Yuki and M. B. Brewer (eds.), *Culture and Group Processes* (pp. 38–65). New York: Oxford University Press.

Yutang, L. (1936). *My Country and My People*. London: William Heinemann.

Zaki, J., Schirmer, J., and Mitchell, J. P. (2011). Social influence modulates the neural computation of value. *Psychological Science* 22 (7), 894–900.

Zeng, T. C., Aw, A. J., and Feldman, M. W. (2018). Cultural hitchhiking and competition between patrilineal kin groups explain the post-Neolithic Y-chromosome bottleneck. *Nature Communications* 9 (1), 1–12.

Zhou, X., Alysandratos, T., and Naef, M. (2017). Rice farming and the emergence of cooperative behavior. Working paper, sites.google.com/site/xiaoyuzhouresearch/r.

Zimmer, C. (2018). *She Has Her Mother's Laugh: The Powers, Perversions, and Potential of Heredity*. New York: Penguin Random House.

INDEX

74; MFP and, 165–66; monogamous, 254, 267–68, 273, 278, 281, 282, 550*n23*; norms, 73, 74, 75, 82, 275; polyandrous, 261, 548*n8*, 549*n12*; polygamous, 156, 163, 537*n25*; premarital labor period, 190; prohibitions, *178*, 186; punishment and, 167; remarriage, 180, 181; residence after, 106; social norms and, 88; sororate, 171–72, 525*n41*; taboos and, 167; tribal boundaries and, 185; venerable customs, 179; Western (Roman Catholic) Church and, 57, 197; women and, 73, 190, 467; *see also* cousin marriage; polygynous marriage

Marriage and Family Program (MFP), 165–66, *168–70*, 174, 192, 237, 471; Carolingian Empire and, 188, 189; changes wrought by, 458; Christianity and, 176; cities most influenced by, 571*n29*; consolidation of, 225; creation of, 177; dosage of, 194, 226, 230, *236*, 240, 243, 357; Eastern Orthodox Church and, 178, 227; Europe, still in, 235; European tribes and, 186; exposure to, 238; full force of, 233; impact on Europe, 179, 251; implementation of, 175, 485; individualism and, 234; intensive kinship and, 185; milestones in, 491–97; norms of, 540*n58*; psychological effects of, 315; social structure reorganized by, 180; sway of, 334; taboos and, 307

Marriage Law of the People's Republic of China, 251–52

Marshall, Lorna, 75, 131

Martin of Tours, 183

Marx, Karl, 300

maternal-child bonds, 520*n22*

mating psychology, 259

Matsigenka, 99–100; guilt and, 524*n27*; hamlets, 101; individualism and, 102; psychology of, 102; shame and, 102; UG and, 289

maximal lineage, 109, *110*

Maya, 138

meat-sharing norms, 73, 79

mechanical clocks, 360, 365; Late Middle Ages and, 363; monasteries and, 361

Mediterranean, 176

Meiji Restoration, 477

memory, 5, 7

Menlo Park, 439

menopause, 259

mentalizing abilities, 76, 129

Merovingian Dynasty, 177, 553*n53*

Mesopotamia, 151, 306

Mesopotamian gods, 144

Mexico, 255, 257

MFP, *see* Marriage and Family Program

MFQ, *see* Moral Foundations Questionnaire

Middle Ages, 16, 159, 181, 380, 386, 444, 472; agriculture and, 441; banking in, 240; Cistercian Order and, 370; cousin marriage and, 237; cultural evolution during, 396; intergroup competition in, 350; market norms and, 318; MFP exposure during, 238; self-regulation and, 367; universities and, 353; urban centers and, 446; Western Christian Church and, 128; Yiddish and, 175; *see also* Early Middle Ages; High Middle Ages; Late Middle Ages

Middle East, 176, 206, 217, 376, 474, 517*n51*